R. Gupta's®

POPULAR MASTER GUIDE

SSC-CHSL

Combined Higher Secondary Level (10+2)

Data Entry Operator (DEO)

Lower Division Clerk (LDC)

Junior Secretarial Assistant (JSA)

TIER-I

Recruitment Exam

by

RPH Editorial Board

2027
EDITION

RAMESH PUBLISHING HOUSE, NEW DELHI

Published by: O.P. Gupta *for* Ramesh Publishing House

Admin. Office

12-H, New Daryaganj Road, Opp. Officers' Mess,
New Delhi-110002 ☏ 23275224, 23245124

E-mail: info@rameshpublishinghouse.com
For Online Shopping: www.rameshpublishinghouse.com

Showroom

- Balaji Market, Nai Sarak, Delhi-110006 ☏ 23282525 📱 9354373464
- 4457, Nai Sarak, Delhi-110006

Book Code: R-1335

ISBN: 978-93-5012-026-2

Price: ₹ 345

Printed at: J.P. Enterpises, Delhi

CONTENTS

Scheme of Examination

The Computer Based Examination will be conducted in two tiers as Tier-I & Tier-II.

TIER-I

Part	Subject	No. of Questions	Maximum Marks	Total Duration/Timing
I	English Language (Basic Knowledge)	25	50	60 Minutes
II	General Intelligence	25	50	
III	Quantitative Aptitude (Basic Arithmetic Skill)	25	50	
IV	General Awareness	25	50	

- The Tier-I Examination will consists of Objective Type Multiple Choice Questions only. The questions will be set in English, Hindi and any language opted by the candidate in the application form, for Part-II, III & IV of Tier-I examination.
- There will be negative marking of 0.50 marks for each wrong answer.

TIER-II

Session	Subject	Number of Questions	Maximum Marks	Time allowed
Session-I	**Section I:** **Module-I:** Mathematical Abilities **Module-II:** Reasoning and General Intelligence	30 30	60 × 3 = 180	1 hour (for each section)
	Section-II: **Module-I:** English Language and Comprehension **Module-II:** General Awareness	40 20	60 × 3 = 180	
	Section-III: **Module-I:** Computer Knowledge Module	15	15 × 3 = 45	15 Minutes
Session-II	**Section-III** **Module-II:** Skill Test/Typing Test Module			
	Part A: Skill Test for DEOs			15 Minutes
	Part B: Typing Test for LDC/JSA			10 Minutes

Note—• It will be mandatory for the candidate to qualify all the sections of Tier-II. Tier-II will consist of Objective Type, Multiple Choice Questions, except for Module-II of Section-III. The questions will be set in English and Hindi except for Module-II (*i.e.,* English Language and Comprehension module) in Section-II. • There will be negative marking of 1 mark for each wrong answer in Section-I, Section-II and Module-I of Section-III. • Module-I of Section-III i.e., Computer Knowledge Test is mandatory but qualifying in nature. • Skill Test/Typing Test will be of qualifying nature. • Errors in the Skill Test will be calculated up to 2 decimal places.

Previous Years' Paper

SSC—Combined Higher Secondary Level (CHSL : 10 + 2)

Data Entry Operator (DEO)/ Lower Division Clerk (LDC)/ Junior Secretarial Assistant (JSA)

Tier-I, Recruitment Exam-2025

(Exam held on 13-11-2025)

English Language

1. Identify the part of the sentence that contains a grammatical error.
The new manager/is responsible of/the entire marketing/campaign.
A. The new manager
B. is responsible of
C. the entire marketing
D. campaign

2. Fill in the blank with the most appropriate phrase:
As the deadline approached, the team was working ______ to finalize the report.
A. under wraps
B. around the corner
C. against the clock
D. in high spirits

3. Select the **most** appropriate synonym of the word:
Hapless
A. Fortunate B. Lucky
C. Unlucky D. Successful

4. Fill in the blank with the most appropriate idiom :
She took the criticism ______ and used it to improve her performance.
A. at face value
B. with a grain of salt
C. in stride
D. out of context

5. Which of the following sentences uses the word "saw" with the **same meaning** as in the following sentence?
"He saw the car coming too late"
A. She used a hand saw to cut the plank in half.
B. We needed a power saw to cut through the thick branch.
C. I saw a beautiful sunset last night.
D. The lumberjack's saw was very loud.

Directions (Qs.No. 6-10): *Read the following passage and answer the questions based on it :*

Online purchasing, which combines unmatched ease with a distinct set of disadvantages, has completely changed how consumers behave. Accessibility is its main benefit; customers may explore and buy things from almost anywhere at any time, and there is frequently a greater selection than in physical stores. Important lures include competitive pricing, made possible by internet retailer' reduced overhead, and the simplicity of comparing prices from several providers. However, there are significant drawbacks to online shopping's virtual nature. Delivery-related discontent may result from the inability to personally inspect things before purchase. Concerns over shipping delays, unstated expenses, and the effects of packaging and transportation on the environment are becoming more widespread. Additionally, the individualised customer service experience may be weakened by a lack of human interaction.

6. What is the primary advantage of online purchasing according to the text?
- A. It allows for in-person inspection of products
- B. It provides easy access to a wider selection of items from anywhere at any time
- C. It offers higher prices than physical stores
- D. It eliminates the need for shipping

7. What is one of the key benefits of online shopping in terms of pricing?
- A. Higher prices due to store overhead costs
- B. Competitive pricing due to lower overhead costs for online retailers
- C. Fixed prices with no possibility of comparison
- D. Prices that remain constant across all platforms

8. What is a significant drawback of online shopping mentioned in the text?
- A. Lack of variety in products
- B. The inability to inspect products before purchasing
- C. Higher prices for shipping
- D. Limited access to the internet

9. What are some growing concerns related to the environmental impact of online shopping?
- A. Increased store visits
- B. Concerns over shipping delays
- C. Higher fuel consumption from physical stores
- D. Limited product availability

10. What aspect of the customer experience may be weakened by online shopping?
- A. The ability to compare prices easily

B. Personalized customer service due to lack of human interaction

C. The variety of products available

D. Convenience of purchasing from anywhere

11. Choose the correctly spelt word:

A. Beaurocrat

B. Burocrat

C. Bureaucrat

D. Buroucrat

12. Choose the correctly spelt word:

A. Iresistible

B. Irresistable

C. Irresistible

D. Irresistble

13. Choose the correct meaning of the idiom:

As thick as thieves

A. Very close and loyal

B. Very secretive

C. Very sneaky

D. Very quiet

14. Choose the correct one-word substitute for:

A person who studies birds

A. Biologist B. Ornithologist

C. Ecologist D. Zoologist

15. Select the most appropriate antonym of the word:

Felicity

A. Misery B. Despair

C. Sorrow D. Anger

16. Select the most appropriate antonym of the word:

Repudiate

A. Reject B. Disown

C. Deny D. Accept

17. Choose the correct one-word substitute for:

A place where records and documents are stored

A. Archive B. Library

C. Storage D. Depository

18. Change the following sentence into the Active form.

Let the emergency meeting be convened at 10 AM without delay.

A. Convene the emergency meeting at 10 AM without delay.

B. The emergency meeting should be convened at 10 AM without delay.

C. They will convene the emergency meeting at 10 AM without delay.

D. An emergency meeting is convened at 10 AM without delay.

19. Select the option that expresses the given sentence in indirect voice.

The company CEO announced, "We will not be able to meet the deadline for this quarter, which is a great disappointment for all of us, but we will have to work harder next time."

A. The company CEO announced that they will not be able to meet the deadline for this quarter, which is a great disappointment for all of us, but that they will have to work harder next time.

B. The company CEO announced that they would not be able to meet the deadline for this quarter, which was a great disappointment for all of them, but that they would have to work harder the next time.

C. The company CEO announced that they would not be able to meet the deadline for that quarter, which was a great disappointment for all of them, but that they would have to work harder next time.

D. The company CEO announced that they would not be able to meet the deadline for that quarter, which was a great disappointment for all of them, but that they would have to work harder the next time.

20. Choose the most suitable option to replace the highlighted part of the sentence:

I am not one of these people who <u>believes</u> in rumours.

A. believer B. believe

C. believing D. to believe

21. Choose the most suitable option to replace the highlighted part of the sentence :

The organized sellers with the ability to control their price-lines, or pass on any increase in cost to customers, <u>should be able to maintain or improve profit margin</u>.

A. should be able to maintain or improve profit margins

B. will be able to maintains or improve profit margin

C. will be able to maintain or improves profit margin

D. will be abled to maintain or improve profit margin

22. Choose the correct passive voice transformation of the sentence:

The students are completing their assignments.

A. The assignments are being completed by the students.

B. The assignments are completed by the students.

C. The assignments were completed by the students.

D. The assignments have been completed by the students.

23. Select the option that expresses the given sentence in direct voice.

The captain explained that the ship had been sailing for three weeks and they had faced a severe storm the previous night.

A. The captain explained, "The ship was sailing for three weeks, and we faced as severe storm last night."
B. The captain explained, "The ship has been sailing for three weeks, and we had faced a severe storm last night."
C. The captain explained, "The ship has been sailing for three weeks, and we faced a severe storm last night."
D. The captain explained, "The ship had been sailing for three weeks, and we faced a severe storm last night."

24. Rearrange the following sentence parts to form a meaningful and grammatically correct paragraph:

P. But the fleet was caught off guard as a sudden, strong storm blew in from the sea.
Q. Confident in their strategy to blockade the enemy port, the admiral gave the order for the ships to proceed.
R. The conflict became a desperate struggle for survival due to the unanticipated weather.
S. Without firing a shot, they were to cut off supplies and compel a surrender.

A. P, S, Q, R
B. S, R, P, Q
C. Q, S, P, R
D. R, S, P, Q

25. Rearrange the following sentence parts to form a meaningful and grammatically correct paragraph:

P. However, as the Empire grew, a series of internal and external pressures began to mount.
Q. The Roman Empire was the most powerful civilisation in history at its height.
R. Its gradual decline was caused by a confluence of political corruption, military overstretch, and economic instability.
S. Its vast network of roads, laws, and military outposts brought a period of peace and prosperity.

A. R, S, P, Q
B. P, S, Q, R
C. R, P, S, Q
D. Q, S, P, R

General Intelligence

26. If HARMONY is coded as KDUPRQB, then what would BALANCE be?

A. EDODQFH
B. EDLDQFH
C. EDLDQGI
D. EDFDRFH

27. In a particular code language, if ARCHAEOLOGICAL is coded as BSDIBFPMPHJDBM and

ANTHROPOLOGICAL is coded as BOUISPQPMPHJDBM, then what is the code for PSYCHOLOGICAL?

A. QTZDIPMPHJDBM
B. QSZDIPMPHJDBM
C. QTZDIPMPHJCBM
D. QTZDIPMPGJDBM

28. In a specific coding system, if MATHEMATICS is coded as NBUIFNBUJDT and GEOGRAPHY is coded as HFPHSBQUIZ, then what is the code for CHEMISTRY?

A. DIFNJTUSZ
B. DIFNJTVRZ
C. DIFNJTRSZ
D. DIFNJTTRZ

29. Here some problem or solution of the problem is given in the statement you have to choose the appropriate logical deduction for given statement.

Statement :

Advancements in surveillance technology have improved national security and crime prevention. However, concerns about mass surveillance and privacy violations have sparked debates on ethical boundaries and government overreach. Critics demand transparent policies and public oversight.

Conclusions :

I. Surveillance technology has both benefits and risks.

II. Public oversight and clear policies are needed to balance privacy and security.

III. Surveillance should be completely banned to protect individual freedom.

Which conclusion necessarily follows?

A. Only I follows
B. I and II follow
C. Only III follows
D. All follow

30. Each item describes a situation and is followed by four possible responses. Indicate the response you find most appropriate. Choose only one response for each item. The responses will be evaluated based on the level of appropriateness for the given situation.

A student has only 3 days left before an exam. She hasn't completed half the syllabus. What's the best strategy?

A. Watch motivational videos to calm nerves
B. Sleep less and cover all topics
C. Focus on high-weightage and familiar topics
D. Give up and skip the exam

31. In this type of questions, question is provided with substitutes for various mathematical symbols, followed by a question involving calculation of an expression or choosing the correct/incorrect equation. You have to put the real signs in the given equation and then solve the questions as required.

If '^' stands for '×', '%' stands for '–', '&' stands for '÷', '*' stands for '+', then find the value of : 13%9*12%14 = ?

A. 5 B. 2
C. 3 D. 1

32. In this type of questions, question is provided with substitutes for various mathematical symbols, followed by a question involving calculation of an expression or choosing the correct/incorrect equation. You have to put the real signs in the given equation and then solve the questions as required.

If '–' stands for '÷', '?' stands for '+', '%' stands for '–', '$' stands for '×', then find the value of : 4%13?9$14 = ?

A. 117 B. 114
C. 118 D. 116

33. Your colleague shares personal problems affecting their work. You are not their manager. Best social intelligence response?

A. Spread their issues as office gossip to get sympathy
B. Offer to help them prioritize tasks and suggest they talk to HR or supervisor
C. Tell them to leave work at home
D. Ignore since it's not your concern

34. In a line of 40 children, Sita is 15th from the beginning and Rita is 18th from the end. How many children are there between. Sita and Rita?

A. 6 B. 7
C. 8 D. 9

35. In a temple, 25 oil lamps are lit in a row. What is the position of the 9th lamp from left when counted from the right?

A. 16th B. 17th
C. 18th D. 15th

36. In each question below is given a statement followed by two courses of action numbered I and II. You have to assume everything in the statement to be true and on the basis of the information given in the statement, decide which of the suggested courses of action logically follow(s) for pursuing.

Statement:

A high number of accidents are occurring at a railway crossing due to lack of proper signalling systems.

Course of action:

I. Install automated signalling systems at the crossing immediately.
II. Ban train services on that route permanently.

A. Only I follows
B. Only II follows
C. Both follow
D. Either I or II follows

37. Each question given below consists of a statement, followed by two arguments numbered

I and II. You have to decide which of the arguments is a 'strong' argument and which is a 'weak' argument.

Statement:

Should voting be made compulsory?

Argument:

I. Yes, it ensures better representation.

II. No, people should have freedom of choice.

A. Only I is strong
B. Only II is strong
C. Both I and II are strong
D. Neither I nor II is strong

38. Few of the letters are given followed by a question mark (?) these letters are following a specific pattern you have to give the correct option which can replace question mark.

What comes next: C, G, L, R, ?

A. Y B. Z
C. A D. B

39. Few of the letters are given followed by a question mark (?) these letters are following a specific pattern you have to give the correct option which can replace question mark.

In the sequence U, Q, M, I, ?

A. D B. E
C. F D. G

40. In this question some conditions or circumstances is provided to you, you have to make logical judgement according to mentioned circumstances and mark the correct judgement for question.

A municipal council must allocate a limited budget for infrastructure. The council has the choice to repair an old bridge, build a new park, improve water supply, or enhance local transportation. What action is most justified if the town has recently faced water shortages?

A. Repair the old bridge
B. Build a new park
C. Improve the water supply
D. Enhance local transportation

41. Four meaningful words are given in the options you have to check that which of the following words cannot be formed from the letters.

'MANAGEMENT'

A. AGENT B. MEANT
C. MANGE D. MANTLE

42. In this type of questions, question is provided with some issues/disputes/problem, followed by few methods to resolve the problem in statement choosing the appropriate problem solving method that can be implemented.

An employee claims a colleague took credit for his idea. HR must resolve. Best step?

A. Investigate by collecting evidence from both sides
B. Ignore to avoid conflict

C. Promote the claimant to appease

D. Fire the colleague immediately

43. In each of the following questions, there is a certain relationship between two given letter pairs on one side of (::) and pair is given on another side of (::) where another pair is to be found from the given alternatives, having the same relationship with this pair as the pairs of the given pair bear. Choose the best alternative.

UV : ST :: QR : ?

A. OO B. OP
C. ON D. PP

44. In each of the following questions, there is a certain relationship between two given letters pairs on one side of (::) and pair is given on another side of (::) where another pair is to be found from the given alternatives, having the same relationship with this pair as the pairs of the given pair bear. Choose the best alternative.

AE : EI :: IO : ?

A. OS B. OU
C. IU D. OA

45. Find the next element that replace the ? Logically

56, 71, 88, 107, ?

A. 136 B. 123
C. 128 D. 143

46. Find the next element that replace the ? Logically

0, 7, 26, 63, ?

A. 131 B. 123
C. 124 D. 140

47. Find the next element that replace the ? Logically

2, 14, 38, 86, ?

A. 182 B. 191
C. 194 D. 175

48. In three of the following pairs are same by same pattern except one pair. Which pair does not follow this pattern?

A. 18 : 27 B. 36 : 45
C. 54 : 63 D. 72 : 80

49. Select the option that represents the correct order of the given words as they would appear in an English dictionary.

1. Circulation
2. Circumference
3. Circumscribed
4. Circumstance
5. Circumstantial

A. 1, 2, 3, 4, 5
B. 2, 3, 1, 4, 5
C. 1, 2, 4, 3, 5
D. 2, 1, 3, 4, 5

50. Select the option that represents the correct order of the given words as they would appear in an English dictionary.

1. Memory 2. Method
3. Middle 4. Modern
5. Moment 6. Monday

A. 1, 2, 3, 4, 5, 6
B. 1, 3, 2, 4, 5, 6
C. 1, 2, 3, 4, 6, 5
D. 1, 3, 2, 4, 6, 5

Quantitative Aptitude

51. A, B and C enter into a partnership. A invests ₹ 80,000, B invests ₹ 60,000, and C invests ₹ 40,000. After 6 month's B increases his capital by 25%, while C decreases his capital by 10%. At the end of 1 year, the total profit is ₹ 1,20,000. What is C's share in the profit?

A. ₹ 20,000 B. ₹ 24,582
C. ₹ 30,000 D. ₹ 35,789

52. If $\sin A = \frac{7}{25}$ and $\cos B = \frac{24}{25}$, find $\sin A \cos B + \cos A \sin B$:

A. $\frac{168}{625}$ B. $\frac{13}{25}$
C. $\frac{336}{625}$ D. $\frac{24}{25}$

53. A trader buys 50 kg of rice at ₹ 50 per kg and 30 kg of a different variety at ₹ 60 per kg. He mixes the two varieties and sells the entire mixture at ₹ 55 per kg. What is his total profit or loss?

A. ₹ 100 profit
B. ₹ 100 loss
C. ₹ 200 profit
D. ₹ 200 loss

54. Two numbers are respectively 20% less and 30% more than a third number. What is the ratio of the two numbers?

A. 8 : 13 B. 2 : 3
C. 4 : 5 D. 7 : 9

55. The average of 8 numbers is 45. If each of the first 4 numbers is increased by 5 and each of the last 4 numbers is decreased by 3, what will be the new average?

A. 45 B. 47
C. 46 D. 48

56. The HCF of $24 \times 3^2 \times 5^3 \times 7$ and $23 \times 5 \times 7 \times 11$ is:

A. 23 B. 5
C. 7 D. 35

57. The population of a town increases by 20% in the first year, decreases by 10% in the second year, and again increases by 25% in the third year. If the population at the beginning was 40,000, what will it be after 3 years?

A. 24,000 B. 43,200
C. 48,000 D. 54,000

58. A thief escapes from a bank at 10:00 AM at a speed of 20 km/h. A police car starts chasing him at 10:30 AM at a speed of 30 km/h. At what time will the police car catch the thief?

A. 11:00 AM
B. 11:30 AM
C. 12:00 PM
D. 12:30 PM

59. A can do a work in 15 days, B in 30 days. They start together but A leaves after 5 days. In how many more days will B complete the remaining work?

A. 15 days B. 6 days
C. 7 days D. 8 days

60. A jeweller marks a necklace at 30% above its cost price. She gives a cash discount of ₹ 150 on the marked price. If the necklace is sold for ₹ 1800 and she earns a profit of 20%, what is the cost price of the necklace?

A. ₹ 1500
B. ₹ 1200
C. ₹ 1450
D. ₹ 1600

61. A sum of money doubles itself in 8 years at a certain rate of simple interest. In how many years will it become five times itself at the same rate?

A. 16 years B. 24 years
C. 32 years D. 40 years

62. Rohan invests a portion of a total sum of ₹ P in Scheme A for 4 years and the remaining amount in Scheme B for 5 years. Scheme A offers a simple interest rate of r% per annum, while Scheme B offers a simple interest rate of $(r+2)\%$ per annum. The amount invested in Scheme A is 50% more than the amount invested in Scheme B. If the total interest earned from both schemes is ₹ 1,920 and the amount invested in Scheme A is ₹ 2,400, what is the simple interest rate r?

A. 10% B. 15%
C. 5% D. 12%

63. What is the value of $a^2 + b^2 + c^2$ if $a + b + c = 12$ and $ab + bc + ca = 40$?

A. 84 B. 64
C. 44 D. 144

64. Which of the following numbers can possibly be a perfect square?

A. 245982
B. 496838
C. 178343
D. 571536

65. A shopkeeper mixes 4 litres of a milk solution containing 25% fat with 6 liters of another milk solution containing 40% fat. What is the fat percentage in the final mixture?

A. 30% B. 32%
C. 34% D. 35%

66. If the radius of a sphere is increased by 20 per cent, by what percentage will its volume increase?

A. 76.6 B. 60.5
C. 72.8 D. 78.4

67. The total surface area of a solid hemisphere is 300π cm^2. Find its volume.

A. 500π cm^3

B. 125π cm^3

C. $\frac{333}{2}\pi$ cm^3

D. $\frac{2000}{3}\pi$ cm^3

68. Which of the following is in ascending order?

A. 1/2, 0.55, 3/5, 0.625

B. 1/2, 3/5, 0.55, 0.625

C. 0.55, 1/2, 0.625, 3/5

D. 1/2, 0.55, 0.625, 3/5

69. The area of a circle is 144π cm^2. What is the length of the circumference of the circle?

A. 82.5 cm

B. 19.8 cm

C. 22.5 cm

D. 75.4 cm

70. If $27^3 \div 3^5 = 3^n$, find n.

A. 3 B. 6

C. 5 D. 4

71. If $x - y = 8$ and $xy = 5$, what is the value of $x^3 - y^3 + 8(x + y)^2$.

A. 1256 B. 1304

C. 3456 D. 3245

72. Simplify : $\dfrac{(\sin(x)+\cos(x))^2}{1+\sin(x)\cos(x)}$

A. $\dfrac{6+5\sin(x)\cos(x)}{1+\sin(x)\cos(x)}$

B. $\dfrac{7+8\sin(x)\cos(x)}{3+\sin(x)\cos(x)}$

C. $\dfrac{9+2\sin(x)\cos(x)}{7+\sin(x)\cos(x)}$

D. $\dfrac{1+2\sin(x)\cos(x)}{1+\sin(x)\cos(x)}$

73. If $\sin A = \frac{5}{13}$, find tanA.

A. $\frac{7}{13}$ B. $\frac{5}{12}$

C. $\frac{8}{15}$ D. $\frac{9}{13}$

74. In a right triangle ABC, right-angled at B, if $\tan A = \frac{1}{\sqrt{3}}$, what is the value of $2\sin A \cos A$?

A. $\frac{\sqrt{3}}{2}$

B. $\frac{\sqrt{3}}{5}$

C. $\frac{\sqrt{3}}{7}$

D. $\frac{\sqrt{3}}{8}$

75. The equation of a line is $5x - 2y = 10$. What is the slope of a line perpendicular to this line?

A. –8 B. $\frac{-2}{5}$

C. $\frac{6}{7}$ D. 7

General Awareness

76. Who was the first woman Director-General of the Archaeological Survey of India?
A. Kamala Das
B. Debala Mitra
C. Anna Chandy
D. Chitra Ramkrishna

77. Who took oath as the Chief Minister of Andhra Pradesh in June 2024?
A. Revanth Reddy
B. N. Chandrababu Naidu
C. Mohan Yadav
D. Vishnu Deo Sai

78. In February 2025, who launched a policy report titled 'Expanding Quality Higher Education through States and State Public Universities'?
A. NITI Aayog
B. Ministry of Education
C. NGO Pratham
D. Azad Foundation

79. Which ministry launched the Swavalambini initiative in March 2025 to promote women entrepreneurship in India?
A. Ministry of Women and Child Development
B. Ministry of Rural Development
C. Ministry of Commerce and industry
D. Ministry of Skill Development and Entrepreneurship

80. In India, which of the following is a report published under **MoSPI?**
I. Periodic Labour Force Survey
II. Monthly infrastructure Performance Review Report
A. Only I
B. Only II
C. Both I and II
D. Neither I nor II

81. The Sudasari Great Indian Bustard Breeding centre is in which of the following state?
A. Rajasthan B. Tamil Nadu
C. Kerala D. Karnataka

82. Who is the author of a travel book 'From Heaven Lake: Travels Through Sinkiang and Tibet', which won the Thomas Cook Travel Book Award?
A. Sarah Joseph
B. Rohit Lal
C. Kanchana Banerjee
D. Vikram Seth

83. The 'Vamsi', a traditional instrument of Tamil Nadu, is a ______.
A. Flute B. Drum
C. Sarod D. Manjira

84. 'Swang' dance is performed in which of the following Indian state of India?
A. Goa B. Kerala
C. Karnataka D. Uttar Pradesh

85. In the context of Indian satellite, the INSAT is used for which of the following purpose?
I. Television broadcasting
II. Weather Forecasting

A. Only I
B. Only II
C. Both I and II
D. Neither I nor II

86. Newton's third law of motion states that _____.
A. For every action, there is an equal and opposite reaction
B. For every action, the reaction is opposite but greater in magnitude
C. The rate of change of momentum of an object is proportional to the applied unbalanced force in the direction of force
D. An object in motion remains in motion unless acted upon by a force

87. What is the formula for pressure?
A. Pressure = force/area
B. Pressure = force × area
C. Pressure = area/force
D. Pressure = (force × force)/area

88. The uncrewed Gaganyaan-G1 mission, scheduled for December 2025, will carry a female-looking half-humanoid robot to test human functions and onboard systems. What is the name of this robot?
A. Manavi B. Vyommitra
C. Bumika D. Rokshak

89. In August 2025, which organisation received an order worth ₹ 62000 crores for 97 LCA Mk1A fighter jets from the Indian government?
A. HAL B. AWE Indi
C. DRDO D. AVANI

90. In 1722, Sawai Raja Jai Singh was given the governorship of which of the following regions?
A. Bengal B. Awadh
C. Agra D. Odisha

91. Which of the following tax are imposed on goods imported into and exported out of India?
A. Excise duty
B. Customs duty
C. Wealth tax
D. Estate duty

92. The target of National Logistics Policy is to improve India's Logistics performance index ranking to among top 25 countries by ________.
A. 2027 B. 2030
C. 2040 D. 2047

93. In which year was the Special Economic Zones (SEZs) policy was launched in India?
A. 1998 B. 2002
C. 1999 D. 2000

94. An Indian state can be divided or its boundary altered by which of the following?
A. The State Legislature
B. Parliament
C. President
D. Supreme Court

95. Which of the following is NOT constitute the hinterland of Marmagao port?
A. Karnataka
B. Goa
C. Southern Maharashtra
D. Himachal Pradesh

96. What is a capital goods industry?
A. Industry that deals in external commercial borrowings.
B. Industry that exports food products.
C. Industry that process raw agricultural product.
D. Industry producing machines and tools.

97. In the context of trade policy tools, which of the following is considered as tariff measure?
I. Export taxes
II. Import taxes
A. Only I
B. Only II
C. Both I and II
D. Neither I nor II

98. As of February 2025, Scheduled Tribe (ST) individuals comprising _______ of the total population in India.
A. 8.6% B. 5.5%
C. 9.8% D. 12.2%

99. What is the process called when organisms acquire oxygen from outside the body to break down food sources?
A. Respiration
B. Digestion
C. Photosynthesis
D. Fermentation

100. The 'Charaksamhita' is a treatise on which of the following subjects?
A. Medicine B. Astronomy
C. Architecture D. Mathematics

ANSWERS

1	2	3	4	5	6	7	8	9	10
B	C	C	C	C	B	B	B	B	B
11	**12**	**13**	**14**	**15**	**16**	**17**	**18**	**19**	**20**
C	C	A	B	A	D	A	A	D	B
21	**22**	**23**	**24**	**25**	**26**	**27**	**28**	**29**	**30**
A	A	C	C	D	A	A	A	B	C
31	**32**	**33**	**34**	**35**	**36**	**37**	**38**	**39**	**40**
B	A	B	B	B	A	C	A	B	C
41	**42**	**43**	**44**	**45**	**46**	**47**	**48**	**49**	**50**
D	A	B	B	C	C	A	D	A	A
51	**52**	**53**	**54**	**55**	**56**	**57**	**58**	**59**	**60**
B	C	A	A	C	D	D	B	A	A
61	**62**	**63**	**64**	**65**	**66**	**67**	**68**	**69**	**70**
C	A	B	D	C	C	D	A	D	D
71	**72**	**73**	**74**	**75**	**76**	**77**	**78**	**79**	**80**
B	D	B	A	B	B	B	A	D	C
81	**82**	**83**	**84**	**85**	**86**	**87**	**88**	**89**	**90**
A	D	A	D	C	A	A	B	A	C
91	**92**	**93**	**94**	**95**	**96**	**97**	**98**	**99**	**100**
B	B	D	B	D	D	C	A	A	A

Explanatory Answers

1. The error is the preposition used after "responsible." Standard usage is "responsible for" something, not "responsible of." So it should read: "The new manager is responsible for the entire marketing campaign."
2. The phrase "against the clock" means working with great urgency because time is limited. Since the sentence mentions that the deadline was approaching, it implies that the team was working quickly to finish before time ran out. The other options do not express urgency related to time pressure, so "against the clock" is the most appropriate choice.
3. "Hapless" means unfortunate, unlucky, or ill-fated. Among the options, Unlucky matches the meaning most accurately.
4. The idiom "take something in stride" means to accept criticism or difficulty calmly and handle it well. The sentence means she accepted the criticism positively and used it to improve.
5. In "He saw the car coming too late," "saw" means noticed/observed with the eyes. The matching usage is "I saw a beautiful sunset last night," where "saw" also means observed visually.
6. The passage clearly states that the main benefit of online purchasing is its accessibility, allowing customers to explore and buy products from almost anywhere at any time, often with a wider selection than physical stores.
7. The text explains that online retailers often have reduced overhead costs compared to physical stores, which enables them to offer competitive pricing, making this a key pricing-related advantage.
8. A major drawback highlighted in the passage is that customers cannot personally inspect products before buying them, which can lead to dissatisfaction related to delivery and product quality.
9. The passage mentions growing concerns linked to online shopping such as shipping delays, unstated expenses, and environmental effects of packaging and transportation, making shipping delays a valid concern mentioned in the text.
10. The passage notes that the absence of direct human interaction in online shopping can weaken the individualized customer service experience, making this the correct choice.
11. Among the given options, "Bureaucrat" is the only word spelled correctly. The others contain incorrect letter arrangements that do not conform to standard English spelling.
12. The correct spelling requires double *r* and double *s*, followed by -ible. All other options miss or misplace essential letters, making them incorrect.
13. The idiom "as thick as thieves" means that people share a very close bond, trust each other deeply, and are strongly loyal to one another. It does not primarily refer to secrecy, sneakiness, or silence.
14. An ornithologist is a specialist who studies birds. The other options refer to broader or different fields of biological study and therefore do not precisely match the definition.

15. Felicity means happiness or great joy. The most direct and accurate opposite among the given options is misery, which denotes extreme unhappiness.

16. The verb repudiate means to reject, deny, or refuse to accept something. Therefore, its most appropriate antonym is accept, which conveys the opposite sense of agreeing to or approving something.

17. An archive is specifically a place where historical records, documents, and official files are systematically stored and preserved. The other options are either broader or not precise one-word substitutes in this context.

18. The given sentence is in passive form using "Let ... be convened." Converting it into active voice requires a direct imperative form, which is correctly achieved by "Convene the emergency meeting at 10 AM without delay."

19. In indirect speech, future tense "will" changes to "would," "this quarter" changes to "that quarter," and present tense "is" changes to "was." Pronoun "us" changes to "them," and "next time" appropriately becomes "the next time." Option D correctly applies all these necessary changes.

20. The relative clause "who believes in rumours" refers to people, which is plural. Therefore, the verb must also be plural. Replacing the highlighted part with "believe" maintains grammatical agreement and correctness.

21. The noun "profit margin" in this context refers to the margins of organized sellers in general, so it should be in the plural form "profit margins." Option A corrects this by using the proper plural noun and keeps the verb structure grammatically correct. The other options contain verb form errors ("maintains," "improves") or incorrect usage ("abled"), making them grammatically unsuitable.

22. The active sentence is in the present continuous tense ("are completing"), so the correct passive transformation must also be in the present continuous form, which is accurately expressed by "are being completed."

23. In converting indirect to direct speech, past perfect continuous ("had been sailing") becomes present perfect continuous ("has been sailing"), and "the previous night" correctly changes to "last night." This option maintains correct tense and meaning.

24. The logical flow begins with the admiral's decision (Q), followed by the planned strategy (S). Then comes the unexpected storm (P), and finally the resulting struggle for survival (R), making this the most coherent sequence.

25. The paragraph logically starts with the Roman Empire at its height (Q), followed by its achievements and prosperity (S). Then the shift introduced by "However" signals rising pressures (P), concluding with the causes of its decline (R).

26. Given,

H	A	R	M	O	N	Y
+3↓	+3↓	+3↓	+3↓	+3↓	+3↓	+3↓
K	D	U	P	R	Q	B

Similarly,

B	A	L	A	N	C	E
+3↓	+3↓	+3↓	+3↓	+3↓	+3↓	+3↓
E	D	O	D	Q	F	H

Hence, the coded form is EDODQFH.

27. In ARCHAEOLOGICAL → BSDIBFPMPHJDBM, every letter

is shifted +1 (A→B, R→S, C→D, ..., L→M).

The same +1 rule also matches ANTHROPOLOGICAL → BOUISPQPMPHJDBM.

Therefore, PSYCHOLOGICAL coded with +1 becomes: P→Q, S→T, Y→Z, C→D, H→I, O→P, L→M, O→P, G→H, I→J, C→D, A→B, L→M = QTZDIPMPHJDBM.

28. MATHEMATICS → NBUIFNBUJDT shows a consistent +1 shift for each letter (M→N, A→B, T→U, ..., S→T).

GEOGRAPHY → HFPHSBQUIZ confirms the same +1 pattern (G→H, E→F, ..., Y→Z).

So CHEMISTRY becomes C→D, H→I, E→F, M→N, I→J, S→T, T→U, R→S, Y→Z = DIFNJTUSZ.

29. The statement clearly says surveillance improves security/crime prevention but also raises privacy/ethical concerns, so I necessarily follows (both benefits and risks exist). It also states critics demand transparent policies and public oversight, so II necessarily follows (need oversight and clear rules to balance). III does not follow because the passage discusses regulation and debate, not a complete ban.

30. With only 3 days left and half the syllabus pending, the most appropriate approach is smart prioritization rather than trying to do everything. High-weightage and familiar areas give the best score-return per hour and reduce panic. This also leaves some time for quick revision and practice, which is crucial near an exam.

31. Replace the symbols as given: % → –, * → +.

So, 13 % 9 * 12 % 14

= 13 – 9 + 12 – 14

= 25 – 23 = 2

32. Replace the symbols as given: % → –, ? → +, $ → ×.

So, 4 % 13 ? 9 $ 14

= 4 – 13 + 9 × 14

= 4 – 13 + 126

= 130 – 13

= 117

33. This response shows empathy without gossiping, gives practical support to manage work impact, and guides them to the right formal support channel (HR/supervisor) since you are not their manager.

34. Sita is 15th from the beginning. Rita is 18th from the end, so from the beginning Rita's position is:

40 – 18 + 1 = 23.

Children between them:

23 – 15 – 1 = 7.

35. Total lamps = 25.

The 9th lamp from the left will be from the right:

25 – 9 + 1 = 17.

36. The problem stated is accidents due to lack of proper signalling. Installing automated signalling directly addresses the cause and is a practical preventive measure, so Course I logically follows. Permanently banning train services is an extreme step, not required by the statement, and it does not logically follow as the necessary action when the issue can be solved through safety upgrades.

37. Argument I is strong because compulsory voting can increase participation and lead to better representation of the population in election outcomes. Argument II is also strong because voting involves individual liberty, and forcing it can be seen as violating freedom of choice. Both arguments are relevant, logical, and directly address the question.

38. Given,

C G L R [Y]

+4 +5 +6 +7

Hence, next term is Y.

39. Given,

U Q M I [E]

−4 −4 −4 −4

Hence, next term is E.

40. Since the town has recently faced water shortages, the most justified budget allocation is the one that addresses the immediate essential need affecting health and daily life. Improving water supply directly solves the pressing shortage problem, making it the most logical and justified choice among the options.

41. From "MANAGEMENT", letter counts are: M(2), A(2), N(2), G(1), E(2), T(1). There is no L available.

So MANTLE cannot be formed because it requires the letter L, which is absent.

The other words (AGENT, MEANT, MANGE) can be formed using available letters within the counts.

42. This is a workplace dispute involving credit/ownership of an idea, so HR should follow a fair process: hear both parties, check e-mails/meeting notes/witnesses, and then decide appropriately. Ignoring, promoting to appease, or firing immediately are unjustified and can worsen conflict or create unfairness.

43. UV → ST means each letter is shifted back by 2 (U→S, V→T).

Apply the same to QR: Q→O, R→P. So the required pair is OP.

44. AE → EI shows a forward shift of +4 for each letter (A→E, E→I). Apply the same to IO: I→M and O→S, giving MS. Since MS is not present, check the vowel-sequence relationship instead: AE are consecutive vowels (A, E) and become the next two consecutive vowels (E, I). Similarly IO are consecutive vowels (I, O) and should become the next two consecutive vowels (O, U). Hence OU fits the intended pattern.

45. The given sequence is 56, 71, 88, 107. Find the differences between consecutive terms:

$$71 - 56 = 15$$
$$88 - 71 = 17$$
$$107 - 88 = 19$$

The differences are increasing by 2 each time (15, 17, 19).

So, the next difference will be 21.

Next term = 107 + 21 = 128

Hence, the correct next element in the series is 128.

46. The pattern is $n^3 - 1$.

$1^3 - 1 = 0$,

$2^3 - 1 = 7$,

$3^3 - 1 = 26$,

$4^3 - 1 = 63$.

Next is $5^3 - 1 = 125 - 1 = 124$.

47. The pattern is:

2 14 38 86 [182]

×2+10 ×2+10 ×2+10 ×2+10

Hence, next term is 182.

48. Checking options:

A. 18 27 (+9) B. 36 45 (+9)

C. 54 63 (+9) D. 72 80 (+8)

Hence, option (D) does not follow the pattern.

49. All begin with "Circu...". After "Circu", compare next letters: Circulation (l) comes before Circum... (*m*), so 1 first.

Among "Circum...": Circumference (*f*) comes before Circums... (*s*), so 2 next.
Then among Circums...: Circumscribed (*c*) comes before Circumst... (*t*), so 3 next.
Between Circumstance and Circumstantial: the shorter base word comes first, so 4 then 5.

50. Arrange the words in strict alphabetical (dictionary) order by comparing letters from left to right.

- All words start with M.
- Next letter comparison: Memory (Me...), Method (Me...), Middle (Mi...), Modern (Mo...),
- Moment (Mo...), Monday (Mo...).
- Among Memory and Method: compare memo vs meth → *m* comes before *t*, so Memory comes first, followed by Method.
- Middle (Mi...) comes after Me... words.
- Among Modern (Mod...), Moment (Mom...), Monday (Mon...): $d < m < n$, so the order is Modern, then Moment, then Monday.

Thus, the correct dictionary order is: Memory, Method, Middle, Modern, Moment, Monday
= 1, 2, 3, 4, 5, 6.

51. A's investment for 12 months
= 80,000 × 12 = 9,60,000
B's investment
First 6 months:
60,000 × 6 = 3,60,000
Next 6 months (25% increase):
60,000 + 25% of 60,000 = 75,000
75,000 × 6 = 4,50,000
Total for B
= 3,60,000 + 4,50,000
= 8,10,000
C's investment
First 6 months:
40,000 × 6 = 2,40,000
Next 6 months (10% decrease):
40,000 – 10% of 40,000 = 36,000
36,000 × 6 = 2,16,000
Total for C = 2,40,000 + 2,16,000
= 4,56,000
Capital ratio
9,60,000 : 8,10,000 : 4,56,000
= 160 : 135 : 76
Total ratio = 160 + 135 + 76
= 371
C's share
= 1,20,000 × 76/371
= 24,582 (approx.)

52. $\sin A = \frac{7}{25} \Rightarrow \cos A = \frac{24}{25}$

$\cos B = \frac{24}{25} \Rightarrow \sin B = \frac{7}{25}$

$\sin A \cos B + \cos A \sin B$

$= \frac{7}{25} \cdot \frac{24}{25} + \frac{24}{25} \cdot \frac{7}{25}$

$= 2 \times \frac{168}{625} = \frac{336}{625}$

53. Cost price
50 × 50 = 2,500
30 × 60 = 1,800
Total CP = 2,500 + 1,800
= 4,300
Total quantity
50 + 30 = 80 kg
Selling price
80 × 55 = 4,400
Profit
4,400 – 4,300 = 100

54. Let the third number = x
First number = 80% of x = $0.8x$
Second number = 130% of x = $1.3x$
Ratio 0.8x : 1.3x
= 0.8 : 1.3 = 8/10 : 13/10
= 8 : 13

55. Original sum
8 × 45 = 360
Increase in first 4 numbers
4 × 5 = 20
Decrease in last 4 numbers
4 × 3 = 12
New sum
360 + 20 – 12 = 368
New average
368/8 = 46

56. **Step 1:** Prime factorisation

$24 = 2^3 \times 3$

So first number:

$24 \times 3^2 \times 5^3 \times 7$

$= (2^3 \times 3) \times 3^2 \times 5^3 \times 7$

$= 2^3 \times 3^3 \times 5^3 \times 7$

Second number:

$23 \times 5 \times 7 \times 11$

(23 and 11 are prime numbers.)

Step 2: Common prime factors

Compare:

$2^3 \times 3^3 \times 5^3 \times 7$

$23 \times 5 \times 7 \times 11$

Common primes are: 5 and 7

Step 3: Take lowest powers

$5^{\min(3,1)} = 5$

$7^{\min(1,1)} = 7$

$HCF = 5 \times 7 = 35$

57. $40{,}000 \times 1.20 = 48{,}000$

$48{,}000 \times 0.90 = 43{,}200$

$43{,}200 \times 1.25 = 54{,}000$

58. Head start time

10:30 – 10:00 = 0.5 h

Head start distance

$20 \times 0.5 = 10$ km

Relative speed

30 – 20 = 10 km/h

Catch time after 10:30

$$\frac{10}{10} = 1 \text{ h}$$

10:30 + 1 h = 11:30 AM

59. Rate of A $= \dfrac{1}{15}$

Rate of B $= \dfrac{1}{30}$

Work done in 5 days together

$$5\left(\frac{1}{15}+\frac{1}{30}\right) = 5\left(\frac{2}{30}+\frac{1}{30}\right)$$

$$= 5\left(\frac{3}{30}\right) = 5\left(\frac{1}{10}\right) = \frac{1}{2}$$

Remaining work

$$1-\frac{1}{2} = \frac{1}{2}$$

Time for B:

$$\frac{1/2}{1/30} = 15$$

60. $1800 = CP \times 1.20$

$$CP = \frac{1800}{1.20} = 1500$$

61. SI in 8 years

= P(because P + SI = 2P)

For 5P, SI = 5P – P = 4P

SI in 8 years ⇒ 4P

When SI is P, time = 8 years

So, when SI is 4P,

time = 8 × 4 = 32 years

62. A = 2400, A = 1.5B

⇒ B = 2400/1.5 = 1600

$$SI_A = \frac{2400 \times r \times 4}{100} = 96r$$

$$SI_B = \frac{1600 \times (r+2) \times 5}{100}$$

$= 80(r + 2)$

$= 80r + 160$

$96r + (80r + 160) = 1920$

$176r + 160 = 1920$

$176r = 1760$

$r = 10$

63. $(a + b + c)^2$

$= a^2 + b^2 + c^2 + 2(ab + bc + ca)$

$12^2 = a^2 + b^2 + c^2 + 2(40)$

$144 = a^2 + b^2 + c^2 + 80$

$a^2 + b^2 + c^2 = 144 - 80 = 64$

64. $756^2 = 756 \times 756$

$= 756(700 + 50 + 6)$

$= 756 \cdot 700 + 756 \cdot 50 + 756 \cdot 6$

$= 529200 + 37800 + 4536$

$= 571536$

65. Fat $= 4 \times 25\% + 6 \times 40\%$

$= 4 \times 0.25 + 6 \times 0.40$

$= 1 + 2.4$

$= 3.4$

Total volume = 4 + 6 = 10

$$\text{Fat \%} = \frac{3.4}{10} \times 100 = 34\%$$

66. $V = \frac{4}{3}\pi r^3$

$r' = r + 0.20r = 1.2r$

$$\frac{V'}{V} = \frac{\frac{4}{3}\pi(1.2r)^3}{\frac{4}{3}\pi r^3} = (1.2)^3 = 1.728$$

$$\% \text{ increase} = (1.728 - 1) \times 100 = 72.8\%$$

67. The total surface area of a solid hemisphere is

$$3\pi r^2 = 300\pi$$
$$r^2 = 100$$
$$\Rightarrow \quad r = 10 \text{ cm}$$

The volume of a hemisphere is

$$V = \frac{2}{3}\pi r^3 = \frac{2}{3}\pi(10^3)$$
$$= \frac{2000}{3}\pi \text{ cm}^3$$

Thus, the required volume is $\frac{2000}{3}\pi \text{ cm}^3$

68. Convert all numbers into decimal form for proper comparison:

$$\frac{1}{2} = 0.50$$
$$0.55 = 0.55$$
$$\frac{3}{5} = 0.60$$
$$0.625 = 0.625$$

Arrange in ascending order:
$0.50 < 0.55 < 0.60 < 0.625$
Thus, the correct ascending sequence is 1/2, 0.55, 3/5, 0.625.

69. Given area of circle:

$$\pi r^2 = 144\pi$$
$$r^2 = 144$$
$$r = 12 \text{ cm}$$

Circumference formula:

$$C = 2\pi r = 2\pi(12)$$
$$= 24\pi$$

Using $\pi \approx 3.1416$:

$$C = 24 \times 3.1416$$
$$= 75.3984$$
$$\approx 75.4 \text{ cm}$$

Hence, the circumference is 75.4 cm.

70.

$$27^3 \div 3^5 = 3^n$$
$$27 = 3^3$$
$$(3^3)^3 \div 3^5 = 3^n$$
$$3^9 \div 3^5 = 3^n$$
$$3^{9-5} = 3^n$$
$$3^4 = 3^n$$
$$n = 4$$

71. Given, $x - y = 8$ and $xy = 5$.

$$(x + y)^2 = (x - y)^2 + 4xy$$
$$= 8^2 + 4(5)$$
$$= 64 + 20 = 84$$
$$x^2 + y^2 = (x + y)^2 - 2xy$$
$$= 84 - 10 = 74$$
$$x^2 + xy + y^2 = 74 + 5 = 79$$
$$x^3 - y^3 = (x-y)(x^2 + xy + y^2)$$
$$= 8 \times 79 = 632$$
$$8(x + y)^2 = 8 \times 84$$
$$= 672$$
$$x^3 - y^3 + 8(x + y)^2$$
$$= 632 + 672 = 1304.$$

72.

$$\frac{(\sin x + \cos x)^2}{1 + \sin x \cos x}$$
$$= \frac{\sin^2 x + \cos^2 x + 2\sin x \cos x}{1 + \sin x \cos x}$$
$$= \frac{1 + 2\sin x \cos x}{1 + \sin x \cos x}$$

73. $\sin A = \frac{5}{13}$

$$\cos A = \sqrt{1 - \sin^2 A}$$
$$= \sqrt{1 - \left(\frac{5}{13}\right)^2}$$
$$= \sqrt{\frac{169 - 25}{169}} = \frac{12}{13}$$

$$\tan A = \frac{\sin A}{\cos A} = \frac{\frac{5}{13}}{\frac{12}{13}} = \frac{5}{12}$$

74. $\tan A = \frac{1}{\sqrt{3}} \Rightarrow A = 30°$

$$\sin A = \frac{1}{2},\ \cos A = \frac{\sqrt{3}}{2}$$

$$2\sin A\cos A = 2\left(\frac{1}{2}\right)\left(\frac{\sqrt{3}}{2}\right) = \frac{\sqrt{3}}{2}$$

75. $5x - 2y = 10$

$$-2y = -5x + 10$$

$$y = \frac{5}{2}x - 5$$

$$\Rightarrow \quad m = \frac{5}{2}$$

$$m_{\perp} = -\frac{1}{m} = -\frac{1}{\frac{5}{2}} = -\frac{2}{5}$$

76. Debala Mitra was the first woman to serve as the Director-General of the Archaeological Survey of India. She held the position in the 1980s and is noted for her contributions to Indian archaeology and heritage conservation.

77. N. Chandrababu Naidu took oath as the Chief Minister of Andhra Pradesh in June 2024 after the Telugu Desam Party's victory in the state assembly elections.

78. The policy report titled "Expanding Quality Higher Education through States and State Public Universities" was launched in February 2025 by NITI Aayog, focusing on strengthening state-level higher education systems and public universities.

79. The Swavalambini initiative, launched in March 2025, was introduced by the Ministry of Skill Development and Entrepreneurship to promote women entrepreneurship through skill training, mentoring, and enterprise support.

80. The Periodic Labour Force Survey (PLFS) is a flagship statistical report published by the Ministry of Statistics and Programme Implementation (MoSPI), providing regular estimates on employment and unemployment indicators in India.

The Monthly Infrastructure Performance Review Report (also referred to as the Review of Infrastructure Industries) is also released under MoSPI and tracks the performance and growth trends of core infrastructure sectors such as coal, power, steel, cement, and refinery products.

Hence, both statements I and II are correct.

81. The Sudasari Great Indian Bustard Breeding Centre is located i[illegible] Rajasthan, near the Desert Nationa[illegible] Park in Jaisalmer district, whic[illegible] is a key habitat for the critical[illegible] endangered Great Indian Bustard.

82. *Travels Through Sinkiang and T*[illegible] is a well-known travel book auth[illegible] by Vikram Seth, and it won [illegible] prestigious Thomas Cook T[illegible] Book Award.

83. The Vamsi is a traditional [illegible] commonly associated with the [illegible] traditions of Tamil Nadu an[illegible] parts of South India.

84. Swang is a traditional fol[illegible] drama form mainly associ[illegible] Haryana and western Utta[illegible] Among the given optio[illegible] Pradesh is the correct an[illegible]

85. The INSAT (Indian Natio[illegible] System) is used for multi[illegible] including television bro[illegible] weather forecasting, [illegible] statements correct.

86. Newton's third law of motion states that forces in nature occur in pairs. When one object exerts a force on another, the second object simultaneously exerts a force of equal magnitude but in the opposite direction on the first object.

87. Pressure is defined as the force applied per unit area. Mathematically, it is expressed as P = F/A, meaning that for the same force, pressure increases when the area of contact decreases.

88. The half-humanoid robot Vyommitra, developed by ISRO, is designed to simulate human functions and test life-support systems during the uncrewed Gaganyaan missions, including the Gaganyaan-G1 mission scheduled for December 2025.

The order worth ₹ 62,000 crores for 97 LCA Mk1A fighter jets was ıwarded to Hindustan Aeronautics imited (HAL), which is India's emier aerospace and defence ufacturing company responsible roducing the Tejas aircraft.

2, Sawai Raja Jai Singh II, r of Jaipur and a noted ıer-administrator, was the governor of Agra by emperor. This position increased his influence ghal administration.

the tax imposed on are imported into of India. Excise ds manufactured vhile wealth tax to assets and

olicy (NLP) Logistics ranking ountries with roving

93. India's Special Economic Zones (SEZs) policy was launched in 2000 as part of the Export–Import (EXIM) Policy 2000–2001, with the objective of promoting exports, investment, and employment.

94. Under Article 3 of the Indian Constitution, the Parliament has the power to form new states, alter the boundaries or names of existing states, or divide a state, subject to certain procedural requirements.

95. The hinterland of Marmagao Port includes Goa, Karnataka, and southern Maharashtra. Himachal Pradesh is geographically distant and not connected to the port's trade influence, so it is not part of its hinterland.

96. A capital goods industry produces goods such as machines, tools, equipment, and plants that are used in the production of other goods. These industries form the backbone of industrial and economic development.

97. Tariff measures are taxes imposed on cross-border trade. Both export taxes and import taxes involve duties levied on goods when they are exported or imported, so both are considered tariff measures.

98. As per Census-based demographic data used officially (and referenced up to 2023–25), Scheduled Tribes constitute about 8.6% of India's total population.

99. Respiration is the biological process in which organisms take in oxygen from the external environment and use it to break down food substances to release energy.

100. The Charaka Samhita is a foundational ancient Indian text of Ayurveda, dealing primarily with medicine, including diagnosis, treatment, pharmacology, and principles of health and disease.

Previous Years' Paper

-Combined Higher Secondary Level (CHSL : 10 + 2)

Operator (DEO)/ Lower Division Clerk (LDC)/ ...r Secretarial Assistant (JSA)

...ecruitment Exam-2024

...ld on 11-07-2024)

... is to baked the ...m, "Who ... ...ically

...propriate ...nk number

...such as ... D. for as

...most appropriate ...M of the underlined

...aters of Germany are ...ant in fish, but there are ...genera and species in them.

... deficient B. flourish

... allay D. discord

Select the most appropriate synonym of the given word.

Revolution

A. Stagnation B. Gyration

C. Harmony D. Order

12. Select the most appropriate ANTONYM for the given word.

Ghastly

A. Agitated B. Bitter

C. Relaxing D. Pleasant

...on (2).

... be ... be

...iate option ...umber (3).

...A **8.** B **9.** B **10.** A **11.** B

Directions (Q.No. 5-9): *In the following passage, some words have been deleted. Read the passage carefully and select the most appropriate option to fill in each blank.*

Teachers ___(1)___ given continuous opportunities for self-improvement and to learn the latest innovations and advances in their professions. Each teacher ___(2)___expected to participate in at least 50 hours of CPD opportunities every year for their own professional development, driven ___(3)___ their own interests. CPD opportunities will, in particular, ___(4)___ cover the latest pedagogies regarding foundational literacy and numeracy, formative and adaptive assessment of learning outcomes, competency-based learning and related pedagogies, ___(5)___ experiential learning, arts-integrated, sports-integrated and storytelling-based approaches, etc.

5. Select the most appropriate option to fill in blank number (1).
A. shall be B. will be
C. can be C. would be

6. Select the most appropriate opt
to fill in blank number
A. shall be B. would
C. can be D. will

7. Select the most approp
to fill in blank n

A. by B. from
C. at D. for

8. Select the most appropriate option
to fill in blank number (4)
A. carelessly
B. systematically
C. roughly
D. partially

9. Select the most ap
option to fill in bla
(5).
A. same as B
C. from as

10. Select the
ANTONYM
word.
The w
abund
few
A
C

11.

5. B 6. D

13. Select the most appropriate option that can substitute the underlined segment in the given sentence. If there is no need to substitute it, select 'No substitution required'.

I opened the box beneath the table and took of a book, the Materia Medica.

A. took out
B. take off
C. took in
D. No substitution required

14. Parts of the following sentence have been given as options. Select the option that contains a spelling error.

I was alarmed lest we should be wreked.

A. I was B. be wreked.
C. we should D. alarmed lest

15. Based on the situation in the sentence, select the most appropriate idiom.

After many years of rivalry, the two schools decided to ______ and participate in a National Event together.

A. bell the cat
B. bury the hatchet
C. go cold turkey
D. be in the doldrums

16. Choose the option that best describes the meaning of the idioms and phrases underlined in the given sentence.

A jack of all trades cannot survive in the world of specialisation.

A. A good communicator
B. A person who can do many things but is not an expert in any
C. An expert of many jobs
D. A businessman

17. Select the most appropriate option that can substitute the underlined segment in the given sentence.

Do not later about the street.

A. loiter around
B. litre about
C. litter about
D. latter about

18. Select the most appropriate ANTONYM of the given word.

Compulsory

A. Optional B. Reliable
C. Factional D. Full-fledged

19. Select the most appropriate option that can substitute the underlined segment in the given sentence.

Well, I prefer eating at home from eating out.

A. and eating out
B. than eating out
C. while eating out
D. to eating out

13. A **14.** B **15.** B **16.** B **17.** A **18.** A **19.** D

20. Rectify the sentence by selecting the correct spelling from the options.

The advertisement of vacencies in education sector has received **huge** response.

A. Vecencies B. Vacansies
C. Vecancies D. Vacancies

21. Select the most appropriate ANTONYM of the underlined word in the given sentence.

The athlete looked unsettled before the race.

A. Confident B. Reticent
C. Triumphant D. Tangent

22. Select the most appropriate synonym of the given word.

Candid

A. Cruel B. Bright
C. Top D. Honest

23. Select the most appropriate option to fill in the blank.

The artist received a __________ from the audience.

A. handful of applause
B. round of applause
C. bunch of applause
D. plenty of applause

24. Select the most appropriate option that can substitute the underlined word in the given sentence.

The experienced surgeon handled the delicate procedure with care and precision.

A. seasoned B. amateur
C. untrained D. unskilled

25. Select the most appropriate ANTONYM of the underlined word in the following sentence.

I have left it to his discretion to accept or decline my offer.

A. Wisdom B. Calculation
C. Inattention D. Judgement

General Intelligence

26. Select the option figure in which the given figure (X) is embedded as its part (rotation is NOT allowed).

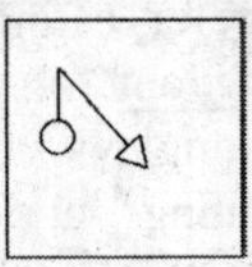

(X)

A. 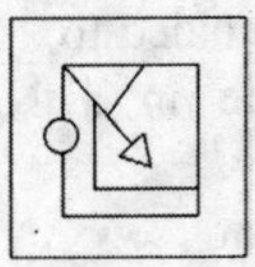

B. 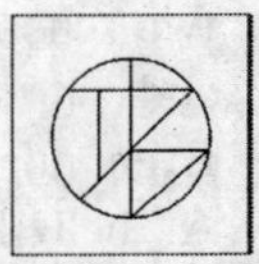

C. 

D. 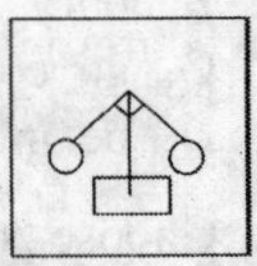

20. D **21.** A **22.** D **23.** B **24.** A **25.** C **26.** A

27. Each of the letters in the word FRANCHISE are arranged from left to right in alphabetical order to form a new word. How many letters are there in the English alphabetical series between the alphabet which is fifth from the left and the one which is third from the right in the newly formed word?

A. Seven B. Five
C. Four D. Six

28. CYRF is related to NJCQ in a certain way based on the English alphabetical order. In the same way, GBUM is related to RMFX. To which of the following is CZKP related, following the same logic?

A. NKVA B. NAKV
C. NKAV D. NAVK

29. If 'A' stands for '÷', 'B' stands for '×', 'C' stands for '+' and 'D' stands for '–', then the resultant of which of the following will be 421?

A. 63 B 7 A 125 D 5 C 5
B. 63 A 7 D 125 B 5 C 5
C. 63 B 7 D 125 A 5 C 5
D. 63 C 7 D 125 A 5 B 5

30. In this question, three statements are given, followed by three conclusions numbered I, II and III. Assuming the statements to be true, even if they seem to be at variance with commonly known facts, decide which of the conclusion(s) logically follows/follow from the statements.

Statements:

No rose is an orchid.
All roses are lilies.
All lilies are lotuses.

Conclusions:

I. Some lilies are orchids.
II. Some lotuses are orchids.
III. All lilies are orchids.

A. Both conclusions I and III follow
B. Neither conclusions I, II nor III follows
C. Both conclusions I and II follow
D. Both conclusions II and III follow

31. What would be the Roman numeral on the opposite side of 'V' if the given sheet is folded to form a cube?

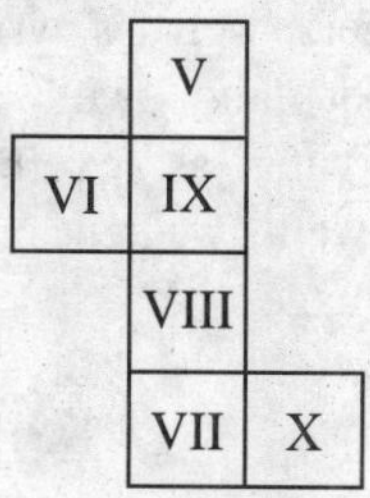

A. VII B. X
C. VIII D. VI

27. B **28.** A **29.** C **30.** B **31.** C

32. Select the correct mirror image of the given figure when the mirror is placed at AB as shown below.

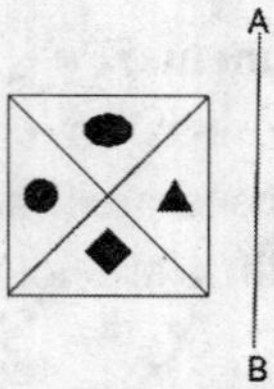

A. 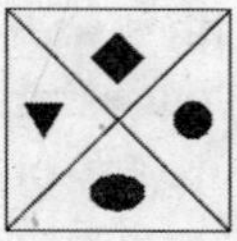 B. 

C. 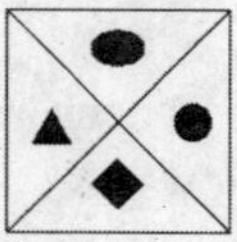 D. 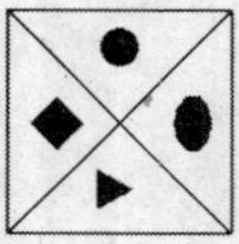

33. What should come in place of ? in the given series based on the English alphabetical order?

QRS MXB IDK EJT ?

A. PCA B. CPA

C. APC D. AAC

34. In a certain code language, 'mix jaggery well' is written as 'rb co ot' and 'well done boss' is written as 'cx rb op'. How is 'well' written in the given language?

A. co B. cx

C. ot D. rb

35. Find the number of triangles in the given figure:

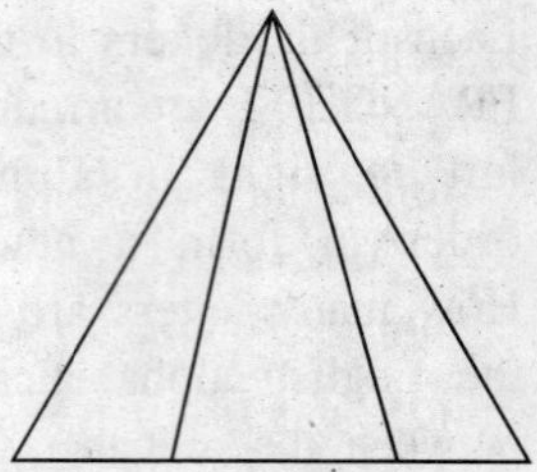

A. 8 B. 6

C. 4 D. 5

36. Which of the following letter-clusters can replace the question mark (?) in the given series to make it logically complete?

JMD, OHJ, ? , YXV, DSB

A. RST

B. AOZ

C. TCP

D. VCP

37. What should come in place of the question mark (?) in the given series?

86, 88, 90, 92, 94, ?

A. 99

B. 96

C. 97

D. 98

38. 78 is related to 30 following a certain logic. Following the same logic, 67 is related to 26.

To which of the following is 54 related, following the same logic?

A. 18 B. 20

C. 16 D. 28

32. C **33.** C **34.** D **35.** B **36.** C **37.** B **38.** A

39. What will come in the place of the question mark (?) in the following equation, if '+' and '–' are interchanged and '×' and '÷' are interchanged?

$125 \div 5 + 19 - 190 \times 19 = ?$

A. 606 B. 636
C. 616 D. 626

40. In a certain language, 'protect your health' is written as 'Df Bk Tu' and 'health is wealth' is written as 'Po Tu Le'. How is 'health' written in the given language?

A. Df B. Po
C. Bk D. Tu

41. IJLO is related to GHJM in a certain way based on the English alphabetical order. In the same way, HIKN is related to FGIL. To which of the following is EFHK related, following the same logic?

A. CEDI B. CDFI
C. CDEF D. CEFI

42. Three of the following four are alike in a certain way and thus form a group. Which is the one that does NOT belong to that group?

(Note: The odd one out is not based on the number of consonants/vowels or their position in the letter cluster.)

A. UXY B. JMN
C. DGH D. ORT

43. What will come in the place of the question mark (?) in the following equation, if '+' and '–' are interchanged and '×' and '÷' are interchanged?

$87 \div 3 + 35 - 88 \times 11 = ?$

A. 231 B. 233
C. 234 D. 232

44. If 25 August 2006 was Friday, then what was the day of the week on 25 August 2018?

A. Saturday B. Sunday
C. Thursday D. Wednesday

45. Identify the figure given in the options that when put in place of the question mark (?) will logically complete the series.

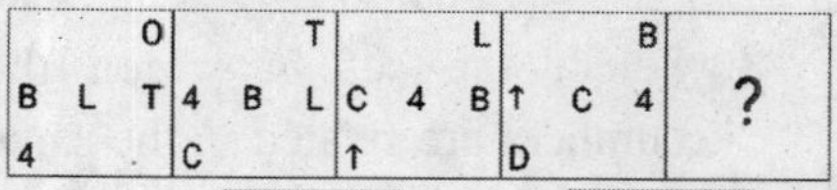

A. 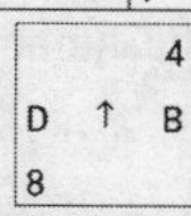

B. 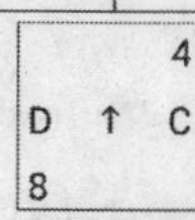

C. 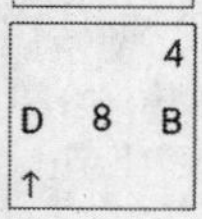

D. 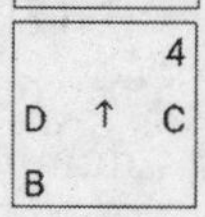

46. Which of the following numbers will replace the question mark (?) in the given series?

$\left[\frac{5}{9}\right], \left[\frac{14}{9}\right], \left[\frac{23}{9}\right], \left[\frac{32}{9}\right], \left[\frac{41}{9}\right], ?$

A. $\left[\frac{44}{9}\right]$ B. $\left[\frac{51}{9}\right]$

C. $\left[\frac{47}{9}\right]$ D. $\left[\frac{50}{9}\right]$

39. C **40.** D **41.** B **42.** D **43.** C **44.** A **45.** B **46.** D

47. A square sheet of paper is folded along the dotted line successively along the directions shown and is then punched in the last. How would the paper look when unfolded?

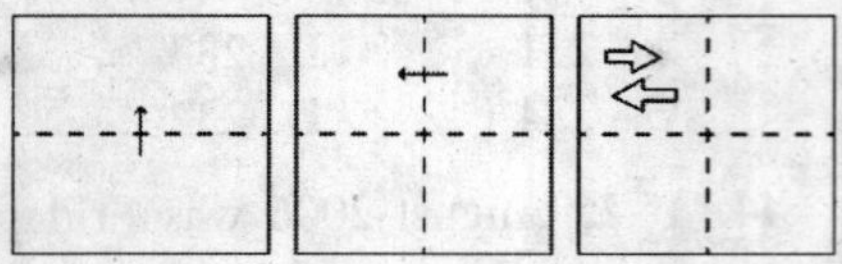

A. 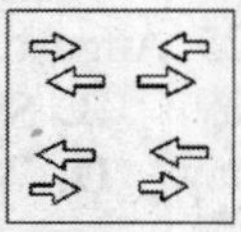

B. 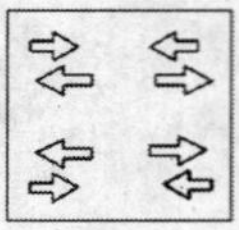

C. 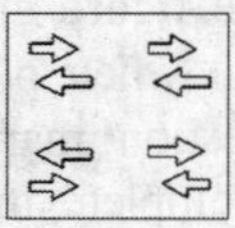

D. 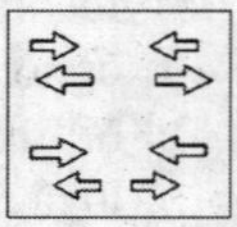

48. Select the set in which the numbers are related in the same way as are the numbers of the following sets.

(NOTE: Operations should be performed on the whole numbers, without breaking down the numbers into their constituent digits. E.g. 13 – Operations on 13 such as adding/subtracting/multiplying etc. to 13 can be performed. Breaking down 13 into 1 and 3 and then performing mathematical operations on 1 and 3 is not allowed.)

(4, 8, 32)
(7, 14, 56)

A. (11, 22, 88)
B. (11, 33, 88)
C. (11, 33, 77)
D. (11, 22, 77)

49. In a certain code language,

A % B means 'A is the mother of B'

A # B means 'A is the brother of B'

A @ B means 'A is the wife of B'

A & B means 'A is the father of B'

Based on the above, how is P related to T if 'P & Q % R # S @ T'?

A. Wife's father
B. Wife's mother's father
C. Wife's mother's brother
D. Wife's brother

50. What would be the letter on the opposite side of 'P' if the given sheet is folded to form a cube?

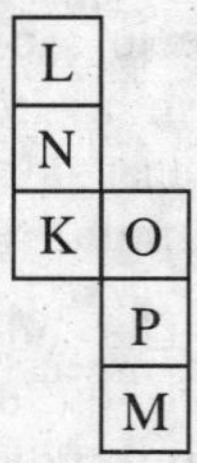

A. L B. N
C. M D. K

47. B **48.** A **49.** B **50.** B

Quantitative Aptitude

51. The following bar graph represents the total number of students enrolled and the number of students who got campus placement in six different engineering colleges A, B, C, D, E, and F. Study the graph carefully and answer the question given below:

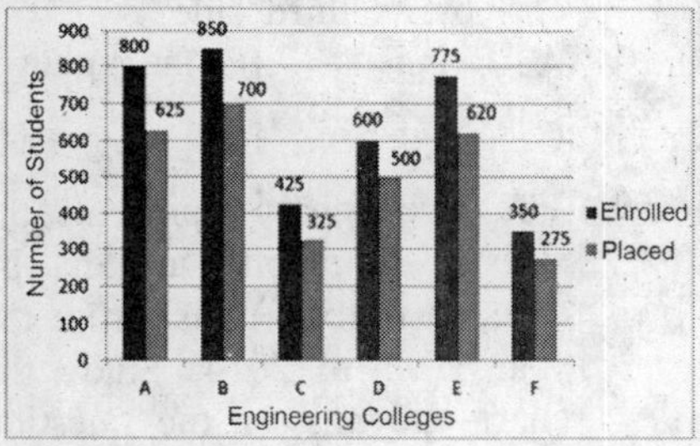

What per cent (correct up to two decimal places) of total enrolled students have got campus placements in colleges A, C, and F?

A. 86.67%
B. 77.78%
C. 82.78%
D. 79.67%

52. The following table gives the percentage of marks obtained by seven students in six different subjects in an examination. The numbers in the brackets give the maximum marks in each subject.

Student	Subject (Max. Marks)					
	Maths	Chem	Phy	Geo	His	Com. Sci
	(150)	(130)	(120)	(100)	(60)	(40)
Ayush	90	50	90	60	70	80
Aman	100	80	80	40	80	70
Sajal	90	60	70	70	90	70
Rohit	80	65	80	80	60	60
Muskan	80	65	85	95	50	90
Tanvi	70	75	65	85	40	60
Tarun	65	35	50	77	80	80

How many students secured a raw score of 135 in Maths?

A. 0
B. 2
C. 1
D. 3

53. If L is the mid-point of side BC of Δ ABC and the area of Δ ABL is 15 cm^2, then the area (in sq cm) of Δ ABC is:

A. 32
B. 30
C. 27
D. 25

54. In Δ ABC, D and E are points on sides AB and AC, such that DE || BC. If AD = x, DB = $x - 3$, AE = $x + 3$ and EC = $x - 2$, then the value of x is:

A. 5.2
B. 4.0
C. 4.5
D. 4.2

51. B **52.** B **53.** B **54.** C

55. X, Y and Z can do a work in 24 days, 5 days and 12 days, respectively. In how many days can they do the same work if they work together?

A. 4 days B. $3\frac{1}{13}$ days

C. $\frac{1}{24}$ days D. $\frac{7}{24}$ days

56. If $\frac{15}{8}+\left[\left\{\frac{4}{5}\text{ of }\frac{5}{12}\div\left(1\frac{1}{15}\right)\right\}\times 1\frac{7}{12}\right]$ is expressed in the form of $\frac{a}{b}$ where a and b are integers and relatively prime to each other, the value $4b - a$ is:

A. 313 B. 225
C. 164 D. 189

57. If the price of a commodity is increased by 36%, by what percentage (rounded off to 1 decimal place) should its consumption be decreased so that the expenditure of the commodity stays the same?

A. 26.5% B. 36%
C. 29.5% D. 32%

58. In an obtuse-angled triangle ABC, the length of its longest side AB is 50 cm and one of the other two sides is 42 cm. If the area of the triangle is 294 cm^2, what is the length (in cm) of its third side?

A. $8\sqrt{35}$ B. $15\sqrt{21}$
C. $2\sqrt{58}$ D. $12\sqrt{43}$

59. The given chart represents the sales of automobiles in India (by type, in million units) from the year 2011 to 2014. Study the chart and answer the question that follows.

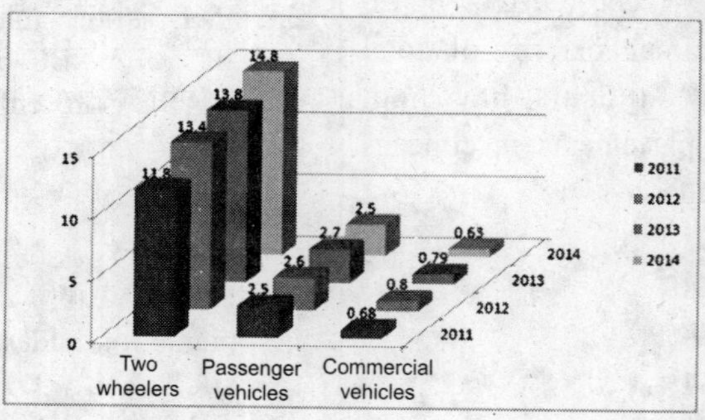

The percentage increase in the sales in 2013 over the previous year was the maximum for which of the categories of vehicles?

A. Two wheelers
B. Commercial vehicles
C. Passenger vehicles
D. Two wheelers and Passenger vehicles

55. B	**56.** A	**57.** A	**58.** C	**59.** C

60. Tom travelled 285 km in 6 hours. In his total travelling, he travelled the first part by bus at 40 km/hr and the remaining part by train at 55 km/hr. How much distance has he travelled by train?
A. 155 km
B. 120 km
C. 165 km
D. 135 km

61. The average of 50 numbers is 23. If each number is multiplied by 13, then the new average is:
A. 219 B. 299
C. 650 D. 88

62. What should be added to each term of the ratio 5 : 11 so that the ratio becomes 3 : 5?
A. 6 B. 4
C. 2 D. 5

63. A cylindrical candle, 14 cm in diameter and length 2 cm is melted to form a cuboid candle dimensions 7 cm × 11 cm × 2 cm. How many cuboidal candles can be obtained?
A. 4 B. 5
C. 2 D. 3

64. A right angled triangle of areas 600 m^2 is to be made such that the hypotenuse is double the base. For the triangle, the hypotenuse is .... more than the base.
A. 20.36 m B. 22.32 m
C. 24.36 m D. 26.32 m

65. How much simple interest will ₹ 5,000 earn in 14 months at a 12% interest rate per annum?
A. ₹ 600 B. ₹ 800
C. ₹ 700 D. ₹ 500

66. Refer to the bar graph below and answer the question that follows.

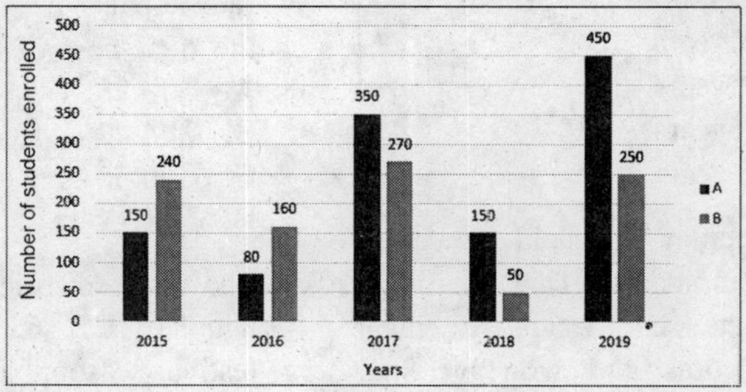

What is the difference between the number of students enrolled in Institute A in 2015 and 2017 and that in Institute B in 2016, 2018 and 2019?
A. 40 B. 150 C. 75 D. 100

60. C	61. B	62. B	63. C	64. D	65. C	66. A

67. If 10% of 24% of x is 240, then x = ?

A. 100 B. 1000
C. 10000 D. 100000

68. If tan A + sin A = x, tan A – sin A = y, what is the value of $x^2 - y^2$?

A. $\sqrt[2]{\frac{x}{y}}$ B. $\sqrt[4]{\frac{x}{y}}$

C. $\sqrt{xy}$ D. $\sqrt[4]{xy}$

69. The number 611611611611 is:
(*a*) divisible by both 6 and 11
(*b*) neither divisible by 6 nor by 11
(*c*) divisible by 6 only
(*d*) divisible by 11 only

A. (*d*) B. (*c*)
C. (*b*) D. (*a*)

70. My father is presently 25 years older than me. The sum of our ages 5 years ago was 39 years. Find my present age.

A. 13 years
B. 12 years
C. 15 years
D. 20 years

71. An election was held between two candidates. The winning candidate scored 54% of the valid votes and won by 88 votes. If 58 votes were declared invalid, then find the total number of votes polled in the election.

A. 1850 B. 1158
C. 1156 D. 2000

72. The salary of employees in a factory was reduced by 20% due to economic crisis. In order to have their salary back to original amount, it must be raised by:

A. 20%
B. 12.5%
C. 40%
D. 25%

73. What is the area (in square units) of the sector if the radius of the circle is given to be 24 units and the arc length is 7.5 units?

A. 135 B. 180
C. 45 D. 90

74. The volume of rectangular block is 12288 m^3. Its dimension are in the ratio of 4 : 3 : 2. If the entire surface is polished at the rate 2 paise per m^2, then find the total cost of polishing.

A. ₹ 33.28
B. ₹ 44.42
C. ₹ 66.56
D. ₹ 11.14

75. The marked price of a table lamp is ₹ 2,165. During the festive season, it is sold for ₹ 1,710.35. Find the percentage discount offered.

A. 21% B. 20.5%
C. 18% D. 22.5%

67. C **68.** D **69.** A **70.** B **71.** B **72.** D **73.** D **74.** C **75.** A

General Awareness

76. Which of the following is the fastest way to open the Help window in Microsoft Word?

A. Type 'help' in the search bar and then, press Enter
B. Click the Microsoft Office button and then, click Help
C. Press F1
D. Click the Help button on the ribbon

77. Which star is also known as the 'Pole Star'?

A. The West star
B. The South star
C. The North star
D. The East star

78. According to Census 2011, which union territory recorded the highest female literacy rate in India?

A. Delhi
B. Lakshadweep
C. Chandigarh
D. Puducherry

79. In Equestrian sports, ______ occurs when a horse or rider lowers an element of a jump that establishes the height of an obstacle.

A. canter
B. curb
C. clean round
D. knockdown

80. Which group of states was concentrated in the cotton production in the early years to develop textile industry?

A. West Bengal and Odisha
B. Bihar and West Bengal
C. Maharashtra and Gujarat
D. Punjab and Haryana

81. Which of the following hills is located in the Eastern-most part of India?

A. Patkai Bum Hills
B. Jaintia Hills
C. Khasi Hills
D. Garo Hills

82. Who among the following is NOT associated with the Green Revolution?

A. M.S. Swaminathan
B. P. Chidambaram
C. Norman Borlaug
D. Chidambaram Subramaniam

83. Who among the following is related to Hindustani classical singing?

A. Mallikarjun Mansur
B. Srinavasa Iyer
C. Aruna Sairam
D. Ramanuj Iyengar

76. C **77.** C **78.** B **79.** D **80.** C **81.** A **82.** B **83.** A

84. The original constitution did NOT mention any fundamental duty because:
A. initially fundamental duties were not expected to be performed
B. it was expected that the citizens of the country would perform their duties willingly
C. it was expected that the citizens of the country would perform their duties forcefully
D. initially fundamental duties were punishable as per the constitution

85. Which of the following measures can be adopted by the government to reduce revenue deficit?
A. Offering freebies
B. Increasing subsidies
C. Increasing money supply
D. Tax reforms

86. Every year in the month of February, this camel festival is organised by Rajasthan Tourism Development Corporation in _____.
A. Barmer B. Bikaner
C. Jaisalmer D. Jodhpur

87. MLAs in which of the following states/UTs received an increase of about 66% in salaries and allowances w.e.f. 14 February 2023?
A. Tamil Nadu
B. Lakshadweep
C. Delhi
D. Bihar

88. From which book is the national song of India compiled?
A. Anandmath
B. Mandukya Upanishad
C. Katha Upanishad
D. Bharat Bharti

89. With reference to 'Saila dance' consider the following statements and select the correct option.
(*a*) A group comprising of male performers.
(*b*) The dance is performed with bamboo sticks.
(*c*) It is performed after the cutting of crops.
A. (*a*), (*b*), (*c*)
B. Both (*b*) and (*c*)
C. Both (*a*) and (*c*)
D. Both (*a*) and (*b*)

90. Who was the first person to conduct a systematic study of chromosomes during division and called this process mitosis?
A. Friedrich Miescher
B. Thomas Hunt Morgan
C. Antonie van Leeuwenhoek
D. Walther Flemming

91. In cricket, a fast, head-high delivery of the ball is referred to as ________.
A. grubber B. leg-bye
C. duck D. bouncer

84. B **85.** D **86.** B **87.** C **88.** A **89.** A **90.** D **91.** D

92. According to the Census of India 2011, which of the following states has the largest Buddhist population?
A. Uttar Pradesh
B. Maharashtra
C. Madhya Pradesh
D. West Bengal

93. Who captained India to victory in the 2011 Cricket World Cup final win over Sri Lanka?
A. Sourav Ganguly
B. Mahendra Singh Dhoni
C. Sachin Tendulkar
D. Rahul Dravid

94. Which function is used to calculate the maximum value in a selected column in MS Excel?
A. Auto max
B. High
C. Max
D. Auto high

95. Which British colonel is remembered as the Butcher of Amritsar for his role in the Jallianwala Bagh massacre in 1919?
A. Reginald Dyer
B. Robert Clive
C. William Birdwood
D. William Slim

96. Thee 42nd Constitutional Amendment Act of Indian Constitution was passed in the year:
A. 1976 B. 1977
C. 1978 D. 1979

97. In which of the following liquids would anthracene dissolve easily?
A. Benzene
B. Sodium chloride
C. Methane
D. Water

98. In March 2023, the Uttarakhand government had approved how much horizontal reservation for statehood activists in state government jobs?
A. 10% B. 15%
C. 8% D. 5%

99. The Press and Registration of Books (PRB) Act was enacted in which year?
A. 1887
B. 1877
C. 1867
D. 1857

100. Who amongst the following Delhi Sultanate rulers sent his army under Malik Kafur's command to conquer South India?
A. Ghiyas-ud-din Balban
B. Iltutmish
C. Alauddin Khilji
D. Qutub-al-din Aibak

92. B **93.** B **94.** C **95.** A **96.** A **97.** A **98.** A **99.** C **100.** C

Explanatory Answers

1. **(D):** The error in option D, "Geeta was working now," is due to the incorrect use of the present progressive tense "was working" in conjunction with "now," which typically requires the simple present or present continuous tense without a past form. A more appropriate construction would be "Geeta is working now," aligning the tense with the immediacy implied by "now."

2. **(C):** The segment "among you is to baked the" contains a grammatical error in the form of the verb "baked," which is incorrectly used in its past participle form. The correct form should be the infinitive "bake," following the construction "is to + base form of the verb," making the correct phrase "among you is to bake the."

3. **(C):** "They quite meet each other" is grammatically incorrect because the adverb "quite" does not properly modify the verb "meet" in this context. "Quite" is typically used to modify adjectives or other adverbs and is not used in standard English to directly modify verbs in this way. The sentence would be correct if transformed into "They meet each other quite often" or using another modifier appropriate for the verb.

4. **(D):** The error in "does not likes" is due to the incorrect verb form. With the auxiliary "does," the main verb should be in the base form; hence, the correct form is "like," making the correct phrase "does not like."

5. **(B):** "Will be" is the most appropriate modal verb for this blank, indicating a future certainty or planned action regarding the teachers being given opportunities. This aligns with the typical use of "will" to express decisions and promises about the future.

6. **(D):** "Will be" correctly suggests a future certainty or expectation that each teacher is expected to participate in professional development activities. It is used here to denote a definitive obligation or policy.

7. **(A):** The preposition "by" is correctly used to indicate the agent or cause in passive constructions. Here, it fits to show that the teachers' participation in CPD opportunities is driven by their own interests.

8. **(B):** "Systematically" fits properly to describe the manner in which CPD opportunities will cover the various pedagogies. It implies a thorough, methodical approach to the inclusion of new teaching methods in the program.

9. **(B):** "Such as" is the correct conjunction to introduce examples. It is used to specify instances like "experiential learning, arts-integrated, sports-integrated and storytelling-based approaches," following the introduction of the general category of CPD opportunities.

10. **(A):** The antonym of "abundant," which means plentiful or in large quantities, is "deficient," indicating a lack or shortage. This contrasts directly with the idea of abundance, making it the appropriate antonym.

11. **(B):** "Revolution" typically refers to a drastic and significant change or the movement in a circular path. "Gyration," which means the act of rotating or whirling, closely aligns with the second meaning, making it a synonym in the context of movement.

12. **(D):** "Ghastly" means causing great horror or fear; something that is unpleasant or shocking. The antonym "pleasant" directly opposes this, as it refers to something enjoyable and agreeable.

13. **(A):** "Took of" is incorrect and likely a typographical error for "took off," but in the context of removing something like a book from a box, the correct phrase is "took out," which means to remove or extract from a place.

14. **(B):** The spelling error is in "be wreked," where "wreked" should be spelled as "wrecked." The correction is necessary to conform to standard spelling conventions.

15. **(B):** "Bury the hatchet" is an idiom meaning to make peace with someone or settle differences, fitting the situation where two schools decide to end their rivalry and collaborate.

16. **(B):** "Jack of all trades" refers to a person who is competent in many skills but not necessarily outstanding in any particular one, which is perfectly described by Option B.

18. **(A):** The antonym of "compulsory," which means required or mandatory, is "optional," indicating something that is not obligatory but rather left to personal choice or discretion.

19. **(D):** The correct phrase to use when expressing preference between two options is "prefer [first option] to [second option]." Thus, "to eating out" is the

appropriate substitution for "from eating out," making the sentence grammatically correct as "Well, I prefer eating at home to eating out."

20. (D): The correct spelling of the word referring to open positions or opportunities is "Vacancies." This conforms to standard English spelling rules, differentiating it from the incorrect alternatives presented.

22. (D): "Candid" means being truthful and straightforward, often in a refreshingly honest way. The synonym "honest" directly aligns with this definition, reflecting a similar meaning of openness and sincerity.

23. **(B):** A "round of applause" is a common phrase used to describe a form of applause that is given by an entire audience, typically in a circular or unanimous manner, indicating approval or praise. This phrase fits contextually and is widely recognized as the standard expression.

25. **(C):** "Discretion" means the freedom to decide what should be done in a particular situation. Its antonym would be "inattention," which implies a lack of consideration or disregard, contrasting directly with the thoughtful and deliberate nature of discretion.

28. **(A):** Given,

C Y R F
+11↓ +11↓ +11↓ +11↓
N J C Q

and

G B U M
+11↓ +11↓ +11↓ +11↓
R M F X

Similarly,

C Z K P
+11↓ +11↓ +11↓ +11↓
N K V A

Hence, CZKP related to NKVA as same logic.

29. **(C):** 63 B 7 D 125 A 5 C 5

After substituting the given symbols, the new expression will be:

$63 \times 7 - 125 \div 5 + 5$

$= 441 - 25 + 5 = 441 - 20$
$= 421.$

37. **(B):**

86 →(+2)→ 88 →(+2)→ 90 →(+2)→ 92 →(+2)→ 94 →(+2)→ [96]

Hence, 96 will come at the place of question mark.

38. **(A):** Given,

$78 \Rightarrow 7 + 8 = 15 \times 2 = 30$

and

$67 \Rightarrow 6 + 7 = 13 \times 2 = 26$

Similarly,

$54 \Rightarrow 5+4 = 9 \times 2 = 18$

Hence, 54 is related to 18.

39. (C): Given,

$125 \div 5 + 19 - 190 \times 19 = ?$

After interchanging,

$125 \times 5 - 19 + 190 \div 19 = ?$

$\Rightarrow 625 - 19 + 10 = ?$

$\Rightarrow 625 - 9 = ?$

$\Rightarrow ? = 616$

Hence, 616 will come at the place of question mark.

43. (C): Given,

$87 \div 3 + 35 - 88 \times 11 = ?$

After interchanging,

$87 \times 3 - 35 + 88 \div 11 = ?$

$\Rightarrow 261 - 35 + 8 = ?$

$\Rightarrow 269 - 35 = ?$

$\Rightarrow ? = 234$

Hence, 234 will come at the place of question mark.

44. (A): Total number of days = 4383

$365 \times 12 + 3$ days $= 4383$

$$4383 \div 7 = 626\frac{1}{7}$$

No. of odd days = 1

Hence, the day on 25 August 2018 was Saturday.

46. (D):

$$\left[\frac{5}{9}\right], \left[\frac{14}{9}\right], \left[\frac{23}{9}\right], \left[\frac{32}{9}\right], \left[\frac{41}{9}\right], \left[\frac{50}{9}\right]$$

+1 +1 +1 +1 +1

Hence, $\left[\frac{50}{9}\right]$ will come at the place of question mark.

48. (A): Given, 4 8 32

×2 ×4

and 7 14 56

×2 ×4

Similarly, 11 22 88

×2 ×4

51. (B): Required %

$$= \frac{1225}{1575} \times 100 = 77.777 = 77.78\%$$

52. (B): Ayush = 90% of 150

$$= \frac{90}{100} \times 150 = 135$$

Sajal = 90% of 150

$$= \frac{90}{100} \times 150 = 135$$

Hence, required no. of students = 2.

53. (B):

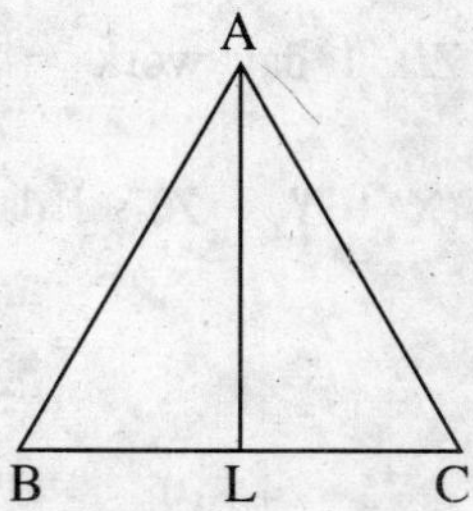

$\because$ AL is median of Δ ABC

$\therefore$ ar Δ ABL = ar Δ ACL

ar Δ ABL = 15 cm^2

$\therefore$ area of Δ ABC = 15×2

$= 30$ cm^2.

54. (C):

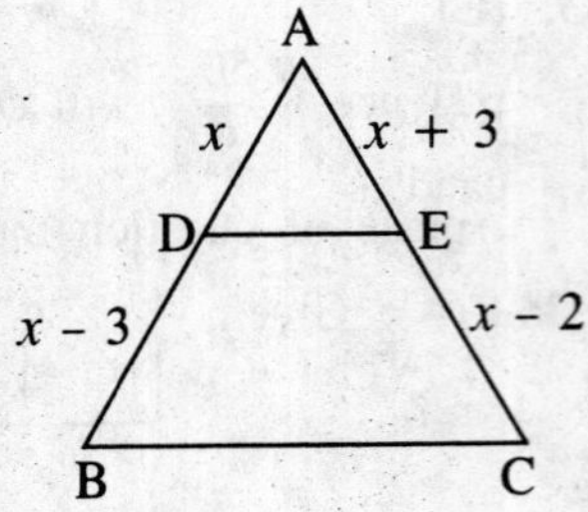

$\because$ DE || BC

$\therefore \dfrac{AD}{DB} = \dfrac{AE}{EC}$

$\Rightarrow \dfrac{x}{x-3} = \dfrac{x+3}{x-2}$

$\Rightarrow x^2 - 2x = x^2 - 9$

$\Rightarrow 2x = 9$

$\Rightarrow x = \dfrac{9}{2} = 4.5.$

55. (B): X's 1 day work $= \dfrac{1}{24}$

Y's 1 day work $= \dfrac{1}{5}$

Z's 1 day work $= \dfrac{1}{12}$

(X + Y + Z)'s 1 day work

$= \dfrac{1}{24} + \dfrac{1}{5} + \dfrac{1}{12}$

$= \dfrac{5+24+10}{120} = \dfrac{39}{120} = \dfrac{13}{40}$

Hence, they can do whole work together in $\dfrac{40}{13}$ days $= 3\dfrac{1}{13}$ days.

56. (A):

$\because \dfrac{15}{8} + \left[\left\{\dfrac{4}{5} \text{ of } \dfrac{5}{12} \div \dfrac{16}{15}\right\} \times \dfrac{19}{12}\right]$

$= \dfrac{15}{8} + \left[\left\{\dfrac{4}{5} \times \dfrac{5}{12} \div \dfrac{16}{15}\right\} \times \dfrac{19}{12}\right]$

$= \dfrac{15}{8} + \left[\left\{\dfrac{1}{3} \times \dfrac{15}{16}\right\} \times \dfrac{19}{12}\right]$

$= \dfrac{15}{8} + \left[\dfrac{5}{16} \times \dfrac{19}{12}\right]$

$= \dfrac{15}{8} + \dfrac{95}{192} = \dfrac{24 \times 15 + 95}{192}$

$= \dfrac{360+95}{192} = \dfrac{455}{192} = \dfrac{a}{b}$

$\therefore$ Value of $4b - a$

$= 4 \times 192 - 455$

$= 768 - 455 = 313.$

57. (A): Price increase % = 36%

To stay remain in expenditure of the commodity, consumption should be decreased by

$= \left(\dfrac{100 \times 36}{100 + 36}\right)$

$= \dfrac{100 \times 36}{136}$

$= 26.4705\%$

$= 26.5\%.$

60. (C): Let Tom travelled by bus for t_1 hrs.

and by train for t_2 hrs.

$\because \quad t_1 = \frac{x}{40}$

and $\quad t_2 = \frac{285 - x}{55}$

$\therefore \quad t_1 + t_2 = 6$ hrs.

$\therefore \frac{x}{40} + \frac{285 - x}{55} = 6$

$\Rightarrow \frac{11x + 8(285 - x)}{440} = 6$

$\Rightarrow 11x + 2280 - 8x = 440 \times 6 = 2640$

$\Rightarrow 3x = 2640 - 2280 = 360$

$\Rightarrow x = 120$ km

Hence, distance travelled by train

$= 285 - 120 = 165$ km.

61. **(B):** Total number $= 50 \times 23$

$= 1150$

Required new average

$= \frac{1150 \times 13}{50}$

$= 23 \times 13 = 299.$

62. **(B):** Let x should be added to each term

$$\frac{5+x}{11+x} = \frac{3}{5}$$

$\Rightarrow 25 + 5x = 33 + 3x$

$\Rightarrow 2x = 33 - 25$

$\Rightarrow 2x = 8$

$\therefore x = 4.$

63. **(C):** $r = 7$ cm

Required no. of cuboidal candles

$= \frac{\text{Volume of cylinder}}{\text{Volume of each cuboid}}$

$= \frac{\frac{22}{7} \times 7 \times 7 \times 2}{7 \times 11 \times 2} = 2.$

65. **(C):** S.I. $= \frac{5000 \times 12 \times 14}{12 \times 100}$

$= ₹\,700$

66. **(A):** Required difference

$= 500 - 460 = 40.$

67. **(C):** $\frac{10}{100} \times \frac{24}{100} x = 240$

$\Rightarrow x = \frac{240 \times 100 \times 100}{10 \times 24} = 10000.$

69. **(A):** Given number = 611611611611

$6 + 1 + 1 + 6 + 1 + 1 = 16$

$1 + 6 + 1 + 1 + 6 + 1 = 16$

Difference $= 16 - 16 = 0$

Then, the given number is divisible by 11.

$\because$ Last digit is not even

$\therefore$ Given number is not divisible by 6

Hence, the given number is divisible by 11 only.

70. (B): Let, my present age = x years

$\therefore$ Father's present age

$= (x + 25)$ years

5 years ago,

$x - 5 + x + 25 - 5 = 39$

$\Rightarrow 2x + 15 = 39$

$\Rightarrow 2x = 39 - 15 = 24$

$\Rightarrow x = 12$

Hence, my present age = 12 yrs.

71. (B): 54% of x – 46% of x = 88

$$\Rightarrow \frac{8}{100}x = 88$$

$\Rightarrow x = 1100$

$\because$ Number of invalid votes = 58

Hence, total votes polled

$= 1100 + 58 = 1158$

72. (D): Original amount must be raised

$$= \frac{20}{100-20}\times 100$$

$$= \frac{20}{80}\times 100 = 25\%.$$

73. (D): $\theta = \frac{l}{r} = \frac{7.5}{24} = \frac{5}{16}$ radian

$\pi r = 180°$

$$\frac{5}{16}r = \frac{180}{\pi}\times\frac{5}{16}$$

$$= \frac{225°}{4\pi}$$

Area of sector

$$= \frac{225}{4\pi\times 360}\times\pi\times 24\times 24$$

$= 6 \times 3 \times 5$

$= 90$ square units.

74. (C): $4x \times 3x \times 2x = 12288$

$\Rightarrow x^3 = 512$

$\Rightarrow x = 8$

$l = 32$ m, $b = 24$ m and $h = 16$ m

Total surface area

$= 2(768 + 384 + 512)$

$= 2 \times 1664 = 3328\ m^2$

$\because$ Cost of 1 m^2 = 2 paise

$$\therefore \text{Cost of } 3328\ m^2 = ₹\ \frac{2\times 3328}{100}$$

$$= ₹\ \frac{6656}{100} = ₹\ 66.56.$$

75. (A): Discount = 2165 – 1710.35

= ₹ 454.65

$$\text{Discount }\% = \frac{454.65}{2165}\times 100$$

$= 21\%.$

76. (C): Pressing F1 is a universally recognized shortcut for opening the Help window in many software applications, including Microsoft Word.

77. (C): The North Star, also known as Polaris, is widely recognized as the Pole Star. It is very close to the North Celestial Pole, making it an essential celestial marker for navigation in the Northern Hemisphere.

78. (B): According to the 2011 Census of India, Lakshadweep recorded the highest female literacy rate among the Union Territories.

79. (D): In equestrian sports, a "knockdown" occurs when a horse or rider causes a jump's rail (or another element that establishes the height of an obstacle) to fall.

80. (C): Maharashtra and Gujarat have been key states in the development of India's textile industry, primarily due to their significant cotton production.

81. (A): The Patkai Bum Hills are located in the easternmost part of India, extending along the India-Myanmar border.

82. (B): P. Chidambaram is not associated with the Green Revolution, which was primarily an agricultural advancement initiative.

83. (A): Mallikarjun Mansur is a renowned figure in Hindustani classical music, specifically known for his exceptional contributions to the Jaipur-Atrauli gharana.

84. (B): The original Indian Constitution did not mention any fundamental duties because it was expected that the citizens would perform their duties willingly without the need for specific enumeration in the constitution.

86. (B): The camel festival referred to is the Bikaner Camel Festival, organised annually in the city of Bikaner, Rajasthan.

87. (C): The MLAs of Delhi received an increase of about 66% in salaries and allowances effective from 14 February 2023.

88. (A): The national song of India, "Vande Mataram," is compiled from "Anandmath," a novel written by Bankim Chandra Chattopadhyay.

90. (D): Walther Flemming was the first person to conduct a systematic study of chromosomes during cell division, and he coined the term "mitosis" to describe this process. His work laid the foundations for modern cellular genetics and significantly advanced the understanding of cell biology.

91. (D): In cricket, a "bouncer" is a type of delivery where the ball

is bowled fast and reaches the batsman at around head height.

92. **(B):** According to the Census of India 2011, Maharashtra has the largest Buddhist population among Indian states.

93. **(B):** Mahendra Singh Dhoni captained the Indian cricket team during the 2011 Cricket World Cup. Under his leadership, India won the final against Sri Lanka, securing their second World Cup victory.

94. **(C):** In MS Excel, the function used to calculate the maximum value from a range of cells is "MAX". This function can be applied to any group of numbers, and it returns the highest value among them, making it essential for data analysis tasks where determining the greatest numeric value is necessary.

95. **(A):** Colonel Reginald Dyer is historically remembered as the Butcher of Amritsar due to his role in the Jallianwala Bagh massacre in 1919.

96. **(A):** The 42nd Constitutional Amendment Act, often referred to as the "Mini-Constitution," was passed in 1976. This act brought about extensive changes to the Indian Constitution, including amendments to the preamble and the alteration of numerous constitutional provisions.

97. **(A):** Anthracene, an organic compound, dissolves easily in non-polar solvents due to its non-polar nature. Benzene, a non-polar solvent, is ideal for dissolving substances like anthracene, which are composed of large polycyclic aromatic hydrocarbons.

98. **(A):** In March 2023, the Uttarakhand government approved a 10% horizontal reservation for statehood activists in state government jobs.

99. **(C):** The Press and Registration of Books (PRB) Act was enacted in the year 1867. This legislation was designed to regulate the printing and publication of books in India, mandating the registration of all printing presses and books published in the country.

100. **(C):** Alauddin Khilji, a ruler of the Delhi Sultanate, sent his general Malik Kafur to the southern part of India to extend his empire's territory.

Previous Years' Paper

SSC—Combined Higher Secondary Level (CHSL : 10 + 2)

Data Entry Operator (DEO)/ Lower Division Clerk (LDC)/ Junior Secretarial Assistant (JSA)

Tier-I, Recruitment Exam-2023

(Exam held on 17-08-2023)

English Language

1. Select the most appropriate synonym of the given word.

Dynamic

A. Famous B. Halt
C. Innate D. Energetic

2. Choose the correct meaning of the underlined word in the given sentence.

The museum's <u>archive</u> is a great place to find valuable artifacts such as ancient manuscripts.

A. A collection of essays
B. A room to store lots of books
C. A room to store important official documents
D. A collection of historical documents or records

3. Select the most appropriate ANTONYM of the given word.

Guile

A. Deceit B. Treachery
C. Honesty D. Terseness

4. Select the most appropriate homophone to fill in the blank.

Ants ________food during the summer and save it for winter.

A. horde B. hoard
C. heard D. herd

5. The following sentence has been divided into parts. One of them may contain an error. Select the part that contains the error from the given options. If you don't find any error, mark 'No error' as your answer.

A owl was / hooting throughout / the night.

A. A owl was
B. the night
C. No error
D. hooting throughout

1. D **2.** D **3.** C **4.** B **5.** A

6. Select the option that can be used as a one-word substitute for the given group of words.

One who studies the evolution of mankind

A. Anarchist
B. Amateur
C. Anthropologist
D. Antagonist

7. Select the most appropriate ANTONYM for 'redeem' in the given sentence.

Shantanu violated the rules of the college when he started screaming and shouting in the premises.

A. Screaming
B. Violated
C. Premises
D. Shouting

8. Select the option that can be used as a one-word substitute for the given group of words.

Something to be easily carried or moved

A. Robust B. Stagnant
C. Portable D. Fragile

9. Select the option that can be used as a one-word substitute for the given group of words.

An imagined place or state of things in which everything is perfect

A. Dwarf
B. Utopia
C. Chronology
D. Octogenarian

10. Select the option that can be used as a one-word substitute for the given group of words.

Poor physical or mental condition.

A. Ill nature
B. Illicit
C. Ill-fated
D. Ill health

11. The following sentence has been split into four segments. Identify the segment that contains a grammatical error.

They were laid / in the sun / the entire morning / till Sudharshan came.

A. till Sudharshan came
B. They were laid
C. the entire morning
D. in the sun

12. Select the correct spelling of the underlined word in the given sentence.

The feeling of weightlessness while skydiving is known to <u>exilarete</u> many people.

A. exilairate
B. exhilarete
C. exilarate
D. exhilarate

6. C	**7.** B	**8.** C	**9.** B	**10.** D	**11.** B	**12.** D

13. Select the option that expresses the given sentence in active voice.

I was never supported by my family.

A. My family have never supported me.
B. My family had never supported me.
C. My family never supported me.
D. My family never supports me.

14. The following sentence has been split into four segments. Identify the segment that contains a spelling error.

The famous author / clearly mentioned / all the names of his friends / in the acknolledgments of the book.

A. in the acknolledgments of the book
B. The famous author
C. clearly mentioned
D. all the names of his friends

15. Select the most appropriate ANTONYM of the given word.

Mean

A. Minute B. Noble
C. Notorious D. Novel

16. Select the most appropriate idiom for the underlined segment in the following sentence.

Nitish's promotion is <u>due</u>.

A. On the cards
B. Not worth his salt
C. With due respect
D. Done to death

17. Parts of a sentence are given below in jumbled order. Select the option that arranges the parts in the correct order to form a meaningful sentence.

(*a*) in social evolution by imitation
(*b*) by reason of its higher standard of living
(*c*) the royal style is the agent
(*d*) and cultural patterns are similarly transmitted by the dominant caste

A. (*c*), (*d*), (*a*), (*b*)
B. (*c*), (*a*), (*d*), (*b*)
C. (*b*), (*c*), (*d*), (*a*)
D. (*b*), (*a*), (*c*), (*d*)

18. Select the option that expresses the following sentence in passive voice.

An agitated gathering of workers in the company disturbed the meeting.

A. Meeting of the company was disturbed.
B. An agitated meeting of workers in the company disturbed the gathering.
C. The meeting was disturbed by an agitated gathering of workers in the company.
D. The gathering agitated the meeting of the company.

13. C	**14.** A	**15.** B	**16.** A	**17.** B	**18.** C

19. Select the most appropriate meaning of the given idiom.
Costs an arm and a leg
A. To be affordable
B. To be moderately priced
C. To be free of charge
D. To be very expensive

20. Select the most appropriate option to fill in the blank.
The ___________ of the company's CEO was widely praised for her innovative leadership.
A. rein B. rayne
C. rain D. reign

Directions (Qs. No. 21-25): *In the following passage, some words have been deleted. Read the passage carefully and select the most appropriate option to fill in each blank.*

Globalisation is not a new _____1_____. Traders travelled vast distances in ancient times to buy commodities that were _____2_____and expensive for sale in their homelands. The Industrial Revolution brought _____3_____ in transportation and communication in the 19th century that eased trade across borders. The think tank, Peterson Institute for International Economics (PIIE), states globalisation _____4_____ after World War I and nations moved toward _____5_____ as they launched import taxes to more closely guard their industries in the aftermath of the conflict.

21. Select the most appropriate option to fill in blank number 1.
A. power
B. variation
C. design
D. concept

22. Select the most appropriate option to fill in blank number 2.
A. plentiful
B. common
C. preserved
D. rare

23. Select the most appropriate option to fill in blank number 3.
A. chaos
B. advances
C. issues
D. a decline

24. Select the most appropriate option to fill in blank number 4.
A. trooped
B. soared
C. de-escalated
D. stalled

25. Select the most appropriate option to fill in blank number 5.
A. protectionism
B. integration
C. liberalisation
D. diversification

19. D **20.** D **21.** D **22.** D **23.** B **24.** D **25.** A

5

General Intelligence

26. A square sheet of paper is folded along the dotted line successively along the directions shown and is then punched in the end. How would the paper look when unfolded?

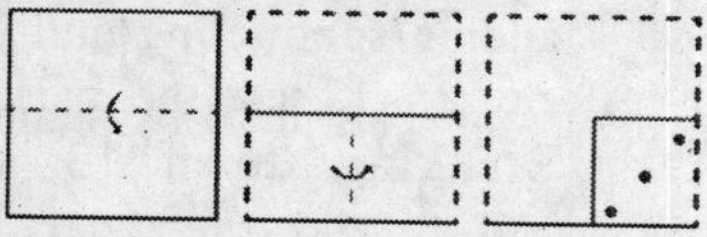

A. 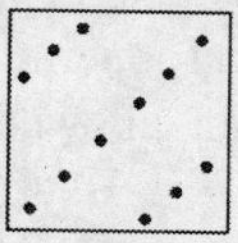
B. 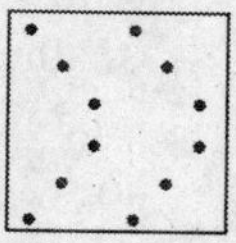

C. 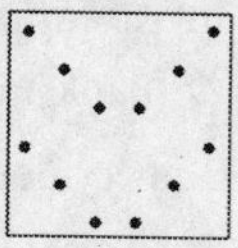
D. 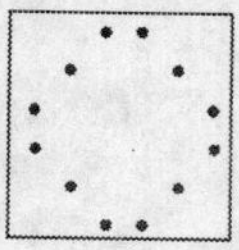

27. Read the given statements and conclusions carefully. Assuming that the information given in the statements is true, even if it appears to be at variance with commonly known facts, decide which of the given conclusions logically follow[s] from the statements.

Statements:

Some houses are trees.

All flowers are houses.

No vegetable is a flower.

Conclusions:

I. Some vegetables are houses is a possibility.

II. Some flowers are trees is a possibility.

III. No vegetable is a house.

A. Both conclusions II and III follow

B. Only conclusion II follows

C. Both conclusions I and II follow

D. Only conclusion III follows

28. If 'A' stands for '÷', 'B' stands for '×', 'C' stands for '+' and 'D' stands for '–', what will come in place of the question mark '?' in the following equation?

4 B 18 D 5 C 9 A 9 = ?

A. 88 B. 58

C. 78 D. 68

29. What will come in the place of '?' in the following equation, if '+' and '–' are interchanged with '÷' and '×' respectively?

$88 + 8 - 17 \times 16 \div 40 = ?$

A. 203 B. 197

C. 200 D. 211

30. In a certain code language, 'BALD' is coded as '7680' and 'DRAB' is coded as '8097'. What is the code for 'L' in the given code language?

A. 8 B. 6

C. 0 D. 7

26. D **27.** C **28.** D **29.** D **30.** B

31. Select the combination of letters that when sequentially placed in the blanks of the given series will complete the series.

A_DE FGI_ _LNO PQ_T UV_Y

A. CJKSX B. CJKRW
C. BJKRW D. BJKSX

32. Select the wood-pair that best represents a similar relationship to the one expressed in the pair of words given below. (The words must be considered as meaningful English words and must not be related to each other based on the number of letters/consonant/vowels in the word.)

Heat : Cold

A. Encourage : Motivate
B. Compete : Success
C. Sustain : Persist
D. Demolish : Build

33. RSPT is related to VWTX in a certain way based on the English alphabetical order. In the same way, MNKO is related to QROS. Which of the following is GHEI related to, following the same logic?

A. KLHI B. KLJM
C. KLIM D. JKHL

34. Three of the following four are alike in a certain way and thus form a group. Which is the one that does NOT belong to that group?

(NOTE: Operations should be performed on the whole numbers, without breaking down the numbers into its constituent digits. E.g. 13- Operations on 13 such as adding/subtracting/multiplying etc. to 13 can be performed. Breaking down 13 into 1 and 3 and then performing mathematical operations on 1 and 3 is not allowed)

A. 2 – 6 B. 4 – 20
C. 5 – 30 D. 8 – 75

35. In a certain code language, 'QUEZAL' is coded as '82' and 'LUCKY' is coded as '72'. What is the code for 'ADVERSE' in the given code language?

A. 68 B. 78
C. 74 D. 62

36. GIEK is related to OQMS in a certain way based on the English alphabetical order. In the same way, KMIO is related to SUQW. To which of the following is EGCI related to following the same logic?

A. MQOK
B. MOKQ
C. PRNT
D. UWSY

31. D 32. D 33. C 34. D 35. C 36. B

37. The second number in the given number pairs is obtained by performing certain mathematical operations(s) on the first number. The same operation(s) are followed in all the number pairs except one. Find that odd number pair.
A. 5 : 20   B. 4 : 12
C. 7 : 42   D. 6 : 36

38. Based on the alphabetical order, three of the following four letter-clusters are alike in a certain way and thus form a group. Which of the following does NOT belong to that group?
A. WZB   B. UWX
C. ORT   D. GJL

39. In a certain code language,
A + B means 'A is the sister of B'
A – B means 'A is the husband of B'
A × B means 'A is the son of B'
A ÷ B means 'A is the mother of B'
Based on the above, how is F related to J if 'F × G – H ÷ I + J'?
A. Brother
B. Mother's brother
C. Father
D. Father's brother

40. If 9 July, 1978 is Sunday, then what will be the day of the week on 19 September 1983?
A. Monday   B. Friday
C. Tuesday   D. Sunday

41. How many triangles are there in the given figure?

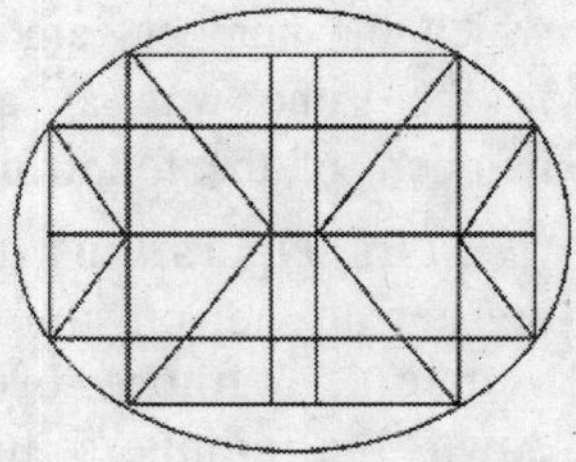

A. 24   B. 28
C. 22   D. 30

42. N is the brother of X, X is the wife of M, S is the daughter of M, K is the brother of S, P is the mother of N. How is K related to P?
A. Son's son
B. Daughter's son
C. Mother's brother
D. Sister's son

43. What should come in place of X in the given series?
23 31 47 71 103 X
A. 153   B. 147
C. 150   D. 143

44. Select the number from among the given options that can replace the question mark (?) in the following series.
136, 135, 137, 136, 138, 137, ?
A. 136   B. 140
C. 138   D. 139

37. D	38. B	39. A	40. A	41. B	42. B	43. D	44. D

45. In the following number-pairs, the second number is obtained by applying certain mathematical operations to the first number. Select the set in which the numbers are related in the same way as are the numbers of the following sets.

(NOTE: Operations should be performed on the whole numbers, without breaking down the numbers into its constituent digits. E.g. 13 - Operations on 13 such as adding/subtracting/multiplying etc. to 13 can be performed. Breaking down 13 into 1 and 3 and then performing mathematical operations on 1 and 3 is not allowed.)

(15, 96)
(35, 216)

A. (41, 250) B. (18, 102)
C. (29, 180) D. (21, 122)

46. The position of how many letters will remain unchanged if each of the letter in the word 'ACQUIRE' is arranged in alphabetical order?

A. Three B. Four
C. Two D. One

47. Select the correct mirror image of the given figure when the mirror is placed at MN as shown.

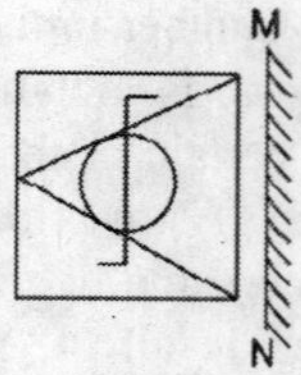

A. 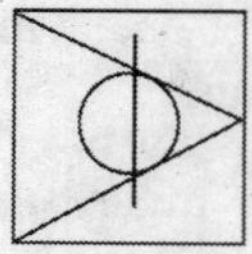 B. 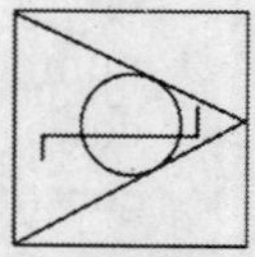

C. 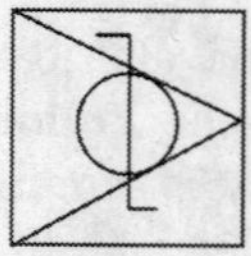 D. 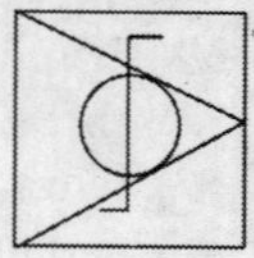

48. Select the combination of letters that when sequentially placed in the blanks of the given series will complete the series.

A_CD_CDAC_AB_ABC

A. AACD B. AABB
C. BBDD D. BDBD

49. Identify the figure given in the options which when put in place of the question mark (?) will logically complete the series.

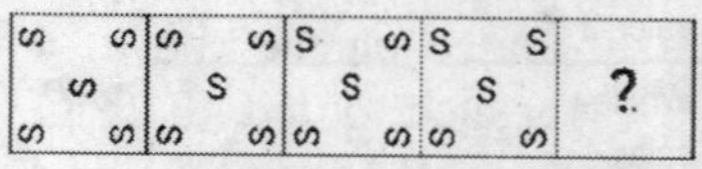

A. 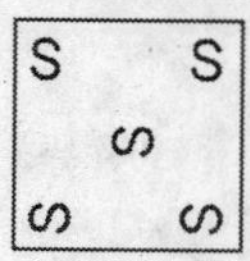 B. 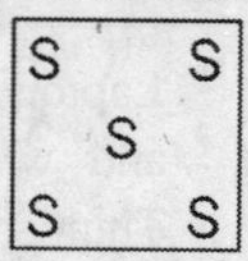

C. 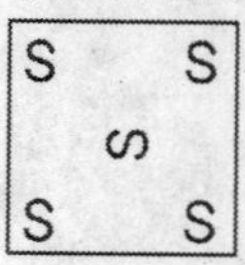 D. 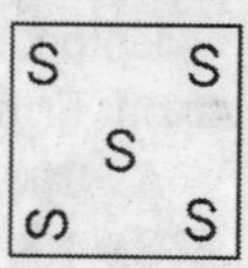

45. C	**46.** A	**47.** C	**48.** C	**49.** D

50. Select the set in which the numbers are related in the same way as are the numbers of the given sets.

(NOTE: Operations should be performed on the whole numbers, without breaking down the numbers into their constituent digits. E.g. 13— Operations on 13 such as adding/deleting/multiplying etc. to 13 can be performed. Breaking down 13 into 1 and 3 and then performing mathematical operations on 1 and 3 is not allowed.)

11 : 87 : 34

6 : 28 : 8

A. 9 : 25 : 54

B. 7 : 35 : 12

C. 8 : 19 : 47

D. 12 : 81 : 63

Quantitative Aptitude

51. The table below shows the laptop sold on different days by different wholesalers. Study the table and answer the questions that follow.

	Mon	Tues	Wed	Thurs	Fri
Whole-saler 1	22	20	14	24	10
Whole-saler 2	46	45	06	14	8
Whole-saler 3	18	40	07	15	19
Whole-saler 4	23	30	32	06	26

Laptop sold by wholesaler 1 and wholesaler 2 together on Thursday is what per cent of laptop sold by wholesalers 3 on Friday?

A. 200% B. 150%

C. 100% D. 50%

52. Find the area of a right-angled triangle whose base is 12 cm and hypotenuse is 13 cm.

A. 30 cm^2 B. 55 cm^2

C. 65 cm^2 D. 22 cm^2

53. Find the value of tan (50 + θ) – cot (40 – θ).

A. $\frac{1}{2}$ B. –1

C. 0 D. 1

54. In 2021, Sam received an annual increment in his salary by 40% but due to recession in 2022, the company started taking cost-cutting measures and his salary was reduced by 15%. What was the net change in his salary?

A. 17% increase

B. 19% increase

C. 9% decrease

D. 11% increase

50. D **51.** A **52.** A **53.** C **54.** B

55. A rod of 5 cm radius and 52 c n length is converted into a wire of 100 cm length of uniform thickness. The radius of the wire (in cm) is:

A. $\sqrt{13}$ B. $\sqrt{15}$

C. $\sqrt{23}$ D. $\sqrt{17}$

56. If $\left(y^2+\frac{1}{y^2}\right) = 74$ and $y > 1$, find the value of $\left(y-\frac{1}{y}\right)$.

A. $6\sqrt{2}$ B. $-2\sqrt{19}$

C. $2\sqrt{19}$ D. $-6\sqrt{2}$

57. If a sum of money at simple interest becomes 45 times in 110 years, then in how many years will that sum become 23 times?

A. 48 B. 60

C. 55 D. 50

58. Two trains 320 m and 205 m in length are running towards each other on parallel lines. One train runs at the rate of 70 kmph and the other train runs at the rate of 56 kmph. Find the time they will take to cross each other (in seconds).

A. 10 B. 20

C. 12 D. 15

59. A can complete a task in the same time in which B and C work together. If A and B could complete it jointly in 10 days and C alone in 50 days, then B could complete it independently in:

A. 26 days B. 27 days

C. 25 days D. 23 days

60. What is the value of $(1 - \sin^2 A)\,\mathrm{cosec}^2 A$? Given A is an acute angle.

A. $\cot^2 A$ B. $\cos^2 A$

C. $\tan^2 A$ D. $\sin^2 A$

61. If $3x - 2y = 3$ and $xy = 9$, then find the value of $3x + 2y$.

A. 16 B. 13

C. 14 D. 15

62. Study the table given below and answer the question that follows. The table below shows the total number of students studying different subjects in a college and the percentage of boys and girls.

Subject	Number of Students	Percentage of Girls	Percentage of Boys
Hindi	110	60	40
English	70	50	50
Physics	50	30	70
Chemistry	40	80	20
Mathematics	80	20	80
Computers	90	40	60

What is the ratio of the total number of girls in all the subjects to that of boys in all the subjects?

A. 5 : 6 B. 7 : 9

C. 6 : 7 D. 2 : 3

55. A **56.** A **57.** C **58.** D **59.** C **60.** A **61.** D **62.** A

63. Simplify the following:

18 × [24 ÷ 70 × {25 × 49 ÷ {5 × 7}}]

A. 218 B. 216
C. 215 D. 220

64. A 40-litre mixture of milk and water contains milk and water in the ratio of 7 : 3. How many litres of water should be added to the mixture so that the resulting mixture has 60% of water in it?

A. 30 B. 35
C. 20 D. 25

65. ΔABC inscribe in a circle with center O. If AB = 9 cm, BC = 40 cm and AC = 41 cm, then what is the circum-radius of a triangle?

A. $20\frac{1}{2}$ cm B. $12\frac{1}{2}$ cm

C. $18\frac{1}{2}$ cm D. $16\frac{1}{2}$ cm

66. The compound interest accrued on a sum of ₹ 20,000 at the end of 2 years compounded annually is ₹ 2,050. Find the compound interest at the end of the 3rd year.

A. ₹ 3,153.50
B. ₹ 2,852.50
C. ₹ 3,152.50
D. ₹ 3,154.50

67. If tan 15° = $2-\sqrt{3}$, then the value of tan 15° cot 75° + tan 75° cot 15° is:

A. 6 B. 10
C. 8 D. 14

68. A certain sum was to be divided between A and B in the ratio 8 : 5. However by mistake, it was divided in the ratio 5 : 8. Thus, A gets ₹ 300 less than his original share. Find the sum.

A. ₹ 2,600 B. ₹ 1,500
C. ₹ 1,300 D. ₹ 600

69. Akash sold a motorcycle to Navin at a profit of 10%. Navin sold it to Vinay at a profit of 20%. Vinay sold it to Vishal at a loss of 5%. If Vishal paid ₹ 62,700 for the motorcycle, then what was the cost of the motorcycle (in ₹) for Akash?

A. 48,000 B. 48,500
C. 52,500 D. 50,000

70. The perimeters of two similar triangles XYZ and PQR are respectively 62 cm and 42 cm. If PQ = 21 cm, find XY:

A. 27 cm B. 28 cm
C. 29 cm D. 31 cm

71. If $px + qy = 1$ and $qx + py = \frac{2pq}{p^2+q^2}$, then $(x^2 + y^2)(p^2 + q^2)$ is equal to:

A. 2 B. 3
C. 0 D. 1

63. B **64.** A **65.** A **66.** C **67.** D **68.** C **69.** D **70.** D **71.** D

72. The radii of two circles are 9 cm and 4 cm, the distance between their centres is 13 cm, then the length of the direct common tangent is:
A. 8 cm B. 14 cm
C. 12 cm D. 16 cm

73. If an electricity bill is paid before the due date, one gets a reduction of 13% on the amount of the bill. By paying the bill before the due date, Ravi got a reduction of ₹ 260.39. The amount of his electricity bill (in ₹) was:
A. 2,003 B. 2,580
C. 2,230 D. 2,064

74. A salesman marks his goods 30% above the cost and gives a discount of 10% on them. Find his gain or loss percentage.
A. Loss 7% B. Gain 7%
C. Loss 17% D. Gain 17%

75. Study the given pie-chart and answer the question that follows. Percentage-wise distribution of teachers in six different subjects in a school is given in the pie-chart. The total number of teachers is 600. The ratio of male and female teachers is 3 : 1.

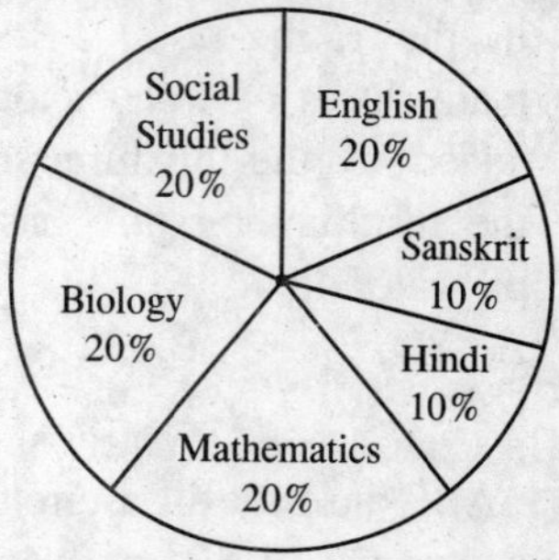

Find the ratio of teachers in English, Sanskrit and Hindi to teachers in Mathematics, Biology and Social Studies.
A. 2 : 5 B. 1 : 2
C. 2 : 3 D. 1 : 5

General Awareness

76. Which is the most powerful river in the world in terms of its volume and extensive drainage into the Atlantic Ocean?
A. Congo B. Amazon
C. Amur D. Nile

77. Which of the following statements about Akshdeep Singh is NOT true?
A. Akshdeep Singh won the National Race Walking Championship.
B. Akshdeep Singh qualified for the Paris 2024 Olympics and World Athletics Championships 2023.
C. Akshdeep Singh won a medal at Nomi in 2023.
D. In the men's 20 km race walk event, Akshdeep Singh clocked 1 hour 19 minutes 55 seconds, a new national record, to win the Silver medal.

72. C	73. A	74. D	75. C	76. B	77. D

78. The law of octaves asserts that every eighth element has comparable properties when grouped in increasing order of their atomic masses and is also known as:

A. Gravity relation
B. Doppler relation
C. Coulomb's relation
D. Newland's relation

79. Which of the following regions in India is nicknamed as the storehouse of minerals?

A. Deccan Plateau
B. Western Ghats
C. Chota Nagpur
D. Himalayas

80. Which of the following is consistent with import substitution policy?

A. Capital account convertibility
B. Flexible exchange rate policy
C. Tariffs and quotas
D. Current account convertibility

81. Which of the following will be considered as normal residents of India?

(*a*) Indians working in foreign embassies in India
(*b*) Ambassador for India in rest of the world

A. Only (*a*)
B. Only (*b*)
C. Both (*a*) and (*b*)
D. Neither (*a*) nor (*b*)

82. Which of the following is the most problematic and primary difficulty of barter exchanges as against money-based exchanges?

A. Bartered exchanges involve difficulty in preserving value.
B. Barter exchanges may result in an incorrect valuation of the goods transacted.
C. Barter exchanges may be imperfectly divisible.
D. Barter exchanges require a double coincidence of wants.

83. Who among the following personalities is a professional Kuchipudi Dancer?

A. Radha Sridhar
B. Surupa Sen
C. Anupama Hoskere
D. Kaushalya Reddy

84. Which region has the maximum concentration of Iron and Steel industries?

A. Shillong Plateau
B. Deccan Plateau
C. Chota Nagpur Plateau
D. Malwa Plateau

85. Who among the following has been accused of committing the judicial murder of Raja Nand Kumar?

A. Lord Wellesly
B. Lord Dalhousie
C. Lord Cornwallis
D. Warren Hastings

78. D **79.** C **80.** C **81.** C **82.** D **83.** D **84.** C **85.** D

86. In which year did Swami Dayanand Saraswati establish Arya Samaj?
A. 1875 B. 1867
C. 1828 D. 1887

87. Which of the following is a transfer payment?
(*a*) Unemployment allowances
(*b*) Scholarships
(*c*) Retirement pension
A. Only (*a*)
B. All of (*a*), (*b*) and (*c*)
C. Only (*a*) and (*b*)
D. Only (*c*)

88. Which equation was verified by American scientists Nichols and Hull in 1903 by measuring the radiation pressure of visible light?
A. Pr = C/N B. P = L/M
C. P = F/A D. P = U/C

89. Match the items in List-I with those in List-II.

Measure of Money Supply	Formula
(*i*) M_1	(*a*) $M_1 + T_d$
(*ii*) M_2	(*b*) $C_p + D_d + O_d$
(*iii*) M_3	(*c*) $M_3 + TPO_d$
(*iv*) M_4	(*d*) $M_1 + POSB_d$

	(*i*)	(*ii*)	(*iii*)	(*iv*)
A.	(*d*)	(*a*)	(*c*)	(*b*)
B.	(*b*)	(*d*)	(*a*)	(*c*)
C.	(*a*)	(*d*)	(*b*)	(*c*)
D.	(*c*)	(*b*)	(*a*)	(*d*)

90. Sheorinarayan fair is held in which of the following states?
A. West Bengal
B. Jharkhand
C. Chhattisgarh
D. Madhya Pradesh

91. Where is Bhimrao Ambedkar Multipurpose Stadium situated?
A. Faizabad B. Ghaziabad
C. Kanpur D. Patna

92. Which of the following Articles of the Indian Constitution has the idea that 'No child below the age of fourteen years shall be employed to work in any factory or mine or engaged in any other hazardous employment'?
A. Article 22
B. Article 24
C. Article 19
D. Article 20

93. Totaram Sharma is associated with which of the following instruments?
A. Tanpura
B. Panchavadyam
C. Pakhawaj
D. Sarangi

94. The founders of Vijayanagara Empire were the feudatories of which of the following dynasties?
A. Hoysala B. Pandya
C. Kakatiya D. Chola

86. A **87.** B **88.** D **89.** B **90.** C **91.** A **92.** B **93.** C **94.** C

95. The Pakhawaj syllables are primarily used to conclude which of the following Indian classical dances?
A. Manipuri B. Kathak
C. Odissi D. Kathakali

96. Who among the following was a member of the Drafting Committee of the Constituent Assembly?
A. Dr. K.M. Munshi
B. B.N. Rao
C. T.T. Krisknamachari
D. N. Madhav Rau

97. In the 2023 Women's World Boxing Championship gold medal match, Lovlina Borgohain defeated Australia's Caitlin Parker in the ________ kg weight category.
A. 70 B. 75
C. 80 D. 85

98. In March 2023, the Pension Fund Regulatory and Development Authority (PFRDA) amended the 2015 PFRDA Regulation to increase the age limit for the Ombudsman from 65 to ______ years.
A. 77 B. 80
C. 70 D. 90

99. The literacy rate of Andhra Pradesh state as per the Census of 2011 is ______ .
A. 66.48% B. 67.02%
C. 66% D. 68.5%

100. In which year did Rudolf Ludwig Karl Virchow formulate his famous aphorism 'Omnis cellula-e cellula' which became a part of the foundation of cell theory?
A. 1855 B. 1869
C. 1840 D. 1835

Explanatory Answers

1. **(D):** Dynamic refers to something characterized by constant change, activity, or progress. Energetic is the most appropriate synonym because it conveys a similar sense of vigor, activity, and movement. Both words suggest a high level of activity and motion, making energetic a suitable choice as a synonym for dynamic.

2. **(D):** In the context of the sentence, the term "archive" refers to a collection of historical documents or records that are preserved for research, reference, or historical purposes. Archives typically contain a wide range of materials such as manuscripts, letters, photographs, maps, and other documents that provide insight into the past.

95. C	**96.** A	**97.** B	**98.** C	**99.** B	**100.** A

3. (C): Guile refers to cunning, slyness, or craftiness, often used to deceive or manipulate others. The most appropriate antonym for "guile" would be an attribute or quality that suggests honesty, straight-forwardness, or sincerity.

4. (B): "Hoard" is a verb that means to accumulate or store something in a large quantity, especially for future use. In this context, it refers to ants collecting and storing food during the summer to use during the winter months.

5. (A): The error is in part A. "A owl was" should be corrected to "An owl was" because "owl" begins with a vowel sound, so it requires the article "an" instead of "a."

6. (C): An anthropologist is a social scientist who specializes in the study of humanity, particularly the study of human societies and cultures throughout history. This includes the study of human evolution, behaviour, and culture. Therefore, an anthropologist is someone who studies the evolution of mankind.

7. (B): When someone violates rules, they fail to uphold or follow them. So, the opposite of "violated" in this context would be to uphold or follow the rules. "Redeem" can mean to make up for a fault or mistake, to restore someone's reputation or honor, or to fulfill a promise or obligation.

Therefore, the most appropriate antonym for "redeem" in this context would be the word that signifies the opposite of violating rules.

8. (C): "Portable" refers to something that is easy to carry or move from one place to another. It implies that the object is lightweight, compact, and designed for easy transportation. Portable items are often convenient for travel, commuting, or temporary use in different locations.

9. (B): It describes an imagined or idealized place or state where everything is perfect, often in terms of politics, society, laws, and customs. In a utopian society, there is typically equality, peace, harmony, and happiness among its inhabitants. The concept of utopia is often used in literature, philosophy, and political discourse to explore ideas about the ideal society and human aspirations.

10. (D): "Ill health" succinctly encapsulates the state of being in poor physical or mental condition. It encompasses a range of ailments, diseases, and conditions that impair one's well-being. Whether it's a physical illness or a mental health issue, "ill health" describes the condition of being unwell or suffering from discomfort or impairment.

11. **(B):** The error lies in segment B, "They were laid." The verb "were laid" is in the past tense and passive voice, suggesting that someone else laid them down.

However, the context of the sentence implies that the subjects ("they") laid themselves down in the sun, which requires the active voice.

12. **(D):** Exhilarate is the correct spelling for the word that means to make someone feel happy and excited.

13. **(C):** "My family never supported me," accomplishes this by placing the subject ("my family") at the beginning of the sentence and the verb "supported" indicates the action performed by the subject.

This construction presents the sentence in active voice, making it clear that the family is the one not providing support.

14. **(A):** in the acknolledgments of the book

The correct spelling should be "acknowledg-ments." Therefore, the corrected segment is: in the acknowledgments of the book.

15. **(B):** The antonym "noble" suggests qualities such as honorable, generous, or possessing high moral principles. It stands in contrast to "mean," as it implies characteristics that are virtuous and commendable. Therefore noble is the most appropriate antonym for mean in this context.

16. **(A):** The idiom "on the cards" means that something is likely to happen or is expected to occur in the future.

In the context of the sentence "Nitish's promotion is due," it suggests that Nitish's promotion is expected to happen soon or is very likely to occur.

17. **(B):** The sentence talks about the transmission of cultural patterns.

(*c*) "the royal style is the agent" introduces the concept of something influencing social evolution.

(*a*) "in social evolution by imitation" explains how the royal style acts as an agent (through imitation).

(*d*) "and cultural patterns are similarly transmitted by the dominant caste" adds another layer, suggesting dominant castes also influence cultural patterns.

(*b*) "by reason of its higher standard of living" provides a potential reason why the royal style might be imitated (because of a perceived better lifestyle).

18. (C): In the given sentence, the action of disturbing the meeting is performed by the subject "an agitated gathering of workers in the company." To transform this active sentence into passive voice, the object of the active sentence ("the meeting") becomes the subject of the passive sentence, and the subject of the active sentence ("an agitated gathering of workers in the company") becomes the agent, introduced by the preposition "by."

19. (D): The idiom "costs an arm and a leg" is used to emphasize that something is very expensive. It implies that the price of the item or service is so high that it feels as though one would have to pay a significant, perhaps exaggerated, amount—equivalent to the loss of a limb—to obtain it.

20. (D): In the given sentence, the word **that best fits in** the blank is reign. **Reign refers** to the period **during which** someone, particularly a monarch or ruler, holds power or authority. In this context, it suggests the period of leadership or authority of the company's CEO.

21. (D): Concept is the most fitting because it refers to a general idea, which aligns with the idea of globalization being a broad phenomenon.

22. (D): Rare makes sense because the passage talks about commodities that were not readily available and therefore valuable for trade.

23. (B): Advances is the most suitable choice because it signifies progress and improvement, which is what the Industrial Revolution brought to transportation and communication.

24. (D): Stalled indicates a halt or pause in progress, which aligns with the information that globalization slowed down after World War I.

25. (A): Protectionism refers to government policies that aim to shield domestic industries from foreign competition. This aligns with the passage mentioning nations raising import taxes to protect their industries.

27. (C): From given statements: Conclusions:

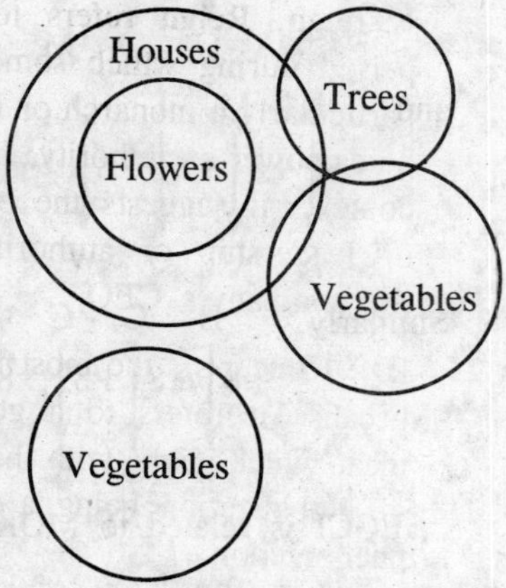

I. Some vegetables are houses is a possibility. (True)

II. Some flowers are trees is a possibility. (True)

III. No Vegetable is a house. (False)

Here, Both conclusions I and II follow.

28. (D): Given, A = ÷, B = ×, C = +, D = –

∴ 4B18D5C9A9

= 4 × 18 – 5 + 9 ÷ 9

= 4 × 18 – 5 + 1

= 72 + 1 – 5

= 73 – 5

= 68.

29. (D): Given, + and – are interchanged with ÷ and × respectively

∴ 88 + 8 – 17 × 16 ÷ 40

= 88 ÷ 8 × 17 – 16 + 40

= 11 × 17 – 16 + 40

= 187 – 16 + 40

= 227 – 16

= 211.

30. (B): Given,

BALD = 7680 ...(*i*)

and DRAB = 8097 ...(*ii*)

From (*i*) and (*ii*), we get,

AD = 80

BL = 67

and BR = 79

Here, B = 7,

L = 6

and R = 9

Hence, 6 is code for 'L' in the given code language.

31. (D): BJKSX

+2 +2 +2 +2 +2

AB, DEFG, I J KL, NOPQ, STUV, XY

Here, Option (D) will complete the series.

33. (C): Given,

R S P T

+4 +4 +4 +4

V W T X

and M N K O

+4 +4 +4 +4

Q R O S

Similarly,

G H E I

+4 ↓ +4 ↓ +4 ↓ +4 ↓

K L I M

∴ GHEI is related to KLIM.

34. (D): (A) 2 – 6

$\Rightarrow 2 \times 2 + 2 = 4 + 2$
$= 6$

(B) 4 – 20

$\Rightarrow 4 \times 4 + 4 = 16 + 4$
$= 20$

(C) 5 – 30

$\Rightarrow 5 \times 5 + 5 = 25 + 5$
$= 30$

(D) 8 – 75

$\Rightarrow 8 \times 8 + 8 = 64 + 8$
$= 72$

Here, option (D) does not belong to that group.

35. (C): Given, QUEZAL = 82

$\Rightarrow 17 + 21 + 5 + 26 + 1 + 12 = 82$

LUCKY = 72

$\Rightarrow 12 + 21 + 3 + 11 + 25 = 72$

Similarly,

ADVERSE = ?

$\Rightarrow 1 + 4 + 22 + 5 + 18 + 19 + 5$

$= 74$

∴ 74 is the code for 'ADVERSE' in the given code language.

36. (B): Given,

G I E K

+8 ↓ +8 ↓ +8 ↓ +8 ↓

O Q M S

and

K M I O

+8 ↓ +8 ↓ +8 ↓ +8 ↓

S U Q W

Similarly,

E G C I

+8 ↓ +8 ↓ +8 ↓ +8 ↓

M O K Q

∴ EGCI is related to MOKQ.

37. (D): (A) $5 : 20 \Rightarrow 5 : 5 \times 4$

(B) $4 : 12 \Rightarrow 4 : 4 \times 3$

(C) $7 : 42 \Rightarrow 7 : 7 \times 6$

(D) $6 : 36 \Rightarrow 6 : 6 \times 6$

Here, option (D) is the odd number-pair.

38. (A):

(A) W Z B (W →+3→ Z →+2→ B)

(B) U W X (U →+2→ W →+1→ X)

(C) O R T (O →+3→ R →+2→ T)

(D) G J L (G →+3→ J →+2→ L)

Here, option (B) does not belong to that group.

39. (A): F × G – H ÷ I + J

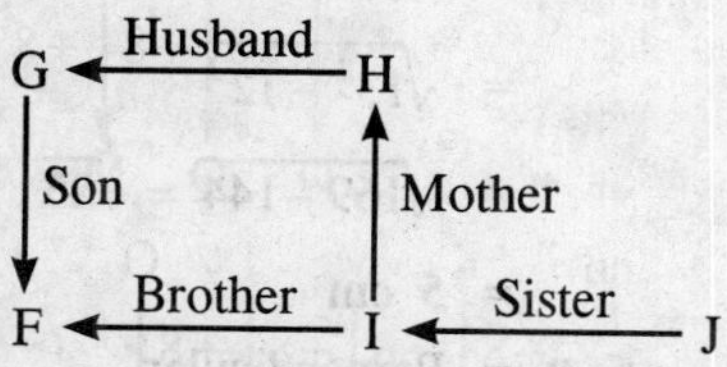

Here, F is the brother of J.

40. (A): Given, 9 July 1978 = Sunday

Number of odd day from 9 July, 1978 to 9 July, 1983
= (1 + 2 + 1 + 1 + 1) = 6

On 9 July 1983, it was Saturday

Now, Number of day from 10 July to 19 September, 1983
= 22 + 31 + 19
= 72 days
= 10 weeks + 2 days
= 2 odd days

Hence, 19 September, 1983
= Saturday + 2 days
= Monday

Hence, it was Monday.

42. (B): From given question,

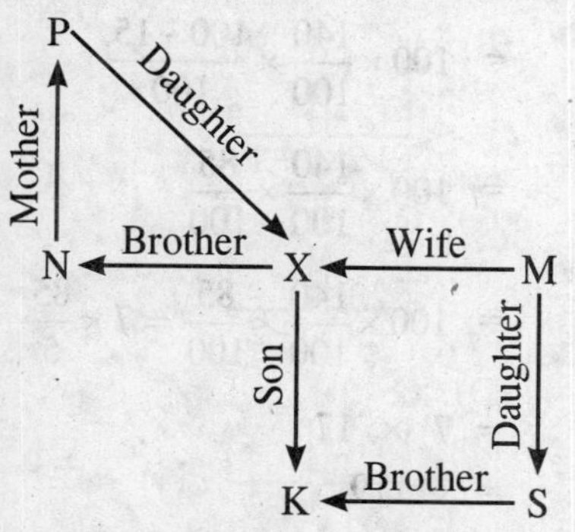

Here, K is the daughter's son of P.

43. (D):

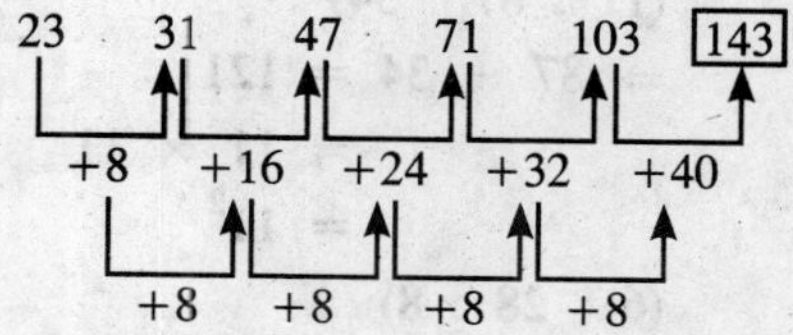

Here, 143 should come in place of X in the given series.

44. (D):

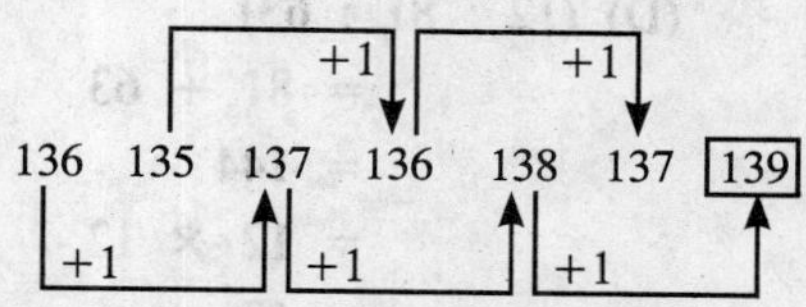

Here, ? = the next number
= 139.

45. (C): Given, number of pairs

(15, 96)
⇒ 15 × 6 + 6 = 90 + 6
= 96

(35, 216)
⇒ 35 × 6 + 6 = 210 + 6
= 216

Similarly, (C) (29, 180)
⇒ 29 × 6 + 6 = 174 + 6
= 180

∴ Option (C) are related in the same way as are the numbers of the given sets.

48. (C): BBDD

∴ A<u>B</u>CD, <u>B</u>CDA, C<u>D</u>AB, <u>D</u>ABC

Here, option (C) will complete the series.

50. (D): Given, sets,

(11 : 87 : 34)

$\Rightarrow 87 + 34 = 121$

$= 11 \times 11$

$= 11^2$

(6 : 28 : 8)

$\Rightarrow 28 + 8 = 36 = 6 \times 6$

$= 6^2$

Similarly,

(D) (12 : 81 : 63)

$= 81 + 63$

$= 144$

$= 12 \times 12$

$= 12^2$

$\therefore$ Option (D) are related in the same way as are the numbers of the given sets.

51. (A): From given table,

Laptop sold by wholesaler 1 and wholesaler 2 together on Thursday

$= 24 + 14$

$= 38$

and laptop sold by wholesalar 3 on Friday = 19

$$\therefore \quad 19 \times \frac{x}{100} = 38$$

$$\Rightarrow x = \frac{38 \times 100}{19} = 200\%$$

Here, required per cent = 200%.

52. (A): Given, a right-angled-triangle

Base = 12 cm

and hypotenuse = 13 cm

$$\therefore \; p = \sqrt{h^2 - b^2}$$

$$= \sqrt{13^2 - 12^2}$$

$$= \sqrt{169 - 144} = \sqrt{25}$$

$$= 5 \text{ cm}$$

$\Rightarrow p$ = Perpendicular

= 5 cm

$\therefore$ The area of a right-angled-triangle

$$= \frac{1}{2} \times \text{base} \times \text{perpendicular}$$

$$= \frac{1}{2} \times 12 \times 5$$

$$= 30 \text{ cm}^2.$$

53. (C): $\tan (50 + \theta) - \cot (40 - \theta)$

$= \tan (50 + \theta) - \cot [90 - (50 + \theta)]$

$= \tan (50 + \theta) - \tan (50 + \theta)$

$= 0.$

54. (B): Let original Salary

= ₹ 100

Then, New salary

$$= 100 \times \frac{140}{100} \times \frac{100 - 15}{100}$$

$$= 100 \times \frac{140}{100} \times \frac{85}{100}$$

$$= 100 \times \frac{140}{100} \times \frac{85}{100} = 7 \times \frac{85}{5}$$

$= 7 \times 17$

= ₹ 119

Hence, the net change in his salary = 19% increase.

55. (A): Let the radius of the wire be r cm

Then, Volume of a rod

= Volume of the wire

$\Rightarrow \pi(5)^2 \times 52 = \pi r^2 \times 100$

$\Rightarrow 25 \times 52 = 100r^2$

$\Rightarrow r^2 = \frac{25 \times 52}{100} = 13$

$\Rightarrow r = \sqrt{13}$ cm

Hence, the radius of the wire $= \sqrt{13}$ cm.

56. (A): Given, $y^2 + \frac{1}{y^2} = 74$

and $y > 1$

$\because \left(y - \frac{1}{y}\right)^2 = y^2 + \frac{1}{y^2} - 2y.\frac{1}{y}$

$= y^2 + \frac{1}{y^2} - 2$

$= 74 - 2$

$= 72$

$\Rightarrow \left(y - \frac{1}{y}\right) = \sqrt{72} = \sqrt{36 \times 2}$

$\Rightarrow \left(y - \frac{1}{y}\right) = 6\sqrt{2}$.

57. (C): $r = \frac{(n-1) \times 100}{t}$

and $t = \frac{(n-1) \times 100}{r}$

$\therefore r = \frac{(45-1) \times 100}{110}$

$= \frac{44 \times 100}{110} = 40\%$

and $t = \frac{(23-1) \times 100}{40}$

$= \frac{22 \times 5}{2}$

= 55 years

$\therefore$ Required years = 55 years.

58. (D): Relative speed of train

= (70 + 56) km/h

$= 126 \times \frac{5}{18}$

$= 21 \times \frac{5}{3}$

$= 7 \times 5$

= 35 m/s

and the length of two trains

= (320 + 205) m

= 525 m

$\therefore$ Time taken by train to cross each-other

$= \frac{525}{35}$

= 15 seconds.

59. (C): Let A can complete a task in x day's

= (B + C) can complete it in x days

Then, A's 1 day's work

= (B + C)'s 1 day's work

$= \frac{1}{x}$

and given, (A + B)'s 1 day's work

$= \frac{1}{10}$

and C's 1 day's work $= \frac{1}{50}$

$\therefore$ (A + B + C)'s 1 day's work

$= \frac{1}{10} + \frac{1}{50}$

$\Rightarrow \frac{1}{x} + \frac{1}{x} = \frac{5+1}{50}$

$\Rightarrow \quad \frac{2}{x} = \frac{6}{50}$

$\Rightarrow \quad \frac{1}{x} = \frac{3}{50}$

A's 1 day's work

= (B + C)'s 1 day work

$= \frac{3}{25}$

B's 1 day's work = (A + B)'s 1 day work − A's 1 day work

$= \frac{1}{10} - \frac{3}{50}$

$= \frac{5-3}{50} = \frac{2}{50} = \frac{1}{25}$

Hence, B could complete it independently in 25 days.

60. (A): $(1 - \sin^2 A) \operatorname{cosec}^2 A$

$= \cos^2 A . \frac{1}{\sin^2 A} = \cot^2 A.$

61. (D): Given, $3x - 2y = 3$ and $xy = 9$

$\Rightarrow \quad (3x - 2y)^2 = 3^2$

$\Rightarrow 9x^2 + 4y^2 - 2 \times 3x \times 2y = 9$

$\Rightarrow 9x^2 + 4y^2 - 12xy = 9$

$\Rightarrow 9x^2 + 4y^2 - 12xy + 24xy$
$= 9 + 24xy$

$\Rightarrow 9x^2 + 4y^2 + 12xy$
$= 9 + 24 \times 9$

$\Rightarrow (3x + 2y)^2 = 9(1 + 24)$
$= 9 \times 25$

$\Rightarrow (3x + 2y)^2 = 225 = (15)^2$

$\Rightarrow \quad 3x + 2y = 15.$

62. (A): From given table:

The total number of girls in all subjects

$= 110 \times \frac{60}{100} + 70 \times \frac{50}{100}$
$+ 50 \times \frac{30}{100} + 40 \times \frac{80}{100}$
$+ 80 \times \frac{20}{100} + 90 \times \frac{40}{100}$

$= 66 + 35 + 15 + 32 + 16 + 36 = 200$

and the total number of boys in all subjects

$= 110 \times \frac{40}{100} + 70 \times \frac{50}{100}$
$+ 50 \times \frac{70}{100} + 40 \times \frac{20}{100}$
$+ 80 \times \frac{80}{100} + 90 \times \frac{60}{100}$

$= 44 + 35 + 35 + 8 + 64 + 54$

$= 240$

Hence, required ratio

$= 200 : 240$

$= 5 : 6.$

63. (B): $18 \times [24 \div 70 \times \{25 \times 49 \div (5 \times 7)\}]$

$$= 18 \times \left[24 \div 70 \times \left\{25 \times 49 \times \frac{1}{5 \times 7}\right\}\right]$$

$= 18 \times [24 \div 70 \times \{5 \times 7\}]$

$= 18 \times [24 \div 70 \times 35]$

$$= 18 \times \left[24 \times \frac{1}{70} \times 35\right]$$

$$= 18 \times \left[24 \times \frac{1}{2}\right]$$

$= 18 \times 12$

$= 216.$

64. (A): $\because$ Quantity of milk in mixture

$$= 40 \times \frac{7}{7+3}$$

$$= 40 \times \frac{7}{10}$$

$= 28$ litres

and quantity of water in mixture

$$= 40 \times \frac{3}{10}$$

$= 12$ litres

Let x litres of water should be added

Then,

$$12 + x = (40 + x) \times \frac{60}{100}$$

$$\Rightarrow \quad 12 + x = (40 + x) \times \frac{3}{5}$$

$\Rightarrow 5(12 + x) = 3(40 + x)$

$\Rightarrow 60 + 5x = 120 + 3x$

$\Rightarrow 2x = 60$

$\Rightarrow x = 30$ litres

Hence, required water = 30 litres.

66. (C): Compound interest

$$= P\left(1 + \frac{r}{100}\right)^n - P$$

$\Rightarrow$ ₹ 2050

$$= ₹\ 20,000\left[\left(1 + \frac{r}{100}\right)^2 - 1\right]$$

$$\Rightarrow \left(1 + \frac{r}{100}\right)^2 - 1 = \frac{2050}{20,000}$$

$$\Rightarrow \left(1 + \frac{r}{100}\right)^2 = 1 + \frac{41}{400} = \frac{441}{400}$$

$$\Rightarrow \left(1 + \frac{r}{100}\right)^2 = \left(\frac{21}{20}\right)^2$$

$$\Rightarrow 1 + \frac{r}{100} = \frac{21}{20}$$

$$\Rightarrow \frac{r}{100} = \frac{21}{20} - 1 = \frac{1}{20}$$

$\therefore \quad r = 5\%$

Now, compound interest at the end of 3rd year

$$= P\left(1 + \frac{r}{100}\right)^n - P$$

$$= P\left[\left(1 + \frac{r}{100}\right)^n - 1\right]$$

$$= 20,000\left[\left(1+\frac{5}{100}\right)^3 - 1\right]$$

$$= 20,000\left[\left(\frac{21}{20}\right)^3 - 1\right]$$

$$= 20,000\left[\frac{9261}{8000} - 1\right]$$

$$= 20,000\left[\frac{1261}{8000}\right]$$

$$= 20 \times \frac{1261}{8} = \frac{5 \times 1261}{2} = \frac{6305}{2}$$

= ₹ 3152.50.

67. (D): Given,

$\tan 15° = 2 - \sqrt{3}$

$\therefore \tan 15° \cot 75° + \tan 75° \cot 15°$

$= \tan 15° \cot (90 - 15°) + \tan (90 - 15) \cot 15°$

$= \tan 15° \tan 15° + \cot 15° \cot 15°$

$= \tan^2 15° + \cot^2 15°$

$$= \tan^2 15° + \frac{1}{\tan^2 15°}$$

$$= \left(2-\sqrt{3}\right)^2 + \frac{1}{\left(2-\sqrt{3}\right)^2}$$

$$= 4+3-4\sqrt{3} + \frac{1}{4+3-4\sqrt{3}}$$

$$= \left(7-4\sqrt{3}\right) + \frac{1}{\left(7-4\sqrt{3}\right)}$$

$$= \frac{(7-4\sqrt{3})^2 + 1}{7-4\sqrt{3}}$$

$$= \frac{49+48-56\sqrt{3}+1}{7-4\sqrt{3}}$$

$$= \frac{98-56\sqrt{3}}{7-4\sqrt{3}}$$

$$= \frac{14\left(7-4\sqrt{3}\right)}{\left(7-4\sqrt{3}\right)} = 14.$$

68. (C): Let a certain sum = ₹ x

Then, A's share $= \frac{8x}{13}$

B's share $= \frac{5x}{13}$

By Mistake,

A's share $= \frac{5x}{13}$

and B's share $= \frac{8x}{13}$

According to question,

$$\frac{5x}{13} = \frac{8x}{13} - 300$$

$$\Rightarrow \frac{8x}{13} - \frac{5x}{13} = 300$$

$$\Rightarrow \frac{3x}{13} = 300$$

$\Rightarrow$ x = ₹ 1300

Hence, The sum = x

= ₹ 1300.

69. (D): Let the C.P. of motorcycle for Akash be ₹ x

Then, C.P. of Motorcycle for Vishal

$$= x \times \frac{110}{100} \times \frac{120}{100} \times \frac{95}{100}$$

$$\Rightarrow ₹\ 67{,}800 = x \times \frac{11}{10} \times \frac{6}{5} \times \frac{19}{20}$$

$$\Rightarrow \quad x = \frac{62700 \times 10 \times 5 \times 20}{11 \times 6 \times 19}$$

$$= \frac{62700 \times 1000}{66 \times 19}$$

$$= \frac{3300 \times 1000}{66}$$

$$= 50 \times 1000$$

$$= 50{,}000$$

Hence, the cost of the motorcycle for Akash = ₹ 50,000.

70. (D): Given, $\Delta XYZ \sim \Delta PQR$

$$\therefore \frac{\text{Perimeter of } \Delta XYZ}{\text{Perimeter of } \Delta PQR} = \frac{XY}{PQ}$$

$$\Rightarrow \quad \frac{64}{42} = \frac{XY}{21}$$

$$\Rightarrow \quad XY = \frac{62 \times 21}{42}$$

$$\Rightarrow \quad XY = 31 \text{ cm.}$$

73. (A): Let the amount of electric bill was ₹ x

Then, $\quad x \times \frac{13}{100} = 260.39$

$$\Rightarrow \quad x = \frac{26039}{13}$$

$$\Rightarrow \quad x = ₹\ 2{,}003.$$

74. (D): Let C.P. of goods = ₹ 100

Then, M.P. = ₹ 130

$$\therefore \quad S.P. = 130 \times \frac{90}{100} = 117$$

$$\therefore \quad \text{Gain} = S.P. - C.P.$$

$$= 117 - 100$$

$$= ₹\ 17$$

and gain % = 17%.

75. (C): From given pie-chart:

The total number of teachers = 600

The total number of teachers in English, Sanskrit and Hindi

$$= 600 \times \frac{20 + 10 + 10}{100}$$

$$= 6 \times 40 = 240$$

and the total number of teachers in Mathematics, Biology and Social Studies

$$= 600 \times \frac{(20 + 20 + 20)}{100}$$

$$= 6 \times 60 = 360$$

$$\therefore \quad \text{Required ratio} = 240 : 360$$

$$= 2 : 3.$$

76. (B): The Amazon River is widely considered the most powerful river in the world based on its volume of water discharge and extensive drainage basin. It carries more water than any other river, accounting for approximately 20% of the total freshwater discharge into the oceans globally. The Amazon River originates in the Andes Mountains of South America and flows across the continent, draining into the Atlantic Ocean.

77. (D): This statement is not correct as Akshdeep Singh actually set a new national record while winning the gold medal (not silver) at the National Open Race Walking competition, clocking 1 hour 19 minutes and 38 seconds, not 1 hour 19 minutes and 55 seconds.

78. (D): The law of octaves, proposed by English chemist John Newlands in 1864, is also known as Newland's relation. It observed a recurring pattern in the properties of elements when arranged by their atomic masses. Newlands found that elements with similar chemical properties tended to appear every eight elements. Newlands' work is recognized as an important step in the history of chemistry.

79. (C): The Chota Nagpur Plateau, located in the eastern part of India, is often referred to as the "storehouse of minerals." This region is rich in mineral resources such as coal, iron ore, copper, mica, bauxite, manganese, and limestone, among others. The presence of these minerals has led to significant industrial development in the area, particularly in sectors such as mining, steel production, and manufacturing.

80. (C): Tariffs and quotas are consistent with import substitution policy because they impose barriers to imports, making foreign goods more expensive or restricting their quantity. By implementing tariffs (taxes on imports) and quotas (limits on the quantity of imports), countries can protect domestic industries from foreign competition, encourage domestic production, and stimulate economic growth.

81. (C):

(*a*) Indians working in foreign embassies in India are considered normal residents of India because they reside in India, even though they may be working for a foreign embassy.

(*b*) Ambassadors for India in the rest of the world are considered normal residents of India because they are representing India in other countries and are likely residing in those countries rather than India.

82. (D): Barter exchanges require a double coincidence of wants, which means that for a transaction to occur, both parties involved must have a desired good or service that the other party wants. This can be highly problematic and is considered the primary difficulty of barter exchanges compared to money-based exchanges. It often leads to inefficiencies and difficulties in finding suitable trading partners.

83. (D): Kaushalya Reddy is a well-known Kuchipudi dancer. Kuchipudi is a classical Indian dance form that originated in the state of Andhra Pradesh. Kaushalya Reddy has dedicated her career to practicing and promoting this traditional dance form. As a professional Kuchipudi dancer, she has likely undergone extensive training in Kuchipudi dance techniques, repertoire, and performance styles.

84. (C): The region in India with the maximum concentration of Iron and Steel industries is Chota Nagpur Plateau. This eastern Indian plateau spreads across the states of Jharkhand, Chhattisgarh, Odisha, and West Bengal.

It's known for its rich mineral resources, including coal, iron ore, copper, bauxite, mica, and manganese. These minerals provide the raw materials necessary for the iron and steel industry, making Chota Nagpur Plateau a hub for steel production in India.

85. (D): Warren Hastings, who served as the Governor-General of India from 1773 to 1785, faced accusations of committing the judicial murder of Raja Nand Kumar. Raja Nand Kumar was a prominent Indian nobleman and diwan (chief minister) of Bihar during the time of the British East India Company's rule in India.

He was arrested by Hastings on charges of corruption and forgery in 1775. Nand Kumar was tried in Calcutta (now Kolkata) and ultimately sentenced to death, despite many believing that the charges against him were politically motivated.

86. (A): Swami Dayanand Saraswati founded Arya Samaj in 1875 in Bombay, India. Arya Samaj is a Hindu reform movement that aimed to promote the values of Vedas (ancient Indian scriptures) and to counteract what Dayanand perceived as the corruptions that had crept into Hindu society over time.

Arya Samaj emphasized the principles of monotheism, social equality, and the rejection of idol worship, caste system, and rituals that were not in line with Vedic teachings.

87. (B): Transfer payments are payments made by the government to individuals or entities that are not in exchange for goods or services currently provided. They are a form of redistribution of wealth.

(*a*) Unemployment allowances are provided to people who are unemployed to help them financially during their job search.

(*b*) Scholarships are financial aid awarded to students to help cover the cost of education.

(*c*) Retirement pensions are regular payments made to individuals after they retire, typically from a fund to which they contributed during their working life.

88. (D): For the equation related to radiation pressure measured by Nichols and Hull, P = U/C. This equation expresses the relationship between the pressure exerted by electromagnetic radiation (light) and the energy density of that radiation. It essentially states that the pressure exerted by light is directly proportional to the energy density of the light and inversely proportional to the speed of light.

90. (C): The Sheorinarayan fair is held in the state of Chhattisgarh, India. It takes place in the town of Sheorinarayan, which is located in the Janjgir-Champa district of Chhattisgarh.

This fair is significant as it celebrates the cultural and religious heritage of the region. It usually occurs during the Hindu festival of Maghi Purnima, which falls in the month of January or February.

91. (A): Bhimrao Ambedkar Multipurpose Stadium, also known as Faizabad Stadium, is located in Faizabad, Uttar Pradesh, India. It is named after Bhimrao Ambedkar, an Indian jurist, economist, politician, and social reformer who is known as the chief architect of the Indian Constitution and a champion of social justice. The stadium serves as a multipurpose sports complex, hosting various sporting events, including cricket matches, football matches, athletic competitions, and cultural events.

92. (B): Article 24 of the Indian Constitution prohibits the employment of children in hazardous occupations. This provision reflects the commitment of the Indian Constitution to protect the rights and welfare of children and ensure their safety and well-being. By prohibiting the employment of children in hazardous occupations, Article 24 aims to prevent child exploitation, protect their health and development, and promote their right to education and a safe childhood.

93. **(C):** Totaram Sharma is a renowned master of the pakhawaj, which is a traditional Indian percussion instrument. It is commonly used in classical Indian music, particularly in the accompaniment of vocal and instrumental performances. Totaram Sharma is celebrated for his mastery of this instrument, known for his skillful playing technique, intricate rhythms, and deep understanding of classical music traditions.

94. **(C):** The founders of the Vijayanagara Empire, Harihara I and Bukka Raya I, were initially feudatories of the Kakatiya dynasty. The Kakatiyas ruled parts of present-day Telangana and Andhra Pradesh in South India. Harihara I and Bukka Raya I served as governors under the Kakatiya dynasty until its decline. Taking advantage of the weakening Kakatiya rule, they established their own kingdom in the region, eventually founding the Vijayanagara Empire around 1336 AD.

95. **(C):** Odissi is a classical dance form originating from Odisha, India. Traditionally, the Pakhawaj was the preferred percussion instrument for Odissi performances. While other instruments are now used as well, the Pakhawaj's rhythmic syllables ("bols") are still incorporated into Odissi dance to create a distinct musical and rhythmic vocabulary for the dance.

96. **(A):** Dr. K.M. Munshi, was a prominent Indian independence activist, politician, and scholar. He was a key figure in the drafting and framing of the Constitution of India. Dr. Munshi was appointed as a member of the Drafting Committee of the Constituent Assembly, which was tasked with the monumental responsibility of preparing the draft of the Indian Constitution. The committee was appointed on August 29, 1947, and was chaired by B. R. Ambedkar.

97. **(B):** The 2023 Women's World Boxing Championship gold medal match in the 75 kg weight category saw Lovlina Borgohain from India competing against Caitlin Parker from

Australia. Lovlina Borgohain emerged victorious in this match, securing the gold medal. This achievement highlights Lovlina Borgohain's skill, determination, and prowess in the sport of boxing.

98. (C): In March 2023, the Pension Fund Regulatory and Development Authority (PFRDA) made amendments to the 2015 PFRDA Regulation regarding the age limit for the Ombudsman. Previously, the age limit for the Ombudsman was set at 65 years. However, with the amendment, the age limit was increased to 70 years, allowing individuals up to the age of 70 to serve as Ombudsman.

99. (B): The literacy rate of Andhra Pradesh state as per the Census of 2011 is 67.02%. This indicates the percentage of the population aged 7 and above who can read and write in any language. It reflects the level of education and literacy attainment within the state.

100. (A): Rudolf Virchow formulated his famous aphorism "Omnis cellula-e cellula" in 1855. This phrase, which translates to "every cell from a cell," became a pivotal part of the foundation of the cell theory. The cell theory states that all living organisms are composed of cells, and that cells arise from pre-existing cells.

Previous Paper (Solved)

SSC-Combined Higher Secondary Level–CHSL (10+2) Tier–1, Online Recruitment Exam–2022

(Exam held on 21-03-2023)

ENGLISH LANGUAGE

1. Choose the sentence with no spelling error.

A. I was rently at a literary festival

B. I was recently at a litrary festival

C. I was recently at a literary festival

D. I was recently at a literery fstival

2. Improve the underlined part of the sentence. Choose 'No improvement' as an answer if the sentence is grammatically correct.

There has been a noticeable fall in the number of children dying from malnutrition.

A. noticeable falling

B. No improvement

C. noticeably falling

D. noticeably falls

3. Rearrange the parts of the sentence in correct order.

P. application, which can also be used to log complaints about

Q. littering or caused by the animals, according to officials

R. registered with the local authority through a mobile phone

S. the residents of Noida can now get their pets like dogs or cats

A. QRPS B. SRPQ

C. PRQS D. RQPS

4. Find the part of the given sentence that has an error in it. If there is no error, choose 'No error'.

Near 800 million people world-wide lack updated sanitation.

A. updated sanitation.

B. people worldwide lack

C. No error

D. Near 800 million

5. Improve the underlined part of the sentence. Choose 'No improvement' as an answer if the sentence is grammatically correct.

Scientists have predicted that the cultivation of rice will be affected severe.

A. affect severe

B. No improvement

C. effecting severely

D. affected severely

6. The given sentence is in active voice. Change the voice of the sentence. Select the correct option from the sentences given in options. She used the aerobic ball during workout.

A. During workout the aerobic ball were to be used by her.

B. During workout the aerobic ball will be used by her.

C. During workout the aerobic ball had been used by her.

D. During workout the aerobic ball was used by her

7. Choose the word that can substitute the given group of words.

A child born after the death of his father

A. Orphan B. Pseudonym

C. Posthumous D. Bigot

8. Select the option that will improve the bracketed part of the sentence. In case no improvement is needed, select 'No improvement'.

Dad said that, "She would have been a great sister if she was just a bit more careful".

A. No improvement

B. that, "She would have been a great sister if she were just a bit more careful"

C. "She would have been a great sister if she were just a bit more careful"

D. "She would have been a greatest sister if she was just a bit more careful"

9. Choose the word that means the same as the given word.

Fad

A. Sensation B. Standard

C. Classic D. Deviant

10. Select the most appropriate option to fill in the blank.

In space it is possible to identify and .... some unique characteristics of human physiology and biology.

A. isolate B. excess

C. replete D. partition

11. Choose the word that is opposite in meaning to the given word.

Devious

A. Outspoken B. Circuitous

C. Clandestine D. Serpentine

12. Choose the word that means the same as the given word.

Nacreous

A. Monochromatic

B. Pale

C. Gloom

D. Iridescent

13. Improve the underlined part of the sentence. Choose 'No improvement' as an answer if the sentence is grammatically correct.

Mary doesn't like cartoons because they are loud, so she <u>doesn't watched them</u>.

A. do not watched this

B. doesn't watch them

C. No improvement

D. does watching them

14. In the following question, out of the given four alternatives, select the alternative which best expresses the meaning of the Idiom/Phrase.

To play with fire

A. Feel sick

B. To take foolish risk

C. To abuse

D. Show disappointment

15. Choose the incorrectly spelt word.

A. Flufy B. Gifted

C. Juggler D. Struggler

16. Parts of the following sentence are given as options. Identify the part that contains a grammatical error. If there is no error, select 'No error'.

That was a good/conversation, I look forward/to meet you.

A. That was a good

B. to meet you.

C. conversation, I look forward

D. No error

17. Select the correct indirect form of the given sentence.

Nandini said, "I bought a pen yesterday."

A. Nandini said she did bought a pen the previous day.

B. Nandini said that she had bought a pen the previous day.

C. Nandini said that she had bought a pen yesterday.

D. Nandini says that she had bought a pen the previous day

18. Select the most appropriate meaning of the given idiom.

Backseat driver

A. A person who offers unsolicited advice.

B. To miss an appointed meeting

C. Attempt to get control over someone

D. To conclude proceedings

19. Choose the word that means the same as the given word.

Corrective

A. Commuting

B. Restorative

C. Compensatory

D. Sluggish

20. Rearrange the parts of the sentence in correct order.

Research shows

P. that medium-skilled employees who work

Q. in front of a computer and work beyond

R. 4.6 effective hours a day produce smaller

S. quantities of output per hour due to fatigue

A. RQSP B. PQSR

C. SQRP D. PQRS

Directions (Qs. No. 21-25): *In the following passage, some words have been deleted. Read the passage carefully and select the correct answer for the given blank out of the four alternatives.*

Rock candy is actually a collection of large sugar crystals that are "grown" from a sugar-water (1) ....

Crystals form when the smallest particles of a substance, the molecules, arrange themselves in a/an (2) .... and repetitive pattern. Molecules are too small for us to see moving around and (3) .... themselves, but you can get a rough idea of what this would look like by taking a small shallow tray and filling it with marbles, ball bearings, or other spheres. As you (4) .... more spheres, the bottom of the tray becomes covered, then the spheres must form layers on top of (5) ...., and a structure or pattern emerges.

21. Select the most appropriate option to fill in blank number 1.
A. convergence
B. ramification
C. disposition
D. solution

22. Select the most appropriate option to fill in blank number 2.
A. orderly B. vastly
C. wholly D. adeptly

23. Select the most appropriate option to fill in blank number 3.
A. summarizing B. shielding
C. arranging D. dividing

24. Select the most appropriate option to fill in blank number 4.
A. add B. curse
C. please D. toil

25. Select the most appropriate option to fill in blank number 5.
A. others B. one
C. one another D. every other

GENERAL INTELLIGENCE

26. In the following question below are given some statements followed by some conclusions based on those statements. Taking the given statements to be true even if they seem to be at variance from commonly known facts. Read all the conclusions and then decide which of the given conclusion logically follows the given statements.

Statements:
I. Some A are T.
II. Some T are H.

Conclusions:
I. No T is A.
II. No H is T.
III. No A is H
A. Only conclusion I follows
B. All conclusion follow
C. Only conclusion II follows
D. Neither conclusion follows

27. In the following question, four number pairs are given. In each pair the number on left side of (–) is related to the number of the right side of (–) with some Logic/Rule/Relation. Three pairs are similar on basis of same Logic/Rule/Relation. Select the odd one out from the given alternatives. (NOTE: Operations should be performed on the whole numbers, without breaking down the numbers into its constituent digits. E.g.13 – Operations on 13 such as adding/subtracting/multiplying etc. to 13 can be performed. Breaking down 13 into 1 and 3 and then performing mathematical operations on 1 and 3 is not allowed)

A. 56885 – 11377
B. 38515 – 7701
C. 74235 – 14847
D. 82695 – 16539

28. A series is given with one term missing. Select the correct alternative from the given ones that will complete the series.

TRAP, MMRE, FHIT, YCZI, ?

A. RYQY B. RXQX
C. RYQX D. RXQY

29. In the following question, select the missing number from the given series.

34, 71, 108, 145, ?, 219

A. 160 B. 182
C. 180 D. 172

30. Words given on the left side of (::) are related with each other by some Logic/Rule/Relation. Select the missing word/word pair on the right side of (::) from the given alternatives based on the same Logic/Rule/Relation.

Six : Hexagon :: ?

A. Four : Rectangle
B. Four : Pentagon
C. Three : Square
D. Seven : Octagon

31. Pointing towards a lady in a photo, Rinku said, "She is my son's sister's mother". How that lady is related to Rinku?

A. Daughter B. Daughter in law
C. Sister D. Wife

32. In the following question, select the odd letter/letters from the given alternatives.

A. KLIO B. RSPT
C. VWTX D. HIFJ

33. Select the option figure in which the given figure is embedded. (Rotation is NOT allowed)

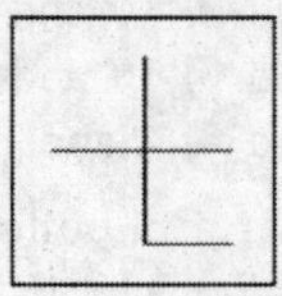

A. 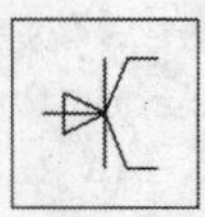 B. 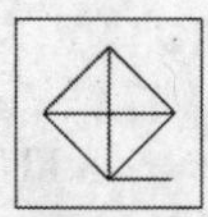

C. 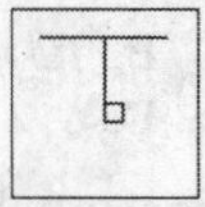 D. 

34. Select the option figure in which the given figure is embedded. (Rotation is NOT allowed)

A.  B. 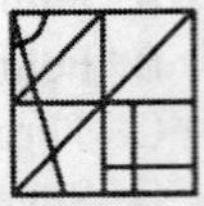

C. 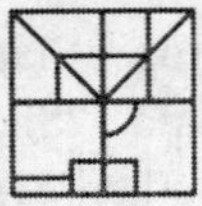 D. 

35. In the following question, select the related letters from the given alternatives.

PM : RO :: BC : ?

A. DE B. ZA
C. JK D. XY

36. After interchanging which two signs and two numbers (Not digits), the value of the given expression will be '45'?

10 × 8 ÷ 6 – 2 + 4

A. + and –, 8 and 6
B. + and ×, 10 and 4
C. ÷ and –, 10 and 8
D. ÷ and –, 4 and 8

37. In a certain code language, 'ONLINE + THEIR' is coded as '11', 'FREE + NEW' is coded as '7'. What is the code for 'HELP + STUDENTS' in that code language?

A. 10 B. 12
C. 8 D. 6

38. Select the option in which the numbers shares the same relationship in set as that shared by the numbers in the given set. (NOTE: Operations should be performed on the whole numbers, without breaking down the numbers into its constituent digits. E.g.13 – Operations on 13 such as adding /subtracting / multiplying etc. to 13 can be performed. Breaking down 13 into 1 and 3 and then performing mathematical operations on 1 and 3 is not allowed)

(182, 79, 378)
(345, 16, 604)

A. (79, 18, 178)
B. (53, 72, 82)
C. (68, 79, 193)
D. (84, 64, 84)

39. How many cycles are not pedals?

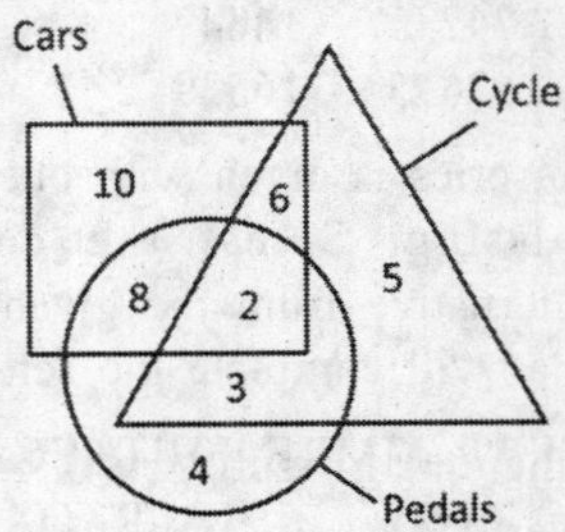

A. 8 B. 11
C. 7 D. 5

40. In a certain code language, 'PRINTS' is coded as 'QRLHQO'. What is the code for 'STRICT' in that code language?

A. RAGSQR B. RAGQSR
C. RAQGSR D. RGAQSR

41. In the following question, four number pairs are given. In each pair the number on left side of (–) is related to the number of the right side of (–) with some Logic/Rule/Relation. Three pairs are similar on basis of same Logic/Rule/Relation. Select the odd one out from the given alternatives. (NOTE: Operations should be performed on the whole numbers, without breaking down the numbers into its constituent digits. E.g.13 – Operations on 13 such as adding/subtracting/multiplying etc. to 13 can be performed. Breaking down 13 into 1 and 3 and then performing mathematical operations on 1 and 3 is not allowed)

A. 9 – 810

B. 11 – 1452

C. 7 – 392

D. 13 – 2368

42. If 13 @ 2 # 5 = 10 and 43 # 9 @ 16 = 50, then 8 @ 6 # 3 = ?

A. 7 B. 11

C. 10 D. 8

43. Select the option figure in which the given figure is embedded. (Rotation is NOT allowed)

A. 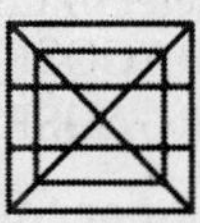 B. 

C. 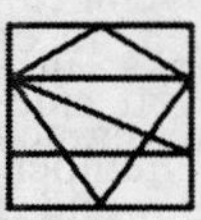 D. 

44. Words given on the left side of (::) are related with each other by some Logic/Rule/Relation. Select the missing word/word pair on the right side of (::) from the given alternatives based on the same Logic/Rule/Relation.

Uttar Pradesh : Lucknow :: ?

A. Sikkim : Trivandrum

B. Rajasthan : Sikar

C. West Bengal : Kolkata

D. Chennai : Tamil Nadu

45. In the following question, select the odd word pair from the given alternatives.

A. Ottawa – Canada

B. Karachi – Pakistan

C. Rome – Italy

D. Canberra – Australia

46. Select the option figure in which the given figure is embedded. (Rotation is NOT allowed)

A. 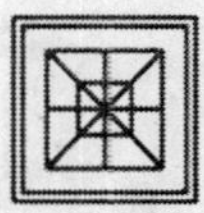 B. 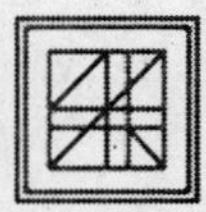

C. 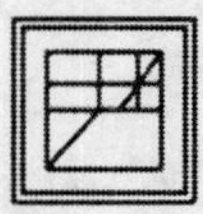 D. 

47. Select the correct option that indicates the arrangement of the given words in the order in which they appear in an English dictionary

1. Lean 2. League

3. Lecture 4. Layout

5. Leftist

A. 4, 2, 3, 1, 5
B. 2, 1, 5, 3, 4
C. 4, 2, 1, 3, 5
D. 4, 2, 1, 5, 3

48. Select the option that is related to the sixth number in the same way as the first number is related to the second number and third number is related to fourth number.

319 : 552 :: 146 : 379 :: ? : 774

A. 535 B. 639
C. 541 D. 479

49. Select the figure from the given options that can replace the question mark (?) in the following series:

A. 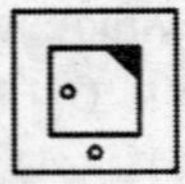 B. 

C.  D. 

50. How many quadrilaterals are there in the given figure?

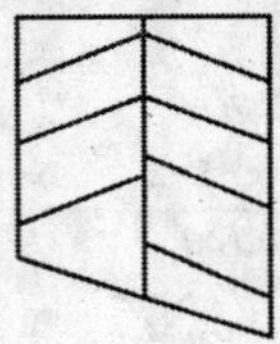

A. 24 B. 26
C. 22 D. 20

QUANTITATIVE APTITUDE

51. If tan $\tan A = \frac{3}{7}$, then what is the value of cosec A?

A. $\frac{2\sqrt{10}}{3}$ B. $\frac{7\sqrt{10}}{20}$

C. $\frac{\sqrt{58}}{3}$ D. $\frac{3}{\sqrt{58}}$

52. A 1800 metres long train crosses a man walking in opposite direction in 10 seconds. If the speed of train is 8 times to the speed of man, then what is the speed of train?

A. 576 km/hr
B. 640 km/hr
C. 596 km/hr
D. 570 km/hr

53. Distance of a chord RS from the centre is 20 cm. If the length of the this chord is 30 cm, then what will be the diameter of this circle?

A. 45 cm B. 55 cm
C. 60 cm D. 50 cm

54. The bar graph given below shows the sales of books (in thousand number) from six branches—B1, B2, B3, B4, B5 and B6 of a publishing company during two consecutive years 2000 and 2001.

Find the percentage (approximate) of the average sales of branches B2, B4 and B6 in the year 2001 to the average sales of branches B1, B3 and B5 in the year 2001.

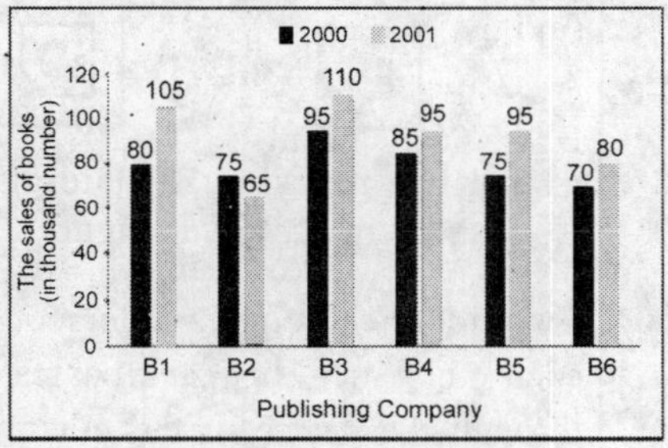

A. 97.95% B. 82.26%
C. 77.42% D. 92%

55. If $\frac{(17)^3-(7)^3}{(17^2+7^2+k)}=10$, then what is the value of k?

A. 102 B. 119
C. 136 D. 85

56. What is the value of $4^2-3^2+6^2-5^2+8^2-7^2+\ldots\ldots.\ 92^2-91^2$?

A. 4272 B. 4280
C. 4278 D. 4275

57. ₹ 43,120 is divided among P, Q and R such that P's share is $\frac{4}{7}$ of total share of Q and R together and Q's share is $\frac{2}{5}$ of total share of P and R together. What is the share of R?

A. ₹ 15120 B. ₹ 14220
C. ₹ 16400 D. ₹ 18050

58. The bar graph given below shows the number of girls in 7 schools.

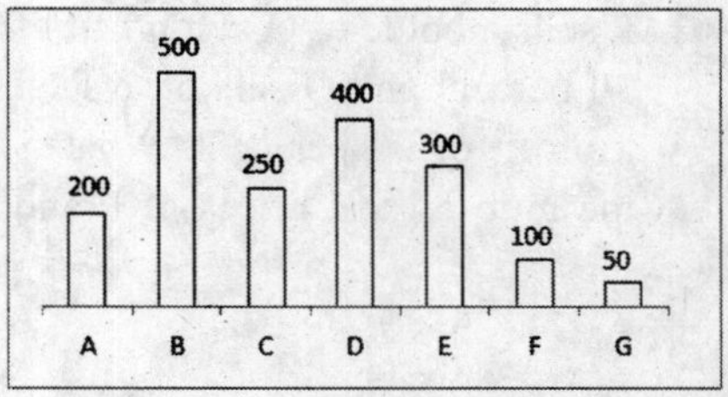

The number of girls in A is what per cent of the number of girls in F?

A. 100 per cent B. 200 per cent
C. 150 per cent D. 50 per cent

59. A merchant marks the price of his article 20 per cent above the cost price. If he allows 10 per cent discount, then what is the profit or loss percentage?

A. 8 per cent profit
B. 3.33 per cent loss
C. 6 per cent loss
D. 5 per cent profit

60. Three metallic cubes whose sides are 6 cm, 8 cm and 10 cm respectively are melted and converted into a single cube. If there is no loss of metal in this process, then what is the length of the side of the new cube?

A. 16 cm B. 14 cm
C. 12 cm D. 20 cm

61. The average of marks obtained by X and Y is 35 less than the average marks obtained by Y and Z. If the marks obtained by Z is 85, what is the marks obtained by X?

A. 155 B. 15
C. 35 D. 25

62. P sells a bottle to Q at a profit of 30 percent and Q sells it to R at a profit of 20 per cent. What is the ratio of cost prices of P and R?

A. 24 : 35
B. 25 : 39
C. 12 : 17
D. 13 : 19

63. A man borrows a sum of ₹ 12,000 which amounts to ₹ 13,200 in 2 years on simple interest. What would have been the amount if the rate of interest was doubled?

A. ₹ 13,400
B. ₹ 14,400
C. ₹ 12,400
D. ₹ 14,000

64. What is the value of

$\frac{\tan\theta - \sec\theta + 1}{\tan\theta + \sec\theta - 1}$?

A. $\sec\theta + \tan\theta$
B. $\frac{(1+\sin\theta)}{\cos\theta}$
C. $2\sec\theta$
D. $\frac{\cos\theta}{(1+\sin\theta)}$

65. If $A = \frac{18 \div 9 \times 4}{15 \div 3 \times 5}$ and

$B = \frac{18 \div 36 \times 3 + 5 \times 1 - 6}{18 \div 6 \times 20 - 3 \times 4 + 12}$,

then what is the value of (A + B)?

A. $\frac{137}{600}$ B. $\frac{23}{100}$
C. $\frac{187}{600}$ D. $\frac{197}{600}$

66. Raman spends 50 per cent of his income. If his income increases by 10 per cent and the expenditure also increases by 10 per cent, then what will be the percentage increase in his savings?

A. 20 per cent
B. 16.66 per cent
C. 10 per cent
D. 8.33 per cent

67. Two identical circles intersect each other such that each passes through the centre of the other. Length of common chord is $16\sqrt{3}$ cm. What is the radius of each circle?

A. 16 cm
B. $16\sqrt{3}$ cm
C. $16\sqrt{2}$ cm
D. $8\sqrt{3}$ cm

68. A alone can complete the project in 10 days; B alone can complete it in 20 days while C alone can complete it in 30 days. They together earn ₹ 1,100 for the project. By how much do the total earnings of A and C exceed the earnings of B?

A. ₹ 600
B. ₹ 900
C. ₹ 700
D. ₹ 500

69. The line chart given below shows the number of girls in 7 schools.

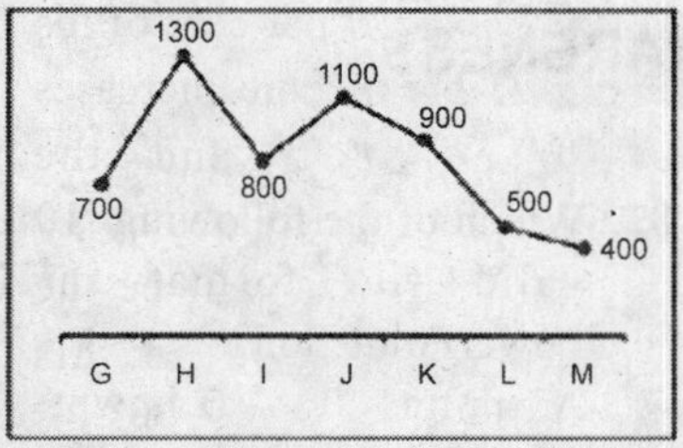

What is the difference between number of girls in school G, H and I together and the number of girls in school J, K, L and M together?

A. 400 B. 50

C. 100 D. 200

70. What is the value of $\dfrac{\cot 60° - \cot 30°}{1+\cot 60°.\cot 30°}$?

A. $\dfrac{1}{\sqrt{3}}$ B. $\sqrt{3}$

C. $-\sqrt{3}$ D. $-\dfrac{1}{\sqrt{3}}$

71. The pie chart given below shows the number of girls in six schools. The total number of girls in all these six schools are 4000. Number of girls in a particular school is shown as a percentage of total number of girls in all these six schools.

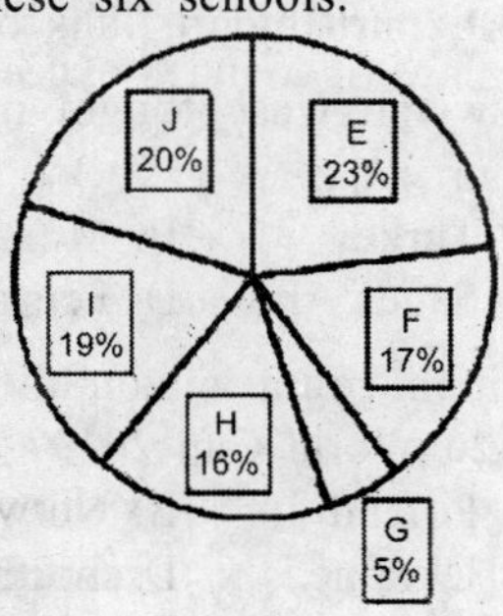

What is the value of central angle formed by sector F?

A. 48.4 degree

B. 72.3 degree

C. 31.4 degree

D. 61.2 degree

72. Angle subtended by a chord AB on the circumference is 90 degree. If radius of this circle is 8 cm, then what is the length of AB?

A. 16 cm

B. 18 cm

C. 14 cm

D. 12 cm

73. In ΔSTU, SE and TF are medians intersect each other at O. If UT = 34 cm, TF = 22.5 cm and SE = 24 cm, then what is the value of ∠TOE?

A. 75 degree

B. 60 degree

C. 45 degree

D. 90 degree

74. Which of the following is largest among $(125)^{\frac{1}{6}}, (11)^{\frac{1}{3}}, (12)^{\frac{1}{6}}, (5)^{\frac{1}{4}}$?

A. $(12)^{\frac{1}{6}}$ B. $(11)^{\frac{1}{3}}$

C. $(125)^{\frac{1}{6}}$ D. $(5)^{\frac{1}{4}}$

75. If $a+\dfrac{1}{a}=4$, then what is the value of $a^4+\dfrac{1}{a^4}$?

A. 206 B. 194

C. 204 D. 198

GENERAL AWARENESS

76. As per Global Hunger Index (GHI) 2022, India ranks at .... position.

A. 57th B. 77th
C. 97th D. 107th

77. What is the full form of EPROM?

A. Erasable Permanent Read Only Memory
B. Entire Programmable Read Only Memory
C. Erasable Programmable Read Only Memory
D. Entire Permanent Read Only Memory

78. Which of the following is monoatomic?

A. Nitrogen B. Oxygen
C. Chlorine D. Helium

79. Which of the following persons has been awarded the Nobel Peace Prize?

A. C. V. Raman
B. Kailash Satyarthi
C. Amartya Sen
D. Rabindranath Tagore

80. Gandhiji, aged ...., arrived in India in 1915 from South Africa.

A. 52 B. 46
C. 28 D. 34

81. Which among the following is a viral disease?

A. Chicken pox
B. Tuberculosis
C. Whooping Cough
D. Malaria

82. Which of the following is NOT a valid file format in MS-PowerPoint 365?

A. .pptm B. .pwpt
C. .ppt D. .pptx

83. The First Amendment Act, 1951 of the Indian constitution added which of the following schedules?

A. Tenth schedule
B. Ninth schedule
C. Eleventh schedule
D. Seventh schedule

84. The asteroid belt lies between which two planets?

A. Jupiter and Saturn
B. Mars and Jupiter
C. Saturn and Uranus
D. Mercury and Venus

85. Which among the following is not an All India Financial Institution?

A. ICICI Bank
B. National Bank for Agriculture and Rural Development
C. National Housing Bank
D. Export-Import Bank of India

86. Qawwali was brought in India from ....

A. Turkey B. Mongolia
C. Saudi Arabia D. Persia

87. Which country won the FIFA U-20 World Cup 2019?

A. Poland B. Norway
C. Ukraine D. South Korea

88. The approximate length of the Great Himalayan range, also known as the central axial range, is .... km from east to west.

A. 2800 B. 2500
C. 3000 D. 2100

89. What is the name of the mascot for 36th National Games, 2022?

A. Chanakya
B. Kojima
C. Manikarnika
D. Savaj

90. Identify the person from the given statements.

He founded e-commerce giant Amazon in 1994 out of his garage in Seattle. He stepped down as CEO to become executive chairman in July 2021.

A. Jack Ma B. Steve Jobs
C. Jeff Bezos D. Elon Musk

91. Western ghats are locally known as .... in Maharashtra.

A. Sahyadri B. Vindhya
C. Khadar D. Gondwana

92. If there are N firms in the economy, each assigned with a serial number from 1 to N, then as per the product method, GDP can be written as ....

A. $GVA_1 - GVA_2 ..... - GVA_N$
B. $NVA_1 + NVA_2 ..... + NVA_N$
C. $GVA_1 + GVA_2 ..... + GVA_N$
D. $GVA_1 + NVA_2 + GVA_3 + NVA_4 .....$

93. National Highways Infra Trust (NHAI InvIT) bonds introduced by Union Minister of Transport and Highways in October 2022 will provide a effective yield of .... per cent each year.

A. 6.05 B. 9.05
C. 7.05 D. 8.05

94. India won the only bronze medal in which team sports at Tokyo Olympics 2020 held in 2021?

A. Table Tennis
B. Basketball
C. Field hockey
D. Badminton

95. What is the average height of inner Himalayas?

A. 6000 metres B. 4500 metres
C. 5200 metres D. 7100 metres

96. Article 350A of the Indian constitution is related with ....

A. Special officers for linguistic minorities
B. Facilities for instruction in mother-tongue at primary stage
C. Direction for development of the Hindi language
D. Language to be used in Supreme Court and High Courts of India

97. What is the percentage of carbon dioxide in the air exhaled by human lungs?

A. 3.2 per cent
B. 5.9 per cent
C. 2.3 per cent
D. 4.4 per cent

98. Which Indian cricketer is also known as Little Master?

A. Umesh Yadav

B. Virat Kohli

C. Sunil Gavasker

D. Kapil Dev

99. When was Alluri Sitarama Raju arrested ending a two-year armed tribal struggle?

A. May 1924

B. January 1921

C. April 1919

D. December 1929

100. Which Indian festival celebrates the birth anniversary of spiritual leader Padmasambhava, founder of Tibet Tantric Buddhism?

A. Bakrid B. Losar

C. Gurpurab D. Hemis

ANSWERS

1. **(C)** **2.** **(B)** **3.** **(B)**

4. **(D)** **5.** **(D)** **6.** **(D)**

7. **(C)** **8.** **(C)** **9.** **(A)**

10. **(A)** **11.** **(A)** **12.** **(D)**

13. **(B)** **14.** **(B)** **15.** **(A)**

16. **(B)** **17.** **(B)** **18.** **(A)**

19. **(B)** **20.** **(D)** **21.** **(D)**

22. **(A)** **23.** **(C)** **24.** **(A)**

25. **(C)**

26. **(D):** According to given statement

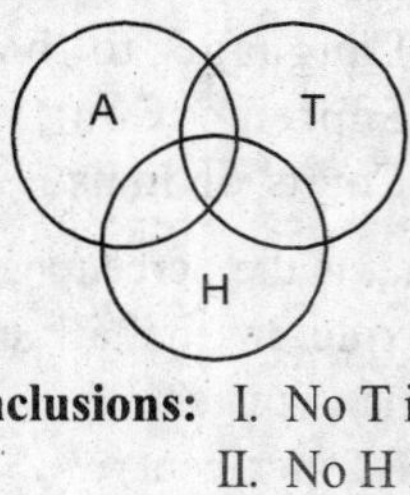

Conclusions: I. No T is A (false)

II. No H is T (false)

III. No A is H (false)

Hence, neither conclusion follows.

27. **(B)**

28. **(B):**

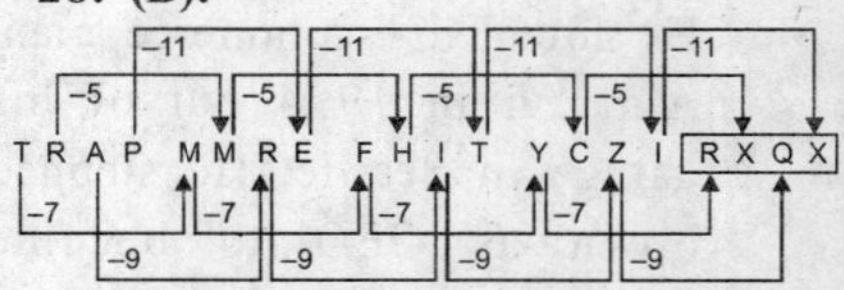

Hence, missing term = RXQX.

29. **(B):**

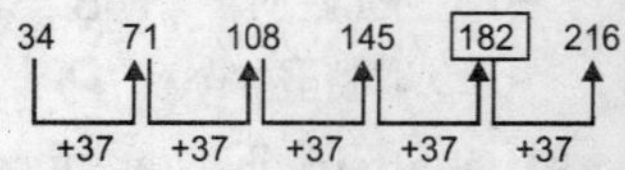

Hence, missing term = 182.

30. **(A)**

31. **(D):**

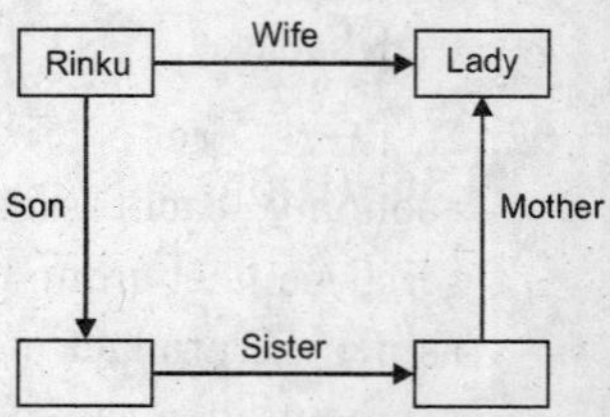

Here, lady is the wife of Rinku.

32. **(A):**

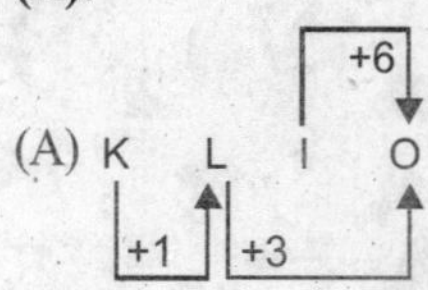

(B) 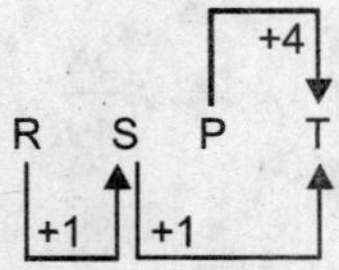

(C) 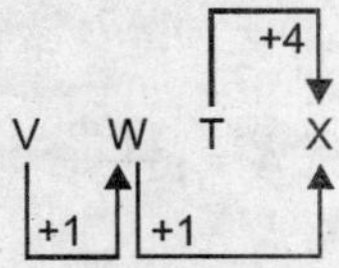

(D) 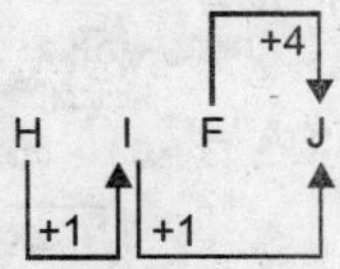

Here, option (A) is the odd letters from the given alternatives.

33. (B)

34. (C)

35. (A): 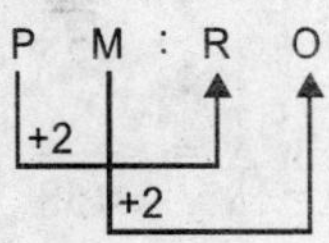

Similarly,

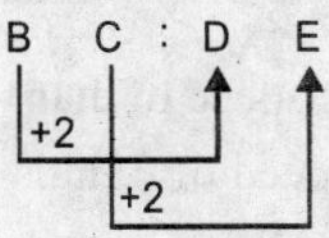

∴ PM : RO :: BC : DE

36. (D): ÷ and –, 4 and 8

∴ 10 × 8 ÷ 6 – 2 + 4

= 10 × 4 – 6 ÷ 2 + 8

= 10 × 4 – 3 + 8

= 40 – 3 + 8

= 48 – 3

= 45

Here, option (D) is correct.

37. (B): Given,

ONLINE + THEIR = 11

⇒ 6 + 5 = 11

(Sum of letters in words)

FREE + NEW = 7

⇒ 4 + 3 = 7

(Sum of letters in words)

Similarly,

HELP + STUDENTS = 4 + 8 = 12

∴ 12 is the code for HELP + STUDENTS.

38. (A) **39. (B)**

40. (B): Given,

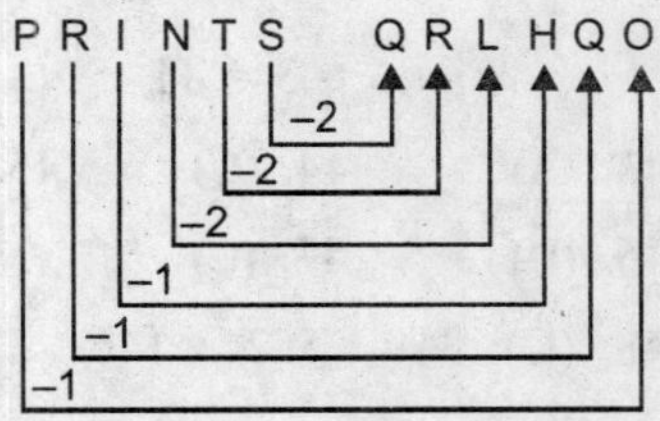

Similarly,

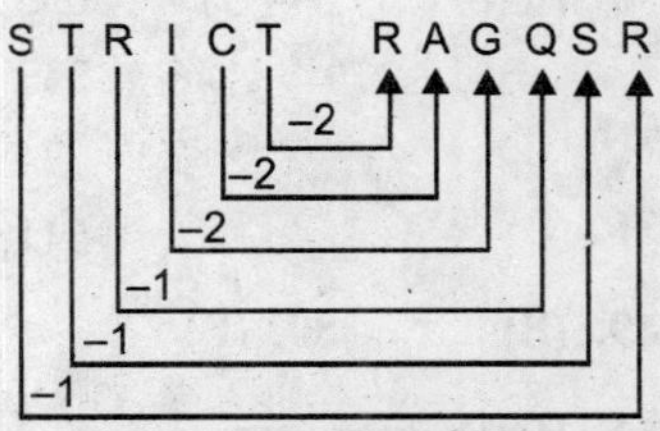

∴ STRICT is coded as RAGQSR.

41. (D): (A) 9 – 810

⇒ 9 × 9 × 10 = 810

(B) 11 – 1452

⇒ 11 × 11 × 12 = 1452

(C) 7 – 392

⇒ 7 × 7 × 8 = 392

(D) 13 – 2368

$\Rightarrow 13 \times 13 \times 14 = 2366$

Here, in option (D) 2366 is not equal to 2368.

$\therefore$ Option (D) is the odd pair.

42. (B): Given, 13 @ 2 # 5 = 10

$\Rightarrow 13 + 2 - 5 = 10$

and 43 # 9 @ 16 = 50

$\Rightarrow 43 - 9 + 16 = 50$

Then, 8 @ 6 # 3

$= 8 + 6 - 3$

$= 14 - 3$

$= 11$

$\therefore$ 8 @ 6 # 3 = 11

43. (A) **44. (C)** **45. (B)**

46. (D) **47. (C)**

48. (C): 319 : 552 :: 146 : 379 :: ? : 774

Here, $552 - 319 = 233$

$379 - 146 = 233$

$\therefore \quad ? = 774 - 233$

$= 541.$

49. (B) **50. (B)**

51. (C): Given, $\tan A = \dfrac{3}{7}$,

$$\therefore \quad \sec A = \sqrt{1 + \tan^2 A}$$

$$= \sqrt{1 + \left(\frac{3}{7}\right)^2}$$

$$= \sqrt{1 + \frac{9}{49}}$$

$$= \sqrt{\frac{58}{49}}$$

$$= \frac{\sqrt{58}}{7}$$

$$\Rightarrow \quad \sec A = \frac{\sqrt{58}}{7}$$

$$\Rightarrow \quad \cos A = \frac{7}{\sqrt{58}}$$

$$\therefore \quad \sin A = \sqrt{1 - \cos^2 A}$$

$$= \sqrt{1 - \frac{49}{58}}$$

$$= \sqrt{\frac{9}{58}}$$

$$= \frac{3}{\sqrt{58}}$$

$$\Rightarrow \quad \sin A = \frac{3}{\sqrt{58}}$$

$$\therefore \text{ cosec } A = \frac{\sqrt{58}}{3}$$

52. (A): Let the speed of man is x m/s

Then, the speed of train is $8x$ m/s

$\because$ Man walking in opposite direction

$\therefore$ Relative speed $= x + 8x$

$= 9x$ m/s

Now, $\dfrac{\text{distance}}{\text{speed}} = \text{time}$

$$\Rightarrow \frac{1800}{9x} = 10$$

$$\Rightarrow \frac{200}{x} = 10$$

$\Rightarrow x = 20$ m/s

∴ The speed of train = $8x$

$= 8 \times 20$

$= 160$ m/s

$= 160 \times \frac{18}{5}$ km/h

$= 32 \times 18$ km/h

$= 576$ km/h.

53. (D): Given, chord RS = 30 cm

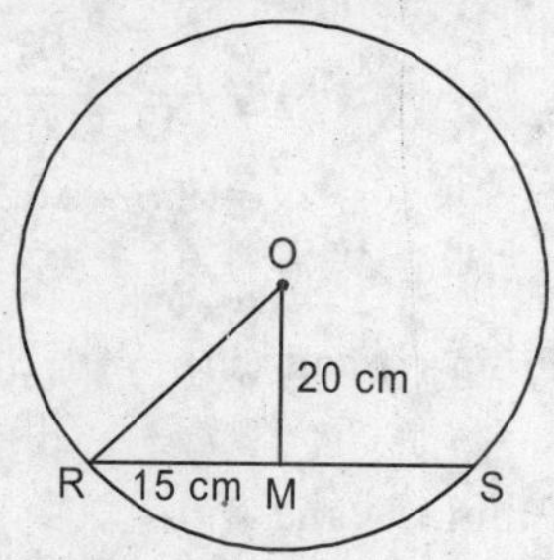

Let OM ⊥ RS

Then, OM = 20 cm

∴ RM = MS = 15 cm

Let OR = Radius

In ΔOMR,

$OR^2 = OM^2 + MR^2$

$\Rightarrow OR^2 = (20)^2 + (15)^2$

$\Rightarrow OR^2 = 400 + 225$

$\Rightarrow OR^2 = 625$

$\Rightarrow OR^2 = (25)^2$

$\Rightarrow OR = 25$ cm

∴ The diameter of the circle = $2r$

$= 2$ (OR)

$= 2 \times 25$

$= 50$ cm.

54. (C)

55. (B): $[a^3 - b^3 = (a - b)(a^2 + b^2 + ab)]$

Given, $\frac{(17)^3 - (7)^3}{(17^2 + 7^2 + k)} = 10$

$\Rightarrow \frac{(17-7)(17^2 + 7^2 + 17 \times 7)}{(17^2 + 7^2 + k)} = 10$

$\Rightarrow \frac{10(17^2 + 7^2 + 119)}{(17^2 + 7^2 + k)} = 10$

$\Rightarrow \frac{(17^2 - 7^2 + 119)}{(17^2 + 7^2 + k)} = 1$

$\Rightarrow 17^2 + 7^2 + 119 = 17^2 + 7^2 + k$

$\Rightarrow k = 119.$

56. (D): $4^2 - 3^2 + 6^2 - 5^2 + 8^2 - 7^2 + \ldots\ldots 92^2 - 91^2$

$= 7 + 11 + 15 + \ldots + 183$

Here, $a = 7$, $d = 4$, th = 183

∵ th $= a + (n - 1)d$

∴ $183 = 7 + (n - 1) \times 4$

$\Rightarrow 4(n - 1) = 183 - 7 = 176$

$\Rightarrow n - 1 = 44$

$\Rightarrow n = 45$

Let $S_n = 7 + 11 + 15 + \ldots + 183$ then,

$S_n = \frac{n}{2}[2a + (n-1)d]$

$= \frac{45}{2}[2 \times 7 + (45 - 1) \times 4]$

$= \frac{45}{2} \times 2\,[7 + 44 \times 2]$

$= 45[7 + 88]$

$= 45 \times 95$

$= 4275.$

57. (A)

58. (B): From given bar-graph

$A = F \times \frac{x}{100}$

$\Rightarrow \quad 200 = 100 \times \frac{x}{100}$

$\Rightarrow \quad x = 200\%$

$\therefore$ Required per cent = 200%.

59. (A): Let cost price of an article is ₹ 100

Then, marked price = ₹ 120

Given, discount = 10%

$\therefore$ Selling Price $= 120 \times \frac{100-10}{100}$

$= 120 \times \frac{90}{100}$

= ₹ 108

$\therefore$ Profit = SP − CP

= 108 − 100

= ₹ 8

Profit percentage = 8%.

60. (C): Here, volume of 3 metallic cubes

$\therefore \quad V_1 = (\text{side})^3$

$= (6)^3$

$= 216 \text{ cm}^3$

$V_2 = (8)^3$

$= 64 \times 8$

$= 512 \text{ cm}^3$

$V_3 = (10)^3$

$= 1000 \text{ cm}^3$

$\therefore$ Volume of new cube = 216 + 512 + 1000

$\Rightarrow V = 1728 \text{ cm}^3$

$\Rightarrow V = 12 \times 144 = 12 \times 12 \times 12$

$\Rightarrow (\text{side})^3 = (12)^3 \text{ cm}^3$

$\Rightarrow$ side = 12 cm

$\therefore$ Length of the side of the new cube = 12 cm.

61. (B): Let the average marks obtained by Y and Z is a

$\Rightarrow \quad Y + Z = 2a \quad ...(i)$

Then the average marks obtained by X and Y

$= a - 35$

$\Rightarrow \quad X + Y = 2(a - 35)$

$= 2a - 70 \quad ...(ii)$

and $\quad Z = 85 \quad ...(iii)$

From (*i*) and (*iii*), $Y = 2a - 85 \quad ...(iv)$

From (*ii*) and (*iv*),

$X = 2a - 70 - 2a + 85$

$= 15$

$\therefore$ The marks obtained by X is 15.

62. (B): Let cost price for P = ₹ x

Then, CP for Q $= x \times \frac{130}{100} = \frac{13}{10}x$

and CP for R

$= \frac{13}{10}x \times \frac{120}{100} = \frac{13}{10} \times \frac{12}{10}x$

$\therefore$ The ratio of cost prices of P and R

$= x : \frac{13}{10} \times \frac{12}{10}x$

$= 1 : \frac{156}{100}$

$= 1 : \frac{39}{25}$

$= 25 : 39.$

63. (B): Here,

P = ₹ 12000, A = ₹ 13200,

t = 2 years

$\therefore$ Simple Interest = A − P

= 13200 − 12000

= ₹ 1200

$\because$ Rate $= \dfrac{SI \times 100}{P \times t}$

$= \dfrac{1200 \times 100}{12000 \times 2}$

= 5%

Given, the rate of interest was doubled

$\therefore$ Simple Interest $= \dfrac{prt}{100}$

$= \dfrac{12000 \times 2 \times 5 \times 2}{100}$

= 2400

$\therefore$ Amount = P + SI

= 12000 + 2400

= ₹ 14400.

64. (D): $\dfrac{\tan\theta - \sec\theta + 1}{\tan\theta + \sec\theta - 1}$

$$= \frac{\tan\theta - \sec\theta + 1}{\tan\theta + \sec\theta - (\sec^2\theta - \tan^2\theta)}$$

$$= \frac{\tan\theta - \sec\theta + 1}{(\tan\theta + \sec\theta) - (\sec\theta - \tan\theta)(\sec\theta + \tan\theta)}$$

$$= \frac{\tan\theta - \sec\theta + 1}{(\tan\theta + \sec\theta)(1 - \sec\theta - \tan\theta)}$$

$$= \frac{1 - \sec\theta + \tan\theta}{(\tan\theta + \sec\theta)(1 - \sec\theta + \tan\theta)}$$

$$= \frac{1}{\tan\theta + \sec\theta}$$

$$= \frac{1}{\dfrac{\sin\theta}{\cos\theta} + \dfrac{1}{\cos\theta}}$$

$$= \frac{1}{\dfrac{\sin\theta + 1}{\cos\theta}}$$

$$= \frac{\cos\theta}{(1 + \sin\theta)}$$

65. (D): Given,

$$A = \frac{18 \div 9 \times 4}{15 \div 3 \times 5} = \frac{2 \times 4}{5 \times 5} = \frac{8}{25}$$

and $B = \dfrac{18 \div 36 \times 3 + 5 \times 1 - 6}{18 \div 6 \times 20 - 3 \times 4 + 12}$,

$$= \frac{18 \times \frac{1}{36} \times 3 + 5 \times 1 - 6}{18 \times \frac{1}{6} \times 20 - 3 \times 4 + 12}$$

$$= \frac{\frac{3}{2} + 5 - 6}{60 - 12 + 12}$$

$$\Rightarrow B = \frac{\frac{3}{2} - 1}{60} = \frac{\frac{1}{2}}{60} = \frac{1}{120}$$

$$\Rightarrow B = \frac{1}{120}$$

$$\therefore (A + B) = \frac{8}{25} + \frac{1}{120}$$

$$= \frac{192 + 5}{600}$$

$$= \frac{197}{600}$$

$$\Rightarrow \ (A + B) = \frac{197}{600}$$

66. (C): Let Raman's income = ₹ 100

Then, expenditure $= 100 \times \frac{50}{100}$

$= ₹\ 50$

$\therefore$ Saving = 100 – 50 = ₹ 50

Again, increased income

$= 100 \times \frac{110}{100}$

$= ₹\ 110$

and expenditure $= 50 \times \frac{110}{100}$

$= ₹\ 55$

$\therefore$ New saving = 110 – 55 = ₹ 55

Percentage increase in saving

$= \frac{55-50}{50} \times 100$

$= 5 \times 2$

$= 10\%$.

67. (A): Let two identical circles intersect each other at A and B such that both passes through the centre of the others. Its centres are O and O′.

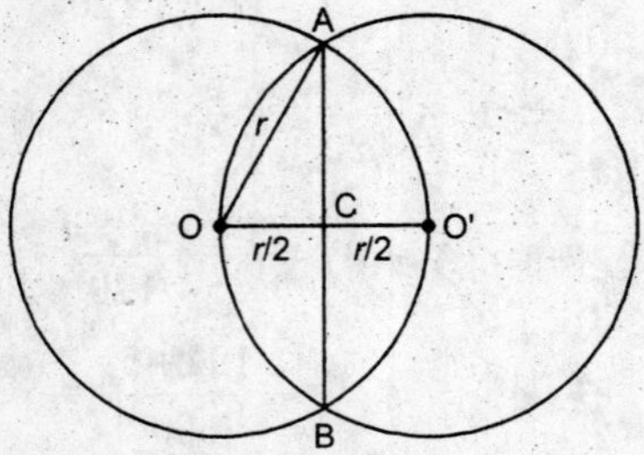

Then, common chord = AB

$= 16\sqrt{3}$ cm

$\Rightarrow AC = BC = 8\sqrt{3}$

$OA = OO' = r,\ OC = O'C = \frac{r}{2}$

In ΔACO,

$$r^2 = \left(8\sqrt{3}\right)^2 + \left(\frac{r}{2}\right)^2$$

$$\Rightarrow r^2 - \frac{r^2}{4} = 64 \times 3$$

$$\Rightarrow \quad 3r^2 = 64 \times 3 \times 4$$

$$\Rightarrow \quad r^2 = 64 \times 4$$

$$\Rightarrow \quad r = 8 \times 2 = 16$$

Hence, the radius of each circle = 16 cm.

68. (D): A's 1 days work $= \frac{1}{10}$

B's 1 days work $= \frac{1}{20}$

C's 1 days work $= \frac{1}{30}$

Ratio of work A : B : C

$= \frac{1}{10} : \frac{1}{20} : \frac{1}{30}$

$= 6 : 3 : 2$

Given, total earning for the project = ₹ 1100

$\therefore$ Earning of A and C

$= 1100 \times \frac{6+2}{6+3+2}$

$= 1100 \times \frac{8}{11}$

$= ₹\ 800$

and earning of B $= 1100 \times \frac{3}{11}$

$= ₹\ 300$

Hence, (A + C) – B = 800 – 300 = ₹ 500.

69. (C): From the line chart

Number of girls in school G, H and I

$= 700 + 1300 + 800$

$= 2800$

and number of girls in school J, K, L and M

$= 1100 + 900 + 500 + 400$

$= 2900$

$\therefore$ Required difference

$= 2900 - 2800$

$= 100.$

70. (D): $\dfrac{\cot 60° - \cot 30°}{1 + \cot 60°.\cot 30°}$

$$= \frac{\frac{1}{\sqrt{3}} - \sqrt{3}}{1 + \frac{1}{\sqrt{3}}.\sqrt{3}}$$

$$= \frac{\frac{1-3}{\sqrt{3}}}{1+1}$$

$$= \frac{-2}{\sqrt{3} \times 2}$$

$$= \frac{-1}{\sqrt{3}}$$

71. (D): From given pie-chart

The total number of girls in all these six school = 4000

$\because \quad 100\% = 360°$

$\therefore \quad 1\% = \dfrac{360°}{100}$

$= \dfrac{18°}{5}$

$\therefore$ Value of central angle formed by sector F

$= 17\%$

$= 17 \times \dfrac{18°}{5}$

$= 17 \times 3.6°$

$= 61.2$ degree.

72. (A)

73. (D)

74. (C): Here, LCM of 6, 3, 6 and 4 = 12

(A) $(12)^{\frac{1}{6}} = (12)^{\frac{1}{6} \times 12}$

$= (12)^2$

$= 144$

(B) $(11)^{\frac{1}{3}} = (11)^{\frac{1}{3} \times 12}$

$= (11)^4$

$= 14641$

(C) $(125)^{\frac{1}{6}} = (125)^{\frac{1}{6} \times 12}$

$= (125)^2$

$= 15625$

(D) $(5)^{\frac{1}{4}} = (5)^{\frac{1}{4} \times 12}$

$= (5)^3$

$= 125$

$\therefore 15625 > 14641 > 144 > 125$

$\Rightarrow (125)^{\frac{1}{6}} > (11)^{\frac{1}{3}} > (12)^{\frac{1}{6}} > (5)^{\frac{1}{4}}$

Hence, $(125)^{\frac{1}{6}}$ is largest among all.

75. (B): $a+\frac{1}{a}=4$

$$\Rightarrow \left(a+\frac{1}{a}\right)^2 = (4)^2$$

$$\Rightarrow a^2+\frac{1}{a^2}+2a\frac{1}{a} = 16$$

$$\Rightarrow a^2+\frac{1}{a^2} = 16-2$$

$$\Rightarrow a^2+\frac{1}{a^2} = 14$$

Again, $\left(a^2+\frac{1}{a^2}\right)^2 = (14)^2$

$$\Rightarrow a^4+\frac{1}{a^4}+2a^2.\frac{1}{a^2} = 196$$

$$\Rightarrow a^4+\frac{1}{a^4}+2 = 196$$

$$\Rightarrow a^4+\frac{1}{a^4} = 194.$$

76. (D)	**77. (C)**	**78. (D)**
79. (B)	**80. (B)**	**81. (A)**
82. (B)	**83. (B)**	**84. (B)**
85. (A)	**86. (D)**	**87. (C)**
88. (B)	**89. (D)**	**90. (C)**
91. (A)	**92. (C)**	**93. (D)**
94. (C)	**95. (A)**	**96. (B)**
97. (D)	**98. (C)**	**99. (A)**
100. (D)		

Previous Paper (Solved)

SSC-Combined Higher Secondary Level–CHSL (10+2) Tier–1, Online Recruitment Exam–2021

(Exam held on 02-06-2022)

ENGLISH LANGUAGE

1. Parts of the given sentence have been given as options. One of them contains a grammatical error. Select the option that has the error.

When you have worked out this sum, you may went out to play.

A. When you have worked out
B. went out to play
C. this sum
D. you may

2. The following sentence has been split into four segments. Identify the segment that contains a grammatical error.

Going to the weekly market / in every Tuesday / is a ritual that has been followed / by generations in my family.

A. is a ritual that has been followed
B. by generations in my family
C. in every Tuesday
D. Going to the weekly market

3. Select the most appropriate ANTONYM of the given word.

Despair

A. Vile
B. Hope
C. Annoy
D. Definite

4. Select the INCORRECTLY spelt word.

A. Audience
B. Comprehension
C. Competence
D. Attendence

5. Select the most appropriate ANTONYM of the given word.

Wax

A. Wane
B. Mourn
C. Error
D. Insolent

6. Select the most appropriate option to substitute the underline segment in the given sentence.

It was apparent that the girl was <u>heading into</u> a serious disaster.

A. heading along
B. heading for
C. heading down
D. heading out

7. Select the INCORRECTLY spelt word.

A. kengaroo
B. Vivacious
C. Ambiguous
D. Itinerary

8. Select the option that can be used as a one-word substitute for the underlined group of words.

He requested the bank to give him more time as at present he was unable to pay his debts.
A. Destitute
B. Meticulous
C. Reckless
D. Bankrupt

9. Select the most appropriate meaning of the given idiom.

Dark horse
A. A person criticised
B. Loved person
C. An unexpected winner
D. A champion

10. Select the option that expresses the given sentence in passive voice. The people will make him the leader.
A. He had been made the leader by people.
B. He will be made the leader by the people.
C. He was made leader by the people.
D. People made him the leader.

11. Select the option that expresses the given sentence in passive voice.

I know him.
A. I am known to him.
B. He is known to myself.
C. He is known to me.
D. Let him be known to me.

12. Select the option that will improve the underlined part of the given sentence.

Mahatma Gandhi is undoubtedly one of the much popular authors of our times.

A. best B. total
C. most D. better

13. Select the most appropriate option that can substitute the underlined segment in the given sentence. If there is no need to substitute it, select 'No substitution required'. Sheela is trying for a job since last year.
A. was trying
B. have been trying
C. No substitution required
D. has been trying

14. In the following passage, a word has been deleted. Read the passage carefully and select the most appropriate option to fill in the blank.

Gifting is generally taken to be the easiest act to ________, if only you have the heart to part with something in your ________.
A. forsake, capacity
B. perform, possession
C. forgive, discretion
D. observe, control

15. Select the most appropriate option to fill in the blank.

He is a ______ in shining armour
A. knit B. nite
C. night D. knight

16. Sentences of a paragraph are given below in jumbled order. Arrange the sentences in the correct order to form a meaningful and coherent paragraph.

(*a*) However, after studying the myths scientifically, only a simpleton would find them irrational or worthless.

(*b*) Moreover, it is wrong to analyse myths on the yardstick of their factual accuracy as they were designed to serve a greater, deeper purpose.

(*c*) Myths have always been regarded as a complex and intriguing aspect in human life

(*d*) In modern scientific world, they are essentially seen as something unscientific and meaningless.

A. (*d*), (*c*), (*a*), (*b*)
B. (*d*), (*a*), (*c*), (*b*)
C. (*a*), (*c*), (*d*), (*b*)
D. (*c*), (*d*), (*a*), (*b*)

17. Select the most appropriate meaning of the given idiom.

Be like chalk and cheese

A. Be absolutely lonely
B. Be absolutely rich
C. Be absolutely deceptive
D. Be absolutely different

18. Select the most appropriate ANTONYM of the word 'Lead' from the given sentence. All the class monitors were asked to follow the guide who was there to manage and control their visit to Yamuna Biodiversity Park.

A. Control
B. Follow
C. Guide
D. Manage

19. Select the most appropriate option that can substitute the underlined segment in the given sentence.

I had get back from Hyderabad last month.

A. got back from
B. had got back
C. get back from
D. had got back from

20. Select the most appropriate synonym of the given word.

Salubrious

A. Beneficial B. Vicarious
C. Insidious D. Septic

Directions (Qs. No. 21-25): *In the following passage, some words have been deleted. Read the passage carefully and select the most appropriate option to fill in each blank.*

While I was sitting there (1)_________ over my failure to keep from having to spend (2) glistering _________ summer months on the freaking Cote of Azur, Grandmere started (3)_________ me from the phone. She kept (4)_________ her fingers on the phone to catch my attention. I just sat there blinking at her until finally she put her hand over the receiver and (5)_________ (so that nobody listens), "Amelia! In my bedroom, there is something for you".

21. Select the most appropriate option to fill in blank number 1.

A. smirking B. sulking
C. grinning D. clapping

22. Select the most appropriate option to fill in blank number 2.

A. ours B. me

C. my D. mine

23. Select the most appropriate option to fill in blank number 3.

A. disconcerting B. beckoning

C. upsetting D. dismissing

24. Select the most appropriate option to fill in blank number 4.

A. piquing B. snapping

C. peering D. tapping

25. Select the most appropriate option to fill in blank number 5.

A. commended B. cheered

C. lauded D. hissed

GENERAL INTELLIGENCE

26. Study the given pattern carefully and select the number that can replace the question mark (?) in it.

First row- 5, 39, 8

Second row- 7, 36, 5

Third row- 11, ?, 9

(NOTE: Operations should be performed on the whole numbers, without breaking down the numbers into its constituent digits. E.g. 13 – Operations on 13 such as adding /deleting / multiplying etc. to 13 can be performed. Breaking down 13 into 1 and 3 and then performing mathematical operations on 1 and 3 is NOT allowed)

A. 60 B. 40

C. 50 D. 70

27. Select the option that is related to the fifth number in the same way as the second number is related to the first number and the fourth number is related to the third number.

6 : 96 : : 8 : 144 : : 5 : ?

A. 70 B. 90

C. 85 D. 75

28. Select the option that represents the correct order of the given words as they would appear in an English dictionary.

1. Catalyst 2. Carrot
3. Calcium 4. Calculate
5. Calendar

A. 4, 3, 5, 2, 1

B. 4, 5, 3, 2, 1

C. 3, 4, 5, 2, 1

D. 3, 2, 1, 4, 5

29. Three Statements are given followed by Three conclusions numbered I, II and III. Assuming the statements to be true, even if they seem to be at variance with commonly known facts, decide which of the conclusions logically follow(s) from the statements.

Statements:

All moons are suns.

No moon is a star.

Some stars are planets.

Conclusions:
I. Some suns are planets.
II. No sun is a star.
III. No planet is a moon.

A. Both conclusions I and II follow.
B. None of the conclusions follow.
C. Both conclusions I and III follow.
D. Only conclusion II follows.

30. The second number in the given number pairs is obtained by performing certain mathematical operation(s) on the first number. The same operation(s) are followed in all the number pairs except one. Find that odd number pair.

A. 43 : 84 B. 21 : 40
C. 15 : 210 D. 19 : 36

31. Select the correct combination of mathematical signs to replace the * signs and to balance the given equation.

16*6*69*81*3

A. −, +, ×, = B. ×, −, =, ÷
C. ÷, +, =, × D. +, =, ×, −

32. Which of the following letter-clusters will replace the question mark (?) in the given series to make it logically complete?

TVX, SUW, RTV, QSU, ?

A. TRP B. RPT
C. TPR D. PRT

33. Select the option that is related to the third term in the same way as the second term is related to the first term and the sixth term is related to the fifth term.

19 : 90 :: 25 : ? :: 13 : 60

A. 120 B. 100
C. 115 D. 110

34. Select the option that is related to the third word in the same way as the second word is related to the first word. (The words must be considered as meaningful English words and must NOT be related to each other based on the number of letters/number of consonants/vowels in the word)

Golf : Stick :: Cricket : ?

A. Bat B. Stadium
C. Ball D. Wicket

35. Select the correct combination of mathematical signs to replace the * signs and to balance the given equation.

127*13*3*129*41

A. +, =, +, −
B. −, ×, =, −
C. ÷, −, =, −
D. −, −, =, +

36. How many squares are there in the given figure?

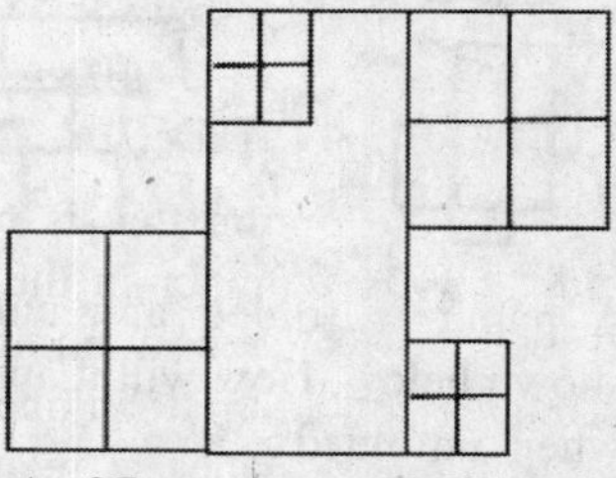

A. 37 B. 21
C. 36 D. 20

37. If A denotes '+', B denotes '×', C denotes '–' and D denotes '÷', then what will come in place of '?' in the following equation?

17 A (31 B 3) C (64 D 8) A 41 C (21 B 4) = ?

A. 69 B. 59
C. 61 D. 55

38. In a certain code language, 'MOTHER' is written as 'LNSGIV' and 'FATHER' is written as 'ZUSGIV'. How will 'WONDER' be written in that language?

A. DLWMIV B. DLMWIV
C. LDWMIV D. LDMWVI

39. Select the option that is embedded in the given figure as its part (rotation is NOT allowed).

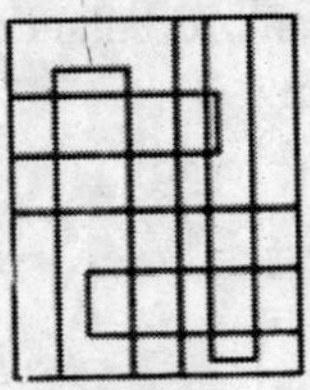

A. 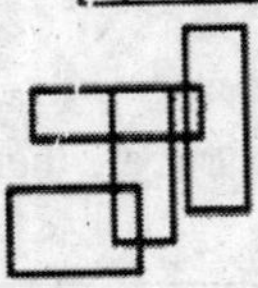
B. 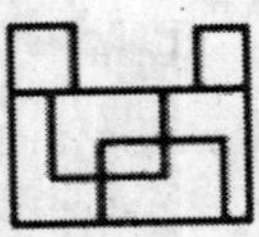
C. 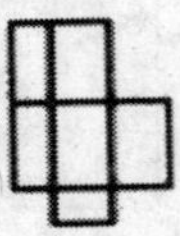
D. 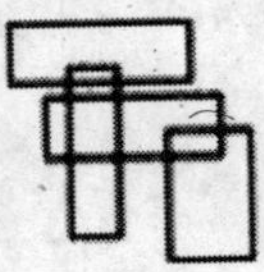

40. A paper is folded and cut as shown below. How will it appear when unfolded?

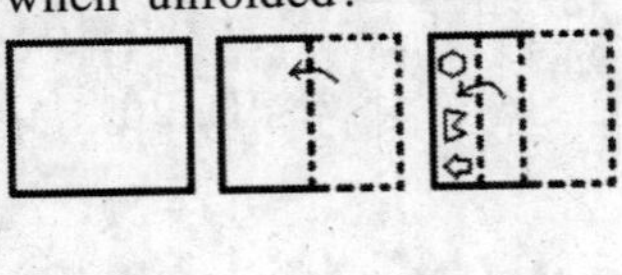

A. 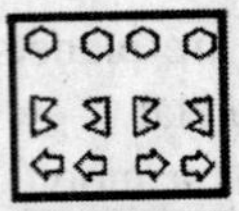
B. 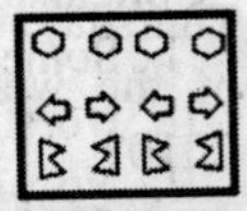
C. 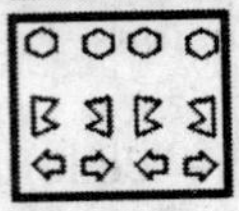
D. 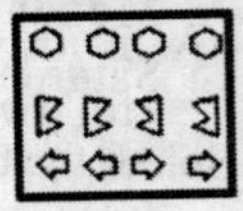

41. Select the correct mirror image of the given combination when the mirror is placed at MN as shown.

A. 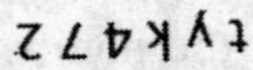
B. 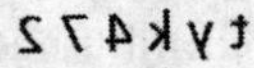
C. 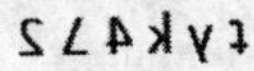
D. 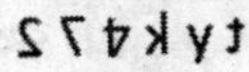

42. Select the correct mirror image of the given combination when the mirror is placed at 'PQ' as shown.

A. 
B. 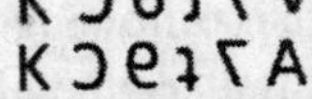
C. 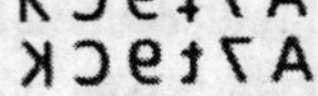
D. 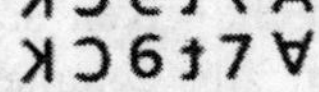

43. Select the correct combination of mathematical signs to replace the * signs and to balance the given equation.

99*25*10*12*7

A. –, =, +, × B. +, =, +, ×
C. –, +, =, × D. –, =, +, +

44. If 31 December 2009 was Thursday, then what was the day of the week on 25 December 2010?

A. Monday B. Sunday
C. Saturday D. Tuesday

45. Select the correct combination of mathematical signs to sequentially replace the * signs and to balance the given equation.

16*4*8*10*2*43

A. ÷, ×, –, +, = B. ÷, ×, +, –, =
C. ×, ÷, –, +, = D. +, ×, –, ÷, =

46. In a certain code language, 'ACTOR' is written as '136812' and 'HEROINE' is written as '95128745'. How will 'HERO' be written in that language?

A. 95128 B. 95768
C. 95218 D. 95378

47. Which of the following numbers will replace the question mark (?) in the given series?

314, 285, 308, ?, 306, 293, 304

A. 277 B. 298
C. 287 D. 289

48. Which letter-cluster will replace the question mark (?) to complete the given series?

CIEO, JAAU, QSWA, XKSE,?

A. FCOI B. ECOI
C. ECRI D. FCRI

49. Two different positions of the same dice are shown, the six faces of which are marked from A to F. Select the letter that will be on the face opposite to the one showing 'D'.

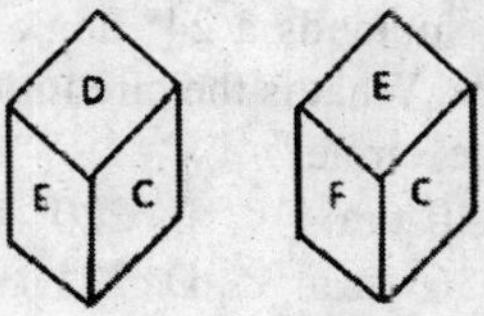

A. F B. C
C. B D. E

50. Select the option that is related to the fifth word in the same way as the second word is related to the first word and the fourth word is related to the third word. (The words must be considered as meaningful English words and must NOT be related to each other based on the number of letters/number of consonants/vowels in the word)

Elephant : Trunk :: Fish : Gill :: Kangaroo : ?

A. Antlers B. Pouch
C. Blowhole D. Muzzle

QUANTITATIVE APTITUDE

51. Ruksana travelled at 60 km/h while going from point A to point B, and returned via the same route at a different speed. If Ruksana's overall average speed during the two-way journey was 48 km/h, what was her speed while travelling from B to A?

A. 42 km/h B. 40 km/h
C. 45 km/h D. 36 km/h

52. What distance will be covered by a bus moving at 108 km/h in 40 seconds?
A. 1 km 600 m B. 1 km 400 m
C. 1 km 800 m D. 1 km 200 m

53. An arc on a circle that is 15 cm long subtends a 24° angle at the centre. What is the circumference of the circle?
A. 240 cm B. 220 cm
C. 236 cm D. 225 cm

54. The ratio of the radii of two right circular cylinders is 2 : 3. If their heights are in the ratio 5 : 3, find the ratio of their volumes.
A. 16 : 19 B. 3 : 4
C. 3 : 1 D. 20 : 27

55. An article is sold at a discount of 10% and an additional discount of 40% is allowed on cash payment. If Anita purchased an article by paying ₹ 2,700 in cash, the marked price of the article was:
A. ₹ 5,000 B. ₹ 2,500
C. ₹ 2,000 D. ₹ 5,500

56. A dealer allows his customers a discount of 15% and still gains 15%. If an article cost ₹ 2,500 to the dealer, then its marked price is (correct to nearest integer):
A. ₹ 3,382 B. ₹ 4,382
C. ₹ 1,312 D. ₹ 3,182

57. The lengths of a pair of parallel sides of a trapezium are 20 cm and 25 cm, respectively, and the perpendicular distance between these two sides is 14 cm. What is the area (in cm^2) of the trapezium?
A. 512 B. 250
C. 300 D. 315

58. The average of six integers is 48. The average of the first five integers is 70% of the sixth integer. The sixth integer is.
A. 64 B. 62
C. 68 D. 58

59. Two numbers X and Y are such that the sum of 18% of X and 8% of Y is one-third of the sum of 22% of X and 36% of Y. Find the ratio of X and Y.
A. 2 : 5 B. 3 : 11
C. 3 : 8 D. 8 : 3

60. Simplify the following expression.
$79 - [6 - \{4 - (8 \times (6 + 3))\}] \div 2$
A. 11.5 B. 2.5
C. 37 D. 42

61. Find θ, if $\cos\theta = -\frac{\sqrt{3}}{2}$.
A. $\frac{3\pi}{2}$ B. $\frac{5\pi}{6}$
C. $\frac{2\pi}{3}$ D. $\frac{4\pi}{3}$

62. What is the compound interest on ₹ 10,625 for 2 years at 8% interest per annum, if interest is compounded annually?
A. ₹ 1,768 B. ₹ 1,698
C. ₹ 1,625 D. ₹ 1,528

63. The smallest four-digit number which is divisible by 4, 8, 12 and 16 is:

A. 1010 B. 1008
C. 1006 D. 1012

64. If $\left(x - \frac{1}{x}\right) = 7.5$, what is the value of $\left(x^2 + \frac{1}{x^2}\right)$?

A. 54.25 B. 58.25
C. 60.25 D. 56.25

65. Which among the below option can be a square root of?

$(x^2 - 14x + 49)(x^2 + 6x + 9)$

A. $(x - 4)(x + 9)$
B. $(x - 1)(x + 17)$
C. $(x - 7)(x + 3)$
D. $(x - 3)(x + 8)$

66. If $(x^3 + y^3)^{2/3} = (x^2 + y^2)$, then the value of $\frac{x^2 + y^2}{xy}$ $x \neq 0, y \neq 0$, is:

A. $\frac{2}{3}$ B. $x^2 + y$
C. 1 D. $x + y^2$

67. Study the given graph and answer the following question.

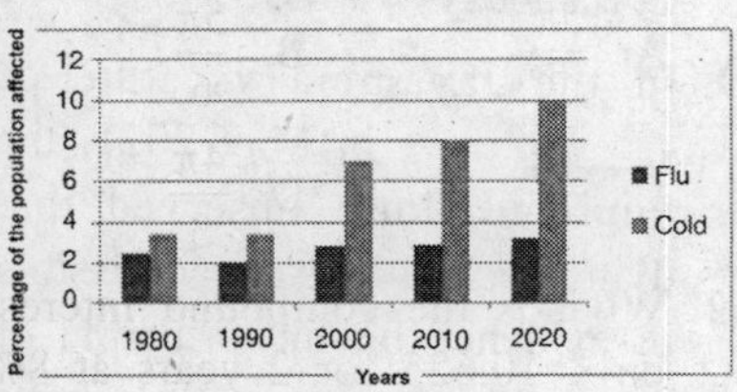

As per data available above in which of the given years was the percentage of the population affected by cold the minimum?

A. 1980 B. 1990
C. 2010 D. 2000

68. Study the given table and answer the question that follows.

Given that the total number of students is 100.

Subject	Marks out of 100				
	80 and above	60 and above	40 and above	20 and above	0 and above
A	9	31	81	92	100
B	4	20	67	81	100
C	7	26	74	87	100

The number of students who scored less than 80% marks in A is:

A. 73 B. 83
C. 91 D. 71

69. A man sold a radio set and gained one-eighth of its cost price. What is the profit per cent?

A. 20% B. 12.5%
C. 15.5% D. 18%

70. The table below gives the percentage of females and males in different professions, out of total 10000 people.

Profession	% of People	% of males	% of females
Teaching	20	50	50
Law	15	65	35
Medical	20	60	40
Engineering	24	55	45
Banking	21	52	48

On the basis of the information provided in the table, find the total number of males who are in the teaching profession.

A. 1000 B. 2000
C. 500 D. 1500

71. The radius of a hemispherical bowl is given as 7 cm. What is the capacity of the bowl? $\left(\pi = \frac{22}{7}\right)$

A. $718\frac{2}{3}$ cm^3 B. $812\frac{1}{3}$ cm^3

C. $618\frac{1}{3}$ cm^3 D. $518\frac{2}{3}$ cm^3

72. A pipe can fill a tank in 15 hours. Due to leakage in the bottom it is filled in 20 hours. If the tank is full, and the pipe is closed, how much time will the leak take to empty the entire tank?

A. 60 hrs B. 50 hrs

C. 40 hrs D. 30 hrs

73. Find the 4th proportional to 5, 10 and 12.

A. 8 B. 24

C. 48 D. 20

74. A man borrowed some money and returned it in two equal instalments of ₹ 3,025 each. If the rate of interest is 10% per annum, compound annually, find the sum borrowed.

A. ₹ 5,575 B. ₹ 6,250

C. ₹ 6,525 D. ₹ 5,250

75. In an election between two candidates, one of the candidates secured 35% of the votes cast and was defeated by the other candidate by 1296 votes. If there were no invalid votes, then the total number of votes polled was:

A. 4546 B. 4230

C. 4456 D. 4320

GENERAL AWARENESS

76. Which of the following instruments is played by P Mani Iyer?

A. Sarangi B. Violin

C. Mridangam D. Mandolin

77. Who among the following authors won the Kamaladevi Chattopadhyay NIF Book Prize in the year 2019?

A. Ornit Shani

B. Jairam Ramesh

C. Milan Vaishnav

D. Dinyar Patel

78. The election of the next Vice-President is to be held within _____ of the expiry of the term of office of the outgoing Vice-President.

A. 90 days B. 60 days

C. 120 days D. 75 days

79. In the Jayamma vs state of _____ case, in May 2021, the Supreme Court observed that dying declarations are admissible in evidence on the principle of necessity, as there is little hope of the maker surviving.

A. Andhra Pradesh

B. Karnataka

C. Tamil Nadu
D. Kerala

80. Which method of calculating the national income is also known as 'Industrial Origin Method'?
A. Expenditure Method
B. Income Method
C. Value Added Method
D. Monetary Measures Method

81. The famous folk musician Bhupen Hazarika belongs to which of the following states?
A. Assam
B. Odisha
C. Madhya Pradesh
D. Karnataka

82. Ustad Amjad Ali Khan, a renowned musician from India is known for playing which of the following instruments?
A. Sarod B. Jaltarang
C. Sarangi D. Veena

83. Which of the following dance forms is performed by Guru Vempati Chinna Satyam?
A. Manipuri
B. Odissi
C. Bharatanatyam
D. Kuchipudi

84. Modhera Dance Festival is an annual cultural phenomenon in the ______ district of the state of Gujarat.
A. Junagadh B. Mehsana
C. Amreli D. Anand

85. How many passenger trains are there as per 2021 data?
A. 19169 B. 11169
C. 13169 D. 16169

86. Kalamandalam Kshemavathy Pavithran was conferred the Padma Shri award for her contribution to which of the following dance forms?
A. Kuchipudi
B. Bharatanatyam
C. Kathak
D. Mohiniyattam

87. Which of the following novels is written by Kiran Desai?
A. The Ministry of Utmost Happiness
B. The Inheritance of Loss
C. Midnight's Children
D. The Golden House

88. C.V. Chandra Shekhar was conferred the Padma Bhushan for his contributions to which of the following forms of Dance?
A. Bharatanatyam
B. Kathakali
C. Manipuri
D. Kathak

89. In 1857, who was the first to experimentally demonstrate that the yeast responsible for making alcohol from sugar, and contaminating microorganisms found in normal air, could sour fermentation?
A. Alexander Fleming
B. Louis Pasteur
C. Fanny Hesse
D. Martinus Willem Beijerinck

90. Which of the following Carnatic instruments is performed by Rajna Swaminathan?
A. Violin B. Flute
C. Veena D. Mridangam

91. Who among the following sportspersons is one of the Arjuna Award 2021 winners?
A. Vikas Kumar
B. Nishad Kumar
C. Bajrang Punia
D. P.V. Sindhu

92. Which phylum of the plant kingdom consists of vascular plants, leaves (known as fronds), roots and sometimes true stems and entire trunks in tree ferns?
A. Angiosperm
B. Pteridophyta
C. Bryophyta
D. Gymnosperm

93. Who observed that in a mixture of non-reactive gases, the total gas pressure is equal to the sum of the partial pressures of the individual gases?
A. Antoine Lavoisier
B. John Dalton
C. Amedeo Avogadro
D. Robert Boyle

94. Which cycle shows the movement of water?
A. Carbon cycle
B. Nitrogen cycle
C. Geological cycle
D. Hydrological cycle

95. Which of the following pairs is NOT correctly matched?
A. Arun Jaitley cricket stadium – Bengaluru
B. Bharat Ratna Atal Bihari Vajpayee cricket stadium – Lucknow
C. Narendra Modi cricket stadium – Ahmedabad
D. Eden Garden – Kolkata

96. The autobiography 'My Experiments with Truth' was originally written in which language?
A. English B. Bengali
C. Gujarati D. Marathi

97. Who among the following secured one of the two silver medals for India at the Tokyo Olympics 2020?
A. Ravi Kumar Dahiya
B. Sushil Kumar
C. Bajrang Punia
D. KD Jadhav

98. Which chemical compound is composed of magnesium, sulphur and oxygen and is commonly used in detox bath to relax muscles and relieve pain in the shoulders, neck, back and scalp?
A. Epsom salt
B. Potash alum
C. Rock salt
D. Glauber's salt

99. The term 'dribble' is used in which of the following sports?
A. Basketball B. Baseball
C. Badminton D. Tennis

100. Which climate zone has an average temperature of over 64°F (18°C) throughout the year and more than 59 inches of rainfall each year?
A. Tropical zone
B. Temperate zone
C. Dry zone
D. Continental zone

ANSWERS

1. (B)	**2. (C)**	**3. (B)**
4. (D)	**5. (A)**	**6. (B)**
7. (A)	**8. (D)**	**9. (C)**
10. (B)	**11. (C)**	**12. (C)**
13. (D)	**14. (B)**	**15. (D)**
16. (D)	**17. (D)**	**18. (B)**
19. (A)	**20. (A)**	**21. (B)**
22. (C)	**23. (B)**	**24. (D)**
25. (D)		

26. (A): First row → 5, 39, 8
$\Rightarrow (5 + 8) \times 3 = 13 \times 3 = 39$
Second row → 7, 36, 5
$\Rightarrow (7 + 5) \times 3 = 12 \times 3 = 36$
Third row → 11, ?, 9
$\Rightarrow (11 + 9) \times 3 = 20 \times 3 = 60$
Hence, ? = Missing number = 60.

27. (D): $(6 + 10) \times 6 = 16 \times 6 = 96$
$(8 + 10) \times 8 = 18 \times 8 = 144$
and $(5 + 10) \times 5 = 15 \times 5 = 75$
Hence, 6 : 96 : : 8 : 144 : : 5 : $\boxed{75}$
Hence ? = Missing number = 75.

28. (C): Order of the given word According to English dictionary
Calcium → Calculate → Calendar → Carrot → Catalyst.

29. (B): According to given statements

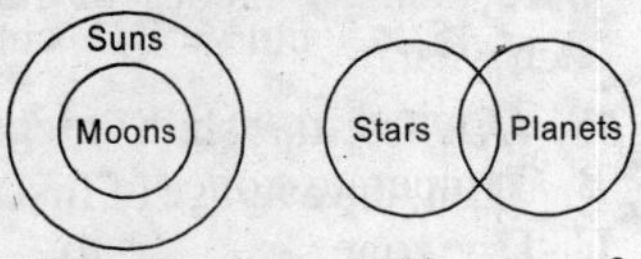

Conclusions: None of the conclusions follows.

30. (C): (A) 43 : 84 $\Rightarrow$ 84 – 43 = 41
(B) 21 : 40 $\Rightarrow$ 40 – 21 = 19
(C) 15 : 210 $\Rightarrow$ 210 – 15 = 195
(D) 19 : 36 $\Rightarrow$ 36 – 19 = 17
Hence, 41, 19 and 17 are prime numbers and 210 is non-price number
Hence, (C) 15 : 210 is odd number pair.

31. (B)	**32. (D)**	**33. (A)**
34. (A)		

35. (B): 127*13*3*129*41
(A) +, =, ÷, –
$\Rightarrow 127 + 13 = 3 \div 129 - 41$
$\Rightarrow \quad 140 = \frac{1}{43} - 41$
(Incorrect combination)
(B) –, ×, =, –
$\Rightarrow 127 - 13 \times 3 = 129 - 41$
$\Rightarrow 127 - 39 = 88$
$\Rightarrow \quad 88 = 88$
(Correct combination)
(C) ÷, –, =, –
$\Rightarrow 127 \div 13 - 3 = 129 - 41$
$\Rightarrow \frac{127}{13} - 3 = 88$
(Incorrect combination)
(D) –, –, =, +
$\Rightarrow 127 - 13 - 3 = 129 + 41$
$\Rightarrow 127 - 26 = 170$
$\Rightarrow \quad 101 = 170$
(Incorrect combination)

36. (D)	**37. (B)**	**38. (C)**
39. (C)	**40. (C)**	**41. (B)**

42. **(C)** **43.** **(C)**

44. **(C):** Given, 31 December 2009 was Thursday

$\Rightarrow$ 25 December 2009 was Friday

$\because$ The year 2010 is an ordinary year

$\therefore$ It has 1 odd day

25 December 2009 was Friday

$\Rightarrow$ 25 December 2010 will be 1 day beyond Friday

Hence, It will be Saturday.

45. **(D)** **46.** **(A)**

47. **(D):**

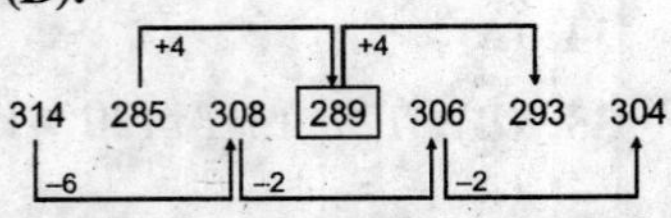

Hence, ? = The missing number.

48. **(B):**

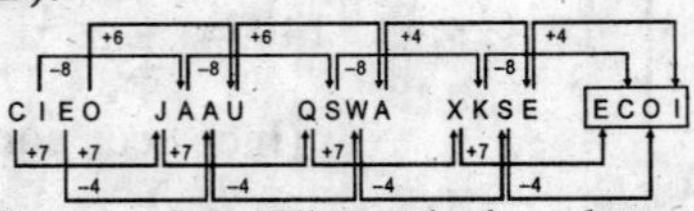

Hence, ? = The missing letter cluster = ECOI

49. **(A):** Here, E and C are common in both position of the dice.

$\therefore$ The face opposite to D = F.

50. **(B)**

51. **(B):** Average speed $= \dfrac{2xy}{x+y}$

$\Rightarrow \quad 48 = \dfrac{2 \times 60 \times y}{60 + y}$

$\Rightarrow 48(60 + y) = 120y$

$\Rightarrow 48 \times 60 + 48y = 120y$

$\Rightarrow 48 \times 60 = 120y - 48y$

$\Rightarrow 48 \times 60 = 72y$

$\Rightarrow \quad y = \dfrac{48 \times 60}{72} = \dfrac{48 \times 5}{6}$

$\Rightarrow \quad = 8 \times 5 = 40$

$\Rightarrow \quad y = 40$ km/h

Hence, Ruksana's speed was 40 km/h while travelling from B to A.

52. **(D):** Here, Speed = 108 km/h

$= 108 \times \dfrac{5}{18}$ m/s

$= 6 \times 5 = 30$ m/s

and time = 40 seconds

$\therefore$ Distane = Speed × time

$= 30 \times 40$ m

$= 1200$ m

$= 1000$ m + 200 m

$= 1$ km 200 m.

53. **(D):** Given, An arc on a circle that is 15 cm long subtends at 24° angle at the centre.

$\because \quad 24° = 15$ cm

$\therefore \quad 1° = \dfrac{15}{24}$

$\Rightarrow \quad 360° = \dfrac{15}{24} \times 360$

$= 15 \times 15 = 225$ cm

Hence, the required circumference of the circle = 225 cm.

54. **(D)** **55.** **(A)** **56.** **(A)**

57. **(D):** The area of the trapezium

$= \dfrac{1}{2} \times$ (Sum of parallel side) × height

$= \dfrac{1}{2} \times (20 + 25) \times 14 \text{ cm}^2$

$= 45 \times 7 \text{ cm}^2 = 315 \text{ cm}^2$.

58. **(A):** Let the sixth integer is x

Then, the average of first 5 integer

$= x \times \dfrac{70}{100} = \dfrac{7}{10}x$

$\Rightarrow$ Sum of first 5 integer

$$= \frac{7}{10}x \times 2 = \frac{7}{2}x$$

and sum of 6 integer = 6 × 48

$$\therefore 6 \times 48 - \frac{7}{2}x = x$$

$$\Rightarrow x + \frac{7}{2}x = 6 \times 48$$

$$\Rightarrow \frac{9}{2}x = 6 \times 48$$

$$\Rightarrow x = 6 \times 48 \times \frac{2}{9}$$

$$= 2 \times 16 \times 2 = 64$$

Hence, the sixth integer is 64.

59. (C)

60. (D):

$79 - [6 - \{4 - (8 \times (6 + 3))\}] \div 2$
$= 79 - [6 - \{4 - (8 \times 9)\}] \div 2$
$= 79 - [6 - \{4 - 72\}] \div 2$
$= 79 - [6 - \{-68\}] \div 2$
$= 79 - [6 + 68] \div 2$
$= 79 - [74] \div 2$
$= 79 - 37 = 42.$

61. (B): Given, $\cos\theta = \frac{-\sqrt{3}}{2}$

$$\Rightarrow \cos\theta = -\cos\frac{\pi}{6}$$

$$\Rightarrow \cos\theta = \cos\left(\pi - \frac{\pi}{6}\right)$$

$$\Rightarrow \cos\theta = \cos\frac{5\pi}{6}$$

$[\cos(\pi - x) = -\cos x]$

$$\Rightarrow \theta = \frac{5\pi}{6}.$$

62. (A): Given, P = ₹ 10,625,

$n = 2$ years

and $r = 8\%$ per annum

$\therefore$ Compound interest

$$= P\left(1+\frac{r}{100}\right)^n - P$$

$$= P\left[\left(1+\frac{r}{100}\right)^n - 1\right]$$

$$= P\left[\left(1+\frac{8}{100}\right)^2 - 1\right]$$

$$= P\left[\left(1+\frac{2}{25}\right)^2 - 1\right]$$

$$= P\left[\left(\frac{27}{25}\right)^2 - 1\right]$$

$$= P\left[\frac{729}{625} - 1\right]$$

$$= 10625\left(\frac{104}{625}\right)$$

$$= 17 \times 104 = ₹\ 1768.$$

63. (B): Here,

LCM of 4, 8, 12 and 16 = 48

$\because$ Smallest 4-digit number = 1000

$$\therefore \frac{1000}{48} = 20.8333$$

and21 × 48 = 1008

Hence, the required smallest 4-digit number = 1008.

64. (B) **65. (C)** **66. (A)**

67. (B): From the given graph

The percentage of the population affected by cold

(A) 1980 $\Rightarrow$ 3.7%
(B) 1990 $\Rightarrow$ 3.6%
(C) 2010 $\Rightarrow$ 8%
(D) 2000 $\Rightarrow$ 10%

Hence, year 1990 was the % of the population affected by cold the minimum.

68. (C) **69. (B)**

70. (A):

According to given information The total number of people

$= 10000$

$\therefore$ The total number of people who are in the teaching profession

$= 10000 \times \frac{20}{100}$

$= 2000$

Hence, the total number of males who are in the teaching profession

$= 2000 \times \frac{50}{100}$

$= 1000.$

71. (A)

72. (A): Work done by the leak in 1 hour

$= \frac{1}{15} - \frac{1}{20}$

$= \frac{4-3}{60} = \frac{1}{60}$

Hence, Leak will empty the tank in 60 hours.

73. (B) **74. (D)**

75. (D): Let the total number of votes polled was x.

Then, $x \times \frac{65}{100} - x \times \frac{35}{100} = 1296$

$\Rightarrow x\left(\frac{65-35}{100}\right) = 1296$

$\Rightarrow x\left(\frac{30}{100}\right) = 1296$

$\Rightarrow \quad x = \frac{1296 \times 10}{3}$

$\Rightarrow \quad x = 4320.$

76. (C) **77. (A)** **78. (B)**

79. (B) **80. (C)** **81. (A)**

82. (A) **83. (D)** **84. (B)**

85. (C) **86. (D)** **87. (B)**

88. (A) **89. (B)** **90. (D)**

91. (B) **92. (B)** **93. (B)**

94. (D) **95. (A)** **96. (C)**

97. (A) **98. (A)** **99. (A)**

100. (A)

Previous Paper (Solved)

SSC-Combined Higher Secondary Level–CHSL (10+2) Tier–1, Online Recruitment Exam–2020

(Exam held on 04-08-2021)

ENGLISH LANGUAGE

1. Select the most appropriate option to substitute the underlined segment in the given sentence. If there is no need to substitute it, select 'No substitution'.

If he doesn't reach the station in time, he would sure miss the train.

A. would surely miss
B. No substitution
C. will sure missing
D. will surely miss

2. Select the most appropriate option to fill in the blank.

It is claimed that if you take a certain homeopathic medicine, it will ______ you against the coronavirus.

A. shelter B. immune
C. reinforce D. fortify

3. Select the most appropriate synonym of the given word.

WRY

A. straight B. frank
C. forthright D. crooked

4. In the given sentence, identify the segment which contains the grammatical error.

My mother generally read the local newspaper to keep abreast of the local news.

A. the local newspaper
B. of the local news
C. My mother generally read
D. to keep abreast

5. Select the most appropriate ANTONYM of the given word.

SUSTENANCE

A. refreshment B. livelihood
C. starvation D. nourishment

6. Select the INCORRECTLY spelt word.

A. superior B. superstition
C. superflous D. supreme

7. Select the option that will improve the underlined segment in the given sentence. In case no improvement is needed, select 'No improvement'

What a palace home!

A. pushy
B. palatial
C. palatable
D. No improvement

8. Select the most appropriate synonym of the given word.

MALIGNANT

A. vicious B. beneficial
C. loving D. healthy

9. Select the most appropriate meaning of the given idiom.

Under wraps

A. under estimate
B. double layered
C. secretly
D. underhand

10. Select the most appropriate ANTONYM of the given word.

DEVIOUS

A. Deceitful B. shrewd
C. straight D. calculating

11. Select the correct indirect form of the given sentence.

Anju said to Vijaya, "You can stay with us whenever you are in Delhi."

A. Anju told Vijaya that she could stay with them whenever she was in Delhi.
B. Anju told Vijaya that she could stay with them whenever you were in Delhi.
C. Anju told Vijaya that she can stay with us whenever she is in Delhi.
D. Anju told Vijaya that you can stay with us whenever you are in Delhi.

12. Select the option which means the same as the group of words given.

A government run by the wealthy people

A. oligarchy B. monarchy
C. plutocracy D. aristocracy

13. Select the correct passive form of the given sentence.

The Central Board of Secondary Education has launched a new helpline for students.

A. A new helpline for students is launched by the Central Board of Secondary Education.
B. A new helpline for students will be launched by the Central Board of Secondary Education.
C. A new helpline for students had been launched by the Central Board of Secondary Education.
D. A new helpline for students has been launched by the Central Board of Secondary Education.

14. Given below are four jumbled sentences. Out of the given options, pick the one that gives their correct order.

(*a*) He lived in a small house near the main road of a village.
(*b*) As both, he and his wife, worked hard, they made a small fortune.
(*c*) But one thing caused them great sorrow: they had no children.
(*d*) After he got married, he started a tailor's shop.

A. (*a*)(*b*)(*d*)(*c*) B. (*b*)(*d*)(*a*)(*c*)
C. (*a*)(*d*)(*b*)(*c*) D. (*b*)(*a*)(*c*)(*d*)

15. Select the most appropriate word to fill in the blank.

Debjyoti's short animation film ______ highlights the stark contrast between the rich and the poor in India.

A. poignantly B. strictly
C. carelessly D. sweetly

16. Select the most appropriate meaning of the given idiom.
On tenterhooks

A. Very sad B. Very tense
C. Very happy D. Very angry

17. Select the INCORRECTLY spelt word.

A. disappear B. until
C. twelth D. temperature

18. Examine the four jumbled sentences. Out of the given options, pick the one that gives their correct order.

(*a*) We gently put the fledgling back into the nest.
(*b*) One morning, we found one of the four fallen on the ground.
(*c*) The robin couple built a nest in our verandah and laid four eggs.
(*d*) Once they had hatched, they busily took turns feeding the four.

A. (*c*)(*d*)(*b*)(*a*) B. (*a*)(*c*)(*d*)(*b*)
C. (*b*)(*a*)(*d*)(*c*) D. (*d*)(*a*)(*b*)(*c*)

19. Select the word which means the same as the group of words given.
That which is incapable of being read or understood

A. Indelible B. Illegible
C. Illegal D. Intelligible

20. The following sentence has been split into four segments. Identify the segment which contains a grammatical error.
Deepu's mother / has repeated asked him / to lower the volume / of his mobile.

A. has repeated asked him
B. to lower the volume
C. of his mobile
D. Deepu's mother

Directions (Qs. No. 21-25): *In the following passage, some words have been deleted. Fill in the blanks with the help of the alternatives given. Select the most appropriate option for each blank.*

A year is hardly sufficient time for a Master to (1) ______ about a new school, leave alone absorb a distinct tradition like (2) ______. Most of the new appointees had not served in a residential school and (3) ______ time to learn. But the short tenure did not allow (4) ______. They could not develop understanding of the student and his (5) ______.

21. Select the most appropriate option for blank No. 1.

A. learnt B. learn
C. learns D. learning

22. Select the most appropriate option for blank No. 2.

A. ourselves B. himself
C. mine D. ours

23. Select the most appropriate option for blank No. 3.

A. needing B. need
C. needed D. needs

24. Select the most appropriate option for blank No. 4.

A. them B. those
C. these D. that

25. Select the most appropriate option for blank No. 5.

A. environmentalist
B. environmental
C. environment
D. environmentally

GENERAL INTELLIGENCE

26. Read the given statements and conclusions carefully. Assuming that the information given in the statements is true, even if it appears to be at variance with commonly known facts, decide which of the given conclusions logically follow(s) from the statements.

Statements:

All computers are machines.

No television is a computer.

All televisions are instruments.

Conclusions:

I. Some instruments are machines.

II. Some machines are computers.

III. Some televisions are machines.

A. Only conclusion II follows.

B. Only conclusion I follows.

C. Only conclusions II and III follow.

D. None of the conclusions follow.

27. Select the combination of letters that when sequentially placed in the blanks of the given letter series will complete the series.

a_ _bcde_ _abbcd_ _aabb_ _ee

A. aeaebecd B. aeecdbea

C. abeaeecd D. abecdeae

28. Select the option in which the words share the same relationship as that shared by the given pair of words.

Ammeter : Electric current

A. Density : Lactometer

B. Pressure : Barometer

C. Hygrometer : Humidity

D. Polarimeter : Steps

29. 'Straw' is related to 'Nest' in the same way as 'Cotton' is related to '______'.

A. Textile industry

B. Thread

C. Sewing

D. Wool

30. Select the figure from among the given options that can replace the question mark (?) in the following series.

A. 

B. 

C. 

D. 

31. The sales boy of a washing machine store charges his customers 24% more than the cost price. If a customer paid ₹ 6,200 for a washing machine, then what was the cost price of the washing machine?

A. ₹ 5,500 B. ₹ 5,000

C. ₹ 6,200 D. ₹ 7,200

32. Study the given pattern carefully and select the number that can replace the question mark (?) in it.

28	16	27
44	16	15
84	?	24

A. 27 B. 30

C. 28 D. 29

33. Select the option that is related to the third number in the same way as the second number is related to the first number.

12 : 150 : : 14 : ?

A. 203 B. 502
C. 302 D. 205

34. The sequence of folding a piece of paper and the manner in which the folded paper has been cut is shown in the following figures. How would this paper look when unfolded?

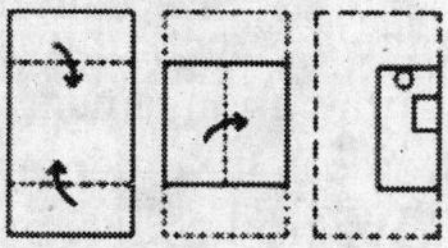

A. 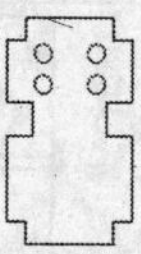
B. 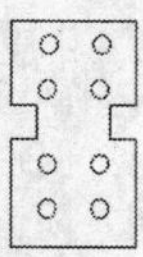
C. 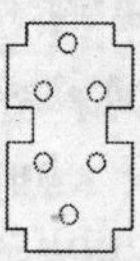
D. 

35. Select the number from among the given options that can replace the question mark (?) in the following series.

3, 5, 15, 41, ?, 173

A. 91 B. 112
C. 78 D. 106

36. Four letter-clusters have been given, out of which three are alike in some manner and one is different. Select the letter-cluster that is different.

A. NRJQ B. DHSZ
C. TXCJ D. GKPW

37. Select the option in which the given figure is embedded (rotation is NOT allowed).

A. 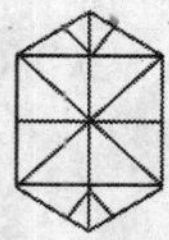
B. 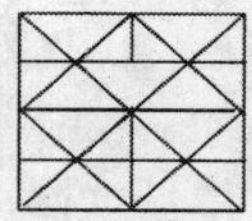
C. 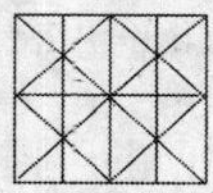
D. 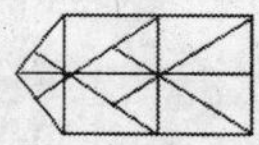

38. Find the number of triangles in the given figure.

A. 15 B. 11
C. 14 D. 13

39. In a certain code language, FORWARD is written as CSZXQPE. How will NUMERAL be written in that language?

A. MZSDNTO B. KZQDLTL
C. KBQFLVM D. MUNELAR

40. Which two signs should be interchanged to make the following equation correct?

$12 - 8 + 4 \div 2 \times 8 = 4$

A. – and × B. × and +
C. ÷ and – D. × and ÷

41. In a certain code language, HAMPER is coded as 17212322036 and INSULT is coded as 16286421340. How will SAFETY be coded in that language?

A. 621910550 B. 612195030
C. 629101350 D. 610195320

42. Select the option that is related to the third letter-cluster in the same way as the second letter-cluster is related to the first letter-cluster.

BYDW : UFSH : : CXFU : ?

A. TGQJ B. SHQJ
C. RIPK D. RIOL

43. Four words have been given, out of which three are alike in some manner and one is different. Select the word that is different.

A. Integrity B. Joviality
C. Honesty D. Truthfulness

44. A cube is made by folding the given sheet. In the cube so formed, how many dots lie opposite to the face having 4 dots?

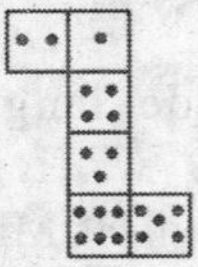

A. 2 B. 5
C. 6 D. 1

45. Select the Venn diagram that best represents the relationship between the following classes.

Women, Professors, Widows

A.  B. 

C. 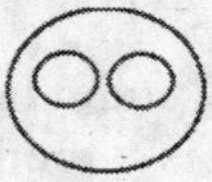 D. 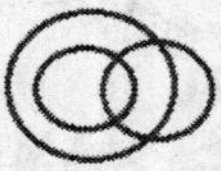

46. Snigda said that she met her mother's only brother's son's mother's father-in-law. Whom did she meet?

A. Father B. Uncle
C. Grandfather D. Brother

47. Four numbers have been given, out of which three are alike in some manner and one is different. Select the number that is different.

A. 6341 B. 6138
C. 5423 D. 1652

48. Select the option in which the numbers are related in the same way as are the numbers of the following set.

{9, 12, 18}

A. {7, 13, 27} B. {21, 29, 44}
C. {5, 12, 24} D. {13, 19, 31}

49. Select the correct option that indicates the arrangement of the given words in the order in which they appear in an English dictionary.

1. Multifocal 2. Movement
3. Multinomial 4. Moviemaker
5. Mutual fund

A. 4, 2, 3, 1, 5 B. 1, 5, 2, 3, 4
C. 4, 2, 1, 3, 5 D. 2, 4, 1, 3, 5

50. Select the correct mirror image of the given figure when the mirror is placed at the right side of the figure.

A.  B. 

C.  D. 

QUANTITATIVE APTITUDE

51. A solid metallic hemisphere of radius 6.3 cm is melted and recast into a right circular cylinder of radius 9 cm. What is the height (in cm, correct to one decimal place) of the cylinder?

A. 1.9 B. 2.7
C. 2.5 D. 2.1

52. If $\cos\theta = \frac{4x}{1+4x^2}$, then what is the value of sin θ?

A. $\frac{1+4x^2}{1-4x^2}$ B. $\frac{1+4x^2}{4x^2}$
C. $\frac{1-4x^2}{1+4x^2}$ D. $\frac{1-4x^2}{4x}$

53. In a triangle ABC, ∠BAC = 90° and AD is perpendicular to BC. If AD = 8.4 cm and BD = 4.8 cm, then the length of BC is:

A. 19.5 cm B. 15 cm
C. 18 cm D. 18.5 cm

54. Tap P can fill a cistern in 6 hours and tap Q can empty the full cistern in 10 hours. If both taps P and Q are kept open simultaneously, then in how many hours will the empty cistern be completely full?

A. 15 B. 18
C. 16 D. 12

55. One dozen notebooks quoted at ₹ 125 are available at 20% discount. How many notebooks can be bought for ₹ 75?

A. 10 B. 6
C. 9 D. 8

56. A man invests ₹ 7,000 at 8% per annum simple interest for 2 years and ₹ 10,000 at compound interest at the same rate for the same period, compounded annually. What will be the total interest and the total amount (in ₹) respectively, on maturity?

A. 19,748 and 2,874
B. 2,748 and 19,784
C. 19,784 and 2,784
D. 2,784 and 19,784

57. If (sin A – cos A) = 0, then what is the value of cot A?

A. $\frac{\pi}{6}$ B. 0
C. 1 D. $\frac{\pi}{4}$

58. A boat can travel with a speed of 19 km/h in still water. If the speed of the stream is 3 km/h, then what will be the total time (in hours) taken by the boat to go 88 km downstream and 24 km upstream?

A. 4.5 B. 5
C. 4 D. 5.5

59. A is 150% of B and B is 40% of C. If A + B + C = 20, then the value of 2B + 3C – 4A is equal to:

A. 16 B. 14
C. 20 D. 15

60. The following histogram represents the distribution of household expenditure (in ₹) of 200 manual workers in a city.

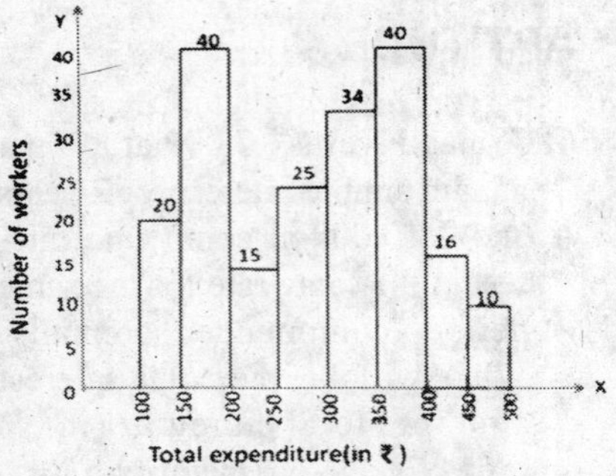

The ratio of the number of workers whose household expenditure is less than ₹ 200 to the number of workers whose household expenditure is ₹ 300 and above is:

A. 3 : 5 B. 2 : 5
C. 4 : 5 D. 3 : 4

61. Using algebraic identities, simplify the following expression.

$$\frac{(x^4 + x^2 + 1)}{(x^2 + x + 1)}$$

A. $(x^2 - 2x + 1)$
B. $(x^2 + x + 1)$
C. $(x^2 + 2x + 1)$
D. $(x^2 - x + 1)$

62.

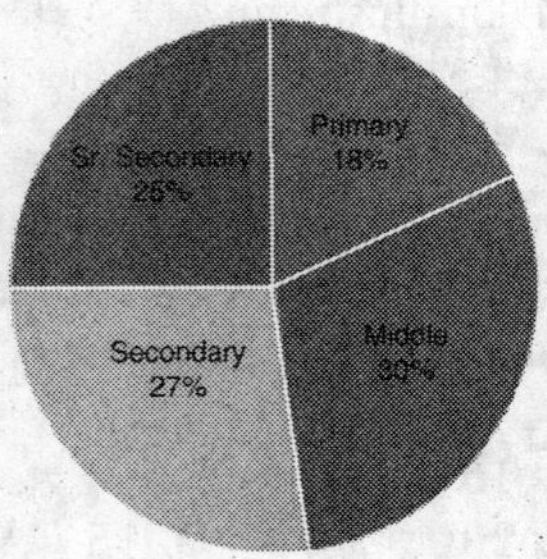

Students of Primary, Middle, Secondary and Sr. Secondary classes collected donation for a Relief Fund as shown in the pie chart. If the donation collected from Middle classes was ₹ 6,750, then how much money was collected by the Primary classes?

A. ₹ 4,050 B. ₹ 4,005
C. ₹ 4,500 D. ₹ 3,960

63. One-quarter of a circular pizza of diameter 28 cm was removed from the whole pizza. What is the perimeter (in cm) of the remaining pizza? (Take π = 22/7)

A. 88 B. 94
C. 80 D. 66

64. The inner and outer radii of two concentric circles are 6.7 cm and 9.5 cm respectively. What is the difference between their circumferences (in cm)?

Take π = 22/7.

A. 20.5 B. 10.4
C. 6.5 D. 17.6

65. Study the given graph and answer the question that follows.

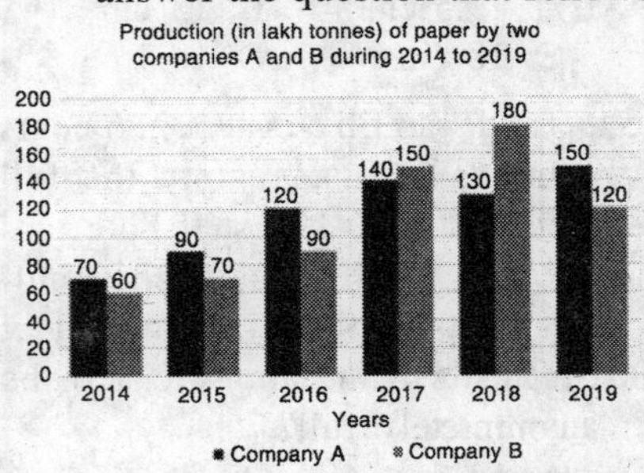

The average production of paper by company B in 2014, 2017 and 2018 was $13\frac{1}{3}\%$ less than the production of paper by company A in the year:

A. 2016 B. 2018
C. 2017 D. 2019

66. What is the perimeter (in cm) of an equilateral triangle whose height is 3.46 cm? Take $\sqrt{3} = 1.73$.

A. 10.4 B. 9

C. 6 D. 12

67. The value of

$$[\{(232 \div 29 \text{ of } 2) + 77 \times 10\} \div 18] - \frac{18 \times 8 \div 4 \text{ of } 3 - 4}{2 \times (8-6) + 1 - 2 \times 3 \div 4 \text{ of } \frac{1}{2}}$$

is:

A. 39 B. 44

C. 33 D. 47

68. The string of a kite is 158 m long and it makes an angle of 30° with the horizontal. What is the height (in m) of the kite? Assume there is no slack in the string.

A. 100 B. 99

C. 79 D. 80

69. If $\left(x + \frac{1}{x}\right)^3 = 27$, then what is the value of $\left(x^2 + \frac{1}{x^2}\right)$? Given that x is real.

A. 11 B. 25

C. 7 D. 9

70. Study the given pie-chart and answer the question that follows.

The pie-chart represents the consumption of fuel (in million litres) by various modes of transport of a country X in the year 2015. The total consumption of fuel by various modes of transport of the country is 800 million litres.

(The data shown here is only for mathematical exercise. They do not represent the actual figures of the country.)

Consumption of fuel (in million litres) by various modes of transport of a country X in the year 2015

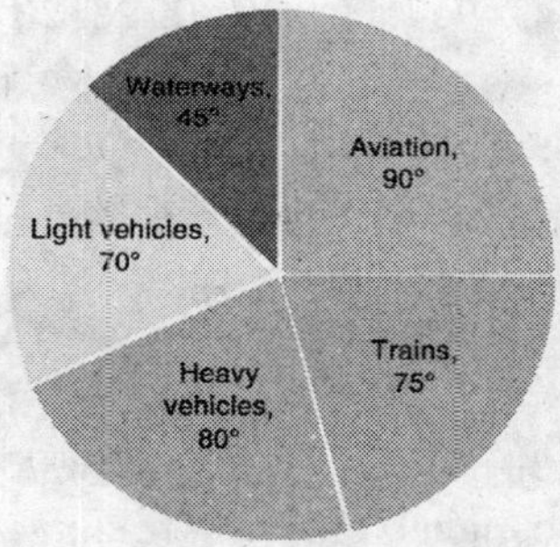

To obtain fuel, energy is required to run the machinery, which is to be produced by burning coal.

If 1 tonne of coal is burnt to produce 0.4 million litres of oil, then approximately what is the requirement of coal (in tonnes) for the Trains sector?

A. 417 B. 415

C. 418 D. 420

71. One-fifth of a journey is covered at a speed of 30 km/h, one-fourth of the journey at a speed of 25 km/h and the rest at 60 km/h. What is the average speed (in km/h, correct to one decimal place) for the whole journey?

A. 38.7 B. 30.6

C. 40.5 D. 25.4

72. If $a + b = p$, $ab = q$, then $(a^4 + b^4)$ is equal to:

A. $p^4 - 2p^2q^2 + q^2$

B. $p^4 - 4p^2q^2 + 2q^2$

C. $p^4 - 4p^2q + q^2$

D. $p^4 - 4p^2q + 2q^2$

73. What is the greatest five-digit number that is completely divisible by 8, 15, 16, 21 and 5?

A. 92680 B. 99120

C. 95760 D. 98320

74. By selling an article for ₹ 1,170, Elisa suffers as much loss as she would have gained by selling it at a profit of 22%. If she sells it for ₹ 1,450, then her profit loss per cent (correct up to one decimal place) is:

A. Profit, 3.3 B. Loss, 3.3

C. Loss, 26.2 D. Profit, 26.2

75. If A : B = 11 : 7 and B : C = 5 : 19, then what is A : B : C?

A. 55 : 35 : 133

B. 35 : 55 : 133

C. 35 : 133 : 55

D. 55 : 133 : 35

GENERAL AWARENESS

76. Who among the following is the first Indian pistol shooter to reach number one in world rankings by the International Shooting Sport Federation?

A. Heena Sidhu

B. Kajal Saini

C. Tejaswini Sawant

D. Suma Shirur

77. Who among the following has become the first woman umpire to officiate in a men's Test match in January 2021?

A. Danielle Wyatt

B. Jess Jonassen

C. Suzie Bates

D. Claire Polosak

78. Which part of soil has organic materials incorporated with the mineral matter, nutrients and water?

A. Horizon D B. Horizon C

C. Horizon A D. Horizon B

79. In which of the following states is Sabarimala Sree Dharma Sastha Temple located?

A. Karnataka

B. Telangana

C. Andhra Pradesh

D. Kerala

80. Identify the Indian state which was known as 'Pragjyotisha' during the epic period.

A. Assam B. Odisha

C. Kerala D. Bihar

81. What is the SI unit for measuring pressure?

A. Pascal B. Candela

C. Ampere D. Kelvin

82. Who among the following was appointed by AIFF (All India Football Federation) as its first Deputy General Secretary in January 2021?

A. Abhishek Yadav

B. Praful Patel

C. Umesh Sinha

D. Kushal Das

83. Kabartal Wetland was designated as a Ramsar site in 2020. In which of the following states is it located?

A. Haryana
B. Bihar
C. Himachal Pradesh
D. Punjab

84. ______ are gently sloping areas of the ocean basins.
A. Deep sea plains
B. Continental shelfs
C. Continental slopes
D. Oceanic deeps

85. Who among the following was appointed as the Chief Justice of the Andhra Pradesh High Court in January 2021?
A. Sharad Arvind Bobde
B. Hima Kohli
C. Rajan Datta
D. Arup Kumar Goswami

86. Who among the following Indian nationals got the 'Legion of Merit' Award 2020 from the US?
A. Dr Manmohan Singh
B. Narendra Modi
C. Dr K Sivan
D. General Bipin Rawat

87. Who among the following became the first Lokpal of India?
A. Dilip B Bhosale
B. Pradip Kumar Mohanty
C. Pinaki Chandra Ghose
D. Ajay Kumar Tripathi

88. In which of the following states did the Land Grabbing (Prohibition) Act, 2020 come into force in December 2020?
A. Punjab
B. Maharashtra
C. Gujarat
D. Madhya Pradesh

89. What happens to Indian exports when Indian rupee is devalued?
A. Export prices fluctuate
B. Exports become cheaper
C. Export prices remain stable
D. Exports become dearer

90. ______ is the process of turning on a computer and powering up the system.
A. Booting
B. Loading
C. Saving
D. Execution

91. What do you call a key on a computer keyboard that is used to move the pointer (cursor) around on the screen?
A. Navigation key
B. Numeric key
C. Function key
D. Control key

92. Vitamin B12 is generally NOT present in ______.
A. milk products
B. plant foods
C. fish products
D. poultry products

93. Who among the following is considered as the 'Father of Modern Atomic Theory'?
A. Robert Boyle
B. John Dalton
C. Willard Gibbs
D. Otto Hahn

94. ______ plains are formed due to the weathering of soluble rocks such as limestone and dolomite.
A. Glacial B. Karst
C. Deposition D. Desert

95. Which of the following state governments unveiled a Braille version of the Constitution of India in January 2021?
A. Haryana
B. Andhra Pradesh
C. Punjab
D. Maharashtra

96. In which of the following cities is the corporate centre of State Bank of India (SBI) situated?
A. Hyderabad B. Kolkata
C. Mumbai D. Bengaluru

97. In which of the following years was the Vijayanagar empire founded?
A. 1456 B. 1229
C. 1412 D. 1336

98. In which of the following years did Telangana become the 29th state of India after the reorganisation of the state of Andhra Pradesh?
A. 2014 B. 1994
C. 2010 D. 1998

99. 'Kati Bihu' in Assam is celebrated by lighting a lamp in front of a ______ tree/plant.
A. banyan B. tulsi
C. banana D. neem

100. Who among the following was awarded the Rabindranath Tagore Literary Award 2020?
A. Ashraf Patel
B. Ranjitsingh Disale
C. Vidyut Mohan
D. Raj Kamal Jha

ANSWERS

1	2	3	4	5	6	7	8	9	10
D	D	D	C	C	C	B	A	C	C
11	**12**	**13**	**14**	**15**	**16**	**17**	**18**	**19**	**20**
A	C	D	C	A	B	C	A	B	A
21	**22**	**23**	**24**	**25**	**26**	**27**	**28**	**29**	**30**
B	D	C	D	C	A	C	C	B	C
31	**32**	**33**	**34**	**35**	**36**	**37**	**38**	**39**	**40**
B	D	A	A	A	A	C	C	C	B
41	**42**	**43**	**44**	**45**	**46**	**47**	**48**	**49**	**50**
A	D	B	C	D	C	B	D	D	D
51	**52**	**53**	**54**	**55**	**56**	**57**	**58**	**59**	**60**
D	C	A	A	C	D	C	D	B	A
61	**62**	**63**	**64**	**65**	**66**	**67**	**68**	**69**	**70**
D	A	B	D	D	D	A	C	C	A
71	**72**	**73**	**74**	**75**	**76**	**77**	**78**	**79**	**80**
A	D	B	B	A	A	D	C	D	A
81	**82**	**83**	**84**	**85**	**86**	**87**	**88**	**89**	**90**
A	A	B	A	D	B	C	C	B	A
91	**92**	**93**	**94**	**95**	**96**	**97**	**98**	**99**	**100**
A	B	B	B	D	C	D	A	B	D

EXPLANATORY ANSWERS

26. According to given statements:

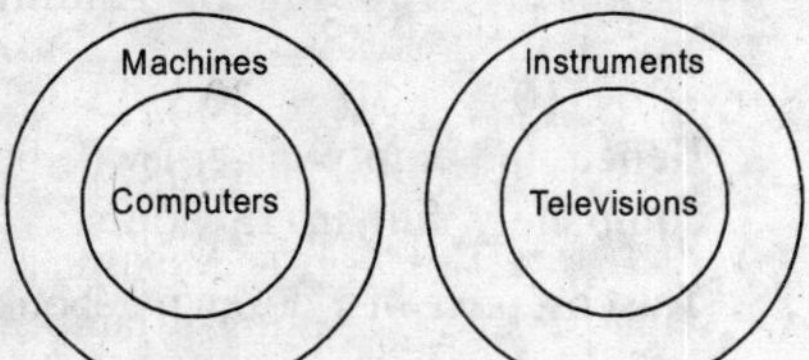

Conclusions: II. Some machines are computers.

31. The cost price of the washing machine

$$= ₹\ 6200 \times \frac{100}{100+24}$$

$$= ₹\ 6200 \times \frac{100}{124} = 100 \times \frac{100}{2}$$

$$= 50 \times 100 = ₹\ 5000$$

33. $12 \times 12 + \frac{12}{2} = 144 + 6 = 150$

and similarly,

$14 \times 14 + \frac{14}{2} = 196 + 7 = 203$

Hence, 12 : 150 : : 14 : 203.

35.

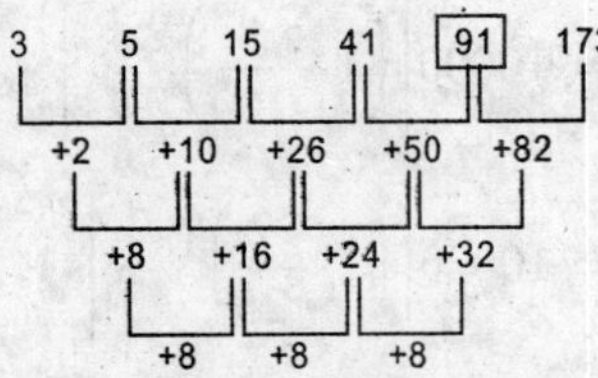

Hence, ? = the missing number = 91.

36. A. 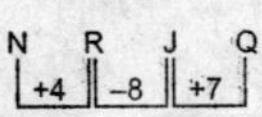

B. 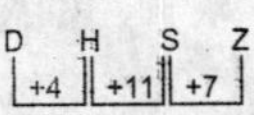

C. 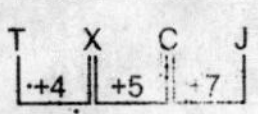

D. 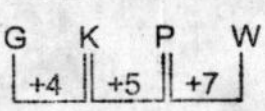

Hence, option (A) is different.

42. As,

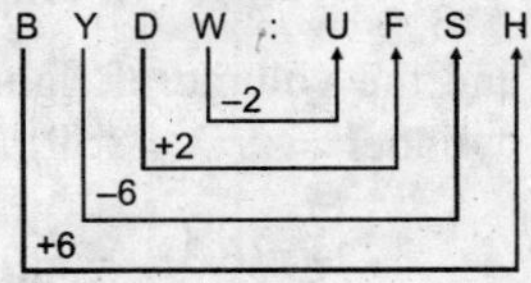

Similarly,

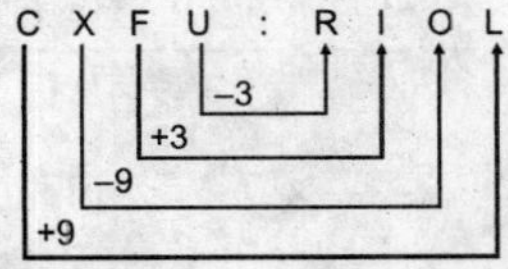

Hence,

BYDW : UFSH : : CXFU : RIOL.

46.

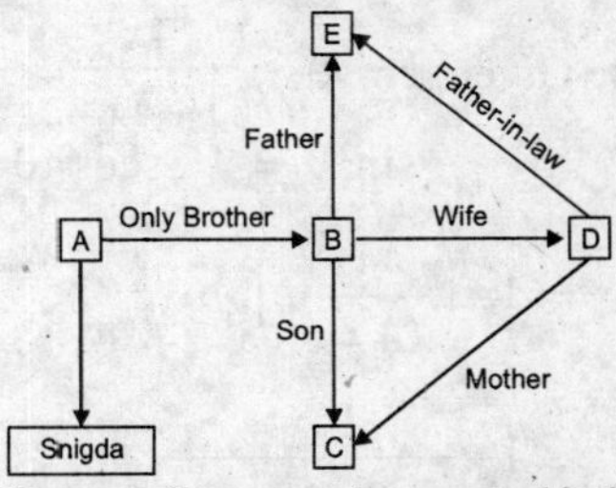

Hence, She met her grandfather.

47. A. 6341 ⇒ 6 + 3 + 4 + 1 = 14
B. 6138 ⇒ 6 + 1 + 3 + 8 = 18
C. 5423 ⇒ 5 + 4 + 2 + 3 = 14
D. 1652 ⇒ 1 + 6 + 5 + 2 = 14
Hence, option (B) is different.

48.

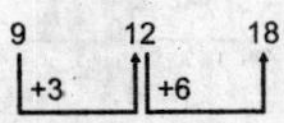

A. 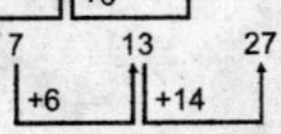

B. 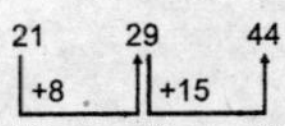

C. 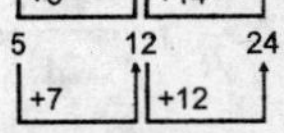

D. 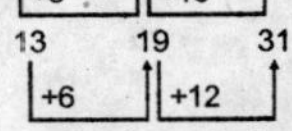

Hence, option (D) is related in the same way as the given set.

49. According to English dictionary Movement → Moviemaker → Multifocal → Multinomial → Mutual fund.

51. Volume of hemispher

$= \frac{2}{3}\pi r^3 = \frac{2}{3}\pi(6.3)^3$ cm^3

and the volume of right circular cylinder $= \pi r^2 h = \pi(9)^2 h$ cm^3

$\therefore \quad \frac{2}{3}\pi(6.3)^3 = \pi(9)^2 h$

$\Rightarrow \quad h = \frac{2}{3} \times \frac{6.3 \times 6.3 \times 6.3}{9 \times 9}$

$= \frac{2}{3} \times .7 \times .7 \times 6.3$

$= 2 \times .7 \times .7 \times 2.1$

$= 2.058 = 2.1$ cm.

52. Given, $\cos\theta = \frac{4x}{1+4x^2}$

$\because \quad \sin^2\theta = 1 - \cos^2\theta$

$= 1 - \left(\frac{4x}{1+4x^2}\right)^2$

$= 1 - \frac{16x^2}{1+8x^2+16x^4}$

$= \frac{1+8x^2+16x^4-16x^2}{1+8x^2+16x^4}$

$= \frac{1-8x^2+16x^4}{1+8x^2+16x^4}$

$\therefore \quad \sin^2\theta = \frac{(1-4x^2)^2}{(1+4x^2)^2}$

$\Rightarrow \quad \sin^2\theta = \left(\frac{1-4x^2}{1+4x^2}\right)^2$

$\Rightarrow \quad \sin\theta = \frac{1-4x^2}{1+4x^2}$.

54. Part filled in 1 hour by tap P $= \frac{1}{6}$ and part empted in 1 hour by tap

$Q = \frac{1}{10}$

$\therefore$ The net part filled in 1 hour

$= \frac{1}{6} - \frac{1}{10} = \frac{5-3}{30} = \frac{2}{30} = \frac{1}{15}$

Hence, the empty cistern will be completely full in 15 hours.

55. The cost price of 1 dozen notebook

$= ₹\ 125 \times \frac{80}{100} = ₹\ 125 \times \frac{4}{5}$

$= 25 \times 4 = ₹\ 100$

Hence, the number of notebooks can be bought for ₹ 75

$= \frac{12}{100} \times 75 = \frac{3}{25} \times 75$

$= 3 \times 3 = 9.$

56. Simple interest

$= \frac{P \times r \times t}{100} = ₹\ \frac{7000 \times 8 \times 2}{100}$

$= ₹\ 1120$

$\therefore \quad$ Amount = P + S.I.

$= 7000 + 1120 = ₹\ 8120$

Compound Interest

$= P\left[\left(1+\frac{r}{100}\right)^n - 1\right]$

$= 10000\left[\left(1+\frac{8}{100}\right)^2 - 1\right]$

$= 10000\left[\left(1+\frac{2}{25}\right)^2 - 1\right]$

$= 10000\left[\left(\frac{27}{25}\right)^2 - 1\right]$

$= 10000\left[\frac{729}{625} - 1\right]$

$= 10000 \times \frac{104}{625}$

$= 16 \times 104 = 1664$

Amount = P + C.I.

$= 10000 + 1664 =$ ₹ 11664

Hence, the total interest

= ₹ 1120 + ₹ 1664 = ₹ 2784

and the total amount

= ₹ 8120 + ₹ 11664 = ₹ 19784.

57. Given, $\sin A - \cos A = 0$

$\Rightarrow \quad \sin A = \cos A$

$\Rightarrow \quad \frac{\cos A}{\sin A} = 1$

$\Rightarrow \quad \cot A = 1.$

58. Here, speed in downstream

= 19 + 3 = 22 km/hr

and speed in upstream

= 19 – 3 = 16 km/hr

Total time will be taken by the boat to go 88 km downstream and 24 km upstream

$= \frac{88}{22}\text{hr} + \frac{24}{16}\text{hr} = \left(4 + \frac{3}{2}\right)\text{hr}$

$= \frac{11}{2}\text{hr} = 5.5$ hours.

60. From the given histogram

Required ratio

= (20 + 40) : (34 + 40 + 16 + 10)

= 60 : 100 = 3 : 5.

62. From the given Pie-chart

Let the total donation collected

= ₹ x

Then, $\quad x \times \frac{30}{100} = 6750$

$\Rightarrow \quad x = \frac{67500}{3}$

Hence, donation collected by the primary classes

$= \frac{67500}{3} \times \frac{18}{100}$

= ₹ 675 × 6 = ₹ 4050.

63. Given, diameter of a circular pizza = 28 cm

$\Rightarrow \quad 2r = 28 \text{ cm} \Rightarrow r = 14 \text{ cm}$

∴ Perimeter of a circular pizza

$= 2\pi r = 2 \times \frac{22}{7} \times 14$

$= 22 \times 4 = 88$ cm

∵ One-quarter of a circular pizza was removed from the whole pizza

∴ The perimeter of the remaining pizza

$= 88 - \frac{88}{4} + 14 + 14$

= 88 – 22 + 28 = 66 + 28 = 94.

64. Given, the inner and outer radii of two concentric circles are 6.7 cm and 9.5 cm

Hence, the difference between their circumference

= 2π × 9.5 cm – 2π × 6.7 cm

= 2π(9.5 – 6.7) cm = 2π × 2.8 cm

$= 2 \times \frac{22}{7} \times 2.8$ cm $= 2 \times 22 \times 0.4$

= 0.8 × 22 = 17.6 cm

66. Let the side of an equilateral triangle (ΔABC) is x cm

Given, height = 3.46 cm

$\therefore \quad h = AD = 3.46$ cm

In ΔADC,

$AD^2 + DC^2 = AC^2$

$\Rightarrow h^2 + \left(\frac{x}{2}\right)^2 = x^2$

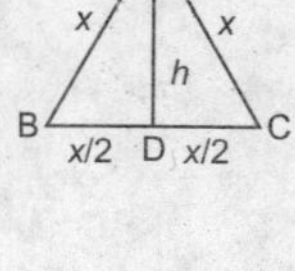

$\Rightarrow \quad h^2 = x^2 - \dfrac{x^2}{4}$

$\Rightarrow \quad h^2 = \dfrac{3}{4}x^2 \Rightarrow x^2 = \dfrac{4h^2}{3}$

$\Rightarrow \quad x = \dfrac{2h}{\sqrt{3}} = \dfrac{2 \times 3.46}{1.73}$

$\Rightarrow \quad x = \dfrac{6.92}{1.73} \Rightarrow x = 4$ cm

Hence, the perimeter of an equilateral triangle

$= 3x = 3 \times 4 = 12$ cm.

68. Let AC = string of a kite = 158 m

$\angle ACB = 30°$

AB = height of the kite

In ΔABC, $\sin 30° = \dfrac{AB}{AC}$

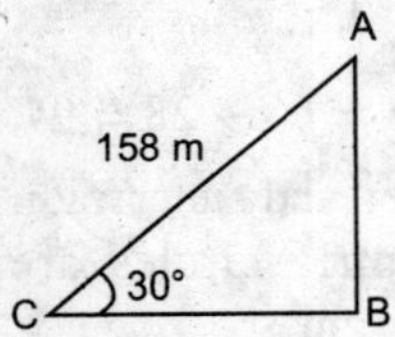

$\Rightarrow \dfrac{1}{2} = \dfrac{AB}{158}$

$\Rightarrow AB = \dfrac{158}{2} = 79$

$\Rightarrow AB = 79$ m.

69. Given, $\left(x + \dfrac{1}{x}\right)^3 = 27$

$\Rightarrow \left(x + \dfrac{1}{x}\right)^3 = (3)^3 \Rightarrow \left(x + \dfrac{1}{x}\right) = 3$

Squaring both sides, we get,

$\left(x + \dfrac{1}{x}\right)^2 = 9$

$\Rightarrow x^2 + \dfrac{1}{x^2} + 2.x.\dfrac{1}{x} = 9$

$\Rightarrow \quad x^2 + \dfrac{1}{x^2} + 2 = 9$

$\Rightarrow \quad x^2 + \dfrac{1}{x^2} = 9 - 2 = 7.$

71. Let the distance of Journey = x km

$\because$ Speed $= \dfrac{\text{Distance}}{\text{Time}}$

$\therefore$ Total time in whole journey

$= \dfrac{\frac{x}{5}}{30} + \dfrac{\frac{x}{4}}{25} + \dfrac{x - \left(\frac{x}{5} + \frac{x}{4}\right)}{60}$

$= \dfrac{x}{150} + \dfrac{x}{100} + \dfrac{x - \frac{9x}{20}}{60}$

$= \dfrac{x}{150} + \dfrac{x}{100} + \dfrac{11x}{1200}$

$= \dfrac{8x + 12x + 11x}{1200} = \dfrac{31x}{1200}$ hours

Hence, the average speed in the whole journey

$= \dfrac{x}{\frac{31x}{1200}} = \dfrac{1200}{31} = 38.\dot{7}$ km/hr.

72. Given, $\quad a + b = p,\ ab = q$

$a^4 + b^4 = (a^2 + b^2)^2 - 2a^2b^2$

$= [(a + b)^2 - 2ab]^2 - 2a^2b^2$

$= (p^2 - 2q)^2 - 2q^2$

$= p^4 + 4q^2 - 4p^2q - 2q^2$

$= p^4 - 4p^2q + 2q^2.$

73. Here, the greatest 5-digit number

= 99999

LCM of 8, 15, 16, 21 and 5 = 1680

$\because \quad 99999 = 1680 \times 59 + 879$

$= 99120 + 879$

Hence, 999120 is the greatest five digit number which is completely divisible by 8, 15, 16, 21 and 5.

75. Given, A : B = 11 : 7 = 55 : 35

and B : C = 5 : 19 = 35 : 133

$\therefore$ A : B : C = 55 : 35 : 133.

Previous Paper (Solved)

SSC-Combined Higher Secondary Level–CHSL (10+2) Tier–1, Online Recruitment Exam–2019*

1. Select the most appropriate word to fill in the blank.

The police used tear gas to _____ the crowd.

A. disburse B. collect
C. attack D. disperse

2. Select the most appropriate meaning of the given idiom.

Take something with a pinch of salt

A. To take long to understand what is being said
B. To think of oneself as always right
C. To consider everyone a liar
D. To believe only part of something

3. Select the word that means the same as the given group of words.

A person weak and disabled by illness

A. Activist B. Invalid
C. Athlete D. Petitioner

4. Select the INCORRECTLY spelt word.

A. Preamble
B. Pnemonia
C. Miscellaneous
D. Deviation

Directions (Qs. No. 5-9): *In the following passage some words have been deleted. Fill in the blanks with the help of the alternatives given. Select the most appropriate option for each blank.*

All her life Ms. Foster had a great fear of missing a train, a plane, a boat or __(1)__ a theatre curtain. In other respects, she was not a __(2)__ nervous woman. But the mere thought of __(3)__ on occasions like these would throw her __(4)__ such a nervous state that a tiny muscle in the corner of her left eye would __(5)__ twitch. This would disappear once she had boarded the plane etc.

5. Select the most appropriate option for blank No. 1.

A. quite B. extremely
C. even D. hardly

6. Select the most appropriate option for blank No. 2.

A. usual B. general
C. particular D. particularly

7. Select the most appropriate option for blank No. 3.

A. be later B. being late
C. be late D. being later

8. Select the most appropriate option for blank No. 4.

A. into B. up
C. away D. in

* *Online exam held on 21/10/2020.*

9. Select the most appropriate option for blank No. 5.

A. begun over B. begun to

C. begin to D. begin over

10. Select the INCORRECTLY spelt word.

A. Conscentious B. Constraint

C. Resultant D. Expanse

11. In the sentence identify the segment which contains the grammatical error.

Subhash Gidwani is selling dolls, which are type of Madhya Pradesh's village culture, at the Annual Dastakar Bazaar, held in January every year in Delhi.

A. Subhash Gidwani is selling dolls

B. in the annual Dastakar Bazaar

C. held in January every year in Delhi

D. which are type of Madhya Pradesh's village culture

12. Given below are four jumbled sentences. Pick the option that gives their correct order.

(*a*) Finally, she takes the decision to go searching for livelihood in the nearby town.

(*b*) They are: Lakua and his wife, Nathuni.

(*c*) The latter, burdened with a paralytic husband and two children, battles to survive.

(*d*) The film 'Wayfarers' narrates the journey of a poor couple in Jharkhand.

A. *cdab* B. *dbac*

C. *dbca* D. *bacd*

13. Given below are four jumbled sentences. Pick the option that gives their correct order.

(*a*) The Emperor would view the comic acts from the jharokha, a special window of his palace.

(*b*) On the festival of Holi, the Emperor was entertained with mimicry, impersonation and play-acting.

(*c*) Bahadur Shah Jafar's life and times are described in a book called 'City of my heart.'

(*d*) Finally, the most talented of the performers would be generously awarded by the king.

A. *cbad* B. *cdba*

C. *adbc* D. *dacb*

14. Select the most appropriate option to substitute the underlined segment in the given sentence. If there is no need to substitute it, select 'No improvement'.

The Delhi Birla International School <u>alumnus occupy</u> leading positions in different areas of profession and service.

A. alumnus occupies

B. alumnus occupying

C. No improvement

D. alumni occupy

15. Select the correct indirect form of given sentence.

The foreigner said to the farmer, "Can you tell me the way to the nearest hotel?"

A. The foreigner told the farmer if he could tell him the way to the nearest hotel.
B. The foreigner suggested the farmer if he could tell him the way to the nearest hotel.
C. The foreigner exclaimed with the farmer if he could tell him the way to the nearest hotel.
D. The foreigner enquired of the farmer if he could tell him the way to the nearest hotel.

16. Select the most appropriate synonym of the given word.

CONGENIAL

A. Compatible B. Servile
C. Aloof D. Bombastic

17. Select the most appropriate ANTONYM of the given word.

PACIFIST

A. Orator B. Warmonger
C. Nihilist D. Peace-maker

18. Select the most appropriate meaning of the given idiom.

Full of sound and fury

A. A fiery and effective speaker
B. Someone who gets angry very quickly
C. Merely loud and angry words but ineffective
D. An angry and unruly mob

19. In the sentence identify the segment which contains the grammatical error.

You must make a choice immediately because there is few time left.

A. because there is
B. You must make
C. few time left
D. a choice immediately

20. Select the most appropriate word to fill in the blank.

Ritu is an ______ reader. I always find her with a book.

A. irritated B. erratic
C. avid D. inattentive

21. Select the most appropriate synonym of the given word.

PEDIGREE

A. Forbidden B. Illegitimate
C. Mongrel D. Lineage

22. Select the most appropriate option to substitute the underlined segment in the given sentence. If there is no need to substitute it, select 'No improvement'.

For the last two years Shweta has being diligently working with Rohingya refugees to create colourful table mats using their local weaving techniques.

A. have been
B. has been
C. No improvement
D. have being

23. Select the most appropriate ANTONYM of the given word.

PROLIFIC

A. Unproductive B. Rich
C. Abundant D. Several

24. Select the correct passive form of the given sentence.

Chhattisgarh organised the first ever 'All India Folk Dance Festival' in January 2020.

A. The first ever 'All India Folk Dance Festival' was organised by the Chhattisgarh State in January 2020.
B. The first ever 'All India Folk Dance Festival' was being organised by the Chhattisgarh State in January 2020.
C. The first ever 'All India Folk Dance Festival' will be organised by the Chhattisgarh State in January 2020.
D. The first ever 'All India Folk Dance Festival' had been organised by the Chhattisgarh State in January 2020.

25. Select the word that means the same as the given group of words.

Happening every two years
A. Centennial
B. Biennial
C. Biannual
D. Triennial

26. Four letter-cluster have been given, out of which three are alike in some manner and one is different. Select the odd letter-cluster.

A. BEYV B. MONL
C. NOPE D. HJSQ

27. The sequence of folding a paper and the manner in which the folded paper has been cut is shown in the following figures. How would this paper look when unfolded?

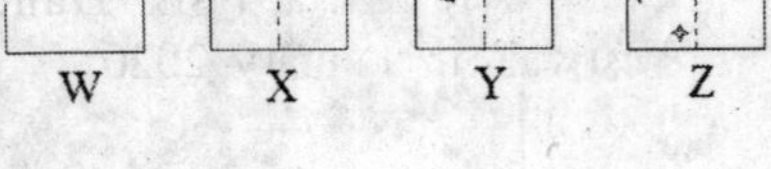

W X Y Z

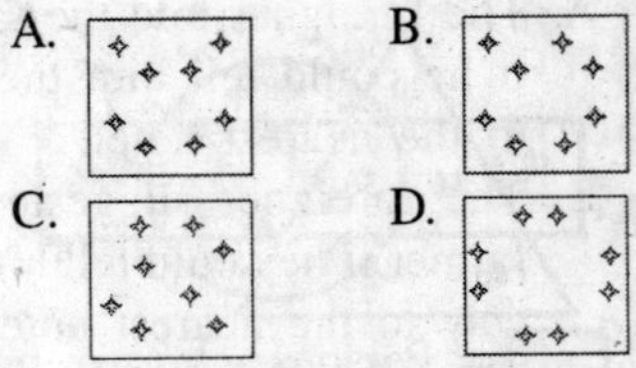

28. Select the number that can replace the question mark (?) in the following figure series.

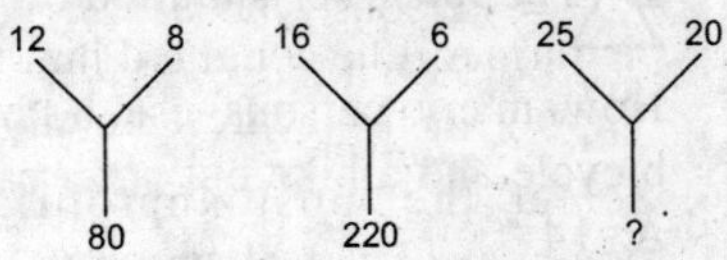

A. 241 B. 225
C. 210 D. 425

29. The rate of onion increased from ₹ 70 per kilogram to ₹ 120 per kilogram within a month. By what percentage (approximate) did the rate of onion increase?

A. 71.5% B. 80%
C. 65% D. 75.2%

30. Introducing a boy, I said, "His mother is the only daughter of my mother in law." How am I related to the boy?

A. Brother
B. Father
C. Brother-in-law
D. Nephew

31. How many triangles are there in the following figure?

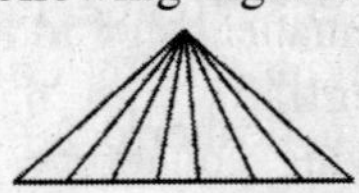

A. 28 B. 24
C. 14 D. 20

32. Study the given Venn diagram carefully and answer the following question.

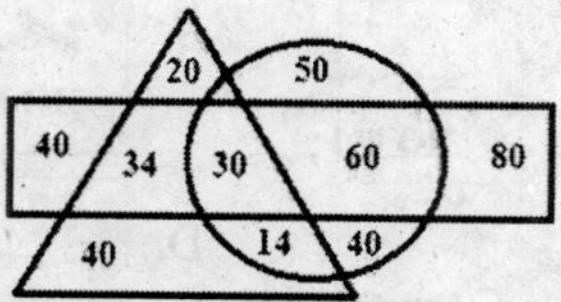

 = Persons who use bike

 = Persons who use car

 = Persons who use bicycle

How many persons use both a bicycle and a bike but not a car?

A. 14 B. 30
C. 34 D. 40

33. Two different positions of the same dice shown here. Select the letter that will be on the face opposite to the one showing the letter 'C'.

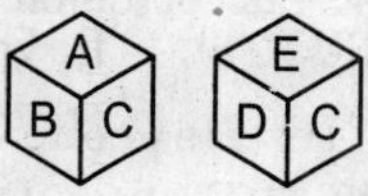

A. F B. A
C. E D. B

34. Four words have been given, out of which three are alike in some manner and one is different. Select the odd one.

A. Paris B. Istanbul
C. Maputo D. London

35. Select the correct combination of mathematical sign to replace 'A' sequentially and balance the following equation.

40 A 2 A 3 A 4 A 15

A. ÷, ×, =, × B. ×, ÷, +, =
C. ×, =, –, ÷ D. ÷, ×, = , –

36. Select the option that is related to the third letter-cluster in the same way as the second letter-cluster is related to the first letter-cluster.

COAT : APZV :: ROAD : ?

A. TNCC B. PQZF
C. SPBE D. PPZF

37. Four numbers have been given, out of which three are alike in some manner and one is different. Select the one that is different.

A. 729 B. 125
C. 216 D. 676

38. Select the Venn diagram best represents the relationship between the following classes.

Dirham, USD, Currency

A.  B. 

C.  D. 

39. Read the given statements and conclusions carefully. Assuming that the information given in the statements is true, even if it appears to be at variance with commonly known facts, decide which of the given conclusions logically follows from the statements.

Statements:

1. All malls are kings.
2. No king is a heater.

Conclusions:

I. No mall is a heater.
II. All kings are malls.

A. Neither conclusion I nor II follows.

B. Only conclusion II follows.
C. Either conclusion I or II follows.
D. Only conclusion I follows.

40. In a certain code language, 'TELEVISION' is written as 'OPJTJWFMFU'. How will 'REMOTE' be written as in that language?
A. FUPNFS B. ETOMER
C. PUPFNS D. SFNPUF

41. Select the option in which the given figure is embedded. (Rotation is not allowed)

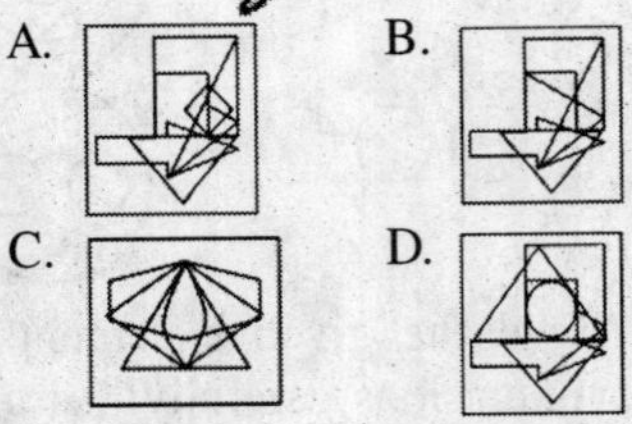

42. Select the option in which the numbers share the same relationship as that shared by the given number-pair.

4 : 25
A. 11 : 170 B. 6 : 49
C. 12 : 120 D. 6 : 36

43. Select the correct mirror image of the given figure.

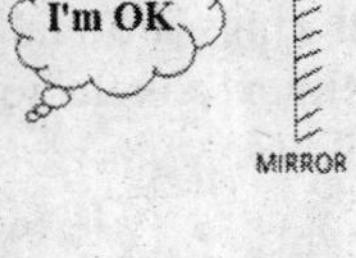

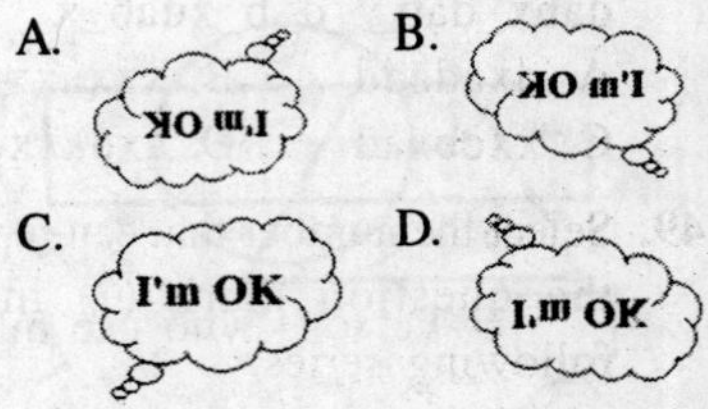

44. Select the option that is related to the third word in the same way as the second word is related to the first word.

Time : Second :: Length : ?
A. Meter B. Distance
C. Long Rule D. Measuring

45. 'TQUS' is related to 'UPVR' in the same way as 'FIRE' is related to ______.
A. GIRG B. GHSD
C. GIRF D. GHRD

46. In a certain code language 'TRAFFIC' is written as 'VTCHHKE'. How will 'POLICE' be written as in that language?
A. RMNGEC B. ONKHBD
C. RQNKEG D. RMJGEC

47. Select the number that can replace the question mark (?) in the following figure series.

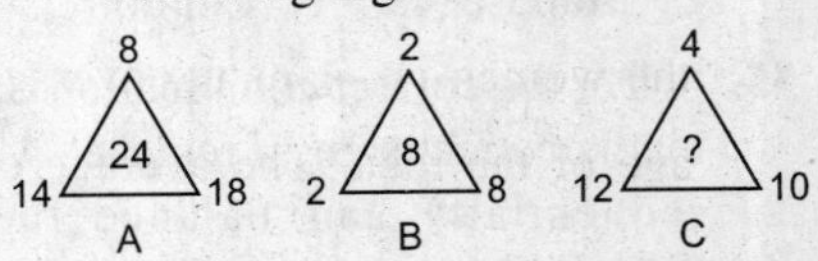

A. 2 B. 18
C. 22 D. 6

48. Select the combination of letters that when sequentially placed in the blanks of the given letter series will complete the series.

dabx_dab_ _d_b_xdab_x_

A. dxadadd B. xxxaxxd

C. xxcbxad D. axdaxxd

49. Select the number that can replace the question mark (?) in the following series.

6, 7, 16, 51, 208, ?

A. 2000 B. 2570

C. 1045 D. 1250

50. Arrange the given words in a logical and meaningful sequence.

1. Earth 2. Saturn
3. Jupiter 4. Mercury
5. Venus 6. Mars

A. 5, 4, 3, 2, 1, 6

B. 4, 5, 1, 6, 3, 2

C. 6, 3, 4, 1, 2, 5

D. 3, 1, 4, 2, 5, 6

51. If $\sqrt{x} = \sqrt{3} - \sqrt{5}$, then the value of $x^2 - 16x + 6$ is :

A. 0 B. 4

C. 2 D. −2

52. In a group of 150 people, $\frac{2}{5}$ are men, $\frac{1}{3}$ are women and the rest are children. The average age of the women is $\frac{4}{5}$ of the average age of the men. The average of the children is $\frac{1}{5}$ of the average age of the men. If the average age of the men is 50 years, then the average age of all the people in the group is :

A. 32 years B. 36 years

C. 35 years D. 28 years

53. The areas of three adjacent faces of a cuboid are 30 cm², 20 cm² and 24 cm². The volume of the cuboid is :

A. 120 cm³ B. 150 cm³

C. 200 cm³ D. 180 cm³

54. The speed of a train is 220% of the speed of a car. The car covers a distance of 950 km in 19 hours. How much distance will the train cover in $3\frac{1}{2}$ hours?

A. 385 km B. 380 km

C. 285 km D. 375 km

55. The side BC of a triangle ABC is extended to the point D. If $\angle ACD = 132°$ and $\angle B = \frac{4}{7}\angle A$, then the measure of $\angle A$ is equal to :

A. 60° B. 80°

C. 50° D. 84°

56. The pie-chart shows the percentage-wise distribution of the number of students in five different schools P, Q, R, S and T. The total number of students in all five schools together is 10,500.

Study the pie-chart and answer the question.

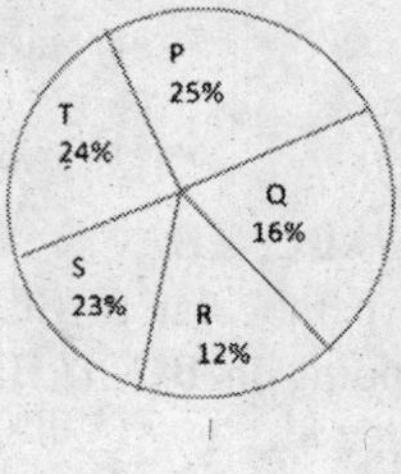

The number of students in school R is what per cent of the total number of students in schools Q and T together?

A. 30% B. 35%

C. 25% D. 40%

57. Study the following graph and answer the given question.

The graph shows the time (in minutes) taken by the pipes (A, B), (C, D), (E, F), (G, H) and (P, Q) to fill a tank.

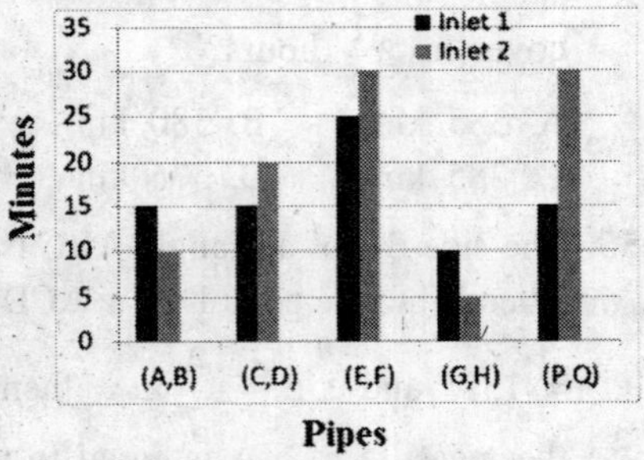

In how many minutes is an empty tank filled completely if pipe D fills it for half the time and then for the other half time, pipes C and D fill it together?

A. 15 minutes B. 18 minutes

C. 12 minutes D. 10 minutes

58. If $x = \frac{\sqrt{3}}{2}$, then the value of $\frac{\sqrt{1+x}+\sqrt{1-x}}{\sqrt{1+x}-\sqrt{1-x}}$ is equal to :

A. 3 B. $\sqrt{3}$

C. 2 D. $\sqrt{2}$

59. In a ΔABC, $\angle BAC = 90°$ and AD is perpendicular to BC where D is a point on BC. If BD = 4 cm and CD = 5 cm, then the length of AD is equal to :

A. 6 cm B. 4.5 cm

C. $2\sqrt{5}$ cm D. $5\sqrt{2}$ cm

60. Study the following graph and answer the given question.

The graph shows the time (in minutes) taken by the pipes (A, B), (C, D), (E, F), (G, H) and (P, Q) to fill a tank.

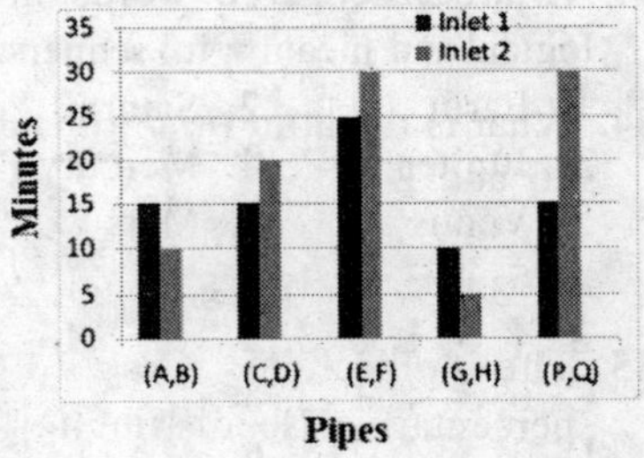

Two pipes P and Q are inlet pipes. If they are opened at alternate minutes and if pipe P is opened first, then in how many minutes will the tank be full?

A. 18 minutes B. 20 minutes

C. 16 minutes D. 30 minutes

61. The circles of same radius 13 cm intersect each other at A and B. If AB = 10 cm, then the distance between their centres is :

A. 18 cm B. 12 cm

C. 24 cm D. 26 cm

62. On selling 26 balls ₹ 1,350, there is a loss equal to the cost price of eight balls. The cost price of a ball is :

A. ₹ 70 B. ₹ 65

C. ₹ 60 D. ₹ 75

63. in the figure, a circle touches all the four sides of a quadrilateral

ABCD whose sides AB = 6.5 cm, BC = 5.4 cm and CD = 5.3 cm. The length of AD is :

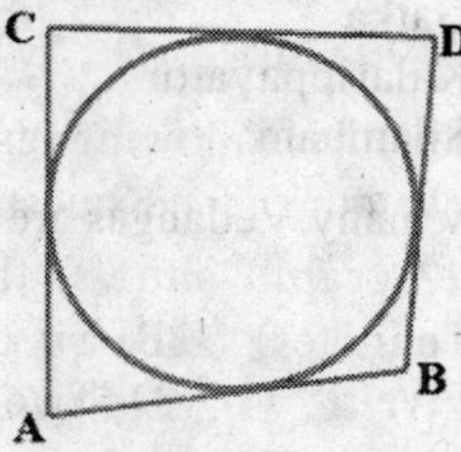

A. 4.6 cm B. 6.4 cm
C. 5.8 cm D. 6.2 cm

64. What is the third proportional to 16 and 24?
A. 36 B. 28
C. 34 D. 32

65. The pie-chart shows the percentage-wise distribution of the number of students in five different schools P, Q, R, S and T. The total number of students in all five schools together is 10,500.
Study the pie-chart and answer the question.

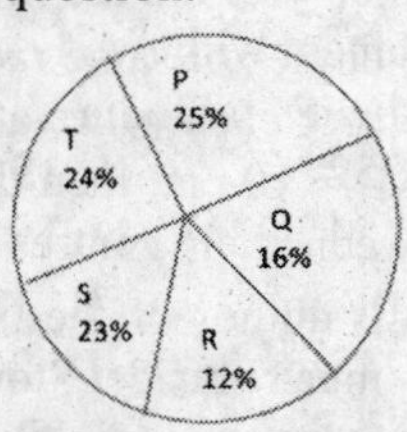

The difference between the central angles corresponding to schools T and R is :
A. 34.5° B. 44°
C. 43.2° D. 42.8°

66. If $a^3 + b^3 = 62$ and $a + b = 2$, then the value of ab is :
A. –9 B. 9
C. –6 D. 6

67. When a number is divided by 14, the remainder is 9. If the square of the same number is divided by 14, then the remainder will be :
A. 11 B. 9
C. 10 D. 8

68. If $\dfrac{\sec\theta+\tan\theta}{\sec\theta-\tan\theta} = 5$ and θ is an acute angle, then the value of $\dfrac{3\cos^2\theta+1}{3\cos^2\theta-1}$ is :
A. 3 B. 2
C. 1 D. 4

69. A sum at simple interest becomes two times is 8 years at a certain rate of interest p.a. The time in which the same sum will be 4 times at the same rate of interest at simple interest is :
A. 30 years B. 25 years
C. 24 years D. 20 years

70. If the price an eraser is reduced by 25%, a person can buy three more erasers for ₹ 2. How many erasers can be bought for ₹ 2 as the original price?
A. 8 B. 10
C. 12 D. 9

71. If $\sin(\theta + 30°) = \dfrac{3}{\sqrt{12}}$, then the value of θ is equal to :
A. 60° B. 15°
C. 45° D. 30°

72. The value of

$$\frac{33}{40}+\frac{1}{5}\left[\frac{4}{5}-\frac{1}{5}\times\left(\frac{7}{8}-\frac{5}{4}\right)\right] \text{ is :}$$

A. 5 B. 0
C. 10 D. 1

73. The marked price of an article is 25° more than its cost price. If 10% discount is given on the marked price, then what is the profit percentage?

A. 12% B. 11.5%
C. 10% D. 12.5%

74. If $\sin(A - B) = \frac{1}{2}$ and $\cos(A + B) = \frac{1}{2}$, where $A > B > 0°$ and $A + B$ is an acute angle, then the value of A is :

A. 45° B. 30°
C. 15° D. 60°

75. A is twice as good a workman as B and together they finish a piece of work in 22 days. In how many days will A alone finish the same work?

A. 11 days B. 44 days
C. 30 days D. 33 days

76. Which instrument is used to measure the level of humidity?

A. Fathometer
B. Galvanometer
C. Hygrometer
D. Hydrometer

77. The first barcode system was developed by:

A. Norman Joseph Woodland
B. John Mc Carthy
C. John Barger
D. David Bradley

78. Which of the following forms of martial arts is from Kerala?

A. Paika Akhada
B. Gatka
C. Kalarippayattu
D. Silambam

79. How many Vedangas are there in total?

A. Ten B. Six
C. Five D. Two

80. Which of the following characteristics of sound is measured in hertz (Hz)?

A. Frequency of the sound
B. Intensity of the sound
C. Wavelength of the sound
D. Loudness of the sound

81. In which year did NITI Aayog come into existence?

A. 2014 B. 2013
C. 2015 D. 2016

82. The term 'monsoon' is derived from a/an:

A. Italian word B. Latin word
C. Arabic word D. Greek word

83. In which year did the first Elected Parliament with two houses come into being in India?

A. 1952 B. 1953
C. 1954 D. 1955

84. Who is author of the book 'The Judgement: Inside Story of the Emergency in India'?

A. KM Munshi
B. Indira Gandhi
C. Kuldip Nayar
D. Jawaharlal Nehru

85. Who among the following is nicknamed the 'Baltimore Bullet'?

A. Tom Jager
B. Ian Thorpe
C. Matt Biondi
D. Michael Phelps

86. In January 2020, who among the following launched the first girder of the Mumbai Trans-Harbour Link (MTHL)?
A. Raj Thackeray
B. Uddhav Thackeray
C. Aaditya Thackeray
D. Bal Thackeray

87. Who Inaugurated the National Tribal Festival "Aadi Mahotsav" in New Delhi in November 2019?
A. Smriti Irani
B. Amit Shah
C. N. Sitharaman
D. Narendra Modi

88. Which country ranked first in the 2019 Human Development India Index?
A. Ireland B. Germany
C. Norway D. Switzerland

89. Who won the International Hockey Federation's (FIH) Player of the Year award in 2019?
A. Dhyan Chand
B. Pargat Singh
C. Dilip Tirkey
D. Manpreet Singh

90. The Hornbill Festival is celebrated in which state?
A. Assam
B. Meghalaya
C. Nagaland
D. Arunachal Pradesh

91. Telangana became the 29th state of India in which year?
A. 2015 B. 2014
C. 2016 D. 2017

92. Which of the following was invented by Walter Hunt?
A. Ship B. Safety pin
C. Scooter D. Safety lamp

93. Who among the following was a leader from Allahabad (now Prayagraj) in the revolt against the British in 1857?
A. Tatya Tope
B. Maulvi Liaquat Ali
C. Khan Bahadur Khan
D. Rani Laxmi Bai

94. The Bomdila Pass is located in which state?
A. Nagaland
B. Arunachal Pradesh
C. Sikkim
D. Himachal Pradesh

95. Trackball is which of the following devices?
A. Input device
B. Touchpad
C. Output device
D. Barcode reader

96. Which country is the 2019 ICC Cricket World Cup champion?
A. England B. Pakistan
C. India D. Australia

97. The Tropic of Cancer does NOT pass through which of the following Indian states?
A. Madhya Pradesh
B. West Bengal
C. Andhra Pradesh
D. Gujarat

98. Who among the following is one of the Deputy Operations Director of the Mars Orbiter Mission (MOM)?

A. Moumita Dutta
B. Nandini Harinath
C. Seetha Somasundaram
D. Minal Rohit

99. Which of the following is the second largest artificial lake in Asia?

A. Chilika Lake in Odisha
B. Chandubi Lake in Assam
C. Kolleru Lake in Andhra Pradesh
D. Dhebar Lake in Rajasthan

100. In October 2019, which of the following pairs of Indian cities was included by UNESCO in its network of 'Creative Cities' on the occasion of World Cities Day 2019?

A. Pune & Hyderabad
B. Jodhpur & Kolkata
C. Hyderabad & Mumbai
D. Delhi & Mumbai

ANSWERS

1	2	3	4	5	6	7	8	9	10
D	D	B	B	C	D	B	A	C	A
11	**12**	**13**	**14**	**15**	**16**	**17**	**18**	**19**	**20**
D	C	A	D	D	A	B	C	C	C
21	**22**	**23**	**24**	**25**	**26**	**27**	**28**	**29**	**30**
D	B	A	A	B	C	D	B	A	B
31	**32**	**33**	**34**	**35**	**36**	**37**	**38**	**39**	**40**
A	C	A	B	A	D	D	D	D	A
41	**42**	**43**	**44**	**45**	**46**	**47**	**48**	**49**	**50**
B	B	B	A	B	C	B	B	C	B
51	**52**	**53**	**54**	**55**	**56**	**57**	**58**	**59**	**60**
C	B	A	A	D	A	C	B	C	B
61	**62**	**63**	**64**	**65**	**66**	**67**	**68**	**69**	**70**
C	D	B	A	C	A	A	D	C	D
71	**72**	**73**	**74**	**75**	**76**	**77**	**78**	**79**	**80**
D	D	D	A	D	C	A	C	B	A
81	**82**	**83**	**84**	**85**	**86**	**87**	**88**	**89**	**90**
C	C	A	C	D	B	B	C	D	C
91	**92**	**93**	**94**	**95**	**96**	**97**	**98**	**99**	**100**
B	B	B	B	A	A	C	B	D	C

EXPLANATORY ANSWERS

26. (A) B E Y V
+3 –3

(B) M O N L
+2 –2

(C) N O P E
+1 –11

(D) H J S Q
+2 –2

Hence Option (A), (B) and (D) are alike in some Manner and (C) is different.

28.

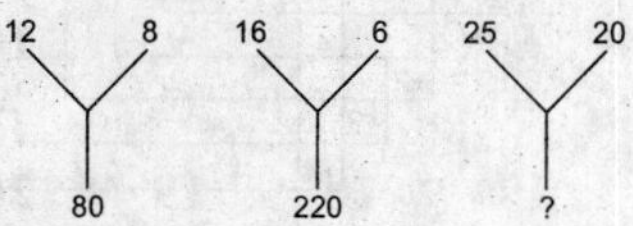

Here,

$(12 + 8) \times 4 = 20 \times 4 = 80$

$(16 + 6) \times 10 = 22 \times 10 = 220$

$(25 + 20) \times 5 = 45 \times 5 = 225$

29. Required rate of onion increasing %

$$= \frac{120-70}{70} \times 100\%$$

$$= \frac{50}{70} \times 100\% = \frac{500}{7}\%$$

$$= 71.4285\% = 71.5\%$$

30.

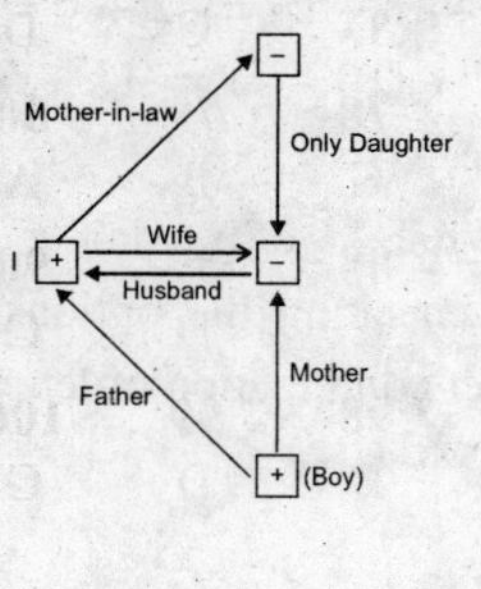

Here, I related to the boy as a father.

31. Here,

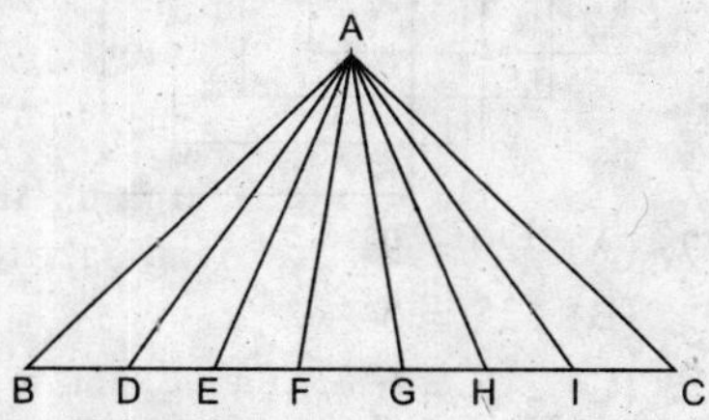

Triangles are

ΔABC, ΔABD, ΔADE, ΔAEF, ΔAFG, ΔAGH, ΔAHI, ΔAIC, ΔABE, ΔABF, ΔABG, ΔABH, ΔABI, ΔADF, ΔADG, ΔADH, ΔADI, ΔADC, ΔAEG, ΔAEH, ΔAEI, ΔAEC, ΔAFH, ΔAFI, ΔAFG, ΔAGI, ΔAGC, ΔAHC

Hence, The number of triangles = 28

33. Taking clockwise from letter C.

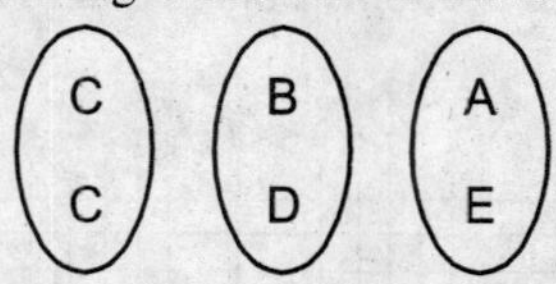

Here, opposite to the letter C = F, Opposite to the letter B = D and Opposite to the letter A = E

35. 40 A 2 A 3 A 4 A 15

After checking the options correct combination (A) ÷, ×, =, ×

∴ 40A2A3A4A15

$\Rightarrow\ 40 \div 2 \times 3 = 4 \times 15$

$\Rightarrow\ 20 \times 3 = 60$

$\Rightarrow\ 60 = 60$

36. 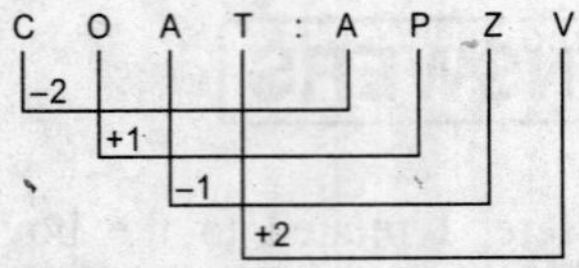

Similarly,

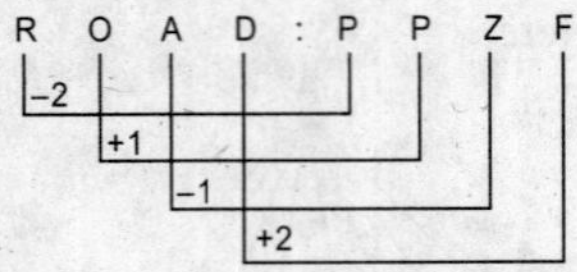

37. (A) $729 = 9^3$

(B) $125 = 5^3$

(C) $216 = 6^3$

(D) $676 = (26)^2$

39. Statements:

1. All malls are kings.
2. No king is a heater.

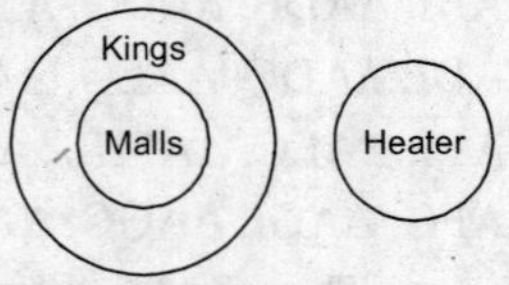

Conclusion:

I. No mall is a heater

Hence, only conclusion I follows.

40.

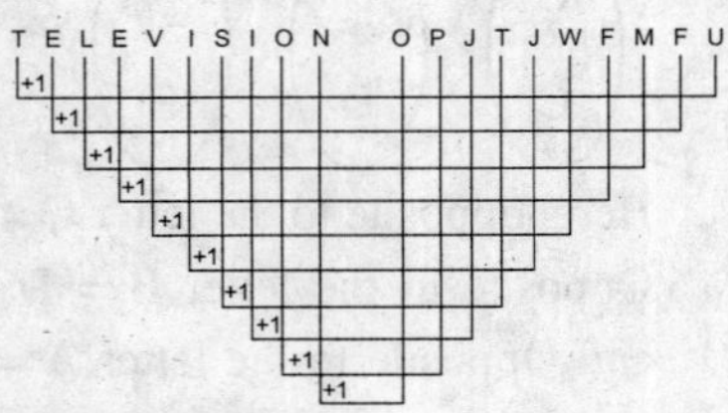

Similarly,

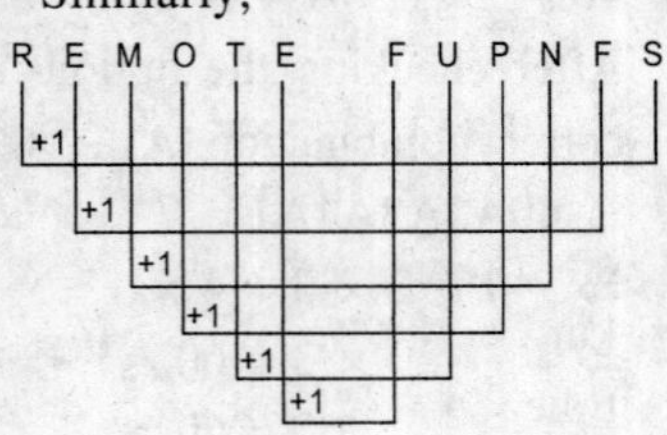

42. $4 : 25 \Rightarrow 4 : (4 + 1)^2$

$\because (4 + 1)^2 = 5^2 = 25$

$6 : 49 \Rightarrow 6 : (6 + 1)^2$

$\Rightarrow 6 : 7^2 = 6 : 49$

45. 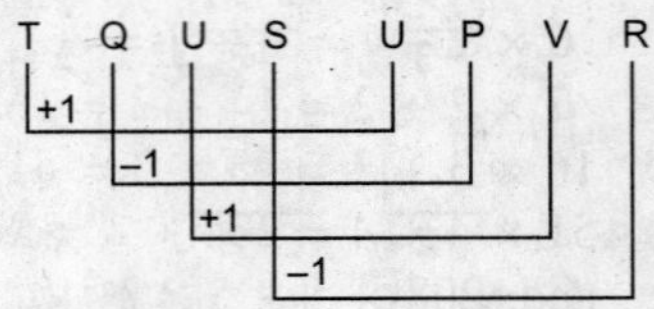

Similarly,

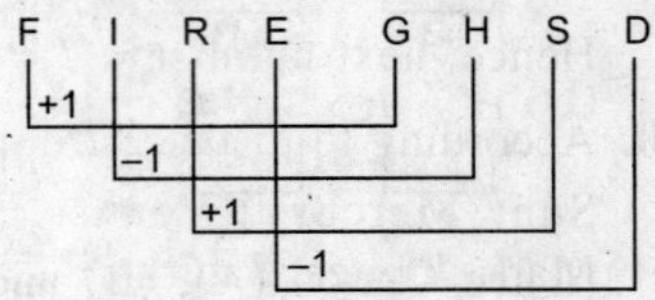

46. 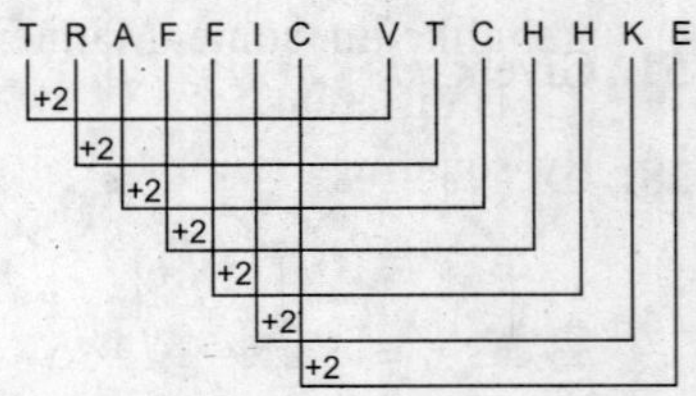

Similarly,

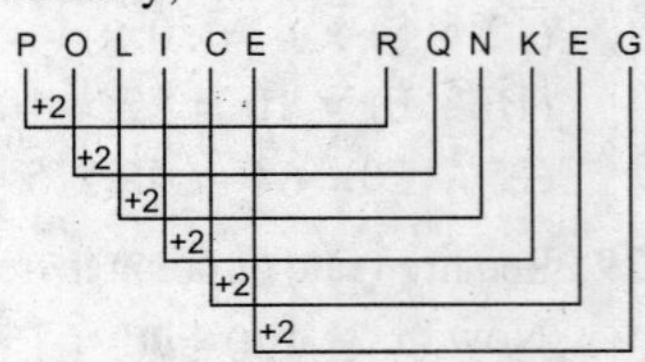

47. 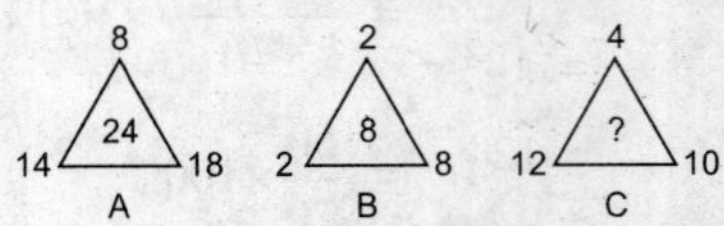

$\Rightarrow 14 + (18 - 8) \Rightarrow 14 + 10 = 24$

$\Rightarrow 2 + (8 - 2) \Rightarrow 2 + 6 = 8$

$\Rightarrow 12 + (10 - 4) \Rightarrow 12 + 6 = 18$

Hence, ? = 18

48. dabx_dab_ _d_b_xdab_x_

after checking the options, correct combination of letters (B) xxxaxxd d a b x x d a b x x d a b x x d a b x x d

49. 6, 7, 16, 51, 208, ?

Here,

$6 \times 1 + 1 = 6 + 1 = 7,$

$7 \times 2 + 2 = 14 + 2 = 16,$

$16 \times 3 + 3 = 48 + 3 = 51,$

$51 \times 4 + 4 = 204 + 4 = 208$

and, $208 \times 5 + 5 = 1040 + 5 = 1045$

Hence, next number = ? = 1045

50. According to distance from Sun.

Sun: Mercury, Venus, Earth, Mars, Jupiter, Saturn

51. Given, $\sqrt{x} = \sqrt{3} - \sqrt{5}$

By squaring, $(\sqrt{x})^2 = (\sqrt{3} - \sqrt{5})^2$

$\Rightarrow \quad x = 3 + 5 - 2\sqrt{3}\sqrt{5}$

$\Rightarrow \quad x = 8 - 2\sqrt{15}$

$\Rightarrow \quad x^2 = (8 - 2\sqrt{15})^2$

$\Rightarrow \quad x^2 = 64 + 60 - 2 \times 8 \times 2\sqrt{15}$

$\Rightarrow \quad x^2 = 124 - 32\sqrt{15}$

Now, $x^2 - 16x + 6$

$= 124 - 32\sqrt{15} - 16(8 - 2\sqrt{15}) + 6$

$= 124 - 32\sqrt{15} - 128 + 32\sqrt{15} + 6$

$= -4 + 6 = 2$

52. Given, The number of people in group = 150

$\therefore$ The number of men

$= 150 \times \frac{2}{5} = 60$

The number of women

$= 150 \times \frac{1}{3} = 50$

and the number of children

$= 150 - (60 + 50)$

$= 150 - 110 = 40$

Given, the average age of the men = 50 years

$\therefore$ The average age of the women

$= \frac{4}{5} \times 50 = 40$ years

and the average age of the children

$= \frac{1}{5} \times 50 = 10$ years

Hence, the average age of all the people in the group

$= \frac{60 \times 50 + 50 \times 40 + 40 \times 10}{150}$ years

$= \frac{3000 + 2000 + 400}{150}$ years

$= \frac{5400}{150}$ years

= 36 years

53. Given, The area of three adjacent faces of a cuboid

$l \times b = 30 \text{ cm}^2 = 6 \times 5 \text{ cm}^2$

$b \times h = 20 \text{ cm}^2 = 5 \times 4 \text{ cm}^2$

and $l \times h = 24 \text{ cm}^2 = 6 \times 4 \text{ cm}^2$

$\therefore$ Here, $l = 6$ cm, $b = 5$ cm and $h = 4$ cm

$\therefore$ The volume of the cuboid

$= l \times b \times h$

$= 6 \times 5 \times 4 \text{ cm}^3$

$= 120 \text{ cm}^3$

54. Here, distance cover by car = 950 km

time = 19 hours

$\therefore$ Speed of a car $= \dfrac{\text{distance}}{\text{time}}$

$= \dfrac{950}{19}$ km/hr = 50 km/hr

$\therefore$ The speed of a train

$= 50 \times \dfrac{220}{100}$ km/hr = 110 km/hr

Hence, the distance will the train cover in $3\frac{1}{2}$ hours

= Speed × time

$= 110$ km/hr $\times 3\frac{1}{2}$ hr.

$= 110 \times \frac{7}{2}$ km

= 55 × 7 km = 385 km

55. Given, $\angle ACD = 132°$

and $\angle B = \frac{4}{7}\angle A$

By exterior angle theorem,

The exterior angle = the sum of the two interior opposite angles.

$\angle ACD = \angle B + \angle A$

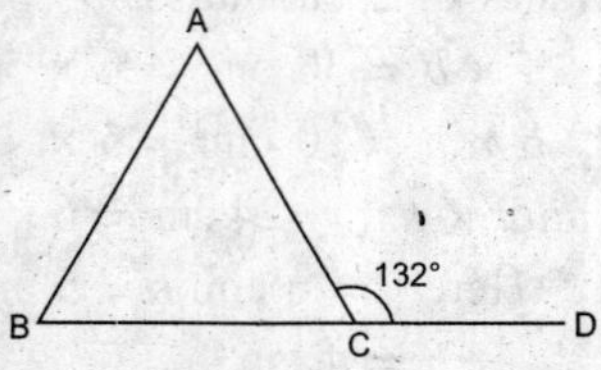

$\Rightarrow 132° = \frac{4}{7}\angle A + \angle A$

$\Rightarrow 132° = \frac{11}{7}\angle A$

$\Rightarrow \angle A = 132° \times \frac{7}{11} = 12° \times 7$

$= 84°$

Hence, $\angle A = 84°$

56. By given the pie-chart

The number of students in school R

$= 10,500 \times \frac{12}{100}$

= 105 × 12 = 1260

and, the total number of students in school Q and T

$= 10,500 \times \frac{16+24}{100}$

$= 10,500 \times \frac{40}{100}$

= 105 × 40 = 4200

Hence, the required per cent

$= \frac{1260 \times 100}{4200}\%$

$= \frac{1260}{42}\% = 30\%$

75. Ratio of work efficiency of A and B

$\therefore A : B = 2x : x$

Ratio of day(time) of A and B

$\therefore A : B = x : 2x$

$\because$ (A + B)'s 1 day's work $= \frac{1}{22}$

$\therefore \frac{1}{x} + \frac{1}{2x} = \frac{1}{22}$

$\Rightarrow \frac{2+1}{2x} = \frac{1}{22}$

$\Rightarrow \frac{3}{2x} = \frac{1}{22} \Rightarrow 2x = 3 \times 22$

$\Rightarrow x = \frac{3 \times 22}{2} \Rightarrow x = 33$

Hence, A alone will finish the same work in x days = 33 days

Previous Paper (Solved)

SSC-Combined Higher Secondary Level–CHSL (10+2) Tier–1, Online Recruitment Exam–2018*

1. In a code language, GOURD is written as IQSTF. How will APHID be written as in that language?

A. CRJKF B. CRFLF
C. CRFKF D. CREKF

2. 'ENGINEER' is related to 'BUILDING' in the same way as 'WRITER' is related to '________'.

A. BOOK B. PAPER
C. PEN D. INK

3. Three of the following four letter-clusters are alike in a certain way and one is different. Pick the odd one out.

A. QSUV B. DFHJ
C. JLNP D. CEGI

4. Three of the following four words are alike in a certain way and one is different. Pick the odd word out.

A. Car B. Jeep
C. Truck D. Ship

5. Arrange the following words in the sequence as they appear in English dictionery order.

1. Mercury 2. Earth
3. Jupiter 4. Venus
5. Mars

A. 1, 4, 2, 3, 5 B. 2, 3, 1, 5, 4
C. 4, 2, 5, 3, 1 D. 2, 3, 5, 1, 4

6. Which letter-pair will replace the question mark (?) in the following series?

FJ, HL, ? , LP, NR

A. JM B. JN
C. GM D. IN

7. Select the set in which the numbers are related in the same way as are the numbers of the following set.

(16, 36, 64)

A. (6, 36, 80) B. (10, 30, 58)
C. (9, 25, 62) D. (12, 32, 50)

8. Select the correct mirror image of the given figure when the mirror is placed to the right of the figure.

A.  B. 

C.  D. 

9. Three statements are given, followed by three conclusions numbered I, II and III. Assuming the statements to be true, even if

---

**Online exam held on 11 July, 2019.*

they seem to be at variance with commonly known facts, decide which of the conclusions logically follow(s) from the statements.

Statements: All hens are eggs.
All birds are eggs.
All eggs are lions.

Conclusions:

I. All hens are lions.
II. Some lions are eggs.
III. All birds are lions.

A. Only conclusions II and III follow
B. Only conclusions I and II follow
C. Only conclusion I follows
D. All the conclusions follow

10. Anil and Abhay are brothers. Swati is the daughter of Samir and sister of Anil. How is Abhay's mother related to Samir?

A. Sister B. Wife
C. Sister-in-law D. Mother

11. Three different positions of the same dice are shown. Select the pattern that will be on the face opposite to the one having .

A. 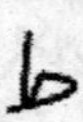 B. 
C.  D. 

12. Select the option in which the given figure (X) is embedded.

X

A.  B. 
C.  D. 

13. Select the number-pair in which the two numbers are related in the same way as are the two numbers of the following number-pair.

29, 31

A. 15, 17 B. 23, 25
C. 11, 13 D. 20, 21

14. Select the Venn diagram that best illustrates the relationship between the following classes.
Rats, Frogs, Snakes

A. 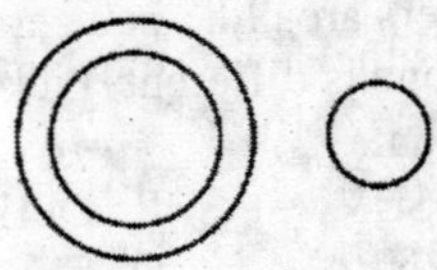

B. 

C. 

D. 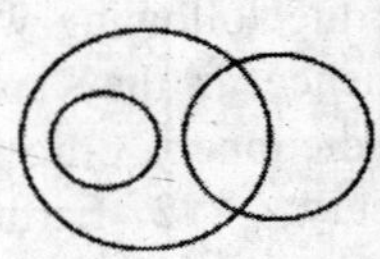

15. Select the word-pair in which the two words are related in the same way as are the two words in the following word-pair.

Cement : Building

A. Wire : Electricity
B. Wood : Furniture
C. Book : Author
D. Pen : Pencil

16. How many triangles are present in the following figure?

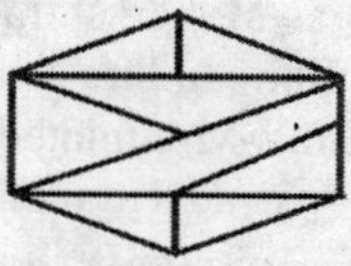

A. 11 B. 9
C. 10 D. 13

17. Which number will replace the question mark (?) in the following series?

2, 4, 7, 12, 19, 30, ?

A. 47 B. 38
C. 43 D. 36

18. What was the day of the week on 15 August 2013?

A. Thursday B. Monday
C. Wednesday D. Tuesday

19. Select the Answer Fig. that will come next in the following Problem Fig. series.

Problem Figure

A.  B. 

C.  D. 

20. Select the option that is related to the third letter-pair in the same way as the second letter-pair is related to the first letter-pair.

DJ : HT : : HM : ?

A. PY B. JK
C. LW D. LP

21. A paper is folded and cut as shown in the following figures (X, Y and Z). Select the option that depicts how this paper will appear when unfolded?

X Y Z

A.  B. 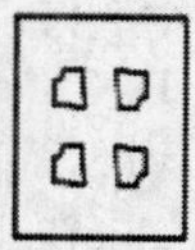

C.  D. 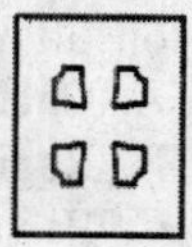

22. Select the set in which the numbers are related in the same way as are the numbers of the following set.

(49, 81, 121)

A. (9, 4, 8) B. (16, 25, 49)
C. (36, 64, 100) D. (16, 64, 100)

23. Which two signs should be interchanged in the following equation to make it correct?

5 + 8 – 30 × 10 ÷ 2 = 240

A. × and ÷ B. + and ÷
C. + and – D. × and –

24. Three of the following four numbers are alike in a certain way and one is different. Pick the number that is different from the rest.

A. 65 B. 95
C. 75 D. 85

25. If BARBER is coded as 116 and GLINT is coded as 73, then how will LIZARD be coded as?
A. 92 B. 93
C. 91 D. 90

26. Who among the following was included in Facebook 'Hall of Fame 2019' for detecting a Whatapp Bug that violated privacy of a user?
A. Sonam Wangchuk
B. Jeje Lalpekula
C. Baichung Bhutia
D. Zonel Sougaijam

27. Who was sworn in as the new chief minister of Andhra Pradesh on 30th May 2019?
A. Chandrababu Naidu
B. Raghuveera Reddy
C. Pawan Kalyan
D. YS Jagan Mohan Reddy

28. In the context of the banking system in India, what does IFSC stand for?
A. Indian Financial Structural Code
B. Indian Functional System Calculation
C. Indian Financial System Code
D. Indian Financial Social Code

29. Which country has become the second country in the world to declare a climate and biodiversity emergency?
A. Bhutan B. Ireland
C. Norway D. Canada

30. Hypokalaemia is caused by the deficiency of ....
A. Iodine B. Potassium
C. Iron D. Calcium

31. Which one of the following lakes and their locations is INCORRECTLY matched?
A. Lonar-Maharashtra
B. Chilika-Andhra Pradesh
C. Loktak-Manipur
D. Roopkund-Uttarakhand

32. In the context of the Internet, what is the full form of MAN?
A. Master Area Network
B. Makeshift Area Network
C. Massive Area Network
D. Metropolitan Area Network

33. Who among the following was re-elected as the Prime Minister of Israel in April 2019?
A. Imad Khamis
B. Benjamin Netanyahu
C. Ranil Wickremesinghe
D. Sheikh Hasina

34. In the cabinet of the 17th Lok Sabha, who has been appointed as the Finance Minister?
A. Amit Shah
B. Nirmala Sitharaman
C. Smriti Irani
D. Rajnath Singh

35. In May 2019, the kilogram was redefined for the first time in 130 years. It will now be redefined by a fundamental property of nature known as:
A. Planck's Constant
B. Electric Constant
C. Gravitational Constant
D. Magnetic Constant

36. Rovers Cup is associated with which of the following sports?
A. Swimming B. Lawn Tennis
C. Snooker D. Football

37. Justice Rajinder Sachar Committee was set up to study ________.
A. the socio-economic status of Muslim community in India
B. the impact of globalisation on India
C. the standards maintained by government hospitals in India
D. the environmental issues of the western ghats in India

38. Which one of the following is NOT a tributary of river Kaveri?
A. Vaigai B. Kabini
C. Bhavani D. Amravati

39. Which of the following classical dances and their places of origin is INCORRECTLY matched?
A. Kuchipudi-Odisha
B. Bharatanatym-Tamilnadu
C. Mohiniattam-Kerala
D. Sattriya-Assam

40. According to which Article of the Constitution of India shall the council of ministers be collectively responsible to the Lok Sabha?
A. Article 29 B. Article 75
C. Article 35 D. Article 302

41. The Salal Project is constructed on the river:
A. Chenab B. Bhima
C. Krishna D. Manjra

42. Which of the following is a western flowing river?
A. Sabarmati B. Gomti
C. Mahanadi D. Krishna

43. The head quarter of Federation Internationale de Football Association (FIFA) is located in ______.
A. Madrid B. Amsterdam
C. Zurich D. Paris

44. Which of the following dances is in UNESCO's Intangible Heritage List?
A. Fugdi B. Chhau
C. Jhoomar D. Dalkhai

45. Who was the founder of Bahujan Samaj Party?
A. Munshi Ram
B. Devi Lal
C. Kanshi Ram
D. Lakshman Singh

46. Which of the following texts gives a detailed account of the kings of Kashmir?
A. Rajatarangini
B. Dipavamsa
C. Vinaya Pitaka
D. Katha Sarit Sagar

47. The Samkhaya School of Philosophy was founded by ....
A. Patanjali
B. Kapila
C. Kumarila Bhatta
D. Gautama

48. The headquarters of computer technology giant, Intel is in ....
A. London B. Tokyo
C. California D. Frankfurt

49. Which of the following is an example of terrestrial habitat?
A. Grassland B. Lagoon
C. Pond D. Swamp

50. Pullela Gopichand is the chief national coach of the Indian

.... team as of June 2019.

A. Badminton B. Basketball
C. Archery D. Table tennis

51. The platform of a station 400 m long starts exactly where the last span of a bridge 1.2 km long ends. How long will a train 200 m long and travelling at the speed of 72 km/h take to cover the distance between the starting point of the span of the bridge and the far end of the platform?

A. 1.6 min B. 1.5 min
C. 1.8 min D. 1.2 min

52. An article having marked price, ₹ 900, was sold for ₹ 648 after two successive discounts. The first discount was 20%. What was the percentage rate of the second discount?

A. 5 B. 15
C. 10 D. 12.5

53. A purchased two articles for ₹ 200 and ₹ 300 respectively and sold at gains of 5% and 10% respectively. What was his overall gain percentage?

A. 6 B. 9
C. 5 D. 8

54. If $\frac{10}{7}(1-2.43\times10^{-3})=1.417+x$, then x is equal to:

A. 0.0417 B. 0.417
C. 0.0081 D. 0.81

55. The full marks for a paper is 300. The break-up of the marks into theory (X), practical (Y) and project (Z), which are the three components of evaluation is 6 : 5 : 4. In order to pass one has to score at least 40%, 50% and 50% respectively in X, Y, Z and 60% in aggregate. The marks scored by four students A, B, C and D are shown in the given Bar Graph.

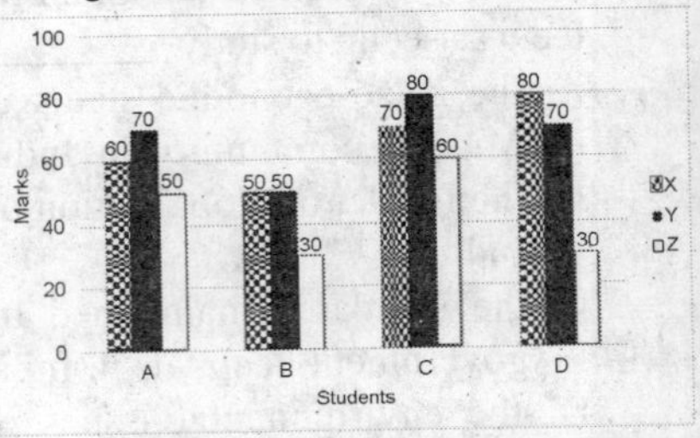

How much percentage marks more than B has C scored in practical?

A. 40 B. 30
C. 60 D. 20

56. The simplified value of

$$\left\{1\frac{1}{4}\text{ of }\left(2\frac{1}{3}\div1\frac{2}{5}\right)-1\frac{5}{12}\right\}+\frac{1}{9}\div2\frac{1}{3}+\frac{2}{7}+\frac{1}{6}$$ is

A. $\frac{7}{3}$ B. $\frac{3}{2}$
C. $\frac{7}{6}$ D. 1

57. The full marks for a paper is 300. The break-up of the marks into theory (X), practical (Y) and project (Z), which are the three components of evaluation is 6 : 5 : 4. In order to pass one has to score at least 40%, 50% and 50% respectively in X, Y, Z and 60% in aggregate. The marks scored by four students A, B, C and D are shown in the given Bar Graph.

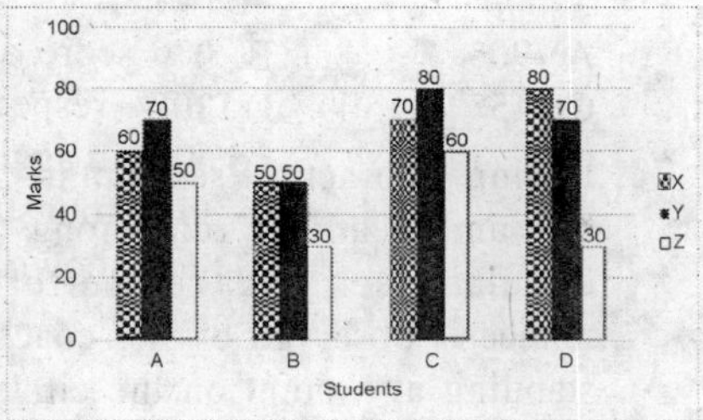

Arrange the students B, C and D according to the ascending order of the aggregate marks scored by them.

A. B, D, C B. B, C, D
C. C, D, B D. D, B, C

58. The full marks for a paper is 300. The break-up of the marks into theory (X), practical (Y) and project (Z), which are the three components of evaluation is 6 : 5 : 4. In order to pass one has to score at least 40%, 50% and 50% respectively in X, Y, Z and 60% in aggregate. The marks scored by four students A, B, C and D are shown in the given Bar Graph.

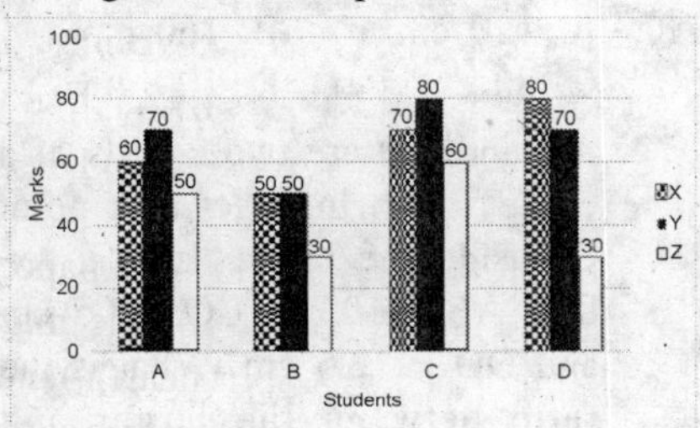

What is the average marks of the four students in theory?

A. 60 B. 65
C. 70 D. 68

59. With reference to a number greater than one, the difference between itself and its reciprocal is 25% of the sum of itself and its reciprocal. By how much percentage (correct one decimal place) is the fourth power of the number greater than its square?

A 57.8 B. 62.5
C. 64.5 D. 66.7

60. For all $\alpha_i' s, (i = 1, 2, 3, ..., 20)$ lying between 0° and 90°, it is given that, $\sin \alpha_1 + \sin \alpha_2 + \sin \alpha_3 + ... + \sin \alpha_{20} = 20$

What is the value (in degrees) of $(\alpha_1 + \alpha_2 + \alpha_3 + ... + \alpha_{20})$?

A. 1800 B. 900
C. 0 D. 20

61. The ten digit number 2x600000y8 is exactly divisible by 24. If $x \neq 0$ and $y \neq 0$, then the least value of $(x + y)$ is equal to:

A. 5 B. 8
C. 9 D. 2

62. The value of

$$\frac{18.43 \times 18.43 - 6.57 \times 6.57}{11.86} \text{ is:}$$

A. 23.62 B. 25
C. 26 D. 24.12

63. O, G, I and H are respectively the circumcentre, centroid, incentre and orthocentre of an equilateral triangle. Which of these points are identical?

A. O and I only
B. O and G only
C. O, G, I and H
D. O, G and H only

64. A certain sum was invested on simple interest. The amount to which it had grown in five years was $1\frac{1}{4}$ times the amount to which it had grown in three years. The percentage rate of interest was:

A. 10% B. 20%

C. 25% D. 15%

65. A can complete a piece of work in 20 days and B can complete 20% of the work in 6 days. If they work together in how many days can they finish 50% of the work?

A. 12 B. 6

C. 8 D. 9

66. What is the value of $\text{cosec}^2 30° + \sin^2 45° + \sec^2 60° + \tan^2 30°$?

A. $\frac{53}{6}$ B. 8

C. $\frac{25}{3}$ D. 9

67. $\Delta ABC \sim \Delta DEF$ and their perimeters are 64 cm and 48 cm respectively. What is the length of AB, if DE is equal to 9 cm?

A. 17.5 cm B. 16 cm

C. 12 cm D. 18 cm

68. If $(3x + 1)^3 + (x - 3)^3 + (4 - 2x)^3 + 6(3x + 1)(x - 3)(x - 2) = 0$, then x is equal to:

A. –1 B. $-\frac{1}{2}$

C. 1 D. $\frac{1}{2}$

69. For $0° \leq \theta \leq 90°$, what is θ, when $\sqrt{3}\cos\theta + \sin\theta = 1$?

A. 90° B. 0°

C. 45° D. 30°

70. During a practice session in a stadium an athlete runs along a circular track and her performance is observed by her coach standing at a point on the circle and also by her physiotherapist standing at the centre of the circle. The coach finds that she covers an angle of 72° in 1 min. What will be the angle covered by her in 1 second according to the measurement made by her physiotherapist?

A. It depends on the position of the coach on the circular track

B. 4.8°

C. 1.2°

D. 2.4°

71. The two diagonals of a rhombus are respectively, 14 cm and 48 cm. The perimeter of the rhombus is equal to:

A. 120 cm B. 160 cm

C. 80 cm D. 100 cm

72. AB and CD are two chords of a circle which intersect at a point O inside the circle. It is given that, AB = 10 cm, CO = 1.5 cm and DO = 12.5 cm. What is the ratio between the larger and smaller among AO and BO?

A. 7 : 3 B. 3 : 2

C. 3 : 1 D. 4 : 1

73. The ratio of the square of a number to the reciprocal of its cube is $\frac{243}{16807}$

What is the number?

A. $\frac{2}{7}$ B. $\frac{7}{3}$

C. $\frac{3}{7}$ D. $\frac{5}{7}$

74. The average of 1088 real numbers is zero. At most how many of them can be negative?

A. 100 B. 88

C. 544 D. 1087

75. The full marks for a paper is 300. The break-up of the marks into theory (X), practical (Y) and project (Z), which are the three components of evaluation is 6 : 5 : 4. In order to pass one has to score at least 40%, 50% and 50% respectively in X, Y, Z and 60% in aggregate. The marks scored by four students A, B, C and D are shown in the given Bar Graph.

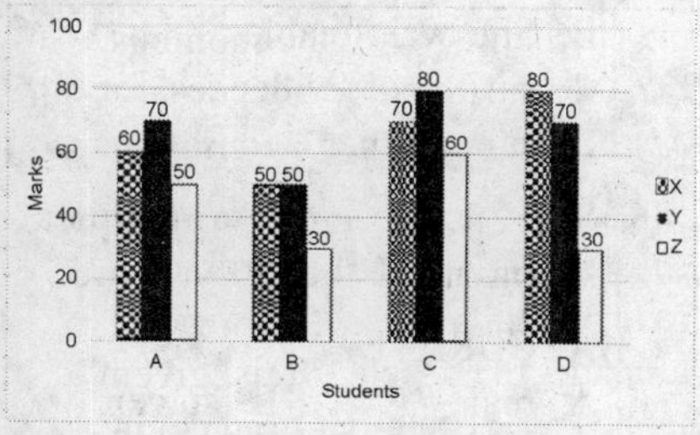

Who among the students could not pass?

A. A only B. B and C

C. B only D. B and D

76. Select the most appropriate option to substitute the underlined segment in the given sentence. If there is no need to substitute it, select No improvement.

The minister <u>promise to looked into</u> the matter of fuel emissions and air pollution.

A. promise to looks into

B. No improvement

C. promised to look into

D. promises to looking at

77. Select the most appropriate antonym of the given word.

ABSTRACT

A. elusive B. concrete

C. intangible D. vague

78. Select the most appropriate meaning of the given idiom.

make no headway

A. check if the head can pass through

B. unable to progress ahead

C. unable to overtake anyone

D. forced to fix a new goal

79. Select the most appropriate word to fill in the blank.

Once again, higher food inflation, in combination with fuel and power, provided .... to the wholesale inflation.

A. impression B. inspiration

C. insight D. impetus

80. Given below are four jumbled sentences. Out of the given options pick the one that gives their correct order.

(*a*) Using matches however came much later.

(*b*) The first great discovery that man probably made was that of fire.

(*c*) In olden times fires were made by rubbing two flints against each other till a spark was produced.

(*d*) And this spark set fire to dry straw, leaves or wood.

A. (*c*)(*b*)(*d*)(*a*) B. (*b*)(*d*)(*a*)(*c*)
C. (*a*)(*d*)(*b*)(*c*) D. (*b*)(*c*)(*d*)(*a*)

81. Select the most appropriate antonym of the given word.

HOPE

A. daring B. courage
C. despair D. confidence

82. Select the correct indirect form of the given sentence.

The interviewer asked Ramesh, "Do you have any idea about our products?"

A. The interviewer asked Ramesh that if he had any idea about the products.
B. The interviewer asked Ramesh if he have any idea about their products.
C. The interviewer asked Ramesh if he had any idea about their products.
D. The interviewer asked Ramesh if they had any idea about his products.

83. Select the correct passive form of the given sentence.

Someone gave him a new case for his credit cards.

A. He is given a new case for his credit cards.
B. He had given a new case for his credit cards.
C. He was given a new case for his credit cards.
D. He has given a new case for his credit cards.

84. Given below are four jumbled sentences. Out of the given options pick the one that gives their correct order.

(*a*) We had already covered half the distance when we reached a three-road junction.
(*b*) I was worried it might pounce on us.
(*c*) But thankfully we picked up speed and it got left behind.
(*d*) Suddenly, a barking dog began to chase the bike for some distance.

A. (*a*)(*b*)(*d*)(*c*) B. (*d*)(*a*)(*c*)(*b*)
C. (*b*)(*d*)(*a*)(*c*) D. (*a*)(*d*)(*b*)(*c*)

85. Identify the segment in the sentence which contains the grammatical error.

She was unable to produce sufficient evidences for support her accusations.

A. to produce
B. She was unable
C. sufficient evidences for
D. support her accusations

86. Select the most appropriate synonym of the given word.

ACCURATE

A. real B. sincere
C. precise D. genuine

87. Select the most appropriate synonym of the given word.

DEDICATION

A. contentment
B. trepidation
C. determination
D. commitment

88. Select the most appropriate option to substitute the underlined segment in the given sentence. If there is no need to substitute it, select No improvement.

My professor <u>gave me a lot of useful advices</u> when I was writing my research paper.

A. gave me a lots of useful advices
B. gave me a lot of useful advice
C. No improvement
D. give me lots of useful advices

89. Select the most appropriate word for the given group of words.

A person who sells and arranges cut flowers

A. nutritionist B. agriculturist
C. florist D. botanist

90. Select the most appropriate meaning of the given idiom.

make short work of something

A. reduce the size
B. dispose of quickly
C. edit carefully
D. shorten some dress

91. Select the correctly spelt word.

A. manegeable B. managable
C. manageble D. manageable

92. Select the most appropriate word for the given group of words.

One who draws or produces maps

A. cartographer B. photographer
C. designer D. draftsman

93. Select the most appropriate word to fill in the blank.

As he crossed the desert he nearly .... to thirst when he was forced to go without water for four days and five nights.

A. succumbed B. subsisted
C. survived D. submerged

94. Select the wrongly spelt word.

A. fourtieth B. seventeenth
C. fifteenth D. fourteenth

95. Identify the segment in the sentence which contains the grammatical error.

The team began searching for reasons for their poor performance in the tournament.

A. The team began
B. in the tournament
C. searching for reasons
D. for their poor performance

Directions (Qs. No. 96-100): *In the following passage some words have been deleted. Fill in the blanks with the help of the alternatives given. Select the most appropriate option for each blank.*

If winter seems to be the season for migratory birds to flock to warmer climates, summer time is ideal for wetland birds. (1) ______ fifty kilometers from Warangal in Telangana, Pakhal lake (2) ______ to be playing host to (3) ______ wide variety of flora and fauna (4) ______ season. Wetland birds from North and Central India come (5) ______ the south in search of larger water bodies.

96. Select the most appropriate option to fill in blank No. 1.

A. Totally B. But
C. Nearly D. Not

97. Select the most appropriate option to fill in blank No. 2.
A. will seems B. seems
C. was seemed D. seem

98. Select the most appropriate option to fill in blank No. 3.
A. one B. a
C. the D. an

99. Select the most appropriate option to fill in blank No. 4.
A. their B. these
C. this D. that

100. Select the most appropriate option to fill in blank No. 5.
A. below B. towards
C. away D. about

ANSWERS

1	**2**	**3**	**4**	**5**	**6**	**7**	**8**	**9**	**10**
C	A	A	D	D	B	B	C	D	B
11	**12**	**13**	**14**	**15**	**16**	**17**	**18**	**19**	**20**
D	C	C	C	B	A	C	A	D	C
21	**22**	**23**	**24**	**25**	**26**	**27**	**28**	**29**	**30**
D	C	D	C	A	D	D	C	B	B
31	**32**	**33**	**34**	**35**	**36**	**37**	**38**	**39**	**40**
B	D	B	B	A	D	A	A	A	B
41	**42**	**43**	**44**	**45**	**46**	**47**	**48**	**49**	**50**
A	A	C	B	C	A	B	C	A	A
51	**52**	**53**	**54**	**55**	**56**	**57**	**58**	**59**	**60**
B	C	D	C	B	C	A	B	D	A
61	**62**	**63**	**64**	**65**	**66**	**67**	**68**	**69**	**70**
A	B	C	B	B	A	C	A	A	D
71	**72**	**73**	**74**	**75**	**76**	**77**	**78**	**79**	**80**
D	C	C	D	D	C	B	B	D	D
81	**82**	**83**	**84**	**85**	**86**	**87**	**88**	**89**	**90**
C	C	C	D	C	C	D	B	C	B
91	**92**	**93**	**94**	**95**	**96**	**97**	**98**	**99**	**100**
D	A	A	A	D	C	B	B	C	B

EXPLANATORY ANSWERS

1. As,

G	O	U	R	D
+2↓	+2↓	−2↓	+2↓	+2↓
I	Q	S	T	F

Similarly,

A	P	H	I	D
+2↓	+2↓	−2↓	+2↓	+2↓
C	R	F	K	F

2. As Engineer's profession is to make a building similarly, writer's profession is to write a book.

3. (A) Q S U V

+2 +2 +1

(B) D F H J

+2 +2 +2

(C) 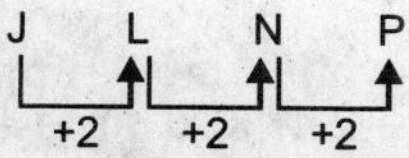

(D) 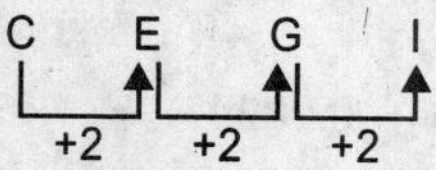

Hence, option (A) is odd-one.

4. Except (D) all other are road transport vehicle.

6. 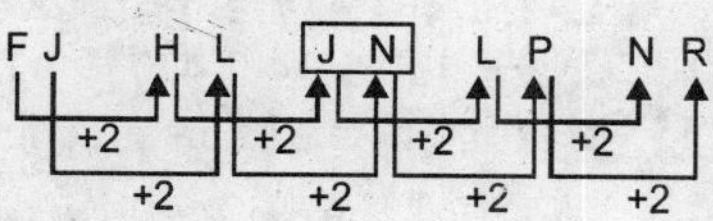

7. As,

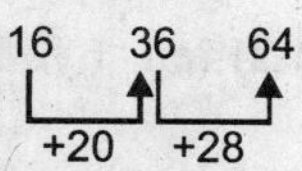

Similarly,

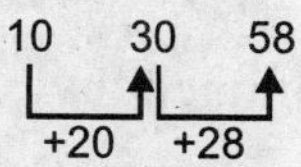

9. 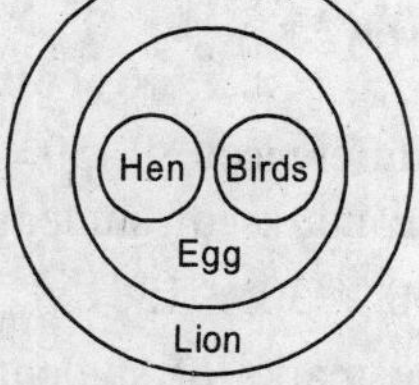

Clearly from Venn diagram

I. All Hens are Lion.

II. All Lions are Eggs.

III. All Birds are Lions.

Hence, all the conclusions follow.

10. 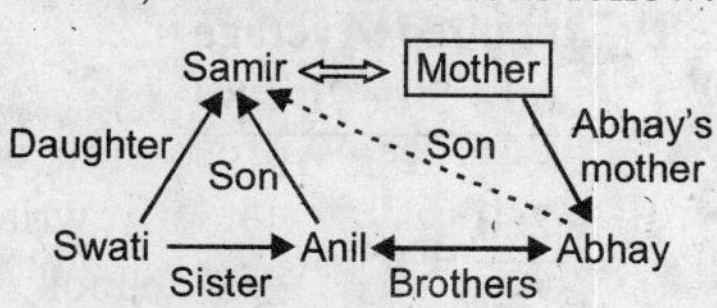

Hence, Abhay's mother is the wife of Samir.

13. As, 29, 31 → Consecutive prime numbers

Similarly,

11, 13 → Consecutive prime numbers.

14. 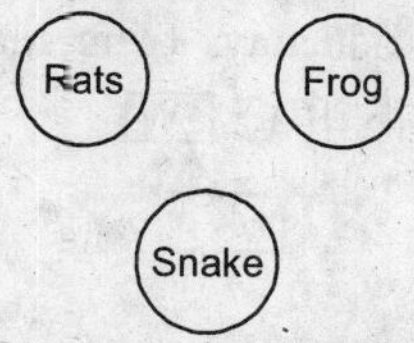

15. As cement is used to make a Building, similarly, wood is used to make Furniture.

16. 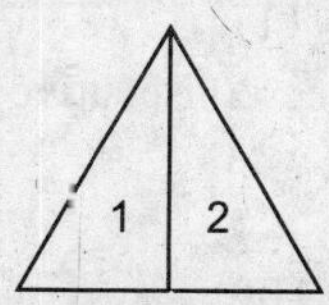

Total triangle = 1 + 2 = 3

There are three figures of this type in the given figure.

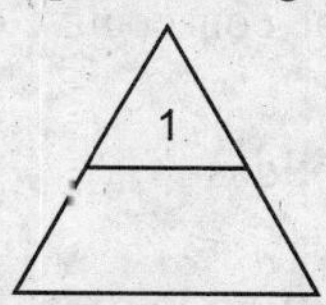

Total triangle = 2

Hence, the total triangle in the given figure

= 3 × 3 + 2 = 9 + 2 = 11.

17. 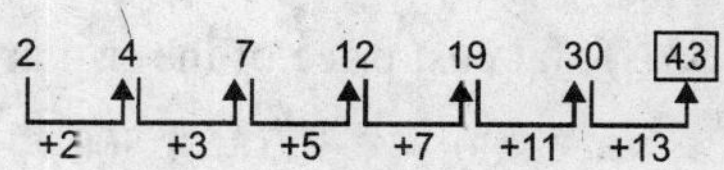

18. 15 August 2013

We have to find odd days

∴ 2012 + Jan + Feb + March + April + May + June + July + 15 days

(2000 + 3 leap year + 9 ordinary year) + Jan + Feb + March + April + May + June + July + 15

$= 0 + 3 \times 2 + 9 \times 1 + 3 + 0 + 3 + 2 + 3 + 2 + 3 + 1$

$= 32 = 4$ odd days (Thursday).

20. DJ : HT :: HM : LW

(D → H: +4; J → T: +10) (H → L: +4; M → W: +10)

22. As,

49	81	121
↓	↓	↓
$(7)^2$	$(9)^2$	$(11)^2$

Square of three consecutive odd numbers.

Similarly,

36	64	100
↓	↓	↓
$(6)^2$	$(8)^2$	$(10)^2$

Square of three consecutive even numbers.

23. Check the options

(D) × and –

$5 + 8 \times 30 - 10 \div 2 = 240$

According to BODMAS Rule

$= 5 + 8 \times 30 - 5 = 5 + 240 - 5$

$= 245 - 5 = 240$ (RHS)

53. Total cost price of the two article

$=$ ₹ 200 + ₹ 300 = ₹ 500

Total selling price of the two article

$=$ 105% × ₹ 200 + 110% × 300

$=$ ₹ 210 + ₹ 330 = ₹ 540

∴ Overall gain percentage

$$= \frac{540 - 500}{500} \times 100 = \frac{40}{500} \times 100$$

$$= \frac{40}{5} = 8\%.$$

54. $\frac{10}{7}(1 - 2.43 \times 10^{-3}) = 1.417 + x$

$\frac{10}{7}(1 - 0.00243) = 1.417 + x$

$\frac{10}{7}(0.99757) = 1.417 + x$

$1.4251 = 1.417 + x$

$\therefore x = 1.4251 - 1.417 = 0.0081.$

55. Maximum marks in practical

$$= 300 \times \frac{5}{6 + 5 + 4} = 100$$

% marks obtained by B in practical

$$= \frac{50}{100} \times 100 = 50\%$$

% marks obtained by C in practical

$$= \frac{80}{100} \times 100 = 80\%$$

Required difference $= 80 - 50 = 30\%$.

57. Aggregate marks of student B

$= 50 + 50 + 30 = 130$

Aggregate marks of student C

$= 70 + 80 + 60 = 210$

Aggregate marks of student D

$= 80 + 70 + 30 = 180$

Required order is B < D < C.

58. Required Average

$$= \frac{60 + 50 + 70 + 80}{4}$$

$$= \frac{260}{4} = 65\%.$$

60. We have

$0° \le (\alpha_1, \alpha_2, \alpha_3, \alpha_4, ..., \alpha_{20}) \le 90°$

and $\sin \alpha_1 + \sin \alpha_2 + \sin \alpha_3 + ... + \sin \alpha_{20} = 20$

This is true only at

$\alpha_1 = \alpha_2 = \alpha_3 = \alpha_4 = ... = \alpha_{20} = 90°$

[$\because$ sin 90° = 1]

$\therefore \alpha_1 + \alpha_2 + \alpha_3 + \alpha_4 + ... + \alpha_{20}$

$= (90 + 90 + 90 + ... + 90)_{20 \text{ term}}$

$= 20 \times 90° = 1800°.$

62. $\dfrac{18.43 \times 18.43 - 6.57 \times 6.57}{11.86}$

Let $a = 18.43$, $b = 6.57$

$a - b = 18.43 - 6.57 = 11.86$

$\therefore \dfrac{a \times a - b \times b}{a - b} = \dfrac{a^2 - b^2}{a - b}$

$= \dfrac{(a+b)(a-b)}{a-b}$

$= a + b = 18.43 + 6.57 = 25.$

63. In an equilateral triangle Circumcentre (O), Centroid (G), Incenter (I) and Orthocentre (H) lie on the same point, hence, all these points are identical.

64. Let the sum and the rate were ₹ x and $r\%$ respectively

Amount after five years

$= x + \dfrac{x \times r \times 5}{100} = \dfrac{x \times r}{20} + x$

Amount after three years

$= \dfrac{x \times r \times 3}{100} + x$

According to the question,

$\dfrac{x \times r}{20} + x = \dfrac{5}{4}\left(\dfrac{x \times r \times 3}{100} + x\right)$

$\dfrac{x \times r}{20} + x = \dfrac{3xr}{80} + \dfrac{5}{4}x$

$\dfrac{r}{20} - \dfrac{3r}{80} = \dfrac{5}{4} - 1$

$\dfrac{4r - 3r}{80} = \dfrac{1}{4}$

$\therefore r = \dfrac{80}{4} = 20\%$

Hence, the percentage rate of interest was 20%.

65. B complete the whole work

$= \dfrac{6}{20\%} \times 100\% = 30$ days

Both (A + B) together complete the whole work

$= \dfrac{20 \times 30}{20 + 30} = \dfrac{600}{50} = 12$ days

$\therefore$ 50% work completed by A and B together = 6 days.

66. $\text{cosec}^2 30° + \sin^2 45° + \sec^2 60° + \tan^2 30°$

$= (2)^2 + \left(\dfrac{1}{\sqrt{2}}\right)^2 + (2)^2 + \left(\dfrac{1}{\sqrt{3}}\right)^2$

$= 4 + \dfrac{1}{2} + 4 + \dfrac{1}{3}$

$= \dfrac{24 + 3 + 24 + 2}{6} = \dfrac{53}{6}.$

67. $\because \Delta ABC \sim \Delta DEF$

$\dfrac{\text{Perimeter of } \Delta ABC}{\text{Perimeter of } \Delta DEF} = \dfrac{AB}{DE}$

$\dfrac{AB}{9} = \dfrac{64}{48}$

$\therefore \quad AB = \dfrac{64 \times 9}{48} = 12$

Hence, the length of AB is 12 cm.

68. We have,

$(3x + 1)^3 + (x - 3)^3 + (4 - 2x)^3 + 6(3x + 1)(x - 3)(x - 2) = 0$

We can write this as,

$(3x + 1)^3 + (x - 3)^3 + (4 - 2x)^3 - 3(3x + 1)(x - 3)(4 - 2x) = 0$

We know that,

If $a^3 + b^3 + c^3 - 3abc = 0$

then $a + b + c = 0$

$\therefore\ 3x + 1 + x - 3 + 4 - 2x = 0$

$2x + 2 = 0 \qquad \Rightarrow 2x = -2$

$\therefore\ x = -1.$

69. We have,

$\sqrt{3}\cos\theta + \sin\theta = 1\ [0° \le \theta \le 90°]$

Divide by 2 both side, we get

$\frac{\sqrt{3}}{2}\cos\theta + \frac{1}{2}\sin\theta = \frac{1}{2}$

$\cos 30° \cos \theta° + \sin 30° \sin \theta°$

$= \frac{1}{2}$

$\cos(\theta° - 30°) = \cos 60°$

$[\because \cos(A - B) = \cos A \cos B + \sin A \sin B]$

$\theta - 30° = 60°$

$\theta = 90°.$

71. We know that,

In a Rhombus,

$$d_1^2 + d_2^2 = 4a^2$$

$$\therefore \quad 4a^2 = (14)^2 + (48)^2$$

$$4a^2 = 196 + 2304$$

$$4a^2 = 2500$$

$$a^2 = 625$$

$$a = 25$$

Hence, perimeter of Rhombus

$= 4 \times a = 4 \times 25 = 100$ cm.

73. Let the number be x

Then, $\frac{x^2}{\left(\frac{1}{x^3}\right)} = \frac{243}{16807}$

$$x^5 = \frac{243}{16807}$$

$$x^5 = \left(\frac{3}{7}\right)^5$$

$$x = \frac{3}{7}$$

Hence, the number be $\frac{3}{7}$.

74. The average of 1088 real number is zero it means the sum of 1088 real numbers will be zero. So at most 1087 real numbers of them can be negative and one number can be positive.

75. Maximum marks in theory (X)

$= 300 \times \frac{6}{6+5+4} = 120$

Maximum marks in practical (Y)

$= 300 \times \frac{5}{6+5+4} = 100$

Maximum marks in project (Z)

$= 300 \times \frac{4}{6+5+4} = 80$

Passing marks in theory (X)

$= 120 \times 40\% = 48$

Passing marks in practical (Y)

$= 100 \times 50\% = 50$

Passing marks in project (Z)

$= 80 \times 50\% = 40$

Aggregate passing marks

$= 300 \times 60\% = 180.$

B and D students do not follow the all criteria hence, B and D students could not pass.

GENERAL INTELLIGENCE & REASONING

VERBAL

1
Series

Letter Series

In letter series the letters follow a definite order. The given series of letters can be in natural order or in reverse order or combination of both. The letters may be skipped or repeated or consecutive. The given series may be single or may even comprise of two different series merged at alternate positions. While attempting questions on letter series one should note the pattern of alphabet series.

Alphabets in natural series are :

A	B	C	D	E	F	G	H	I	J	K	L	M	N	O	P	Q	R	S	T	U	V	W	X	Y	Z
↓				↓					↓					↓					↓					↓	
1st				5th					10th					15th					20th					25th	

Alphabets in reverse series are :

Z	Y	X	W	V	U	T	S	R	Q	P	O	N	M	L	K	J	I	H	G	F	E	D	C	B	A
↓				↓					↓					↓					↓					↓	
1st				5th					10th					15th					20th					25th	

Note : On reaching Z, the series restarts from A and on reaching A, it restarts from Z.

Example

Directions : *Which of the given options will complete the given series?*

BDFHJ?

(*a*) L (*b*) O (*c*) M (*d*) K

Ans. *(a)* : The series follows the pattern of moving the letters two steps forward.

B →(+2) D →(+2) F →(+2) H →(+2) J →(+2) L

EXERCISE

Directions : *In each of the following series determine the order of the letters. Then from the given options select the one which will complete the given series.*

1. B Y C X D W E ?
(*a*) S (*b*) T
(*c*) U (*d*) V

2. A D C G E ?
(*a*) G (*b*) J
(*c*) I (*d*) L

3. X O I F ?
(*a*) D (*b*) F
(*c*) B (*d*) E

4. Z A A Y B B X C ?
(*a*) W (*b*) C
(*c*) V (*d*) D

5. A Z Y B X W C V U D T S E ?
(*a*) R S (*b*) S T
(*c*) R Q (*d*) Q R

6. R K F ? B
(*a*) D (*b*) C
(*c*) E (*d*) B

7. R Z J K S B C ?
(*a*) W (*b*) K
(*c*) L (*d*) X

8. A L W B M X C N ?
(*a*) V (*b*) W
(*c*) Y (*d*) X

9. LAZ, NEX, PIV, ?
(*a*) SLS (*b*) QNS
(*c*) RMT (*d*) RMS

10. EJOT, DHLP, CFIL, ?
(*a*) BDFH (*b*) DGKL
(*c*) DEIJ (*d*) BLHM

ANSWERS

1	2	3	4	5	6	7	8	9	10
(*d*)	(*b*)	(*b*)	(*b*)	(*c*)	(*b*)	(*b*)	(*c*)	(*c*)	(*a*)

SOME SELECTED EXPLANATORY ANSWERS

1. There are two alternate series.

Series I : BCDE (natural order)
Series II : YXWV (reverse order)

3. The series follows the sequence of the difference decreasing by 3 *i.e.*

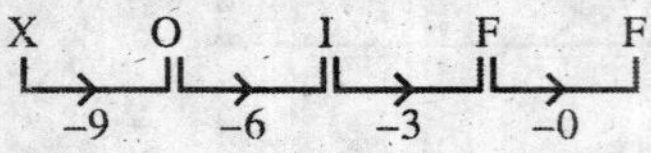

5. There are two alternate series.

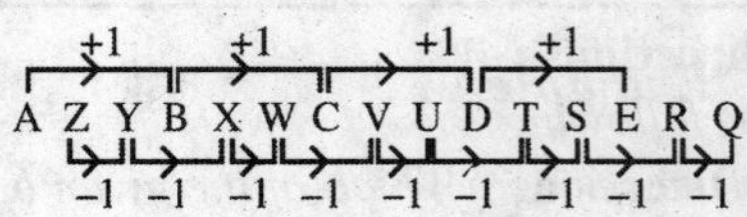

Series I : ABCDE (in natural series).
Series II : ZY XW VU TS RQ (double letter in reverse series)

6. The difference between the letters is reduced by two at each step.

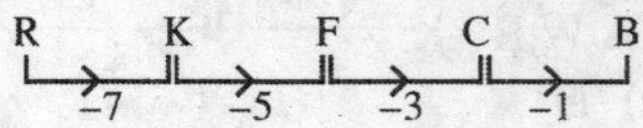

8. There are three alternate series.

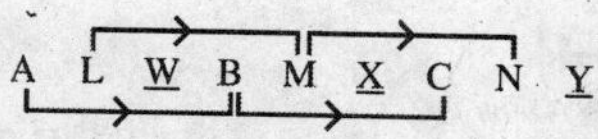

Series I : ABC
Series II : LMN
Series III : WXY

10. The letters in each group correspond to the letters in the next group in the manner –1, –2, –3, –4 respectively.

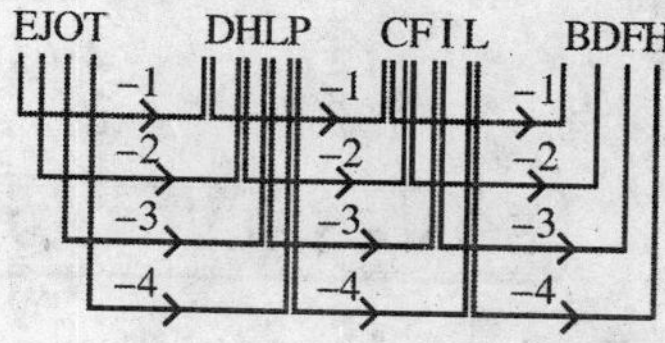

Wrong Letter Series

In this type of series the candidates are not required to find the letter or group of letters which will complete the given series but, they have to identify the letter or number which is wrong or misfit in the given series.

Example

Which of the following letters in the given series is wrong?

J M P T V Y

(*a*) J (*b*) P (*c*) T (*d*) Y

Ans. (*c*) : The letters in this series are moved three steps forward, *i.e.*,

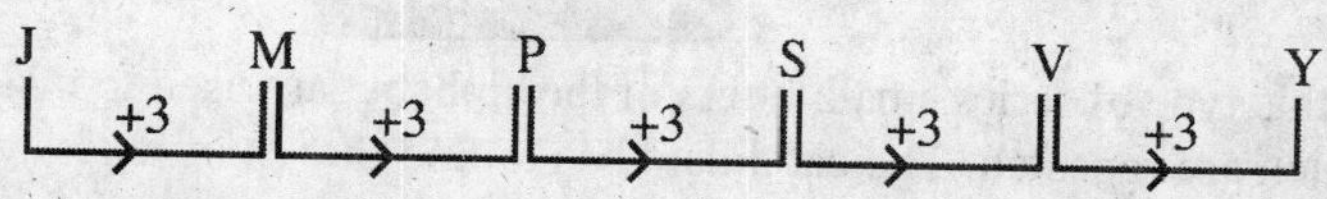

Letter 'T' should have been 'S'.

EXERCISE

Directions : *Which letter(s) in each of the following series is wrong or is misfit in the series?*

1. C H M S W B
(*a*) C
(*b*) S
(*c*) B
(*d*) W

2. Z A W B X C
(*a*) D (*b*) C
(*c*) X (*d*) W

3. D K R Y F L
(*a*) L
(*b*) D
(*c*) R
(*d*) Y

4. XW, DC, CB, NM, PQ
(*a*) NM (*b*) CB
(*c*) PQ (*d*) XW

5. Z T P K H F
(*a*) Z (*b*) P
(*c*) T (*d*) F

ANSWERS

1	2	3	4	5
(*b*)	(*d*)	(*a*)	(*c*)	(*b*)

SOME SELECTED EXPLANATORY ANSWERS

1. The letters in the series are moved five steps forward.

C H M R W B

+5 +5 +5 +5 +5

R should be in place of S.

3. The pattern in this series in moving the letters seven steps forward.

D K R Y F M

+7 +7 +7 +7 +7

M should be in place of L.

4. The series is made with any two consecutive letters written backwards.

XW DC CB NM QP

← ← ← ← ←

Q should come before P in the series.

Repeat Series

In this type of series small letters of the alphabet are used to make a set of letters which are repeated. The candidate has to find the set of letters which will fit the blanks left in the given series in such a manner that one section of the series is further repeated in the same manner.

Example

Which of the following groups of letters will complete the given series?

ba-b-aab-a-b

(*a*) baab (*b*) abba (*c*) abaa (*d*) babb

Ans. (*b*) : The series is baab, baab, baab. Here the section 'baab' is repeated in the series.

***Solving steps* :** The candidate has to look for clues to solve such series pattern. 'aab' in the Series indicates that 'b' in this series is preceded by two 'a' so, the first blank and the last blank will be filled by 'a'. Now the first set is formed, *i.e.*, 'baab' in the beginning. This set is repeated, so the second and third blanks will have 'b' filling them. Now, solve the exercise given below to know the different ways in which these series are formed.

EXERCISE

Directions : *Which of the following groups of letters will complete the given series?*

1. b-abbc-bbca-bcabb-ab
   (*a*) acba (*b*) acaa
   (*c*) cacc (*d*) cabc
2. aca-ac--a-ac
   (*a*) babc (*b*) aaac
   (*c*) cacc (*d*) caca
3. ba-cb-b-bab-?
   (*a*) acbb (*b*) bcaa
   (*c*) cabb (*d*) bacc
4. ab-aa-caab-aab-a
   (*a*) bcbc (*b*) bbca
   (*c*) cbcc (*d*) caba
5. -bbcaa-bcaa-bc-a-bca
   (*a*) bacab (*b*) abbab
   (*c*) abcba (*d*) bcaab

EXPLANATORY ANSWERS

1. (*d*) : The series is bcab, bcab, bcab, bcab, bcab

2. (*c*) : The series is ac, ac, ac, ac, ac, ac

3. (*d*) : The series is babc, babc, babc

4. (*c*) : The series is abca, abca, abca, abca

5. (*b*) : The series is abbca, abbca, abbca, abbca

Number Series

In this type of series, the set of given numbers in a series are related to one another in a particular pattern or manner. The relationship between the numbers may be (i) consecutive odd/even numbers; (ii) consecutive prime numbers; (iii) squares/cubes of some numbers with/without variation of addition or subtraction of some number; (iv) sum/product/difference of preceding numbers; (v) addition/subtraction/multiplication/division by some number; and (vi) many more combinations of the relationships given above.

Example

Complete the given series.

2, 14, 98, 686, ?

(*a*) 1976 (*b*) 2548
(*c*) 980 (*d*) 4802

Ans. (*d*) : The numbers are multiplied by 7 to obtain the next numbers.

2 →(×7)→ 14 →(×7)→ 98 →(×7)→ 686 →(×7)→ 4802

EXERCISE

Directions : *In the following questions, select the number(s) from the given options for completing the given series.*

1. 1, 8, 27, 64, 125, ?
(*a*) 172 (*b*) 176
(*c*) 216 (*d*) 189

2. 2, 3, 5, 7, 11, 13, ?
(*a*) 19 (*b*) 57
(*c*) 31 (*d*) 17

3. 80, 64, 48, 32, 16, ?
(*a*) 4 (*b*) 0
(*c*) 8 (*d*) 1

4. 3, 8, 13, 24, 41, ?
(*a*) 65 (*b*) 75
(*c*) 70 (*d*) 80

5. 9, 81, 90, 810, 819, ?
(*a*) 7371 (*b*) 900
(*c*) 8100 (*d*) 1638

6. 0, 8, 24, 48, 80, ?
(*a*) 110 (*b*) 96
(*c*) 120 (*d*) 140

7. 2, 4, 8, 3, 9, 27, 4, 16, ?
(*a*) 64 (*b*) 32
(*c*) 48 (*d*) 24

8. 27, 28, 25, 25, 23, 22, 21, ?
(*a*) 20 (*b*) 21
(*c*) 19 (*d*) 18

9. 80, 63, 72, 72, 64, 81, 56, ?
(*a*) 96 (*b*) 98
(*c*) 89 (*d*) 90

10. 0, 5, 22, 57, ?, 205
(*a*) 198 (*b*) 116
(*c*) 172 (*d*) 92

ANSWERS

1	2	3	4	5	6	7	8	9	10
(*c*)	(*d*)	(*b*)	(*c*)	(*a*)	(*c*)	(*a*)	(*c*)	(*d*)	(*b*)

SOME SELECTED EXPLANATORY ANSWERS

1. The sequence in the series is cube of numbers in their natural order.

2. The series consists of prime numbers in increasing order.

3. The numbers in the series are decreasing with the difference of 16 at each step.

5. The sequence in the series is × 9, + 9 which is repeated.

7. In this series 3 numbers form a set. The first number is in natural order. The second number is the square of above number. The third number is the cube of first number.

10. The series follows this sequence : cube of natural numbers starting from 1 minus odd numbers starting from 1.

0	5	22	57	116	205
↓	↓	↓	↓	↓	↓
1^3-1	2^3-3	3^3-5	4^3-7	5^3-9	6^3-11

Wrong Number Series

In this type of series the given series may be complete but what needs to be identified is the number in the given completed series which is disturbing the sequential pattern of that series and does not fit in with the relationship shared between the other numbers.

Example

Directions : *In each of the following series, one number is wrong. Select the answer from the given options.*

2, 4, 8, 16, 30, 64, 128

(*a*) 8 (*b*) 128 (*c*) 30 (*d*) 4

Ans. (*c*) : The numbers in the series are multiplied by 2.

2 4 8 16 32 64 128

×2 ×2 ×2 ×2 ×2 ×2

∴ 32 should be in place of 30.

EXERCISE

Directions : *In the given series find the number which is wrong.*

1. 5, 12, 16, 24, 27

(*a*) 12 (*b*) 16

(*c*) 24 (*d*) 27

2. 27, 36, 45, 60, 71, 99

(*a*) 27 (*b*) 45

(*c*) 60 (*d*) 71

3. 81, 64, 49, 35, 25, 16

(*a*) 64 (*b*) 35

(*c*) 25 (*d*) 16

4. 625, 125, 25, 5, 0

(*a*) 0 (*b*) 125

(*c*) 5 (*d*) 625

5. 25, 19, 17, 13, 11, 7

(*a*) 25 (*b*) 17

(*c*) 13 (*d*) 7

EXPLANATORY ANSWERS

1. (*c*) : The sequence in the series is +7, +4 which is repeated, *i.e.,*

5 12 16 23 27

+7 +4 +7 +4

∴ 23 should be in place of 24.

2. (*d*) : All other numbers are divisible by 3.

3. (*b*) : The sequence is the square of the number in decreasing order starting from 9, *i.e.,*

$9^2 = 9 \times 9 = 81$

$8^2 = 8 \times 8 = 64$

$7^2 = 7 \times 7 = 49$

$6^2 = 6 \times 6 = 36$

$5^2 = 5 \times 5 = 25$
$4^2 = 4 \times 4 = 16$
$\therefore$ 36 should be in place of 35.

4. (*a*) : The number in the series are divided by 5 to get the next number

625 125 25 5 1

$\div 5$ $\div 5$ $\div 5$ $\div 5$

$\therefore$ 1 should be in place of 0 digit.

5. (*a*) : Other numbers are prime numbers.

Mixed Series

Mixed series comprises of the combination of letters and numbers. In this type of series the letters and numbers may have a common sequence pattern or may have separate sequence patterns.

Example

What should come in the place of question mark in the following letter-number combination?

F6, H8, J10, L12, ?

(*a*) N15 (*b*) O14 (*c*) N14 (*d*) O13

Ans. (*c*) : The letters are moved two steps forward and the number indicates the position of the letter in the alphabet series.

F6 H8 J10 L12 N14

+2 +2 +2 +2

EXERCISE

Directions : *In each series given below, what would come in place of the question-mark?*

1. 2B, 4C, 8E, 14H, ?
(*a*) 20L
(*b*) 22L
(*c*) 21I
(*d*) 16K

2. C(1)L, F(4)O, I(9)R, L(16)U, ?
(*a*) P(27)W
(*b*) N(24)Y
(*c*) M(23)X
(*d*) O(25)X

3. 3F, 6G, 11I, 18L, ?
(*a*) 27P
(*b*) 21O
(*c*) 27Q
(*d*) 25N

4. W(1)A, X(4)Z, Y(9)Y, ?, A(25)W
(*a*) X(11)Z
(*b*) Z(21)A
(*c*) Z(16)X
(*d*) Z(14)X

5. 81Y, 27S, 9N, 3J, ?
(*a*) 0H (*b*) 1G
(*c*) 0F (*d*) 1E

EXPLANATORY ANSWERS

1. (*b*) : The sequence of numbers is +2, +4, +6 +8 and sequence of letters is +1, +2, +3, +4.

2. (*d*) : The corresponding letters are moved 3 steps forward and the sequence of numbers is +3, +5, +7, +9.

3. (*a*) : The sequence of numbers is +3, +5, +7, +9 and the letters are moved 1, 2, 3, 4 steps forward.

4. (*c*) : The letters on the left are in reverse series, the letters on the right are in natural series, and the numbers are squares of numbers in natural order starting from 1.

5. (*b*) : The numbers are divided by 3 at each step and the letters are moved 6, 5, 4, 3 steps backward.

❑❑❑

2

Analogies or Relationships

Wrong Analogy

In Analogy Tests the relationship between two given words is established and then applied to the other words. The type of relationship may vary, so while attempting such questions the first step is to identify the type of relationship.

EXERCISE

Directions : *In the questions given below establish the relationship between the two words. Then from the given options select one which has the same relationship as of the given two words.*

1. *Guilt* is to *Past* as *Hope* is to.....
(*a*) Present (*b*) Future
(*c*) Today (*d*) Despair

2. .... is to *Liquid* as *Mile* is to *Distance*.
(*a*) Unit (*b*) Kilo
(*c*) Scale (*d*) Litre

3. *Bench* is to *Judges* as *Chair* is to.......
(*a*) Attorney (*b*) President
(*c*) Lawyer (*d*) Ruler

4. *Psychology* is to *Emotions* as *Philosophy* is to.....
(*a*) Knowledge (*b*) Scholar
(*c*) Research (*d*) Wisdom

5. *Surgeon* is to *Scalpel* as *Sculptor* is to....
(*a*) Pastle (*b*) Chisel
(*c*) Pallet (*d*) Engraving

6. .... is to *Dumb* as *Light* is to *Blind*.
(*a*) Voice (*b*) Language
(*c*) Speech (*d*) Tongue

7. *Physicist is to Physics as .... is to Anatomy.*
(*a*) Botany (*b*) Botanist
(*c*) Body (*d*) Biologist

8. *Frequently* is to *Always* as *Seldom* is to......
(*a*) Often
(*b*) Rarely
(*c*) Occasionally
(*d*) Never

9. *Tailor* is related to *Cloth* in the same way as *Cobbler* is related to ....

(*a*) Machine (*b*) Leather
(*c*) Stiching (*d*) Mending

10. *Millionaire* is related to *Wealth* in the same way as *Genius* is related to........

(*a*) Capability (*b*) Smartness
(*c*) Intelligence (*d*) Awareness

EXPLANATORY ANSWERS

1. (*b*) : Feeling of guilt comes with mistakes in past and that of hope for a good future.

2. (*d*) : Liquid is measured in litres and distance in miles.

3. (*b*) : The seat of judges is bench and that of President a chair.

4. (*d*) : Psychology is the study of emotions as philosophy is of wisdom.

5. (*b*) : As scalpel is an instrument used by a surgeon so is chisel of a sculptor.

6. (*c*) : Blind cannot see the light and dumb cannot give speech.

7. (*d*) : Physicist deals with the subject Physics and biologist with subject anatomy.

8. (*d*) : The related words are near opposites.

9. (*b*) : Tailor makes clothes from cloth, cobbler makes shoes from leather.

10. (*c*) : A millionaire has lots of wealth, a genius has lots of intelligence.

Letter Analogy

In this type of analogy the relationship between two given set of letters is established and then applied to the other set to obtain the required set of letters as the answer. These letters can be moved some steps backward or forward; reversed in whole or in sections or have some common identity between each other.

EXERCISE

Directions : *In the questions given below one term is missing. Based on the relationship of the two given words find the missing term from the given options.*

1. GFC : CFG : : RPJ : ?

(*a*) JRP (*b*) JPR
(*c*) PJR (*d*) RJP

2. BCF : DEG : : MNQ : ?

(*a*) OPR (*b*) PQS
(*c*) OPP (*d*) QRT

3. UVW : SXU : : LMN : ?

(*a*) JOL (*b*) KNM
(*c*) JKL (*d*) MLO

4. BCDA : STUR : : KLMJ : ?

(*a*) VWXU (*b*) EFHG
(*c*) SRTU (*d*) QSRP

5. AEI : LPT : : CGK : ?

(*a*) OSV (*b*) RUY
(*c*) TXC (*d*) FJN

6. RUX : TRP :: BEH : ?
(*a*) SQN (*b*) QON
(*c*) QOM (*d*) QNL

7. RRS : XMW :: ITB : ?
(*a*) PNE (*b*) NOG
(*c*) RSW (*d*) OOF

8. LOM : NMK :: PKI : ?
(*a*) RNK (*b*) RSM
(*c*) RMP (*d*) RIG

9. ARQ : DTR :: JNG : ?
(*a*) MPH (*b*) PHJ
(*c*) LPI (*d*) GLE

10. BYDW : FVHT :: GQIO : ?
(*a*) JLNP
(*b*) QSTR
(*c*) KMOL
(*d*) KNML

ANSWERS

1	2	3	4	5	6	7	8	9	10
(*b*)	(*a*)	(*a*)	(*a*)	(*d*)	(*c*)	(*d*)	(*d*)	(*a*)	(*d*)

SOME SELECTED EXPLANATORY ANSWERS

1. The letters of the first group are reversed.

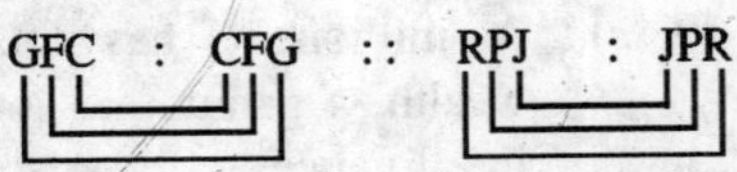

3. The three letters are moved –2, +2 and –2 steps respectively.

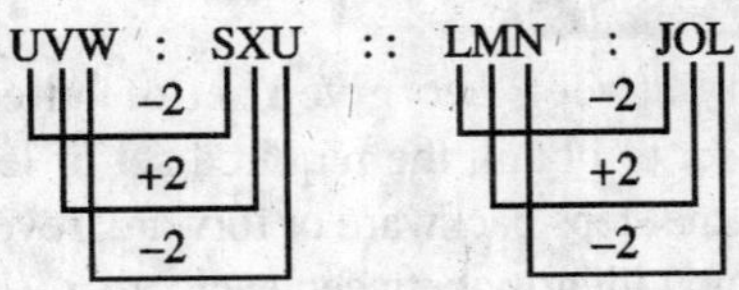

4. In each group the first three letters are consecutive and they follow the fourth letter.

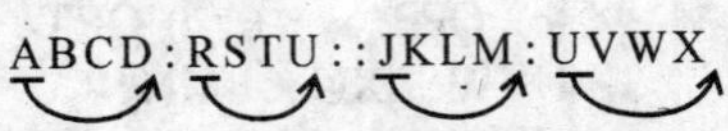

5. In each group the letters jump three letters between them, *i.e.*, they are moving to the fourth letter.

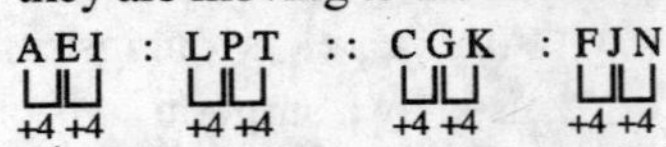

9. The three letters are moved 3, 2 and 1 step forward respectively.

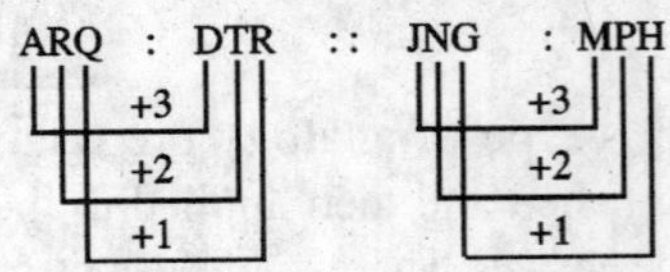

10. The letters are moved +4, –3, +4, –3 steps respectively

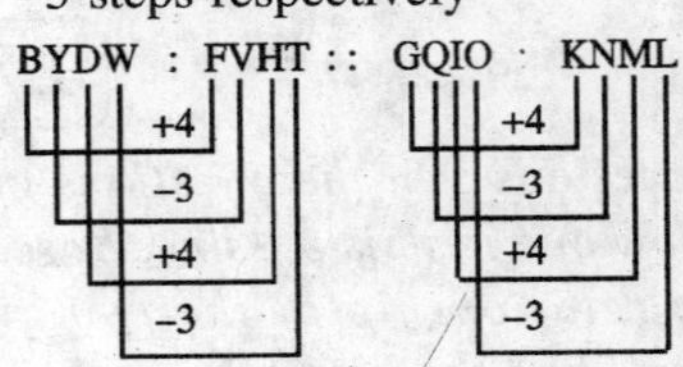

Number Analogy

In number analogy also, the relationship between the given numbers is detected and then applied to the second part to find the missing numbers.

Example

Directions : *Which number will come in the place of question mark?*

25 : 81 : : 36 : ?

(*a*) 121 (*b*) 93 (*c*) 65 (*d*) 103

Ans. (*a*) : All the numbers are squares of different numbers.

25	:	81	: :	36	:	121
↓		↓		↓		↓
5^2		9^2		6^2		11^2

EXERCISE

Directions : *In the following questions, select the number from the given options which follows the same relationship as shared between the first two numbers.*

1. 18 : 27 : : 22 : ?

(*a*) 42 (*b*) 39
(*c*) 33 (*d*) 54

2. 14 : 20 : : 16 : ?

(*a*) 23 (*b*) 10
(*c*) 48 (*d*) 32

3. 8 : 27 : : 64 : ?

(*a*) 277 (*b*) 125
(*c*) 250 (*d*) 99

4. $\frac{1}{7} : \frac{1}{14} :: \frac{1}{9} : ?$

(*a*) $\frac{1}{88}$ (*b*) $\frac{1}{80}$
(*c*) $\frac{1}{81}$ (*d*) $\frac{1}{18}$

5. 0.16 : 0.0016 : : 1.02 : ?

(*a*) 10.20 (*b*) 0.102
(*c*) 0.0102 (*d*) 1.020

EXPLANATORY ANSWERS

1. (*c*) : In the given set, the numbers are multiples of 9 and in the second set, multiples of 11.

18	:	27	: :	22	:	33
↓		↓		↓		↓
9 × 2		9 × 3		11 × 2		11 × 3

2. (*a*) : The relationship between the numbers is :

14	:	20	: :	16	:	23
↓		↓		↓		↓
7 × 2		(7×3)−1		8×2		(8×3)−1

3. (*b*) : The numbers are cubes of different numbers

8	:	27	: :	64	:	125
↓		↓		↓		↓
2^3		3^3		4^3		5^3

4. (*d*) : The first fraction is multiplied by half to obtain the second fraction.

$$\frac{1}{7} : \frac{1}{14} :: \frac{1}{9} : \frac{1}{18}$$

(each pair: $\times \frac{1}{2}$)

5. (*c*) : The decimals are divided by 100.

0.16 : 0.0016 : : 1.02 : 0.0102

(each pair: ÷ 100)

3

Classification

Odd One Out–Words

In this type of classification, five words are given out of which four are almost same in matter or meaning and only one word is different from the common four. One has to find out the word which is different from the rest.

Example

Directions : *In the following questions spot the odd one out.*

(*a*) Father (*b*) Mother (*c*) Friend (*d*) Brother

Ans. *(c)* : All other are blood relations.

EXERCISE

Directions : *In each of the following questions, four words are alike in some manner. Spot the odd one out.*

1. (*a*) Ornate (*b*) Pleasant (*c*) Decorate (*d*) Beautify

2. (*a*) Polo (*b*) Chess (*c*) Ludo (*d*) Squash

3. (*a*) Tutor (*b*) Principal (*c*) Pupil (*d*) Professor

4. (*a*) Pond (*b*) River (*c*) Stream (*d*) Brook

5. (*a*) Quotation (*b*) Duty (*c*) Tax (*d*) Octroi

EXPLANATORY ANSWERS

1. *(b)* : All other words have the same meaning.

2. *(a)* : All others are indoor games.

3. *(c)* : All others are instructors. Pupil learns from the instructor.

4. *(a)* : All others are running forms of water.

5. *(a)* : All others are forms of taxes.

Odd One Out–Letters

In this classification of letters, four groups of letters or a series of letters is given as options. One has to select the option as answer which does not share the commonness of the others.

Example

Directions : *Find the odd one out in the following letters :*

(*a*) NOP (*b*) RTU (*c*) JKL (*d*) EFG

Ans. (*b*) : In each group the letters are consecutive. In this option the first two letters jump one letter (S) inbetween.

EXERCISE

Directions : *Three of the following four in each question are alike in a certain way and so form a group. Select the group of letters that does not belong to that group.*

1. (*a*) ACE (*b*) LOR (*c*) GIK (*d*) VXZ
2. (*a*) TSR (*b*) LKJ (*c*) PQO (*d*) HGF
3. (*a*) EF LM (*b*) KJ SR (*c*) XW HG (*d*) ED YX
4. (*a*) JOPK (*b*) BOPC (*c*) QOPR (*d*) TOPS
5. (*a*) DfH (*b*) MoQ (*c*) UwY (*d*) lnO

EXPLANATORY ANSWERS

1. (*b*) : The sequence in each group is +2. Only option B has sequence in +3, *i.e.*,

ABCDE (+2 +2) LMNOPQR (+3 +3)

GHIJK (+2 +2) VWXYZ (+2 +2)

2. (*c*) : The sequence of alphabet in each group is in reverse order. Only option C has sequence in disturbed order.

3. (*a*) : Two consecutive alphabet in each group are in reverse sequence (–1), *i.e.*,

KJ SR; XW HG; (–1 –1 –1 –1)

ED YX (–1 –1)

Only in option (a) the sequence is in natural order (+1), *i.e.*,

E F L M (+1 +1)

4. (d) : In each group, letters 'OP' are common. The two corner alphabet are in natural order (+1); *i.e.*,

JOPK ; BOPC ; QOPR
+1 +1 +1

Only in option (d) they are in reverse order (–1); *i.e.*,

TOPS
–1

5. (d) : In other groups, only the alphabet in the centre is of lower case. In this option letter 'L' on the left is also in lower case.

Odd One Out–Numbers

In this type of classification, different numbers are given as options. These numbers have some commonness; except one which is the odd one. One has to identify the similarity and then strike the odd one out as answer option.

Example

Directions : *Find the odd number from the given options.*

(*a*) 62 (*b*) 121 (*c*) 36 (*d*) 256

Ans. (*a*) : The other numbers are squares of : 11, (= 121), 6 (= 36) and 16 (= 256)

EXERCISE

Directions : *In each of the following questions, there are four options. Three numbers, in these options, are alike in certain manner. Only one number does not fit in. Choose the one which is different from the rest.*

1. (*a*) 1948 (*b*) 2401 (*c*) 966 (*d*) 1449

2. (*a*) 129 (*b*) 130 (*c*) 131 (*d*) 132

3. (*a*) 3215 (*b*) 9309 (*c*) 4721 (*d*) 2850

4. (*a*) 64 (*b*) 84 (*c*) 16 (*d*) 36

5. (*a*) 24 (*b*) 90 (*c*) 54 (*d*) 36

EXPLANATORY ANSWERS

1. (*a*) : Other numbers are divisible by 7.

2. (*c*) : 131 is a prime number.

3. (*b*) : In other numbers, no digit is repeated.

4. (*b*) : All other numbers are perfect squares.

5. (*a*) : In other numbers, the sum of both the digits is 9.

□□□

4

Coding and Decoding

Part-I

Coding is a secretive language which is used to change the representation of the actual term/word/value. This coded language can be framed by *(i)* moving the letters one or more steps forward or backward; *(ii)* substituting numbers for letters and vice–versa; *(iii)* writing the letters of the given word in reverse order in part or in whole; and *(iv)* replacing the letters in their natural series by the same positioned letters in their reverse series.

Alphabet in natural series are :

A B C D E F G H I J K L M N O P Q R S T U V W X Y Z

A ↓ 1st, E ↓ 5th, J ↓ 10th, O ↓ 15th, T ↓ 20th, Y ↓ 25th

Alphabet in reverse series are :

Z Y X W V U T S R Q P O N M L K J I H G F E D C B A

Z ↓ 1st, V ↓ 5th, Q ↓ 10th, L ↓ 15th, G ↓ 20th, B ↓ 25th

Note : On reaching Z, the series restarts from A and on reaching A, it restarts from Z.

Example

If FACE is coded as GBDF, then BADE will be coded as :

(*a*) CBEF (*b*) CEBF (*c*) CFBE (*d*) CBFE

Ans. *(a)* : The word is coded by moving the letters one step forward.

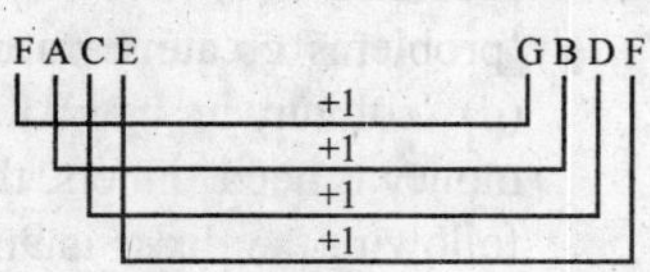

Similarly,

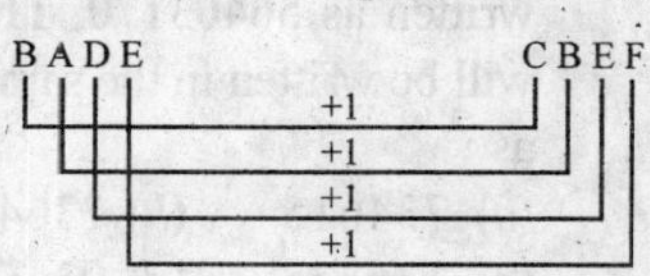

EXERCISE

Directions (Qs. 1 to 10): *In the following questions select the right option which indicates the correct code for the word or letter given in the question.*

1. If CHAIR is coded as FKDLU then RAID is coded as :
   (*a*) ULGD (*b*) ULKG
   (*c*) ULDG (*d*) UDLG

2. In a code language COME is written as XLNV and ABLE as ZYOV. How will MOLLY be written in that code?
   (*a*) NLOBO (*b*) NLBOO
   (*c*) LNOOB (*d*) NLOOB

3. If ACTION is coded as ZXGRLM, then HEALTH will be coded in the same way as :
   (*a*) SVZOGS (*b*) TVZOGT
   (*c*) RUZPGR (*d*) QVGOZQ

4. If 'w' is coded as 'a', 's' as 'r' and 'r' as 'w', how will 'answer' be written?
   (*a*) wnsaes (*b*) anraew
   (*c*) anrwas (*d*) wnraes

5. If MUSK is coded as 146816, then ZERO will be coded as :
   (*a*) 113811 (*b*) 122912
   (*c*) 15915 (*d*) 2651815

6. In a certain code LIBERATE is written as 56403170, TRIBAL will be written in the same code as :
   (*a*) 734615 (*b*) 736415
   (*c*) 136475 (*d*) 034615

7. If 341782 denotes MONKEY and 0596 denotes RAGS, then 75195044 will denote.
   (*a*) KANGAROO
   (*b*) PALMANTT
   (*c*) HANGAMEE
   (*d*) KARNAGOO

8. If ADD is coded as WOO, SUM as QJM and TOTAL as KPKWX, then TOADS will be coded as :
   (*a*) KPOWQ (*b*) KPWQO
   (*c*) KPWOQ (*d*) KPWOJ

9. If BOOK is coded as CNPJ, then MOON will be coded as :
   (*a*) MPNN (*b*) NNPM
   (*c*) PNMN (*d*) NMPN

10. DAZE is written as 41265 in a certain code. How will BOY be written in the same code?
    (*a*) 41425 (*b*) 5120
    (*c*) 21525 (*d*) 359

Directions (Qs. 11 to 15): *In the following questions study the coded patterns and then select the right option from the given alternatives.*

11. In a certain language, (a) 'go ju mi' stands for 'plenty of money'; (b) pao ju go nei vu' for 'money creates lots of problems'; (c) 'kol vu nei' for 'problems create tension'; and (d) 'sol tun ju haw' for 'still money is needed'. Which of the following words stand for 'money'?

(*a*) nei (*b*) ju
(*c*) haw (*d*) go

12. In a certain language, (a) 'FOR' stands for 'old is gold'; (b) 'ROT' stands for 'gold is pure'; (c) 'ROM' stands for 'gold is costly'. How will 'pure old gold is costly' be written?
(*a*) TFROM (*b*) FOTRM
(*c*) FTORM (*d*) TOMRF

13. In a certain code '415' means 'milk is hot'; '18' means 'hot soup'; and '895' means 'soup is tasty'. What number will indicate the word 'tasty'?
(*a*) 9 (*b*) 8
(*c*) 5 (*d*) 4

14. In a certain code '643' means 'she is beautiful', '593' means 'he is handsome', and '567' means 'handsome meets beautiful'. What number will indicate the word 'meets'?
(*a*) 5 (*b*) 3
(*c*) 7 (*d*) 6

15. In a certain code language, (a) 'dugo hui mul zo' stands for 'work is very hard'; (b) 'hui dugo ba ki' for 'Bingo is very smart'; (c) 'nano mul dugo' for 'cake is hard', and (d) 'mul ki qu' for 'smart and hard'. Which of the following words stand for 'Bingo'?
(*a*) jalu (*b*) dugo
(*c*) ki (*d*) ba

Directions (Qs. 16 to 20): *Read the given coded information and choose the correct answer from the given options.*

16. If 'water' is called 'blue', 'blue' is called 'red', 'red' is called 'white', 'white' is called 'sky', 'sky' is called 'rain', 'rain' is called 'green', 'green' is called 'air' and 'air' is called 'table', which of the following is the colour of milk?
(*a*) white (*b*) rain
(*c*) sky (*d*) green

17. If 'light' is called 'dark', 'dark' is called 'green', 'green' is called 'blue', 'blue' is called 'red', 'red' is called 'white' and 'white' is called 'yellow', what is the colour of blood?
(*a*) red (*b*) dark
(*c*) white (*d*) yellow

18. If 'sky' is called 'sea', 'sea' is called 'water', 'water' is called 'air', 'air' is called 'cloud' and 'cloud' is called 'river', then what do we drink when thirsty?
(*a*) sky (*b*) air
(*c*) water (*d*) sea

19. If 'yellow' means 'red', 'white' means 'green', 'red' means 'orange', 'blue' means 'white' and 'green' means 'blue', then the colour of sky is :
(*a*) white (*b*) green
(*c*) blue (*d*) yellow

20. If 'land' is called 'sky', 'sky' is called 'air', 'air' is called 'water', 'water' is called 'sand' and 'sand' is called 'solid', where do fishes swim?
(*a*) air (*b*) sky
(*c*) water (*d*) sand

ANSWERS

1	2	3	4	5	6	7	8	9	10
(*d*)	(*d*)	(*a*)	(*b*)	(*b*)	(*b*)	(*a*)	(*c*)	(*b*)	(*c*)
11	**12**	**13**	**14**	**15**	**16**	**17**	**18**	**19**	**20**
(*b*)	(*a*)	(*a*)	(*c*)	(*d*)	(*c*)	(*c*)	(*b*)	(*a*)	(*d*)

SOME SELECTED EXPLANATORY ANSWERS

4. Alphabet whose codes are given

w → a
s → r
r → w

All other alphabet will remain unchanged, so, 'answer' will be coded as :

a n s w e r   a n r a e w

5. The coded number signifies the position of the alphabet in its reverse order of the alphabetical series (ZYXW...)

M U S K → MUSK
↓ ↓ ↓ ↓
14th 6th 8th 16th → 146816

Similarly,

Z E R O → ZERO
↓ ↓ ↓ ↓
1st 22nd 9th 12th → 122912

6. The letters of the word TRIBAL are picked from LIBERATE. So will be the coded numbers.

L I B E R A T E → given word
5 6 4 0 3 1 7 0 → codes

Similarly,

T R I B A L → word to be coded
7 3 6 4 1 5 → answer codes

7. The numbers represent letters and to find the answer, select the respective letters.

3 4 1 7 8 2 0 5 9 6 → codes
M O N K E Y R A G S → letters

So,

7 5 1 9 5 0 4 4 → codes
K A N G A R O O → answer letters

8. The letters of the words are coded by substituted letters. To find the answer codes, select the respective substituted letters.

A D D S U M T O T A L → letters
W O O Q J M K P K W X → sub-stituted letters codes

So,

T O A D S → letters
K P W O Q → substituted answer letter codes

10. The letters of the word are coded by the numbers representing their position in the natural series.

D A Z E → letters
4 1 26 5 → position of letters in natural series

Similarly,
BOY → letters
2 15 25 → position of letters in natural series

11. *Code* / *Sentence*

Code	Sentence
1. go *ju* mi	plenty of *money*
2. pao *ju* go nei vu	*money* creates lots of problems
3. kol vu nei	problems create tension
4. sol tun *ju* haw	still *money* is needed

In 1st, 2nd and 4th codes and their sentences the word 'ju' is repeated and so is 'money'.

13.

Code	Sentence
1. 415	milk is hot
2. 18	hot soup
3. 895	soup is *tasty*

From 3rd code and its sentence neither number '9' is repeated nor the word 'tasty'.

15.

Code	Sentence
1. *dugo hui* mul zo	work *is very* hard
2. *hui dugo* **ba** *ki*	**Bingo** *is very smart*
3. nano mul *dugo*	cake is *hard*
4. mul *ki* qu	*smart* and hard

From 2nd code and its sentence, neither 'ba' nor 'Bingo' is repeated. (Words repeated are in italics)

16. Colour of milk is 'white' and 'white' is called 'sky'.

17. Colour of blood is 'red' and 'red' is called 'white'.

18. We drink 'water' when we are thirsty and 'water' is called 'air'.

19. Colour of sky is 'blue' and 'blue' means 'white'.

20. Fishes swim in 'water' and 'water' is called 'sand'.

❑❑❑

5

Direction Sense

In these type of tests, the directions in questions needs to be perceived. Such questions are based on the direction chart.

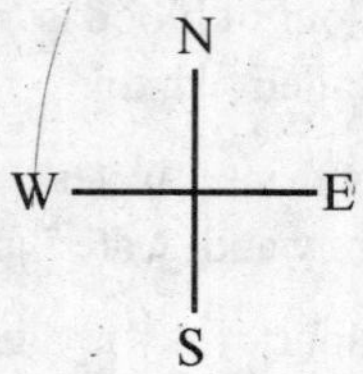

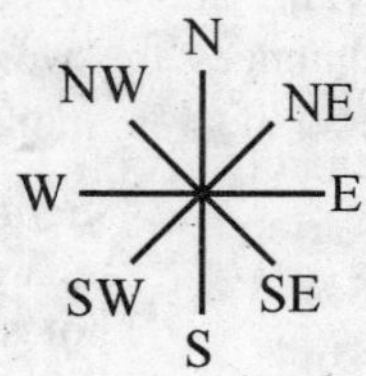

N = North S = South E = East W = West

The sense of the different directions are guided by the left and right turns or angular turns.

EXERCISE

Directions : *In the following questions, select the right answer from the given options to depict the correct direction/ distance.*

1. A man travels 100 km towards South. From there he turns right and travels 100 km and again turns right to travel 50 km. Which direction is he in from his starting point?
(*a*) North (*b*) North-East
(*c*) East (*d*) South-West

2. A train runs 120 km in West direction, 30 km in South direction and then 80 km in east direction before reaching the station. In which direction is the station from the train's starting point?
(*a*) South-West (*b*) North-West
(*c*) South-East (*d*) South

3. Facing the West direction, Priya jogs for 20 m, turns left and goes further 40 m. She turns left again and jogs for 20 m. Then she turns right to go 20 m to reach the park. How far is the park from her starting point and in which direction?

(*a*) 20 m South (*b*) 40 m West
(*c*) 60 m South (*d*) 100 m East

4. If all the directions are rotated, *i.e.,* if North is changed to West and East to North and so on, then what will come in place of North-West?
(*a*) South-West (*b*) North-East
(*c*) East-North (*d*) East-West

5. A and B start together from one point. They walk 10 km towards North. A turns left and covers 5 km whereas B turns right and covers 3 km. A turns left again and covers 15 km whereas B turns right and covers his 15 km. How far is A from B?
(*a*) 18 km (*b*) 10 km
(*c*) 5 km (*d*) 8 km

6. Tarun is walking towards East. What direction he should not follow if he should walk towards North?
(*a*) right, right, left, right, right
(*b*) right, right, left, left, left
(*c*) right, right, right
(*d*) right, left, right, left

7. Sony and Moni start walking from a point. Sony walks in West direction and Moni in South direction. After covering 20 km, Soni turns left and walks 15 km. Moni walks 10 km, turns left and walks 5 km. Soni, then turns left again and walks 25 km, whereas Moni turns right and walks 5 km. How far are Sony and Moni from each other?
(*a*) 5 km
(*b*) They are back at the starting point
(*c*) They are at same place at the finishing point
(*d*) Data is insufficient

8. I was walking in South-East direction. After a while I turned 90° to the right and walked ahead. Later I turned 45° to the right. In which direction am I walking now?
(*a*) North (*b*) North-East
(*c*) South-West (*d*) East

9. Two friends Jack and Bunny start a race, and together they run for 50 mts. Jack turns right and runs 60 mts while Bunny turns left and runs 40 mts. Then Jack turns left and runs 50 mts while Bunny turns right and runs 50 mts. How far are the two friends now from each other?
(*a*) 60 mts (*b*) 100 mts
(*c*) 20 mts (*d*) 150 mts

10. A policeman left his police post and proceeded south 4 km, after hearing a loud sound from point A. On reaching the place he heard another sound and proceeded 4 km to his left to the point B, only to find that the sound was coming from left of B. From B he proceeded left to reach that place 4 km away. In which direction he has to go to reach his police post?
(*a*) North (*b*) South
(*c*) East (*d*) West

ANSWERS

1	2	3	4	5	6	7	8	9	10
(*d*)	(*a*)	(*c*)	(*a*)	(*d*)	(*d*)	(*c*)	(*a*)	(*b*)	(*d*)

SOME SELECTED EXPLANATORY ANSWERS

2.

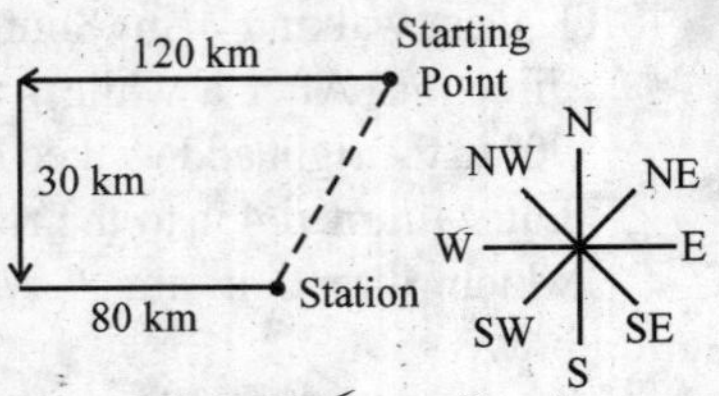

3. $(40 + 20) = 60$ metres South

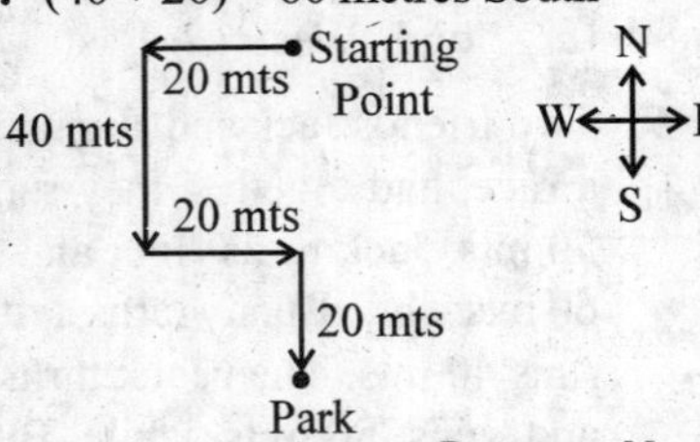

5.

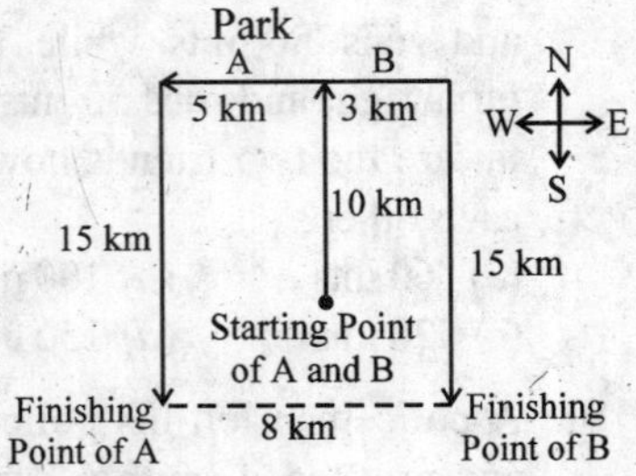

6.

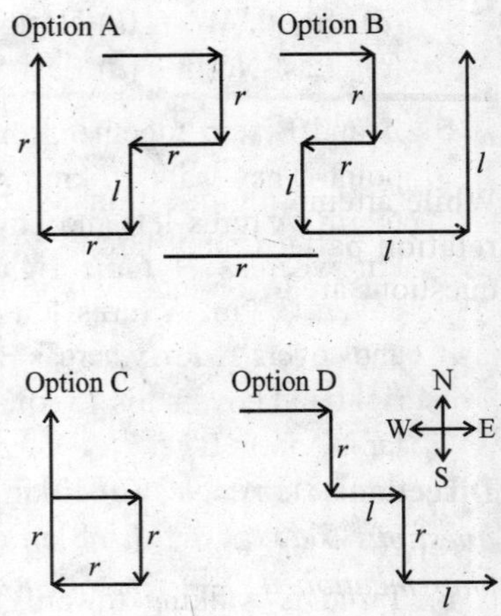

10.

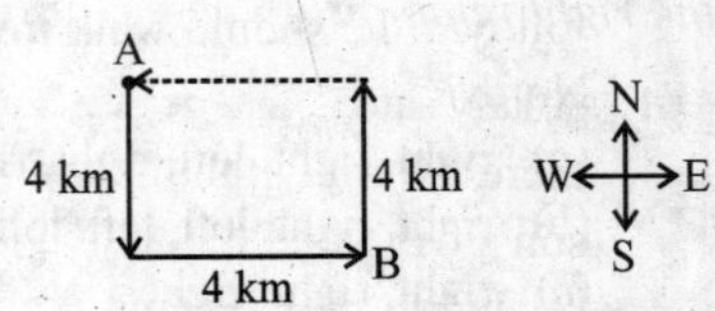

6

Blood Relations

While attempting questions on blood relations, one should be clear of all the relation patterns that can exist between any two individuals. These type of questions are given mainly to test one's relationship ability.

EXERCISE

Directions : *In each of the following questions keenly study the relationship mentioned between the persons, and then from the given options select the right relationship as the answer.*

1. A lady said, "The person standing there is my grandfather's only son's daughter". How is the lady related to the standing person?
(*a*) Sister (*b*) Mother
(*c*) Aunt (*d*) Cousin

2. Ajay is the brother of Vijay. Mili is the sister of Ajay. Sanjay is the brother of Rahul and Mehul is the daughter of Vijay. Who is Sanjay's Uncle?
(*a*) Rahul
(*b*) Ajay
(*c*) Mehul
(*d*) Data inadequate

3. A man introduced the boy coming with him as "He is son of the father of my wife's daughter". What relation did the boy bear to the man?
(*a*) Son-in-law (*b*) Son
(*c*) Brother (*d*) Father

4. If Amit's father is Billoo's father's only son and Billoo has neither a brother nor a daughter, what is the relationship between Amit and Billoo?
(*a*) Uncle — Nephew
(*b*) Father — Daughter
(*c*) Father — Son
(*d*) Cousins

5. Pointing to a woman in the photograph a man said, "She is the daughter of my grandmother's only son. How is the woman related to the man?

(*a*) Mother
(*b*) Daughter
(*c*) Sister-in-law
(*d*) Sister

6. Pointing to a photograph, a woman said, "She is the only daughter of my mother's father." How is the woman related to the person in the photograph?
(*a*) Mother
(*b*) Grandmother
(*c*) Daughter
(*d*) Cannot be determined

7. Ram is the brother of Shyam and Mahesh is the father of Ram. Jagat is the brother of Priya and Priya is daughter of Shyam. Who is the uncle of Jagat ?
(*a*) Shyam
(*b*) Mahesh
(*c*) Ram
(*d*) Data insufficient

8. Introducing a man, a woman said, "His wife is the only daughter of my father". How is the man related to the woman?
(*a*) Husband
(*b*) Father
(*c*) Father-in-law
(*d*) Brother

9. If Maya is the only daughter of Richa's grandmother's brother, how is Maya's daughter related to Richa?
(*a*) Niece (*b*) Cousin
(*c*) Aunt (*d*) Mother

10. Pointing to a woman, a man said, "Her husband's mother is the wife of my father's only son". How is the man related to the woman?
(*a*) Son
(*b*) Brother-in-law
(*c*) Uncle
(*d*) Father-in-law

ANSWERS

1	2	3	4	5	6	7	8	9	10
(*a*)	(*d*)	(*b*)	(*c*)	(*d*)	(*c*)	(*c*)	(*a*)	(*b*)	(*d*)

SOME SELECTED EXPLANATORY ANSWERS

2. 1. Mili —(sister)→ Ajay —(brother)→ Vijay
Vijay ↓ Mehul (daughter)

2. Sanjay —(brother)→ Rahul

There are two sets of relationship. Information given is incomplete and no relation can be established between the two sets.

3. The relationship chart based on problem is :

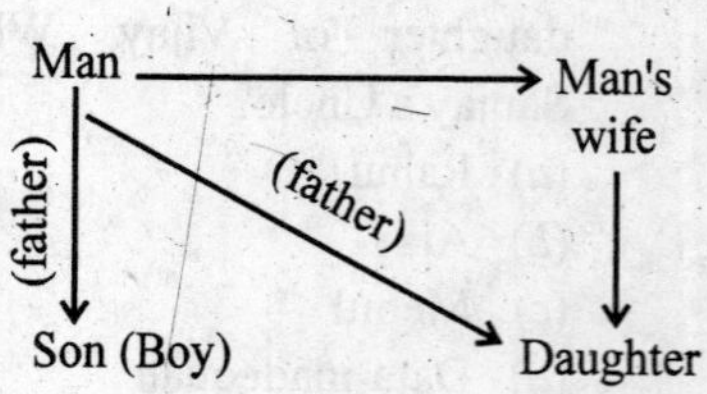

'Father of the man's wife's daughter' is the man himself and the boy in question is the man's son.

5.

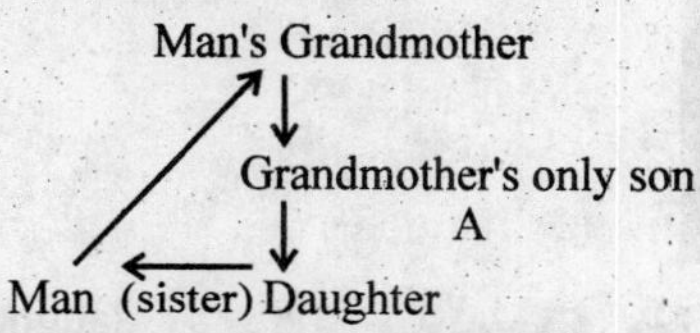

'My grandmother's only son' is the father of the man, and 'daughter of my grandmother's only son' is the sister of the man.

6.

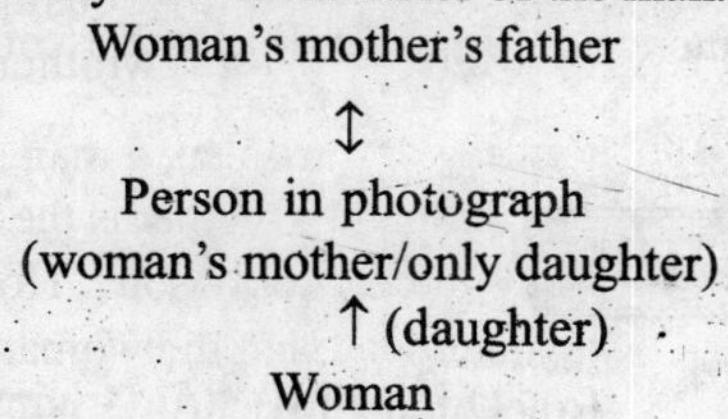

'Only daughter of my mother's father' is the person in the photograph and she is also the mother of the woman. So, the woman is the daughter of the person in the photograph.

8.

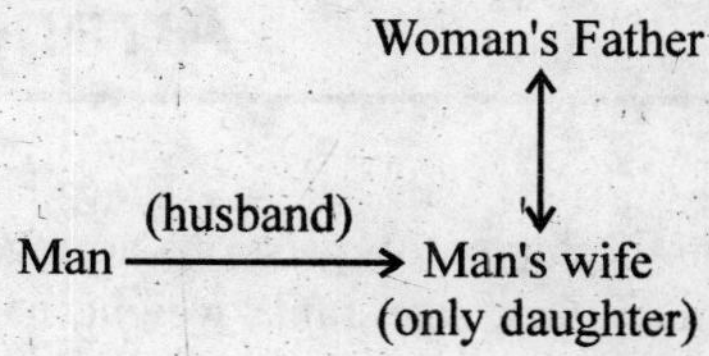

'Only daughter of my father' is the woman herself and the man is her husband.

❑❑❑

7

Arranging in Order

In these type of questions arrangement of given options is done on the basis of dictionary, size, rank, weight, natural sequence etc in ascending or descending order.

EXERCISE

1. If the following words are arranged in natural order, what will come in the last place in ascending order?

1. Captain
2. Brigadier
3. Major
4. Lieutenant-General
5. Lieutenant

(*a*) Lientenant-General
(*b*) Brigadier
(*c*) Captain
(*d*) Major

2. If these words are arranged according to dictionary then what word will come in the third place?

1. Originality
2. Originally
3. Originator
4. Original
5. Originate

(*a*) Originality (*b*) Originator
(*c*) Originate (*d*) Originally

3. What will be the natural order of the following?

1. Independence Day
2. Christmas
3. Diwali
4. Holi
5. Republic Day

(*a*) 5 4 1 3 2 (*b*) 5 1 4 3 2
(*c*) 4 1 5 3 2 (*d*) 2 3 4 1 5

4. If the following words are arranged in ascending order what word will be in the fourth place?

1. Air commodore
2. Wing Commander
3. Pilot Officer
4. Squadron Leader
5. Air Marshal

(*a*) Air Marshal
(*b*) Air Commodore

(*c*) Wing Commander
(*d*) Pilot Officer

5. What will be the natural order of the following words according to size?

1. Dog 2. Horse
3. Ant 4. Giraffe
5. Mouse

(*a*) 3 5 1 2 4 (*b*) 3 1 5 2 4
(*c*) 3 5 1 4 2 (*d*) 3 5 2 1 4

ANSWERS

1	2	3	4	5
(*a*)	(*d*)	(*a*)	(*b*)	(*a*)

SOME SELECTED EXPLANATORY ANSWERS

1. The arrangement of ranks in ascending order is—Lieutenant, Captain, Major, Brigadier, **Lieutenant-General.**

2. The dictionary order of words is–Original, Originality, **Originally,** Originate, Originator.

3. The natural order of National Holidays in Calendar is—Republic Day (January), Holi (March), Independence Day (August), Diwali (October/November), Christmas (December).

4. The arrangement of ranks in ascending order is—Pilot Officer, Squadron Leader, Wing Commander, **Air Commodore,** Air Marshal.

5. The natural order of living beings according to increasing size is—Ant, Mouse, Dog, Horse, Giraffe.

□□□

8

Calendar, Clock & Time

These are mathematical problem based on calculations of time by a clock or calendar and computations of speed or distances.

EXERCISE

1. If the day before yesterday was Thursday, when will Sunday be?
   (*a*) Tomorrow
   (*b*) Day after tomorrow
   (*c*) Today
   (*d*) Two days after today
2. Radha remembers that her father's birthday is after 16th but before 21st of March, while her brother Mangesh remembers that his father's birthday is before 22nd but after 19th of March. On which date is the birthday of their father?
   (*a*) 19th
   (*b*) 20th
   (*c*) 21st
   (*d*) Cannot be determined
3. A clock is so placed that at 12 noon its minute hand points towards north-east. In which direction does its hour hand point at 1.30 P.M.?
   (*a*) East (*b*) West
   (*c*) North (*d*) South
4. A couple married in 1980 had two children, one in 1982 and the other in 1984. Their combined ages will equal the years of the marriage in?
   (*a*) 1986 (*b*) 1985
   (*c*) 1987 (*d*) 1988
5. Manoj left home for the bus stop 15 minutes earlier than the usual time. It takes 10 minutes to reach the stop. He reached the stop at 8.40 a.m. What time does he usually leave home for the bus stop?
   (*a*) 8.30 a.m.
   (*b*) 8.55 a.m.
   (*c*) 8.45 p.m.
   (*d*) None of these
6. If the third day of a month is Monday, which of the following

will be the fifth day from 21st of that month?

(*a*) Tuesday (*b*) Monday
(*c*) Wednesday (*d*) Thursday

7. Keshav runs a factory in three shifts of eight hours each with 210 employees. In each shift minimum of 80 employees are required to run the factory effectively. No employee can be allowed to work for more than 16 hours a day. At least how many employees will be required to work for 16 hours every day?

(*a*) 30
(*b*) 60
(*c*) Data inadequate
(*d*) None of these

8. A clock shows the time as 3 : 30 p.m. If the minute hand gains 2 minutes every hour, how many minutes will the clock gain by 4 a.m.?

(*a*) 23 Minutes (*b*) 24 Minutes
(*c*) 25 Minutes (*d*) 26 Minutes

9. A train started from station 'A' and proceeded towards station 'B' at a speed of 48 km/hr. Forty-five minutes later another train started from station 'B' and proceeded towards station 'A' at 50 km/hr. If the distance between the two stations is 232 km, at what distance from station 'A' will the trains meet?

(*a*) 132 km (*b*) 144 km
(*c*) 108 km (*d*) 160 km

10. My uncle shall visit me after 64 days of my father's birthday. If my father's birthday falls on Tuesday, what shall be the day on my Uncle's visit?

(*a*) Wednesday (*b*) Sunday
(*c*) Tuesday (*d*) Monday

ANSWERS

1	2	3	4	5	6	7	8	9	10
(*a*)	(*b*)	(*a*)	(*a*)	(*d*)	(*c*)	(*d*)	(*c*)	(*a*)	(*a*)

SOME SELECTED EXPLANATORY ANSWERS

1. Thursday – Day-before-yesterday
Friday – Yesterday
Saturday – Today
Sunday – Tomorrow

4. 1982 – 2 years later – 1st child
1984 – 4 years later – 2nd child
Total age of children — 2 years.
1985 — 5 years later — Total age of children : 4 years.
1986 — 6 years later — Total age of children : 6 years.

5. Manoj reached the bus stop at 8.40 a.m. He left his home at 8:40 – 10 minutes = 8:30 a.m. He left 15 minutes earlier than usual, so his actual time of leaving home is 8:30 am + 15 minutes = 8:45 a.m.

6. 3rd day of the month is Monday
5th day from 21st is 26th
$26 - 3 = 23$ days
23 days later, 23/7 leaves 2 days.
So, two days ahead of Monday will be Wednesday.

8. Hours between 3:30 p.m. and 4 a.m. are — 12½ hours. Number of minutes gained will be $12\frac{1}{2} \times 2 = 25$ minutes.

9. $\xleftarrow{\quad d \quad}\!\!\!\rightarrow | \xleftarrow{\quad 232 - d \quad}\!\!\!\rightarrow$

i.e., $\dfrac{d}{48} = \dfrac{232 - d}{50} + \dfrac{3}{4}$

$$\frac{d}{48} = \frac{464 - 2d + 75}{100}$$

$$100\,d = (539 - 2d)\,48$$

$$100\,d = 25872 - 96\,d$$

$$196\,d = 25872$$

$$d = 25872 \div 196 = 132 \text{ km.}$$

10. My father's birthday is on Tuesday.
$64 \div 7$ gives 1 as remainder
So, 63rd day will be Tuesday and one day ahead is the day when uncle shall visit *i.e.,* on Wednesday.

□□□

9

Rows and Ranks

These type of problems need easy calculations to find out the number of objects in a row, lane or queue or to find a person's rank in a class of certain number of students; or to find the total number of students.

EXERCISE

1. Mahesh and Suresh are ranked 11th and 12th respectively from the top in a class of 41 students. What will be their respective ranks from the bottom?
   (*a*) 32nd and 33rd
   (*b*) 29th and 30th
   (*c*) 30th and 31st
   (*d*) 31st and 30th
2. Uma ranked 8th from the top and 37th from bottom in a class. How many students are there in the class?
   (*a*) 47 (*b*) 46
   (*c*) 45 (*d*) None of these
3. In a queue, Sadiq is 14th from the front and Joseph is 17th from the end, while Jane is in between Sadiq and Joseph. If Sadiq be ahead of Joseph and there be 48 persons in the queue, how many persons are there between Sadiq and Jane?
   (*a*) 5 (*b*) 6
   (*c*) 7 (*d*) 8
4. Rohan ranked eleventh from the top and twenty-seventh from the bottom among the students who passed the annual examination in a class. If the number of students who failed in the examination was 12, how many students appeared for the examination?
   (*a*) 48
   (*b*) 49
   (*c*) 50
   (*d*) Cannot be determined
5. Some boys are sitting in a row. P is sitting fourteenth from the left and Q is seventh from the right. If there are four boys between P and Q, how many boys are there in the row?
   (*a*) 19 (*b*) 21
   (*c*) 25 (*d*) 23

ANSWERS

1	2	3	4	5
(*d*)	(*d*)	(*c*)	(*b*)	(*c*)

SOME SELECTED EXPLANATORY ANSWERS

2.

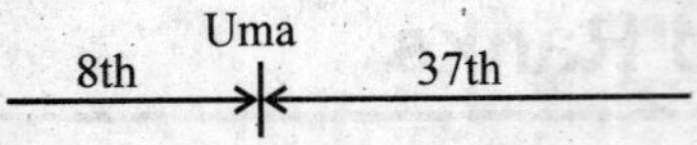

Total number of students in the class are :
$(8 + 37) - 1 = 44.$

4.

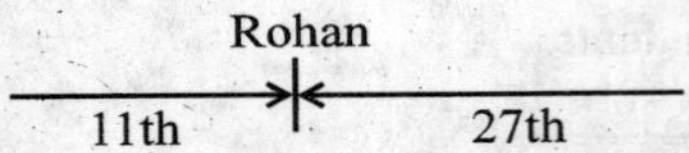

Number of students who passed the examination $(11 + 27) - 1 = 37$

Those who failed = 12

Total number of students who appeared in the examination
$= 37 + 12 = 49.$

5.

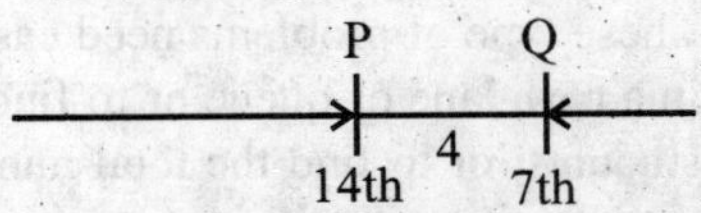

The number of boys in the row are :
$(14 + 4 + 7) = 25.$

□□□

10

Symbol Substitution

Questions in these category are easy to attempt. Candidates must be quick in substituting symbols and calculations. The common pattern of questions asked are given below.

EXERCISE

1. If '✱' denotes '×', 'Δ' denotes '÷', '□' denotes '–', '●' denotes '+', 'α' denotes '=' and 'β' denotes ≠, then which of the following euations is correct?

(*a*) 2 □ 10 ✱ 4 Δ 5 α 5 ● 12 Δ 6
(*b*) 27 Δ 9 ● 6 β 3 ✱ 6 □ 9
(*c*) 4 Δ 2 ✱ 0 α 7 Δ 1 ✱ 0
(*d*) 5 ● 6 Δ 3 □ 2 α 8 Δ 4 ✱ 3

2. If ↓ stands for '÷', ↑ stands for '×', → stands for '+' and ← stands for '–', then

25 ↓ 5 → 3 ↑ 6 ← 8 = ?

(*a*) 9 (*b*) 12
(*c*) 16 (*d*) 15

3. If the + and × signs of the following equations are interchanged, which will be the correct equation?

(*a*) $7 \times 5 + 3 = 20$
(*b*) $4 + 9 \times 1 = 42$
(*c*) $6 \times 5 + 8 = 46$
(*d*) $2 + 11 \times 4 = 28$

4. If '+' stands for multiplication, '×' stands for addition, '÷' stands for subtraction and '–' stands for division, then what will be the result of the following equation?

$7 \times 4 \div 10 \times 2 + 5 = ?$

(*a*) 7 (*b*) 0
(*c*) 11 (*d*) 15

5. If 'A' means '÷', 'B' means '+', 'C' means '×' and 'D' means '–', then

12 C 4 A 24 D 10 B 1 = ?

(*a*) $11\frac{1}{3}$ (*b*) 23
(*c*) –7 (*d*) $16\frac{4}{5}$

Directions (Qs. 6 to 8): *Find out the one word among the options which* *cannot be formed by using the letters of the word as given in each question.*

6. ROTATION
(*a*) TORN (*b*) NOTE
(*c*) TART (*d*) RAIN

7. PHILOSOPHY
(*a*) SOIL (*b*) SHIP
(*c*) SOLO (*d*) SPIN

8. SLAVATION
(*a*) SNORT (*b*) LATVIA
(*c*) SALIVA (*d*) AVAIL

Directions (Qs. 9 and 10): *Find out the one word among the options which can be formed by using the letters of the word as given in each question.*

9. INVESTIGATE
(*a*) INVERT (*b*) GLIDE
(*c*) STING (*d*) ACTED

10. MAJORITY
(*a*) MORE (*b*) JURY
(*c*) READ (*d*) TRAY

ANSWERS

1	2	3	4	5	6	7	8	9	10
(*c*)	(*d*)	(*c*)	(*c*)	(*c*)	(*b*)	(*d*)	(*a*)	(*c*)	(*d*)

SOME SELECTED EXPLANATORY ANSWERS

2. $25 \div 5 + 3 \times 6 - 8$
$5 + 18 - 8 = 15$

3. After interchanging the signs the equations are :
(*a*) $7 + 5 \times 3 = 22$ which is wrong
(*b*) $4 \times 9 + 1 = 37$ which is wrong
(*c*) $6 + 5 \times 8 = 46$ which is correct
(*d*) $2 \times 11 + 4 = 26$ which is wrong

4. $7 + 4 - 10 + 2 \times 5$
$7 + 4 - 10 + 10 = 11$

5. $12 \times 4 \div 24 - 10 + 1$
$2 - 10 + 1 = -7$

□□□

11

Statement Analysis

In these type of questions, a few statements are given. Certain facts are broken up and mentioned in these statements. What is required is to analyse the statements, arrange and sort out the given facts and then answer the questions related to the given statements.

EXERCISE

1. Among five friends, A is heavier than B; C is lighter than D; B is lighter than D but heavier than E. Who among them is the heaviest?
   (*a*) B (*b*) C
   (*c*) A (*d*) Can't say
2. Pune is bigger than Jhansi, Sitapur is bigger than Chittor. Raigarh is not as big as Jhansi, but is bigger than Sitapur. Chittor is not as big as Sitapur. Which is the smallest?
   (*a*) Jhansi (*b*) Pune
   (*c*) Chittor (*d*) Sitapur
3. Ajay works more than Ram. Alok works as much as Raju. Pankaj works less than Alok. Ram works more than Alok. Who works the most of all?
   (*a*) Ajay (*b*) Ram
   (*c*) Alok (*d*) Raju
4. Among five friends P, Q, R, S and T, who is the youngest? To arrive at the answer which of the following information given in the statements (A) and (B) is sufficient?
   (A) R is younger than P and T.
   (B) S is younger than Q.
   (*a*) Only A alone is sufficient
   (*b*) Either A or B is sufficient
   (*c*) Both A and B together are needed
   (*d*) Both A and B together are not sufficient
5. A is elder to B while C and D are elder to E who lies between A and B. If C be elder to B, which one of the following statements is necessarily true?
   (*a*) E is elder to B
   (*b*) A is elder to C
   (*c*) C is elder to D
   (*d*) D is elder to C

Directions (Qs. 6 and 7) : *Read the following directions and answer the questions given below :*

There are five persons in a group. Out of these two are men. Only three persons know swimming, of which one is a man. There is a couple, of which the husband knows swimming. A is the younger sister of D and B is the husband of E. C is a swimming champion.

6. The two women who know how to swim are:

(*a*) A and C (*b*) C and D
(*c*) D and E (*d*) A and E

7. The two persons who do not know how to swim are :

(*a*) B and D (*b*) D and E
(*c*) A and E (*d*) A and D

Directions (Qs. 8 to 10) : *Read the following statements and answer the questions given below :*

Rajat, Sushil and Nagesh play football, hockey and cricket. Rajat, Ramu and Nagesh play hockey, cricket and basketball. Rajat, Sushil, Mayank and Nagesh play football and cricket.

8. Which game is played by all the boys?

(*a*) Hockey (*b*) Basketball
(*c*) Football (*d*) Cricket

9. Who does not play football?

(*a*) Rajat (*b*) Nagesh
(*c*) Sushil (*d*) Ramu

10. Which of the following two boys play all the games?

(*a*) Nagesh, Rajat
(*b*) Mayank, Ramu
(*c*) Ramu, Nagesh
(*d*) Sushil, Mayank

Directions (Qs. 11 to 15) : *Read the following information and answer the questions given below:*

(*i*) P, Q, R, S, T and U are six members in a family in which there are two married couples.
(*ii*) T a teacher is married to the doctor who is mother of R and U.
(*iii*) Q the lawyer is married to P.
(*iv*) P has one son and one grandson.
(*v*) Of the two married ladies one is a housewife.
(*vi*) There is also one student and one male engineer in the family.

11. Who among the following is the housewife?

(*a*) Q (*b*) P
(*c*) S (*d*) T

12. Which of the following represents the group of females in the family?

(*a*) QTR
(*b*) PSR
(*c*) PSU
(*d*) Data inadequate

13. Which of the following is true about the granddaughter in the family?

(*a*) She is a student
(*b*) She is an engineer
(*c*) She is a lawyer
(*d*) Data Inadequate

14. How R is related to U?
(*a*) Brother
(*b*) Sister
(*c*) Brother and Sister
(*d*) Data inadequate

15. How is P related to R?
(*a*) Grandfather
(*b*) Mother
(*c*) Sister
(*d*) Grandmother

ANSWERS

1	2	3	4	5	6	7	8	9	10
(*d*)	(*c*)	(*a*)	(*d*)	(*a*)	(*a*)	(*b*)	(*d*)	(*d*)	(*a*)
11	**12**	**13**	**14**	**15**					
(*b*)	(*d*)	(*a*)	(*c*)	(*d*)					

SOME SELECTED EXPLANATORY ANSWERS

1. The five friends in descending order of weight are : A/D, B/C, E or A/D, B, C/E. Either A or D is the heaviest.

2. The order of cities in descending order of size is : Pune, Jhansi, Raigarh, Sitapur, Chittor.

3. On the basis of doing work, the descending order will be : Ajay, Ram, Alok/Raju, Pankaj.

4. Statements are not inter-related.

5. The order in descending seniority will be : A/C/D, E, B.

Chart for Answers 8 to 10

Boy	*Games Played*
Rajat	Football, Hockey, Cricket, Basketball
Sushil	Football, Hockey, Cricket, Basketball
Nagesh	Football, Hockey, Cricket, Basketball
Ramu	Hockey, Cricket, Basketball
Mayank	Football, Cricket

Chart for Answers 11 to 15

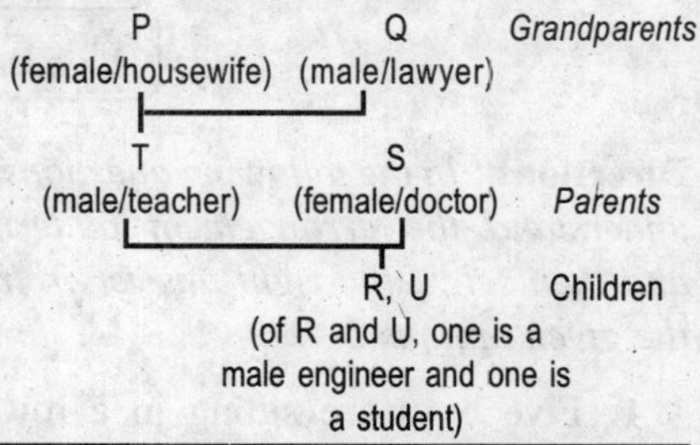

11. One married lady S who is mother of R and U is a doctor. Q the lawyer is married to P. Of the two married ladies one is a house-wife. As Q is a lawyer the other married lady who is a housewife should be P.

12. Sex of R and U is not given.

13. P has one son T and one grandson either R or U one of whom is an engineer. So, the granddaughter is a student.

14. Sex of R and U is not given, but as both are children of S and one is a male engineer, the relationship between the two is of brother and sister.

□□□

12

Place Arrangement

Place arrangement generally refers to the positioning of persons or objects in a manner indicated by set of information given. One has to understand the order of placement and then attempt questions following the given information.

EXERCISE

Directions : *In the following questions, understand the arrangement pattern and then select the right answer from the given options :*

1. Five boys are sitting in a row. Raghu is not adjacent to Shyam or Amit. Ajay is not adjacent to Shyam. Raghu is adjacent to Mayank. If Mayank is at the middle in the row, then Ajay is adjacent to whom out of the following?
   (*a*) Amit (*b*) Raghu
   (*c*) Mayank (*d*) Shyam
2. Mini is to the right of Rajni but to the left of Ananta. Saya is to the right of Mini but to the left of Jaya. Who is on the extreme left if all the girls are facing North?
   (*a*) Jaya (*b*) Mini
   (*c*) Rajni (*d*) Saya
3. O, P, Q, R, S and T are standing on a bench according to their height. P is taller than O but shorter than S. Only S is taller than T. R is shorter than P but taller than Q. Who is the shortest?
   (*a*) O
   (*b*) Q
   (*c*) P
   (*d*) Cannot be said
4. Five personalities are living in a multistoried building. Mr. Effortless lives in a flat above Mr. Active, Mr. Charge lives in a flat below Mr. Diligent, Mr. Active lives in a flat above Mr. Diligent and Mr. Behaved lives in a flat below Mr. Charge. Who lives in the topmost flat?

(*a*) Mr. Charge
(*b*) Mr. Diligent
(*c*) Mr. Effortless
(*d*) Mr. Behaved

5. Six friends are sitting in a circle and playing cards. Kenny is to the left of Danny. Michael is in-between Bob and John. Roger is in between Kenny and Bob. Who is sitting to the right of Michael?
(*a*) Danny (*b*) John
(*c*) Kenny (*d*) Bob

6. Four girls A, B, C and D are sitting in a circle. B and C are facing each other. Which of the following is definitely true?
(*a*) A is to the left of C
(*b*) D is to the left of C
(*c*) A and D are facing each other
(*d*) A is not between B and C

7. Brijesh, Jayesh, Amar and Praveer are playing a game of cards. Amar is to the right of Jayesh who is to the right of Brijesh. Who is to the right of Amar?
(*a*) Brijesh
(*b*) Praveer
(*c*) Brijesh or Praveer
(*d*) Jayesh

8. In a pile of 10 books there are 3 of History, 3 of Hindi, 2 of Maths, and 2 of English. Taking from above there is an English book between a History and Maths book, a History book between a Maths and an English book, a Hindi book between an English and a Maths book, a Maths book between two Hindi books, and two Hindi books between a Maths and a History book. Book of which subject is at the sixth position from the top?
(*a*) English (*b*) Hindi
(*c*) History (*d*) Maths

9. Five persons A, B, C, D and E are sitting in a row facing you such that D is on the left of C and B is on the right of E. A is on the right of C and B is on the left of D. If E occupies a corner position, then who is sitting in the centre?
(*a*) A (*b*) B
(*c*) C (*d*) D

10. Six friends A, B, C, D, E and F are standing in a circle. B is between F and C; A is between E and D; F is to the left of D. Who is between A and F?
(*a*) C (*b*) B
(*c*) D (*d*) E

ANSWERS

1	2	3	4	5	6	7	8	9	10
(*b*)	(*c*)	(*d*)	(*c*)	(*d*)	(*c*)	(*b*)	(*b*)	(*d*)	(*c*)

SOME SELECTED EXPLANATORY ANSWERS

1. The order of sitting is :
Amit, Shyam, Mayank, Ajay, Raghu

or

Ajay, Raghu, Mayank, Amit, Shyam

4. The personalities living in flats in multi-storied building are in order given below :

Mr. Effortless

Mr. Active

Mr. Diligent

Mr. Charge

Mr. Behaved

6. The sitting positions are :

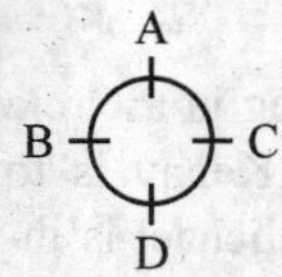

or

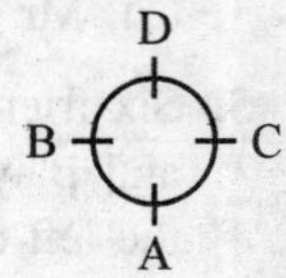

7. The order from left to right is :
Brijesh, Jayesh, Amar, Praveer

9. Sitting order while facing us is :
A, C, D, B, E

10. The pattern of standing is :

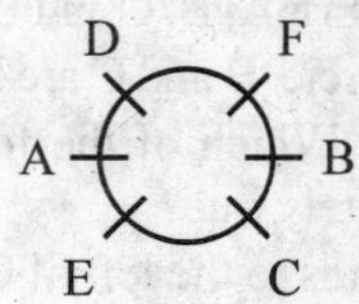

□□□

13

Missing Numbers

Playing with numbers and mathematical skills are needed to attempt these type of tests. The candidates have to work out the right combination of arithmetical symbols to arrive at the answer options which will take the place of the interrogation sign in the given questions.

EXERCISE

Directions : *In each question given below which one number can be placed at the sign of interrogation?*

1. 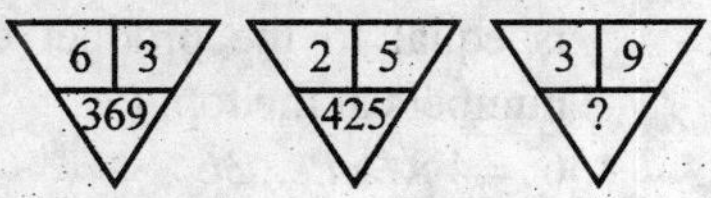

(*a*) 693 (*b*) 939
(*c*) 981 (*d*) 993

2. 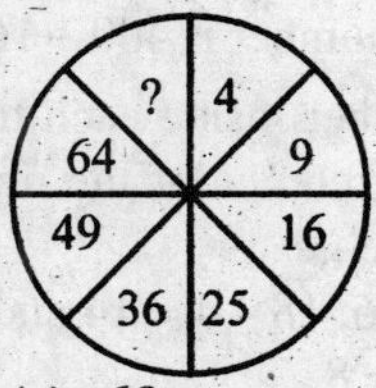

(*a*) 68 (*b*) 100
(*c*) 72 (*d*) 81

3. 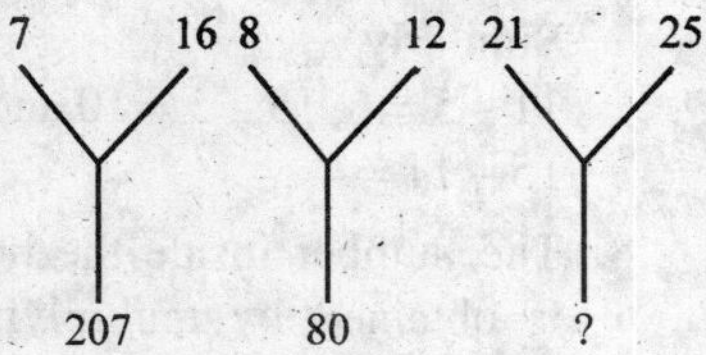

(*a*) 425 (*b*) 184
(*c*) 241 (*d*) 210

4.

14	9	4
12	7	2
10	5	0
16	11	?

(*a*) 9 (*b*) 6
(*c*) 3 (*d*) 7

5. 

(*a*) 69 (*b*) 49
(*c*) 50 (*d*) 60

6. 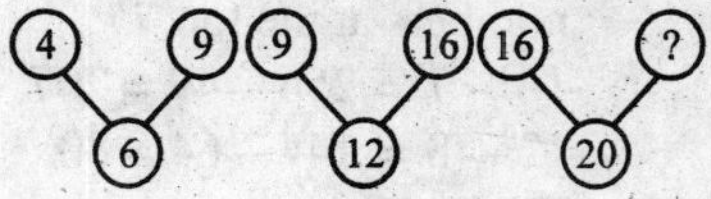

(*a*) 21 (*b*) 25
(*c*) 50 (*d*) 60

7. 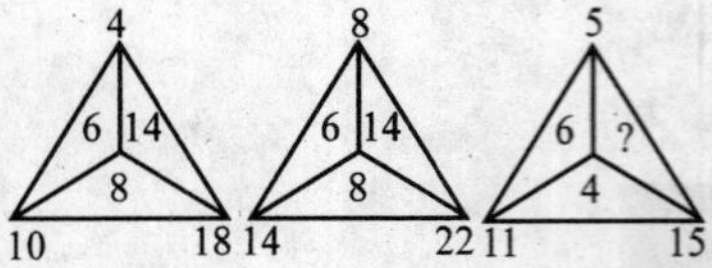

(*a*) 8 (*b*) 14
(*c*) 10 (*d*) 6

8. 42 (21) 22
78 (?) 84
162 (18) 99

(*a*) 12 (*b*) 13
(*c*) 60 (*d*) 72

9. 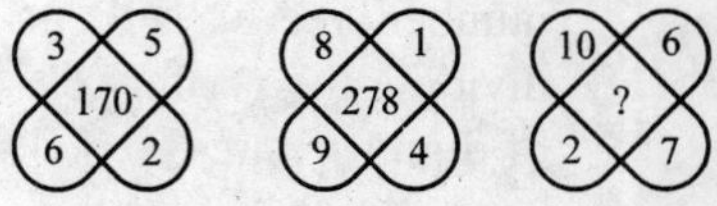

(*a*) 960 (*b*) 628
(*c*) 830 (*d*) 492

10. 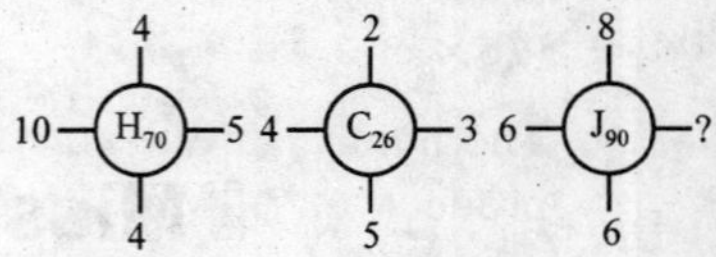

(*a*) 5 (*b*) 4
(*c*) 2 (*d*) 1

ANSWERS

1	2	3	4	5	6	7	8	9	10
(*c*)	(*d*)	(*b*)	(*b*)	(*a*)	(*b*)	(*c*)	(*b*)	(*c*)	(*b*)

SOME SELECTED EXPLANATORY ANSWERS

1. The squares of two numbers on the top placed side by side gives the number inside the bottom triangle, *i.e.*,
6^2 and $3^2 = 369$
2^2 and $5^2 = 425$, similarly
3^2 and $9^2 = 981$.

2. Starting from number 4 the numbers are the squares of numbers in natural order *i.e.*, $2^2 = 4, 3^2 = 9, 4^2 = 16 \ldots\ldots 9^2 = 81$.

3. The number at the bottom is the difference of the squares of two numbers at the top, *i.e.*,
$16^2 - 7^2 = 256 - 49 = 207$
$12^2 - 8^2 = 144 - 64 = 80$,
Similarly
$25^2 - 21^2 = 625 - 441 = 184$.

6. Square of number at the bottom is equal to the product of two numbers at the top, *i.e.*,
$6^2 = 4 \times 9$, *i.e.*, 36
$12^2 = 9 \times 16$, *i.e.*, 144, similarly
$20^2 = 16 \times ?$, *i.e.*, 400. The missing number is $400 \div 16 = 25$.

7. The number inside each triangle is the difference of the numbers at its base *i.e.*
$10 - 4 = 6$, $18 - 4 = 14$ and
$18 - 10 = 8$
$14 - 8 = 6$, $22 - 8 = 14$ and
$22 - 14 = 8$,
Similarly
$11 - 5 = 6$, $15 - 5 = 10$ and
$15 - 11 = 4$.

8. The number inside the brackets is obtained by multiplying the number on the left by 2 and then dividing the product by the sum of digits of number on the right, *i.e.*,

$(42 \times 2) \div (2 + 2) = 21$

$(162 \times 2) \div (9 + 9) = 18$, similarly

$(78 \times 2) \div (8 + 4) = 13$.

9. The number in the centre is the product of all the 4 numbers minus 10, *i.e.*,

$(3 \times 5 \times 2 \times 6) - 10 = 170$

$(8 \times 1 \times 4 \times 9) - 10 = 278$, Similarly,

$(10 \times 6 \times 7 \times 2) - 10 = 830$.

10. Letter H is 8th in order of alphabetical series. Taking the sum of numbers placed vertically outside the circle + 8; multiplying it by the number on the right; then subtracting from the product the number on the left, gives the number inside the circle, *i.e.*,

Step I $\rightarrow$ $4 + 8 + 4 = 16$

Step II $\rightarrow$ $16 \times 5 = 80$

Step III $\rightarrow$ $80 - 10 = 70$

Letter C is 3rd in order, so

Step I $\rightarrow$ $2 + 3 + 5 = 10$

Step II $\rightarrow$ $10 \times 3 = 30$

Step III $\rightarrow$ $30 - 4 = 26$

Similarly, J is 10th in order, so

Step I $\rightarrow$ $8 + 10 + 6 = 24$

Step II $\rightarrow$ $24 \times ?$

Step III $\rightarrow$ $(24 \times ?) - 6 = 90$

Simplifying the above equation :

$24 \times ? = 90 + 6$, *i.e.*, 96

$? = 96 \div 24 = 4$.

□□□

14

Matrices

In these type of questions, a set of numbers or letters are given in a figure which is divided into different cells. Some logic is applied to form a pattern in rows or columns. One of the cells is left empty. The candidates are required to analyse the logic and from the given options select one which will complete the given incomplete matrix.

EXERCISE

Directions (Qs. 1 to 5) : *In each question given below which one number when placed at the sign of interrogation shall complete the number matrix.*

1.

4	5	6
2	3	7
1	8	3
21	98	?

(*a*) 16 (*b*) 73
(*c*) 76 (*d*) 94

2.

3	6	8
5	8	4
4	7	?

(*a*) 9 (*b*) 8
(*c*) 7 (*d*) 6

3.

1	4	9	?
1	2	3	4
2	4	6	?

(*a*) 16 and 8 (*b*) 25 and 5
(*c*) 36 and 4 (*d*) 49 and 7

4.

7	16	9
5	21	16
9	?	4

(*a*) 29 (*b*) 21
(*c*) 13 (*d*) 42

5.

6	6	8
5	7	5
4	3	?
120	126	320

(*a*) 12 (*b*) 16
(*c*) 8 (*d*) 4

Directions (Qs. 6 to 10) : *In questions given below, a word is represented by only one set of numbers as given in any one of the alternatives. The sets of numbers given in the alternatives are represented by two classes of alphabets as in the 2 matrices given below. The columns and rows of matrix I are numbered from 0 to 4 and that of matrix II from 5 to 9. A letter from these matrices can be represented first by its row and next by column number. Identify the set for the word given in each question.*

6.

	0	1	2	3	4
0	E	A	T	S	H
1	A	H	T	A	S
2	E	H	A	S	T
3	H	E	A	T	S
4	S	H	T	A	E

	5	6	7	8	9
5	O	R	K	L	P
6	L	P	O	R	K
7	O	K	R	P	L
8	P	R	K	L	O
9	R	L	K	O	P

REAP

(*a*) 56, 00, 22, 59
(*b*) 68, 21, 22, 86
(*c*) 96, 00, 01, 99
(*d*) 86, 34, 24, 69

7.

	0	1	2	3	4
0	C	A	F	E	D
1	C	D	A	E	D
2	D	E	C	F	E
3	A	D	D	D	C
4	D	C	A	C	A

	5	6	7	8	9
5	T	R	R	S	M
6	S	T	M	R	S
7	R	S	P	T	P
8	P	S	T	R	T
9	P	M	P	M	S

FARM

(*a*) 02, 30, 85, 65
(*b*) 20, 31, 76, 68
(*c*) 23, 12, 68, 96
(*d*) 44, 43, 87, 57

8.

	0	1	2	3	4
0	C	H	H	N	N
1	I	N	C	B	B
2	N	E	C	H	I
3	I	C	N	E	I
4	B	B	E	C	I

	5	6	7	8	9
5	Y	P	S	P	K
6	K	T	S	R	R
7	K	Y	R	Y	Y
8	P	R	K	P	R
9	S	Y	S	T	S

PREY

(*a*) 82, 76, 34, 77
(*b*) 80, 70, 43, 12
(*c*) 94, 87, 43, 56
(*d*) 88, 77, 33, 79

9.

	0	1	2	3	4
0	D	K	A	E	C
1	C	D	K	A	E
2	K	C	E	A	D
3	K	C	D	E	A
4	E	D	A	K	C

	5	6	7	8	9
5	P	L	O	T	N
6	T	P	N	L	O
7	P	N	T	O	L
8	O	N	T	P	L
9	L	O	P	N	T

COLD

(*a*) 10, 85, 79, 24
(*b*) 31, 99, 77, 22
(*c*) 30, 66, 86, 43
(*d*) 44, 96, 95, 22

10.

	0	1	2	3	4
0	M	M	R	M	R
1	O	F	R	F	N
2	R	N	O	R	O
3	F	O	F	M	O
4	F	M	R	R	F

	5	6	7	8	9
5	T	G	J	T	G
6	P	J	G	G	U
7	U	T	P	T	J
8	U	T	T	J	P
9	G	U	G	T	P

TURF

(*a*) 57,86, 44, 11
(*b*) 86, 75, 20, 32
(*c*) 77, 68, 41, 44
(*d*) 89, 97, 12, 30

ANSWERS

1	2	3	4	5	6	7	8	9	10
(*d*)	(*d*)	(*a*)	(*c*)	(*c*)	(*a*)	(*c*)	(*d*)	(*a*)	(*b*)

SOME SELECTED EXPLANATORY ANSWERS

1. $4^2+2^2+1^2=21$, *i.e.,* $16+4+1=21$
$5^2+3^2+8^2=98$, *i.e.,* $25+9+64=98$
$6^2+7^2+3^2=36+49+9=94$.

2. Sum of numbers in each row is 17, *i.e.,*
$3+6+8 = 17$
$5+8+4 = 17$
So, $17-(4+7) = 6$.

4. $7+9 = 16$
$5+16 = 21$
$9+4 = 13$.

6. R is represented by row 5, column 6
E by row 0, column 0
A by row 2, column 2
P by row 5, column 9.

8. P is represented by row 8, column 8
R by row 7, column 7
E by row 3, column 3
Y by row 7, column 9.

9. C is represented by row 1, column 0
O by row 8, column 5
L by row 7, column 9
D by row 2, column 4.

❑❑❑

15

Venn Diagrams & Logical Diagram

In these type of questions, diagrammatic representation presents a logical illustration of particular class or statements based on which the questions are asked. A clear view of the diagram makes the concepts clear for attempting such questions.

EXERCISE

1. What is the number which is common to only two geometrical figures?

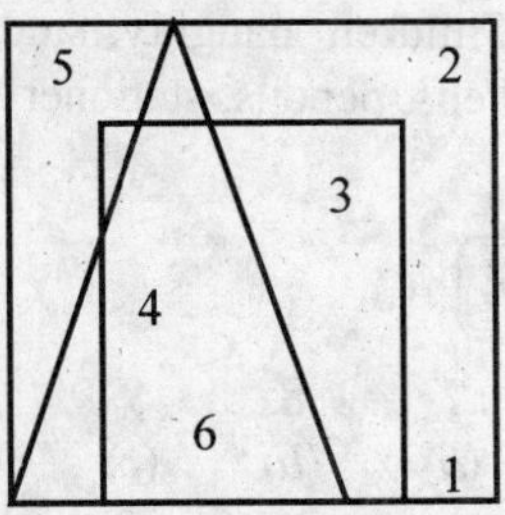

(*a*) 4 (*b*) 3
(*c*) 5 (*d*) 2

Directions (Qs. 2 & 3) : *In the following diagram, rectangle represents Hindi Announcers, circle represents English Announcers, square represents French Announcers, and triangle represents German Announcers.*

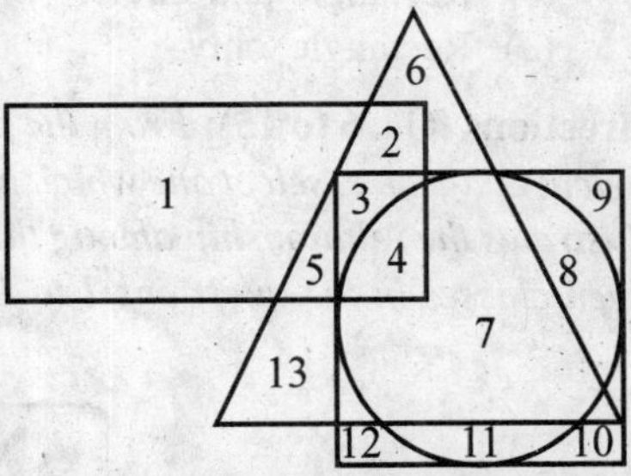

2. Which area represents those announcers who can present programmes in Hindi, French and German only?

(*a*) 1 (*b*) 2
(*c*) 3 (*d*) 4

3 Which area represents those announcers who can present programmes in French and English only?

(*a*) 7 (*b*) 9
(*c*) 11 (*d*) 13

Directions (Qs. 4 & 5): *Study the diagram to answer these questions.*

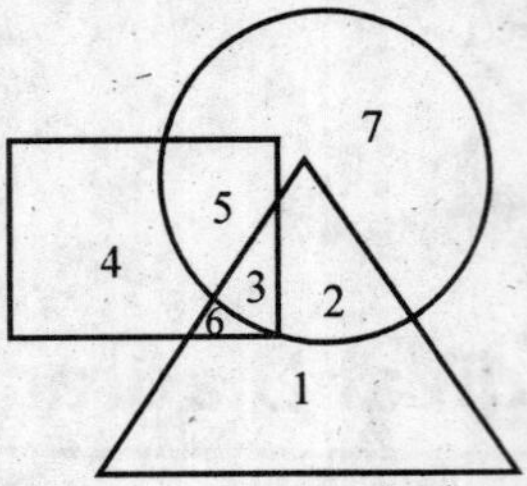

4. Which number is in all the geometrical figures?
(*a*) 5 (*b*) 6
(*c*) 2 (*d*) 3

5. Number 6 is in :
(*a*) Rectangle and triangle
(*b*) Circle and traingle
(*c*) Rectangle and circle
(*d*) Rectangle only

Directions (Qs. 6 to 15): *From the five logical Diagrams, select one which best illustrates the relationship among three given classes in the questions 1 to 10.*

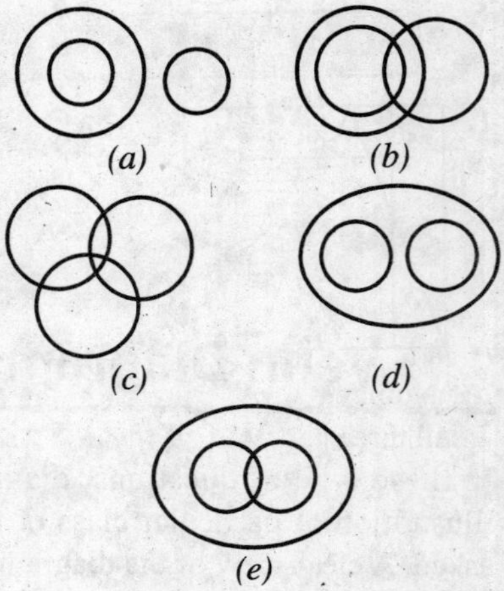

6. Birds, fruits, mangoes
7. Criminals, lawyers, bandits
8. Swimmers, bachelors, men
9. Smart, engineers, women
10. Vegetables, potatoes, brinjals
11. Grapes, sweet, fruit
12. Doctors, architects, humans
13. Scholars, people, Indians
14. Children, naughty, studious
15. Pens, pencils, stationery

ANSWERS

1	**2**	**3**	**4**	**5**	**6**	**7**	**8**	**9**	**10**
(*b*)	(*c*)	(*c*)	(*d*)	(*a*)	(*a*)	(*a*)	(*b*)	(*c*)	(*d*)
11	**12**	**13**	**14**	**15**					
(*b*)	(*d*)	(*e*)	(*c*)	(*d*)					

SOME SELECTED EXPLANATORY ANSWERS

1.

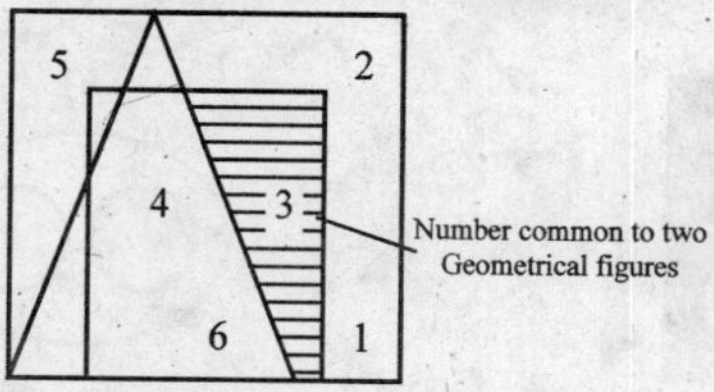

Note : Numbers 4 and 6 are common to all three geometrical figures.

2–3.

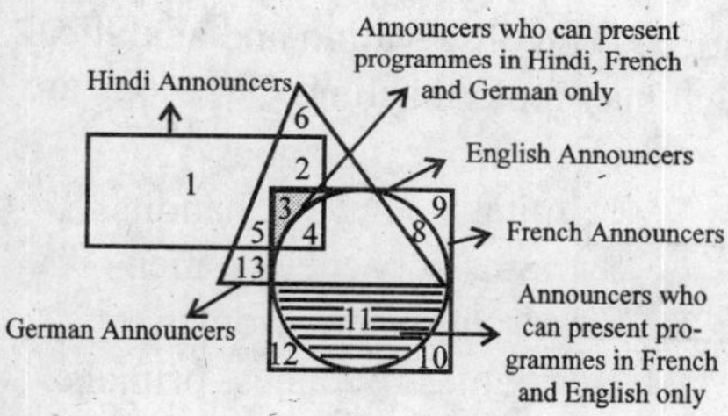

4–5.

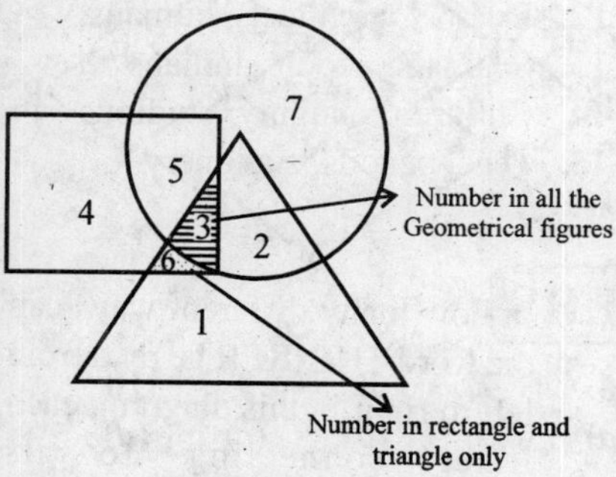

6.

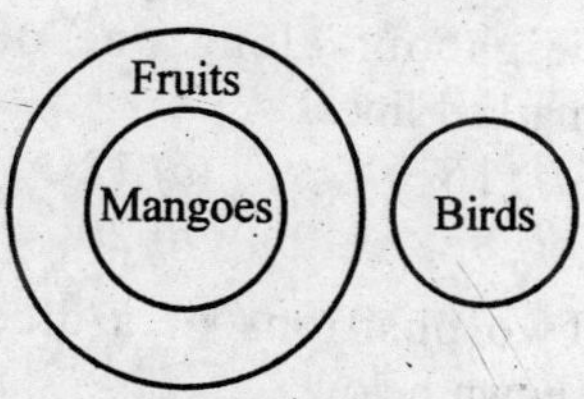

All mangoes are fruits, but neither fruits, nor mangoes can be birds.

8.

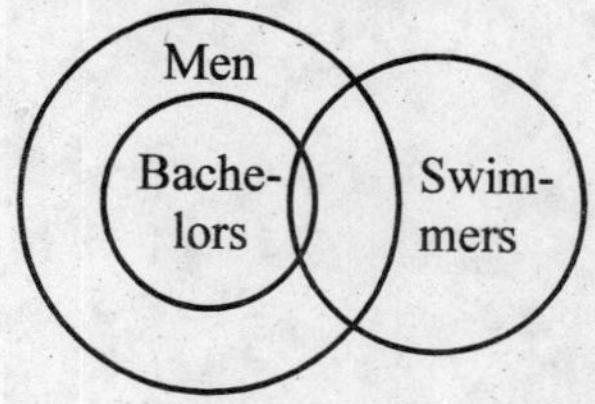

All bachelors are men and some men and bachelors can be swimmers.

9.

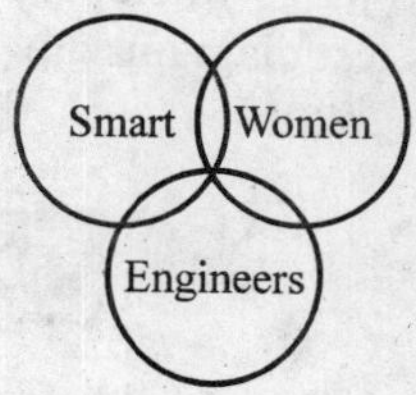

Some women can be smart and some women can be engineers and vice–versa. Some engineers can be women and some engineers can be smart and vice–versa.

13.

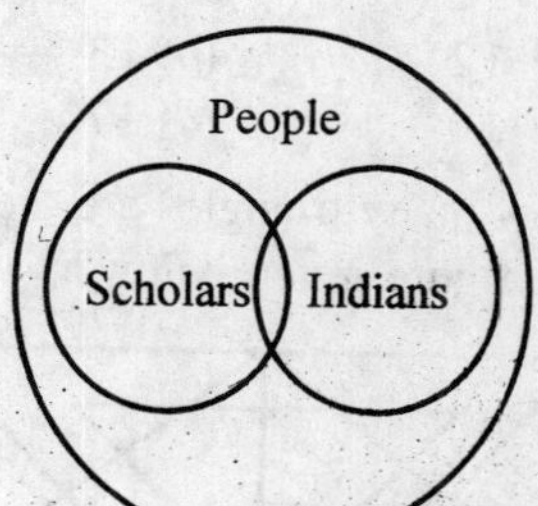

Some Indians can be scholars and some scholars can be Indians. All scholars and Indians are people.

16

Diagrammatic Puzzle

This test aims to judge your space visualisation, keen observation and analytical aptitude. In this test diagrams are given which may look puzzling. Questions are asked on the diagrams.

EXERCISE

1. How many squares are there in the figure given below?

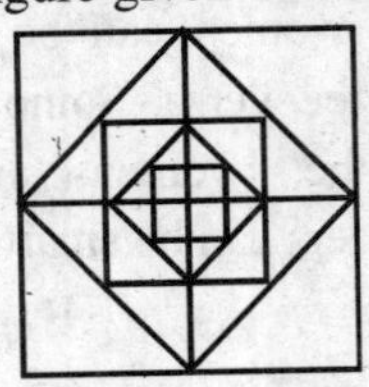

(*a*) 12 (*b*) 13
(*c*) 16 (*d*) 17

2. How many triangles are there in the figure given below?

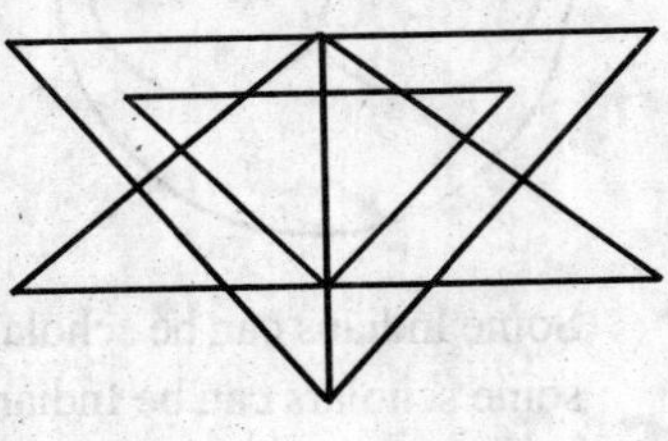

(*a*) 25 (*b*) 23
(*c*) 21 (*d*) 27

3.

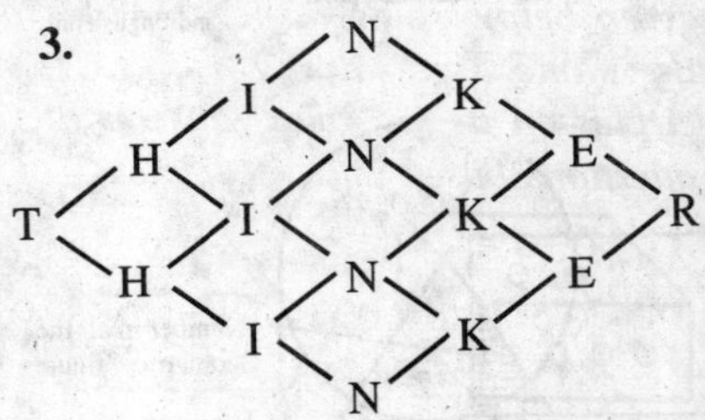

In how many different ways can the word THINKER be read from left to right in this diagram, each letter connecting to its neighbour along one of the marked lines.

(*a*) 16 (*b*) 12
(*c*) 8 (*d*) 20

4. Two positions of a dice are shown below.

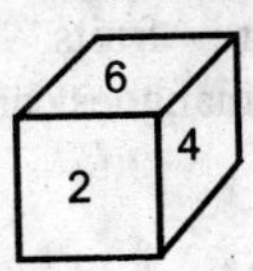

and
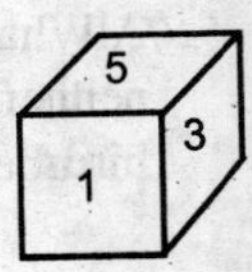

When 2 is at the bottom, what number will be at the top?

(a) 1 (b) 3
(c) 4 (d) 5

5. Six sides of a block are coloured Green, Blue, Red, Yellow, Orange and White in the following manner:

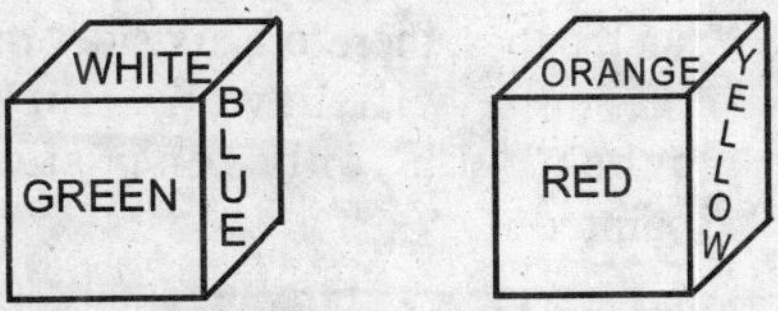

When Blue is on the top, which colour will be at the bottom?

(a) Orange (b) Red
(c) White (d) Yellow

Directions (Qs. 6 to 8): *The figures given below show three positions of the same dice having 1, 2, 3, ...6 circles on its six faces. Answer these questions based on this dice.*

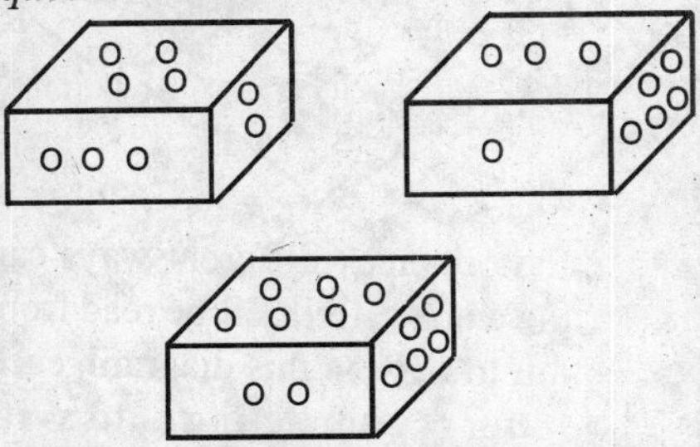

6. The number of circles on the face opposite to the one having three circles is:

(a) 6 (b) 5
(c) 7
(d) None of these

7. What is the number of circles on the face at the bottom of the first cube?

(a) 6
(b) 1
(c) 5
(d) None of these

8. How many circles will be there on the top face in the figure shown?

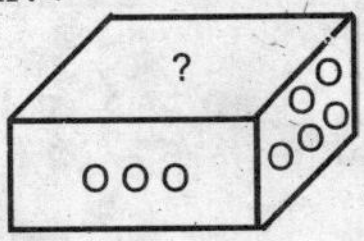

(a) 2 (b) 1
(c) 6 (d) 4

Directions (Qs. 9 & 10): *A toy cube has pictures of different fruits on its six faces. The top face has the picture of orange. Banana is adjacent to melon and orange. Apple is not at the bottom of the cube and melon is opposite the peach.*

9. A cube is coloured with different colours on each side. Red is at the base and white at the top. The colours green, yellow, blue and purple respectively are painted on the four sides of the cube, in the clockwise direction. When the yellow side is changed as the base of the cube, which colour will be on the top?

(a) BLUE (b) GREEN
(c) PURPLE (d) RED

10. A four centimetre cube has been painted blue on all its sides. It is then cut into one cm cubes. How many cubes will be there with only one side painted?

(a) 24 (b) 16
(c) 8 (d) 32

ANSWERS

1	2	3	4	5	6	7	8	9	10
(*d*)	(*d*)	(*d*)	(*b*)	(*b*)	(*a*)	(*c*)	(*a*)	(*c*)	(*a*)

SOME SELECTED EXPLANATORY ANSWERS

6. 2, 4, 1 and 5 circles are neighbouring faces of 3.

7. 5 circles' face has neighbouring faces with 1, 3, 2 and 6 circles. Hence 4 and 5 circles faces form opposite pairs.

9. The sides are painted green, yellow, blue and purple respectively. So the colour opposite each will be the alternate one, *i.e.*, when yellow colour is at the base purple colour will be at the top.

10. One side of the cube has four such cubes, therefore six sides of the cube will have 24 such cubes with only one side painted.

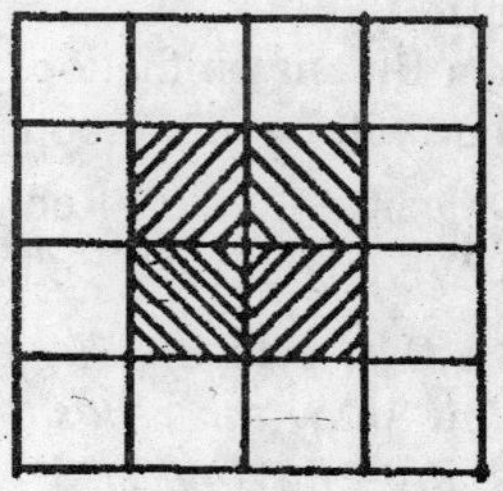

□□□

17

Assertion and Reason

Questions of this pattern are based on facts and are given to judge the candidate's general knowledge and intelligence along with his ability to reason out correctly. In this test two statements labelled as Assertion (A) and the other lebelled as Reason (R) are given. In the context of these two statements the candidate has to choose the correct option from the given options.

EXERCISE

Directions : *In each question given below there are two statements labelled as Assertion (A) and the other labelled as Reason (R). Of these statements which one of the following is correct?*

(a) Both A and R are true and R is the correct explanation of A.

(b) Both A and R are true but R is not the correct explanation of A.

(c) A is true but R is false.

(d) A is false but R is true.

1. **Assertion (A) :** Eggs of mosquitoes being very light in weight, float on water and water bodies.

   Reason (R) : Surface tension of water balances the weight of eggs.

2. **Assertion (A) :** Gun powder is an example of a mixture.

   Reason (R) : The components of gun powder are not present in a fixed ratio.

3. **Assertion (A) :** In cold wintry nights, the valleys in high mountainous areas are colder than the higher slopes.

   Reason (R) : The cold, moist heavy air descends down the slopes of the mountain.

4. **Assertion (A) :** The sponsor and the most prominent figure of the Chisti order of Sufis in India is Khwaja Moinuddin Chisti.

   Reason (R) : The Chisti order takes its name from a village Chisti in Ajmer.

5. **Assertion (A) :** The reservation of thirty–three percent of seats for women in Partiament and

State legislature does not require constitutional amendment.

Reason (R) : Political parties contesting elections can allocate thirty-three percent of seats they contest to women candidates without any constitutional amendment.

6. **Assertion (A) :** Comets always have their tails away from the Sun.

   Reason (R) : Solar winds drive the gaseous tail away from the Sun as the comet approaches the Sun.

7. **Assertion (A) :** Human figure was the pivot of the sculpture of the Gupta period.

   Reason (R) : In the Gupta period, the artists lost interest in nature.

8. **Assertion (A) :** Diamond and graphite are allotropic forms of carbon.

   Reason (R) : Diamond and graphite have different types of bonding between the carbon atoms.

9. **Assertion (A) :** The percentage share of tea exports from India has been declining considerably.

   Reason (R) : There has been a substantial increase in the consumption of other beve-rages in the importing countries.

10. **Assertion (A) :** Oxides of nitrogen illustrate the law of multiple proportions.

    Reason (R) : Nitrogen forms five oxides. The weight of Oxygen combining with a fixed weight of Nitrogen is in the simple ratio 1 : 2 : 3 : 4 : 5.

ANSWERS

1	2	3	4	5	6	7	8	9	10
(*a*)	(*c*)	(*a*)	(*b*)	(*d*)	(*a*)	(*c*)	(*a*)	(*c*)	(*a*)

SOME SELECTED EXPLANATORY ANSWERS

1. Both the statements are true and R explains the reason why eggs float.
3. Both A and R are true and R explains the climate of cold wintry night in A.
4. Both the statements are true but R is not the explanation of A.
6. Both A and R are correct and R is the correct explanation of A.
8. Both statements are true and the type of bonding explains why diamond & graphite are allotropic forms of carbon.
9. Statement A is true but R is based on assumption and therefore it is false.
10. Both the statements are correct and R is the correct explanation of A.

□□□

NON-VERBAL

1

Series

In this form of non-verbal series, which are the most common, four or five consecutive problem figures form a definite sequence and one is required to select the one figure from the given set of Answer Figures that will continue the same sequence.

One has to try different set of moves, changes, replacements, rotations, repetitions and a lot more variations to arrive at the logical pattern making the series. Practising alone will sharpen one's skill of solving such sequences.

Example

Directions : *Which of the given options will complete the given series?*

Problem Figures

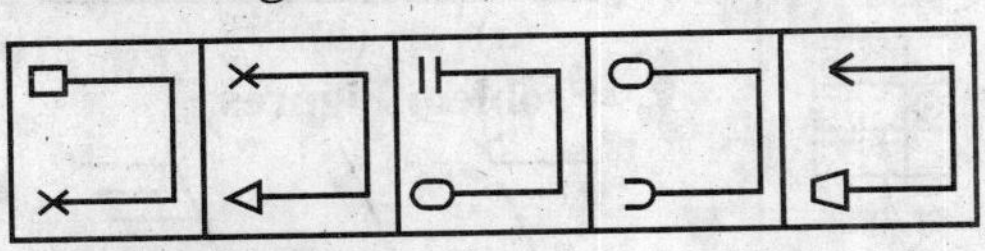

Answer Figures

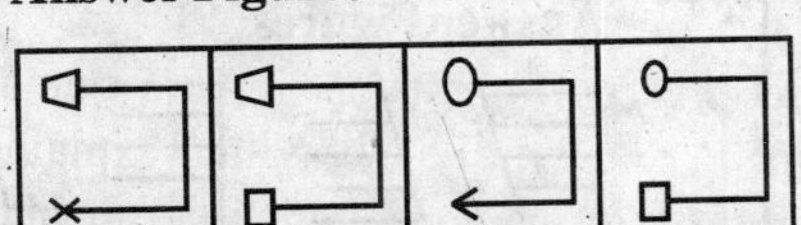

(*a*) (*b*) (*c*) (*d*)

Answer (*b*) : Observe the series. Figure one corelates to figure two in the manner that the places of both the elements on the left are inter changed and then the element at the bottom is replaced by a new element. Similarly, Figure three corelates to figure four and answer figure 'B' corelates to figure five.

EXERCISE

Direction : *Each of the following questions consist of problem figures followed by answer figures. Select a figure from amongst the answer figures which will continue the same series or pattern as established by the problem figures.*

1. Problem Figures

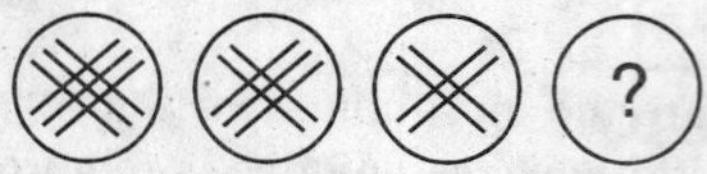

Answer Figures

(a) (b) (c) (d)

2. Problem Figures

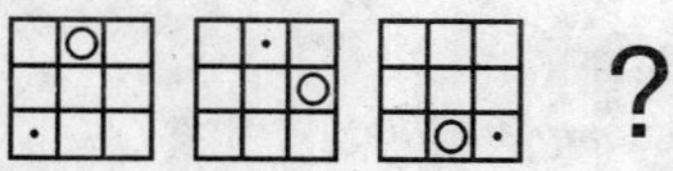

Answer Figures

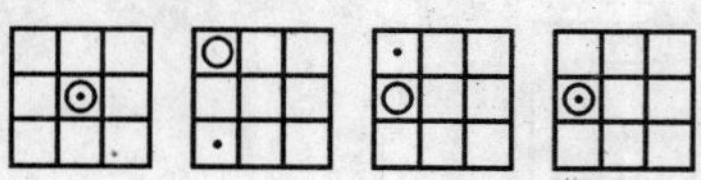

(a) (b) (c) (d)

3. Problem Figures

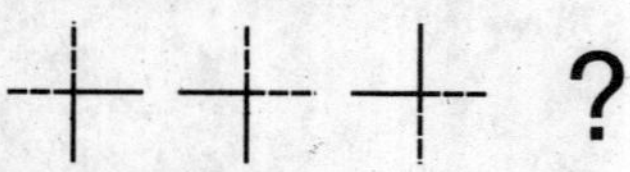

Answer Figures

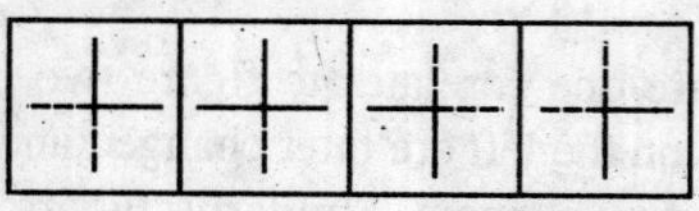

(a) (b) (c) (d)

4. Problem Figures

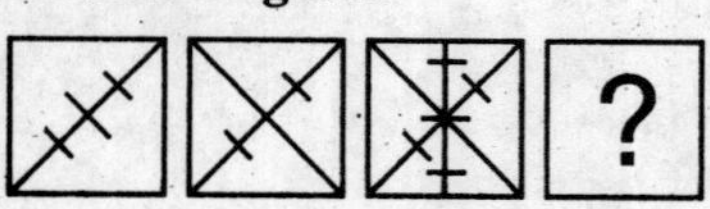

Answer Figures

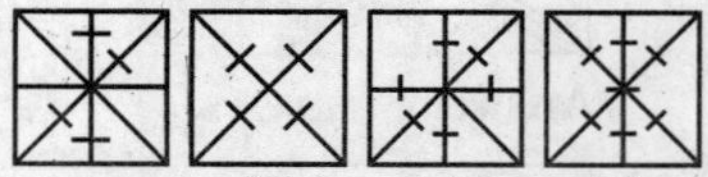

(a) (b) (c) (d)

5. Problem Figures

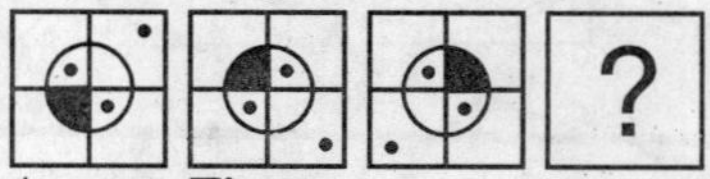

Answer Figures

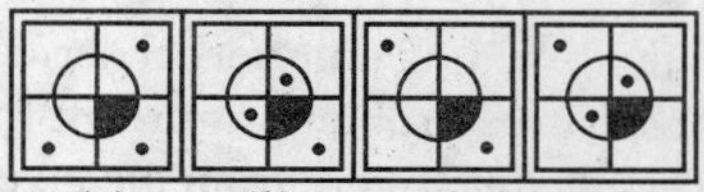

(a) (b) (c) (d)

6. Problem Figures

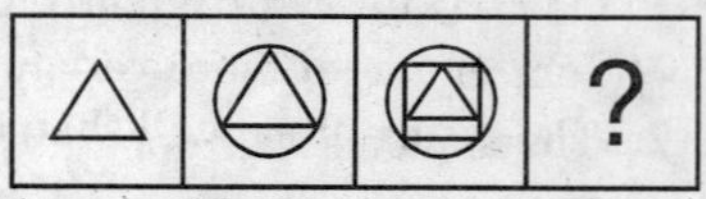

Answer Figures

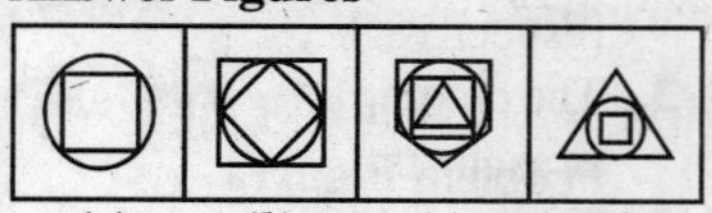

(a) (b) (c) (d)

7. Problem Figures

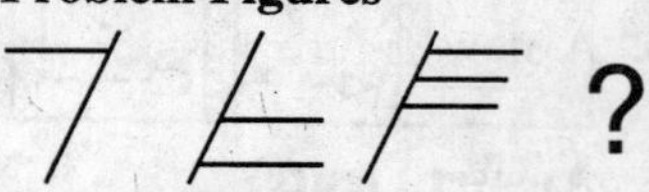

Answer Figures

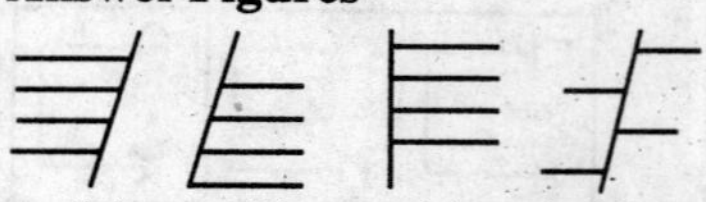

(a) (b) (c) (d)

8. Problem Figures

Answer Figures

(a) (b) (c) (d)

9. Problem Figures

Answer Figures

(*a*) (*b*) (*c*) (*d*)

10. Problem Figures

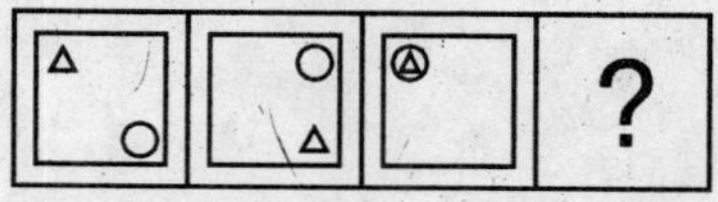

Answer Figures

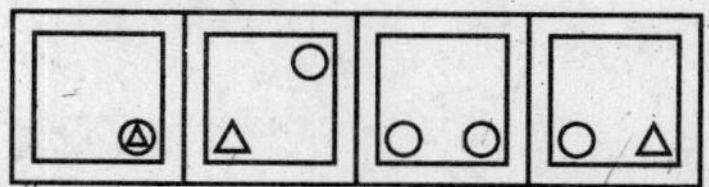

(*a*) (*b*) (*c*) (*d*)

ANSWERS

1	2	3	4	5	6	7	8	9	10
(*d*)	(*d*)	(*a*)	(*a*)	(*d*)	(*c*)	(*a*)	(*d*)	(*d*)	(*d*)

SOME SELECTED EXPLANATORY ANSWERS

2. The circle and the dot are moved two and three sections clockwise respectively.

3. The cross is turned 90° clockwise at each step.

5. The complete figure is turned 90° clockwise at each step.

6. A new figure is added to the previous set of figures at each step.

8. The star shape is rotated 90° anticlockwise at each step.

10. The triangle is moved diagonally to and fro and the circle one step anticlockwise to get the next figure.

2

Analogy

Analogy is a process of reasoning between two parallel cases. It relates to agreement or correspondence in certain respects between two things. It is a process whereby the underlying relationship that exists between two figures, designs or patterns is determined. Under the process, one has to discover the features common to the two figures or designs. This common feature is a model or base. The question seeks solution on the basis of this model or base.

Example

Directions : *Which of the given options will complete the given series?*

Problem Figures

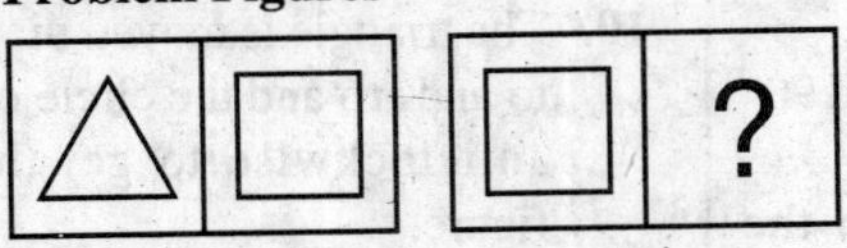

Answer Figures

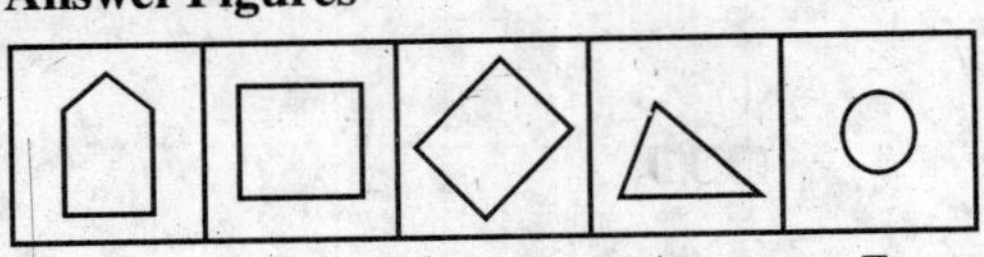

A B C D E

Answer A : Study the two figures in the first part of the Problem Figures. They are a triangle and a square. The first figure (a triangle) has three angles and three sides, while the second figure (a square) has four angles and four sides. The relationship between them is—the second figure has one angle and one side more than what the first figure has.

On this analogy the figure to suit in the space marked by ? should be one with 5 angles and 5 sides (one angle and one side more than what the first figure of the second part of the Problem Figures has).

EXERCISE

Directions : *The second figure in the first unit of the Problem Figures bears a certain relationship to the first figure. Similarly, one of the figures in the Answer Figures bears the same relationship to the first figure in the second unit of the Problem Figures. Locate the figure which would fit the question mark.*

1. Problem Figures

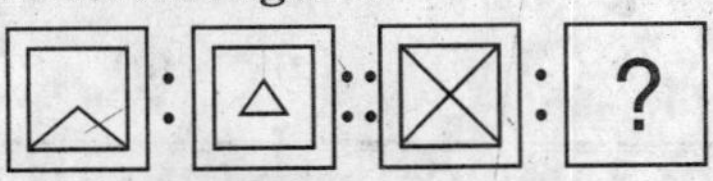

Answers Figures

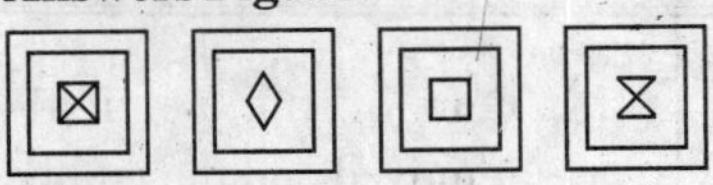

(a) (b) (c) (d)

2. Problem Figures

Answer Figures

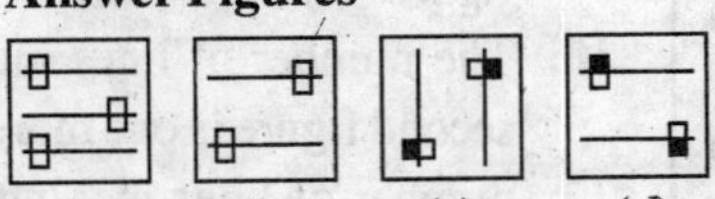

(a) (b) (c) (d)

3. Problem Figures

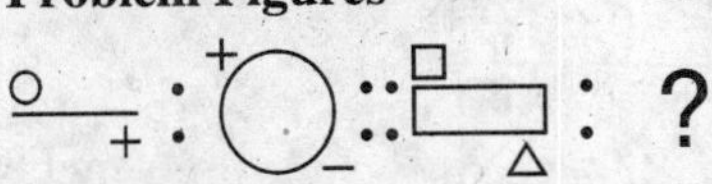

Answer Figures

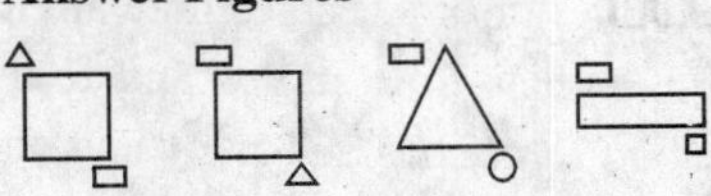

(a) (b) (c) (d)

4. Problem Figures

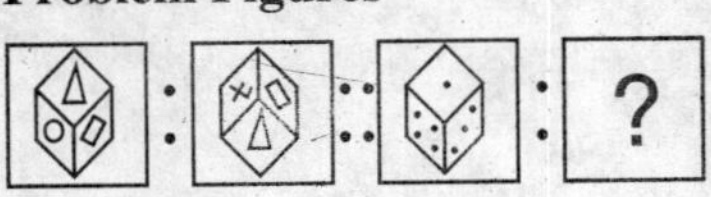

Answer Figures

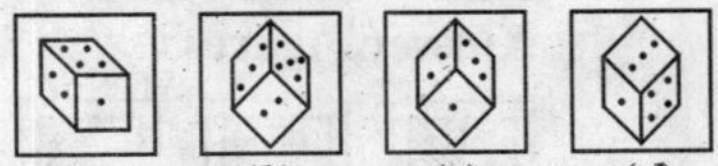

(a) (b) (c) (d)

5. Problem Figures

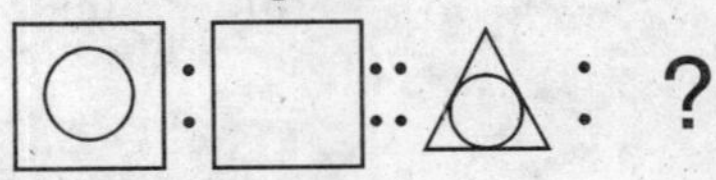

Answer Figures

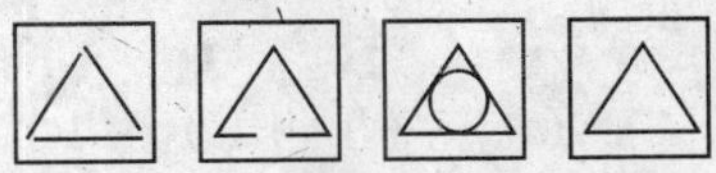

(a) (b) (c) (d)

6. Problem Figures

Answer Figures

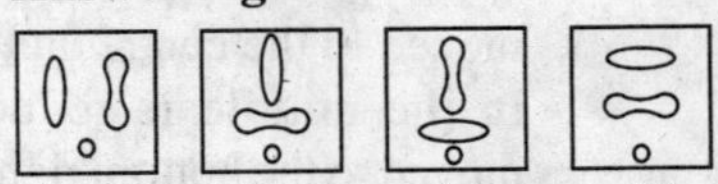

(a) (b) (c) (d)

7. Problem Figures

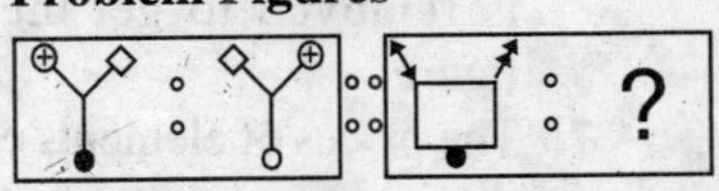

Answer Figures

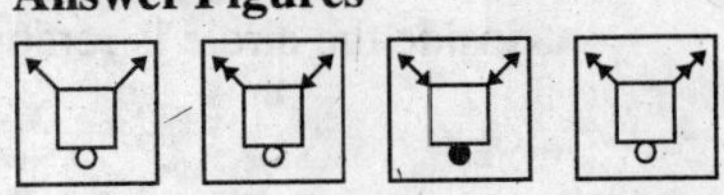

(a) (b) (c) (d)

8. Problem Figures

Answer Figures

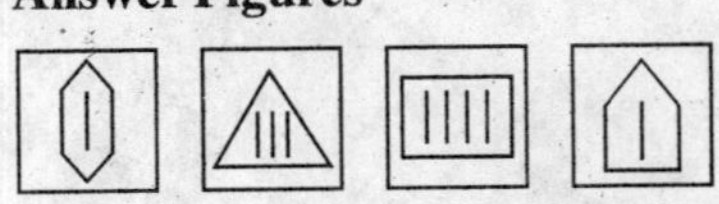

(a) (b) (c) (d)

9. **Problem Figures**

Answer Figures

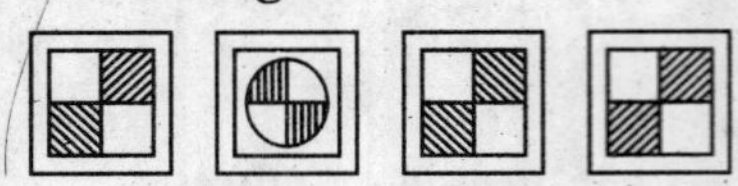

(*a*) (*b*) (*c*) (*d*)

10. **Problem Figures**

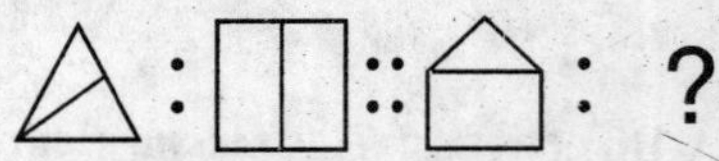

Answer Figures

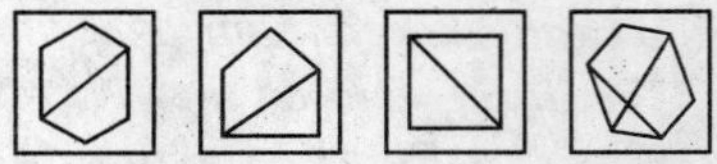

(*a*) (*b*) (*c*) (*d*)

ANSWERS

1	2	3	4	5	6	7	8	9	10
(*d*)	(*d*)	(*a*)	(*c*)	(*d*)	(*b*)	(*b*)	(*a*)	(*a*)	(*a*)

SOME SELECTED EXPLANATORY ANSWERS

3. The element at the bottom is moved to the diagonal corner, the element in the top is enlarged and moved to the centre and element in the middle is reduced and moved to the bottom right corner.

5. The inner shape in the first figure is removed to get the second figure.

7. The places of elements on the top are interchanged and the shade inside the circle is removed.

8. One of the vertical lines is removed and the number of lines making the second figure is increased by one.

9. First figure is rotated 90° anticlockwise to get the second figure.

10. The number of lines making the second figure is one more than the number of lines making the first figure.

☐☐☐

3

Classification

Classification means arranging the given content in groups or classes having qualities of same kind. In classification type questions, the figures or items are sorted out in groups on the basis of their similarities in qualities in shapes, size, pattern, structure, genus, order, species, grade, style, constituents and other specifications, and thus the answer is found out.

Example

Directions : *Find the figure which is different from all given figure?*

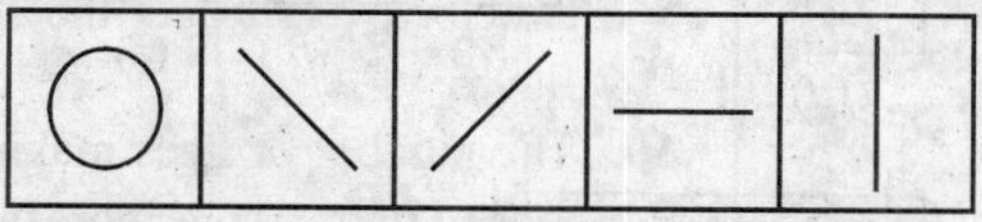

(*a*) (*b*) (*c*) (*d*) (*e*)

Answer (*a*) : A is a circle, whereas B, C, D and E are straight lines pointing to different directions. Note that the common characteristic in each of the four figures B, C, D and E is that they are straight lines. Thus, they belong to a class. As against these figures, A is a circle and does not belong to that class.

Therefore, the figure that does not belong to the class is A.

EXERCISE

Directions : *In each of the following questions one of the figures is different from the rest. Spot the figure.*

1. 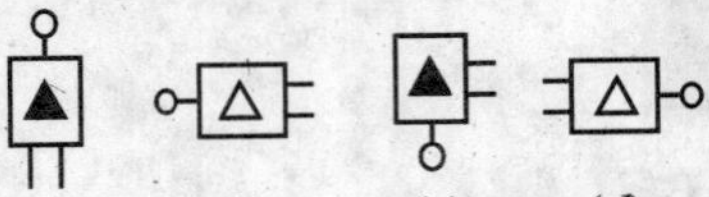

(a) (b) (c) (d)

2. 

(a) (b) (c) (d)

3. 

(a) (b) (c) (d)

4. 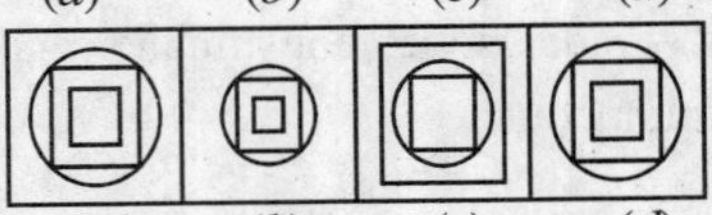

(a) (b) (c) (d)

5. 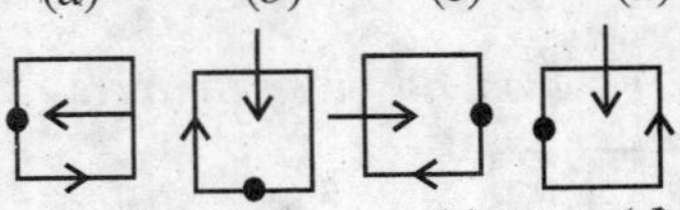

(a) (b) (c) (d)

6. 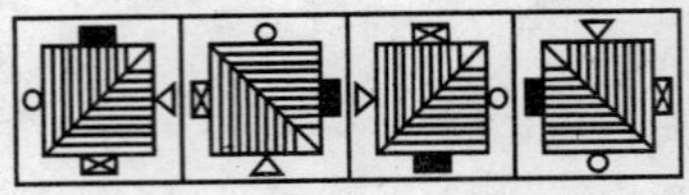

(a) (b) (c) (d)

7. 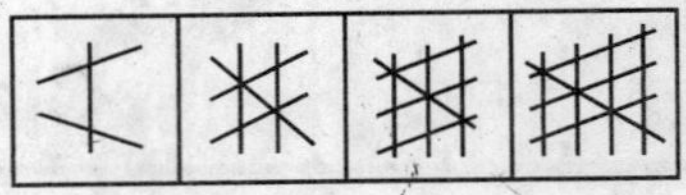

(a) (b) (c) (d)

8. 

(a) (b) (c) (d)

9. 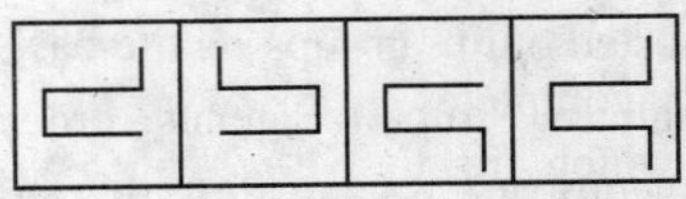

(a) (b) (c) (d)

10. 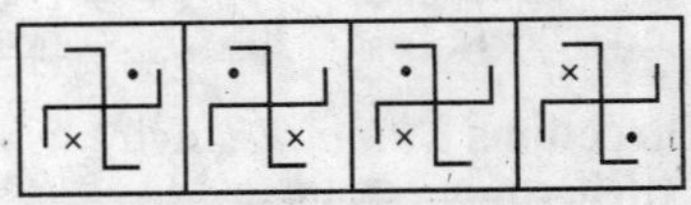

(a) (b) (c) (d)

ANSWERS

1	2	3	4	5	6	7	8	9	10
(c)	(c)	(d)	(c)	(a)	(c)	(d)	(a)	(d)	(c)

SOME SELECTED EXPLANATORY ANSWERS

2. All other figures are divided into four parts.

3. Only in this figure the middle and the centre shapes are opposite to each other.

4. In all other figures the middle and the centre designs are identical.

6. All other figures can be rotated into each other.

8. In all other figures the cuts are identical along the two sides of the square.

9. Only in this figure both ends of the design are drawn further.

10. In all other figures the dot and the cross are in diagonally opposite sections of the shape.

□□□

4

Complete an Incomplete Pattern

This test aims at judging the ability to comprehend correlations between geometric figures and diagrams and to perceive the structure of the design in its totality in order to select the appropriate part from amongst the answer figures for completion of each incomplete pattern.

In this test, a pattern/figure is given, a portion of which is left blank or incomplete. From the answer figures, you are required to select the figure which fits into the blank space in the incomplete figure.

EXERCISE

Directions (Qs. 1 to 10): *In each of the following questions a figure or a pattern or a design is given. A portion of that figure/pattern/design is blank or shown with a question mark. Below it are given four alternative figures. Choose a figure from the alternative figures which complete the given figure/pattern or design.*

1.

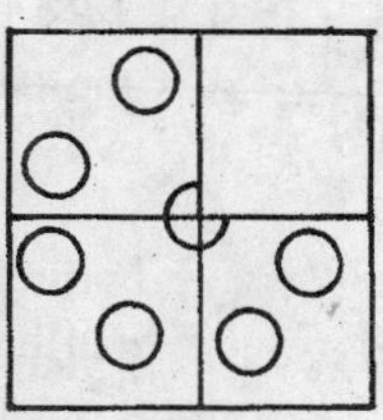

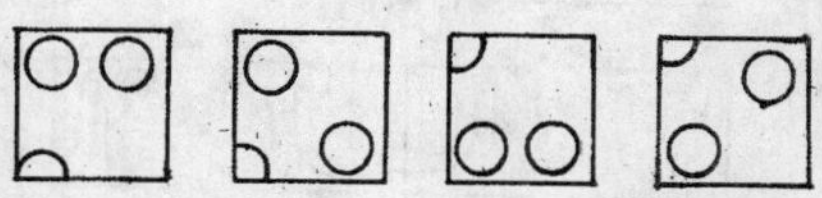

(*a*) (*b*) (*c*) (*d*)

2.

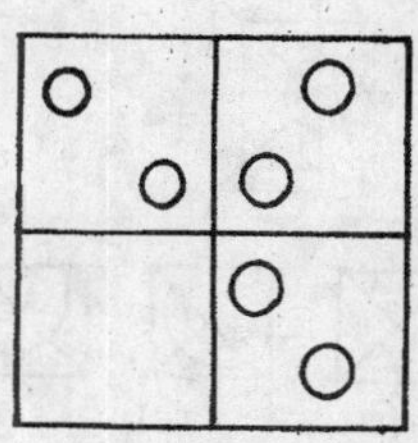

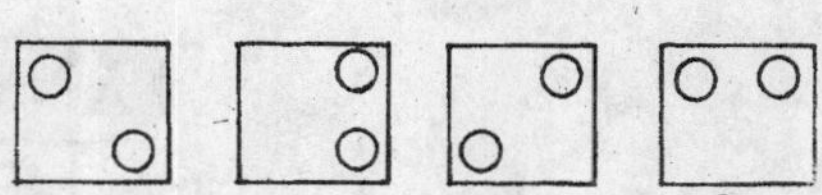

(*a*) (*b*) (*c*) (*d*)

3.

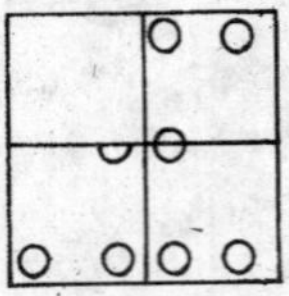

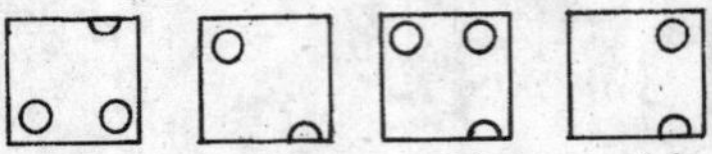

(a) (b) (c) (d)

4.

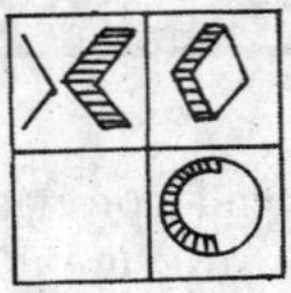

(a) (b) (c) (d)

5.

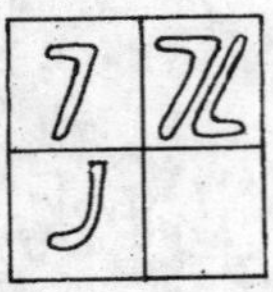

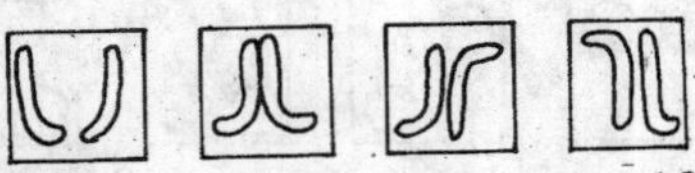

(a) (b) (c) (d)

6.

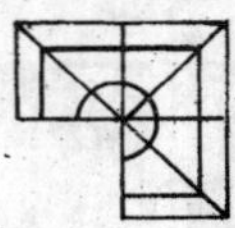

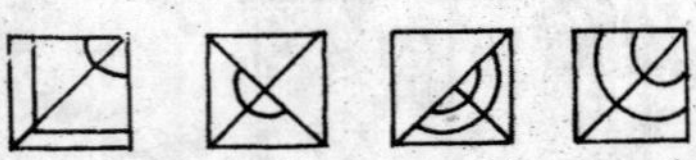

(a) (b) (c) (d)

7.

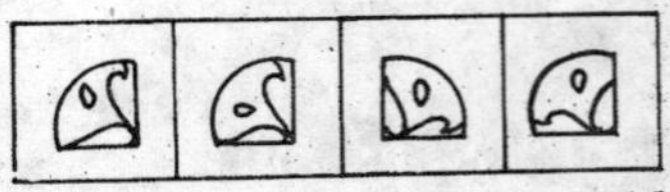

(a) (b) (c) (d)

8.

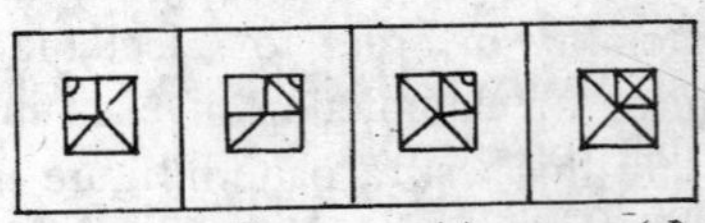

(a) (b) (c) (d)

9.

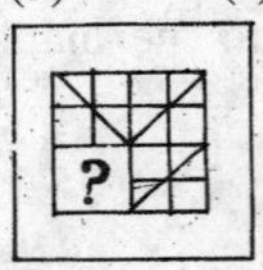

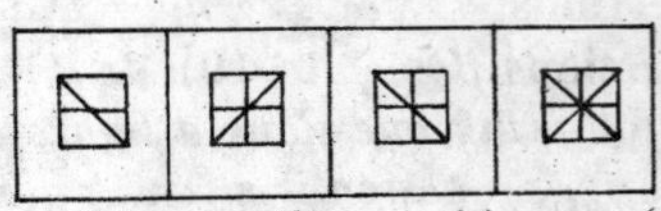

(a) (b) (c) (d)

10.

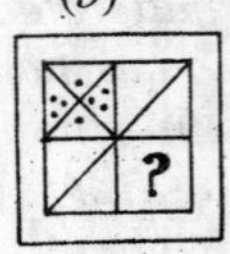

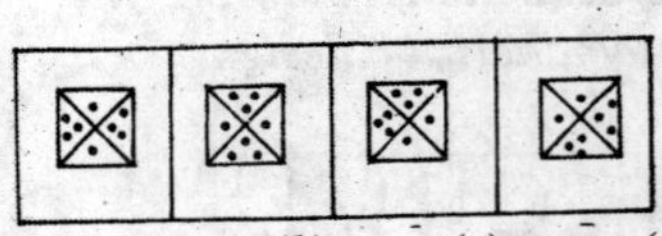

(a) (b) (c) (d)

ANSWERS

1	2	3	4	5	6	7	8	9	10
(b)	(c)	(c)	(b)	(c)	(a)	(d)	(c)	(c)	(a)

5

Spotting Hidden Pattern

In this test, the problem figure comprises just one figure.

Below it are given four alternative figures. Of these four alternative figures, one figure is such that the problem figure is hidden into it. Candidates must observe very keenly the problem figure. They must then try to make a search of that (problem figure) among the alternative figures. It requires undiluted shape perception and sharp analytical capability to pin point the hiddern figure/design out of a large and jumbled figure.

EXERCISE

Directions: *In each of the following questions a figure is given at the top. Below it are given four figure alternatives. In each question, the figure given at the top is hidden in one of the four alternatives. Choose that alternatives.*

1. Question Figure:

Alternative Figures:

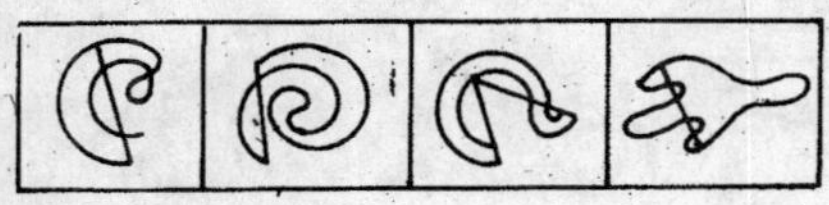

(*a*) (*b*) (*c*) (*d*)

2. Question Figure:

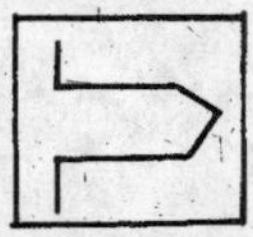

Alternative Figures:

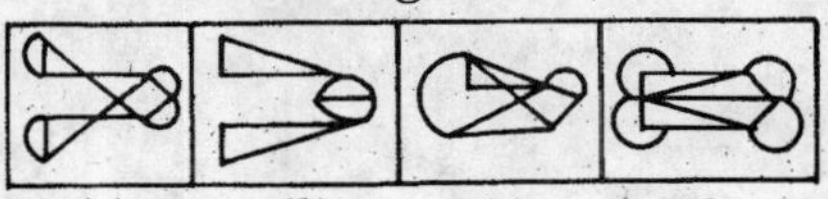

(*a*) (*b*) (*c*) (*d*)

3. Question Figure:

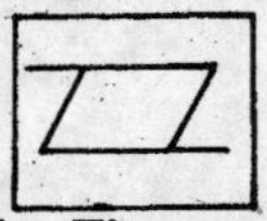

Alternative Figures:

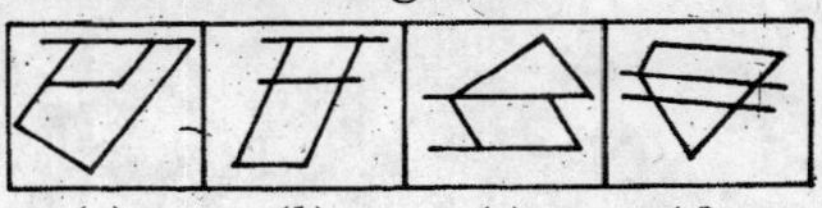

(*a*) (*b*) (*c*) (*d*)

4. Question Figure:

Alternative Figures:

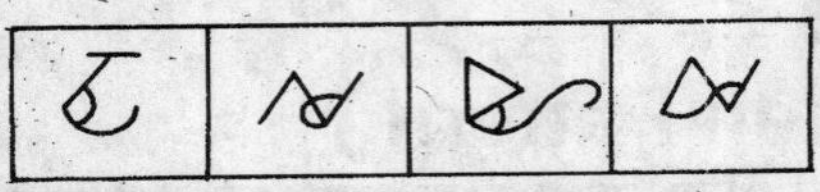

(*a*) (*b*) (*c*) (*d*)

5. Question Figure:

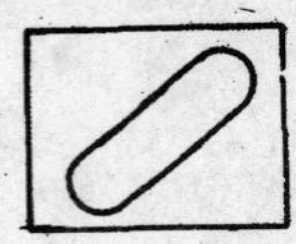

Alternative Figures:

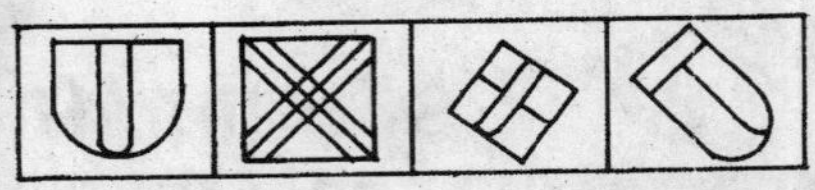

(*a*) (*b*) (*c*) (*d*)

ANSWERS

1	2	3	4	5
(*b*)	(*a*)	(*c*)	(*d*)	(*b*)

□□□

6

Folded or Unfolded Pattern

In this test, the problem figures show how a piece of paper or cardboard is folded and cut or punched. From the answer figures, you are required to choose the correct shape of the paper or cardboard when it is unfolded.

EXERCISE

Directions (Qs. 1 to 3): *In these questions, a piece of square paper is folded as shown below and a cut is made as marked. How would the paper look like when unfolded?*

1. Problem Figures:

Answer Figures:

(*a*) (*b*) (*c*) (*d*)

2. Problem Figure:

Answer Figures:

(*a*) (*b*) (*c*) (*d*)

3. Problem Figures:

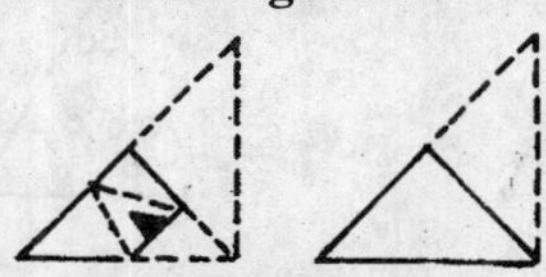

Answer Figures:

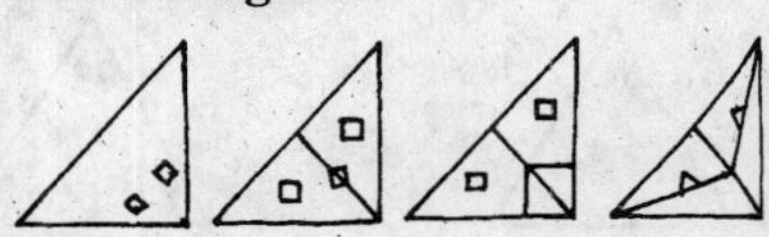

(*a*) (*b*) (*c*) (*d*)

Directions (Qs. 4 to 8): *As shown below, a paper is folded and then cut. How will the paper look like, when unfolded?*

4. **Problem Figures:**

Answer Figures:

(*a*)

(*b*)

(*c*)

(*d*)

5. **Problem Figures:**

Answer Figures:

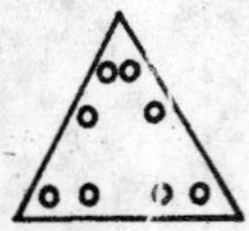

(*a*)

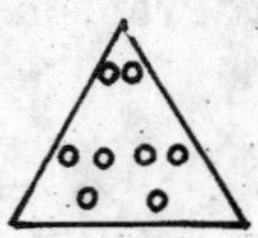

(*b*)

(*c*)

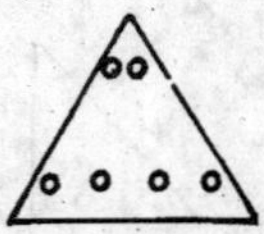

(*d*)

6. **Problem Figures:**

Answer Figures:

(*a*)

(*b*)

(*c*)

(*d*)

7. **Problem Figures:**

Answer Figures:

(*a*)

(*b*)

(*c*)

(*d*)

8. **Problem Figures:**

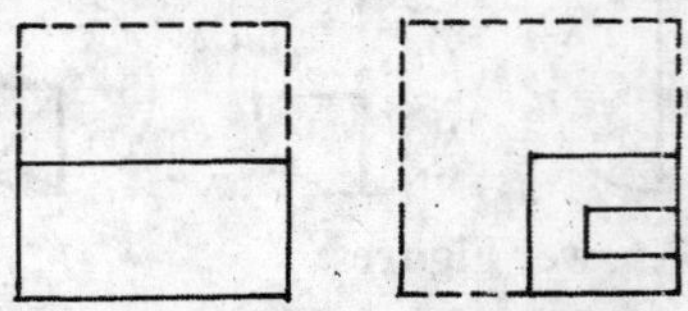

Answer Figures:

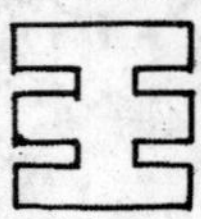

(*a*)

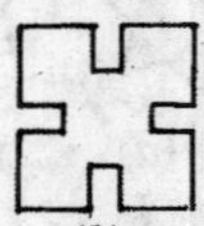

(*b*)

(*c*)

(*d*)

Directions (Qs. 9 & 10): *In these questions, a square/hexagonal sheet of paper has been folded and punched as shown by the top figures. You have to find out from amongst the four response figures how it will appear when opened?*

9. Problem Figures:

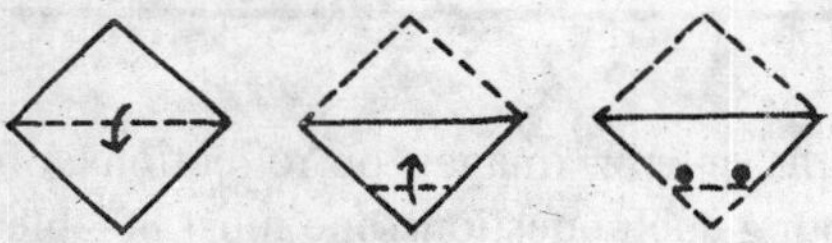

Answer Figures:

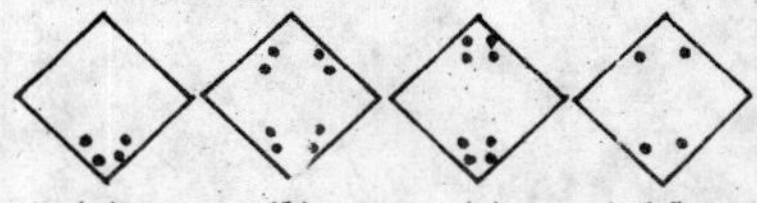

(*a*) (*b*) (*c*) (*d*)

10. Problem Figures:

Answer Figures:

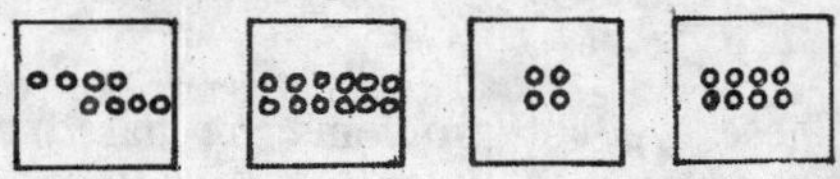

(*a*) (*b*) (*c*) (*d*)

ANSWERS

1	2	3	4	5	6	7	8	9	10
(*d*)	(*a*)	(*a*)	(*b*)	(*a*)	(*b*)	(*d*)	(*a*)	(*c*)	(*b*)

❑❑❑

7

Mirror Image

These type of problems are based on the mirror images or reflections of number, letters and figures. While attempting such questions one must be able to visualise clearly the questioned reflections, be they on vertical plane or on horizontal plane.

EXERCISE

Directions (Qs. 1 to 4) : *In each question below which is the exact mirror image if the mirror is held vertically?*

1. CHIDE

A. CHIᗡƎ B. CHIDƎ

C. CHIDE D. ƆHIDƎ

2. 4320

A. ᔭ3Ƨ0 B. ᔭƐ20

C. ᔭƐƧ0 D. ᔭ3Ƨ0

3. MJ7KL

A. MႱ⅃K⅃ B. MႱ⅃KΓ

C. MႱ⅃ꓘL D. MႱΓꓘL

4. ↓OF2xq

A. ↑OꟻƧxd B. ↑OᖷƧxd

C. ↑OᖷƧxp D. ↑OƧᖷxd

Directions (Qs. 5 to 10) : *In each question given below which one would be the mirror image of the given figure when the mirror is placed along the line shown in each figure.*

5. Problem Figure

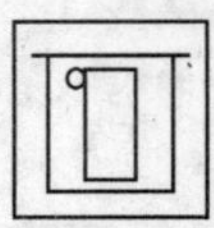

Answer Figures

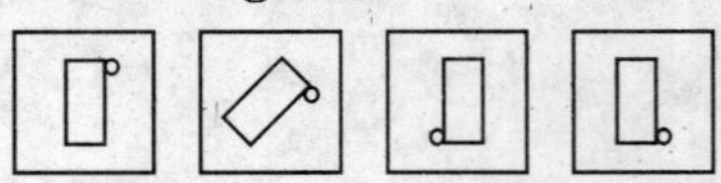

(a) (b) (c) (d)

6. Problem Figure

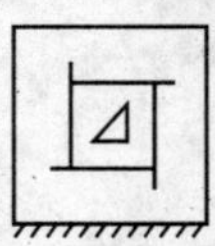

Answer Figures

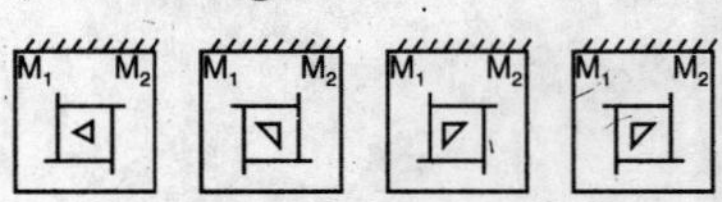

(a) (b) (c) (d)

7. Problem Figure

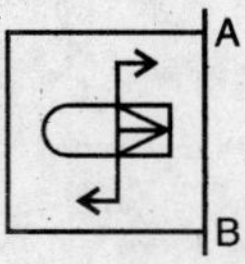

Answer Figures

(*a*) (*b*) (*c*) (*d*)

8. Problem Figure

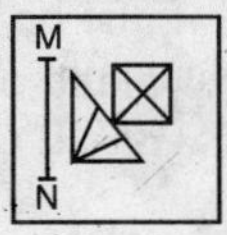

Answer Figures

(*a*) (*b*) (*c*) (*d*)

9. Problem Figure

Answer Figures

(*a*) (*b*) (*c*) (*d*)

10. Problem Figure

Answer Figures

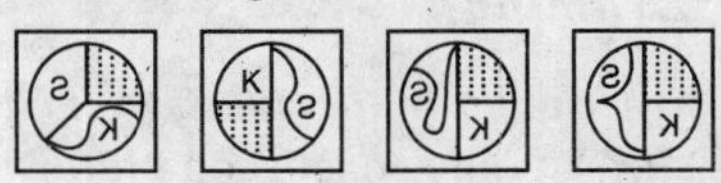

(*a*) (*b*) (*c*) (*d*)

ANSWERS

1	2	3	4	5	6	7	8	9	10
(*c*)	(*a*)	(*b*)	(*b*)	(*c*)	(*b*)	(*b*)	(*c*)	(*d*)	(*b*)

□□□

8

Syllogism

In this reasoning pattern the two premises are followed by two conclusions drawn from them. Four options (*a*), (*b*), (*c*) and (*d*) are given as answers. Based on the two statements the candidate has to select the right option as answer.

Example

Directions : *In the questions below the answer is given as :*

(*a*) if only conclusion I follows.

(*b*) if only conclusion II follows.

(*c*) if neither I nor II follows, and

(*d*) if both I and II follows.

Q. *Statements* *I :* All officers are lazy.

II : Some men are officers.

Conclusions *I :* All lazy are men.

II : Some men are lazy.

Ans. *(b)* : When all officers are lazy and some men are officers then some men must be lazy. Therefore, conclusion II is correct.

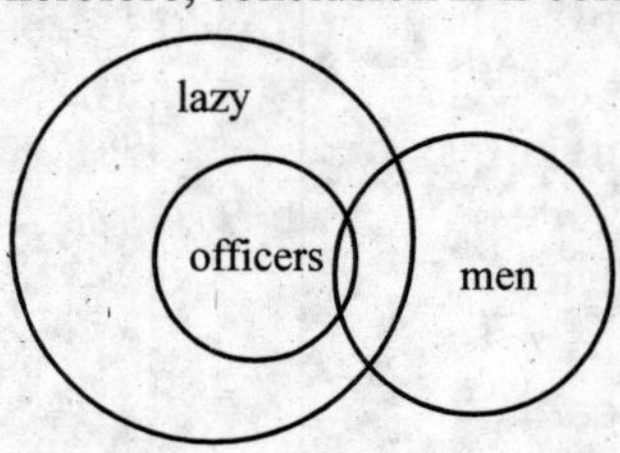

EXERCISE

Directions : *In each question below are given two statements followed by two conclusions numbered I and II. You have to take the two given statements to be true even if they seem to be at variance from commonly known facts and then decide which of the given conclusions logically follows from the two given statements, disregarding commonly known facts. Read both the statements and—*

Give answer (a) if only conclusion I follows; give answer (b) if only conclusion II follows; give answer (c) if neither I nor II follows and give answer (d) if both I and II follows.

1. **Statements**
   I. All tomatoes are red.
   II. All grapes are tomatoes.
   Conclusions
   I. All grapes are red.
   II. Some tomatoes are grapes.
2. **Statements**
   I. All painters are smilling.
   II. Some authors are painters.
   Conclusions
   I. All smiling authors are painters.
   II. Some authors are smiling.
3. **Statements**
   I. All peons in this office are efficient.
   II. Ramu is not efficient.
   Conclusions
   I. Ramu is not peon in this office.
   II. Ramu should be more efficient.
4. **Statements**
   I. All weavers are hard working.
   II. No hard working men are foolish.
   Conclusions
   I. No weavers are foolish.
   II. Some foolish are weavers.
5. **Statements**
   I. All fishes are cars.
   II. All cars are vegetables.
   Conclusions
   I. Some vegetables are cars.
   II. Some vegetables are fishes.
6. **Statements**
   I. Some dogs are pups.
   II. All horses are pups.
   Conclusions
   I. Some dogs are horses.
   II. Some horses are dogs.
7. **Statements**
   I. All beautiful women are mothers.
   II. All mothers are understanding.
   Conclusions
   I. All beautiful women are understanding.
   II. All mothers are beautiful women.
8. **Statements**
   I. Some toys are tables.
   II. No table is black.
   Conclusions
   I. Some toys are black.
   II. Some toys are not black.

9. Statements

I. All rivers are mountains.

II. Some rivers are deserts.

Conclusions

I. Some mountains are deserts.

II. Some deserts are not mountains.

10. Statements

I. All men are horses.

II. All horses are elephants.

Conclusions

I. All men are elephants.

II. All elephants are men.

11. Statements

I. All talented persons are trustworthy.

II. Some trustworthy are musicians.

Conclusions

I. All talented persons are musicians.

II. Some musicians are not talented person.

12. Statements

I. Alcoholic drinks are injurious to health.

II. All old women drink whisky.

Conclusions

I. All old women have poor health.

II. All young women are in good health.

13. Statements

I. All students are employed.

II. No employed are babies.

Conclusions

I. No students are babies.

II. Some employed are students.

14. Statements

I. Some engineers are teachers.

II. Some engineers are efficient.

Conclusions

I. Some teachers are efficient.

II. All efficient are engineers.

15. Statements

I. Some foods are sweet.

II. Some foods are sour.

Conclusions

I. All foods are either sweet or sour.

II. Some sweet are sour.

ANSWERS

1	2	3	4	5	6	7	8	9	10
(*d*)	(*b*)	(*a*)	(*a*)	(*d*)	(*c*)	(*a*)	(*c*)	(*d*)	(*a*)
11	**12**	**13**	**14**	**15**					
(*b*)	(*c*)	(*d*)	(*c*)	(*c*)					

SOME SELECTED EXPLANATORY ANSWERS

1. When all tomatoes are red and all grapes are tomatoes, then all grapes are also red. When all grapes are tomatoes, then some tomatoes must be grapes. Therefore, both conclusions I and II are correct.

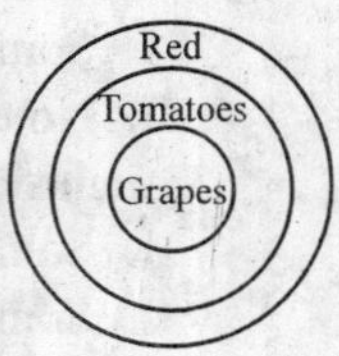

2. When all painters are smiling and some authors are painters, then some authors are smiling. Therefore, only conclusion II is correct.

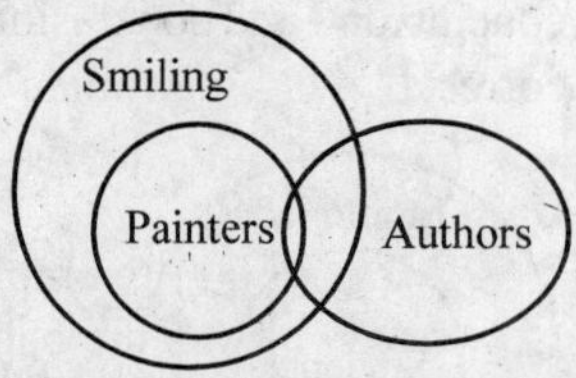

3. When all the peons of the office are efficient, then Ramu cannot be a peon in this office. Therefore, only conclusion I is correct.

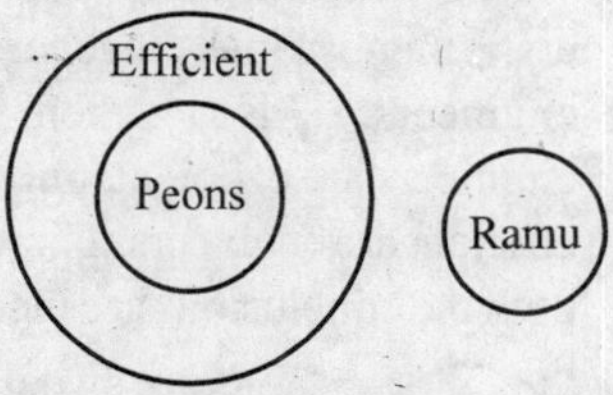

4. When all weavers are hardworking and no hardworking men are foolish, then no weavers are foolish. Therefore, only conclusion I is correct.

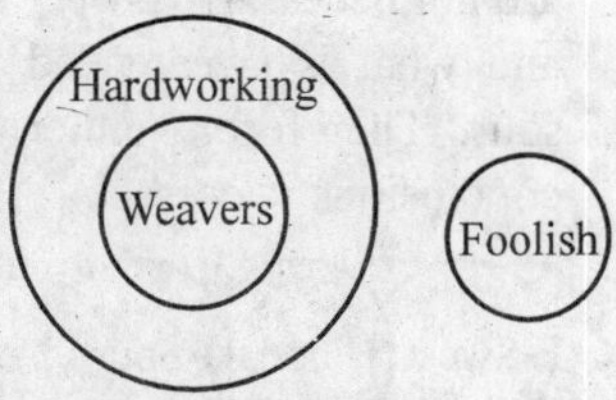

5. When all fishes are cars and all cars are vegetables, then all fishes will naturally be vegetables. This means that some vegetables are fishes. And when all cars are vegetables, then some vegetables will be cars naturally. Therefore, both the conclusions I and II are correct.

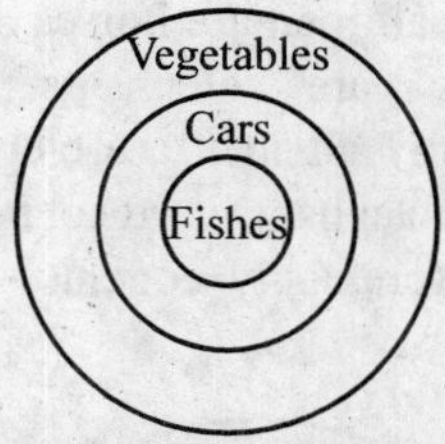

7. When all beautiful women are mothers and all mothers are understanding, then naturally all beautiful women are understanding. All mothers need not be beautiful women. Therefore, only conclusion I is correct.

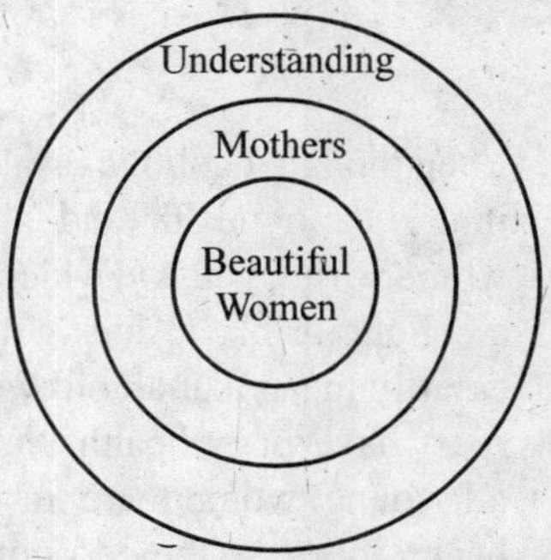

8. When some toys are tables and no table is black, then it is indicated that some toys can be black, as all toys are not tables. On the other hand, some toys may not be black. Therefore, there is a possibility that some toys may or may not be black. As such, either conclusion I or conclusion II can be correct.

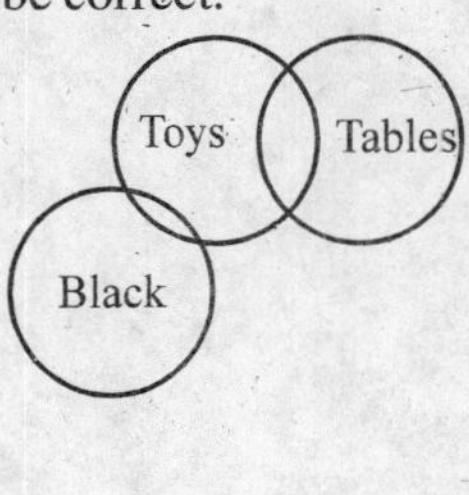

10. When all men are horses and all horses are elephants then, naturally all men are elephants, but all elephants need not be men. Therefore, only conclusion I is correct.

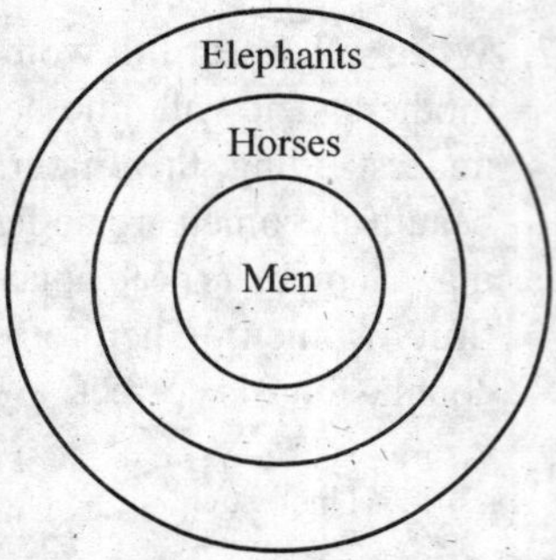

12. Even though alcoholic drinks are injurious to health and all old women drink whisky, which is an alcoholic drink, it does not necessarily mean that all old women must have poor health and that all young women are in good health, because they do not take alcoholic drinks. Therefore, neither conclusion I nor conclusion II is correct.

13. When all students are employed, then some employed must be students. And when no employed are babies, then no student can be a baby, as all students are employed. Therefore, both conclusion I and conclusion II are correct.

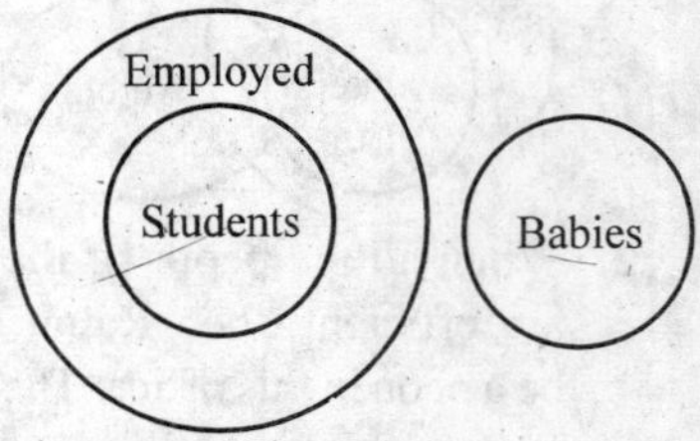

14. When some engineers are teachers, then some teachers are engineers. Also, when some engineers are efficient, only some efficient are engineers. Thererfore, both the conclusions are incorrect.

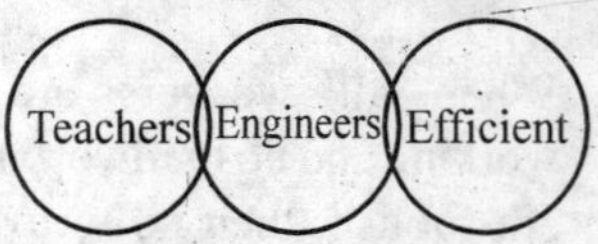

15. When some foods are sweet and some foods are sour, then all foods are not necessarily sweet or sour and what is sweet need not be sour. Therefore, neither of the conclusions is correct.

❑❑❑

General English

1 Spelling Errors

The most common errors in English are of spellings of words. Even the most learned men are sometimes confused about the correct spellings of some words. One must keep and use a dictionary religiously. Never ignore and let pass a new word casually.

A number of question to test your knowledge of spellings are compiled here. Try to solve as many as you can.

MULTIPLE CHOICE QUESTIONS

Directions: *Find the correctly spelt word out of the four options in each question.*

1. A. Accompalish
   B. Ackmplesh
   C. Acomplush
   D. Accomplish
2. A. Acommodation
   B. Acomodation
   C. Accomodation
   D. Accommodation
3. A. Astonished
   B. Astronished
   C. Astoneshed
   D. Asstonished
4. A. Benefeted
   B. Benefitted
   C. Benifited
   D. Benefited
5. A. Belligerent
   B. Beligirent
   C. Belligarant
   D. Belligerrent
6. A. Chancelery
   B. Chancellery
   C. Chancellary
   D. Chancelary
7. A. Discriminate
   B. Discremineta
   C. Discrimenate
   D. Discriminat
8. A. Damage B. Dammage
   C. Damaige D. Dammege
9. A. Efficiant B. Effecient
   C. Efficient D. Eficient
10. A. Extravagant
    B. Extreragent
    C. Extreregant
    D. Extravegent
11. A. Efflorascence
    B. Eflorescene
    C. Effllorescence
    D. Efflorescence

12. A. Equinimity
B. Equanimmity
C. Equannimity
D. Equanimity

13. A. Farmament B. Farmement
C. Fermament D. Fremament

14. A. Grieff B. Grief
C. Grieef D. Grrief

15. A. Guarantee B. Garuntee
C. Guaruntee D. Gaurantee

16. A. Hypocritical
B. Hypocretical
C. Hypocriticel
D. Hypocirticel

17. A. Humurous B. Humorous
C. Humoreus D. Humorrous

18. A. Itenerary B. Itinarery
C. Itinarary D. Itinerary

19. A. Indipenseble
B. Indispansible
C. Indispensable
D. Indipensable

20. A. Imprecticability
B. Impracticebility
C. Impracticibility
D. Impracticability

21. A. Incradulous
B. Incredulous
C. Incridulous
D. Incredalous

22. A. Juddicious B. Judiceous
C. Judicious D. Judiceus

23. A. Kleptomonia
B. Kleptemonia
C. Kleptomania
D. Klaptomania

24. A. Lackdaisical
B. Lackadaisical
C. Lckadaisicle
D. Lackadisical

25. A. Licentious B. Licontious
C. Licenttious D. Licientious

26. A. Meddicine B. Medicine
C. Medicene D. Medicinne

27. A. Meritricious
B. Merefrecious
C. Meretricious
D. Merritricious

28. A. Missunderstood
B. Miesunderstood
C. Misunderstood
D. Misunderstod

29. A. Occurad B. Occurred
C. Ocurred D. Occured

30. A. Osttentatious
B. Ostentetious
C. Ostentatious
D. Ostenttatious

31. A. Obnosious B. Obnoxeous
C. Obnoxious D. Obnoseous

32. A. Omenous B. Ominous
C. Ommineous D. Omineous

33. A. Pecification
B. Pacification
C. Pecifacation
D. Pecefication

34. A. Prograssive B. Progressive
C. Progresive D. Prograsive

35. A. Pasiveness B. Passiveness
C. Passeveniss D. Passivines

36. A. Polyendry B. Poliendry
C. Pollyendry D. Polyandry

37. A. Puerille B. Puerrile
C. Puerile D. Purrile

38. A. Pesanger B. Passenger
C. Pessenger D. Pasanger

39. A. Querrelsome
B. Quarrelsame
C. Quarrelsome
D. Querralsome

40. A. Rigourous B. Rigerous
C. Rigorous D. Regerous

41. A. Survellance
B. Surveilance
C. Surveillance
D. Survaillance

42. A. Schedule B. Schdule
C. Schedale D. Schedeule

43. A. Sepalchrle B. Sepalchral
C. Sepulchrle D. Sepulchral

44. A. Sympathetic
B. Smypathetic
C. Sympothetic
D. Sympethetic

45. A. Sincerely B. Sencerely
C. Sincerelly D. Sincerrely

46. A. Satellite B. Sattellite
C. Satelite D. Sattelite

47. A. Teracherous
B. Treacherous
C. Treacheraus
D. Treachereans

48. A. Uncivilized
B. Uncevilized
C. Uncivillized
D. Uncevelized

49. A. Vainglorious
B. Vaniglorious
C. Vaniglerious
D. Vaingloreus

50. A. Vulnarable B. Valnerable
C. Velnerable D. Vulnerable

ANSWERS

1	2	3	4	5	6	7	8	9	10
D	D	A	B	A	C	A	A	C	A
11	**12**	**13**	**14**	**15**	**16**	**17**	**18**	**19**	**20**
D	D	C	B	A	A	B	D	C	D
21	**22**	**23**	**24**	**25**	**26**	**27**	**28**	**29**	**30**
B	C	C	B	A	B	C	C	B	C
31	**32**	**33**	**34**	**35**	**36**	**37**	**38**	**39**	**40**
C	B	B	B	B	D	C	B	C	C
41	**42**	**43**	**44**	**45**	**46**	**47**	**48**	**49**	**50**
C	A	D	A	A	A	B	A	A	D

❑❑❑

2 Spotting Errors

The most common errors in English are of spellings, grammar and usage of words. By regular practice, the errors can be easily spotted and minimised.

Common Errors with Nouns and Noun-Phrases

	Incorrect	Correct
1.	I have bought new *furnitures.*	I have bought new *furniture.*
2.	The wages of sin *are* death.	The wages of sin *is* death.
3.	She told these *news* to her mother.	She told her mother this *news.*
4.	He took *troubles* to do his work.	He took *trouble* (or pains) over his work.
5.	The *cattles* were grazing.	The *cattle* were grazing.
6.	He showered *many abuses* on me.	He showered *much abuse* on me.
7.	I spent the holidays with my *family members.*	I spent the holidays with my *family.*
8.	There is no *place* in this compartment.	There is no *room* in this compartment.
9.	Write this new *poetry* in your *copy.*	Write this new *poem* in your *notebook.*
10.	He took *insult* at this.	He took *offence* at this.
11.	Put your *sign* here.	Put your *signatures* here.
12.	She is my *cousin sister.*	She is my *cousin.*
13.	*Sunil's* my *neighbour's* house was burgled.	*Sunil* my *neighbour's* house was burgled.
14.	I lost a *ten-rupees* note.	I lost *a ten-rupee* note.
15.	Road closed for *repair.*	Road closed for *repairs.*
16.	His house is out of *repairs.*	His house is out of *repair.*
17.	What is the *reason* of an earthquake?	What is the *cause* of an earthquake?
18.	This building is made of *stones.*	This building is made of *stone.*
19.	I disapprove of *these kinds* of games.	I disapprove of *this kind* of games.

20. Veena's and Sheela's father is ill.	Veena and Sheela's father is ill.
21. His *son-in-laws* are doctors.	His *sons-in-law* are doctors.
22. *Alms* is given to the *poor.*	*Alms* are given to the poor.
23. He always keeps his words.	He always keeps his *word.*
24. I carried the *luggages.*	I carried the *luggage.*
25. *Two-third* of the work is left.	*Two-thirds* of the work is left.

Common Errors with Pronouns

Incorrect	*Correct*
1. Both did not go.	Neither went.
2. We all did not go.	None of us went.
3. Each of these boys play.	Each of these boys plays.
4. Whoever does best he will get a prize.	Whoever does best will get a prize.
5. One should not waste his time.	A man should not waste his time.
6. I and she are sisters.	She and I are sisters.
7. He is wiser than me.	He is wiser than I.
8. Between you and I, Anil is not to be trusted.	Between you and me, Anil is not to be trusted.
9. Nobody was there but I.	Nobody was there but me.
10. Who is there ? It is me.	Who is there ? It is I.
11. Only he and me can use this card.	Only he and I can use this card.
12. Let you and I go now.	Let you and me go now.
13. Everyone got one's pay.	Everyone got his pay.
14. Everyone is frightened when they see a tiger.	Everyone is frightened when he sees a tiger.
15. These two friends are fond of one another.	These two friends are fond of each other.
16. I did not like him coming at that hour.	I did not like his coming at that hour.
17. Who do you think I met?	Whom do you think I met?
18. You should avail this opportunity.	You should avail yourself this opportunity.
19. When you have read these books, please return the same to me.	When you have read the books, please return them to me.
20. They that are humble need fear no fall.	Those that are humble need fear no fall.

Common Errors with Adjectives

	Incorrect	Correct
1.	These all oranges are good.	All these oranges are good.
2.	He held the book in the both hands.	He held the book in both hands.
3.	Both men have not come.	Neither man has come.
4.	That man should do some or other work.	That man should do some work or other.
5.	He is elder than I.	He is older than I.
6.	Shakespeare is greater than any other poets.	Shakespeare is greater than any other poet.
7.	He is a coward man.	He is a cowardly man.
8.	Many villagers cannot write his own name.	Many villagers cannot write their own name.
9.	Each of us loves our home.	Each of us loves his home.
10.	Much efforts bring their reward.	Much effort brings its reward.
11.	He found hundred rupees.	He found a hundred rupees.
12.	He had leave of four days.	He had four days leave.
13.	This is a worth seeing sight.	This is a sight worth seeing.
14.	He will spend his future life here.	He will spend the rest of his life here.
15.	There is a best teacher in that class.	There is a very good teacher in that class.
16.	Of the two plans this is the best.	Of the two plans this is the better.
17.	He is becoming strong every day.	He is becoming stronger every day.
18.	He is worst than I.	He is worse than I.
19.	Jaipur is hot than Delhi.	Jaipur is hotter than Delhi.
20.	In our library the number of books is less.	In our library the number of books is small.

Common Errors with Verbs

	Incorrect	Correct
1.	He asked had we taken our luggage.	He asked if we had taken our luggage.
2.	She asked what are you doing.	She asked what we were doing.
3.	Rama asked to Anil why he is angry.	Rama asked Anil why he was angry.
4.	He does not care for his money.	He does not take care of his money.
5.	He does not care for his work.	He takes no care over his work.

	Incorrect	Correct
6.	No one cared for him after his mother died.	No one took care of him after his mother died.
7.	He got angry before I said a word.	He got angry before I had said a word.
8.	I met a man who was my tutor 20 years ago.	I met a man who had been my tutor twenty years ago.
9.	I had been for walking yesterday.	I went for a walk yesterday.
10.	If I shall do this I shall be wrong.	If I do this I shall be wrong.
11.	I have left trekking.	I have given up trekking.
12.	I came to know as to how he did this.	I learnt how he did this.
13.	I came to know why he was sad.	I found out why he was sad.
14.	He knows to swim.	He knows how to swim.
15.	The criminal's head was cut.	The criminal's head was cut off.
16.	I said to him to go.	I told him to go.
17.	I told the teacher to excuse me.	I asked the teacher to excuse me.
18.	He is troubling me.	He is giving me trouble.
19.	I have got a hurt on my leg.	I have hurt my leg.
20.	She gave a speech.	She made a speech.

Common Errors in Subject-Verb Agreement

	Incorrect	*Correct*
1.	The owners of this factory *is* very rich.	The owners of this factory *are* very rich.
2.	The pleasures of nature that one can experience at Shimla *is* beyond description.	The pleasures of nature that one can experience at Shimla *are* beyond description.
3.	There *is* no street lights in our colony.	There *are* no street lights in our colony.
4.	He and I *am* entrusted with the job.	He and I *are* entrusted with the job.
5.	Rice and curry *are* his favourite dish.	Rice and curry *is* his favourite dish.
6.	The honour and glory of our country *are* at stake.	The honour and glory of our country *is* at stake.
7.	Time and tide *waits* for none.	Time and tide *wait* for none.
8.	All the passengers with the driver *was* killed.	All the passengers, with the driver, *were* killed.
9.	The teacher, with her students, *were* going out.	The teacher, with her students, *was* going out.

10.	I as well as they *am* tired.	I as well as they *are* tired.
11.	Not only the soldiers but their captain also *were* captured.	Not only the soldiers but their captain also *was* captured.
12.	Neither you nor I *were* selected.	Neither you nor I *was* selected.
13.	Either of these two applicants *are* fit for the job but neither want to accept it.	Either of these two applicants *is* fit for the job but neither wants to accept it.
14.	One of these students are sure to stand first.	One of these students *is* sure to stand first.
15.	Everyone of these workers want a raise.	Everyone of these workers wants a raise.
16.	None of these letters has been answered so far.	None of these letters *have* been answered so far.
17.	None of the girls were present at the party.	None of the girls *was* present at the party.
18.	Many a battle were fought on Indian soil.	Many a battle *was* fought on Indian soil.
19.	A lot of work remain to be done.	A lot of work *remains* to be done.
20.	The majority of these girls likes music.	The majority of these girls *like* music.

Common Errors in the Use of Modals/Auxiliary Verbs

	Incorrect	*Correct*
1.	When I shall see him I shall tell. him this	When I *see* him, I shall tell him this.
2.	If I should do wrong, he would punish me.	If I *did* wrong, he would punish me.
3.	Until he will have confessed his fault, he will be kept in prison.	Until he *has* confessed his fault, he will be kept in prison.
4.	She will obey me.	She *shall* obey me.
5.	You would work hard.	You *should* work hard.
6.	You shall find him in the garden.	You *will* find him in the garden.
7.	He must have died of exposure, but we cannot be certain.	He *might* have died of exposure, but we cannot be certain.
8.	You might not show disrespect to your elders.	You *must* not show disrespect to your elders.
9.	You may take exercise in order to maintain good health.	You *must* take exercise in order to maintain good health.
10.	He must be a crook for all we know.	He *may* be a crook for all we know.

Common Errors in the Use of Adverbs

	Incorrect	Correct
1.	He is very much angry.	He is *very* angry.
2.	She was very good enough to help me.	She was *good enough* to help me.
3.	She runs much fast.	She runs *very* fast.
4.	She runs very faster than Seema.	She runs *much* faster than Seema.
5.	It is bitter cold today.	It is *bitterly* cold today.
6.	He is a much learned man.	He is a very learned man.
7.	She is thinking very hardly.	She is thinking very hard.
8.	To tell in brief the film was boring.	*In short* the film was boring.
9.	He told the story in details.	He told the story *in detail.*
10.	I did it anyhow.	I *managed to do* it somehow.
11.	Aeroplanes reach Europe soon.	Aeroplanes reach Europe quickly.
12.	Before long there were dinosaurs on the earth.	*Long ago,* there were dinosaurs on the earth.
13.	This book is too interesting.	This book is *very* interesting.
14.	He lives miserly.	He lives in *a miserly* way.
15.	Just I had gone when she came.	I had just gone when she came.
16.	He sings good.	He sings *well.*
17.	He sings good than I.	He sings *better* than I.
18.	Really speaking it is cold.	*As a matter of fact* it is cold.
19.	He is enough tall to reach the ceiling.	He is *tall enough* to reach the ceiling.
20.	He went directly to his college.	He went *direct* to his college.

Common Errors in the Use of Conjunctions

	Incorrect	Correct
1.	As he is fat so he runs slowly.	As he is fat *he* runs slowly.
2.	If he is fat then he will run slowly.	If he is fat, he will run slowly.
3.	Though he is fat still he runs fast.	Though he is fat, *he runs* fast.
4.	*As* I pulled the trigger at the sametime he shook my arm.	As I pulled the trigger, he shook my arm.
5.	No sooner I had spoken than he left.	No sooner *had* I spoken than he left.
6.	Not only he will go, but also he will stay there.	Not only *will he* go, but he *will also* stay there.

	Incorrect	Correct
7.	Neither he comes nor he writes.	Neither *does he* come nor *does he* write.
8.	Scarcely he entered the room than the telephone rang.	Scarcely *had* he entered the room *when the* telephone rang.
9.	Hardly she had left the house than it began to rain.	Hardly *had she* left the house *when* it began to rain.
10.	He is the fastest runner and he comes last.	He is the fastest runner *but* he comes last.
11.	She is as innocent as if she looks.	She is as innocent as she looks.
12.	Until he does not try he must be punished.	He must be punished unless he tries.
13.	I want to know as to why you are late.	I want to know why you are late.
14.	I am fond of Chinese food as for example sweet and sour prawns.	I am fond of Chinese food, for example, sweet and sour prawns.
15.	He was angry therefore I ran away.	He was angry so I ran away.
16.	I was trying to work, at that time he was disturbing me.	While I was trying to work, he was disturbing me.
17.	Supposing if he is late, what will happen?	Supposing he is late (or if he is late) what will happen?
18.	He asked me that why I was late.	He asked me why I was late.
19.	Let us catch a taxi lest we should not get late.	Let us catch a taxi lest we should get late.
20.	She dresses herself like the teacher does.	She dresses herself as the teacher does.
21.	Wait while I come.	Wait *until* (or *till)* I come.
22.	Until, there is corruption in India, there can be little progress.	*As long* as there is corruption in India there can be little progress.
23.	I have never told a lie nor cheated anybody.	I have never told a lie *nor have I* cheated anybody.
24.	Both Mohan as well as Arun are responsible for this action.	Both Mohan *and* Arun are responsible for this action.
25.	Hindus and Muslims both are to blame for the riots.	*Both Hindus* and Muslims are to blame for the riots.

Common Errors in the Use of Prepositions

	Incorrect	*Correct*
1.	I will not listen him.	I will not listen *to* him.
2.	Copy this word by word.	Copy this word *for* word.

3.	He enquired from her where she lived.	He enquired *of* her where she lived.
4.	Sign here with ink.	Sign here *in* ink.
5.	Has she come in train or by foot?	Has she come *by* train or *on* foot?
6.	She said this at his face.	She said this *to* his face.
7.	Open the book on page one.	Open the book *at* page one.
8.	I was invited for lunch.	I was *invited to* lunch.
9.	I am ill since three months.	I have been *ill for* three months.
10.	This paper is inferior than that.	This paper is inferior *to* that.
11.	This resembles to that.	This *resembles* that.
12.	My brother is superior than you in strength.	My brother is superior *to* you in strength.
13.	He wrote me.	He wrote *to* me.
14.	I shall explain them this.	I shall explain this *to* them.
15.	Send this letter on my address.	Send this letter *to* my address.
16.	He suggested me this.	He suggested this *to* me.
17.	He goes *on his* work.	He goes *to his* work.
18.	He *reached to* Nagpur.	He *reached* Nagpur.
19.	He told *to me* to go.	He told *me* to go.
20.	The term begins *from* July 1st.	The term begins *on* July 1st.

Miscellaneous Errors

	Incorrect	*Correct*
1.	Many *homes* are lying vacant.	Many *houses* are lying vacant.
2.	It is cool in the *shadow* of the tree.	It is cool in the *shade* of the tree.
3.	She *keeps* good health.	She *enjoys* good health.
4.	My leg is *paining*.	*I am feeling pain* in my leg.
5.	*See* this word in the dictionary.	*Look up* this word in the dictionary.
6.	The train will arrive *just now*.	The train will arrive *shortly*.
7.	They are *pulling* on well.	They are *getting* on well.
8.	The river has *over flown* its bank.	The river has *over flown* its banks.
9.	He was appointed *on* the post.	He was appointed *to* the post.
10.	Last but not *the least,* we have to discuss the problem of over population.	Last but not *least,* we have to discuss the problem of over population.
11.	*Cities* after *cities* fell.	*City* after *city* fell.
12.	What is the use Munir going there?	What is the use of Munir going there?
13.	He *did many mischief.*	He *made much mischief.*

14. It is exact five *in* my watch.	It is exact five *by* my watch.
15. I will dine with them on *next Sunday*.	I will dine with them *Sunday next*
16. Misfortunes when faced bravely and *manly* become less troublesome.	Misfortunes when faced bravely an *manfully* become less troublesome
17. I am *laid down* with fever.	I am *laid up* with fever.
18. He is habituated to smoking.	He is *addicted* to smoking.
19. *According to my opinion* he is right.	*In my opinion* (or according *to me*, he is right.
20. Could you please *open* this knot?	Could you please *untie* this knot

MULTIPLE CHOICE QUESTIONS

Directions: *In this section, each sentence has three parts, indicated by (A), (B) and (C). Read each sentence to find out whether there is an error. If you find an error in any one of the parts (A, B, C), indicate your response by marking the letter related to that part. If a sentence has no error, indicate this by marking '(D)' which stands for "No error". Errors may belong to grammar, usage or idiom. Ignore errors of punctuation, if any.*

1. (A) Beware of/(B) a fair-weather friend/(C) who is neither a friend in need nor a friend indeed/(D) No error.

2. (A) Copernicus proved/(B) that Earth/(C) moves round the Sun./(D) No error.

3. (A) Seldom we have been treated/(B) in such a rude manner/(C) by the police personnel./(D) No error.

4. (A) Some men are born great,/(B) some achieve greatness/(C) and some had greatness thrust on them./(D) No error.

5. (A) The property/(B) wa divided/(C) among the tw brothers./(D) No error.

6. (A) I am quite certain/(B) tha the lady is not only greedy/(C but miserly./(D) No error.

7. (A) The aircraft overloaded/(B there was something wrong o the battery/(C) and the engin was making a queer noise/(D No error.

8. (A) A thorough inquiry of th misappropriation of funds/(B) i now imperative/(C) to bring th guilty to book/(D) No error.

9. (A) The brilliant success in th examination/(B) as well as hi record in sports/(C) deserves hig praise/(D) No error.

10. (A) While travelling by a train (B) on a cold winter night/(C) a argument rose between tw passengers in our compartment (D) No error.

11. (A) I cannot find/(B) where has he gone/(C) though I have tried may best/(D) No error.

12. (A) If I was/(B) the Prime Minister of India/(C) I would work wonders/(D) No error.

13. (A) Amit's severe bout of flu/(B) debilitated him so much/(C) that he was too tired to do for work for a week./(D) No error.

14. (A) This is the crux of the entire problem;/(B) everything centres on/(C) it being resolved./(D) No error.

15. (A) One of the major aims of the Air Force/(B) was the complete demolition of all means of transportation/(C) by the bombing of rail lines and terminals./(D) No error.

16. (A) His strong voice cut over/(B) the hum of conversation/(C) like a knife through butter./(D) No error.

17. (A) Even though they weren't expecting us/(B) they managed to knock up/(C) a marvellous meal./(D) No error.

18. (A) The celebrated singer was/(B) surrounded by the usual crowd/(C) of lackeys and hanger-ons./(D) No error.

19. (A) If it weren't/(B) for you,/(C) I wouldn't be alive today./(D) No error.

20. (A) He looked like a lion/(B) baulked from/(C) its prey./(D) No error.

21. (A) Widespread flooding/(B) is effecting/(C) large areas of the villages./(D) No error.

22. (A) She regards/(B) negotiating prices with customers/(C) as her special preserve./(D) No error.

23. (A) Often in political campaigns, a point is reached at which/(B) the candidates take out their gloves./(C) and start slugging with bare fists./(D) No error.

24. (A) If we really set to/(B) we can get the whole house/(C) cleaned in an afternoon./(D) No error.

25. (A) Pieces of rock plummeted/(B) down the mountainside/(C) in the ground below./(D) No error.

26. (A) Since the two parties each won/(B) the same number of seats,/(C) the minority party holds the balance of power./(D) No error.

27. (A) It's arrogant for you/(B) to assume you'll/(C)win every time./(D) No error.

28. (A) We've paid for our travel and accommodation,/(B) so we need only to take/(C) some pocket-money with us./(D) No error.

29. (A) There's no evidence to show/(B) that information technology secrets are more/(C) vulnerable in India than Britain or the US./(D) No error.

30. (A) It is shameful that hunting/(B) is still considered sport/(C) by some unscrupulous people in the civilized world./(D) No error.

31. (A) The Prime Minister's good looks won him/(B)the election but he has still to prove/(C) that he's not a just pretty face./(D) No error.

32. (A) The two books are the same/ (B) except for the fact that this/ (C) has an answer in the back./ (D) No error.

33. (A) He estimated his income tax bill/(B) by extrapolation over figures/(C) submitted in previous years./(D) No error.

34. (A) The modern office block/(B) sticks out like a sore thumb/(C) among the old buildings in the area./(D) No error.

35. (A) I will try to put over/(B) some feelers to gauge/(C) people's reactions to our proposal./(D) No error.

36. (A) A major contribution of Mathura sculptors/(B)of that period were the creation and popularization/(C) of the Buddha's image in human form./ (D) No error.

37. (A) Amit has been deceiving Mona/(B) for many years but she/ (C) has not still tumbled to it./ (D) No error.

38. (A) Mahavira was an advocate of nonviolence and vegetarianism,/ (B) who revived and reorganized the Jain doctrine/(C) and established rules for their monastic order. (D) No error.

39. (A) Microwaves are the principle carriers/(B) of television, telephone and data transmissions/ (C)between stations on earth and between the earth and satellites./ (D) No error.

40. (A) An unit is an abstract idea,/ (B) defined either by reference to/(C) a randomly chosen material standard or to a natural phenomenon./(D) No error.

41. (A) With the crisis deepening,/ (B) the critics sense an opportunity/(C) about putting in place a more radical strategy./(D) No error.

42. (A) The salesman gave us/(B) a big spiel about why/(C) we should buy his product./(D) No error.

43. (A) I will need several weeks/(B) to invent the lie of the land before/(C) I can make any decision about the future of the business./(D) No error.

44. (A) You should be cautious/(B) and make a few discrete enquiries about/(C) the firm before you sign anything./(D) No error.

45. (A) Your husband doesn't/(B) believe that you are older/(C) than I./(D) No error.

46. (A) We are meeting today afternoon/(B) to discuss the matter/(C) and reach a compromise./(D) No error.

47. (A) Either Ram or/(B) you is responsible/(C) for this action./ (D) No error.

48. (A) The student flatly denied/(B) that he had copied/(C) in the examination hall./(D) No error.

49. (A) By the time you arrive tomorrow/(B) I have finished/(C) my work./(D) No error.

50. (A) The speaker stressed repeatedly on/(B) the importance of improving/(C) the condition of the slums./(D) No error.

51. (A) The captain with the members of his team/(B) are returning/(C) after a fortnight./(D) No error.

52. (A) After returning from/(B) an all-India tour/(C) I had to describe about it/(D) No error.

53. (A) The teacher asked his students/(B) if they had gone through/(C) either of the three chapters included in the prescribed text./(D) No error.

54. (A) Although they are living in the country/(B) since they were married/(C) they are now moving to the town./(D) No error.

55. (A) Do you know/(B) how old were you/(C) when you came here?/(D) No error.

ANSWERS

1	**2**	**3**	**4**	**5**	**6**	**7**	**8**	**9**	**10**
D	B	A	C	C	C	B	A	D	C
11	**12**	**13**	**14**	**15**	**16**	**17**	**18**	**19**	**20**
B	A	C	C	B	A	A	C	C	C
21	**22**	**23**	**24**	**25**	**26**	**27**	**28**	**29**	**30**
C	A	A	A	C	A	A	B	D	B
31	**32**	**33**	**34**	**35**	**36**	**37**	**38**	**39**	**40**
C	C	C	D	A	B	C	C	A	A
41	**42**	**43**	**44**	**45**	**46**	**47**	**48**	**49**	**50**
C	D	D	D	C	A	B	D	B	A
51	**52**	**53**	**54**	**55**					
B	C	C	B	D					

❑❑❑

3 Articles

Definite and Indefinite Articles

(*i*) 'A' and 'an' are Indefinite Articles.

(*ii*) 'The' is Definite Article.

(*iii*) 'A' and 'an' modify a noun in a general way.

(*iv*) 'The' particularises it. *e.g.*,

Mohan has **a pen.**

The pen which you gave me was expensive.

Vowel and Consonant Sounds

(*i*) 'A' is used before words starting with the sound of a consonant.

(*ii*) 'An' is used before a vowel sound (vowels a, e, i, o, u) *e.g.*,

a book, a cat, a useful thing, a European girl, a university,

but an FDR, an MA, an honest boy, an hour, an owl, an egg, an umbrella, etc.

Use of Articles 'A' and 'An'

A cat mews.	(*i.e.,* every cat)
The cat of my neighbour mews day and night.	(*i.e.,* a particular cat)
He gave me **an** egg.	(Here 'an' means 'one')

Use of Article 'The'

1. 'The' is used before names of rivers, mountains, seas, oceans:

   The Himalayas, the Ganga, the Yamuna, the Bay of Bengal, the Indian Ocean, the Nile, the English Channel, *etc.*

2. Names of newspapers and magazines:

   The Times of India, the Tribune, The Sun, *etc.*

3. Names of the famous and holy books:

   The Guru Granth Sahib, The Gita, The Ramayana, *etc.*

4. Names of creations of nature:

   the sun, the earth, the moon, the sky, *etc.*

5. While using Adjectives as Nouns:

   The poor should be helped by **the rich.**

6. Sometimes with the Comparative Degree:

   The more you think, **the more** you worry.

7. With the Superlative Degree:

   She is **the most intelligent** girl in our school.

8. Before the imaginary lines and directions:

   The Latitude, The Equator, the east, the west, etc.

9. Before the names of musical instruments:
the violin, the piano, the flute, etc.
10. While using a Proper Noun as a Common Noun:
Mohan is **the Sachin** of our team.

Omission of Article 'The'

1. Before some Nouns used to convey general sense, articles are not used but are used to particularise them:
Man is mortal.
2. Before Proper Nouns:
Rakesh is an intelligent boy.
3. With Abstract Noun:
Childhood is the prime time of one's life.
The childhood of Sohan was full of sorrow.
4. With Material Nouns:
Milk is an essential food.
The milk of the cow is sweet.
5. Usually no article is used before names of diseases:
Cancer is a fatal disease.
However, when we talk about a disease figuratively, we use an article before its name, *e.g.*
Corruption is a cancer.
6. Names of games and language:
I like football.
I can speak Punjabi, Hindi and English.
7. Gold is a precious metal.

NOTE: As you must have noted above, the definite article 'the' has been used where a noun is particularised.

Double Use of Article 'The'

Read the following sentences carefully to understand this :

1. The poet and novelist has been honoured.
(The same person is the poet as well as novelist)
2. The poet and the novelist have been honoured.
(The poet and the novelist are two different persons).
3. I have a black and white dog.
(that is, one dog)
4. I have a black and a white dog.
(that is, two dogs)

MULTIPLE CHOICE QUESTIONS

Directions : *Fill in the blanks with suitable articles. Mark 'D' if no article required.*

1. Do you know .... boy in white?
A. a B. an
C. the D. No article

2. She is .... girl I am looking for.
A. a B. an
C. the D. No article

3. Have you read .... Mahabharat?
A. a B. an
C. the D. No article

4. ....rich are not always happy.
A. A B. An
C. The D. No article

5. Oranges are sold by .... dozen.
A. a B. an
C. the D. No article

6. Milk is sold by .... litre.
A. a B. an
C. the D. No article

7. .... Amazon is the longest river in the world.
A. A B. An
C. The D. No article

8. .... higher you climb, the colder it gets.
A. A B. An
C. The D. No article

9. She is .... untidy girl.
A. a B. an
C. the D. No article

10. I am .... M.A. is English.
A. a B. an
C. the D. No article

11. I have already spent .... few rupees I had.
A. a B. an
C. the D. No article

12. .... English are very hard-working.
A. A B. An
C. The D. No article

13. April is the fourth month of .... year.
A. a B. an
C. the D. No article

14. Rice is sold by .... kilogram
A. a B. an
C. the D. No article

15. She is .... best of the three girls.
A. a B. an
C. the D. No article

16. .... man in the car is a friend of mine.
A. A B. An
C. The D. No article

17. Brevity is .... soul of wit.
A. a B. an
C. the D. No article

18. .... thing of beauty is a joy for ever.
A. A B. An
C. The D. No article

19. .... little learning is a dangerous thing.
A. A B. An
C. The D. No article

20. .... best sauce for food is hunger.
A. A B. An
C. The D. No article

21. Birds of .... feather flock together.
A. a B. an
C. the D. No article

22. He makes .... living by begging.
A. a B. an
C. the D. No article

23. It is .... pity that he died so young.
A. a B. an
C. the D. No article

24. What .... nuisance it is?
A. a B. an
C. the D. No article

25. Delhi is .... London of India.
A. a B. an
C. the D. No article

26. Where is .... will, there is a way.
A. a B. an
C. the D. No article

27. Her father is .... physician and surgeon.
A. a B. an
C. the D. No article

28. This will benefit .... poor.
A. a B. an
C. the D. No article

29. ....bird in hand is better than two in a bush.
A. A B. An
C. The D. No article

30. As he is hardworking, he will win .... prize.
A. a B. an
C. the D. No article

31. .... water of this well is dirty.
A. A B. An
C. The D. No article

32. Only .... wearer knows where the shoe pinches.
A. a B. an
C. the D. No article

33. .... action will be taken against you.
A. A B. An
C. The D. No article

34. .... sun rises in the east.
A. A B. An
C. The D. No article

35. She was promoted to .... highest post.
A. a B. an
C. the D. No article

36. Did you see .... Taj Mahal?
A. a B. an
C. the D. No article

37. He is .... one-eyed man.
A. a B. an
C. the D. No article

38. This is .... useful book.
A. a B. an
C. the D. No article

39. Cloth is sold by .... metre.
A. a B. an
C. the D. No article

40. The sun sets in .... west.
A. a B. an
C. the D. No article

41. Amar bought ...... umbrella yesterday.
A. a B. an
C. the D. No article

42. Surinder is ...... honest boy.
A. a B. an
C. the D. No article

43. She wrote ...... book in French.
A. a B. an
C. the D. No article

44. ...... lion roars.
A. A B. An
C. The D. No article

45. ..... apple a day keeps the doctor away.
A. A B. An
C. The D. No article

46. John bought ...... car yesterday.
A. a B. an
C. the D. No article

47. His father is ..... engineer in the U.S.A.
A. a B. an
C. the D. No article

48. It is hard for ..... owl to fly during the day times.
A. a B. an
C. the D. No article

49. She had ..... rimmed hat.
A. a B. an
C. the D. No article

50. My uncle is ..... heart specialist.
A. a B. an
C. the D. No article

51. He looks as foolish as .... ass.
A. a B. an
C. the D. No article

52. Did you go to .... prison to visit him?
A. a B. an
C. the D. No article

53. I found .... one-rupee note in the market.
A. a B. an
C. the D. No article

54. It is a pleasure to meet such .... efficient man.
A. a B. an
C. the D. No article

55. The Sanyasi lived in a cave in .... Himalayas.
A. a B. an
C. the D. No article

56. There is .... union in our factory.
A. a B. an
C. the D. No article

57. He hit his wife on the head with .... umbrella.
A. a B. an
C. the D. No article

58. I caught him by .... collar.
A. a B. an
C. the D. No article

59. Child is .... father of man.
A. a B. an
C. the D. No article

60. He gazed at .... moon for two hours.
A. a B. an
C. the D. No article

ANSWERS

1	2	3	4	5	6	7	8	9	10
C	C	C	C	C	C	C	C	B	B
11	**12**	**13**	**14**	**15**	**16**	**17**	**18**	**19**	**20**
C	C	C	C	C	C	C	A	A	C
21	**22**	**23**	**24**	**25**	**26**	**27**	**28**	**29**	**30**
A	A	A	A	C	A	A	C	A	A
31	**32**	**33**	**34**	**35**	**36**	**37**	**38**	**39**	**40**
C	C	B	C	C	C	A	A	C	C
41	**42**	**43**	**44**	**45**	**46**	**47**	**48**	**49**	**50**
B	B	A	A	B	A	B	B	A	A
51	**52**	**53**	**54**	**55**	**56**	**57**	**58**	**59**	**60**
B	C	A	B	C	A	B	C	C	C

4 Prepositions

A Preposition is a word that comes before a Pronoun or a Noun and expresses the relationship between Noun or Pronoun and some part of the remaining sentence.

(*a*) He is busy **with** his work.
(*b*) The boy jumped **into** the river.
(*c*) The birds are chirping **in** the trees.

In these sentences the words **with**, **into** and **in** show the relationship between the verbs **busy, jumped** and **chirping** with the nouns **work, river** and **trees** respectively.

Position of the Preposition

A. A Preposition usually precedes its object.

(*i*) He laughs **at** the poor.
(*ii*) He is angry **with** you.
(*iii*) She agrees **with** me.

B. In the case of Relative Pronouns it comes after the subject.

(*i*) This is the boy whom I was looking **for**.
(*ii*) That is the pen whose mention I was making **of**.

C. In the following cases, the Preposition comes after its object.

(*i*) Where is the boy you were complaining **against**?
(*ii*) What things are there you are looking **for**?
(*iii*) Who is there, you are waiting **for**?

Omission of the Prepositon

In many cases when the sentences contain Nouns of Time or Place, the Prepositions **from**, **in** and **for** are often omitted.

(*i*) He walked many kilometres.
(*ii*) He came to see me last year.
(*iii*) As I could not find my puppy anywhere, I looked here and there.

Prepositions are small words that show the relationship between one word and another. Prepositions in the following sentences show the position of the paper in relation to the desk, the book, hand and the door.

The paper is **on** the desk.
The paper is **under** the book.
The paper is **in** his hand.
The paper is **by** the door.

Common Prepositions

about	at	by
in	onto	toward
above	before	concerning
inside	out	under
across	behind	despite
into	over	until

after	below	down	of	throughout	with
like	since	up	amid	between	for
against	beneath	during	off	till	within
near	through	upon	among	beyond	from
along	beside	except	on	to	without

MULTIPLE CHOICE QUESTIONS

Directions: *Select the most appropriate preposition from the given alternatives to fill in the blanks and make the sentence meaningfully complete.*

1. Don't try to be an advocate ..... these criminals.
   A. for B. with
   C. across D. in
2. The audience admired him ..... his sweet voice.
   A. to B. on
   C. for D. at
3. I want to check your bag ..... fake currency notes.
   A. to B. for
   C. upon D. on
4. The dew drops clung .... the blades of grass.
   A. for B. on
   C. to D. in
5. The thief was chased ..... by the police.
   A. on B. after
   C. into D. at
6. Please carry this bag ..... my room.
   A. on B. for
   C. to D. in
7. A lorry bumped ..... a car.
   A. on B. over
   C. into D. to
8. They were begging ..... food.
   A. for B. on
   C. to D. after
9. She always boasts ..... her wealth.
   A. of B. for
   C. on D. after
10. She banged ..... the door violently.
    A. for B. to
    C. on D. down
11. I applied ..... the post of a clerk.
    A. for B. on
    C. in D. to
12. I applied ..... the Principal for the post of a teacher.
    A. to B. on
    C. with D. for
13. I begged ..... him not to divulge the secret.
    A. for B. of
    C. with D. to
14. You had better borrow a pen ..... Rakesh.
    A. over B. into
    C. from D. by
15. I baked a cake ..... the guests.
    A. to B. for
    C. on D. of
16. She is confident ..... (her) success.
    A. with B. on
    C. of D. for
17. The doctor will cure you ..... malaria.
    A. of B. with
    C. for D. from

18. This law is common ..... all.

A. to B. upon

C. over D. at

19. She was condemned ..... her bad hand writing.

A. on B. for

C. into D. of

20. In summer there will be a great demand ..... desert cooler.

A. on B. with

C. for D. of

21. We shall wait ..... you.

A. on B. for

C. towards D. after

22. Tom displayed his injury ..... all his friends.

A. for B. upon

C. to D. at

23. She distributed the sweets ..... the two brothers.

A. among B. between

C. for D. in

24. Please distribute these apples ..... all.

A. among B. to

C. for D. at

25. It rarely happened that he defended ..... an innocent person.

A. against B. for

C. upon D. at

26. The parents were disappointed ..... the performance of their son.

A. on B. with

C. at D. of

27. Common salt dissolves ..... water.

A. for B. in

C. with D. by

28. This medicare is free ..... sugar.

A. on B. to

C. from D. of

29. The manager granted leave ..... the clerk.

A. to B. on

C. into D. for

30. The air was heavy ..... aroma of perfumes.

A. on B. with

C. into D. from

31. She had a quick glance ..... the magazine.

A. at B. from

C. into D. to

32. The climate of Kashmir is favourable ..... me.

A. with B. in

C. to D. for

33. They hate you ..... your poverty.

A. for B. on

C. in D. of

34. He is eligible ..... this post.

A. for B. to

C. with D. at

35. The smoke was emerging ..... down the foot of the hill.

A. on B. to

C. from D. at

36. The criminal managed to escape ..... the prison.

A. upon B. from

C. with D. of

37. You should educate your friends ..... the benefits of living in villages.

A. on B. towards

C. upon D. in

38. She made a lot of efforts ..... win the match.

A. for B. to

C. upon D. at

39. The new inspector will enquire ..... the murder case.
A. on B. for
C. into D. at

40. The retired soldiers were exempted ..... all taxes.
A. from B. to
C. on D. of

41. She was adept ..... journalism.
A. at B. on
C. with D. in

42. She is afraid ..... snakes.
A. on B. to
C. of D. with

43. I agree ..... your proposal.
A. for B. on
C. to D. with

44. The children were amazed ..... so big a python.
A. at B. on
C. in D. with

45. She was anxious ..... the final match.
A. about B. on
C. with D. for

46. He apologized ..... his being late.
A. towards B. for
C. on D. as

47. The children were amused ..... his jokes.
A. for B. to
C. at D. on

48. She is angry ..... you.
A. to B. with
C. on D. for

49. She is angry ..... your teasing remark.
A. at B. in
C. for D. with

50. A big patch of land was allocated ..... the refugees.
A. to B. for
C. in D. upon

ANSWERS

1	2	3	4	5	6	7	8	9	10
A	C	B	C	B	C	C	A	A	C
11	**12**	**13**	**14**	**15**	**16**	**17**	**18**	**19**	**20**
A	A	B	C	B	C	A	A	B	C
21	**22**	**23**	**24**	**25**	**26**	**27**	**28**	**29**	**30**
B	C	B	A	A	C	B	C	A	B
31	**32**	**33**	**34**	**35**	**36**	**37**	**38**	**39**	**40**
A	C	A	A	C	B	A	B	C	A
41	**42**	**43**	**44**	**45**	**46**	**47**	**48**	**49**	**50**
A	C	C	A	A	B	C	B	A	A

❑❑❑

5 Synonyms & Antonyms

There are thousands of words in English language. No one can remember their meanings easily but with regular practice one can memorise most of them. A number of words with their Synonyms and Antonyms are compiled here. Try to learn as many as you can and answer the questions thereafter.

Words	*Synonyms*	*Antonyms*
Abandon	Cease, Forsake	Continue
Abhor	Hate, Loathe, Detest	Like, Love
Abiding	Enduring, Durable	Fleeting
Able	Proficient, Competent	Incompetent, Unfit
Ability	Skill, Power	Disability, Inability
Abortive	Fruitless, Futile	Fruitful, Successful
Abolish	Destroy, Undo	Restore, Revive
Abridge	Shorten, Curtail	Lengthen, Expand
Absolve	Forgive, Pardon, Excuse	Condemn
Accelerate	Hasten	Retard
Accord	Agreement, Harmony	Discord, Disagreement
Accumulate	Collect, Store, Amass	Distribute, Scatter
Adamant	Hard, Inflexible	Flexible
Adversity	Misfortune, Distress	Prosperity
Adept	Expert, Skilful	Inexpert, Unskillful
Aggravate	Heighten, Intensify	Quell, Suppress
Agile	Nimble	Clumsy, Undeft
Alert	Vigilant	Heedless
Allay	Calm, Soothe, Assuage	Arouse
Ameliorate	Improve, Advance, Amend	Worsen, Deteriorate
Ambiguous	Vague, Unclear	Clear
Amiable	Lovable, Agreeable	Disagreeable
Annihilate	Destroy	Create

Words	*Synonyms*	*Antonyms*
Arduous	Hard, Strenuous	Easy
Attacks	Assault	Defend
Audacity	Boldness	Cowardice
Auspicious	Favourable, Propitious, Lucky	Ominous, Inauspicious, Unlucky
Austere	Harsh, Severe, Rigorous	Easy-going
Authentic	True, Genuine	Spurious, False
Avarice	Greed	Generosity
Averse	Unwilling, Loath, Disinclined	Willing, Inclined
Aversion	Hostility, Hatred	Affinity, Liking
Base	Low, Mean, Ignoble	Noble, Exalted
Boisterous	Noisy, Stormy	Calm, Quiet
Brave	Courageous, Daring, Bold, Plucky	Cowardly, Dastardly, Timid
Brief	Short, Concise, Laconic	Lengthy, Diffuse
Bright	Vivid, Radiant	Dull, Dark
Brutal	Savage, Cruel	Humane, Kindly
Callous	Hard, Cruel, Indifferent	Soft, Tender, Concerned
Cautious	Careful, Wary	Rash, Reckless, Foolhardy
Censure (*n*)	Blame, Condemnation	Praise
Censure (*vb*)	Blame, Condemn	Praise, Commend
Circumscribed	Restricted, Confined, Limited	Unconfined, Unrestricted
Civil	Polite, Courteous, Gracious, Urbane	Rude, Uncivil, Impolite, Ungracious
Coerce	Compel, Force	Volunteer
Compassionate	Pitiful, Sympathetic, Merciful	Unsympathetic, Merciless, Cruel
Compress	Condense, Abbreviate	Expand, Lengthen
Conspicuous	Noticeable, Manifest	Inconspicuous
Constant	Steady, Steadfast, Uniform	Inconstant, Variable
Cordial	Friendly, Warm, Hearty	Cold, Unfriendly
Covert	Hidden, Secret	Overt, Open
Cruel	Savage, Ruthless, Vicious	Kind, Gentle, Benevolent
Cursory	Rapid, Superficial	Thorough, Exhaustive, Intensive
Credible	Believable, Probable, Plausible	Incredible, Unbelievable, Fantastic
Crafty	Cunning, Sly	Artless, Simple, Ingenuous

Words	Synonyms	Antonyms
Costly	Expensive, Dear	Cheap, Inexpensive
Confidence	Trust, Reliance	Distrust, Doubt
Death	Decease, Demise	Existence, Life
Dearth	Scarcity, Lack, Want, Paucity, Shortage	Plenty, Abundance
Decay	Dissolution, Decline, Decomposition, Disintegration	Regeneration
Deference	Respect, Reverence	Disrespect, Irreverence
Deficient	Lacking, Inadequate	Complete, Sufficient
Desolate	Lonely, Deserted	Crowded, Occupied
Destitute	Wanting, Needy	Rich, Affluent
Diligence	Industry, Perseverance	Idleness
Disgrace	Dishonour, Discredit	Honour, Credit
Dwindle	Decrease, Shrink	Grow, Increase
Earthly	Terrestrial, Mundane	Celestial, Heavenly, Unearthly
Eligible	Qualified, Suitable	Ineligible, Unsuitable
Emancipate	Liberate, Free	Enslave
Excited	Impassioned, Stimulated	Composed, Cool, Impassive
Extraordinary	Uncommon, Remarkable, Marvellous	Commonplace, Ordinary
Extravagant	Lavish, Prodigal, Wastrel, Spendthrift	Thrifty, Economical, Frugal
Fabricate	Construct, Make	Destroy
Fabulous	Fictitious, Mythical	Actual, Real
False	Untrue, Mendacious	True, Genuine
Famous	Well-known, Renowned	Obscure, Unknown
Fantastic	Fanciful, Imaginative, Visionary	Practical, Down to earth
Fearful	Nervous, Anxious, Afraid, Scared	Fearless, Dauntless
Felicity	Happiness	Sorrow
Gaiety	Joyousness, Hilarity	Mourning, Dullness
Garrulous	Talkative, Loquacious	Taciturn, Silent, Reserved
Generous	Liberal, Magnanimous	Stingy, Miserly
Gigantic	Huge, Colossal	Minute, Small

Words	Synonyms	Antonyms
Graphic	Vivid, Pictorial, Meaningful	Vague
Guest	Visitor	Host
Guile	Fraud, Trickery	Artlessness, Ingenuousness
Gratitude	Gratefulness	Ingratitude, Ungratefulness
Gratuitous	Voluntary, Spontaneous, Unwarranted	Involuntary, Forced
Hamper	Hinder, Obstruct	Facilitate, Ease
Haughty	Arrogant, Proud	Humble, Modest
Hazardous	Dangerous, Perilous	Safe, Secure Protected
Headstrong	Obstinate, Stubborn	Weak-willed, Flexible
Hope	Belief, Conviction, Expectation	Despair, Hopelessness
Improvident	Prodigal, Carelessness	Provident, Economical
Incessant	Unceasing, Continuous	Discontinuous
Indolent	Slothful, Lethargic	Active, Energetic
Joy	Delight, Pleasure	Sadness, Gloom
Jolly	Jovial, Merry	Gloomy, Sad
Judicious	Discreet, Prudent	Indiscreet, Injudicious
Knowledge	Enlightenment, Learning	Ignorance, Stupidity
Laborious	Industrious, Assiduous	Slothful, Lazy
Laxity	Slackness, Looseness	Firmness
Lenient	Mild, Forbearing	Strict, Stern
Lethal	Deadly, Fatal, Mortal	Life-giving, Vital, Vivifying
Liberal	Generous, Tolerant	Intolerant, Illiberal
Liberty	Freedom, Independence	Slavery, Bondage
Lively	Animated, Active	Dull, Listless
Loyal	Faithful, Devoted	Treacherous, Disloyal, Unfaithful
Lucky	Fortunate	Unlucky, Unfortunate
Lucrative	Profitable	Unprofitable
Magnanimous	Generous, Largehearted	Ungenerous, Stingy
Malady	Illness, Ailment	Health
Manifest	Noticeable, Obvious	Obscure, Puzzling
Meagre	Small	Plentiful, Large
Mean	Low, Abject	Noble, Exalted
Mendacious	False, Untruthful	Truthful
Misery	Sorrow, Distress	Happiness, Joy
Morbid	Sick, Diseased	Healthy
Mournful	Sorrowful, Sad	Joyful, Happy

Words	*Synonyms*	*Antonyms*
Negligent	Careless, Heedless	Careful
Notorious	Infamous, Disreputable	Reputable
Obedient	Submissive, Compliant, Docile	Disobedient, Recalcitrant, Wayward
Obsolete	Antiquated, Out-of-Date	Current, Modern
Opportune	Timely, Seasonable	Inopportune
Opulence	Wealth, Riches	Penury, Poverty
Onerous	Heavy, Burdensome	Light, Easy
Palatable	Tasty, Delicious	Unpalatable
Pathetic	Touching	Joyous, Cheery
Persuade	Urge, Induce	Dissuade
Praise (*vb*)	Applaud, Eulogise	Condemn
Praise (*n*)	Applause, Eulogy	Condemnation
Precarious	Risky, Uncertain	Safe, Certain
Pretence	Pretext, Excuse	Candour, Frankness
Propagate	Breed, Circulate	Terminate, Restrict
Quaint	Odd, Singular	Usual, Ordinary
Quell	Suppress, Subdue	Agitate, Arouse
Rare	Uncommon, Scarce	Common, Ordinary
Refined	Polished, Elegant	Crude, Coarse
Remote	Distant	Near, Close
Renown	Fame, Reputation	Infamy, Notoriety
Rigid	Stiff, Unyielding	Flexible, Yielding
Remorseful	Regretful, Repentant	Unrepentant
Rebellion	Revolt, Mutiny, Insurgency	Loyalty
Scared	Holy, Consecrated	Profane, Unholy
Sane	Sensible, Sound	Insane
Scold	Chide, Rebuke	Praise
Serious	Grave, Earnest	Frivolous
Shy	Bashful	Bold, Impudent
Simple	Plain, Artless	Complex, Cunning, Shrewd
Solitary	Single, Lonely, Secluded	Numerous, Multitude
Shallow	Superficial	Deep
Solace	Comfort, Relief	Discomfort, Grief
Spurious	Sham, False	Genuine, Authentic
Stagnant	Still, Motionless	Moving
Surplus	Excess	Deficit, Shortage
Tame	Gentle, Mild, Domesticated	Savage, Wild

Words	Synonyms	Antonyms
Teacher	Instructor, Educator	Student, Pupil
Tedious	Wearisome, Monotonous	Agreeable, Lively
Temporal	Worldly, Secular	Spiritual
Temperate	Moderate	Immoderate, Intemperate
Tortuous	Winding, Circuitous	Straight, Direct
Tough	Hard, Strong	Tender, Soft, Flexible
Transient	Temporary, Fleeting	Lasting, Durable, Permanent
Trusworthy	Reliable	Unreliable, Untrustworthy
Tranquil	Calm	Agitated
Ugly	Unsightly, Repulsive	Beautiful, Attractive
Useful	Advantageous, Serviceable	Useless
Vehemence	Passion, Force	Apathy, Indifference
Vindictive	Revengeful	Forgiving
Wholesome	Healthy	Unwholesome, Morbid, Unhealthy, Diseased
Wicked	Evil, Impious	Pious, Good
Wise	Sagacious, Erudite	Foolish, Stupid
Wrath	Anger, Fury, Rage	Love, Peace, Calm
Wreck	Ruin, Destroy	Create, Construct
Yield	Surrender, Submit	Resist, Revolt
Yielding	Submissive, Supple	Inflexible, Intractable
Yoke	Oppression, Bondage	Freedom
Zeal	Passion, Fervour	Apathy, Indifference
Zest	Relish, Enthusiasm	Distaste, Disrelish

MULTIPLE CHOICE QUESTIONS

Directions (Qs. 1 to 50): *In the following questions choose the word which best expresses the MEANING of the given word.*

1. TEPID
A. Hot B. Warm
C. Cold D. Boiling

2. MAYHEM
A. Jubilation B. Havoc
C. Excitement D. Defeat

3. TIMID
A. Fast B. Slow
C. Medium D. Shy

4. CANTANKEROUS
A. Quarrelsome B. Rash
C. Disrespectful D. Noisy

5. PRECARIOUS
A. Cautious B. Critical
C. Perilous D. Brittle

6. TACITURNITY
A. Dumbness
B. Changeableness
C. Hesitation
D. Reserve

7. INEBRIATE
A. Dreamy B. Stupefied
C. Unsteady D. Drunken

8. HARBINGER
A. Massenger B. Steward
C. Forerunner D. Pilot

9. INTIMIDATE
A. To hint B. Frighten
C. Bluff D. Harass

10. IRONIC
A. Inflexible
B. Bitter
C. Good-natured
D. Disguisedly sarcastic

11. STRINGENT
A. Tense
B. Stringy
C. Strict
D. Causing to shrink

12. ECSTATIC
A. Animated B. Bewildered
C. Enraptured D. Willful

13. COMMENSURATE
A. Measurable
B. Proportionate
C. Beginning
D. Appropriate

14. DESTITUTION
A. Humility B. Moderation
C. Poverty D. Beggary

15. ASCEND
A. Leap B. Grow
C. Deviate D. Mount

16. UNCOUTH
A. Ungraceful B. Rough
C. Slovenly D. Dirty

17. LYNCH
A. Hang B. Madden
C. Killed D. Shoot

18. LAUD
A. Lord B. Eulogy
C. Praise D. Extolled

19. CORRESPONDENCE
A. Agreements B. Contracts
C. Documents D. Letters

20. VENUE
A. Place B. Agenda
C. Time D. Duration

21. STERILE
A. Barren B. Arid
C. Childless D. Dry

22. SYNOPSIS
A. Index B. Mixture
C. Summary D. Puzzle

23. GERMANE
A. Responsible B. Logical
C. Possible D. Relevant

24. PONDER
A. Think B. Evaluate
C. Anticipate D. Increase

25. CANNY
A. Obstinate B. Handsome
C. Clever D. Stout

26. ABUNDANT
A. Ripe B. Cheap
C. Plenty D. Absent

27. CONSEQUENCES
A. Results
B. Conclusions
C. Difficulties
D. Applications

28. SHIVER
A. Shake B. Rock
C. Tremble D. Move

29. DILIGENT
A. Progressive
B. Brilliant
C. Inventive
D. Hardworking

30. DISTANT
A. Far B. Removed
C. Reserved D. Separate

31. FORAY
A. Excursion B. Contest
C. Ranger D. Intuition

32. FRUGALITY
A. Foolishness B. Extremity
C. Enthusiasm D. Economy

33. GARNISH
A. Paint B. Garner
C. Adorn D. Abuse

34. VIGOUR
A. Strength B. Boldness
C. Warmth D. Enthusiasm

35. CANDID
A. Apparent B. Explicit
C. Frank D. Bright

36. BRIEF
A. Limited B. Small
C. Little D. Short

37. GARRULITY
A. Credulity
B. Senility
C. Loquaciousness
D. Speciousness

38. FURORE
A. Excitement B. Worry
C. Flux D. Anteroom

39. NEUTRAL
A. Unbiased
B. Non-aligned
C. Undecided
D. Indifferent

40. LAMENT
A. Complain B. Comment
C. Condone D. Console

41. ADVERSITY
A. Failure
B. Helplessness
C. Misfortune
D. Crisis

42. TURN UP
A. Land up B. Show up
C. Crop up D. Come up

43. DEIFY
A. Flatter B. Challenge
C. Worship D. Face

44. ERROR
A. Misadventure B. Misgiving
C. Ambiguity D. Blunder

45. SHALLOW
A. Artificial B. Superficial
C. Foolish D. Worthless

46. MASSACRE
A. Murder B. Stab
C. Assassinate D. Slaughter

47. COMBAT
A. Conflict B. Quarrel
C. Feud D. Fight

48. VORACIOUS
A. Wild B. Hungry
C. Angry D. Quick

49. IMPROMPTU
A. Offhand
B. Unimportant
C. Unreal
D. Effective

50. RABBLE

A. Mob B. Noise
C. Roar D. Rubbish

Directions (Qs. 51 to 100): *In the following questions choose the word which is the exact OPPOSITE of the given words.*

51. STRINGENT

A. General
B. Vehement
C. Lenient
D. Magnanimous

52. FLIMSY

A. Frail B. Filthy
C. Firm D. Flippant

53. BUSY

A. Occupied B. Engrossed
C. Relaxed D. Engaged

54. ADAPTABLE

A. Adoptable B. Flexible
C. Yielding D. Rigid

55. LOVE

A. Villainy B. Hatred
C. Compulsion D. Force

56. BALANCE

A. Disbalance B. Misbalance
C. Debalance D. Imbalance

57. RELINQUISH

A. Abdicate B. Renounce
C. Possess D. Deny

58. MOUNTAIN

A. Plain B. Plateau
C. Precipice D. Valley

59. FICKLE

A. Courageous B. Sincere
C. Steadfast D. Humble

60. PERENNIAL

A. Frequent B. Regular
C. Lasting D. Rare

61. RARELY

A. Hardly
B. Definitely
C. Frequently
D. Periodically

62. STARTLED

A. Amused B. Relaxed
C. Endless D. Astonished

63. ADHERENT

A. Detractor B. Enemy
C. Alien D. Rival

64. QUIESCENT

A. Indifferent
B. Troublesome
C. Weak
D. Unconcerned

65. CONDENSE

A. Expand B. Distribute
C. Interpret D. Lengthen

66. BENIGN

A. Malevolent B. Soft
C. Friendly D. Unwise

67. OBSCURE

A. Implicit B. Obnoxious
C. Explicit D. Pedantic

68. HYPOCRITICAL

A. Gentle
B. Sincere
C. Amiable
D. Dependable

69. EVASIVE

A. Free B. Honest
C. Liberal D. Frank

70. INDUSTRIOUS
A. Indifferent B. Indolent
C. Casual D. Passive

71. EXTRICATE
A. Manifest B. Palpable
C. Release D. Entangle

72. LUCID
A. Glory B. Noisy
C. Obscure D. Distinct

73. INSIPID
A. Tasty B. Stupid
C. Discreet D. Feast

74. OBEYING
A. Ordering
B. Following
C. Refusing
D. Contradicting

75. VICTORIOUS
A. Defeated B. Annexed
C. Destroyed D. Vanquished

76. COMMISSIONED
A. Started B. Closed
C. Finished D. Terminated

77. VANITY
A. Pride B. Humility
C. Conceit D. Ostentious

78. ZENITH
A. Acme B. Top
C. Nadir D. Pinnacle

79. TANGIBLE
A. Ethereal B. Concrete
C. Actual D. Solid

80. REPRESS
A. Inhibit B. Liberate
C. Curb D. Quell

81. EPILOGUE
A. Dialogue B. Prelude
C. Post script D. Epigram

82. FRAUDULENT
A. Candid B. Direct
C. Forthright D. Genuine

83. LOQUACIOUS
A. Reticent B. Talkative
C. Garrulous D. Verbose

84. NIGGARDLY
A. Frugal B. Thrifty
C. Stingy D. Generous

85. PERTINENT
A. Irrational B. Irregular
C. Insistent D. Irrelevant

86. FAINT-HEARTED
A. Warm-hearted
B. Full-blooded
C. Hot-blooded
D. Stout-hearted

87. VIOLENT
A. Humble B. Harmless
C. Gentle D. Tame

88. STATIONARY
A. Active B. Mobile
C. Rapid D. Busy

89. HONORARY
A. Dishonourable
B. Reputed
C. Paid
D. Official

90. COMMON
A. Rare B. Small
C. Petty D. Poor

91. REPEL
A. Attend B. Concentrate
C. Continue D. Attract

92. ARTIFICIAL
A. Red B. Natural
C. Truthful D. Solid

93. CAPACIOUS
A. Limited
B. Caring
C. Foolish
D. Changeable

94. PROVOCATION
A. Vocation
B. Pacification
C. Peace
D. Destruction

95. METICULOUS
A. Mutual B. Shaggy
C. Meretricious D. Slovenly

96. ABLE
A. Disable B. Inable
C. Unable D. Enable

97. COMFORT
A. Uncomfort
B. Miscomfort
C. Discomfort
D. None of these

98. GAIN
A. Loose B. Fall
C. Lost D. Lose

99. SYNTHETIC
A. Affable B. Natural
C. Plastic D. Cosmetic

100. ACQUITTED
A. Freed B. Burdened
C. Convicted D. Entrusted

ANSWERS

1	2	3	4	5	6	7	8	9	10
B	B	D	A	B	D	D	C	B	D
11	**12**	**13**	**14**	**15**	**16**	**17**	**18**	**19**	**20**
C	C	B	C	D	A	C	C	D	A
21	**22**	**23**	**24**	**25**	**26**	**27**	**28**	**29**	**30**
A	C	D	A	C	C	A	C	D	A
31	**32**	**33**	**34**	**35**	**36**	**37**	**38**	**39**	**40**
A	D	C	A	C	D	C	A	A	A
41	**42**	**43**	**44**	**45**	**46**	**47**	**48**	**49**	**50**
C	B	C	D	B	D	D	B	A	A
51	**52**	**53**	**54**	**55**	**56**	**57**	**58**	**59**	**60**
C	C	C	D	B	D	C	D	C	D
61	**62**	**63**	**64**	**65**	**66**	**67**	**68**	**69**	**70**
D	B	B	A	C	A	C	B	B	B
71	**72**	**73**	**74**	**75**	**76**	**77**	**78**	**79**	**80**
D	C	A	A	A	D	B	C	A	B
81	**82**	**83**	**84**	**85**	**86**	**87**	**88**	**89**	**90**
B	D	B	D	D	D	C	B	C	A
91	**92**	**93**	**94**	**95**	**96**	**97**	**98**	**99**	**100**
D	B	A	B	D	C	C	D	B	C

❑❑❑

6 One Word Substitutions

There are many words in English language which can be perfectly used for a number of words. These words help in expressing ideas in a short and correct manner for the right occasion. Such words not only enhance the vocabulary but also enable you to economise in the use of words to a great extent. Try to learn as many as you can.

Denoting Numbers

- A collection of poems *anthology*
- A number of merchant ships protected by warships (in war-time) *convoy*
- A number of stars grouped together *constellation*
- A number of hired applauders, *i.e.* persons paid to clap *claque*
- A number of people at church *congregation*
- A number of people gathered together for some common purpose *gathering, assembly, society*
- A group of people who get together to work for some cause of common interest *coterie*
- A number of workmen, prisoners, thieves *gang*
- A number of sheep *flock*
- A number of geese *gaggle*
- A number of leopards *leap*
- A number of lions, monkeys *pride, troop*
- A number of herrings, mackerel *shoal*
- A number of fish taken in a net *catch, haul*
- A number of whales, porpoises *school, gam*
- A number of oxen or horses (two or more) harnessed together *team*
- A number of ships, cars, buses *fleet*

Denoting Places

- A place where bees are kept *apiary*

- A place where birds are kept *aviary*
- A place where fishes are kept *aquarium*
- A dwelling-place of an animal underground *burrow*
- A squirrel's home *drey*
- A nest of a bird of prey *eyrie, aerie*
- A place where spirituous liquors are produced *distillery*
- A place where clothes are washed and ironed *laundry*
- A place where Government records are kept *archives*
- A place where treasures of art, curiosities, etc. are preserved or exhibited *museum*
- A place where fruit trees are grown *orchard*

Pertaining to the Literary Sphere

- A work whose writer is unknown *anonymous*
- A record of one's life written by oneself *autobiography*
- The history of the life of a person *biography*
- The heading or short description of a newspaper article, chapter of a book etc. *caption*
- A humorous play, having a happy ending *comedy*
- A list of books in a library *catalogue, bibliography*
- A book in which the events of each day are recorded *diary*
- A book containing the words of a language with their definitions, in alphabetical order *dictionary*
- A book of names and addresses *directory*
- A short speech by a player at the end of a play *epilogue*
- A brief summary of a book *epitome*
- A book containing information on all branches of knowledge *encyclopedia*
- To remove the offensive portions of a book *expurgate*
- A speech delivered without earlier preparation *extempore*
- A noisy or vehement speech intended to excite passions *harangue*
- A written account, usually in book form of the interesting and memorable experiences of one's life *memoirs*
- A note to help the memory *memorandum*
- A declaration of plans and promises put forward by a candidate for election, political party or a sovereign *manifesto*
- A short speech by a player at the beginning of a play *prologue*
- Literary theft, or passing off an author's original work as one's own *plagiarism*

- Speaking aloud to oneself *soliloquy*
- A play with a sad or tragic end *tragedy*

Pertaining to Religion

- One who believes that man can have no knowledge of God but only of natural phenomena *agnostic*
- One who renounces his religious vows or forsakes his religious principles *apostate*
- One who does not believe in existence of God *atheist*
- One intolerantly devoted to a particular creed *bigot*
- To utter profane language against God or anything holy *blaspheme*
- A breaker of church images *iconoclast*
- Worship of images or idols *idiolatory*
- One who believes in God *theist*
- One who believes in only one God *monotheist*
- One who believes in many Gods *polytheist*

Pertaining to Government

- To give up a throne or other office of dignity *abdicate*
- Absence of government *anarchy*
- Government by Sovereign of uncontrolled authority *autocracy, despotism*
- Government by departments of states *bureaucracy*
- Government of the people, for the people and by the people *democracy*
- Government by the nobility *aristocracy*
- The right of self-government *autonomy*
- Government by a few *oligarchy*
- Government by the wealthy *plutocracy*
- Government by divine guidance *theocracy*
- To decide a political question by the direct vote of the whole electorate *referendum*
- Sweeping governmental change *revolution*
- The science of government *politics*

Pertaining to Professions

- One who attends to the diseases of the eye *oculist*
- One who tests eyesight and sells spectacles *optician*
- One who attends to the teeth *dentist*

- One skilled in the care of hands and feet *chiropodist*
- A physician who assists women at child-birth *obstetrician*
- One who drives a motorcar *chauffeur*
- One who makes or sells candles *chandler*
- One who preserves the skins of animals and mounts them so as to resemble the living animals *taxidermist*
- One who compiles a dictionary *lexicographer*
- One who writes books *author*
- One skilled in the treatment of diseases of animals *veterinarian*
- A tradesman who manages funerals *undertaker*
- One who draws up contracts and lends money on interest *scrivener*
- One who lends money and keeps goods as security *pawnbroker*
- A teacher who travels from place to place to give instruction. *peripatetic*
- One who travels from place to place selling miscellaneous articles *hawker, pedlar*
- One who collects postage stamps *philatelist*
- One who lends money at exorbitant interest *usurer*
- One who takes care of a building *janitor*
- One who sells sweets and pastries *confectioner*
- One who works in a coalmine *collier*
- One who flies an aeroplane *pilot, aviator*
- One who studies rocks and soils *geologist*
- One who shoes horses *farrier*
- A professional rider in horses races *jockey*
- One who deals in silks, cotton, woollen, and linen goods *mercer*
- One who deals in wines *vintner*
- One who deals in fish *fishmonger*
- One who deals in iron and hardware *ironmonger*
- One who sells fruits, vegetables, etc. from a barrow *costermonger*
- One who sets type in a printing office *compositor*

Pertaining to Medicine

- A substance which destroys or weakens germs *antiseptic*
- Any medicine which produces insensibility *anaesthetic*
- A medicine to counteract poison *antidote*
- Want or poorness of blood *anaemia*
- A medicine which alleviates pain *anodyne*
- To cut off a person's body a part which is infected *amputate*
- One who is recovering from illness *convalescent*

- To be able to tell the nature of disease by its symptoms *diagnose*
- A disease affecting many persons at the same place and time *epidemic*
- A disease confined to a particular district or place *endemic*
- To disinfect by smoke *fumigate*
- Free or exempt from infection *immune*
- A person who is sick *invalid*
- A cure for all diseases *panacea*
- A disease widely epidemic *pandemic*
- Confinement to one place to avoid spread of infection *quarantine*

Pertaining to Characteristics and Actions

- One who devotes his life to the welfare and interests of other people *altruist*
- One who can use both hands with equal ease *ambidexterous*
- One who fishes with a rod *angler*
- One who kills secretly or by surprise *assassin*
- A person who collects things belonging to ancient times *antiquary*
- One who is always finding faults *censorious*
- One living at the same time as another *contemporary*
- One who sneers at the aims and beliefs of his fellowmen *cynic*
- One who delights in speaking about oneself *egotist*
- One who exalts his own opinion *egoist*
- One who dies for a noble cause *martyr*
- One who retires from society to live a solitary life *recluse, hermit*
- One who maliciously sets fire to buildings *incendiary*
- One who is banished from his home or his country *exile*
- One who takes refuge in a foreign country *refugee, alien*
- One who runs away from justice or the law *fugitive*
- One who walks in his sleep *somnambulist*
- One who looks on the bright side of things *optimist*
- One who looks on the dark side of things *pessimist*
- A hater of mankind *misanthropist*
- One who knows everything *omniscient*
- One who is all powerful *omnipotent*
- One who is present everywhere *omnipresent*
- One who devotes his service or wealth for the love of mankind *philanthropist*
- One new to anything *novice, tyro, neophyte*
- One who engages in any pursuit for the love of it, and not for gain *amateur*

- One who journeys to a holy place *pilgrim*
- A leader of the people who can sway his followers by his oratory *demagogue*
- One who has special skill in judging art, music, tastes, etc. *connoisseur*
- One whose reasoning is clever yet false *sophist*
- One who makes a display of his learning *pedant*
- One who is indifferent to pain or pleasure *stoic*
- One who loves his country and serves it devotedly *patriot*
- One devoted to the pleasures of eating and drinking *epicure*
- One who poses to be what he is not *hypocrite, impostor*
- One who foretells events *prophet*
- One who pretends to know a great deal about everything *mountebank, charlatan, quack*
- One versed in many languages *linguist*
- One who cannot pay one's debts *insolvent*
- One who takes over after another in office or employment *successor*
- One who has been before another in office or employment *predecessor*
- One who is opposed to intellectual progress *obscurant*
- One who abstains from alcoholic drinks *teetotaller*
- One who hides away on a ship to obtain a free passage *stowaway*
- One who spends very little *miser*
- One who spends too much *spendthrift*

Pertaining to War

- An unprovoked attack by an enemy *aggression*
- Shells, bombs, military stores *ammunition*
- A place where naval or military weapons are made or stored *ordnance*
- An agreement between belligerents to stop fighting *armistice*
- A general pardon of offenders *amnesty*
- To reduce to nothing *annihilate*
- Nations carrying on warfare *belligerents*
- To surround a place with the intention of capturing *besiege*
- To camp in the open air without tents or covering *bivouac*
- To seize for military use *commandeer*
- A person who is forced by law to become a soldier *conscript*
- An order prohibiting ships to leave the ports *embargo*
- A number of firearms being discharged continuously *fusillade*
- To make an examination or preliminary survey of enemy territory for military objectives *reconnoitre*

Pertaining to Marriage and Children

- One who marries a second wife or husband while the legal spouse is alive *bigamist*
- One vowed to a single or unmarried life *celibate*
- One engaged to be married *fiancé, fiancee*
- A child whose parents are dead *orphan*
- A hater of marriage *misogamist*
- One who has more than two wives at a time *polygamist*

Pertaining to Death

- Dead and decaying flesh (esp. of animals) *carrion*
- A monument set up for persons who are buried elsewhere *cenotaph*
- To preserve a dead body from putrefaction *embalm*
- Words inscribed on a tomb *epitaph*
- An examination of dead body *postmortem, autopsy*
- An account in the newspaper of the funeral of one deceased *obituary*
- The property left to someone by a will *legacy*
- Occurring after death *posthumous*
- The act of killing a human being *homicide*
- Murder of a new born child *infanticide*
- Murder of a brother *fratricide*
- Murder of a sister *sororicide*
- Murder of a mother *matricide*
- Murder of a father *patricide*
- Murder of a parent *parricide*
- Murder of a king *regicide*

Pertaining to Sciences and Arts

- The study of all heavenly bodies and the earth in relation to them *astronomy*
- The science of land management *agronomics*
- The study of mankind *anthropology*
- The study of physical life or living matter *biology*
- The study of plants *botany*
- The art of beautiful handwriting *calligraphy*
- The science which deals with the varieties of human race *ethnology*
- The study of the origin and history of words *etymology*
- The study of coins *numismatics*

- The study of human face *physiognomy*
- The art of making fireworks *pyrotechnics*
- The study of birds *ornithology*
- The study of languages *philology*
- At home equally on land or in water *amphibious*
- The inside of a nut *kernel*
- The central or innermost part of fruit *core*
- The animals of a certain region *fauna*
- The plants and vegetation of a certain region *flora*
- Absence of rain for a long time *drought*
- To supply land with water by artificial means *irrigate*
- One who studies plant and animal life *naturalist*
- A cud-chewing animal, *e.g.* the cow *ruminant*
- A gnawing animal, *e.g.* the rat *rodent*
- A four-footed animal *quadruped*
- Animals which carry their young in a pouch, *e.g.* kangaroo *marsupials*
- Soil composed largely of decayed vegetable matter *humus*
- A preparation for killing insects *insecticide*
- A plant or animal growing on another *parasite*
- Living for many years *perennial*

Miscellaneous

- Loud enough to be heard *audible*
- Not distinct enough to be heard *inaudible*
- Fit for food *edible*
- Unfit for human consumption *inedible*
- Fit to be chosen or selected *eligible*
- Not having the qualities for being chosen *ineligible*
- Writing that is easy to read *legible*
- Writing that is difficult to decipher *illegible*
- Able to read *literate*
- Unable to read *illiterate*
- Born of married parents *legitimate*
- Born of unmarried parents *illegitimate*
- To send back a person to his own country *repatriate*
- To banish from one's country *expatriate*
- To move from one country to another *migrate*
- One who leaves his country to settle in another *emigrant*
- One who comes into a foreign country to settle there *immigrant*

- Incapable of being redeemed from evil, *i.e.* beyond correction *incorrigible*
- That which cannot be rubbed out or blotted out *ineffaceable, indelible*
- That which cannot be conquered *invincible*
- Incapable of making errors *infallible*
- That which cannot be avoided or prevented *inevitable*
- Incapable of being burnt *incombustible*
- That which easily catches fire *inflammable, flammable*
- That which cannot be seen *invisible*
- Living for ever *immortal*
- Increase the gravity of an offence *aggravate*
- Ordinary or commonplace remark *platitude*
- That which cannot be satisfied *insatiable*
- That which cannot be repaired *irreparable*
- That which cannot be imitated *inimitable*
- Persons (or efforts) that cannot be wearied *indefatigable*
- One who eats too much *glutton*
- To destroy completely *annihilate*
- A statement open to more than one interpretation *ambiguous*
- A round about way of speaking *circumlocution*
- Cautious observation of events, etc. *circumspection*
- That which cannot be hurt *invulnerable*

MULTIPLE CHOICE QUESTIONS

Directions: *Below are given some statements each of which is capable of being expressed by one word only. Each statement is followed by four such words of which only one is correct. Out of the given alternatives A, B, C and D choose the correct word which very closely fits each definition.*

1. A set of papers giving information about a person or event:
A. editorial B. agenda
C. dossier D. clippings

2. List and explanations of technical, difficult, etc. terms:
A. preface B. glossary
C. bibliography D. appendix

3. One who pays too much care to his clothes and personal appearance:
A. conscious B. dandy
C. cynosure D. leer

4. A child born after death of father:
A. effeminate B. immature
C. fatherless D. posthumous

5. A person who is hard to please:
A. insensible B. hypocrite
C. egoist D. fastidious

6. Complete failure in something attempted:

A. fiasco B. vain
C. falsies D. flop

7. A word which can be interpreted in any way:

A. confusing B. misnomer
C. ambiguous D. precise

8. A group of persons united by common interests:

A. society B. class
C. clique D. coterie

9. A person who is inexperienced and easily deceived:

A. fool B. immature
C. blackhorn D. greenhorn

10. Instruction by question and answer:

A. interrogatory B. catechism
C. bulletin D. alibi

11. Record of events by someone with first hand knowledge:

A. novice B. report
C. memoir D. itinerary

12. A mode of talk familiar to a particular group or profession:

A. jargon B. colloquial
C. slang D. abuses

13. Person who is crazy:

A. lackadaisical B. tarter
C. scrupulous D. loony

14. A person who readily believes others:

A. hasty B. immature
C. credulous D. credible

15. One who eats human flesh:

A. beast B. cannibal
C. maneater D. carnivorous

16. Intentional destruction of racial groups:

A. genocide
B. homicide
C. fratricide
D. communal riot

17. One with weakness of mind caused by old age:

A. dastard B. dotard
C. fop D. philanderer

18. Study of insects:

A. zoology B. philology
C. entomology D. etymology

19. A critical judge of any art particularly fine arts:

A. connoisseur B. veteran
C. philistine D. dilettante

20. One who introduces items of an entertainment:

A. consort B. compere
C. director D. introducer

21. A combination of business firms:

A. enterprise
B. franchise
C. cartel
D. autonomous

22. Freeing of suppressed emotions:

A. catastrophe B. catharsis
C. epilogue D. chagrin

23. One who believes in the power of fate:

A. optimist B. pessimist
C. fearful D. fatalist

24. The murder of brother:

A. genocide B. homicide
C. salvage D. fratricide

25. Additional to proper payment:

A. premium B. overtime
C. ex-gratia D. fringe

26. A person or thing used to tempt somebody into a position of danger:
A. decoy
B. provocateur
C. jinx
D. scapegoat

27. Custom of having more than one husband at the same time:
A. polygamy B. polyandry
C. bigamy D. sexagenary

28. A person of refined taste in food and drink:
A. emeritus B. epicure
C. glutton D. gourmand

29. A tombstone inscription:
A. epithet B. encomium
C. epistle D. epitaph

30. An office which has no work but high salary:
A. fortuitous B. gratuitous
C. sinecure D. ceremonial

31. One who is indifferent to pains and pleasure of life:
A. stoic
B. metaphysical
C. pessimist
D. sceptic

32. List of names of persons showing duties to be performed by each in turn:
A. notice B. bulletin
C. roster D. agenda

33. Long angry speech of criticism or accusation:
A. track record B. tirade
C. taut D. outburst

34. One who is in favour of never drinking alcoholicdrinks:
A. idealist
B. uxorious
C. teetotaller
D. unalcoholic

35. Trying to win favour by flattery and charm:
A. smarmy B. shrewish
C. toady D. loquacious

36. A decision on which one cannot go back:
A. incorrigible
B. irrevocable
C. rigid
D. invulnerable

37. The science that studies the varieties of human race:
A. phrenology B. physiology
C. sociology D. ethnology

38. A person who hates women:
A. philogynist B. philatelist
C. misogamist D. misogynist

39. A group of people in a particular grade in an organisation:
A. colleague
B. staff
C. echelon
D. commission

40. Honourably discharged from service:
A. emeritus
B. latitudinarian
C. infallible
D. meritorious

41. One who does not believe in the existence of God:
A. atheist B. altruist
C. agnostic D. flippant

42. The large money paid for an early retirement:
A. goldmine
B. golden handshake
C. gratuity
D. lion's share

43. A hater of learning and knowledge:
A. misologist
B. misogynist
C. philologist
D. philanthropist

44. One who lives and acts for the welfare of others:
A. misanthrope B. credulous
C. altruist D. gregarious

45. Mental weariness for want of occupation:
A. desperate B. depression
C. fatigue D. ennui

46. That which makes it difficult to recognise the presence in real of somebody or something:
A. cover B. mask
C. make-up D. camouflage

47. To bear a hand in one's new business:
A. partnership B. interfere
C. assist D. join

48. One who renounces the world and practices self-discipline in order to attain salvation:
A. devotee
B. ascetic
C. theist
D. parsimonious

49. A place where gambling is practiced:
A. hotel B. motel
C. casino D. stadium

50. A sad song is a:
A. dirge B. elegy
C. ditty D. knell

ANSWERS

1	2	3	4	5	6	7	8	9	10
C	B	B	D	D	A	C	C	D	B
11	12	13	14	15	16	17	18	19	20
C	A	D	C	B	A	B	C	A	B
21	22	23	24	25	26	27	28	29	30
C	B	D	D	D	A	B	B	D	C
31	32	33	34	35	36	37	38	39	40
A	C	B	C	A	B	D	D	C	A
41	42	43	44	45	46	47	48	49	50
A	B	A	C	D	D	C	B	C	A

❑❑❑

7 Idioms and Phrases

- An idiom is a group of words established by usage as having a meaning different from the individual words.
- A phrase is a small group of words standing together as an idiomatic expression.

  Learn and practise as may as you can.

Idioms and Idiomatic Phrases

✦ **ABC** (basic principles)
She does not know the ABC of photography.

✦ **At one's beck and call** (ready to obey)
He had a dozen men at his beck and call.

✦ **At sixes and sevens** (in disorder)
The drawing room articles were lying at sixes and sevens on the floor.

✦ **A wet blanket** (a discouraging person)
Don't allow Rakesh to accompany you to the hunting trip because he is a wet blanket.

✦ **A big gun** (an important person)
Mr Smith is a big gun in our city.

✦ **At a stone's throw** (at a short distance from)
My school is at a stone's throw from my house.

✦ **A man of word** (a person who keeps his promise)
Mr Sharma is a man of word.

✦ **A man of a few words** (a remarkable person)
Gandhiji was a man of a few words.

✦ **At arm's length** (to keep away)
We should always keep bad boys at arm's length

✦ **A bolt from the blue** (a sudden and unexpected event)
The news of my friend's death came to me like a bolt from the blue.

✦ **A man of letters** (a scholar)
Radha Krishnan was a man of letters.

✦ **A hard nut to crack.** (a puzzling problem)
To get a win over American basket ball team is a hard nut to crack for India.

✦ **A yeoman's service** (service which is beneficial to the human beings)
He did yeoman's service through his life.

✦ **A snake in the grass** (a hidden foe)
Beware of him because he seems to be a snake in the grass.

✦ **Acid test** (hard test)
The election will be an acid test for the ruling party.

✦ **A wolf in sheep's clothing** (a hypocrite)
You should not keep company with him because he is a wolf in sheep's clothing.

✦ **At the eleventh hour** (at the last moment)
The war was about to start but fortunately at the eleventh hour a messenger came to the PM with a message of peace.

✦ **A great card** (an important person)
Mr Sood is a great card in the ministry of finance.

✦ **A fool of the first water** (one completely foolish)
Being a fool of the first water he could not solve even the simplest sum.

✦ **A bone of contention** (to be the cause of quarrel)
Kashmir is the bone of contention between India and Pakistan.

✦ **A green hand** (not very much experienced)
We shall pay a little to a green hand.

✦ **All in all** (completely)
Rajesh is all in all in this office.

✦ **A bed of roses** (a comfort)
Life is not a bed of roses.

✦ **An apple of discord** (to be the cause of)
Kashmir is an apple of discord between India and Pakistan.

✦ **A white elephant** (of no use)
This sort of glib talker always proves a white elephant in the end.

✦ **A red letter day** (An important day)
15th August is a red letter day for the Indians.

✦ **By hook or by crook** (by any means fair or foul)

✦ **Black sheep** (a traitor)
Later on Mr XYZ proved a black sheep.

✦ **By dint of** (by means of)
By dint of hard work, she earned a lot of money.

✦ **Break ones back** (to work hard to get something)
He broke his back to earn his livelihood.

✦ **Break the back of** (accomplish the hardest part of a certain job)
There is nothing to be worried about as we've already broken the back of the problem.

✦ **Beat about the bush** (to go on talking on some worthless topic)
Stop this beating about the bush, come to the main task.

✦ **Beyond one's means** (beyond one's budget)
He is living beyond his means, therefore, he is sure to get ruined.

✦ **Cut loose** (Keep away)
India should cut loose from bad politics.

✦ **Chips of the same block** (having the same taste)
They are the chips of the same block.

✦ **Cut-throat competition** (a stiff competition)

There is a cut-throat competition among the publishers in the market.

- **Come what may** (no matter what happens)
  I'll do it come what may.
- **Drop someone a line** (send a letter, etc.)
  Please drop me a line of your well-being.
- **Dull the edge of** (reduce the intensity of)
  Take this pill and it will dull the edge of pain.
- **From hand to mouth** (without any saving)
  The poor factory worker is living from hand to mouth.
- **Fair and square** (clean)
  One must be fair and square in one's dealing.
- **Hard of hearing** (somewhat deaf)
  She is a bit hard of hearing.
- **In the good books of** (be good in one's mind)
  Jack is in the good books of his teachers.
- **In black and white** (in written)
  Don't give him anything in black and white.
- **In cold blood** (mercilessly)
  The old woman was murdered in cold blood.
- **In a crack** (all of a sudden or rapidly)
  The thief left the place in a crack.
- **In full swing** (in full force)
  The studies of the students are going on in full swing.
- **In the twinkling of an eye** (quickly)
  The monkey ate up grams in the twinkling of an eye.
- **Keep the ball rolling** (to maintain the progress of some activity)
  After the death of his father he had to take the charge of his office to keep the ball rolling.
- **Neck and neck** (even)
  There is a neck and neck fight between the two boxers.
- **Once in a blue moon** (seldom)
  She visits her brother once in a blue moon.
- **Slow and steady** (slowly but continually)
  Slow and steady wins the race.
- **To cut a sorry figure** (present oneself in a bad way)
  She cut a sorry figure on the stage.
- **To give a red carpet reception** (to give a warm welcome)
  The PM was given a red carpet reception in America.
- **To dance one's tune** (to follow someone submissively)
  He always dances to his brother's tune.
- **To turn a deaf ear to** (to disregard)
  She turned a deaf ear to her parents' advice.
- **To call a spade a spade** (to speak the truth)
  Gandhiji always called a spade a spade.

✦ **To bring to book** (to scold)
The naughty boy was brought to book by the teacher.

✦ **To cut short** (to reduce)
Smoking will cut short your life.
He wants to get money by hook or by crook.

✦ **To grease the palm of** (to bribe)
Rohit greased the palm of the clerk and got the file moved.

✦ **Through thick and thin.** (under all circumstances)
We'll stand by you through thick and thin.

✦ **To die by inches** (to die a painful death)
The old man died by inches.

✦ **To eat one's words** (to retract one's statement)
You'll have to eat your words because you have spoken without thinking.

✦ **To burn the midnight oil** (to work hard)
You'll have to burn the midnight oil if you want to get good marks.

✦ **To poke one's nose into** (to meddle with)
It is bad to poke your nose into others' affair.

✦ **To fall flat** (to have no effect)
His father's advice fell flat on him.

✦ **To make a clean breast of** (to confess)
He made a clean breast of his involvement in the bomb blast.

✦ **To get the better of** (overcome)
Anger got the better of him.

✦ **To break somebody's back** (to give too much work to him to do)
She broke his back by giving him so much hard work to do.

✦ **Throw cold water on** (to discourage)
She tried to throw cold water on his plan but he was well-determined.

✦ **The long and short of** (in brief)
The long and short of his lecture is that we should live like brothers.

✦ **To burn one's fingers** (to get oneself in trouble)
You have burnt your fingers by speaking against him.

✦ **To turn over a new leaf** (to change the course of life)
He has turned over a new leaf in his life.

✦ **To have one's own axe to grind** (to have vested interest)
He has his own axe to grind in this matter.

✦ **To take to one's heels** (to run away)
The thief took to his heels as soon as he saw the policeman.

✦ **To move heaven and earth** (to make too much effort)
The young man moved heaven and earth to find a job.

✦ **To be caught red handed** (to be caught at the time of committing a crime)
The clerk was caught red handed when he was accepting bribe from Mr ABC.

- **To receive with open arms** (to give a warm welcome)
  The new president of the club was received with open arms by the members.
- **To be born with a silver spoon in one's mouth** (to be born in a rich family)
  Mr. J.L. Nehru was born with a silver spoon in his mouth.
- **To come to light** (to be known)
  A new disease has recently come to light.
- **To be the apple of one's eye** (be very dear)
  He is the apple of his parent's eye.
- **To make fun of** (laugh at)
  The children made fun of the waiter in the hotel.
- **To let the cat out of the bag** (to divulge secret)
  It was Sohan who let the cat out of the bag by telling the real matter.
- **To open a new chapter** (to start some habit, etc.
  By drinking, you've opened a new chapter in your life.
- **To make the flesh creep** (to terrify)
  The story made my flesh creep.
- **To lose ground** (to retreat)
  After fighting for some time the Pakistani army began to lose ground.
- **To bring to book** (to punish)
  The student was brought to book by the teacher.
- **To show a clean pair of heels** (to run away)
  The thief showed a clean pair of heels as soon as he saw the policeman approaching.
- **To gain ground** (to be established)
  He gained ground in India in a few years.
- **To get wind of** (to get information)
  I got wind of his secret plans.
- **Under a cloud** (be in trouble or in a state of disgrace or suspicion)
  His company seemed to be under a cloud as it had no funds to pay the wages to the workers.

Verbal Phrases

- **Act upon** (to follow)
  I acted upon my father's advice.
- **Act upto** (to perform within limits)
  He acted upto his conscience.
- **Act beyond** (to perform crossing limits)
  We should not act beyond our capacity.
- **Act for** (to perform in place of someone else)
  The vice principal acted for the principal.
- **Back up** (to make a queue)
  The vehicles began to back up.
- **Back down** (withdraw claim in the presence of opposition)
  The leader backed down from his previous statement.
- **Back off** (draw back some plan or action)

They backed off from building a flyover.

✦ **Back out** (withdraw from a promise, etc.)
The government backed out of its promise.

✦ **Break down** (stop working) My car broke down on the highway.

✦ **Break into** (enter in certain premises by breaking the door, etc.)
Last night a thief broke into my neighbour's.

✦ **Break off** (stop all of a sudden)
She broke off and began to think over about her/his hand.

✦ **Break out** (spread)
Cholera has broken out in the town.

✦ **Break out of** (escape from)
A prisoner broke out of the prison last night.

✦ **Break up** (disperse)
The cloud of fog began to break up as the sun rose.

✦ **Break something up** (Cause something to break into small pieces)
She broke up the chocolate to distribute it among the girls.

✦ **Break with** (Cut off connection after quarrelling with someone)
He has broken with his brother.

✦ **Call on** (pay a visit to somebody)
I'll call on Mohan's today.

✦ **Call out** (to start)
The workers have called out a strike.

✦ **Call off** (to stop the strike etc.)
The workers have called off the strike.

✦ **Call at** (to visit someone's house)
I called at his house yesterday.

✦ **Call in** (send for)
Please call in the doctor.

✦ **Carry on** (continue)
Please carry on your work.

✦ **Carry something out** (perform a task)
Our company is carrying out a big deal with a foreign company.

✦ **Carry something over** (postpone)
The fancy dress competition had to be carried over till Monday)

✦ **Carry someone off** (kill somebody)
Cancer carried her off on the day of her 20th birthday.

✦ **Come of age** (get established)
As our company has come of age, so, there is no problem in selling our goods.

✦ **Come of** (belong to)
She comes of a royal family.

✦ **Come over** (surmount)
We at last came over all our problems.

✦ **Come off** (to take place)
The marriage of my brother comes off in the next month.

✦ **Come round** (agree)
At last he came round to my views.

✦ **Come under** (fall in the category of)
All these animals come under the same species.

✦ **Come down with** (suffer from)
She came down with whopping cough.

✦ **Come from** (be the nature of)
She came from London.

✦ **Come about** (happen)
The explosion came about when the worker struck the match to light a cigarette.

✦ **Cut off** (die)
The princess was cut off in the prime of her life.

✦ **Cut down** (reduce)
The prices of consumer goods should be cut down.

✦ **Cut someone out** (exclude someone)
His father cut him out of his will.

✦ **Fall in**
She fell in love with the prince.

✦ **Fall down** (fail)
The deal fell down for lack of transparency.

✦ **Fall out** (quarrel)
She fell out with his elder brother.

✦ **Fall through** (fail)
The project fell through for lack of funds.

✦ **Get away** (escape)
She got away with her life.

✦ **Get by** (to accomplish something with great difficulty)
She is not rich. She has just enough to get by.

✦ **Get on** (perform)
How are you getting on with your studies?

✦ **Get out** (become known)
The news got out that the PM was paying a visit to Russia.

✦ **Get over** (overcome)
At last I got over all obstacles.

✦ **Get up** (rise)
When do you get up in the morning?

✦ **Give up** (stop)
He gave up smoking.

✦ **Give out** (emit)
Garlic gives out a pungent smell.

✦ **Give in** (collapse)
The bridge gave in under the heavy load.

✦ **Give away** (distribute)
The Principal gave away the prizes.

✦ **Give out** (announce)
It was given out that the President of India would visit the place soon.

✦ **Go off** (explode)
The gun went off suddenly.

✦ **Go on** (continue)
She went on about how she flew the aeroplane.

✦ **Go through** (examine)
I'll go through this book later on.

✦ **Go up** (be built)
The construction of the house is going up.

✦ **Grind on** (continue for a long time in a tedious way)
The discussion over political issues ground on.

✦ **Grind something out** (produce something a tedious way)
She will grind some more short stories.

✦ **Look out** (be careful)
Look out! there is a snake.

✦ **Look down upon** (hate)
We should not look down upon the poor.

✦ **Look at** (watch)
Look at the blackboard.

✦ **Look after** (take care of)
We ought to look after our old parents.

✦ **Look into** (investigate)
The new police inspector will look into the matter.

✦ **Look up** (rise)
The prices of consumer goods are looking up.

✦ **Look back** (think of the past)
It made her feel disolate when she looked back on things of the past.

✦ **Make up** (to fulfil)
I'll make up my deficiency in Mathematics.

✦ **Make out** (understand)
I could not make out what she said.

✦ **Make up one' mind** (to resolve)
I have made up my mind to settle in the USA.

✦ **Make off** (leave hurriedly)
She made off without informing anybody.

✦ **Make something over** (transfer)
She should make her property over to her sons.

✦ **Make over** (hand over)
He made over the charge of the file to Mr Robert.

✦ **Pull back** (retreat)
The government has pulled back from its previous policy.

✦ **Pull something down** (demolish)
The authorities concerned pulled down a few building which were illegally built on government land.

✦ **Pull out** (pluck)
The child pulled out a few petals of the flower.

✦ **Pull through** (recover)
The patient will pull through.

✦ **Push on** (continue a journey)
It was getting darker but we pushed on.

✦ **Push at** (exert force)
He pushed at the bell, but it did not ring.

✦ **Push for** (demand persistently)
The workers have been pushing for the installation of new machines for five years.

✦ **Put out** (extinguish)
She put out the light.

✦ **Put on** (wear)
He put on an overcoat.

✦ **Put off** (postpone)
The plan had to be put off.

✦ **Put by** (spare something for future)
We must put by some money for future.

- **Put up with** (stay)
  Your aunt is out of town for a couple of days, you may put up with us till she comes.
- **Put something down** (record something)
  She put a new idea down on the paper.
- **Take after** (resemble)
  He takes after his father.
- **Take off** (remove)
  He took off his shoes.
- **Take something out** (obtain)
  You may take out some money from Rohit if you want to purchase this car.
- **Take to** (fall into the habit of)
  He took to gambling.
- **Turn something down** (reject something)
  The judge turned down his appeal.
- **Turn on** (attack)
  The thief turned on him with a knife.

MULTIPLE CHOICE QUESTIONS

Directions: *Some idioms/phrases are given below with their probable meanings. Select the options with their correct meanings.*

1. Carry out
A. To take from one place to another
B. To continue
C. To obey
D. To make efforts

2. In the same boat
A. A worn out choice
B. Indifferent
C. In identical circumstances
D. Carry off

3. In one's good book
A. A costly book
B. A priceless treasure
C. In one's favour
D. An enchanting beauty

4. Keep a straight face
A. To do make up
B. To change clothes
C. Assume responsibility
D. To remain serious

5. To be above board
A. To have a good height
B. To be honest in any business deal
C. To have no debts
D. To try to be beautiful

6. On the face of it
A. To agree
B. From an action
C. More than enough
D. Apparently

7. Let the bygones be bygones
A. In one's favour
B. To pretend
C. To forget the past
D. Other choice

8. To split hairs
A. Major distinctions
B. Hair with two ends
C. To make minute distinction
D. Without distinction

9. Bread and butter

A. Both bread and butter
B. Something essential
C. Livelihood
D. Relevant things

10. To bell the cat

A. To catch a cat and tie a bell round its neck
B. To make an effort
C. To be quick
D. To face a risk

11. Hard and fast

A. Strict
B. Solid
C. Fast moving
D. Some hard surface

12. Part and parcel

A. The part of a parcel
B. An essential part
C. A missing parcel
D. Some part of a machine sent by parcel

13. Null and void

A. Something invalid
B. Something that can be avoided
C. Something that can be nullified
D. Something evil

14. To make clean breast of

A. To gain prominence
B. To praise oneself
C. To confess without reserve
D. To destroy before it blooms

15. Trump card

A. A powerful means of achieving an object
B. Resourcefulness
C. The best gamble to attain success
D. None of these

16. Tall talk

A. A discussion continued for a long time
B. A high sounding talk
C. A meaningful talk
D. A useless talk

17. Small talk

A. Gossip
B. A discussion carried on for a long time
C. A brief discussion
D. None of these

18. Throw out of gear

A. To replace
B. Hinder, disturb
C. To decide
D. Take up tune

19. To and fro

A. Back and forth
B. Puzzled
C. Amazed
D. Reprove

20. To bell the cat

A. To do an easy job
B. To be indifferent to
C. To undertake a difficult job
D. To clarify

21. To be under cloud

A. Puzzle
B. Enjoy the favour
C. Talk thoughtlessly
D. To be under suspicion

22. A labour of love

A. A tragic end
B. A funny thing

C. Not fruitful
D. Work done without payment

23. Follow suit
A. Follow an example
B. Wear a new dress
C. Irrelevant
D. A gay person

24. Foul play
A. Bad intentions
B. A play not well acted
C. A play not liked by the audience
D. None of these

25. To pick holes
A. To find some reason to quarrel
B. To destroy something
C. To criticise someone
D. To cut some part of an item

26. To smell a rat
A. To see signs of plague epidemic
B. To get bad smell of a dead rat
C. To suspect foul dealings
D. To be in a bad mood

27. To put a spoke in one's wheel
A. To encourage
B. Act without restraint
C. Risk something
D. To obstruct one's progress

28. To pull one's leg
A. To give up
B. Take care of
C. To befool
D. To know

29. To play with fire
A. Grasp the truth
B. To handle something dangerous
C. To ridicule
D. To flee away

30. To reckon with
A. Take up time
B. Make an inventory
C. To deal with
D. Submit to punishment

31. To run short
A. Talk until one is tired at
B. Apply to oneself
C. To get rid of
D. To have or be too little

32. A man of letters
A. A postman
B. A learned man
C. A hypocrite
D. An ignorant man

33. A maiden speech
A. A speech made in the parliament
B. A speech made before unmarried girls
C. A speech made by a political leader
D. A speech made for the first time

34. Order of the day
A. An order passed on a particular day
B. A current law
C. Something common or general
D. None of these

35. To end in smoke
A. To make completely understand
B. To ruin oneself
C. To excite great applause
D. None of these

36. To give vent to
- A. To allow to flow forth
- B. To prove a failure
- C. To amass wealth
- D. To evade

37. To eat humble pie
- A. To apologise or confess
- B. To order
- C. To flatter
- D. To get rid of

38. A black sheep
- A. An unlucky person
- B. A negro
- C. An ugly person
- D. None of these

39. To catch a tartar
- A. To trap wanted criminal with great difficulty
- B. To catch a dangerous person
- C. To meet with disaster
- D. To deal with a person who is more than one's watch

40. Sit on fence
- A. To remain neutral
- B. To show contempt
- C. To enjoy the surroundings
- D. To become fond of

41. Pay off old scores
- A. To repay the debt
- B. To have revenge
- C. To invite
- D. Secretly

42. Turn turtle
- A. To cheat
- B. To be lopsided
- C. To frustrate
- D. To dance to the tune

43. Wash one's hands of
- A. To refuse
- B. To assist
- C. To abuse
- D. To refuse to be

44. Under duress
- A. Under compulsion
- B. Willing
- C. To elicit information
- D. To demand

45. To turn the tables
- A. To ruin someone
- B. To turn the situation to one's own side
- C. To reverse the situation
- D. To move from one point to another

46. On the cards
- A. Possibly
- B. Probably
- C. Openly
- D. Likely

47. To leave someone in the lurch
- A. To come to compromise with someone
- B. Constant source of annoyance to someone
- C. To put someone at ease
- D. To desert someone in his difficulties

48. To play second fiddle
- A. To be happy, cheerful and healthy
- B. To reduce importance of one's senior
- C. To support the role and view of another person
- D. To do back seat driving

49. To yearn for

A. To weep for

B. To remember

C. To admire

D. To long for intensely

50. Call off

A. To finish

B. To withdraw

C. To postpone

D. To cry

ANSWERS

1	2	3	4	5	6	7	8	9	10
C	C	C	D	B	D	C	C	C	D
11	**12**	**13**	**14**	**15**	**16**	**17**	**18**	**19**	**20**
A	B	A	C	C	B	A	B	A	C
21	**22**	**23**	**24**	**25**	**26**	**27**	**28**	**29**	**30**
D	D	A	A	C	C	D	C	B	C
31	**32**	**33**	**34**	**35**	**36**	**37**	**38**	**39**	**40**
D	B	D	C	D	A	A	D	B	A
41	**42**	**43**	**44**	**45**	**46**	**47**	**48**	**49**	**50**
B	B	D	A	C	D	D	C	D	B

❑❑❑

8 Narration

Direct and Indirect Narration/Speech

The exact words spoken by the speaker are known as Direct Speech.

The words spoken by somebody and expressed by someone else with some modification are known as Indirect Speech.

(*a*) Ram says to me, "You do not help me."

(*b*) Ram tells me that I do not help him.

The sentence (*a*) shows the words spoken by Ram. So, it is a sentence of Direct Speech.

The sentence (*b*) shows the words spoken by Ram and expressed by someone else with certain modification. So, it is a sentence of Indirect Speech.

The following points should be noted while changing Direct Speech into Indirect speech:

1. The verb outside the inverted commas is called the Reporting Verb.

2. The verb or sentence inside the inverted commas is called the Reported Speech.

3. If the Reporting verb is in the Present or Future Tense, there is no change in the tense in the Reported Speech.

4. If the Reporting Verb is in the Past Tense, the Tense in the Reported Speech is changed.

5. The Reporting verb may be in any Tense, in it the Pronouns are changed as under:

(*i*) First Person according to Subject

(*ii*) Second Person according to Object

(*iii*) Third Person, No change.

6. If the Reporting verb is in the Past Tense the Adverb will change as under in the Indirect Speech.

Direct	***Indirect***
now	then
here	there
after	before
today	that day
yesterday	the previous day
these	those
tomorrow	the next day
last week	the previous week
this	that

7. Adjectives/Determiners are changed as under:

Direct	***Indirect***
this	that
these	those

Rules for Change of Tense

Reporting Verb	Reporting Speech	Change of Tense
Present Tense	Any Tense	No change
Future Tense	Any Tense	No change
Past Tense	Present/Future Tense	Change into corresponding Past Tense
Past Tense	Past Indefinite Tense	Change into Past Perfect Tense
Past Tense	Past Continuous Tense	Change into Past Perfect Continuous Tense
Past Tense	Past Perfect/Perfect Continuous Tense	No change
Past Tense	Universal Truth	No change
Past Tense	Proverb	No change

Transformation of Speech Based on Special Rules

1. Rule Related to Interrogative Sentence

- If the answer of an interrogative sentence is possible in yes-no manner.

Illustration.

Dhoni said to Sachin, "Will you help me?"

Dhoni asked Sachin whether he would help him.

(**Note :** The answer of R.S. is possible in yes-no manner)

Rule of Transformation from Direct to Indirect speech

Step I : Change R.V. into ask.

Step II : In place of comma use 'if/whether'.

Step III : Change interrogative sentence into assertive sentence.

- If the answer of an interrogative sentence is not possible in yes-no manner.

Illustration:

Sachin said to Dhoni, "What do you want?"

Sachin asked Dhoni what he wanted.

(**Note :** Only in Step II, you have to avoid comma and inverted comma and rest will be same as mentioned above).

2. Rule related to Imperative Sentence

- Imperative sentence is a sentence which shows Order/Advice/Request

Illustration:

My teacher said to me, "Go there".

My teacher ordered me to go there.

Rule of Transformation from Direct to Indirect Speech

Step I : Change R.V. as per meaning/sense of R.S. into order/request/advise.

Step II : In place of comma, use 'to'.

Step III: Rest portion will be same.

3. Rule related to Optative Sentence

- Optative sentence is a sentence which expresses the feeling of bless/curse/pray/wish.

Illustration:

Mother said to me, "May you live long!"

Mother blessed me that I might live long.

Rule of Transformation from Direct to Indirect Speech

Step I : Change R.V. as per meaning/sense of R.S. into bless/curse/pray/wish.

Step II : In place of comma, use 'that'.

Step III: Change optative sentence into assertive sentence.

4. Rule related to Exclamatory Sentence

- Exclamatory sentence is a sentence which takes note of exclamatory (!) mark in that sentence showing inner feeling.

Illustration:

She said, "Alas! I am ruined".

She exclaimed with sorrow that she was ruined.

Rule of Transformation from Direct to Indirect Speech

Step I : Change R.V. as per meaning/sense of R.S. into exclaim/exclaims/exclaimed/will or shall exclaim + joy/sorrow/anger/surprise/applause/contempt.

Step II : Change comma into that.

Step III: Change note of exclamation (!) into full stop (.)

Step IV : Change exclamatory sentence into assertive sentence.

Universal, Historical truth, etc.

If the Reported Speech expresses a Universal or Historical or Habitual truth, its Tense will not change.

1. The teacher said to the students, "The sun rises in the east."

The teacher told the students that the sun rises in the east.

2. My father said to me, "The First Battle of Panipat was fought in 1526."

My father told me that the First Battle of Panipat was fougnt in 1526.

MULTIPLE CHOICE QUESTIONS

Directions (Qs. 1 to 13): *Select the correct Indirect Speech for the following sentences:*

1. I said to him, "I shall help you."
- A. I told him that I can help him.
- B. I told him that I would help him.
- C. I told him that I will help him.
- D. I told him that I shall be helping him.

2. My Teacher said to me, "The earth revolves round the sun."
- A. My teacher told me that the earth revolves round the sun.
- B. My teacher told me that the earth revolve round the sun.
- C. My teacher told me that the earth had been revolving round the sun.
- D. My teacher told me that the earth has been revolving round the sun.

3. I said to my friend, "My father daily goes for a walk."
- A. I told my friend that my father daily goes for a walk.
- B. I told my friend that my father daily went for a walk.
- C. I told my friend that my father has to go for a walk.
- D. I told my friend that my father had gone for a walk.

4. He said to me, "May God bless you!"
- A. He requested that God can bless me.
- B. He prayed that God can bless me.
- C. He prayed that God might bless me.
- D. He prayed that God will bless me.

5. The patient said, "Thank you, doctor."
- A. The patient thanked the doctor.
- B. The patient requested the doctor with thanks.
- C. The patient told the doctor thanks.
- D. The patient suggested the doctor thanks.

6. Satish said, "No, I shall not talk to him."
- A. Satish told that he should not talk to him.
- B. Satish suggested that he would not have talked to him.
- C. Satish exclaimed with sorrow that he would not talk with him.
- D. Satish refused to talk to him.

7. The child said, "What a lovely place!"
- A. The child exclaimed with sorrow that it was a lovely place.
- B. The child thought that the place was lovely.
- C. The child exclaimed with joy that the place was very lovely.
- D. The child suggested that the place was lovely.

8. He said, "What a fool I have been!"

A. He told himself with sorrow that he was a fool.

B. He confessed with regret that he had been a great fool.

C. He said himself a fool.

D. He suggested that he could be a fool.

9. He said, "Alas! I am ruined."

A. He told me that he had been ruined.

B. He exclaimed with joy that he had been ruined.

C. He exclaimed with sorrow that he was ruined.

D. He told me that he should not be ruined.

10. The accused said, "I am not guilty."

A. The accused exclaimed with sorrow that I am not guilty.

B. The accused exclaimed with joy that he was not guilty.

C. The accused stated that he was not guilty.

D. The accused told me that he has not been guilty.

11. My teacher said, "The earth is round".

A. My teacher said that the earth was round.

B. My teacher says that the earth is round.

C. My teacher said that the earth is round.

D. My teacher ordered that the earth is round.

12. He said, "What a place it is!"

A. He said that it was a very fine place.

B. He said that is a very fine place.

C. He said that the place is fine.

D. He exclaimed with joy/ surprise that it was a very fine place.

13. Ria said, "Shall I thread the needle?"

A. Ria asked if she should thread the needle.

B. Ria asked if she shall thread the needle.

C. Ria ordered if she should thread the needle.

D. Ria says that if she would thread the needle.

Directions (Qs. 14 to 33): *Pick out the correct alternative that completes the incomplete sentence which is changed into Indirect Narration.*

14. She said to me, "I shall see you as soon as I get time."
She told me:

A. that she will see me as soon as she will get time.

B. that she would see me as soon as she would get time.

C. she would see me whenever she got time.

D. that she would see me whenever she gets time.

15. My secretary said to me, "Your plane will leave if you do not go at once."
My secretary told me that:

A. her plane would leave if she did not go at that time.

B. her plane would leave if I do not go at once.
C. my plane would leave if I did not go at that very time.
D. my plane will leave if I did not go at that time.

16. My mother said to me, "Don't quarrel among yourselves".
My mother:
A. forbade me to quarrel among ourselves.
B. asked me not to quarrel among ourselves.
C. asked me that not to quarrel among ourselves.
D. asked me to quarrel not among ourselves.

17. Her father said to her mother, "Excuse the daughter."
Her father:
A. requested her mother to excuse the daughter.
B. asked her mother to excuse the daughter.
C. asked her mother to have excused the daughter.
D. asked her mother to have been excused.

18. He said to his friend, "Wait here till father comes."
He requested his friend:
A. to wait here till father had come.
B. that to wait there till his friend came.
C. to wait there till father came.
D. to wait here until his friend came.

19. She said to her maid, "Run and catch the thief."
She ordered her maid:
A. ran and catch the thief.
B. that to run and to catch the thief.
C. ran and caught the thief.
D. to run and catch the thief.

20. Anita said to Sunita, "What are you doing?"
Anita asked Sunita:
A. what she will be doing.
B. that what she is doing.
C. that what she was doing.
D. what she was doing.

21. She said to me, "Are you meeting me today?"
She enquired of me:
A. whether I am meeting her that day.
B. whether I was meeting her today.
C. whether I was meeting her that day.
D. I was meeting her that day.

22. Nitish said to me, "When did you buy this pen?"
Nitish asked me:
A. when I was to buy that pen.
B. when I would buy that pen.
C. when I had bought that pen.
D. when I was buying that pen.

23. She said to me, "Are you going to market?"
She enquired of me:
A. I am going to market.
B. I was going to market.
C. if I was going to market.
D. if I had been going to the market.

24. Damini said, "Why did not you change your clothes?"
Damini asked me:
A. why I had not changed my clothes.
B. why I did not change my clothes.
C. why I would not change my clothes.
D. why I have not been changing my clothes.

25. Umesh said to me, "Have you read that novel?"
Umesh asked me:
A. if he was reading that novel.
B. if he had read that novel.
C. if I had read that novel.
D. if I was reading that novel.

26. She said to me, "I shall forgive you."
She told me:
A. that she will forgive me.
B. that she was going to forgive me.
C. that she will not forgive me.
D. that she would forgive me.

27. I said to her, "It was very hot last night."
I told her:
A. that it had been very hot the previous night.
B. that it was very hot the previous night.
C. that it has been very hot the last night.
D. that it had been very hot this night.

28. She said to me, "I thank you for the help you have given."
She:
A. told me that she thanked me for the help I had given.
B. thanked me for the help I have given.
C. thanked to me for the help I have given.
D. thanked me for the help I had given.

29. Mohini said to me, "Trust in God."
Mohini advised me:
A. that I should trust in God.
B. should trust in God.
C. trusted in God.
D. to trust in God.

30. I said to him, "Let us go to school."
I told him:
A. we would go to school.
B. we shall go to school.
C. that we would go to school.
D. that we should go to school.

31. Rajni said, "May God bless you?"
Rajni:
A. exclaimed with wish that God might bless me.
B. expressed a wish that God might bless me.
C. asked God to bless me.
D. shouted with joy to bless me.

32. My mother said me, "Do not have so many friends."
My mother forbade me:
A. to have so many friends.
B. not to have so many friends.
C. to have been so many friends.
D. to possess so many friends.

33. Ram said, "Pay attention to me."
Ram asked:
A. pay attention to him.
B. paid attention to him.
C. having paid attention to him.
D. to pay attention to him.

Directions (Qs. 34 to 50): *In questions below, the sentences have been given in Direct/Indirect Speech. Out of the four alternatives suggested select the one which best expresses the given sentence in Indirect/Direct Speech.*

34. She said that her brother was getting married
A. She said, "Her brother is getting married."
B. She told, "My brother is getting married"
C. She said, "My brother is getting married".
D. She said, "My brother was married".

35. "Please don't go away", she said.
A. She said to please her and not go away.
B. She told me to go away.
C. She begged me not to go away.
D. She begged that I not go away.

36. "If you don't keep quiet I shall shoot you", he said to her in a calm voice.
A. He warned her to shoot if she didn't keep quiet calmly.
B. He said calmly that I shall shoot you if you don't be quiet.
C. He warned her calmly that he would shoot her if she didn't keep quiet.
D. Calmly he warned her that be quiet or else he will have to shoot her.

37. I told him that he was not working hard.
A. I said to him, "You are not working hard."
B. I told him, "You are not working hard."
C. I said, "You are not working hard."
D. I said to him, "He is not working hard."

38. She said that she would finish the work the next day.
A. She said, "I will finish the work the next day."
B. She said, "I will finish the work tomorrow."
C. She said, "You will finish the work tomorrow."
D. She said, "I finished the work."

39. She said to him, "Why don't you go today?"
A. She asked him why he did not go that day.
B. She said to him that why he don't go today.
C. She asked him not to go today.
D. She asked him why he did not go today.

40. "Are you alone, my son?" asked a soft voice close behind me.
A. A soft voice asked that what I was doing there alone.

B. A soft voice said to me are you alone son.
C. A soft voice from my back asked if I was alone.
D. A soft voice behind me asked if I was alone.

41. My cousin said, "My room-mate had snored throughout the night."
A. My cousin said that her room-mate snored throughout the night.
B. My cousin told me that her room-mate snored throughout the night.
C. My cousin complained to me that her room-mate is snoring throughout the night.
D. My cousin felt that her room-mate may be snoring throughout the night.

42. He asked Rama if he needed his help then.
A. He said to Rama, "Do you need my help?"
B. He told Rama, "Tell me if you need help."
C. He asked Rama, "Do I need your help?"
D. He said to Rama, "Do you need my help now?"

43. Nita ordered her servant to bring her a cup of tea.
A. Nita told her servant, "Bring a cup of tea."
B. Nita said, "Bring me a cup of tea."
C. Nita said to her servant, "Bring me a cup of tea."
D. Nita said to her servant, "Bring her that cup of tea."

44. He exclaimed with joy that India had won the Sahara Cup.
A. He said, "India has won the Sahara Cup."
B. He said, "India won the Sahara Cup."
C. He said, "How! India will win the Sahara Cup."
D. He said, "Hurrah! India has won the Sahara Cup."

45. The boy said, "Who dare call you a thief?"
A. The boy enquired who dared call him a thief.
B. The boy asked who called him a thief.
C. The boy told that who dared call him a thief.
D. The boy wondered who dared call a thief.

46. The little girl said to her mother, "Did the sun rise in the East?
A. The little girl said to her mother that the sun rose in the East.
B. The little girl asked her mother if the sun rose in the East.
C. The little girl said to her mother if the sun rises in the East.
D. The little girl asked her mother if the sun is in the East.

47. Dhruv said that he was sick and tired of working for that Company.

A. Dhruv said, "I am sick and tired of working for this Company."
B. Dhruv said, "He was tired of that Company."
C. Dhruv said to me, "I am sick and tired of working for this Company."
D. Dhruv said, "I will be tired of working for that Company."

48. He said to his father, "Please increase my pocket-money."
A. He told his father, please increase the pocket-money.
B. He pleaded his father to please increase my pocket-money.
C. He requested his father to increase his pocket-money.
D. He asked his father increase his pocket-money.

49. She said to her friend, "I know where is everyone."
A. She told that she knew where was everyone.
B. She told her friend that she knew where was everyone.
C. She told her friend she knew where is everyone
D. She told her friend that she knows where was everyone.

50. His father ordered him to go to his room and study.
A. His father said, "Go to your room and study."
B. His father said to him, "Go and study in your room."
C. His father shouted, "Go right now to your study room."
D. His father said firmly, "Go and study in your room."

ANSWERS

1	2	3	4	5	6	7	8	9	10
B	A	A	C	A	D	C	B	C	C
11	**12**	**13**	**14**	**15**	**16**	**17**	**18**	**19**	**20**
C	D	A	B	C	A	B	C	D	D
21	**22**	**23**	**24**	**25**	**26**	**27**	**28**	**29**	**30**
C	C	C	A	C	D	A	A	A	D
31	**32**	**33**	**34**	**35**	**36**	**37**	**38**	**39**	**40**
B	A	D	C	C	C	A	B	A	D
41	**42**	**43**	**44**	**45**	**46**	**47**	**48**	**49**	**50**
A	D	C	B	A	B	A	C	B	A

❑❑❑

9 Voice

A sentence in active voice focuses on the person or thing doing the action. A sentence in passive voice focuses on the person or thing affected by the action. *e.g.,*

The idol was built.
(Active voice)
Someone built the idol.
(Passive voice)

Transformation of Voice

- Voice and Tense are closely associated with each other.
- Tense plays an important role while transforming the voice.

On the basis of following points, voice can be transformed from active to passive voice.

The Present Indefinite Tense

Active voice: Subject + V_1 + Object

Passive voice: Subject + is, am, are + V_3 + by + Object

1. **Active voice:** He sings sweet songs.
   Passive voice: Sweet songs are sung by him.
2. **Active voice:** She does not cause any hindrance in my work.
   Passive voice: No hindrance in my work is caused by her.
3. **Active voice:** Do they love their country?
   Passive voice: Is their country loved by them?

The Present Continuous Tense

Active voice: Subject + is/am/are + V_1 + ing + Object.

Passive voice: Subject + is/am/are + being + V_3 + by + Object.

1. **Active voice:** She is cooking food.
   Passive voice: Food is being cooked by her.
2. **Active voice:** Rita is not knitting a sweater.
   Passive voice: A sweater is not being knitted by Rita.
3. **Active voice:** Is Meena baking a cake?
   Passive voice: Is a cake being baked by Meena?

The Present Perfect Tense

Active voice: Subject + has/have + V_3 + Object.

Passive voice: Subject + has/have + been + V_3 + by + Object.

1. **Active voice:** I have written an essay.
   Passive voice: An essay has been written by me.

2. **Active voice:** They have not whitewashed the fence.
   Passive voice: The fence has not been whitewashed by them.
3. **Active voice:** Have you cut the cake?
   Passive voice: Has the cake been cut by you?

The Past Indefinite Tense

Active voice: Subject + V_2 + Object
Passive voice: Subject + was/were + V_3 + by + Object

1. **Active voice:** He composed a new song.
   Passive voice: A new song was composed by him.
2. **Active voice:** He did not operate the computer.
   Passive voice: The computer was not operated by him.
3. **Active voice:** Did she catch a fish?
   Passive voice: Was a fish caught by her?

The Past Continuous Tense

Active voice: Subject + was/were + V_1 + ing + Object
Passive voice: Subject + was/were + being + V_3 + by + Object

1. **Active voice:** The farmers were ploughing the fields.
   Passive voice: The fields were being ploughed by the farmers.
2. **Active voice:** He was not administering the new drug to the patient.
   Passive voice: The new drug was not being administered to the patient by him.
3. **Active voice:** Was she sewing a dress?
   Passive voice: Was a dress being sewn by her?

The Past Perfect Tense

Active voice: Subject + had + V_3 + Object.
Passive voice: Subject + had + been + V_3 + by + Object

1. **Active voice:** He had issued me an import licence.
   Passive voice: I had been issued an import licence.
2. **Active voice:** We had not visited the Taj.
   Passive voice: The Taj had not been visited by us.
3. **Active voice:** Who had taught you English?
   Passive voice: By whom had you been taught English?

The Future Indefinite Tense

Active voice: Subject + will/shall + V_1 + Object.
Passive voice: Subject + will/shall + be + V_3 + by + Object.

1. **Active voice:** He will remove the dust from the shelf.
   Passive voice: The dust from the shelf will be removed by him.

2. **Active voice:** He will not open the main gate.
   Passive voice: The main gate will not be opened by him.
3. **Active voice:** Will you help us?
   Passive voice: Shall we be helped by you?

The Future Perfect Tense

Active voice: Subject + will/shall + have + V_3 + Object.
Passive voice: Subject + will/shall + have + been + V_3 + by + Object.

1. **Active voice:** They will have sold their house by then.
   Passive voice: Their house will have been sold by them by then.
2. **Active voice:** He will not have informed the police about it.
   Passive voice: The police will not have been informed about it by him.
3. **Active voice:** Will they have accepted the deal?
   Passive voice: Will the deal have been accepted by them?

Imperative Sentences

1. **Active voice:** Open the window.
   Passive voice: You are ordered to open the window.
   Or
   Let the window be opened.
2. **Active voice:** Please/kindly open the window.
   Passive voice: You are requested to open the window.
3. **Active voice:** Never make a noise.
   Passive voice: A noise should never be made.

Infinitives

1. **Active voice:** It is time to open the shop.
   Passive voice: It is time for the shop to be opened.
2. **Active voice:** He begged the officer to forgive him.
   Passive voice: He begged the officer to be forgiven.
3. **Active voice:** He has to break the door.
   Passive voice: The door has to be broken by him.

Prepositional Verb

1. **Active voice:** She laughed at the beggar.
   Passive voice: The beggar was laughed at by her.
2. **Active voice:** He listened to the news.
   Passive voice: The news was listened to by him.
3. **Active voice:** They called in the doctor.
   Passive voice: The doctor was called in by them.

Double Object

1. **Active voice:** He gave me a pen.
   Passive voice: A pen was given to me by him.

Or

I was given a pen by him.

2. **Active voice:** She told us a story.
   Passive voice: A story was told (to) us by her.
   Or
   We were told a story by her.

Use of Preposition other than 'by'

1. **Active voice:** The jug contains juice.
   Passive voice: Juice is contained in the jug.
2. **Active voice:** The audience thronged the hall.
   Passive voice: The hall was thronged with the audience.
3. **Active voice:** I know her.
   Passive voice: She is known to me.

Quasi Passive Verbs

1. **Active voice:** Quinine tastes bitter.
   Passive voice: Quinine is bitter when tasted.
   Or
   Quinine is bitter when it is tasted.
2. **Active voice:** Sugar is sweet (to taste).
   Passive voice: Sugar is sweet when tasted.
   Or
   Sugar is sweet when it is tasted.

Implied Sentences

1. **Active voice:** The driver drove the bus.
   Passive voice: The bus was driven.
2. **Active voice:** Someone read the news.
   Passive voice: The news was read.
3. **Active voice:** They say work is worship.
   Passive voice: It is said that work is worship.

MULTIPLE CHOICE QUESTIONS

Directions (Qs. 1 to 20): *In the following questions, a sentence has been given in Active/Passive Voice. Out of the four alternatives suggested, select the one that Best Expresses the same sentence in Passive/Active Voice.*

1. Circumstances will oblige me to go.
   A. I will oblige the circumstances and go.
   B. I shall be obliged to go by the circumstances.
   C. Under the circumstances, I should go.
   D. I shall be obliged by the circumstances to go.
2. We waste much time on trifles.
   A. Much time was wasted on trifles.
   B. Much time will be wasted on trifles.

C. Much time is wasted by us on trifles.
D. Much time is wasted on trifles.

3. Mohan gave the beggar an old shirt.
A. An old shirt was given to Mohan by the beggar.
B. An old shirt was given to the beggar by Mohan
C. The begger was gave an old shirt by Mohan.
D. An old shirt was gave to the beggar by Mohan.

4. They have made him a king.
A. A king has been made by him.
B. He was made a king by them.
C. They have been made kings by him.
D. He has been made a king by them.

5. Who taught you English?
A. By whom English was taught to you?
B. By whom you were taught English?
C. By whom was English taught to you?
D. By whom are you taught English?

6. Was he knocking at the door?
A. Was the door being knocked at by him?
B. Was the door being knocked by him?
C. Was the door knocked by him?
D. Was the door knocking at him?

7. What was Rani doing?
A. What was done by Rani?
B. What was Rani being done?
C. What was being done by Rani?
D. What was being doing Rani?

8. Why were you wasting your time?
A. Why was your time being wasted?
B. Why was your time being wasted by you?
C. Why was your time wasted by you?
D. Why was your time wasted?

9. She has laid out a small garden.
A. A small garden has been laid by her.
B. A small garden has laid her.
C. A small garden being laid by her.
D. A small garden has been laid out by her.

10. She had already solved all the sums.
A. All the sums had already been solved by her.
B. All the sums have already been solved by her.
C. All the sums have been solved by her.
D. All the sums are solved by her.

11. He will have posted the letter.
A. The letter has been posted by him.
B. The letter will be posted by him.

C. The letter will have been posted by him.
D. The letter is posted by him.

12. They will have sold all the books by 4 P.M.
A. All the books will be sold by 4 P.M.
B. All the books will have been sold by 4 P.M.
C. All the books were being sold by 4 P.M.
D. All the books must be sold by 4 P.M.

13. Do you speak English?
A. Is English spoken by you?
B. Does English spoken by you?
C. Is English being spoken by you?
D. Does English being spoken by you?

14. Had they seen me before?
A. Had myself been seen by them before?
B. Had me being seen by them before?
C. Had I been seen by them before?
D. Had I being seen by them before?

15. May I take this pen?
A. May this pen will be taken by me?
B. May this pen shall be taken by me?
C. May this pen should be taken by me?
D. May this pen be taken by me?

16. Can we send it by air?
A. Can this be sent by air?
B. Can it be sent by air?
C. Can it go by air?
D. Can it be send by air?

17. Who wrote this book?
A. By whom was this book written?
B. By whom is this book written?
C. By whom was this book being written?
D. By whom is this book being written?

18. What did you buy?
A. What is bought by you?
B. What is being bought by you?
C. What was bought by you?
D. What was being bought by you?

19. Whom do you want?
A. Who is wanted by you?
B. Who is being wanted by you?
C. You are wanted by whom?
D. You are being wanted by whom?

20. When will you raise this question?
A. When this question will be raised by you?
B. When will this question be raised by you?
C. When this question is being raised by you?
D. When is this question being raised by you?

Directions (Qs. 21 to 35): *In each of the following questions, a sentence is given in Active Voice. Below it are given four alternatives suggesting the Passive Voice form of the above sentence. Choose the correct alternative.*

21. Who did this?
A. This was done by whom?
B. By whom was this done?
C. Who has done this?
D. By whom this was done?

22. One should keep ones promises.
A. Promises should be kept.
B. Ones promises should be kept by one.
C. Promises must be kept.
D. Ones promises one should keep.

23. Give the order.
A. Order given.
B. Order be given.
C. Let the order be given.
D. Order may be given by you.

24. You will have to do it.
A. It will be done by you.
B. It will have to be done by you.
C. It has to be done by you.
D. It would have to be done by you.

25. Keep to the left.
A. You are ordered to keep to the left.
B. You ought to keep to the left.
C. You are advised to keep to the left.
D. You must keep to the left.

26. They will arrange a party.
A. A party will have to be arranged by them.
B. A party they will have to arrange.
C. A party will be arranged by them.
D. A party by them will be arranged.

27. Someone has picked my pocket.
A. My pocket is picked.
B. My pocket has picked.
C. My pocket has been picked.
D. My pocket was picked.

28. He kept me waiting.
A. I kept waiting for him.
B. I kept waiting by him.
C. I was waiting for him.
D. I was kept waiting by him.

29. Why do you tell a lie?
A. Why is a lie told by you?
B. Why is told a lie by you?
C. Why is told by you a lie?
D. Why has a lie been told by you?

30. I have written a letter.
A. A letter is written by me.
B. A letter has been written by me.
C. A letter was written by me.
D. A letter had been written by me.

31. They will have helped you.
A. You will have helped by them.
B. You will have been helped by them.
C. You will be helped by them.
D. You will be helped by them.

32. Open the door.
- A. Door may be opened.
- B. Let the door be open.
- C. Let the door be opened.
- D. Door be opened.

33. I am reading a book.
- A. A book is read by me.
- B. A book is being read by me.
- C. A book has been read by me.
- D. A book in been read by me.

34. Why did your brother write such a letter?
- A. Why your brother wrote such a letter?
- B. Why was by brother written such a letter?
- C. Why was such a letter written by your brother?
- D. Why was written such a letter by your brother?

35. Did you run a great risk?
- A. Was a great risk run by you?
- B. Was run a great risk by you?
- C. Was by you run a great risk?
- D. Had you run a great risk?

Directions (Qs. 36 to 45): *In each of the following questions, a sentence is given in Passive Voice. Below it are given four alternatives suggesting the Active Voice form of the above sentence. Choose the correct alternative.*

36. He was made king.
- A. He became king.
- B. They made him king.
- C. They had made him king.
- D. He has been made king.

37. Good news is expected by us.
- A. We are expecting good news.
- B. We have been expecting good news.
- C. We had expected good news.
- D. We expect good news.

38. The child must be looked after.
- A. The child you must look after.
- B. You must look after the child.
- C. You must look the child after.
- D. You may look after the child.

39. What is wanted by you?
- A. What you want?
- B. What did you want?
- C. What do you want?
- D. What you do want?

40. Your father is known to me.
- A. I am known to your father.
- B. I know your father.
- C. I have known your father.
- D. I knew your father.

41. She may be told the story by you.
- A. The story may be told by you to her.
- B. You may tell the story to her.
- C. You may tell her the story.
- D. You may tell to her the story.

42. Duty ought to be done.
- A. Let duty be done.
- B. One ought to do one's duty.
- C. One should do his duty.
- D. Do you duty.

43. Is English spoken by you?
- A. Did you speak English?
- B. Do you speak English?
- C. Have you spoken English?
- D. Do you know how to speak English?

44. Gold coins are contained in this box.
A. This box contains gold coins.
B. This box has contained gold coins.
C. This box is containing gold coins.
D. This box has gold coins.

45. Character is revealed by manners.
A. Manners revealed character.
B. Manners reveal character.
C. Manners have revealed character.
D. Manners do reveal character.

ANSWERS

1	2	3	4	5	6	7	8	9	10
D	C	B	D	C	A	C	B	D	A
11	**12**	**13**	**14**	**15**	**16**	**17**	**18**	**19**	**20**
C	B	A	C	D	B	A	C	A	B
21	**22**	**23**	**24**	**25**	**26**	**27**	**28**	**29**	**30**
B	A	C	B	C	C	C	D	A	B
31	**32**	**33**	**34**	**35**	**36**	**37**	**38**	**39**	**40**
B	C	B	C	A	B	D	B	C	B
41	**42**	**43**	**44**	**45**					
C	B	B	A	B					

❑❑❑

10 Sentence Completion

Filling the blanks is such an exercise that starts with the primary schools and continues at the highest level of competitive examinations. One must practise it regularly to score well.

MULTIPLE CHOICE QUESTIONS

Directions: *Pick out the most effective word(s) from the given words to fill in the blanks and make the sentence meaningfully complete.*

1. One requires great .... to teach and handle little children who are restless.

A. patience
B. attitude
C. determination
D. knowledge

2. The researchers will .... some of the causes of increasing poverty in the state.

A. fund B. investigate
C. promote D. circulate

3. I usually perform .... when nobody is watching me.

A. alone B. good
C. better D. hard

4. It was .... to everyone that the minister had been drinking.

A. observed B. known
C. discovered D. realised

5. I would rather stay indoors .... the rain stops.

A. so B. waiting
C. until D. usually

6. The process should be completed as far as possible within a week, ... which the matter should be brought to notice of the officer concerned.

A. following B. failing
C. realizing D. referring

7. The officers are ..... to regular transfers.

A. free B. open
C. subject D. available

8. All letters received from Government should ..... be acknowledged.

A. suddenly
B. obviously
C. immediately
D. occasionally

9. Mumbai office ..... a meeting of senior officials to discuss the

high incidence of frauds.
A. attended B. convened
C. reported D. registered

10. The note should be ..... to all the concerned departments for their consideration.
A. regulated B. requested
C. carried D. forwarded

11. Your present statement does not .... what you said last week.
A. accord to B. accord in
C. accord with D. accord for

12. I had a vague .... that the lady originally belonged to Scotland.
A. notion B. expression
C. imagination D. theory

13. The prisoner showed no .... for his crimes.
A. hatred B. obstinacy
C. remorse D. anger

14. It is inconceivable that in many schools children are subjected to physical .... in the name of discipline.
A. violation B. exercise
C. violence D. security

15. We have not yet fully realised the .... consequences of the war.
A. happy B. pleasing
C. grim D. exciting

16. Happiness consists in being .... what we have.
A. contented to
B. contented with
C. contented for
D. contented in

17. His rude behaviour is a .... his organization.
A. disgrace for
B. disgrace on
C. disgrace upon
D. disgrace to

18. No child is .... understanding. One has to wait and provide proper guidance.
A. dull to B. dull in
C. dull of D. dull for

19. I am fully .... the problems facing the industry.
A. alive with B. alive to
C. alive for D. alive on

20. The Romans were .... science.
A. bad in B. bad to
C. bad for D. bad at

21. Although I was .... of his plans, I encouraged him, because there was no one else who was willing to help.
A. sceptical B. remorseful
C. fearful D. excited

22. You have no business to .... pain on a weak and poor person.
A. inflict B. put
C. direct D. force

23. Her uncle died in a car accident. He was quite rich. She suddenly .... all her uncle's money.
A. succeeded B. caught
C. gave D. inherited

24. There was a major accident. The plane crashed. The pilot .... did not see the tower.
A. likely B. probably
C. scarcely D. hurried

25. The car we were travelling in .... a mile from home.
A. broke off
B. broke down
C. broke into
D. broke up

26. What are you .... in the kitchen cupboard?
A. looking in B. looking on
C. looking to D. looking for

27. I did not see the point of .... waiting for them, so I went home.
A. hanging around
B. hang on
C. hang together
D. hanging up

28. He lost confidence and .... of the deal at the last minute.
A. backed out
B. backed on
C. backed down
D. backed onto

29. To the dismay of all the students, the class monitor was ..... berated by the principal at a school assembly.
A. critically
B. ignominiously
C. prudently
D. fortuitously

30. All attempts to revive the fishing industry were ..... failure.
A. foredoomed to
B. heading at
C. predicted for
D. estimated to

31. There are ..... parked outside than yesterday.
A. fewer cars
B. few cars
C. less cars
D. a small number of cars

32. The minister had to ..... some awkward questions from reporters.
A. fend B. fend at
C. fend out D. fend off

33. The ..... of evidence was on the side of the plaintiff since all but one of the witnesses testified that his story was correct.
A. propensity
B. force
C. preponderance
D. brunt

34. Attention to detail is ..... of a fine craftsman.
A. hallmark
B. stamp
C. seal of authority
D. authenticity

35. Behaving in a .... and serious way, even in a .... situation, makes people respect you.
A. calm, difficult
B. steady, angry
C. flamboyant, tricky
D. cool astounding

36. Along with a sharp rise in ...., a recession would eventually result in more men, women, and children living in ....
A. crime, apathy
B. fatalities, poor
C. deaths, slums
D. unemployment, poverty

37. The government has .... to provide financial aid to the ones .... by severe floods in the city.

A. desired, troubled
B. promised, havoc
C. failed, affected
D. wanted, struck

38. An airplane with .... passengers on board made an unscheduled .... as the airport to which it was heading was covered with thick fog.

A. imitable, slip
B. faulty, stop
C. variety, halt
D. numerous, landing

39. Deemed universities .... huge fees, but have not been successful in providing .... education to our students.

A. collect, maintaining
B. pay, better
C. ask, good
D. charge, quality

40. If the banks desire to .... profit, they should get rid of .... measures.

A. lose, concentrate
B. increase, populist
C. earn, unhealthy
D. maximise, traditional

41. Leadership defines what the future should look like and ...... people with that vision.

A. aligns B. develops
C. trains D. encourages

42. We upset ourselves by responding in an ...... manner to someone else's actions.

A. unabashed B. irrational
C. arduous D. arguable

43. All the people involved in that issue feel a great ...... to his suggestion.

A. contradiction
B. adherence
C. indifference
D. repugnance

44. These elections will be remembered as much for its anti-incumbency mood as for its ...... mandate.

A. invincible
B. rational
C. unprecedented
D. deliberate

45. How do you expect us to stay in such a ...... building even if it can be hired on a nominal rent?

A. scruffy B. disperate
C. fragmented D. robust

46. ...... efforts from all concerned are required to raise the social and economic conditions of our countrymen.

A. Perpetual B. Dynamic
C. Massive D. Exploring

47. Many companies see technology as a ...... for a whole host of business problems.

A. consideration
B. preference
C. linking
D. panacea

48. Known as devout and serious person, she also has ...... sense of humour.

A. better B. plentiful
C. quick D. good

49. The matter would have become serious if ...... action had not been taken.

A. hasty B. fast
C. timely D. unusual

50. The ...... with which he is able to yield the paint brush is really remarkable.

A. ease B. practice
C. majesty D. sweep

51. You must ensure the correctness of the information before ....

A. drawing B. enabling
C. learning D. jumping

52. The rocket .... the target and did not cause any casualty.

A. sensed B. reached
C. missed D. exploded

53. It is desirable to take .... in any business if you want to make profit.

A. advice B. risk
C. loan D. recourse

54. They wasted all the money on purchase of some .... items.

A. excellent B. important
C. significant D. trivial

55. When he found the wallet his face glowed but soon it faded as the wallet was ....

A. empty B. vacant
C. recovered D. stolen

ANSWERS

1	2	3	4	5	6	7	8	9	10
A	B	C	A	C	B	C	C	B	D
11	**12**	**13**	**14**	**15**	**16**	**17**	**18**	**19**	**20**
C	A	C	C	C	B	D	B	B	D
21	**22**	**23**	**24**	**25**	**26**	**27**	**28**	**29**	**30**
B	C	C	B	C	C	D	A	B	A
31	**32**	**33**	**34**	**35**	**36**	**37**	**38**	**39**	**40**
A	D	D	A	A	D	C	D	C	B
41	**42**	**43**	**44**	**45**	**46**	**47**	**48**	**49**	**50**
A	A	D	C	A	A	D	D	C	A
51	**52**	**53**	**54**	**55**					
A	C	B	D	A					

❑❑❑

11 Sentence Improvement

One may use the same words in many ways but the best way is only one that makes the perfect usage of the words and conveys the proper meaning of the expression. Try it yourself in the following questions.

MULTIPLE CHOICE QUESTIONS

Directions: *In these questions, a part of the sentence is bold. Below are given alternatives to the bold part at A, B and C which may improve the sentence. Choose the correct alternative. In case no improvement is needed, your answer is 'D'.*

1. Discreet salience **is extremely important** to create that 'irresistible-yet-unattainable' image for brands that want to take India seriously
   A. was extremely important
   B. is mainly important
   C. was important extremely
   D. No Improvement

2. This, over a designer outfit that he wanted for a friend's party and **that his sensitive** parents refused him.
   A. which his sensitive
   B. which his insensitive
   C. that his insensitive
   D. No Improvement

3. Goa was full of non-Goa property hunters **rushing about buying up the place** like tomorrow was an expired lease.
   A. rushing in buying up the place
   B. rushed about buying up the place
   C. rushing about to buy up the place
   D. No Improvement

4. Property hunting is a **tired and hungry** making business.
   A. is a tiresome and hungry
   B. is a tiring and hungry
   C. is a tiring and waste
   D. No Improvement

5. Cultural differences aside, **till luxury need speaks** in a manner that befits.
   A. luxury still needs to speak
   B. luxury still need to speak

C. luxury till need to speak
D. No Improvement

6. Indian food—the culinary avatar of the subcontinent's social history presented on a platter—**is without doubt the best food** in the world.
A. is undoubtedly the greatest food
B. is without doubt greatest food
C. is best food without doubt
D. No Improvement

7. It must retain the language of poetry. **It needed to create** stories, and not statements.
A. It needed creating
B. It needs creating
C. It needs to create
D. No Improvement

8. This year, Asia-Pacific has become the first region **to reach aggregate profiting** in biotech.
A. to reach aggregated profitability
B. to reach aggregate profitability
C. to reach aggregate of profit
D. No Improvement

9. India is deviating to embrace the West. If Western luxury brands deviate a little, **albeit selectively**, they will find rich Indian arms open far and wide.
A. though selectively
B. however selectively
C. albeit selectedly
D. No Improvement

10. China and India continued to attract attention and deals, motivated by the desire to increase access to these **largest and growing** drug markets and by the need to lower the costs of drug development.
A. larger and growing
B. large and growing
C. larger and grown
D. No Improvement

11. Luxury brands are **still above of the** clover curve here, with their elite (small) audiences.
A. still ahead of the
B. still in the
C. still far of the
D. No Improvement

12. Agencies **hence needed to be** sure of returns before investing, say admen.
A. hence needs to be
B. so needs to be
C. hence need to be
D. No Improvement

13. India is still a nascent market and that's the spirit everyone's **looking at it**.
A. looking for it
B. looking in it
C. looking with it
D. No Improvement

14. Questioning the state's move to allow women to serve liquor but not dance in bars **of the ground that** dancing aroused physical lust.
A. on the grounds that

B. of the grounds that
C. over the grounds that
D. No Improvement

15. For England the positives from their crushing series lose come in the shape of James Anderson and Kevin Pietersen, **both of which** have made significant strides up the rankings.
A. both of which
B. both of whom
C. both of who
D. No Improvement

16. International campaigns can work well for luxury here, **but context cannot be** ignored.
A. so context cannot be
B. but context cannot
C. but context couldn't
D. No Improvement

17. For one, the 'Indian luxury context, **while evolved rapidly**, still has its own meaning, and its own implications.
A. while evolved rapid
B. which evolving rapidly
C. while evolving rapidly
D. No Improvement

18. But too much of availability can compromise a luxury brand or **made it lose** its lustre.
A. make her lose
B. make him lose
C. make it lose
D. No Improvement

19. Still, it's under-the-upper **layers themselves who** are aspiring for slivers of luxury.
A. layers themselves which
B. layer itself who
C. layers themself which
D. No Improvement

20. It is like saying Hindi movies, with skimpily dressed dancers, would **effect public** order.
A. effect your
B. affect public
C. affected public
D. No Improvement

21. The court held that a few women being involved in prostitution was no **justice to deny other** bar girls the right to livelihood.
A. justification to declare other
B. justification to deny other
C. justice to let other
D. No Improvement

22. All-rounder cricketer has also made some progress **over the** player rankings.
A. above the
B. at the
C. up the
D. No Improvement

23. Former minister on Sunday **joined hands** with a suspended Lok Sabha member to float a new political outfit.
A. folded hands
B. walked hand in hand
C. shaked hands
D. No Improvement

24. Pakistan's former ministers will meet in London on Monday **to ask** a strategy to return home from exile.
A. to chalk out

B. to negotiate
C. to create
D. No Improvement

25. It's a family potboiler, medical thriller and political drama **all in one**—except that it's all too real and all too grim.
A. all 3 in one
B. all coupled into one
C. all rolled into one
D. No Improvement

26. India's efforts to get international support for its civil nuclear energy programme got **a go ahead on** Sunday as Germany indicated it would not come in the way of the India-US nuclear deal.
A. a life in
B. a boost on
C. a boost at
D. No Improvement

27. Is it time for old bungalows to **bite the dust**?
A. go down
B. get down
C. come down
D. No Improvement

28. The bungalows was an outward manifestation of a certain **way in life**, and with that era gone.
A. way for life
B. way of life
C. way at life
D. No Improvement

29. The builder Mittals will reportedly **raise their money**-raking high-rise behind it.
A. highten their money
B. rise their money
C. raise there money
D. No Improvement

30. The impatient present has usually demolished **more of the** past before we wake up to the irretrievable loss.
A. much of
B. much of their
C. much of the
D. No Improvement

31. Preservation is a romantic notion; demolition **quiet** more practical reasons.
A. has many
B. had many
C. have many
D. No Improvement

32. You must get back to your **charming self** and impress the audience with your social skills.
A. own self
B. main self
C. own uniqueness
D. No Improvement

33. Stay focused on your goals and don't **get disturbed by** non-materialistic possessions.
A. get involved by
B. get betrayed by
C. get distracted by
D. No Improvement

34. You may appear more optimistic than your detractors **may want** i. **to be**.
A. want you to be
B. wish yourself to be

C. seek you be
D. No Improvement

35. There are a number of mineral springs in the Czech territory, which **has been used** for medicinal purposes since the early 15th century.
A. have been used
B. had been used
C. has being used
D. No Improvement

36. The picturesque mountains **offer**s excellent bungee jumping spots.
A. shows
B. provides
C. offer
D. No Improvement

37. Begin your **meal with** traditional faves like potato soup, beef soup with liver dumplings or dill soup made from sour milk.
A. meals with
B. meal in
C. meals of
D. No Improvement

38. You can also **go to the** National Museum building and the famous Prague State Opera.
A. went to
B. visit the
C. saw
D. No Improvement

39. If they close the Gulf for a **length of time** to shipping, then certainly we could look at $150, probably higher.
A. larger amount of time
B. larger duration of time
C. larger amount of hours
D. No Improvement

40. **More of them** are owned by the state and even the privately-owned ones are open to the public.
A. Most of which
B. Most of them
C. Most of all
D. No Improvement

41. Constructed in the ninth century by the Prince Booivoj, the castle has transformed **oneself** from a wooden fortress surrounded by earthen bulwarks to the imposing form it has today.
A. himself
B. herself
C. itself
D. No Improvement

42. Apart from frequent art exhibitions, **their are also** permanent collections devoted to archaeology, anthropology, mineralogy, natural history and numismatics.
A. there is also
B. there are also
C. their are also
D. No Improvement

43. You can visit the Czech Museum of Fine Arts, **at a** permanent exhibition on Czech Kubism.
A. with a
B. for a
C. in a
D. No Improvement

44. Tensions **above** Iran come at a time of strong demand for energy.
A. under
B. inside
C. over
D. No Improvement

45. Because its shores line the narrow Straits of Hormuz, Iran **could quickly hit** both military and commercial shipping.
A. will quickly hit
B. shall quickly hit
C. will be quick hitting
D. No Improvement

46. For most people who exercise **at the** morning, there is no getting around the question: Eat and run? Or run and eat later?
A. in the
B. in
C. at the time of
D. No Improvement

47. Are ad agencies even attempting to peer into the keyhole of this indulgence sanctum to garner consumer insights **ahead of** the curve?
A. above
B. over
C. within
D. No Improvement

48. Too many people rush into the world of credit and don't stop to think about how **their actions could affect their** credit score and ability to qualify for credit in the future.
A. their actions may affect their
B. their actions might affect their
C. their actions will affect their
D. No Improvement

49. According to the report, **number of deal with** vaccines were energized by concerns around avian flu, SARS, and biodefence products, while looming patent expirations led to more deals in generics.
A. number of deals in
B. number of deal in
C. number of deals with
D. No Improvement

50. This is how the Bombay High Court responded to the state government's purported **moral stand which** dance bars were causing grave harm to society.
A. moral stand in
B. moral stand at
C. moral stand that
D. No Improvement

51. If you have a high credit limit, use **at least a** third of it.
A. atleast a
B. at last a
C. utmost a
D. No Improvement

52. Fitness experts will say that **first eating provides** fuel for a proper workout.
A. eating in the beginning provides
B. first eat provides
C. eating first provides
D. No Improvement

53. One study that examined the claim directly in 1995 found that a group of people did **burned much calories from fat on days** when they exercised on an empty stomach than on days when they had a small breakfast first.

A. burn more calories from fat on days
B. burn more calorie from fat on days
C. burnt more calories from fat on days
D. No Improvement

54. Carefree children spent their afternoons **to run about barefoot**, their clothes dusty, and telltale twigs of the neighbour's mango tree in their hair.

A. running barefoot in the sun
B. run about barefoot in the sun
C. running about barefoot in the sun
D. No Improvement

55. A year ago, a 13-year-old girl attempted suicide because her mother **refuses to pay his** mobile bills.

A. refuses to pay her
B. refused to pay her
C. refused to pay his
D. No Improvement

ANSWERS

1	2	3	4	5	6	7	8	9	10
D	C	D	B	A	D	C	C	D	B
11	**12**	**13**	**14**	**15**	**16**	**17**	**18**	**19**	**20**
C	C	D	A	C	D	C	C	C	C
21	**22**	**23**	**24**	**25**	**26**	**27**	**28**	**29**	**30**
B	C	C	A	C	B	D	B	D	C
31	**32**	**33**	**34**	**35**	**36**	**37**	**38**	**39**	**40**
A	D	C	A	D	C	A	B	D	B
41	**42**	**43**	**44**	**45**	**46**	**47**	**48**	**49**	**50**
C	B	A	C	D	A	D	C	A	C
51	**52**	**53**	**54**	**55**					
C	C	A	C	B					

❑❑❑

12 Reordering Words & Sentences

Different words form a sentence and convey their meaning only when arranged in a proper order. A Paragraph is formed from sentences, it will convey its true meaning and purpose only when the sentences are arranged in a proper manner. Try and practise it in this exercise.

MULTIPLE CHOICE QUESTIONS

Directions (Qs. 1 to 20): *In the following questions, some parts of the sentence have been jumbled up. You are required to rearrange these parts which are labelled P, Q, R and S to produce the correct sentence. Choose the option with proper sequence.*

1. We are doing
P : to the people
Q : to give relief
R : all we can
S : but more funds are needed
The correct sequence should be
A. P Q R S B. R Q P S
C. Q P R S D. S P Q R

2. The man
P : when he was
Q : in the office last evening
R : could not finish
S : all his work
The correct sequence should be
A. P Q R S B. Q R S P
C. R Q P S D. R S P Q

3. The people decided
P : they were going
Q : how much
R : to spend
S : on the construction of the school building
The correct sequence should be
A. Q P R S B. P Q R S
C. P R Q S D. S Q P R

4. The man said that
P : those workers
Q : would be given a raise
R : who did not go on
S : strike last month
The correct sequence should be
A. P Q R S B. P R S Q
C. Q P R S D. R S P Q

5. I think
P : the members
Q : are basically in agreement
R : of the group
S : on the following points

The correct sequence should be
A. R Q P S B. S Q R P
C. P R Q S D. P Q S R

6. While it was true that
P : I had
Q : to invest in industry
R : some lands and houses
S : I did not have ready cash
The correct sequence should be
A. P Q R S B. P R S Q
C. S Q P R D. Q P R S

7. P : But for your help
Q : to finish this work
R : it would not have been possible
S : in time
The correct sequence should be
A. P R Q S B. S P Q R
C. R P Q S D. P Q R S

8. The boy
P : in the competition
Q : who was wearing spectacles
R : won many prizes
S : held in our college
The correct sequence should be
A. P Q R S B. R P S Q
C. Q R P S D. Q P S R

9. About 200 years ago,
P : in the south of India
Q : an old king
R : ruled over a kingdom
S : called Rajavarman
The correct sequence should be
A. Q S R P B. P Q R S
C. Q P S R D. Q S P R

10. P : his land
Q : a wooden plough
R : the Indian peasant still uses
S : to cultivate
The correct sequence should be
A. R Q P S B. Q P S R
C. S R Q P D. R Q S P

11. He was a man,
P : even if he had to starve
Q : who would not beg
R : borrow or steal
S : from anyone
The correct sequence should be
A. P Q R S B. P R Q S
C. Q R S P D. Q P R S

12. P : in the progress of
Q : universities play a crucial role
R : our civilization
S : in the present age
The correct sequence should be
A. S Q P R B. Q R S P
C. Q R P S D. S Q R P

13. P : far out into the sea
Q : for the next two weeks there were further explosions
R : which hurled
S : ashes and debris
The correct sequence should be
A. Q R P S B. R S P Q
C. Q R S P D. S R P Q

14. William Shakespeare,
P : in his lifetime
Q : the great English dramatist
R : wrote thirty-five plays
S : and several poems
The correct sequence should be
A. P Q R S B. R S P Q
C. Q S R P D. Q R S P

15. Whenever I am,
P : with an old friend of mine
Q : in New Delhi

R : to have dinner
S : I always try
The correct sequence should be
A. S Q P R B. Q S R P
C. R P S Q D. P R Q S

16. P : I don't know
Q : must have thought
R : what people sitting next to me
S : but I came away
The correct sequence should be
A. R S Q P B. R Q S P
C. P Q R S D. P R Q S

17. P : in estimating the size of the earth
Q : but they were hampered by the lack of instruments of precision
R : ancient astronomers
S : used methods which were theoretically valid
The correct sequence should be
A. R P Q S B. P R Q S
C. R S Q P D. R P S Q

18. P : It is a pity that
Q : by offering a handsome dowry
R : a number of parents think that
S : they will be able to ensure the happiness of their daughters
The correct sequence should be
A. S Q R P B. P R S Q
C. P S R Q D. P R Q S

19. The common man
P : in nurturing
Q : a more active role
R : communal harmony
S : should play
The correct sequence should be
A. P R S Q B. S Q P R
C. S Q R P D. P R Q S

20. The doctor
P : able to find out
Q : what has caused
R : the food poisoning
S : has not been
The correct sequence should be
A. S P R Q B. P R Q S
C. P R S Q D. S P Q R

Directions (Qs. 21 to 40): *A number of sentences are given below which when properly sequenced form a coherent paragraph. Each sentence is labelled as abcdef...... Choose the most logical order of sentences from among the given choices to construct a coherent paragraph:*

21. (a) Parts of northern region were pounded by heavy rains today.
(b) Vehicular traffic came to a near halt.
(c) As mid and high altitude areas of Himachal Pradesh were in grip of severe cold wave with snow lashing the tribal areas and mid ranges receiving showers.
(d) As the sky remained heavily overcast with dark clouds reducing the visibility considerably.
(e) A large number of tourists were forced to buy heavy woollens and stay indoors due to inclement weather.

A. ecabd B. adecb
C. edabc D. acbde

22. (a) The idea is that students should be able to find employment for themselves after the course.
(b) The Central Board of Secondary Education is planning a revamp of its vocational courses.
(c) For this it is necessary to tie up with the industry as well as mobilise schools for their support.
(d) While others will be made less academic and more in tune with the needs of the industry.
(e) A number of courses have been identified as 'deadwood' and will be done away with.

A. bedac B. abcde
C. acebd D. baced

23. (a) Clearly, age is not a deterrent in one's choice of learning.
(b) Perhaps, it was because of her childhood desire.
(c) When Rachna came to Delhi eight years back, she had not anticipated a career in the field of art.
(d) She has been successful in the various exhibitions that she has been part of in terms of business.
(e) She had got into expressing her thoughts with the help of a brush and colours only because her daughter refused to get initiated into it.
(f) She feels that her use of colour appeals to people.

A. aedcbf B. cdefba
C. cebadf D. acdebf

24. (a) The rehabilitation record has been dismal.
(b) It has been two years years since the earthquake rudely rattled the people of Gujarat.
(c) And since then, life has been a constant struggle.
(d) The quake set Gujarat's clock back by 10 years.
(e) Things changed forever.

A. bedca B. bcade
C. dbace D. edcba

25. (a) In fact, success in exams depended on rote learning from old notes.
(b) When he was studying civil engineering in a college in Gujarat.
(c) He was detained for lack of attendance.
(d) Lectures were soporific, classes rarely worth attending and 80 per cent attendance compulsory.
(e) The college became a trap he hated.
(f) His is a plight many engineers across India would identify with.
(g) He found the going tough.

A. abcdgef B. bgdacef
C. fabcdge D. abcdefg

26. (a) In a country that has close to 600 recognised engineering colleges, there are only seven IITs.

(b) Barring a few exeptions, the academic atmosphere in these is moribund.

(c) The very best students usually get there.

(d) many waste themselves in frustration.

(e) Most of those who get into engineering are good students.

(f) but about 1.25 lakh others and up in the remaining colleges.

A. aecfbd B. abecdf
C. abcdef D. acfbed

27. (a) Whatever the job market, common wisdom says that IIT graduates will find jobs where others have failed.

(b) The IIT brand name is a ticket to success.

(c) When recruiters go headhunting, the IITs are still top of their list.

(d) Its possessor is understood to have an excellent academic record and the will to succeed.

(e) In the job market, that counts.

A. bdeac B. abcde
C. abdce D. dbace

28. (a) It will pave the way ....

(b) signalling a new beginning in strategic ties......

(c) for a tangible Indian economic presence in Iran and Central Asia.

(d) Iran has offered India valuable road linkages to central Asia ......

(e) aimed at promoting peace and economic cooperation in the region.

A. dbeac B. debca
C. acebd D. abced

29. (a) A good college is essential for a successful career and admissions are based on marks.

(b) The marks-based system followed by all the boards in the country recognises only a small percentage of students as successful.

(c) The marks one scores in the crucial board exams dictate the path his life takes.

(d) Anyone scoring below a certain percentage is automatically branded a 'failure'.

(d) So if you cannot make it into the best college, your career is over even before it has started.

A. abcde B. bcdea
C. bdcae D. abdec

30. (a) The project has already started on an experimental basis in the west district.

(b) A website is soon going to be launched where application forms can be downloaded and submitted.

(c) Standing in a queue at a government office to submit application form will be a thing of the past.
(d) A unique code will be alloted while submitting the form which will help in finding the status of the application.

A. abcd B. dabc
C. cbda D. badc

31. (a) To curb bio-terrorism is a difficult task.
(b) To check these attacks and lessen their impact, we need an impartial team of sincere, strong and dedicated men.
(c) The media can play a strong role in stopping this unnecessary spread of panic.
(d) Since bio-terrorism is not visible or easily detectable, it can be used often.
(e) Men who honour the lives of their fellow countrymen before their own.

A. abcde B. dabce
C. adbec D. acbed

32. (a) He was dying.
(b) No one was ready to touch him as even shifting him from one place to another would lead to profuse bleeding.
(c) He was a five-day old infant, premature and bleeding profusely.
(d) Even if injected one small needle, blood would ooze out and continue to flow for an hour at a stretch.
(e) This small being had haematoma, a thick blood clot in his brain.

A. edbca B. cabde
C. eacdb D. cedba

33. (a) The day I don't treat a patient, I feel ....
(b) I have enough to eat, I crave for blessings now.
(c) But if a financially weak patient gives me only ₹ 50, I don't mind.
(d) Each month I do three to four operations free of cost.
(e) I have lost something in life.
(f) My consultation fee is ₹ 300.

A. fcdeab B. dfcbae
C. fcabde D. bdfcea

34. (a) When he was rushed to the nearby Primary Health Centre after his fall, the doctor referred him to a hospital.
(b) This worsened his injury.
(c) Had a little precaution been exercised after the accident, Tarun would have continued with his gymnastic classes.
(d) He was paralysed from waist downwards when he fell from the vaulting horse while doing gymnastics.
(e) However, the doctor forgot to tell Tarun's parents to take him on a stretcher as he had suffered spinal injuries.
(f) Tarun is wheelchair bound for two years.

A. fdeabc B. abcdef
C. fdcaeb D. fdbcae

35. (a) As the temperature rises, staying hydrated can become a greater challenge for people exercising both indoors and out.

(b) Several things can influence this process, including age, gender, physical conditioning. humidity and a lack of sufficient fluids.

(c) In hot weather, individuals can lose as much as two quarts of sweat per hour.

(d) As we age, we have a lower perceived level of thirst in response to fluid loss and early stages of dehydration.

(e) If not replenished, this can lead to dehydration, heat exhaustion and even heatstroke.

A. abcde B. dbcae
C. cbdea D. acebd

36. (a) The leopard was discovered in the servant quarters of a farmhouse.

(b) The injuries appeared to have been caused by the paws of the leopard, and were not teeth wounds.

(c) It took the wild life officials, Delhi Police and Delhi zoo vets eight hours to capture the leopard that had wandered into a factory in south Delhi.

(d) The leopard then jumped into the factory where the workers managed to lock it in a small generator room before calling in the police.

(e) Before its capture, the leopard attacked two women and a man in the farmhouse.

A. aebdc B. bdaec
C. eadbc D. adbec

37. (a) Police suspect a carpenter working at John's house as he has not reported for work since the day the boy went missing.

(b) John did not return home in the afternoon.

(c) John's mother had herself put the boy on the vehicle in the morning.

(d) John smiled at him and was last seen walking up to him.

(e) His parents called the school and were told John had not been to school at all and had been marked absent.

(f) He was about to enter the school when someone called out his name.

A. cfdbea B. debfca
C. bfdaec D. abcdef

38. (a) However, the mayhem over the last few months is deeply shocking.

(b) Yet I do not agree with the prophets of doom who see nothing but disaster ahead.

(c) When I came back to my motherland India after a stay in Switzerland, I felt I was trading a hotbed of intense religious and political violence for peace and quiet.

(d) I think our nation is searching for an identity.

(e) And a new vision of the future will emerge from this.

A. abcde B. cabde

C. cebad D. bedca

39. (a) An integrated and combined approach was required to reveal the mystery of the brain— its structure, composition and function.

(b) Since the early 80's, scientists were clear that the brain would be the final frontier to conquer.

(c) The initiative was flagged off and came to be known as the Human Brain Project.

(d) But that wasn't easy because understanding the brain involved completely integrating information from the level of the gene to the level of behaviour.

(e) To fulfill this requirement a group of American scientists from various disciplines decided to work together.

A. acbed B. bdaec

C. abdec D. badec

40. (a) A product is something that is made in a factory, a brand is something that is bought by a consumer.

(b) The trick therefore, lies in the brand positioning.

(c) For a consumer, the satisfaction of becoming associated with a name that is the 'best' and the 'leader' is far more important and at times makes him ignore the price factor.

(d) Brands come and go.

(e) Still there are those who manage to stay and develop an affinity with consumers.

A. aebcd B. debac

C. decab D. aecdb

ANSWERS

1	2	3	4	5	6	7	8	9	10
B	D	A	B	C	C	A	C	A	D
11	**12**	**13**	**14**	**15**	**16**	**17**	**18**	**19**	**20**
C	A	C	D	B	D	C	B	B	D
21	**22**	**23**	**24**	**25**	**26**	**27**	**28**	**29**	**30**
D	A	C	A	B	D	A	A	C	C
31	**32**	**33**	**34**	**35**	**36**	**37**	**38**	**39**	**40**
C	D	B	C	D	A	A	B	B	B

❑❑❑

13 Comprehension Passages

Directions: *Read the following passages and answer the questions given below each.*

PASSAGE-1

In the Roman times, defected enemies were generally put to death as criminals for having offended the emperor of Rome. In the middle ages, however, the practice of ransoming of returning prisoners in exchange for money became common. Though some saw this custom as a step towards a most humane society, the primary reasons behind it were economic rather than humanitarian.

In those times, rulers had only a limited ability to raise taxes. They could neither force their subject to fight nor pay them to do so. The promise of material compensation in the form of goods and ransom was therefore the only way of inducing combatants to participate in a war. In the middle ages, the predominant incentive for the individual soldiers was the expectation of spoils. Although collecting ransom clearly brought financial gain, keeping a prisoner and arranging for his exchange had its cost. Consequently, procedures were devised to reduce transaction costs.

One such device was a rule asserting that the prisoner had to assess his own value. This compelled the prisoner to establish a value *without too much distortion;* indicating too low a value would increase, the captive's chances of being killed, while indicating too high a value would either ruin him financially or create a prohibitively expensive ransom that would also result in death.

1. It can be inferred from the passage that a medieval soldier

A. was less likely to kill captured members of opposing armies than was a soldier of the Roman Empire

B. was similar to a 20th century terrorist in that he operated on a basically independent level and was motivated solely by economic incentives

C. had few economic options and chose to fight because it was the only way to earn an adequate living

D. was motivated to spare prisoners' lives by humanitarian rather than economic ideals

2. Which of the following best describes the change in policy from executing prisoners in Roman times to ransoming prisoners in the middle ages?

A. The emperors of Rome demanded more respect than

did medieval rulers and thus Roman subjects went to greater lengths to defend their nation

B. It was a reflection of the lesser degree of direct control medieval ruler had over subjects

C. It became a show of strength and honour warrior of the middles ages to be able to capture and return their enemies

D. Medieval soldiers were not as hum-anitarian as their ransoming practices might have indicated

3. The primary purpose of the passage is to

A. discuss the economic basis of the medieval practice of exchanging prisoners for ransom

B. examine the history of the treatment of prisoner of war

C. emphasize the importance of a warrior's code of honour during the middle ages

D. explore a way of reducing the cost of ransom

4. The author uses the phrase *"without too much distortion"* in order to

A. indicate that prisoners would fairly assess their worth

B. emphasize the important role medieval prisoners played in determining whether they should be ransomed

C. explain how prisoners often paid more than an appropriate ransom in order to increase their chances for survival

D. suggest that captors and captives often had understanding relationships

PASSAGE-2

The world dismisses curiosity by calling it idle or mere idle curiosity—even though curious persons are seldom idle. Parents do their best to extinguish curiosity in their children because it makes life difficult to be faced everyday with a string of unanswerable questions about what makes fire hot or why grass grows. Children whose curiosity survives parental discipline are invited to join our university. With the university, they go on asking their questions and trying to find the answers. In the eyes of a scholar, that is what a university is for. Some of the questions which the scholars ask, seem to the world to be scarcely worth asking, let alone answering. They asked questions too minute specialised for you and me to understand without years of explanation. If the world inquires of one of them why he wants to know the answer to a particular question he may say especially if he is a scientist, that the answer will in some obscure way make possible a new machine or weapon or gadget. He talks that way because he knows that the world understands and respects utility.

But to you who are now part of the university, he will say that he wants to know the answer simply because he does not know it, the way the mountain climber wants to climb a mountain, simply because it is there. Similarly a historian asked by an outsider why he studies history may come out with the argument that he has learnt to repeat on such occasions, something about knowledge of the past making it possible to understand the present and mould the future. But if you really want to know why a historian studies the past, the answer is much simpler, something happened and he would like to know what. All this does not mean that the answers which scholars find to their questions have no consequences. They may have enormous consequences but these seldom form the reason for asking the questions or pursuing the answers. It is true that scholars can be put to work answering questions for the sake of the consequences as thousands are working, now, for example, in search of a cure for cancer. But this is not the primary function of the scholars. For the consequences are usually subordinate to the satisfaction of curiosity.

1. According to the passage, the children make life difficult for their parents
   A. by their ceaseless curiosity
   B. by unceasing bombardment of questions
   C. by asking irrelevant questions
   D. by posing profound questions

2. The common people consider some of the questions that the scholars ask unimportant
   A. as they are too lazy and idle
   B. as they are too modest
   C. as it's beyond their comprehension
   D. as it is considered a waste of time

3. A historian really studies the past
   A. to comprehend the present and to reconstruct the future
   B. to explain the present and plan the future
   C. to understand the present and make fortune
   D. to understand the present and mould the future

4. Children whose curiosity survives parental discipline means
   A. children retaining their curiosity in spite of being discouraged by their parents
   B. children pursuing their mental curiosity
   C. children's curiosity subdued due to parents' intervention
   D. children being disciplined by their parents

5. According to the passage, parents do their best to discourage curiosity in their children
   A. because they have no time
   B. because they have no patience to answer them

C. because they feel that their children ask stupid questions continuously
D. because they are unable to answer all their questions

PASSAGE-3

The factor of geographical distribution is equally, possibly even more, significant that English is spoken as first or native language in at least four continents of the world, Russian in two, Chinese and the Indian languages in one. English is without question the closest approach to a world language today. It goes without saying that no two persons ever have an identical command of their common language. Certainly, they have not precisely the same vocabulary. There are at least minor differences in pronunciation, indeed the same individual will not pronounce his vowels and consonants in absolutely identical fashion everytime he utters them. Everyone possesses, in addition, certain individual traits of grammatical form and syntactical order, constituting that peculiar and personal quality of language which we term as style. All of this is implicit in the well-known phrase, 'Style is the man.' No men are identical, no two styles are the same. If this be true of but two persons, the potential of differences resident in a language spoken by more than 200 million truly staggers imagination.

1. The author argues that English is the closest approach to a world language because
   A. there are more native speakers of English than of any other language
   B. English has less number of mutually unintelligible dialects
   C. the geographical distribution of English covers a much greater area
   D. other languages are much too complex to be world languages
2. The fact that the same individual will not pronounce his vowels and consonants identically everytime shows that
   A. literary style varies from person to person
   B. mutual intelligibility is a myth
   C. vocabulary varies from individual to individual
   D. no two persons speak the same language exactly the same way
3. It is evident from the passage that style is
   A. a strange type of language
   B. a language where one does not have to be particular about correctness and grammar
   C. language used in a particular way by an individual
   D. a question of grammatical and syntactic correctness
4. According to some authorities
   A. more people speak Chinese dialect than English

B. more people speak English as an auxiliary language than as a first language
C. more people speak English in the UK than in England
D. about one-fourth of the world's population speaks English

5. The overall implication of the passage is that
A. to suppose that 230 million people speak English as a native language would certainly be an underestimate
B. the 55 million inhabitants of the British Isles speak like the 30 million inhabitants of the dominions and colonies
C. a little less than half the native English speakers in the world live in the US
D. about one-tenth of the total English-speaking world population lives in British dominions and colonies

PASSAGE-4

What is the future which awaits our children? The underlying assumption of the question, that Indian children have a common future, is itself dubious. It can legitimately be asked whether a student who is well-fed, attending a boarding school in the salubrious climate of the hills and learning to use computers has any future in common with a malnourished child who goes to a school with no blackboards, if indeed he does go to school. The latter may have no worthwhile future at all. And it might be worthwhile to analyse the significance of this marginalisation of more than 75 per cent of the children of this country.

The failure to provide an infrastructure for primary education in the villages of India more than 40 years after independence is in sharp contrast with the sophisticated institutions, for technical institutes of higher education are funded by the government, which essentially means that the money to support them comes from taxes. And, since indirect taxation forms a substantial part of the taxes collected by the government, the financial burden is borne by all the people. L.K. Jha put it graphically when he observed that 25 paise of every rupee spent on educating an IIT student comes from the pockets of men and women whose children may never enter a proper classroom.

1. The author is trying to highlight which of the following?
A. Faulty system of direct taxes
B. The greatness of L.K. Jha
C. Need of sophisticated education for rural poor
D. Need to have common future for Indian children

2. Which of the following pairs have been termed as 'sharp contrast' by the author?
(*i*) Infrastructure for technical education
(*ii*) Lack of infrastructure for rural primary schools
(*iii*) 25 paise of every rupee earned by Government is spent on education

(*iv*) The financial burden of higher technical education is borne by all people

(*v*) 75% of children have limited opportunities

A. (*ii*) and (*iv*)
B. (*ii*) and (*iii*)
C. (*iii*) and (*iv*)
D. (*i*) and (*ii*)

3. Which of the following statements is not true?

(*i*) The author welcomes Govt.'s initiative on primary education

(*ii*) 75% of the children have a bright future

(*iii*) 25% cost of educating a technocrat comes from poor people

A. Only (*i*)
B. Only (*ii*)
C. Only (*iii*)
D. Only (*i*) and (*ii*)

4. According to the author, who among the following does not have a hopeful and prosperous future?

(*i*) All students from technical institutes

(*ii*) All students financially supported by the Government

A. Only (*i*)
B. Only (*ii*)
C. Both (*i*) and (*ii*)
D. Neither (*i*) nor (*ii*)

5. What seems to be the likely answer of the author to the question posed by him in the first sentence of the passage?

(*i*) There is no common future for the Indian children

(*ii*) The future is worthwhile for majority of Indian children

(*iii*) The majority may never enter a proper classroom

A. Only (*i*)
B. Only (*ii*)
C. Only (*iii*)
D. Both (*i*) and (*ii*)

6. What seems to be the purpose of the author in writing this passage?

A. Setting goals for children of upper middle class
B. Questioning the legitimacy of public schools
C. Highlighting lack of infrastructural facilities for primary education
D. Focusing on inequality in educational opportunities

PASSAGE-5

Cyber crime is the branded stigma defacing the culture and magnanimity of computer technology. It is upkeeping the flag with indomitable triumph against developing computer technology worldwide.

Modern age is striding with marching steps of technology revolution beating the past decade of ancestral belief with ultimate care. Computer invention has unfolded the mystery of quick access with the objective of minimum manpower and cutting the time consumption parameters.

As each coin has dual face of its portrait, likewise computer technology is sick of creeping virus. Synthetic manmade dilemma of site hackers activation is causing setback to the expanding anchor of revolutionary device with great loss of time, economy and data profile as suffered by consumers. A recent report from Internet security firm Websense estimates that 85.6 per cent of all the unwanted e-mails contained links to spam sites. The company's data suggests that the number of malicious sites grew 233 per cent in the last six months and saw 671 per cent growth in the number of malicious sites during the last year. In June alone, the total number of e-mails detected as containing viruses increased by 600 per cent compared to May.

Chat rooms, blogs and message-boards where the users post comments have been identified as the top targets of hackers and spammers due to the high traffic these attract. According to Websense, 95 per cent of user-generated comments to blogs, chat rooms and message-boards during the first half of the year were malicious.

It is advisable not to click on spurious links and stay away from keying in passwords at unknown sites as they are most likely to be spammed. Hackers can steal your passwords and log in to your account and access critical information like account numbers and contact details among other things.

1. The above passage is:
   A. an advisory for the computer users.
   B. an advisory for the Internet users.
   C. a warning against possible threat to the Internet users.
   D. related to chat rooms, blogs and message boards.

2. People who use chat rooms and blogs,
   A. are safe and have no threats from spam.
   B. are more prone to malicious e-mails.
   C. create virus and hack the accounts of others.
   D. are unsafe.

3. According to the writer, it is not safe to:
   A. log on to spurious links.
   B. access one's own account frequently.
   C. have essential information stored in a computer.
   D. include data-stealing code.

4. Hackers and spammers, according to the writer, are:
   A. a new threat to the Internet users and the economy.
   B. only pranksters and not serious threat to the system.
   C. trained, professional technocrats who are an asset.
   D. not expert professionals.

5. Which word in the passage is synonym of *weblog*?
   A. blog
   B. password

C. site
D. e-mail

6. Which agency has assessed the data record with spam sites?
A. Microsoft
B. Internet security from Google
C. Websense
D. Spammers

7. Which month dominates the e-mails detection data record?
A. May
B. June
C. Last six months
D. Last year

PASSAGE-6

Progress in life depends a good deal on crossing one threshold after another. Sometime ago, a man watched his little nephew try to write his name. It was hard work, very hard work. The little boy had arrived at an effort threshold. Today he writes his name with comparative ease. No new threshold confronts him. This is the way with all of us. As soon as we cross one threshold, as soon as we conquer one difficulty, a new difficulty appears, or should appear. Some people make the mistake of steering clear of thresholds. Anything that requires genuine thinking and use of energy, they avoid. They prefer to stay in a rut where thresholds are not met. Probably, they have been at their job a number of years. Things are easy for them. They make no effort to seek out new obstacles to overcome. Real progress stops under such circumstances.

Some middle-aged and elderly people greatly enrich their lives by continuing to cross thresholds. One man went into an entirely new business when he was past middle life and made success of it, De Morgan didn't start to write novels until he was past sixty. Psychologists have discovered that man can continue to learn throughout his life. And it is undoubtedly better to try and fail than not to try at all. There one can be placed in the category of the Swiss mountaineer of whom it was said, *"He died climbing"*. When a new difficulty arises to obstruct your path, do not complain. Accept the challenge. Determine to cross this threshold as you have crossed numerous other thresholds in your past. In the words of a poet, do not rest but strive *to pass from dream to grander dream.*

1. What obstructs real progress in life?
A. Remaining at one and the same post
B. Avoiding the thinking and energy
C. Shunning every work
D. Stopping education

2. What does progress in life depend upon?
A. Good habits
B. Hardwork
C. Overcoming one difficulty after another
D. Spirit of service and cooperation

3. What does *'He died climbing'* signify?

A. He died when he was climbing the hill
B. He died before getting at the top
C. He strove hard till the last moment of life
D. He climbed the hill and then died

4. What does *'to pass from dream to grander dream'* mean?
A. Always having greater and greater aspiration in life
B. Seeing one good dream and then greater aspiration in life
C. Making plan after plan
D. Seeing one dream after the other

5. What did the man entering a new business past middle life do of his business?
A. He miserably failed in it
B. He achieved partial success
C. He dropped the business after some time
D. He achieved good success in it

6. How can you accomplish the most difficult tasks?
A. By mobilizing all possible resources
B. By avoiding all obstacles
C. By sticking to hardwork
D. By doing it bit by bit and persisting in the effort

7. What does De Morgan's life teach?
A. That it is futile to learn many things
B. That one is never old in case he has vigour
C. That it is never too late to learn
D. That creative writing can be made even late in life

8. How do middle-aged and elderly people add brilliance to their lives?
A. By overcoming difficulty one after another
B. By getting sycophants to surround them
C. By making fine speeches
D. By acquiring resourcefulness

9. What should we do when a new difficulty obstructs our path?
A. Run away from it
B. Be bold and face it
C. Manoeuvre to get it removed
D. Enlist other people's help to get it over

10. When did De Morgan start to write novels?
A. When he was sixty years old
B. When he was below sixty
C. When he studied psychology
D. None of these

PASSAGE-7

It is *heartening* to know that if one had not had any heart attack earlier and he stops smoking, his chances of having a heart attack *drop* to that of a non-smoker in about six months' time. Stopping of smoking is also the single most effective means of secondary prevention (recurrence of a heart attack) in heart patients.

Smoking leads to pain and stiffness in the legs while walking. No amount of drugs can help. The only remedy is to give up smoking. If women smoke during pregnancy, there is an increased risk of death of the baby in the womb or soon after birth. Even where the baby survives, there is likelihood of delayed physical and intellectual development of the baby till it reaches 11 years of age.

Still worse the fact about smoking is that passive smoking is equally dangerous. Passive smokers are those who do not smoke but being in the company of smokers have to inhale smoke exhaled by the smokers They are equally prone to heart diseases, lung cancer and bronchitis, for no fault of theirs. It is seen that the incidence of these diseases is greater among women whose husbands are *heavy* smokers As such, every non-smoker has a fundamental right to safeguard himself against the danger of passive smoking. "Your smoking is injurious to my health and I have a right to stop you from smoking" could be the slogan against passive smoking. It is a great threat to the health of the individual, the family and the society. In fact one has to choose between health and smoking including passive smoking. *One cannot have both.*

Another matter of *grave concern* about smoking is the long time interval between the start of smoking habit and the manifestation of deadly diseases like cancer, chronic bronchitis and heart attack. People are generally not aware of the link between smoking and the misery they have to undergo years later and younger people often fall victim to this menacing habit under the wrong impression that they are *immune* to its disastrous effects, not realising that they are *heading* towards catastrophe. The prolonged incubation period of many tobacco-related diseases has prevented recognition of the size of the threat and the *grim* picture of chronic and life-threatening diseases.

1. What is "passive smoking"?

A. Giving up the habit of smoking abruptly

B. Exhaling smoke by a non-smoker

C. Unintended intake of smoke exhaled by smokers

D. Smoking cigarettes which are harmless in nature

2. The effects of passive smoking are more and more prominently observed among

A. the children

B. the smokers

C. the wives of smokers

D. the non-smokers

3. Which of the following is a heartening thing, according to the author?

A. People who have had a heart attack stop smoking

B. It takes only six months for any person to quit smoking

C. The smoker carries the risk of heart attack for six months

D. None of these

4. Which of the following statements is/are false in the context of the passage?

(*i*) Passive smokers are not free from risk of heart diseases
(*ii*) Intake of certain medicines helps recover pain and stiffness in legs caused by smoking
(*iii*) Younger people are immune to the disastrous effects if their regular smoking is under control

A. (*i*) and (*ii*) only
B. (*ii*) and (*iii*) only
C. (*ii*) only
D. (*iii*) only

5. Which of the following is not mentioned in the passage as a likely result of smoking by women during pregnancy?

A. Death of baby before birth
B. Death of baby after birth
C. Survival of baby with some abnormality
D. Abnormal delay in the childbirth

6. Which of the following is considered by the author as a matter of "grave concern"?

A. Inordinate delay in appearance of symptoms of hazards of smoking
B. Long time required for giving up the habit of smoking
C. Manifestation of deadly diseases like cancer, bronchitis, etc.
D. Lack of awareness of people regarding the hazards of smoking

7. The youth feel that they are immune to the hazardous effects of smoking because

A. these effects of smoking are not visible within a short time span
B. they do not realise that they are heading towards disaster
C. they feel a great thrill in acquiring the habit of smoking
D. the link between smoking and its disastrous effects cannot be established

8. Which factor prevents people from realising the extent of threat of smoking hazards?

A. Their lack of awareness of civic responsibilities
B. Their firm belief that they are not immune to these hazards
C. The less disastrous effects of tobacco-related diseases
D. None of these

9. The last sentence of the third para *"One cannot have both"* means

A. active smoking and passive smoking
B. smoking and risk of heart diseases
C. threat to the individual and also to the family
D. None of these

Directions (Qs. 10 to 12): *Choose the word which is most nearly the **SAME** in meaning as the word given in bold capitals as used in the passage.*

10. HEADING
A. crowning B. marching
C. adorning D. title

11. HEAVY
A. excessive B. bulky
C. large D. thick

12. DROP
A. roll B. escape
C. remove D. reduce

Directions (Qs. 13 to 15): *Choose the word which is most nearly the **OPPOSITE** in meaning of the word given in bold capitals as used in the passage.*

13. GRIM
A. dim B. dark
C. presentable D. pleasant

14. IMMUNE
A. free B. vulnerable
C. powerful D. weak

15. HEARTENING
A. cheerful B. miserable
C. frightening D. dangerous

PASSAGE-8

The happy man is the man who lives objectively, who has free affections and wide interests, who secures his happiness through these interests and affections and through the fact that they, in turn, make him an object of interest and affection to many others. To be the recipient of affection is a potent cause of happiness, but the man who demands affection is not the man upon whom it is *bestowed*. The man who receives affection is, speaking broadly, the man who gives it. But it is useless to attempt to give it as a calculation, in the way in which one might lend money at interest, for a calculated affection is not genuine and is not felt to be so by the recipient.

What then can a man do who is unhappy because he is encased in self? So long as he continues to think about the causes of his unhappiness, he continues to be self-centred and therefore does not get outside the vicious circle, if he is to get outside it, it must be genuine interests, not by simulated interests adopted merely as a medicine. Although this difficulty is real, there is nevertheless much that he can do if he has rightly diagnosed his trouble. If, for example, his trouble is due to a sense of sin, conscious or unconscious, he can first persuade his conscious mind that he has no reason to feel sinful and then proceed, to plant his rational conviction in his unconscious mind, concerning himself meanwhile with some more or less neutral activity. If he succeeds in *dispelling* the sense of sin, it is possible that genuine objective interests will arise spontaneously. If his trouble is self-pity, he can deal with it in the same manner after first persuading himself that there is nothing extraordinarily unfortunate in his circumstances.

If fear is his trouble, let him practise exercises designed to give courage. Courage has been recognised from time immemorial as an important virtue, and a great part of training of boys and young men has been devoted to producing a type of character capable of fearlessness in battle. But moral courage and intellectual courage have been much less studied, they also, however, have their technique. Admit to yourself everyday at least one painful truth, you will find this quite useful. Teach yourself to feel that life still be worth living even if you were not, as of course you are, immeasurably superior to all your friends in virtue and in intelligence. Exercises of this sort prolonged through several years will at last enable you to admit facts *without flinching* and will, in so doing, free you from the empire of fear over a very large field.

1. Who according to the passage is the happy man?
   A. who is encased in self
   B. who has free affection and wide interests
   C. who is free from worldly passions
   D. who has externally centre passions

2. According to the passage, calculated affection
   A. appears to be false and fabricated
   B. makes other pen-on to love you
   C. turns into permanent affection over a period of time
   D. leads to self-pity

3. Which of the following virtues, according to the passage, has been recognised for long as an important virtue?
   A. Patriotism
   B. Sacrifice
   C. Courage
   D. Self-consciousness

4. Which of the following, according to the passage, has not been studied much?
   A. Feeling of guilt and self-pity
   B. The state of mind of an unhappy man
   C. How to get absorbed in other interests
   D. Moral and intellectual courage

5. If a man is suffering from a sense of sin
   A. he should invite opinion of others
   B. he should admit his sin at once
   C. he should consciously realize that he has no reason to feel sinful
   D. he should develop a fearless character

6. What happens to a man who demands affection?
   A. His feelings are reciprocated by others
   B. He tends to take a calculated risk
   C. He becomes a victim of a viscious circle
   D. None of these

7. What should a man do who is suffering from the feeling of self-pity?
   A. He should control his passions and emotions

B. He should persuade himself that everything is alright in his circumstances
C. He should seek affection from others
D. He should develop a feeling of fearlessness

8. How to get out of the viscious circle mentioned in the passage?
A. By practicing skills of concentration
B. By inculcating the habits of self-absorption
C. Being true to others and one's internal circumstances
D. None of these

9. Which of the following statements is not *true* in the context of the passage?
A. Happy man has wide interests
B. Courage has been recognized as an important virtue
C. Unhappy man is encased in self
D. Issue of intellectual courage has been extensively studied

10. Which of the following words is ***SIMILAR*** in meaning of the word **'bestowed'** as used in the passage?
A. Conferred
B. Accommodated
C. Trusted
D. Withdrawn

11. Which of the following statements is *true* in the context of the passage?
A. All passions stem from unhappiness
B. The happy man lives in subjectively
C. Any virtue has a dark side also
D. One feels happy if one receives affection

12. Which of the following words is ***SIMILAR*** in meaning to the word **'flinching'** as used in the passage?
A. Wincing
B. Convincing
C. Explaining
D. Debating

13. What happens when you think about cause of your unhappiness?
A. You try to introspect and look critically at yourself
B. You realize that the life can be lived in different ways
C. You try to practice exercise designed to give courage
D. You remain a self-centred person

14. What according to the passage is the real cause of happiness?
A. Material rewards and incentives received
B. Critical analysis of the happy state of mind
C. Affection received from others
D. Calculated risks taken

15. Which of the following words is ***OPPOSITE*** in meaning of the word **'dispelling'** as used in the passage?

A. Giving
B. Accumulating
C. Projecting
D. Scattering

PASSAGE-9

Education, particularly higher education, is the obvious but crucially important instrument for nation building. As Confucious has said:

"If you are thinking of one year, plant rice. If you are thinking of a decade, plant trees. If you are thinking of a century, educate the people."

When we set about the task of higher education, we should be absolutely clear in our perception of the goals of education in the specific context of our nation's development. No *doubt,* one of the important aims of education would be to create the required range and nature of trained manpower assessed to be needed by different sectors of national growth. The entire educational apparatus must be geared progressively to fulfill the requirements of different phases of our growth in every sector—primary, secondary and *tertiary.* The aim must be to ensure that our country does not experience either *paucity,* or a *surfeit* of trained manpower in any specific segment of our economy. The requirements of our country, as a free, democratic, secular, socialist, nation, *aspiring* for rapid development, *entail* a specific recipe for our educational institutions. Today's educational institutions must therefore be developed accordingly and must regulate themselves to give the country the precise nature and quantum of trained manpower as projected by the requirements of our planned economy.

1. The author has quoted thoughts of Confucious to stress
A. importance of planting trees for human beings
B. the worthless efforts in planting rice
C. the benefits of investing in education
D. the need for assessing manpower requirement

2. Which statement cannot be made on the basis of the passage?
A. Higher education should keep in view the requirements of national economy
B. Higher education has not been employed for nation building
C. All levels of education have a role to play in nation's growth
D. In our country we need to have a specially planned educational system

3. The writer believes that
A. there are no problems related to higher education
B. investment in education is of long-range
C. higher education should be used to assess manpower needs
D. aims of higher education in India are absolutely clear

4. The author's expectations from higher education, are essentially
A. unrealistic B. confusing
C. critical D. vague

5. The writer indicates that
A. higher education did not play any role in national growth
B. primary education did not play any role in national growth
C. our nation experiences paucity of trained manpower in many sectors
D. today's higher education has no precise goals to achieve

6. Author has used the word 'apparatus' to indicate the
A. scientific nature of education
B. complicated organization demanded by education
C. readily visible benefits of education
D. entire equipment of education to perform particular function

7. Which of the following has not been conveyed by the passage?
A. Education at any level can contribute in nation building
B. Manpower needs in many areas can be fulfilled through higher education
C. Rapid development of our nation is possible through higher education
D. Present higher education does not ensure surfeit of trained manpower

8. This passage is likely to be addressed to
A. politicians only
B. scientists only
C. students only
D. cannot be said

9. Choose a suitable title to the passage:
A. Manpower Planning in India
B. Importance of Higher Education
C. Demands of Higher Education
D. Role of Higher Education in India

Directions (Qs.10 to 12): *Choose the word which is most nearly the **SAME** in meaning as the word given in bold capitals as used in the passage.*

10. DOUBT
A. suspicion B. certain
C. definite D. sure

11. TERTIARY
A. last B. important
C. third D. terminal

12. ASPIRING
A. inquiring B. awaiting
C. involving D. striving

Directions (Qs.13 to 15): *Choose the word which is most **OPPOSITE** in meaning as the word given in bold capitals as used in the passage.*

13. PAUCITY
A. moderate B. enormity
C. mediocrity D. littleness

14. SURFEIT
A. abundance B. redundancy
C. repletion D. lack

15. ENTAIL

A. entitled B. ensure
C. dismiss D. retain

PASSAGE-10

Books are a great treasurehouse of knowledge. They are the living examples of man's *march* on the path to higher and higher civilisation. The great men who died long ago, live in their books. We feel their very personality and existence when we read their books. We feel as if they were conversing with us.

Books not only store civilization but also carry it forward. All coming generations get the light of knowledge from the books written by their ancestors and try to improve upon that knowledge. Civilization cannot make much *headway* in a country where there are not many *great* books. We get through books the latest knowledge in the fields of arts, science, commerce, etc. This knowledge is helpful to us and *enables* us to achieve success in the field of our choice.

Books are never failing friends. They never *desert* us, not even when all fair-weather friends have deserted us. They dispel the dark clouds of gloom from our minds and increase our happiness if we are already happy. Through the ages, the scriptures and other great books have provided immeasurable *solace* to the wounded and strife-torn humanity.

There may be books prescribed for some course or profession, but then there are books for general study. The books of literature—poetry, drama, novel, short stories, etc., are generally highly thrilling and inspiring if they are written by a good author. There may be tragic, comical or humorous books. The question is that of an individual's choice.

To be a lover of books, though not to be bookworm, is a sign of good luck. A voracious reader gets much *more pleasure* from reading books than a miser gets in hoarding money. The knowledge embedded in books is valueless; so is pleasure obtained from reading them. A good book absorbs the whole spirit of man; the reader's pleasure is indescribable.

1. Which of the following, according to the passage, is not true about books?

A. They are source of inspiration
B. They are source of knowledge
C. They are source of happiness
D. They are means of livelihood

2. How do the books help in progress of civilization?

A. Based on the earlier books new knowledge is obtained
B. The books provide solution to many problems
C. The books inspire the scientists
D. Not mentioned in the passage

3. How do the books make people more happy?

A. They help the reader to overcome the shadows of uncertainty

B. They help bring in joy by amusing the reader through their content
C. They help the reader to understand the darker side of life
D. Not mentioned in the passage

4. Which of the following is the author's view about the knowledge and pleasure derived from books?
(*i*) We get more of knowledge and less of pleasure
(*ii*) We get more of pleasure and less of knowledge
(*iii*) We get knowledge and pleasure in equal measure
A. only (*i*)
B. only (*ii*)
C. either (*i*) or (*ii*)
D. only (*iii*)

5. The high quality of books produced by a country indicates:
A. it has a high rate of literacy
B. it has a progressive civilization
C. it is not an industrialised nation
D. it has learned ancestors

6. Why are the books, according to the passage, called never-failing friends?
A. Books do not betray individuals
B. Books are inanimate
C. Books always give companionship to the reader
D. Books are available in the market anytime unlike others

7. How do the books help in bringing peace in the minds of people?
A. Books provide information about the past civilization
B. Books help people learn to take correct steps with the help of the recorded information
C. Books act as a window to the minds of the great men
D. Not mentioned in the passage

8. Which of the following has been described as a sign of good luck?
A. Being a miser
B. Having lot of money
C. Advancing the culture
D. A passion for books

Directions (Qs. 9 to 12): *Choose the word which is most nearly the* ***SAME*** *in meaning as the word given in bold capitals as used in the passage.*

9. SOLACE
A. peace B. tranquillity
C. calmness D. console

10. ENABLES
A. helps B. succeeds
C. promotes D. stops

11. HEADWAY
A. higher B. forge
C. movement D. improve

12. MARCH
A. move B. progress
C. pass D. register

Directions (Qs. 13 to 15): *Choose the word which is most* ***OPPOSITE*** *in meaning of the word given in bold capitals as used in the passage.*

13. GREAT

A. small B. thin
C. short D. ordinary

14. PLEASURE

A. displeasure B. pain
C. happiness D. hardship

15. DESERT

A. waterhole B. bitter
C. accompany D. propel

ANSWERS

PASSAGE-1

1	2	3	4
A	B	A	A

PASSAGE-2

1	2	3	4	5
A	C	D	A	D

PASSAGE-3

1	2	3	4	5
A	D	C	D	A

PASSAGE-4

1	2	3	4	5
D	A	D	A	A
6				
D				

PASSAGE-5

1	2	3	4	5
A	D	A	A	A
6	**7**			
C	B			

PASSAGE-6

1	2	3	4	5
A	C	C	A	D
6	**7**	**8**	**9**	**10**
D	B	A	B	D

PASSAGE-7

1	2	3	4	5
C	C	D	B	D
6	**7**	**8**	**9**	**10**
A	A	D	D	B
11	**12**	**13**	**14**	**15**
A	D	D	B	C

PASSAGE-8

1	2	3	4	5
B	A	C	D	C
6	**7**	**8**	**9**	**10**
D	B	D	D	A
11	**12**	**13**	**14**	**15**
D	D	D	C	B

PASSAGE-9

1	2	3	4	5
D	D	C	D	D
6	**7**	**8**	**9**	**10**
D	A	D	B	A
11	**12**	**13**	**14**	**15**
C	D	B	D	C

PASSAGE-10

1	2	3	4	5
D	A	D	D	B
6	**7**	**8**	**9**	**10**
A	D	D	D	A
11	**12**	**13**	**14**	**15**
D	B	D	B	C

❑❑❑

QUANTITATIVE APTITUDE

1

NUMBERS

A number tells us how many times a unit is contained in a given quantity. It therefore signifies one or more units, or denotes one or more distinct objects of the same kind. For example, *one* rupee, *six* pencils, *nine* cats, *thirty* paise, etc. The words in italics denote numbers.

Whole Numbers: The numbers 0, 1, 2, 3, 4, 5, 6, 7, 8, 9, 10, 11, ... are called whole numbers or integers. So 84 is an integer while 6¼ is not an integer.

Even Numbers: The numbers, which are divisible by two are called even numbers. *For example,* 2, 4, 6, 8, 10, 12, 28, 36, etc.

Odd Numbers: The numbers, which cannot be divided by two are called odd numbers. *For example,* 1, 3, 5, 7, 9, 11, 13, 15, 17, 19, etc.

Prime Numbers: The numbers, which are divisible only by themselves and one are called prime numbers. *For example,* 2, 3, 5, 7, 11, 13, etc.

Composite Numbers: The numbers, which are not prime called composite numbers. Thus, the prime numbers and composite numbers make up the set of natural numbers.

Consecutive Numbers: A collection of numbers is consecutive if each number is the successor of the number which precedes it. *For example,* 4, 5, 6, 7, 8 and 9 are consecutive, but 4, 5, 6, 8, 10 are not. 6, 8, 10, 12 are consecutive even numbers. 11, 13, 17, 19 are consecutive prime numbers.

Any whole number can be written as a product of factors which are prime numbers.

How to write a number as a product of prime factors?

(*i*) Divide the number by 2 if possible; continue to divide by 2 until the factor you get, is not divisible by 2.

(*ii*) Divide the result from (i) by 3 if possible; continue to divide by 3 until the factor you get, is not divisible by 3.

(*iii*) Divide the result from (ii) by 5 if possible; continue to divide by 5 until the factor you get, is not divisible by 5.

(*iv*) Continue this procedure by dividing by 7, 11, 13, and so on; until all the factors are prime.

EXAMPLES :

Example 1. *Express 2310 as a product of prime factors.*

Solution.

2	2310
2	1155
5	385
7	77
	11

$\therefore$ $2310 = 2 \times 3 \times 5 \times 7 \times 11.$

Example 2. *Resolve 1026 into prime factors.*

Solution.

2	1026
3	513
3	171
3	57
	19

$\therefore$ $1026 = 2 \times 3 \times 3 \times 3 \times 19$

A number n is a common multiple of two other numbers a and b if it is a multiple of each of them. For example, 24 is a common multiple of 2 and 3, since $2 \times 12 = 24$ and $3 \times 8 = 24$. But 21 is not a common multiple of 3 and 6, because 21 is not a multiple of 6.

A number *x* is a common factor of two other numbers *a* and *b* if *x* is a factor of *a* and *x* is a factor of *b*.

L.C.M.: The least common multiple of two numbers is the smallest number which is a common multiple of both numbers.

How to find the least common multiple of two numbers *a* and *b*?

(i) Write *a* and *b* as products of *primes* separately.

(ii) If there are any common factors delete them in one of the products.

(iii) Multiply the remaining factors to get L.C.M.

PROPERTIES OF NUMBERS

1. The product of any two consecutive numbers is divisible by 2

For example,	$2 \times 3 = 6$	is divisible by 2
	$3 \times 4 = 12$	is divisible by 2
	$4 \times 5 = 20$	is divisible by 2
	$15 \times 16 = 240$	is divisible by 2

2. The product of any three consecutive numbers is divisible by 6.
For example,

$2 \times 3 \times 4 = 24$ is divisible by 6
$3 \times 4 \times 5 = 60$ is divisible by 6
$4 \times 5 \times 6 = 120$ is divisible by 6
$10 \times 11 \times 12 = 1320$ is divisible by 6
$40 \times 41 \times 42 = 68880$ is divisible by 6

3. The product of any four consecutive numbers is divisible by 24.
For example,

$$2 \times 3 \times 4 \times 5 = 120 \text{ is divisible by } 24.$$
$$4 \times 5 \times 6 \times 7 = 24 \times 5 \times 7$$
$$6 \times 7 \times 8 \times 9 = 3 \times 2 \times 7 \times 8 \times 9$$
$$= 24 \times 2 \times 7 \times 9$$
$$10 \times 11 \times 12 \times 13 = 2 \times 5 \times 11 \times 12 \times 13$$
$$= 24 \times 5 \times 11 \times 13$$

4. The product of any five consecutive numbers is divisible by 120.
For example,

$$2 \times 3 \times 4 \times 5 \times 6 = 120 \times 6$$
$$3 \times 4 \times 5 \times 6 \times 7 = 120 \times 21$$
$$4 \times 5 \times 6 \times 7 \times 8 = 120 \times 56$$

5. Every square number is a multiple of 3 or exceeds of multiple of 3 by unity.
For example,

$$3^2 = 9 = 3 \times 3$$
$$4^2 = 16 = 3 \times 5 + 1$$
$$5^2 = 25 = 3 \times 8 + 1$$
$$6^2 = 36 = 3 \times 12$$
$$7^2 = 49 = 3 \times 16 + 1$$

6. Difference of the squares of any two odd numbers is always divisible by 8.
For example,

$$5^2 - 3^2 = 25 - 9 = 16 = 8 \times 2$$
$$7^2 - 5^2 = 49 - 25 = 24 = 8 \times 3$$
$$9^2 - 5^2 = 81 - 25 = 56 = 8 \times 7$$
$$11^2 - 3^2 = 121 - 9 = 112 = 8 \times 14$$

7. A number is exactly divisible by 11 when the difference between the sums of the digits in the odd and even places respectively is zero or a multiple of 11.
For example, Consider the number 1569942

Sum of the odd digits $= 1 + 6 + 9 + 2 = 18$
Sum of the even digits $= 5 + 9 + 4 = 18$

Difference between the sums of the odd and even digits

$$= 18 - 18 = 0$$

Hence, 1569942 is divisible by 11.

8. The product of two consecutive odd or even numbers increased by unity is a perfect square.

For example,

$$3 \times 5 + 1 = 16 = 4^2$$
$$4 \times 6 + 1 = 25 = 5^2$$
$$5 \times 7 + 1 = 36 = 6^2$$
$$6 \times 8 + 1 = 49 = 7^2$$

9. The sum of any two consecutive numbers is equal to the difference of their squares.

For example,

$$3 + 4 = 7 = 4^2 - 3^2 = 7$$
$$5 + 4 = 9 = 5^2 - 4^2 = 9$$
$$7 + 6 = 13 = 7^2 - 6^2 = 13$$

10. The sum of the cubes of any three consecutive numbers is divisible by the sum of the numbers themselves.

For example, $2^3 + 3^3 + 4^3 = 8 + 27 + 64 = 99 = (2 + 3 + 4)\ 11$

$$4^3 + 5^3 + 6^3 = 64 + 125 + 216 = 405$$
$$= (4 + 5 + 6)\ 27$$

EXERCISE

1. 2, 4, 6, 8, 10, ... are:
A. prime numbers
B. odd numbers
C. even numbers
D. natural numbers

2. 1, 2, 3, 4, ... are :
A. Natural numbers
B. Odd numbers
C. Prime numbers
D. Composite numbers

3. 1, 2, 3, 4, 5, 7, 11 and 13 are:
A. even numbers
B. odd numbers
C. prime numbers
D. natural numbers

4. The prime numbers between 1 to 100 are:
A. 20 B. 22
C. 25 D. 30

5. The only even prime number is:
A. 2 B. 67
C. 79 D. 98

6. Which of the following is not a prime number?
79, 83, 87, 97
A. 79 B. 83
C. 87 D. 97

7. Which of the following is a prime number?
117, 147, 149, 159

A. 117 B. 147
C. 149 D. 159

8. The next number in the sequence 1, 7, 3, 9, 5, 11, ... is :
A. 7 B. 13
C. 15 D. 17

9. In the sequence 4, 9, ...25, 36, the missing number is :
A. 14 B. 16
C. 20 D. 21

10. In the sequence 17, ..., 18, 15, 19, 14, 20, 13, the missing number is:
A. 5 B. 10
C. 12 D. 16

Directions. *For questions 11 to 14, let * means add the first number to twice the second number.*

11. The value of 5*4 is:
A. 20 B. 9
C. 11 D. 13

12. The value of 7*0 is:
A. 7 B. 9
C. 14 D. 0

13. The value of [1*2] * 3 is:
A. 5 B. 7
C. 9 D. 11

14. The value of 3* [0*6] is:
A. 18 B. 23
C. 27 D. 29

Directions. *For questions 15 to 17, let Δ means square the first number and add the second.*

15. The value of 2 Δ 10 is:
A. 12 B. 14
C. 27 D. 102

16. The value of 6 Δ 7 is:
A. 42 B. 43
C. 54 D. 59

17. The value of [3 × 2] Δ 9 is :
A. 42 B. 45
C. 87 D. 91

Directions. *For questions 18 to 20, let ** means increase the first number by 2 and then multiply by the second number.*

18. The value of 5** 3 is :
A. 15 B. 25
C. 21 D. 17

19. The value of [3**3]**4 is:
A. 68 B. 60
C. 54 D. 36

20. The value of [5**0]**3 is :
A. 0 B. 6
C. 15 D. 21

21. The smallest whole number which is divisible by 3 and also by the next two greater prime number is:
A. 15 B. 21
C. 60 D. 105

22. A number is called perfect, when it is equal to the sum of all its divisions excluding the number itself, e.g., 6 = 1 + 2 + 3. The other perfect number less than 32 is:
A. 8 B. 12
C. 16 D. 28

23. The smallest number of four digits is:
A. 1001 B. 0001
C. 0010 D. 1000

24. The largest number of four digits is:

A. 1000 B. 9000
C. 9009 D. 9999

25. If 'a' is an odd number, 'b' is an even number and 'c' is odd then, $a + b + c$ is:

A. odd number
B. even number
C. prime number
D. any number

26. The product of two prime numbers is a :

A. prime number
B. even number
C. odd number
D. composite number

27. Prime factors of a number are 2, 2, 3, 7. The number is :

A. 14 B. 41
C 48 D. 84

28. The largest number which is a factor of 56 as well as 84 is :

A. 2 B. 7
C. 14 D. 28

29. H.C.F. of 72, 108, 56 is :

A. 3 B. 4
C. 6 D. 8

30. L.C.M. of 6, 9, 12, 18 is :

A. 28 B. 36
C. 38 D. 42

31. If 'x' and 'y' are both odd numbers, which of the following numbers must be an even number?

A. $x + y$
B. $x \times y$
C. $xy + 2$
D. $2x + y$

32. 'a' is less than 'b', which of the following numbers is greater than 'a' and less than 'b' :

A. $\frac{a+b}{2}$ B. $\frac{ab}{2}$
C. $b^2 - a^7$ D. ab

33. $a + b + c + d$ is a positive number, a minimum of 'x' of the numbers a, b, c and d must be positive, where 'x' is equal to :

A. 1 B. 2
C. 3 D. 4

34. Which of the following is largest?
$[2 + 2 + 2]^2$, $[(2 + 2)^2]^2$, $[2 \times 2 \times 2]^2$, $[4]^2$

A. $[2 + 2 + 2]^2$
B. $[(2 + 2)^2]^2$
C. $[2 \times 2 \times 2]^2$
D. $[4]^2$

35. The sum of two numbers is 84. If one of them exceeds the other by 12, the numbers are :

A. 62, 22 B. 36, 24
C. 48, 36 D. 35, 47

36. Take a number. Double it and add 15 to it. If the result is 81, the number is :

A. 30 B. 32
C. 33 D. 66

37. Take a number, find its square root and add 20 to it. If the result is 30, the number is :

A. 5 B. 1
C. 20 D. 100

38. There are four numbrs A, B, C and D. Average of the first three, i.e., A, B and C is 15 and that of

B, *C* and *D* is 16. If the last number, i.e. *D* is 19, then the first number is:

A. 15 B. 16
C. 17 D. 18

39. Think of a number, divide it by 9 and add 9 to it, if the result is 27, the number is :

A. 18 B. 21
C. 100 D. 162

40. Of the three numbers, the first is twice the second and thrice the third. If the average of three is 22, the three numbers are:

A. 12, 18, 36 B. 18, 12, 36
C. 36, 12, 18 D. 36, 18, 12

41. The number which when added to itself 10 times gives 264. The number is:

A. 20 B. 22
C. 24 D. 26

42. If a person is standing on the sixth number in the queue from both the ends, the total persons in the queue are:

A. 9 B. 11
C. 12 D. 13

43. A number increased by itself and 5 gives 17. The number is :

A. 2 B. 3
C. 5 D. 6

44. Consider a number '*x*'. Divide it by 4 and add 9. If the result is 15, the value of '*x*' is :

A. 20 B. 24
C. 23 D. 28

45. A number '*x*' when multiplied by 5 and added to three times its own gives 64, the number is:

A. 8 B. 12
C. 14 D. 18

46. If the sum of two numbers '*x*' and '*y*' is equal to twice the first number, the second number '*y*' is:

A. $> x$
B. $< x$
C. $= x$
D. negative number

47. The excess of thrice a certain number over 11 is 19. The number is:

A. 8 B. 9
C. 10 D. 11

48. The difference between the squares of two consecutive numbers is 25. The numbers are:

A. 13, 12 B. 12, 13
C. 15, 14 D. 14, 13

49. The sum of two digits of a number is 15. If 9 is added to the number, the digits are reversed. The number is :

A. 78 B. 87
C. 69 D. 96

50. A number which when multiplied by 11 is as much above 180 as it was originally below it. The number is:

A. 25 B. 30
C. 40 D. 45

51. Divide ₹ 53 among *X*, *Y*, *Z* so that *X* may receive ₹ 7 more than *Y*, and *Y* may receive ₹ 8 more than *Z*.

A. 10, 15, 18 B. 18, 10, 25
C. 20, 12, 27 D. 25, 18, 10

EXPLANATORY ANSWERS

1. **C :** The numbers divisible by 2 are called even numbers since, 4, 6, 8, 10, are divisible by 2, hence these are even numbers.

2. **A :** The numbers written in natural sequence are natural numbers.

3. **C :** The numbers which are not divisible by 2, 3, 5, 7, 11 and 13 (*i.e.*, by any numbers except themselves and one) are called prime numbers.

4. **C :** To find out prime numbers between 1 and 100, write all numbers between 1 to 100.

*	(2)	(3)	4	(5)	6	(7)	8	9	10
(11)	12	(13)	14	15	16	(17)	18	(19)	20
21	22	(23)	24	25	26	27	28	(29)	30
(31)	32	33	34	35	36	(37)	38	39	40
(41)	42	(43)	44	45	46	(47)	48	49	50
51	52	(53)	54	55	56	57	58	(59)	60
(61)	62	63	64	65	66	(67)	68	69	70
(71)	72	(73)	74	75	76	77	78	(79)	80
81	82	(83)	84	85	86	87	88	(89)	90
91	92	93	94	95	96	(97)	98	99	100

(*i*) Cross out 1 which is not a prime number.

(ii) Cross out all numbers divisible by 2, except 2 which is a prime number.

(*iii*) Cross out all numbers divisible by 3, except 3 itself.

(*iv*) Cross out all numbers divisible by 5, except 5 itself.

(*v*) Cross out all numbers divisible by 7, except 7 itself.

The numbers remaining are the prime numbers between 1 and 100 which are circled and are 25 in all.

5. **A :** 2 is the only even prime number.

6. **C :** 87 is divisilble by 3, therefore it is not a prime number.

7. **C :** 149 is not divisible by any number, therefore it is a prime number.

8. **A :** In the sequence 1, 7, 3, 9, 5, 11..... the alternate numbers differ by 2, i.e., first and third number differ by 2, similarly the difference of second and fourth number is 2. Thus, next number in the series should be 5 + 2 = 7.

9. B : The sequence 4, 9, ..., 25, 36 contains the square of natural numbers, *i.e.*, 2^2, 3^2, 4^2, 5^2, 6^2. Thus the missing number is 4^2, *i.e.*, 16.

10. D : In the sequence 17, ..., 18, 15, 19, 14, 20, 13, the next alternate number is one more than the previous alternate number, i.e., 17 + 1 = 18, 18 + 1 = 19, 19 + 1 = 20. Also the second number and fourth number differ by 1, i.e., 13 + 1 = 14, 14 + 1 = 15, 15 + 1 = 16 is the required missing number).

[**means add the first number to the twice of the second number*].

11. D : 5 + [2 × 4] = 5 + 8 = 13

12. A : 7 + [2 × 0] = 7 + 0 = 7.

13. D : [1 * 2]* 3 = [1 + 2 × 2]* 3 = 5* 3 = 5 + 3 × 2 = 11.

14. C : 3 * [0 * 6] = 3 *[0 + 2 × 6] = 3* 12 = 3 + 2 × 12 = 27

[*Δ means square the first number and add the second number.*]

15. B : 2 Δ 10 = 2 × 2 + 10 = 14

16. B : 6 Δ 7 = 6 × 6 + 7 = 43

17. B : [3 × 2] Δ 9 = 6 Δ 9 = 6 × 6 + 9 = 45

[*** *means increase the first number by 2 and then multiply by the second number*].

18. C : 5**3 = [5 + 2] × 3 = 21

19. A : [3**3]**4 = [(3 + 2) × 3]**4 = 15**4 = [15 + 2] × 4 = 68

20. B : [5**0]**3 = [(5 + 2) × 0] = **3 = 0**3 = [0 + 2] × 3 = 6

21. D : The number should be divisible by 3, 5, and 7. Thus L.C.M. of 3, 5, 7 is equal to 105 which is the required number.

22. D : 28 is multiple of 1, 2, 4, 7, 14.
Also 1 + 2 + 4 + 7 + 14 = 28

23. D. 24. D.

25. A : Out of *a, b, c* ; a is odd and *c* is odd while b is even. The sum of two odd numbers is even, *i.e.*, *a* + *c* = even = *d*. Also the sum of two even numbers is even, i.e., d + b = even.
∴ $a + b + c$ = Even number.

26. D : Product of two prime numbers is not a prime number but it is always composite number.

27. D : The number is equal to the product or prime factors.
∴ 2 × 2 × 3 × 7 = 84 is the required number.

28. D : Find H.C.F. of 56, 84 which is equal to 28.

29. B.

30. B.

31. A : Since the sum of two odd numbers is always even number, therefore, $x + y$ is even number.

32. A : Average of two different numbers is always between the two numbers.

33. A : If all the numbers were not positive, then the sum could not be positive. If a, b, c were all –1 and d were 5, then $a + b + c + d$ would be positive, so B, C, D are incorrect.

34. B :

$$(2 + 2 + 2)^2 = 6^2 = 36$$
$$[(2 + 2)^2]^2 = [4^2]^2 = [4 \times 4]^2 = 16 \times 16 = 256$$
$$[2 \times 2 \times 2]^2 = (8)^2 = 64$$
$$(4)^2 = 4 \times 4 = 16.$$

35. C : Let the numbers be x and y

$$x + y = 84$$
$$x + (x + 12) = 84, \text{ or } 2x = 84 - 12 = 72,$$

or $$x = \frac{72}{2} = 36$$
$$y = x + 12 = 36 + 12 = 48.$$

36. C : Let the number be x

$\therefore$ $$2x + 15 = 81, \text{ or } 2x = 81 - 15 = 66$$

$\therefore$ $$x = \frac{66}{2} = 33.$$

37. D : Let the number be x

$\therefore$ $$\sqrt{x} + 20 = 30, \text{ or } \sqrt{x} = 30 - 20 = 10$$

$\therefore$ $$\left(\sqrt{x}\right)^2 = (10)^2, \text{ or } x = 100.$$

38. B :

$$\frac{A+B+C}{3} = 15, \text{ or, } A + B + C = 15 \times 3 = 45 \quad ...(i)$$

$$\frac{B+C+D}{3} = 16, \text{ or } B + C + D = 48 \quad ...(ii)$$

$$D = 19$$

$\therefore$ $B + C + 19 = 48$ or, $B + C = 48 - 19 = 29$

But, $A + B + C = 45$

Putting the value of $B + C = 29$ in the above equationi (i), we get

$$A + 29 = 45$$

$\therefore$ $$A = 45 - 29 = 16$$

39. D : Let the number be x.

$$\therefore \quad \frac{x}{9}+9 = 27 \text{ or, } \frac{x}{9} = 27 - 9 = 18$$

$$\therefore \quad x = 18 \times 9 = 162$$

40. D : Let the third number = x

$$\therefore \quad \text{First number} = 3x, \text{ Second number} = \frac{3x}{2}$$

$$\therefore \quad \frac{1}{3}\left[x+3x+\frac{3x}{2}\right] = 22 \text{ or, } \frac{11}{2}\ x = 66$$

$$\text{or,} \quad x = \frac{66\times 2}{11} = 12 = \text{Third number,}$$

$$12 \times 3 = 36 = \text{First number,}$$

$$\frac{12\times 3}{2} = 18 = \text{Second number.}$$

41. C : Let the number be x.

Then, $\quad x + 10x = 264$

$$\text{or,} \quad 11x = 264, \ \therefore \ x = \frac{264}{11} = 24$$

42. B : If the person is standing at sixth number in the queue from both sides, that means there are five persons ahead and five persons behind him. Hence, total number of person in the queue is 5 + 1 + 5 = 11.

43. D : Let the number is x.

$$\therefore \quad x + x + 5 = 17, \text{ or } 2x = 17 - 5 = 12$$

$$\therefore \quad x = \frac{12}{2} = 6$$

44. B :

$$\frac{x}{4}+9 = 15$$

$$\frac{x}{4} = 15 - 9 = 6$$

$$\therefore \quad x = 6 \times 4 = 24.$$

45. A : $5 \times x + 3x = 64$ or, $8x = 64$, $\quad \therefore x = \frac{64}{8} = 8$

46. C :

$$x + y = 2x$$

$$\therefore \quad y = 2x - x = x$$

47. C : Let the number be x.

$\therefore \quad 3x - 11 = 19, \quad$ or $3x = 19 + 11 = 30$

$\therefore \quad x = \dfrac{30}{3} = 10.$

48. A : Let the numbers are x and $(x + 1)$

$\therefore \quad (x + 1)^2 - x^2 = 25$

or, $\quad x^2 + 1 + 2x - x^2 = 25$

or, $\quad 2x + 1 = 25$

or, $\quad 2x = 25 - 1 = 24, \quad \therefore \ x = \dfrac{24}{2} = 12$

$\therefore \quad x + 1 = 12 + 1 = 13$

Hence, the numbers are 12, 13.

49. A : Let x be the digit in units place. Digit in ten's place is then $15 - x$.

$\therefore$ The number $= 10\,(15 - x) + x$

The new number with reserve digits $= 10 \times x + (15 - x)$

$\therefore \quad 10(15 - x) + x + 9 = 10x + 15 - x$

$150 - 10x + x + 9 = 9x + 15$

or, $\quad 18x = 144, \quad \therefore \ x = \dfrac{144}{18} = 8$

The digit of ten's place $= 15 - 8 = 7$

$\therefore$ The required number = 78

50. B : Let the number is x

$\therefore \quad 180 - x = 11x - 180$

or, $\quad 180 + 180 = 11x + x, \ 360 = 12x,$

or, $\quad x = \dfrac{360}{12} = 30$

51. D : Let Y receives ₹ a.

Then X receives ₹ $a + 7$ and Z receives ₹ $a - 8$.

But, $a + 7 + a + a - 8 =$ ₹ 53

or, $\quad 3a - 1 = 53, \ 3a = 53 + 1$

$\therefore \ 3a = 54, \ $ or, $\ a = \dfrac{54}{3}$

= ₹ 18. = Y's share

X's share= $a + 7 = 18 + 7 =$ ₹ 25,

Z's share= $a - 8 = 18 - 8 =$ ₹ 10.

2

FRACTIONS AND DECIMALS

A fraction is a number that represents a ratio or division of two whole numbers. A fraction is written in the form x/y, the number on the top, 'x' is called numerator; the number on the bottom, 'y' is called denominator. The denominator tells how many equal parts there are; and the numerator tells how many of these equal parts are taken.

> **Sets of equal fractions can be obtained by multiplying, or dividing, the numerator and denominator by the same number.**

For example,

$$\frac{3}{4}=\frac{3\times 2}{4\times 2}=\frac{3\times 2\times 2}{4\times 2\times 2}=\frac{3\times 3}{4\times 3}=\frac{3\times 4}{4\times 4}$$

Mixed Numbers: A mixed number consists of a whole number and a fraction. $3\frac{1}{4}$ is a mixed number, it means $3 + \frac{1}{4}$.

How to change mixed number into fraction?

(*i*) Multiply the whole number by the denominator of the fraction.

(*ii*) Add the numerator of the fraction to the result of step (*i*)

(*iii*) Use the result of step (*ii*) as the numerator and use the denominator of the fractional part of the mixed number as the denominator. This fraction is equal to the mixed number.

> **In calculations involving mixed numbers, always change the mixed numbers into fractions.**

Multiplication of Fractions: While multiplying, two fractions multiply their numerators and divide this by the product of their denominators.

Note: *In word problems,* **of** *always indicates multiplication.*

Division of Fractions: This can be done either by multiplying by the L.C.M. of the denominators of the fractions, or by multiplying by such a number which can make the denominator 1.

It may be noted that one fraction is a reciprocal of another if their product is 1. So $\frac{1}{3}$ and 3 are reciprocals. To find the reciprocal of a fraction, simply interchange the numerator and deno-minator. This is known as inverting fractions. To divide one fraction by another fraction, invert the divisor and multiply. *For example :*

$$\frac{3}{8} \div \frac{1}{2} = \frac{3}{8} \times 2 = \frac{6}{8} = \frac{3}{4}$$

Addition of Fractions: If the fractions have same denominator, then the denominator is called a common denominator. In such cases, add the numerators and use this sum as the new numerator with the common denominator as the denominator of the sum. *For example,*

$$\frac{3}{15} + \frac{7}{15} = \frac{3+7}{15} = \frac{10}{15} = \frac{2}{3}$$

If the fractions have different denominators, then L.C.M. is called the least common denominator and as has been said for the case when the fractions had the same denominator, *For example,*

$$\frac{1}{3} + \frac{9}{4} + \frac{3}{5} = ?$$

In this case, common denominator is L.C.M. of 3, 4, 5, which is equal to 60,

$$\frac{1}{3} = \frac{20}{60}, \frac{9}{4} = \frac{135}{60}, \frac{3}{5} = \frac{36}{60}$$

$$= \frac{20}{60} + \frac{135}{60} + \frac{36}{60} = \frac{191}{60}$$

Subtracting Fractions: When the fractions have the same denominator, subtract the numerators and place the result over the denominator.
For example,

$$\frac{5}{8} - \frac{3}{8} = \frac{5-3}{8} = \frac{2}{8}$$

When the fractions have different denominators,

(*i*) First of all, find the common denominator:

(*ii*) Express the fractions as equivalent fractions with the same denominator.

(*iii*) Subtract as has been said above, *for example,*

$$\frac{5}{8} - \frac{1}{5} = ?$$

Common denominator in this case is 40,

$$\frac{5}{8} = \frac{25}{40}, \frac{1}{5} = \frac{8}{40}$$

$$\frac{25}{40} - \frac{8}{40} = \frac{25-8}{40} = \frac{17}{40}$$

Equivalent Fractions: Two fractions may be equivalent or equal if they represent the same ratio of number. *For example,*

$$\frac{2}{5}=\frac{4}{10}=\frac{6}{15}=\frac{20}{50}$$

Combined Operations: Sometimes in simplifying fractions, we may come across the following signs :

(i) Brackets – ( ), { }, [ ]

(ii) Of – means multiplication

while dealing with such problems,

(i) first of all brackets should be removed,

(ii) then *of* followed by,

(iii) division and multiplicaiton, then

(iv) addition and subtraction.

Note: *Terms enclosed within brackets are to be treated as one quantity.*

When an expression within a bracket is preceded by the sign (+), the bracket may be removed without making any change in the sign of the quantities or terms within the bracket.

When an expression within a bracket is preceded by the sign (–), the bracket may be removed only after changing the sign of every term within it.

Complex Fractions: A fraction whose numerator and denominator are themselves fractions is called a complex fraction.

For example, $\frac{3/8}{4/5}$

It can be simplified by dividing the fractions. Thus,

$$\frac{3/8}{4/5}=\frac{3}{8}\div\frac{4}{5}=\frac{3}{8}\times\frac{5}{4}=\frac{15}{32}$$

DECIMALS

A collection of digits after a period (decimal point) is called decimal fraction. *For example,* .513, .317, .219, .6, etc. Every decimal represents a fraction.

How to find a fraction represented by decimal?

(i) Take a fraction whose denominator is 10, and whose numerator is the first digit to the right of decimal point.

(ii) Take the fraction whose denominator is 100, and whose numerator is the second digit to the right of decimal point.

(iii) Continue the procedure untill all the digits to the right of the decimal point have been used up. The denominator in each case is 10 times the denominator in the previous step.

(*iv*) The sum of the fractions obtained in (i), (ii) and (iii) is the fraction represented by the decimal point. For example, the fraction represened by 0.317 may be found out as follows:

$$\frac{3}{10}+\frac{1}{100}+\frac{7}{1000}=\frac{300}{1000}+\frac{10}{1000}+\frac{7}{1000}=\frac{317}{1000}$$

Any number of zeros may be added to the right of a decimal fraction without changing its value.

Addition and Subtraction of Decimals: While adding decimals we put decimal under decimal, units under units, tens under tens and hundreds under hundreds.

For example, 23.4621 + 102.019 + 0.961 =?

$$\begin{array}{r} 23.4621 \\ 102.0190 \\ 0.9610 \\ \hline 126.4421 \\ \hline \end{array}$$

Multiplicaiton of Decimals: When we multiply the decimal fractions by 10, the hundredths become tenths (10 × 1/100 = 1/10), the tenths become units (10 × 1/10 = 1) and the units become tens (1 × 10 = 10) and so on.

For example, 2.45 × 10 = 24.5.

Decimals are multiplied like whole numbers. The decimal point of the product is placed in such a way that the number of decimal places in the product is equal to the total of the number of decimal places in all the numbers multiplied.

Division of Decimals: While dividing one decimal by another decimal :

(i) Move the decimal point in the divisor to the right until there is no decimal fraction in the divisor.

(ii) Move the decimal point in the dividend the same number of places to the right as you moved the decimal point in step *(i)*.

(iii) Divide the result of *(ii)* by the result of *(i)*.

(iv) The number of decimal places in the result should be equal to the number of decimal places in the result of step *(ii)*.

For example, 66.957 ÷ 0.11

$$=\frac{66.957}{0.11}=\frac{66.957\times 100}{0.11\times 100}=\frac{6695.7}{11}=608.7$$

Relation between Decimal Fraction and Normal Fraction: A fraction can be converted into a decimal fraction by dividing the numerator by denominator.

For example, 1/2 = 1.0/2 = 0.5.

$$\frac{1}{5}=\frac{1.0}{5}=0.2, \qquad \frac{1}{10}=\frac{1\cdot 0}{10}=0\cdot 1$$

$\frac{1}{4} = \frac{1 \cdot 00}{4} = 0 \cdot 25,$

$\frac{3}{4} = \frac{3 \cdot 00}{4} = 0 \cdot 75,$

$\frac{1}{20} = \frac{1 \cdot 00}{20} = 0.05,$

$\frac{1}{16} = \frac{1 \cdot 0000}{16} = 0 \cdot 0625,$

$\frac{1}{100} = \frac{1 \cdot 00}{100} = 0 \cdot 01$

$\frac{1}{1000} = \frac{1 \cdot 000}{1000} = 0.001$

$\frac{3}{8} = \frac{3.000}{8} = 0 \cdot 375$

$\frac{7}{8} = \frac{7 \cdot 000}{8} = 0 \cdot 875$

EXERCISE

1. Which of the following is equivalent to $\frac{15}{25}$?

A. $\frac{150}{25}$ B. $\frac{15}{250}$

C. $\frac{3}{5}$ D. $\frac{60}{75}$

2. Which of the following is not equivalent to $\frac{13}{20}$?

A. $\frac{26}{40}$ B. $\frac{130}{200}$

C. $\frac{39}{60}$ D. $\frac{52}{60}$

3. If $\frac{9*3}{3*7}$ is equivalent to $\frac{9}{7}$, the sign * is replaced by :

A. ÷ B. ×

C. + D. –

4. $\frac{5}{6}$ of an hour is equal to :

A. half an hour B. 40 minutes

C. 50 minutes D. 55 minutes

5. An aircraft uses 2/5 of its fuel in flying 1,250 kilometres. The distance travelled on remaining fuel is :

A. 1875 km B. 2125 km

C. 250 km D. 475 km

6. If $\frac{4}{3} * \frac{3}{4} = \frac{16}{9}$, then * means :

A. + B. –

C. × D. ÷

7. If $\frac{3}{15} * \frac{17}{5} = \frac{51}{75}$, then * means :

A. + B. –

C. × D. ÷

8. If $5x = 1$, then x is equal to :

A. .20 B. .02

C. $\frac{1}{2}$ D. 5

9. Which of the following is the largest fraction?

A. $\frac{3}{15}$ B. $\frac{5}{20}$

C. $\frac{8}{64}$ D. $\frac{25}{1000}$

10. Which of the following is the smallest fraction?

A. $\frac{1}{10}$ B. $\frac{1}{100}$

C. $\frac{9}{1000}$ D. $\frac{500}{10000}$

11. Six times x increased by 12 is equal to :

A. $\frac{x}{2}$ B. $2x$

C. $6x + 12$ D. $12x + 6$

12. Five times y diminished by 20 is equal to :

A. $5y - 20$ B. $5y + 20$

C. $y/4$ D. $4y$

13. The number less than 15 by 7 is:

A. $15x - 7$ B. 15/7

C. 15 D. 8

14. The excess of thrice a certain number over 16 is 32. The number is :

A. 17 B. 16

C. 12 D. 10

15. If 21 is added to four times a number, the result is 57. The number is :

A. 7 B. 8

C. 9 D. 10

16. A number, the sum of whose fourth and fifth parts exceeds their third part by 28, is :

A. 120 B. 240

C. 220 D. 160

17. Which fraction should be added to the sum of $5\frac{3}{4}$, $4\frac{4}{5}$ and $7\frac{3}{8}$ to make the result a whole number?

A. $\frac{1}{40}$ B. $\frac{2}{40}$

C. $\frac{3}{40}$ D. $\frac{4}{40}$

18. $\frac{1}{15}+\frac{3}{15}+\frac{5}{15}+\frac{6}{15}=?$

A. $\frac{10}{15}$ B. $\frac{3}{5}$

C. $\frac{4}{5}$ D. 1

19. A number one-sixth of which exceeds its one-ninth by 100 is :

A. 600 B. 900

C. 1500 D. 1800

20. The sum of $\frac{1}{2}, \frac{1}{4}$ and $\frac{1}{8}$ of a number is 28. The number is :

A. 28 B. 32

C. 36 D. 42

21. The sum of $\frac{1}{9}, \frac{1}{3}, \frac{1}{6}$ and $\frac{7}{18}$ of a number is 150. The number is :

A. 120 B. 130

C. 140 D. 150

22. Which is the greatest? .999, .1011, .1995, .9985

A. .999 B. .1011

C. .1995 D. .9985

23. In decimal system, $9\frac{1}{8}$ may be represented as:

A. 9.18 B. 9.125

C. 9.025 D. 9.225

24. $2.205 \div 0.15 = ?$

A. 1.47 B. 14.7

C. 147 D. 0.147

25. G.C.M. of .24, 3.2 and 16.0 is :
A. 80 B. 8
C. .8 D. .08

26. L.C.M. of .24, 3.2 and 16.0 is :
A. .48 B. 4.8
C. 48 D. 480

27. A pole has 0.5 of its length in mud, 0.25 of its length in water and 2 metres above water. The total length of the pole is :
A. 8 metres B. 5 metres
C. 4 metres D. 2 metres

28. $\sqrt{1/3}$ is equal to :
A. 0.57 B. 0.35
C. 0.30 D. 3.00

29. How many times does 2/3 of 1/2 go into half of one third?
A. 2 B. 1/2
C. 1/3 D. 2/3

30. The eleventh part of $990\frac{990}{990}$ is:
A. 99.0 B. 99.99
C. 90 D. 90.9

31. A train started from Delhi at 6.00 A.M. On the next (second) station 1/3 passengers got down and 96 got in. On the next (third) station, 1/2 of the total passengers present in the train got down and 12 came in. Now there were 248 passengers in the train. When the tain started from Delhi, total number of passengers were :
A. 435 B. 564
C. 654 D. 736

32. 1 ÷ [1 + 1 ÷ {1 + 1 ÷ 1(1 + 1 ÷ 2)}] is equal to:
A. 1 B. 2
C. $\frac{5}{8}$ D. zero

33. L.C.M. of 6, 7, 8 and 10 is equal to :
A. 840 B. 830
C. 820 D. 800

34. By how much does $\frac{6}{7/8}$ exceed $\frac{6/7}{8}$:
A. $6\frac{2}{3}$ B. $6\frac{3}{4}$
C. $7\frac{1}{2}$ D. $8\frac{3}{4}$

35. $\frac{.03}{1000}$ is equal to :
A. 3×10^5 B. 3×10^{-3}
C. 3×10^{-6} D. 3×10^{-5}

36. $10\frac{1}{25}$ is equal to :
A. 10.25 B. 10.125
C. 10.04 D. 10.025

37. 1.25 × 1.25 + 2.75 × 2.75 + 2 × 1.25 × 2.75 is equal to :
A. 4.000 B. 16.000
C. 26.1250 D. 28.3250

38. What fraction of an hour is a second ?
A. $\frac{1}{24}$ B. $\frac{1}{60}$
C. $\frac{1}{120}$ D. $\frac{1}{3600}$

39. G.C.M. of 1.6 and 0.72 is equal to :
A. 8 B. .8
C. .08 D. .008

40. $\frac{4}{5}$ of 0.025 is equal to :
A. 0.0002 B. 0.002
C. 0.02 D. 0.2

EXPLANATORY ANSWERS

1. C : $\frac{15}{25}=\frac{3\times5}{5\times5}=\frac{3}{5}$.

2. D : $\frac{26}{40} = \frac{2\times13}{2\times20} = \frac{13}{20}, \frac{39}{60} = \frac{13\times3}{20\times3} = \frac{13}{20}$

$\frac{130}{200} = \frac{13\times10}{20\times10} = \frac{13}{20}, \frac{52}{60} = \frac{13\times4}{20\times3} = \frac{13}{20}\times\frac{4}{3}$

Hence, $\frac{52}{60}$ is not equal to $\frac{13}{20}$.

3. B : $\frac{9*3}{3*7}=\frac{9}{7}$, or, $\frac{9\times3}{7\times3}=\frac{9}{7}$, $\therefore$ The sign * is $\times$.

4. C : $\frac{5}{6}$ of 1 hr = $\frac{5}{6}\times$ 60 minutes = 50 minutes.

5. A : Remaining fuel = $1-\frac{2}{5}=\frac{5-2}{5}=\frac{3}{5}$

Distance flown by $\frac{2}{5}$ of fuel = 1250 km.

Distance flown by full fuel = $\frac{1250}{2/5} = \frac{1250\times5}{2}$ km.

Distance flown by $\frac{3}{5}$ of fuel = $\frac{1250\times5\times3}{2\times5}=1875$ km.

6. D. **7. C.**

8. A : $5x = 1$, $\therefore x = \frac{1}{5} = .20$.

9. B : $\frac{3}{15}=\frac{1}{5}, \frac{8}{64}=\frac{1}{8}, \frac{5}{20}=\frac{1}{4}, \frac{25}{1000}=\frac{1}{40}$,

$\frac{1}{5},\frac{1}{4},\frac{1}{8},\frac{1}{40}$, $\frac{16,\ 20,\ 10,\ 2}{80}$

$\therefore$ The largest fractin is $\frac{1}{4}=\frac{5}{20}$.

10. C : $\frac{1}{10} = .1, \; \frac{9}{1000} = .009$

$\frac{1}{100} = .01. \; \frac{500}{10000} = \frac{5}{100} = .05$

The smallest of these quantities is $.009 = \frac{9}{1000}$.

11. C : $x \times 6 + 12 = 6x + 12$.

12. A : $5 \times y - 20 = 5y - 20$.

13. D : $15 - 7 = 8$.

14. B : Let the number be x

$$3x - 16 = 32$$

$\therefore \quad 3x = 32 + 16 = 48$, or $x = \frac{48}{3} = 16$.

15. C : Let the number is x

$\therefore 4x + 21 = 57$ or, $4x = 57 - 21 = 36$, or, $x = \frac{36}{4} = 9$.

16. B : Let the number is x.

$\therefore \frac{x}{4} + \frac{x}{5} = \frac{x}{3} + 28, \; \frac{9x}{20} = \frac{x}{3} + 28$, or, $\frac{9x}{20} - \frac{x}{3} = 28$

or, $\frac{27x - 20x}{60} = 28$ or, $7x = 28 \times 60 \; \therefore \; x = \frac{28 \times 60}{7} = 240$.

17. C : $5\frac{3}{4} + 4\frac{4}{5} + 7\frac{3}{8} = \frac{23}{4} + \frac{24}{5} + \frac{59}{8} = \frac{717}{40}$

717/40 becomes whole number when 3/40 is added to it, i.e.,

$\frac{717}{40} + \frac{3}{40} = \frac{720}{40} = 18$ which is a whole number.

18. D : $\frac{1}{15} + \frac{3}{15} + \frac{5}{15} + \frac{6}{15} = \frac{1+3+5+6}{15} = \frac{15}{15} = 1$.

19. D : Let the number is x.

$\frac{x}{6} = \frac{x}{9} + 100$ or, $\frac{x}{6} - \frac{x}{9} = 100$, or, $\frac{x}{18} = 100$

or, $x = 100 \times 18 = 1800$.

20. B : Let the number is x.

$\therefore \frac{x}{2}+\frac{x}{4}+\frac{x}{8}=28$, or, $\frac{7x}{8}=28$ $\therefore$ $7x = 28 \times 8$ or, $x=\frac{28\times 8}{7}=32$.

21. D : Let the number is x.

$\therefore \frac{x}{9}+\frac{x}{3}+\frac{x}{6}+\frac{7x}{18}=150$ or, $\frac{2x+6x+3x+7x}{18}=150 \Rightarrow \frac{18x}{18}=150$

or, $x=\frac{150\times 18}{18}=150$.

22. A : .999 is the greatest.

23. B : $9\frac{1}{8}=9+\frac{1}{8}=9+.125=9.125$.

24. B : $2.205 \div 0.15 = \frac{2.205}{0.15}=\frac{2205}{1000}\times\frac{100}{15}=\frac{2205}{150}=14.7$.

25. D : G.C.M. of .24, 3.2 and 16.0

$=$ G.C.M. of $\frac{24,\ 320 \text{ and } 1600}{100}=\frac{8}{100}=0.08$.

26. C : L.C.M. of .24, 3.2 and 16.0 = L.C.M. of

$\frac{24,\ 320 \text{ and } 1600}{100}=\frac{4800}{100}=48$.

27. A : Let total length of the pole $= x$
Pole above water $= x - [0.5x + 0.25x] = 0.25x$;
$0.25x = 2$ metres

$\therefore x=\frac{2\times 100}{25}=8$ metres.

28. A : $\sqrt{\frac{1}{3}}=\frac{\sqrt{1}}{\sqrt{3}}=\frac{1}{\sqrt{3}}=\frac{1}{1.732}=\frac{1000}{1732}=0.57$.

29. B : $\frac{2}{3}$ of $\frac{1}{2}=\frac{2}{3}\times\frac{1}{2}=\frac{1}{3}$, $\frac{1}{2}$ of $\frac{1}{3}=\frac{1}{6}$ $\therefore$ $\frac{1}{6}\div\frac{1}{3}=\frac{1}{6}\times\frac{3}{1}=\frac{1}{2}$.

30. C : Eleventh part of $990\frac{990}{990}=990\frac{990}{990}\div 11=\frac{991}{11}=90.09$.

31. B : When train started from Delhi let number of passengers was x. On next station, 1/3 got down and 96 got in.

Now passengers in train $= x - \frac{x}{3} + 96 = \frac{2x}{3} + 96$

On next station 1/2 of it got down and 12 got in, i.e.,

$\frac{1}{2}\left[\frac{2x}{3} + 96\right]$ got down and 12 got in

Now passengers in train $= \frac{2x}{3} + 96 - \left[\frac{x}{3} + 48\right] + 12$

$= \frac{2x}{3} - \frac{x}{3} + 96 - 48 + 12 = 248 \quad \therefore x = [248 - 60] \times 3 = 188 \times 3 = 564.$

32. C.

33. A : The L.C.M. of 6, 7, 8 and 10 is calculated as follows :

2	6, 7, 8, 10
3	3, 7, 4, 5
4	1, 7, 4, 5
5	1, 7 1, 5
7	1, 7, 1, 1
	1, 1, 1, 1

L.C.M. = 2 × 3 × 4 × 5 × 7 = 840.

34. B : $6 \div \frac{7}{8} = \frac{6}{1} \times \frac{8}{7} = \frac{48}{7}$ or $\frac{6}{7} \div 8 = \frac{6}{7} \times \frac{1}{8} = \frac{3}{28}$

$\frac{48}{7} - \frac{3}{28} = \frac{192 - 3}{28} = \frac{189}{28} = 6\frac{21}{28} = 6\frac{3}{4}.$

35. D. **36. C.**

37. B : Put 1.25 = a and 2.75 = b, then,
1.25 × 1.25 + 2.75 × 2.75 + 2 × 1.25 × 2.75
$= a^2 + b^2 + 2ab = (a + b)^2 = (1.25 + 2.75)^2 = (4)^2 = 16.000.$

38. D. **39. C.**

40. C : $\frac{4}{5} \times 0.025 = \frac{4}{5} \times \frac{25}{1000} = \frac{1}{50} = 0.02.$

3

POWERS, EXPONENTS AND ROOTS

If 'x' is any number and 'n' is a whole numbr greater than 0, x^n means that the product of n factors each of which is equal to x. Thus,

$$x^n = x \,.\, x \,.\, x \,.\, x \text{ ....} x \; n \text{ times}$$

$$2^4 = 2 \times 2 \times 2 \times 2 = 16$$

$$3^5 = 3 \times 3 \times 3 \times 3 \times 3 = 243$$

$$\left(\frac{x}{y}\right)^n = \frac{x^n}{x^n}$$

$$\left(\frac{3}{7}\right)^2 = \frac{3\times3}{7\times7} = \frac{9}{49}.$$

In the expression x^n, x is called the base and n is called the exponent. The laws of exponents are :

$$x^n \times x^m = x^{n+m}$$

$$\frac{x^n}{x^m} = x^{n-m}$$

$$(x^m)^n = x^{mn}$$

$$(xy)^m = x^m y^m$$

Negative Exponents: $x^0 = 1$, for any non-zero number x. By one of the law of exponents,

$$x^n \times x^0 = x^{n+0} = x^n$$

i.e., $x^0 = 1$

Also, $x^{-n} = \dfrac{1}{x^n}$

Roots : If a number 'x' is raised to nth power and the result is 'a', then 'x' is called the *nth* root of 'a', which is usually written as $\sqrt[n]{a} = x$, *For example,*

$$2^4 = 16, \text{ or } \sqrt[4]{16} = 2$$

The second root is called the square root, the third root is called the cube root.

$$x^{1/n} \times y^{1/n} = (x.y)^{1/n}$$

or,

$$\sqrt[n]{x \times y} = \sqrt[n]{x} \times \sqrt[n]{y}$$

A number which is a prfect square must end in one or another of the digits 0, 1, 4, 5, 6, 9.

It may be noted that the square of,

1 & 9 both end in 1.
2 & 8 both end in 4.
3 & 7 both end in 9.
4 & 6 both end in 6.
5 end in 5.

(1, 9); (2, 8); (3, 7); (4, 6); (5, 5) are pairs of complementary digits, i.e., the sum of the digits in each pair is 10.

If two numbers end in complementary digits, their squares will have the same final digit.

If a number end in zero, its square should contain 2 zero and if a number ends in 2 zeros, its square should end in 4 zeros, and so on.

A number ending in an odd number of zeros cannot be a perfect square.

EXERCISE

1. $\sqrt{\frac{1}{3}} = ?$

A. 0.30
B. 0.57
C 0.89
D. 3.00

2. $\frac{6^4}{3^3} = ?$

A. 24
B. 42
C 48
D. 2

3. $\left(\frac{1}{2}\right)^{-1} = ?$

A. $-\frac{1}{2}$
B. $+\frac{1}{2}$
C. –2
D. + 2

4. 125° = ?

A. 125
B. 1
C. 1250
D. 12.5

5. $8^{1/3} = ?$

A. $\frac{8}{3}$ B. $\frac{3}{8}$

C. 4 D. 2

6. $4^4 \times 4^{17} = ?$

A. 8^{17} B. 4^{21}

C. 8^{21} D. 4^{13}

7. $\frac{10x^8}{5x^4} = ?$

A. $2x^4$ B. $2x^2$

C. $2x^8$ D. $2x^{12}$

8. $2^{3^2} = ?$

A. 2^6 B. 2^9

C. 2^5 D. 8^4

9. $(2^3)^2 = ?$

A. 8 B. 64

C. 312 D. 512

10. $(36)^{1/2} = ?$

A. 18 B. 9

C. 6 D. 3

11. $x^{3/4} . x^{3/4} = ?$

A. $2x^{3/1}$ B. $x^{9/16}$

C. $x^{6/8}$ D. $x^{3/2}$

12. $(x^{3/4})^{1/2} = ?$

A. $x^{3/8}$ B. $x^{4/6}$

C. $x^{2/5}$ D. $x^{3/2}$

13. $\sqrt{32} = ?$

A. 4 B. $2\sqrt{4}$

C. $4\sqrt{2}$ D. $2^3\sqrt{2}$

14. $5\sqrt{3} = ?$

A. $\sqrt{75}$ B. $\sqrt{50}$

C. $\sqrt{25}$ D. $\sqrt[3]{5}$

15. $x^{b-c} \times X^{c-a} \times X^{a-b} = ?$

A. x^{a+b+c} B. x^{a-b-c}

C. $x^{2a-2b-2c}$ D. 1

16. When 16000 is expressed as a product of powers of 4 and 10, then it equals :

A. $4^2 \times 10^2$ B. $4^2 \times 10^3$

C. $4^3 \times 10^3$ D. $4^2 \times 10^4$

17. When 1800 is expressed as a product of powers of prime numbers, then it equals :

A. $2 \times 9 \times 10^2$ B. $2 \times 3^2 \times 10^2$

C. $2 \times 3^2 \times 5^2$ D. $2^3 \times 3^2 \times 5^2$

18. 27×243 is equal to :

A. 3^8 B. 3^9

C. 3^{10} D. 3^{11}

19. The sum of the squares of two numbers is 26 and difference is 8. The numbers are :

A. 9, 17 B. 3, 17

C. $9, \sqrt{17}$ D. $3, \sqrt{17}$

20. $\left[\left(\frac{x}{y}\right)^3\right]^{-2} = ?$

A. $\left(\frac{x}{y}\right)^{-6}$ B. $\left(\frac{x}{y}\right)^{1}$

C. $\left(\frac{x}{y}\right)^{6}$ D. $\left(\frac{x}{y}\right)^{5}$

21. $(x^4)^3$ is equal to :

A. x^{6+2} B. x^{12}

C. $x^{4/13}$ D. x^{4-3}

22. $(27)^{-4/3}$ is equal to :

A. 81 B. 54

C. $\frac{1}{21}$ D. $\frac{1}{81}$

23. $x^{1/8} \div x^{3/4}$ is equal to :

A. $x^{5/8}$ B. $x^{2/4}$

C. $x^{2/3}$ D. $\frac{1}{x^{5/8}}$

24. $\left[27^{-2/3}\right]^{1/2}$ is equal to :

A. $\frac{27}{54}$ B. $\frac{2}{3}$

C. $\frac{1}{3}$ D. $\frac{1}{9}$

25. $\sqrt{72}$ is equal to :

A. $6\sqrt{2}$

B. $4\sqrt{6}$

C. $9\sqrt{6}$

D. $2\sqrt{6}$

EXPLANATORY ANSWERS

1. B : $\sqrt{\frac{1}{3}} = \sqrt{0.3333} = 0.57$.

2. C : $\frac{6^4}{3^3} = \frac{6\times6\times6\times6}{3\times3\times5} = 2\times2\times2\times6 = 48$.

3. D : $\left(\frac{1}{2}\right)^{-1} = (2)^{+1} = 2$.

4. B : Any number raise to power zero = 1.

5. D : (8)1/3 = $(\sqrt[3]{8})^1 = \sqrt[3]{8} = 2$.

6. B : Since, $a^x \times a^x = a^{x+y}$

$\therefore$ $4^4 \times 4^{17} = 4^{4+17} = 4^{21}$.

7. A : $\frac{10x^8}{5x^4} = \frac{2x^8}{x^4} = 2x^8 \times x^{-4} = 2x^{8-4} = 2x^4$.

8. B : $2^{3^2} = 2^{3\times3} = 2^9$.

9. B : $(2^3)^2 = (2\times2\times2)^2 = 2\times2\times2\times2\times2\times2 = 64$.

10. C : $(36)^{1/2} = \sqrt{36} = 6$.

11. D : $x^{3/4}.x^{3/4} = x^{3/4+3/4} = x^{6/4} = x^{3/2}$.

12. A : $(x^{3/4})^{1/2} = x^{3/4.1/2} = x^{3/8}$.

13. C : $\sqrt{32} = \sqrt{4\times4\times2} = \sqrt{(4)^2.2} = 4\sqrt{2}$.

14. A : $5\sqrt{3} = \left(\sqrt{5}\right)^2.\sqrt{3} = \sqrt{5}.\sqrt{5}.\sqrt{3} = \sqrt{5.5.3} = \sqrt{75}$.

15. D : $x^{b-c} \cdot x^{c-a} \cdot x^{a-b} = x[b - c + c - a + a - b] = x^0 = 1$.

16. B : $16000 = 16 \times 1000 = (4)^2 \times (10)^3 = 4^2 \times 10^3$.

17. D : The prime factors of 1800 are, $2 \times 2 \times 2 \times 3 \times 3 \times 5 \times 5$
$= 2^3 \times 3^2 \times 5^2$.

18. A : $27 \times 243 = [3 \times 3 \times 3] \times [3 \times 3 \times 3 \times 3 \times 3] = 3^3 \cdot 3^5 = 3^8$.

19. D : Let the numbers are x and y

$\therefore \qquad x^2 + y^2 = 26 \qquad ...(i)$

$x^2 - y^2 = 8 \qquad ...(ii)$

Adding (*i*) and (*ii*), we get

$$2x^2 + y^2 - y^2 = 26 + 8 = 34$$

or, $\quad 2x^2 = 34, \quad$ or $\quad x^2 = \frac{34}{2} = 17$

$\therefore \quad x = \sqrt{17}$

Since, $\quad x^2 + y^2 = 26$

or, $\quad 17 + y^2 = 26$

$\therefore \quad y^2 = 26 - 17 = 9$

$\therefore \quad y = \sqrt{9} = 3$

Hence, the numbers are 3 and $\sqrt{17}$.

20. A : $\left[\left(\frac{x}{y}\right)^3\right]^{-2} = \left(\frac{x}{y}\right)^{3\times-2} = \left(\frac{x}{y}\right)^{-6}$

21. B : $(x^4)^3 = x^4 \cdot x^4 \cdot x^4 = x^{4+4+4} = x^{12}$.

22. D : $(27)–4/3 = \frac{1}{(27)^{4/3}} = \frac{1}{\sqrt[3]{(27)^4}} = \frac{1}{3^4} = \frac{1}{3\times3\times3\times3} = \frac{1}{81}$.

23. D : $\quad x^{1/8} \div x^{3/4}$

or $\quad x^{1/8\,-\,3/4}$

or $\quad x^{-5/8} = \frac{1}{x^{5/8}}$.

24. C : $[27^{-2/3}]^{1/2} = 27^{-2/3\times1/2} = 27^{-1/3} = \frac{1}{27^{1/3}} = \frac{1}{3}$.

25. A : $\sqrt{72} = \sqrt{36\times2} = \sqrt{6\times6\times2} = 6\sqrt{2}$.

4

PERCENTAGE

Percent, or per centum means 'for every hundred'. A percentage is a fraction expressed with 100 as its denominator and the rate per cent as its numerator. Thus, 5 per cent means 5 out of 100, or it can be expressed as 5/100 = 1/20. The symbol % is used to denote the term 'per cent'.

A decimal is converted to percentage by multiplying the decimal by 100, or by moving the decimal point two places to the right.

A percentage can be converted into decimal by dividing it by 100, or by moving the decimal point two places to the left.

For example, 12.5% = 0.125

and, 25% = .25

A fraction can be converted into a percentage by changing the fraction to a decimal and then changing the decimal to a percentage. A percentage can be changed into a fraction by first converting the percentage into a decimal and then changing the decimal to a fraction. *For example,*

1% = .01 = 1/100, 100% = 1.0 = 1

2% = .02 = 2/100, 120% = 1.2 = 12/10

5% = .05 = 1/20, 12.5% = 0.125 = 1/8

Remember :

1. To change a fraction or mixed number to a per cent; multiply the fraction or mixed number by 100. Reduce, if possible and add % sign.
2. To remove a % sign attached to a decimal and to keep it as decimal, divide the decimal by 100.
3. To remove a % sign attached to a decimal and to change the number to a fraction; divide the decimal by 100, change the result to a fraction, and reduce if necessary.
4. To remove a % sign attached to a fraction or mixed number and to keep it as fraction, divide the fraction or mixed number by 100.
5. To remove a % sign attached to a fraction or mixed number and to change the number to a decimal; divide the fraction by 100 and change the result to decimal.
6. In percentage problems, the whole is 100%. *For example,* if a problem involves 20% of a quantity, the rest of the quantity is 100 – 20 = 80%.

EXERCISE

1. 20% is equal to :

A. $\frac{1}{3}$ B. $\frac{1}{4}$

C. $\frac{1}{5}$ D. $\frac{2}{5}$

2. 5/8 may be expressed as:

A. 50/80%

B. 62.5%

C. 55.5%

D. 70.5%

3. 15% of ₹ 50 is equal to:

A. ₹ 25 B. 12.50

C. ₹ 9.50 D. 7.50

4. What rate per cent is one minute 12 seconds to an hour?

A. 2% B. 3%

C. 4% D. 5%

5. A student has to secure 40 per cent marks to pass. If he gets 20 marks and fails by 20 marks, the maximum marks are:

A. 20 B. 40

C. 80 D. 100

6. A person spends 75% of his salary and saves ₹ 150 per month. His monthly salary is:

A. ₹ 750 B. ₹ 600

C. ₹ 400 D. ₹ 300

7. Standard gold contains 22 parts of pure gold to 2 parts of alloy. The percentage of alloy in a sovereign which is made of standard gold is:

A. 11% B. 12%

C. $8\frac{1}{3}\%$ D. $11\frac{1}{3}\%$

8. The catalogue price of an article is ₹ 250. A reduction of 12% is made for cash purchase. The case price is:

A. ₹ 250

B. ₹ 220

C. ₹ 200

D. ₹ 180

9. 20% of ₹ 5 is :

A. Re. 1 B. ₹ 2

C. ₹ 3 D. ₹ 4

10. 15% of 3 metres is :

A. 30 cm

B. 45 cm

C. 60 cm

D. 25 cm

11. 5% of a number is 15. The number is :

A. 150 B. 200

C. 250 D. 300

12. 75% of what area is 15 square metres?

A. 10 square metres

B. 15 square metres

C. 20 square metres

D. 25 square metres

13. What per cent of ₹ 30 is ₹ 10?

A. 30% B. 33.3%

C. 35% D. 40%

14. What per cent of 6.25 is 1.25?

A. 10% B. 15%

C. 20% D. 25%

15. What per cent of 3 metres is 75 cm?

A. 10% B. 15%

C. 20% D. 25%

16. 62.5% may be written as :

A. $\frac{3}{8}$ B. $\frac{4}{8}$

C. $\frac{5}{8}$ D. $\frac{6}{8}$

17. 125% may be expressed in fractions as :

A. $\frac{4}{5}$ B. $\frac{5}{4}$

C. $\frac{3}{5}$ D. $\frac{6}{5}$

18. 97% of students were present in a school and 18 students were absent. The total number of students in the school is:

A. 400 B. 450

C. 500 D. 600

19. The population of a town increased from 50,000 to 52,000. The increase per cent is:

A. 4%

B. 3%

C. 2%

D. 1%

20. At a clearance sale, goods were sold at a reduction of 20 per cent. A student purchased a pen for ₹ 12 at the clearance sale. The usual price of the pen was:

A. ₹ 12

B. ₹ 13

C. Rs 14

D. ₹ 15

21. In a college election, a candidate who got 40% of total votes was defeated by his rival by 160 votes. the total number of votes polled was:

A. 900 B. 800

C. 700 D. 600

22. In an election, 4000 votes were polled. One of the candidates got 40% votes. He was defeated by:

A. 2400 votes

B. 1600 votes

C. 800 votes

D. 600 votes

23. The selling price of a certain commodity was reduced by 25%. As a result of it, the sales increased by 30%. What was the effect of it on cash collected by daily sales?

A. 5% increase

B. 5% decrease

C. 2.5% increase

D. 2.5 decrease

24. If the price of kerosine be raised by 10%, find by how much per cent a house holder must reduce his consumption of kerosine so that not to increase his expenditure?

A. 10%

B. 9.09%

C. 9.0%

D. 8.25%

25. A towel was 50 cm broad and 100 cm long. When bleached, it was found to have lost 20% of its length and 10% of breadth. The percentage of decrease in area is:

A. 28%

B. 20%

C. 10.08%

D. 10%

EXPLANATORY ANSWERS

1. C : $20\% = \frac{20}{100} = \frac{1}{5}$.

2. B : $\frac{5}{8} \Rightarrow \frac{5}{8} \times 100 = \frac{500}{8} = 62.5\%$.

3. D : 15% of ₹ 50 = $\frac{15}{100}$ × ₹ 50 = ₹ 7.50.

4. A : 1 minute 12 seconds = 60 + 12 = 72 second

1 hour = 60 × 60 = 3600 seconds

$\therefore \quad \frac{72 \times 100}{3600} = 2\%$.

5. D : Marks required to pass = 40% = 20 + 20

$\therefore$ Maximum marks $= \frac{100 \times 40}{40} = 100$.

6. B : Saving = 100% – 75% = 25% = ₹ 150

$\therefore$ Total salary = $\frac{100}{25}$ × 150 = ₹ 600.

7. C : Total parts = 22 parts + 2 parts = 24 parts; 24 parts contain 2 parts alloy

$\therefore$ 100 parts contain $\frac{2}{24} \times 100 = \frac{25}{3} = 8\frac{1}{3}\%$.

8. B : Reduction at 12% on ₹ 250 = $\frac{12}{100}$ × 250 = ₹ 30

$\therefore$ Cash price = Catalogue price – Reduction

= ₹ 250 – ₹ 30 = Rs. 220.

9. A : 20% of ₹ 5 = $\frac{20}{100} \times 5$ = Re. 1.

10. B : 15% of 3 metres = 15% of 300 cm = $\frac{15}{100} \times 300$ = 45 cm.

11. D : Let the number = x

$\therefore$ 5% of $x = 15$

or, $\frac{5}{100} \times x = 15$

$\therefore$ $x = \frac{15 \times 100}{5} = 300.$

12. C : Let the area = x m^2

$\therefore$ 75% of $x = 15$ sq. m

or $\frac{75}{100} \times x = 15$

$\therefore$ $x = \frac{15 \times 100}{75} = 20$ sq. m.

13. B : $\frac{10}{30} \times 100 = 33.3\%.$

14. C : $\frac{1.25}{6.25} \times 100 = 20\%.$

15. D : $\frac{75}{300} \times 100 = 25\%.$

16. C : $62.5\% = \frac{62.5}{100} = \frac{625}{1000} = \frac{5}{8}.$

17. C : $125\% = \frac{125}{100} = \frac{5}{4}.$

18. D : Number of students absent = 100% – 97% = 3% = 18

$\therefore$ $100\% = \frac{18 \times 100}{3} = 600.$

19. A : Increase in population = 52,000 – 50,000 = 2000

$\therefore$ % increase $= \frac{2000}{50,000} \times 100 = 4\%.$

20. D : S.P. = ₹ 12 = 80% of usual price

$\therefore$ Usual price $= \frac{100}{80} \times 12 =$ ₹ 15.

21. B : Candidate who won the election got 100 – 40 = 60% votes;
Difference of votes = 60% – 40% = 20% = 160

$$\therefore \quad \text{Total votes polled} = \frac{160}{20} \times 100 = 800.$$

22. C : Candidates who lost election got 40% of 4000

$$= \frac{40}{100} \times 4000 = 1600 \text{ votes}$$

Candidates who won the election got 60% of 4000

$$= \frac{60}{100} \times 4000 = 2400 \text{ votes}$$

$$\text{Difference of votes} = 2400 - 1600 = 800 \text{ votes}.$$

23. D : Selling price = 100 – 25 = 75%, Daily sales = 100 + 30 = 130%;

$$0.75 \times 1.30 = 0.975 = \text{Cash collected} = 97.5\%;$$

$$100\% - 97.5\% = 2.5\% \text{ decrease}.$$

24. B : Raised price of kerosine is 110/100 of the original price. Hence, the consumption should become 100/110 of the original consumption so as to keep the expenditure same.

$$\therefore \quad \text{Reduction} = \left(1 - \frac{100}{110}\right) \text{ of original consumtion}$$

$$= \frac{10}{110} \text{ of original consumption}$$

$$\text{Reduction } \% = \frac{10}{110} \times 100 = 9.09\%.$$

25. A :

$$\text{Original area} = 100 \times 50 = 5000 \text{ sq. cm.}$$

$$\text{Reduced length} = 80\% \text{ of } 100 \text{ cm} = 80 \text{ cm.}$$

$$\text{Reduced breadth} = 90\% \text{ of } 50 \text{ cm.} = 45 \text{ cm.}$$

$$\text{Reduced area} = 80 \times 45 = 3600 \text{ sq. cm.}$$

$$\text{Reduction in area} = 5000 - 3600 = 1400 \text{ sq. cm.}$$

$$\therefore \quad \% \text{ Reduction} = \frac{1400}{5000} \times 100 = 28\%.$$

5

RATIO AND PROPORTION

Ratio: The relation which one quantity bears to another quantity of the same kind, showing the number of times one quantity is contained in another, is called ratio between the two quantities. Thus, the relation between ₹ 48 and ₹ 6 is the same as the relation between ₹ 8 and Re. 1. This relation or the ratio is written as 8 : 1.

Since, a ratio is a fraction, it is not altered if both of its terms are divided or multiplied by the same number.

For example,

$$\frac{2}{3} = \frac{4}{6} = \frac{8}{12} = \frac{20}{30}$$

Both the quantities are called the terms of the ratio. The quantity in the numerator is called *antecedent* and the quantity in the denominator is called *consequent.*

Inverse Ratio: When antecedent and consequent of one ratio become respectively the consequent and antecedent of the other, the second ratio is called the inverse or reciprocal ratio of the first.

For example, 3/5 or 3 : 5 is the inverse ratio of 5/3 or 5 : 3.

Compound Ratio: When the antecedents and consequents of two or more ratios are multiplied to get a new antecedent and a new consequent, the new ratio formed is called their compound ratio.

For example,

the compound ratio of 2 : 3, 3 : 4, 5 : 6 is

$\frac{2}{3} \times \frac{3}{4} \times \frac{5}{6} = \frac{5}{12}$ or 5 : 12

Proportion: Four quantities may be in proportion when the ratio of first to the second is the same as the ratio of third to the fourth. Thus the ratio 2 : 5 and 12 : 30 are equal and the four numbers 2, 5, 12 and 30 are in proportion and are writen as 2 : 5 : :12 : 30

If four quantities are in proportion, the product of the extremes is equal to the product of the means.

EXERCISE

1. The ratio between two numbers is 3 : 4 and their sum is 490. The numbers are:
   A. 200 and 290
   B. 210 and 280
   C. 220 and 270
   D. 230 and 260

2. The ratio between two numbers is 3 : 4 and the sum of their squares is 625. The numbers are:
   A. 6 and 8 B. 15 and 20
   C. 18 and 24 D. 20 and 25

3. Which of the following is greatest?
   3 : 4, 4 : 5, 5 : 6, 6 : 7
   A. 3 : 4 B. 4 : 5
   C. 5 : 6 D. 6 : 7

4. In an examination, 25 students out of 70 scored less than 50% marks. The ratio of number of students who scored 50% marks or more to the number of students who scored less than 50% marks is:
   A. 1 : 2 B. 3 : 5
   C. 9 : 5 D. 5 : 7

5. The fraction that bears the same ratio to 4/9 that 3/11 does to 5/33 is:
   A. 4 : 5 B. 5 : 6
   C. 6 : 5 D. 7 : 5

6. If the consequent be 15 and the value of the ratio 3/5, then the value of antecedent is:
   A. 7 B. 8
   C 9 D. 10

7. If A : B = 5 : 7 and B : C = 9 : 11, then A : C = ?
   A. 9 : 11 B. 45 : 77
   C. 45 : 66 D. 39 : 77

8. Three numbers are in the ratio of 2 : 3 : 4 and the sum of the squares of the numbers is 116. The numbers are:
   A. 4 : 6 : 8
   B. 5 : 6 : 7
   C. 6 : 9 : 12
   D. 8 : 12 : 16

9. Sides of two squares are in the ratio of 3 : 4. Their perimeters are in the ratio of:
   A. 3 : 4 B. 7 : 8
   C. 5 : 6 D. 6 : 7

10. Two cubical boxes made of card-board have their edges in the ratio of 3 : 4. The ratio of the amounts of card-board in each of them is:
    A. 3 : 4 B. 5 : 6
    C. 6 : 7 D. 9 : 16

11. The angles of a triangle are in the ratio of 1 : 2 : 3. The largest angle is of:
    A. 30º B. 60º
    C. 90º D. 120º

12. The salaries of two persons are in the ratio of 4 : 7. Both of them spend 80 per cent of salaries and save rest of the money. The ratio of their savings is:
    A. 8 : 2
    B. 4 : 7
    C. 7 : 5
    D. 5 : 3

13. The mean proportion between 9 and 25 is:
A. 10 B. 12
C. 15 D. 17

14. The third proportional to 12 and 30 is:
A. 40 B. 45
C. 50 D. 75

15. The fourth proportional to 3, 4 and 15 is:
A. 20 B. 18
C. 17 D. 15

16. 75 : 15 = x : 7, the value of x is:
A. 25 B. 35
C. 40 D. 45

17. x : 7.5 = 7 : 17.5, the value of x is:
A. 1.0 B. 2.5
C. 3.0 D. 3.5

18. The mean proportional to 5 and 125 is:
A. 10 B. 15
C. 20 D. 25

19. The inverse ratio of 12 to 18 is:
A. $\frac{3}{2}$ B. $\frac{2}{3}$
C. $\frac{1}{3}$ D. $\frac{3}{1}$

20. Two numbers are in the ratio of 2: 3 and if 8 is added to each of them, they become in the ratio of 3 : 4. The number are:
A. 2 and 3
B. 4 and 6
C. 8 and 12
D. 16 and 24

21. If $x : y = 3 : 2$, then $(x + y) : (x - y) = ?$
A. 1 : 5 B. 5 : 1
C. 3 : 5 D. 5 : 2

22. If $x : y = y : z$, then $x = ?$
A. z B. $\frac{z}{y^2}$
C. $\frac{y^2}{z}$ D. $\frac{y}{z}$

EXPLANATORY ANSWERS

1. B : Ratio is 3 : 4, sum = 490
If sum is 7, the numbers are 3 and 4.
If sum is 490, the numbers are $\frac{3}{7} \times 490$ and $\frac{4}{7} \times 490$ *i.e.*, 210 and 280.

2. B : Ratio is 3 : 4. Sum of the squares of 3 and 4 is 9 + 16 = 25. If sum of the squares is 25, the squares of numbers are 9 and 16.
If sum of the squares is 625, the squares of numbers are $\frac{9}{25} \times 625$ and $\frac{16}{25} \times 625$ *i.e.,* 225 and 400.
Hence, the numbers are $\sqrt{225}$ and $\sqrt{400}$, *i.e.,* 15 and 20.

3. D : $\frac{3}{4}, \frac{4}{5}, \frac{5}{6}, \frac{6}{7}$

$\frac{315, 336, 350, 360}{420}$. Hence, the ratio 6 : 7 is the greatest.

4. C : Total students = 70.

Number of students scoring less than 50% marks = 25; Number of students scoring 50% or more than 50% marks = 70 – 25 = 45.

∴ The ratio of number of students who scored 50% marks or more to the number of students who scored less than 50% marks

$$= 45 : 25 = 9 : 5.$$

5. A : Let the required fraction is x. Then

$$\frac{x}{4/9} = \frac{3/11}{5/33} = \frac{3}{11} \times \frac{33}{5} = \frac{9}{5}$$

$$\therefore \quad x = \frac{9}{5} \times \frac{4}{9} = \frac{4}{5}, \text{ or }, 4 : 5.$$

6. C :

$$\text{Ratio} = \frac{3}{5} = \frac{\text{Antecedent}}{\text{Consequent}} = \frac{x}{15}$$

$$\therefore \quad x = 9, \text{ only then } \frac{9}{15} = \frac{3}{5}$$

7. B : $A : B = 5 : 7$; $B : C = 9 : 11$; A : C = ?

$$\frac{A}{B} = \frac{5}{7}, \frac{B}{C} = \frac{9}{11}, \frac{A}{C} = x$$

$$\frac{A}{B} \times \frac{B}{C} = \frac{5}{7} \times \frac{9}{11}, \text{ or, } \frac{A}{C} = \frac{45}{77}$$

$$\therefore \quad A : C = 45 : 77$$

8. A : Ratio of numbers = 2 : 3 : 4.

Ratio of squares of numbers = 4 : 9 : 16

If sum of the squares is 29, the squares of the numbers are 4, 9, 16.

If sum of the squares is 116, the squares of the numbers are

$$\frac{4}{29} \times 116, \frac{9}{29} \times 116, \frac{16}{29} \times 116 = 16, 36, 64$$

∴ The numbers are $\sqrt{16}$, $\sqrt{36}$, $\sqrt{64}$ = 4, 6, 8.

9. A : Let the sides of two squares are $3x$ and $4x$.
Their perimeters are $4(3x)$ and $4(4x) = 12x$ and $16x$.
Ratio of permieters $= 12x : 16x = 3 : 4$.

10. D : Let the sides of two cubes are $3x$ and $4x$. Surface areas of two cubes are $6(3x)^2$ and $6(4x)^2$.
Ratio of surface areas $= 6(3x)^2 : 6(4x)^2 = 54x^2 : 96x^2 = 9 : 16$.

11. C : Ratio of the angles of triangle $= 1 : 2 : 3$
Sum of the angles of triangle $= 180°$

$$\text{Largest angle} = \frac{3}{6} \times 180 = 90°$$

12. B : Let the salaries be $4x$ and $7x$.
Savings are $100 - 80 = 20\%$

$$\text{Ratio of savings} = 20\% \text{ of } 4x : 20\% \text{ of } 7x$$

$$= \frac{20}{100} \times 4x : \frac{20}{100} \times 7x = 4 : 7$$

13. C : The mean proportion between any two numbers is equal to the square root of their product.
Let x be the mean proportion between 9 and 25.

$$\therefore \quad 9 : x = x : 25$$

$$\text{or,} \quad x^2 = 25 \times 9, \text{ or, } x = \sqrt{25 \times 9} = \sqrt{225} = 15.$$

14. D : Let x be the third proportional to 12 and 30.

$$\text{Then,} \quad 12 : 30 = 30 : x$$

$$\text{or,} \quad 12x = 30 \times 30$$

$$\therefore \quad x = \frac{30 \times 30}{12} = 75.$$

15. A : Let x be the fourth proportional to 3, 4, 15.
Then, $3 : 4 = 15 : x$
Since, product of the extremes = Product of the means

$$\therefore \quad 3x = 15 \times 4, \text{ or, } x = \frac{15 \times 4}{3} = 20.$$

16. B :

$$75 : 15 = x : 7$$

$$75 \times 7 = 15 \times x \text{ or, } x = \frac{75 \times 7}{15} = 35.$$

17. C : $$x : 7.5 = 7 : 17.5$$
$$x \times 17.5 = 7.5 \times 7.0$$
$$\therefore \quad x = \frac{7.5 \times 7.0}{17.5} = 3.0.$$

18. D : Let x be the mean proportional to 5 and 125.

Then, $5 : x = x : 125$ or, $x^2 = 125 \times 5$

$$\therefore \quad x = \sqrt{125 \times 5} = \sqrt{625} = 25.$$

19. A : The inverse ratio of 12 : 18 *i.e.,*

$\frac{12}{18}$ is $\frac{18}{12} = \frac{3}{2}$.

20. D : Let the numbers be $2x$ and $3x$.

Then we have, $\frac{2x+8}{3x+8} = \frac{3}{4}$, or, $8x + 32 = 9x + 24$

or, $9x - 8x = 32 - 24$, or, $x = 8$

$\therefore$ The numbers are 2×8 and 3×8 *i.e.,* 16 and 24

21. B : $$x : y = 3 : 2, x + y = 3 + 2$$

and $$x - y = 3 - 2$$

$$\therefore \quad (x + y) : (x - y) = 5 : 1$$

22. C : $$x : y = y : z, \text{ or, } \frac{x}{y} = \frac{y}{z}$$

$$\therefore \quad x = \frac{y}{z} . y = \frac{y^2}{z}$$

6

PROFIT AND LOSS

Profit and Loss: The terms profit and loss are largely used in business. When the selling price (S.P.) is greater than cost price (C.P.) there is always some profit. When the selling price is less than the cost price, there is always loss.

> **It should be noted that profit or loss is calculated on the cost price, generally in the form of per cent.**

For example, a man buys an article for ₹ 50 and sells it for ₹ 65. The gain per cent is calculated as follows:

$$\text{Profit} = \text{Selling Price} - \text{Cost Price}$$
$$= ₹\ 65 - ₹\ 50 = ₹\ 15$$

$$\%\ \text{Profit} = \frac{15}{50} \times 100 = 30\%$$

When cost price and profit or loss % are given, then

$$\text{S.P.} = \frac{[100 + \text{gain}\%]}{100} \times \text{C.P.}$$

or

$$\text{S.P.} = \frac{[100 - \text{Loss}\%]}{100} \times \text{C.P.}$$

When selling price and profit or loss % are given,

$$\text{C.P.} = \frac{\text{S.P.} \times 100}{100 + \text{Gain}\ \%} \quad \text{or} \quad \text{C.P.} = \frac{\text{S.P.} \times 100}{100 - \text{Loss}\ \%}$$

(i) To find the cost price when the selling price and the % profit based on cost price is given:

Establish a relation between S.P. and C.P. and solve it to find C.P.

For example, an article is sold for Rs.10 which is a 10% profit of C.P.

In this case, S.P. = ₹ 10 = C.P. + 10% of C.P. (Profit)

∴ S.P. = 100% of C.P.

or,

$$\text{C.P.} = ₹\ \frac{10 \times 100}{110} = ₹\ 9.09.$$

(ii) To find the S.P. when the profit based on S.P. is given:

Establish a relation between the S.P. and C.P. and solve it to find the S.P.

For example, a person buys a book for ₹ 27 and sells it at a profit of 10% of S.P. Find the S.P.

₹ 27 + Profit = S.P.

Since, profit is 10% of S.P., the C.P. must be 90% of S.P.

∴ ₹ 27 = 90% of S.P.

$$\therefore \quad \text{S.P.} = \frac{27 \times 100}{90} = ₹\ 30.$$

(iii) To find S.P. when the % loss on the S.P. is given:

Establish a relation between C.P. and S.P. and solve it to find S.P.

For example, an article was bought for ₹ 10. Due to some breakage, it was sold for 25% loss on the S.P. Find the S.P. of the article.

₹ 10 – Loss = S.P.

Since, the loss is 25% of the S.P., the C.P. must be 125% of S.P.

∴ ₹ 10 = 125% of S.P.

$$\therefore \quad \text{S.P.} = \frac{\text{Rs. } 10 \times 100}{125} = ₹\ 8.$$

(iv) To find S.P. when the list price and % discount are given:

Multiply the list price by % discount to find the discount in terms of money and subtract it from the list price.

For example, the list price of an article is ₹ 90. Find its selling price if it is sold at 10% discount.

List price = ₹ 90.00, Discount = 10% of ₹ 90.00

$$= \frac{10 \times 90}{100} = ₹\ 9.00$$

∴ Selling price = ₹ 90.00 – ₹ 9.00 = ₹ 81.00

(v) To find S.P. when list price and a series of discounts are given:

(a) Multiply the list price by first % discount.

(b) Subtract it from the list price.

(c) Multiply the remainder by second discount.

(d) Subtract the product from the remainder.

(e) Continue the same procedure if more discounts are given.

For example, find the selling price of an article listed at ₹ 200 on which there are discounts of 10% and 20%.

First discount = 10% of ₹ 200

$$= \frac{10 \times 200}{100} = ₹\ 20$$

First selling price = ₹ 200 – ₹ 20 = ₹ 180.

Second discount = 20% of ₹ 180

$$= \frac{20 \times 180}{100} = ₹\ 36$$

Second selling price = ₹ 180 – ₹ 36 = ₹ 144

(vi) To find the single equivalent discount of a series of discounts :

(*a*) Add first two discounts.

(*b*) Multiply first two discounts.

(*c*) Subtract this product from the sum to find the equivalent discount of the first two discounts.

(*d*) If there is third discount, add the equivalent of first two discounts to the third.

(*e*) Multiply the equivalent of first two discounts by third.

(*f*) Subtract this product from the sum to find the equivalent of the three discounts.

(*g*) Continue the same procedure, if there are more discounts.

For example, what is the single discount equivalent to discount series 10%, 20%, 30%.

10% + 20% = 0.1 + 0.2 = 0.3
10% × 20% = 0.1 × 0.2 = 0.02
0.30 – 0.02 = 0.28
0.28 + 30% = 0.28 + 0.3 = 0.580
0.28 × 30% = 0.28 × 0.3 = 0.084
0.580 – 0.084 = 0.496 = 49.6%

Hence, the single equivalent discount of 10%, 20% and 30%, is 49.6%.

EXERCISE

1. A man buys an article for ₹ 25 and sells it for ₹ 30. His profit is:

A. 16.67% B. 20%
C. 25.5% D. 25.67%

2. If an article is sold at 10% profit, then the selling price in terms of cost price is:

A. 10/11 B. 11/10
C. ₹ 110 D. ₹ 90

3. If an article is sold at gain of *x*%, the cost price in terms of selling price is:

A. $\frac{100}{100+x}$ B. $\frac{100+x}{100}$
C. $\frac{100}{100-x}$ D. $\frac{100-x}{100}$

4. If an article is sold at gain of *y*%, the selling price in terms of cost price is:

A. $\frac{100}{100-y}$ B. $\frac{100-y}{100}$
C. $\frac{100}{100+y}$ D. $\frac{100+y}{100}$

5. If an article is sold at a loss of 25%, the selling price in terms of cost price is:

A. $\frac{1}{2}$ B. $\frac{2}{3}$

C. $\frac{3}{4}$ D. $\frac{4}{5}$

6. If an article is sold at a loss of 50%, the cost price in terms of selling price is:

A. $\frac{1}{2}$

B. 2

C. 2.5

D. None of the above

7. If S.P. of an article is 4/3 of C.P., the profit is:

A. $\frac{1}{3}\%$ B. $33\frac{1}{3}\%$

C. $25\frac{1}{5}\%$ D. $20\frac{1}{2}\%$

8. If C.P. of an article is 3/2 of S.P., the profit or loss percentage is:

A. $33\frac{1}{3}\%$ loss B. $33\frac{1}{3}\%$ profit

C. $33\frac{1}{8}\%$ loss D. $33\frac{1}{8}\%$ profit

9. If S.P. of an article is 6 times the loss, the loss percentage is:

A. $14\frac{5}{9}\%$ B. $15\frac{2}{8}\%$

C. $16\frac{3}{5}\%$ D. $14\frac{2}{7}\%$

10. If gain is 1/4 of C.P., the profit percentage is:

A. 4% B. 25%

C. 50% D. 75%

11. If loss is 1/3 of S.P., the loss percentage is:

A. 33% B. 25%

C. 20% D. 17%

12. A man bought certain articles at 8 for ₹ 7 and sold them at 6 for ₹ 5. The gain or loss percentage is:

A. $4\frac{16}{21}\%$ gain

B. $4\frac{16}{21}\%$ loss

C. No profit no loss

D. None of the above

13. A man bought a number of oranges at 3 for a rupee and an equal number at 2 for a rupee. At what price per dozen should be sell them to make a profit of 20%?

A. ₹ 4 B. ₹ 5

C. ₹ 6 D. ₹ 7

14. A machine was bought for ₹ 9000. For how much should it be sold to gain 15%?

A. ₹ 10,150 B. ₹ 10,250

C. ₹ 10,300 D. ₹ 10,350

15. Find the selling price if a fountain pen costing ₹ 6.20 is sold at a loss of 10%?

A. ₹ 6.92 B. ₹ 5.58

C. ₹ 6.00 D. ₹ 5.92

16. A carpet is sold for ₹ 585 at a loss of 10%. The cost price is:

A. ₹ 650 B. ₹ 640

C. ₹ 630 D. ₹ 620

17. A machine is sold at a profit of 20%. If it had been sold at a profit of 25%, it would have fetched ₹ 35 more. The cost price of the machine is:

A. ₹ 650 B. ₹ 700

C. ₹ 750 D. ₹ 800

18. By selling a book for ₹ 31 a person loses 7% of his outlay. If he sells the same book for ₹ 35, the bargain is:

A. 4% loss B. 4% profit

C. 5% loss D. 5% profit

19. The cost price of 12 articles is equal to the selling price of 9 articles. The gain per cent is:

A. 25.0% B. 33.3%

C. 30.0% D. 67.7%

20. At a clearance sale, the prices had been reduced by 20%. If a transistor was being sold at ₹ 150 before reduction, the price at clearance sale was:

A. ₹ 130

B. ₹ 125

C. ₹ 120

D. ₹ 115

EXPLANATORY ANSWERS

1. B : Profit = ₹ 30 – ₹ 25 = ₹ 5, % Profit = $\frac{5}{25} \times 100 = 20\%$.

2. B : If the profit is 10%, then S.P. = 110% of C.P. = $\frac{110}{100}$ of C.P. = $\frac{11}{10}$ of C.P.

3. A : Gain = $x\%$, S.P. = $[100 + x]$ % of C.P. ∴ C.P. = $\frac{100}{100+x}$ S.P.

4. D : Gain = $y\%$, S.P. = $[100 + y]$ % of C.P.

$$\text{S.P.} = \frac{100+y}{100} \times \text{C.P.}$$

5. C : Loss = 25%, C.P. = 100, S.P. = 100 – 25 = 75

or, S.P. = 75% of C.P. = $\frac{3}{4}$ of C.P.

6. B : Let C.P. = 100, Loss = 50%, S.P. = 100 – 50 = 50%;

or, S.P. = 50% of C.P. or, C.P. = 200% of S.P. or, C.P. = 2 × S.P.

7. B : C.P. = 1, S.P. = $\frac{4}{3}$, Profit = $\frac{4}{3} - 1 = \frac{1}{3}$

% Profit = $100 \times \frac{1}{3} = 33\frac{1}{3}\%$.

8. A : C.P. = 1, S.P. = $\frac{2}{3}$ of C.P., Loss = $1 - \frac{2}{3} = \frac{1}{3}$.

% Loss = $\frac{1}{3} \times 100 = 33\frac{1}{3}\%$.

9. D : S.P. = 6 times the Loss or, Loss = $\frac{1}{6}$ of S.P.

$$\text{C.P.} = \text{S.P.} + \text{Loss} = \text{S.P.} + \frac{1}{6} \text{ of S.P.} = \frac{7}{6} \text{ of S.P.}$$

or, $\text{S.P.} = \frac{6}{7}$ of C.P. $\therefore$ Loss $= 1 - \frac{6}{7}$ of C.P. $= \frac{1}{7}$ of C.P.

$$\% \text{ Loss} = 100 \times \frac{1}{7} = 14\frac{2}{7}\%$$

10. B : C.P. = 1, Gain = $\frac{1}{4}$ of C.P. = $\frac{1}{4} \times 1 = \frac{1}{4}$

$$\% \text{ Gain} = \frac{1}{4} \times 100 = 25\%.$$

11. B : Loss = $\frac{1}{3}$ of S.P.

$$\text{C.P.} = \text{S.P.} + \text{Loss} = \text{S.P.} + \frac{1}{3} \text{ of S.P.} = \frac{4}{3} \text{ of S.P.}$$

or, S.P. = $\frac{3}{4}$ of C.P. $\therefore$ Loss = $\frac{1}{4}$ of C.P.

$$\% \text{ Loss} = \frac{1}{4} \times 100 \text{ of C.P.} = 25\% \text{ of C.P.}$$

12. B : C.P. of one article = ₹ $\frac{7}{8}$, S.P. of one article = ₹ $\frac{5}{6}$

$$\text{Loss} = \text{C.P.} - \text{S.P.} = \frac{7}{8} - \frac{5}{6} = \frac{1}{24}$$

$$\% \text{ Loss} = \frac{1}{24} \times \frac{8}{7} \times 100 = \frac{100}{21} = 4\frac{16}{21}\%$$

13. C : Let 1 dozen oranges were bought at 3 for a rupee and one dozen oranges were bought at 2 for a rupee.

$\therefore$ C.P. of 1 dozen = ₹ 4

C.P. of 1 dozen = ₹ 6

C.P. of 2 dozens = ₹ 6 + ₹ 4 = ₹ 10

% Profit 20% = 20% of ₹ 10 = ₹ 2

$\therefore$ S.P. = C.P. + Profit = ₹ 10 + ₹ 2

= ₹ 12

S.P. of 2 dozen oranges = ₹ 12

$\therefore$ S.P. of 1 dozen oranges = ₹ $\frac{12}{2}$ = ₹ 6

14. D : C.P. = ₹ 9000, Gain = 15% of ₹ 9000 = $\frac{15}{100} \times 9000$ = ₹ 1350.

∴ S.P. = ₹ 9000 + ₹ 1350 = ₹ 10,350.

15. B : C.P. = ₹ 6.20, Loss = 10% of C.P. = 10% of ₹ 6.20

$= \frac{10}{100} \times 6.20$ = 62 paise

S.P. = C.P. – Loss = ₹ 6.20 – 62 paise

= ₹ 5.58

16. A : S.P. = ₹ 585, Loss = 10% of C.P.

$$\text{C.P.} = \frac{\text{S.P.} \times 100}{[100 - \text{Loss\%}]} = \frac{585 \times 100}{100 - 10} = \frac{585 \times 100}{90} = ₹\ 650.$$

17. B : Let, C.P. = ₹ 100

Ist S.P. = ₹ 120, IInd S.P. = ₹ 125

Difference = ₹ 125 – ₹ 120 = ₹ 5

If difference is ₹ 5, C.P. = ₹ 100

If difference is ₹ 35, C.P. = $\frac{100}{5} \times 35$ = ₹ 700

18. D : S.P. = ₹ 31, Loss = 7%

∴ C.P. = $\frac{31 \times 100}{93}$ = ₹ $\frac{100}{3}$

IInd S.P. = ₹ 35, Profit = ₹ 35 – ₹ $\frac{100}{3}$ = ₹ $\frac{5}{3}$

∴ % Profit = $\frac{5}{3} \times \frac{3}{100} \times 100$ = 5%.

19. B : Let C.P. of one article = ₹ 1

∴ C.P. of 12 articles = ₹ 12

C.P. of 12 articles = S.P. of 9 articles = ₹ 12

∴ S.P. of 12 articles = $\frac{12}{9} \times 12$ = ₹ 16

Profit = ₹ 16 – ₹ 12 = ₹ 4

% Profit = $\frac{4}{12} \times 100$ = 33.3%

20. C : S.P. before reduction = ₹ 150

S.P. after reduction = 100 – 20 = 80% of ₹ 150

= $\frac{80}{100} \times 150$ = ₹ 120.

7
INTEREST

Interest is the sum which is paid for the use of other's money. If it is payable yearly, it is called rate per cent per annum. Thus, 6% per annum means ₹ 6 paid as interest on each ₹ 100 for one year. The money borrowed is called *Principal.* The sum of the principal and interest is called *Amount.*

In the Case of Simple Interest:

$$\text{Simple Interest} = \frac{\text{Principal} \times \text{Rate\%} \times \text{Time (in years)}}{100}$$

$$\text{Amount} = \text{Principal} + \text{Interest}$$

When time, rate% and interest are given,

$$\text{Principal} = \frac{\text{Interest} \times 100}{\text{Rate} \times \text{Time (in years)}}$$

When principal, interest and time are given,

$$\text{Rate} = \frac{\text{Interest} \times 100}{\text{Principal} \times \text{Time}}$$

When principal, interest and rate are given,

$$\text{Time} = \frac{\text{Interest} \times 100}{\text{Principal} \times \text{Rate}}$$

Example 1. A sum of money amounts to ₹ 6000 in 2 years. If the interest on the sum for that time is ₹ 1000. Find the rate of simple interest.

Solution. Amount = ₹ 6000, Interest = ₹ 1000

Principal = ₹ 6000 – ₹ 1000 = ₹ 5000

Time = 2 years

$$\text{Rate} = \frac{\text{Interest} \times 100}{\text{Principal} \times \text{Time}} = \frac{1000 \times 100}{5000 \times 2} = 10\%$$

Example 2. What principal with yield ₹ 600 as simple interest at 12% per annum in 1 year?

Solution. Interest = ₹ 600, Rate = 12%, Time = 1 year

$$\text{Principal} = \frac{\text{Interest} \times 100}{\text{Rate} \times \text{Time}} = \frac{\text{Rs. } 600 \times 100}{12 \times 1} = ₹\ 5000.$$

Example 3. At what time will the interest on a sum of money will equal to the principal at 10% per annum?

Solution. Let, Principal = x, ∴ Interest = x, Rate = 10%

$$\text{Time} = \frac{\text{Interest} \times 100}{\text{Principal} \times \text{Rate}} = \frac{x \times 100}{x \times 10} = 10 \text{ years.}$$

Example 4. Three years back, a sum of money was remitted in a bank at 12% per annum S.I. The accounts are now cleared, the bank paying a sum of ₹ 6,800. What was the sum originally invested?

Solution. Interest for 3 years = 3 × 12 = 36% of the principal. The amount in 3 years = 100 + 36 = 136% of the principal = ₹ 6800.

$$\therefore \quad \text{Original sum invested} = \frac{6800 \times 100}{136} = ₹\ 5000.$$

In the Case of Compound Interest:

$$\text{Amount} = \text{Principal}\left[1 + \frac{\text{Rate}}{100}\right]^{\text{Time(in year)}}$$

If rate of compound interest differs from year to year, then

$$\text{Amount} = \text{Principal}\left[1 + \frac{\text{Rate}_1}{100}\right]\left[1 + \frac{\text{Rate}_2}{100}\right]\left[1 + \frac{\text{Rate}_3}{100}\right]\text{..........}$$

Example 5. Find the compound interest on ₹ 2000 for 2 years at 10%.

Solution. $\text{Amount} = \text{Principal}\left[1 + \frac{\text{Rate}}{100}\right]^2$

$$= ₹\ 2000\left[1 + \frac{10}{100}\right]^2 = ₹\ 2000 \times \frac{11}{10} \times \frac{11}{10}$$

$$= ₹\ 2420$$

$$\text{Compound Interest} = ₹\ 2420 - ₹\ 2000 = ₹\ 420$$

Example 6. Find the compound interest on ₹ 4000 for 1.5 years at 10% interest payable half- yearly.

Solution. (In such cases, double the time and half the rate)

$$\text{Amount} = 4000\left(1 + \frac{5}{100}\right)^3$$

$$= ₹\ 4000 \times \frac{21}{20} \times \frac{21}{20} \times \frac{21}{20} = ₹\ 4630.50$$

$$\text{Compound Interest} = ₹\ 4630.50 - ₹\ 4000 = ₹\ 630.50$$

Example 7. In what time ₹ 12000 will amount to ₹ 13230 at 5% C.I.?

Solution. Principal $\left[1+\frac{\text{Rate}}{100}\right]^n$ = Amount

$$\therefore \quad ₹\ 13230 = ₹\ 12000\left[1+\frac{5}{100}\right]^n$$

$$\therefore \quad \left[1+\frac{5}{100}\right]^n = \frac{\text{Rs. } 13230}{\text{Rs. } 12000}$$

$$\text{or,} \quad \left[\frac{21}{20}\right]^n = \frac{441}{400} = \frac{21}{20}\times\frac{21}{20} = \left[\frac{21}{20}\right]^2$$

$$\therefore \quad n = 2 \text{ years}$$

When interest is calculated half-yearly, halve the rate and double the time. When interest is calculated quarterly, divide the rate by 4 and multiply the time by 4.

EXERCISE

1. S.I. on ₹ 5000 for 5 years at 10% p.a. is equal to:
A. ₹ 250 B. ₹ 2000
C. ₹ 2500 D. ₹ 2800

2. What principal will yield ₹ 120 as S.I. at 6% p.a. in 10 years?
A. ₹ 100 B. ₹ 125
C. ₹ 150 D. ₹ 200

3. In how many years will the sum of money double itself at 10% per annum S.I.?
A. 4 years B. 5 years
C. 8 years D. 10 years

4. What sum of money will produce an interest of ₹ 80 in 5 years at the rate of 5% per annum?
A. ₹ 320 B. ₹ 380
C. ₹ 420 D. ₹ 500

5. If S.I. on ₹ 5000 in 2 years is ₹ 500, the amount is:
A. ₹ 4500 B. ₹ 5500
C. ₹ 5575 D. ₹ 6000

6. The simple interest on a certain sum of money is ₹ 49 and the rate per cent is equal to the number of years. The rate per cent is:
A. 10% B. 9%
C. 7% D. 6%

7. If the rate of interest is 2 paise per rupee per month, then the interest on ₹ 200 in one year will be:
A. ₹ 4 B. ₹ 24
C. ₹ 48 D. ₹ 50

8. What annual payment will discharge a debt of ₹ 440 due in 5 years? Simple interest reckoned at 5%.
A. ₹ 80 B. ₹ 90
C. ₹ 100 D. ₹ 105

9. Compound interest on ₹ 2000 for 3 years at 5% p.a. is:
A. ₹ 300 B. ₹ 315.25
C. ₹ 325.50 D. ₹ 333.75

10. Find the compound interest on ₹ 1000 is one year at 5% per annum when the interest is calculated half-yearly?

A. ₹ 50.20 B. ₹ 50.62
C. ₹ 50.82 D. ₹ 55.62

11. The difference between C.I. and S.I. on ₹ 2500 for 2 years at 4% p.a. is:

A. ₹ 2 B. ₹ 3
C. ₹ 4 D. ₹ 5

12. What sum lent at C.I. at 5% p.a. will amount to ₹ 441 in 2 years?

A. ₹ 200 B. ₹ 250
C. ₹ 450 D. ₹ 400

13. For a sum of ₹ 1000, during same time at the same rate, highest quantity will be:

A. S.I. B. C.I.
C T.D. D. B.G.

14. S.I. is equal to C.I. for a certain sum when:

A. rate is same
B. time is same
C. interest is computed annually and time is one year
D. None of the above

15. Simple interest on the sum due of a bill for the time from when the bill is discounted to the due date of bill is called:

A. Simple Interest
B. Compound Interest
C. True Discount
D. Banker's Discount

16. A sum becomes double in 15 years at simple interest. It will become triple in:

A. 20 years B. 30 years
C. 35 years D. 40 years

17. In 5 years the interest on certain sum amounts to one-fourth of the sum. The rate of interest per annum is:

A. 4% B. 5%
C. 6% D. 10%

EXPLANATORY ANSWERS

1. C : $\text{S.I.} = \dfrac{\text{Principal} \times \text{Time} \times \text{Rate}}{100} = \dfrac{5000 \times 5 \times 100}{100} = ₹\ 2500.$

2. D : $\text{Principal} = \dfrac{\text{S.I.} \times 100}{\text{Time} \times \text{Rate}} = \dfrac{120 \times 100}{6 \times 10} = ₹\ 200$

3. D : Let Principal = x

$\therefore$ Amount = $2x$, Hence, Interest = $2x - x = x$

$$\text{Rate} = 10\%,\ \text{Time} = \frac{\text{Interest} \times 100}{\text{Principal} \times \text{Rate}} = \frac{x \times 100}{x \times 10} = 10 \text{ years.}$$

4. A : Principal $= \dfrac{\text{Interest} \times 100}{\text{Rate} \times \text{Time}} = \dfrac{80 \times 100}{5 \times 5} =$ ₹ 320.

5. B : Amount = ₹ 5000 + ₹ 500 = ₹ 5500.

6. C : Let the Principal = ₹ 100, Time = x years, Rate = x%

$$\text{S.I.} = \frac{100 \times x \times x}{100} = x^2 = ₹\ 49$$

$$\therefore \quad x = \sqrt{49} = 7 = 7\%$$

7. C : Rate of interest = 2% per month
= 24% per year

$$\therefore \quad \text{Interest} = \frac{200 \times 24 \times 1}{100} = ₹\ 48$$

8. A.

9. B :

$$\text{Amount} = ₹\ 2000 \left(1 + \frac{5}{100}\right)^3$$

$$= ₹\ 2315.25$$

$$\text{C.I.} = \text{Amount} - \text{Principal} = 2315.25 - 2000$$

$$= ₹\ 315.25.$$

10. B : When interest is calculated half-yearly, convert 1 year into 2 half years and take half of the rate.

Thus, rate = 2.5%, $n = 2$

$$\text{Amount} = ₹\ 1000 \left(1 + \frac{2.5}{100}\right)^2$$

$$= ₹\ 1050.62$$

$$\text{Interest} = 1050.62 - 1000 = ₹\ 50.62.$$

11. C. **12. D.** **13. B.** **14. C.** **15. D.** **16. B.**

17. B : Let sum = x, $\therefore$ Interest = $x/4$,

Time = 5 years,

$$\text{Rate} = \frac{\text{Interest} \times 100}{\text{Sum} \times \text{Time}} = \frac{x/4 \times 100}{x \times 5} = 5\%.$$

8

DISCOUNT

Discount in the general term is the reduction or an allowance made from the amount of a bill in lieu of its immediate cash payment. The reduction made in consideration of making immediate payment is called discount or true discount. The immediate cash payment or cash equivalent is called present worth or present value.

$$\text{Sum Due} = \text{Present Worth} + \text{True Discount}$$

$$\text{True Discount} = \text{Sum Due} - \text{Present Worth}$$

$$\text{True Discount on Sum Due} = \text{Interest on Present Worth}$$

$$\text{Present Worth} = \frac{100 \times \text{Sum Due}}{100 + [\text{Rate} \times \text{Time}]}$$

$$\text{True Discount} = \frac{\text{Sum Due} \times \text{Rate} \times \text{Time}}{100 + [\text{Rate} \times \text{Time}]}$$

Example. *Find the present worth and true discount on ₹6000 due 2 years at 10% per annum S.I.*

Solution.

$$\text{P.W.} = \frac{100 \times \text{Sum Due}}{100 + [\text{Rate} \times \text{Time}]}$$

$$= \frac{100 \times 6000}{100 + [10 \times 2]} = \frac{100 \times 6000}{120} = ₹\ 5000$$

$$\text{T.D.} = \frac{\text{Sum Due} \times \text{Rate} \times \text{Time}}{100 + [\text{Rate} \times \text{Time}]}$$

$$= \frac{6000 \times 10 \times 2}{100 + [10 \times 2]} = \frac{6000 \times 10 \times 2}{120} = ₹\ 1000.$$

Banker's Discount: In business when a trader buys goods from a wholesaler, the payment is generally made by a bill of exchange which is a kind of undertaking in writing to pay for the goods after a certain time. When the wholesaler wants money at earlier date, in such case, the bill is sold to the banker for ready money and it is said to be discounted and the amount which the banker deducts is called Banker's discount.

Banker's Discount (B.D.) is the same as the simple interest on the amount of bill for the number of days the bill has yet to run.

$$\text{Banker's Gain (B.G.)} = \text{Banker's Discount} - \text{True Discount}$$

$$\text{Banker's Discount} = \text{True Discount} + \text{Interest on True Discount}$$

$$\text{Sum Due} = \frac{\text{B.D.} \times \text{T.D.}}{\text{B.D.} - \text{T.D.}}$$

$$\text{T.D.} = \sqrt{\text{P.W.} \times \text{B.G.}}$$

Example 1. *True discount on a certain sum of money due 1 year hence is ₹ 48 and interest on the same sum for the same time is ₹ 50. Find the sum and the rate per cent.*

Solution.
$$\text{Sum} = \frac{\text{Interest} \times \text{Discount}}{\text{Interest} - \text{Discount}}$$

$$= \frac{\text{Rs. } 50 \times \text{Rs. } 48}{\text{Rs. } 50 - \text{Rs. } 48} = ₹\ \frac{50 \times 48}{2} = ₹\ 1200$$

Now, ₹ 50 is the interest on ₹ 1200 in one year,

$$\therefore \quad \text{Rate} = \frac{50 \times 100}{1200 \times 1} = 4\frac{1}{6}\%$$

Example 2. The banker's discount and true discount on a certain sum of money at 5% S.I. are ₹ 30 and ₹ 25 respectively. Find the sum.

Solution.
$$\text{Sum} = \frac{\text{B.D.} \times \text{T.D.}}{\text{B.D.} - \text{T.D.}} = \frac{30 \times 25}{30 - 25} = ₹\ 150$$

Example 3. *Find the banker's discount and banker's gain on a bill of ₹ 4000 at 10% if it is cashed 3 months in advance.*

Solution.
$$\text{Banker's discount} = \frac{\text{Rs. } 4000 \times 10 \times 3}{12 \times 100} = ₹\ 100$$

Cash received by the bill holder = ₹ 4000 – ₹ 100 = ₹ 3900

Interest on ₹ 100 = ₹ 2.50

Amount = ₹ 100 + ₹ 2.50 = ₹ 102.50

If amount is ₹ 102.50, T.D. = ₹ 2.50

If amount is ₹ 4000,
$$\text{T.D.} = \frac{2.50}{102.50} \times 4000 = ₹\ 97.56$$

B.G. = B.D. – T.D. = ₹ 100 – ₹ 97.56 = ₹ 2.44.

Example 4. *Banker's gain on a bill is ₹ 18 whose present worth is ₹ 450. Find true discount.*

Solution.
$$\text{T.D.} = \sqrt{\text{P.W.} \times \text{B.G.}}$$

$$= \sqrt{450 \times 18} = \sqrt{8100} = ₹\ 90.$$

Example 5. *True discount on a bill of ₹ 5400 is ₹ 900. Find the banker's discount and also banker's gain.*

Solution. Amount = ₹ 5400, T.D. = ₹ 900,

P.W. = Amount − T.D. = ₹ 5400 − ₹ 900

= ₹ 4500

S.I. on ₹ 4500 = ₹ 900

∴ S.I. on ₹ 5400 = ₹ $\frac{900 \times 5400}{4500}$ = ₹ 1080

∴ B.D. = ₹ 1080

∴ B.G. = B.D. − T.D. = ₹ 1080 − ₹ 900 = ₹ 180.

EXERCISE

1. Present worth of a money is equal to:

A. $\frac{100 \times \text{Sum Due}}{100 + \text{Rate} + \text{Time}}$

B. $\frac{100 \times \text{Sum Due}}{(100 + \text{Rate})\ \text{Time}}$

C. $\frac{100 + (\text{Rate} \times \text{Time})}{100 \times \text{Sum Due}}$

D. $\frac{100 \times \text{Sum Due}}{100 + (\text{Rate} \times \text{Time})}$

2. Find the present worth of ₹ 1248 due 2 years hence at 2% per annum simple interest

A. ₹ 1200 B. ₹ 1210
C. ₹ 1220 D. ₹ 1242

3. Find the present worth of ₹ 460 due 3 years hence at 5% per annum S.I.

A. ₹ 450 B. ₹ 420
C. ₹ 410 D. ₹ 400

4. Find the discount on ₹ 1010 due 3 months hence at 4% p.a. S.I.

A. ₹ 8 B. ₹ 9
C. ₹ 10 D. ₹ 12

5. Find the reduction made on a bill of ₹ 1150 paid 1.25 years before it is due when the rate of interest is 12%

A. ₹ 100 B. ₹ 150
C. ₹ 200 D. ₹ 225

6. Find the difference between S.I. and T.D. on ₹ 5100 for half-year at 4% p.a.

A. Re. 0.50 B. Re. 1.00
C. ₹ 1.50 D. ₹ 2.00

7. If the true discount on a bill due 2 years hence at 5% p.a. is ₹ 25, the amount of the bill is:

A. ₹ 125 B. ₹ 220
C. ₹ 250 D. ₹ 275

8. If the present worth of a bill of ₹ 660 due 2 years hence is ₹ 600, the rate per cent per annum is:

A. 4% B. 5%
C. 6% D. 10%

9. The true discount on a sum of money due 1 year is ₹ 100 and banker's discount on the same sum and for the same time is ₹ 104. The sum is:

A. ₹ 2500 B. ₹ 2550
C. ₹ 2600 D. ₹ 2700

10. The true discount on a sum of money due 12 months is ₹ 200 and banker's discount on the same sum and for the same time is ₹ 208. The rate of interest is:
A. 4% B. 5%
C. 6% D. 7%

11. The true discount on a certain sum of money for 2 years is 3/4 the banker's discount. The rate of interest is:
A. 15% B. 16.67%
C. 20% D. 20.33%

12. The T.D. on a bill is 5/6 of B.D. and the rate is 4%. The time is:
A. 5 years B. 4 years
C. 3 years D. 2 years

13. A trader's terms are 20% discount for cash payment and interest is charged after one year. What rate of interest per annum does the customer get on his money for cash payment?
A. 15% B. 20%
C. 25% D. 30%

14. The T.D. on a bill due 1 year hence at 5% p.a. is ₹ 40. The amount is:
A. ₹ 840 B. ₹ 900
C. ₹ 950 D. ₹ 1000

15. The interest on ₹ 5000 is equal to the true discount on ₹ 5050 at 4% p.a. The latter is due after:
A. 3 months B. 4 months
C. 5 months D. 6 months

EXPLANATORY ANSWERS

1. D : $\text{P.W.} = \dfrac{100 \times \text{S.D.}}{100 + (\text{Rate} \times \text{Time})}$.

2. A : $\text{P.W.} = \dfrac{100 \times \text{S.D.}}{100 + (\text{Rate} \times \text{Time})} = \dfrac{100 \times 1248}{100 + (2 \times 2)} = \dfrac{100 \times 1248}{104} = ₹\ 1200.$

3. D : $\text{P.W.} = \dfrac{100 \times \text{S.D.}}{100 + (\text{Rate} \times \text{Time})} = \dfrac{100 \times 460}{100 + (3 \times 5)} = \dfrac{100 \times 460}{115} = ₹\ 400.$

4. C : $\text{T.D.} = \dfrac{\text{Sum} \times \text{Rate} \times \text{Time}}{100 + (\text{Rate} \times \text{Time})} = \dfrac{1010 \times 1/4 \times 4}{100 + (1/4 \times 4)} = \dfrac{1010}{101} = ₹\ 10$

5. B : $\text{Reduction} = \text{T.D.} = \dfrac{1150 \times 12 \times 5/4}{100 + (12 \times 5/4)} = \dfrac{1150 \times 15}{115} = ₹\ 150.$

6. D :

$$\text{S.I.} = \frac{5100 \times 4 \times 1/2}{100} = ₹\ 102$$

$$\text{T.D.} = \frac{5100 \times 4 \times 1/2}{100 + (4 \times 1/2)} = \frac{5100 \times 2}{102} = ₹\ 100$$

$$\text{S.I.} - \text{T.D.} = ₹\ 102 - ₹\ 100 = ₹\ 2.$$

7. D : Let P.W. = ₹ 100

$$\text{S.I. on ₹ 100 at 5\% for 2 years} = \frac{100 \times 5 \times 2}{100} = ₹\ 10$$

Amount = 100 + 10 = ₹ 110,
₹ 10 is the T.D. on ₹ 110
If T.D. is ₹ 10, amount = ₹ 110

If T.D. is ₹ 25, amount = $\frac{110}{10} \times 25$ = ₹ 275.

8. B : P.W. = ₹ 600, Interest = ₹ 660 – ₹ 600 = ₹ 60,

Time = 2 years, Rate = $\frac{60 \times 100}{600 \times 2} = 5\%$.

9. C : Sum = $\frac{\text{B.D.} \times \text{T.D.}}{\text{B.D.} - \text{T.D.}} = \frac{104 \times 100}{104 - 100} = \frac{104 \times 100}{4}$ = ₹ 2600.

10. A : Sum = $\frac{\text{B.D.} \times \text{T.D.}}{\text{B.D.} - \text{T.D.}} = \frac{208 \times 200}{208 - 200} = \frac{208 \times 200}{8}$ = ₹ 5200.

Now, ₹ 208 is the interest on ₹ 5200 for 1 year.

∴ Rate = $\frac{208 \times 100}{5200 \times 1} = 4\%$.

11. B : If B.D. = x, T.D. = $3/4x$, Sum = $\frac{x \times 3/4x}{x - 3/4x} = 3x$,

Since, B.D. is the interest on sum due, ∴ Rate = $\frac{x \times 100}{3x \times 2} = \frac{100}{6} = 16.67\%$.

12. A : If, B.D. = x, T.D. = $6/5x$, Sum = $\frac{x \times 5/6x}{x - 5/6x} = 5x$

Since, B.D. is the interest on sum due, ∴ Time = $\frac{x \times 100}{5x \times 4}$ = 5 years.

13. C : Let amount of Bill = ₹ 100, Discount for cash payment = 20% = ₹ 20

∴ Cash price = ₹ 100 – ₹ 20 = ₹ 80

i.e., ₹ 20 is interest earned on ₹ 80 for one year.

∴ Rate = $\frac{20 \times 100}{80 \times 1}$ = ₹ 25%.

14. A : T.D. = Interest on P.W. = ₹ 40

Time = 1 year, Rate = 5% P.W. = $\frac{40 \times 100}{5 \times 1}$ = ₹ 800.

∴ Amount = 800 + 40 = ₹ 840

15. A : Interest on P.W. = T.D. on amount

Now, Interest on ₹ 5000 = T.D. on ₹ 5050

∴ ₹ 5000 is the P.W. of ₹ 5050 due at 4%

∴ Interest on ₹ 5000 = Sum due – P.W. = ₹ 5050 – ₹ 5000 = ₹ 50

∴ Time = $\frac{50 \times 100}{5000 \times 4} = \frac{1}{4}$ year = 3 months

9

TIME, WORK AND WAGES

While dealing with problems of time and work, it should be kept in mind that,

(*i*) If a man can do a piece of work in 5 days, It is evident that in one day he will finish 1/5 of his whole work; and vice versa.

(*ii*) If the number of persons engaged to do a certain job be increased in a certain ratio, the time required to do the same job will be decreased in the same ratio, and vice-versa. Thus, if the number of persons be changed in the ratio of 3 : 5, the time required to finish the job will be changed in the ratio of 5 : 3.

(*iii*) If A is twice as good workman as B, then A will take one-half of the time taken by B to do the same job.

(*iv*) While dealing with problems on wages, it may be kept in mind that the money obtained is always divided in the ratio of the work done by each person.

In the problems based on time and work, it is always assumed that a person works at uniform rate, unless and until specified in the problem.

Example. *A can do a piece of work in 4 days and B can do the same work in 6 days. How long will A and B take to do the work together?*

Solution. A's work in one day $= \frac{1}{4}$ of the total work

B's Work in one day $= \frac{1}{6}$ of the total work

$(A + B)$'s work in one day $= \frac{1}{4} + \frac{1}{6} = \frac{5}{12}$ of the total work

$\therefore$ Number of days taken by A + B to finish the work $= \frac{12}{5} = 2.4$ days.

EXERCISE

1. A can do a certain job in 6 days and B can finish the same job in 10 days. A and B together will finish the same job in:

A. less than 10 days but more then 6 days

B. more than 10 days

C. less than 6 days

D. 2 days

2. A can make a table in 3 days while his friend can make it in 6 days. A and his friend together will make the table in:

A. 3 days B. 2 days
C. 1 day D. 1/2 days

3. X and Y together can do a certain job in 10 days while X alone can do the same job in 15 days. Y alone will do the same job in:

A. 15 days B. 20 days
C. 25 days D. 30 days

4. Amit can do 1/2 of a piece of work in 8 days, while Aslam can do 1/3 of the same work in 8 days. In how many days can both do it together?

A. 9.6 days B. 10.5 days
C. 11.2 days D. 16.0 days

5. X, Y and Z together can do a piece of work in 8 days while X and Z together can do it in 12 days. Y alone will do the same work in:

A. 16 days B. 20 days
C. 24 days D. 28 days

6. 24 persons can assemble a machine in 12 days. In how many days 36 persons will assemble the same machine?

A. 8 days B. 12 days
C. 16 days D. 20 days

7. X, Y and Z can do a certain job in 8, 10 and 8 days respectively. How long would they take to complete the same job when all work together?

A. $2\frac{1}{7}$ days B. $2\frac{3}{7}$ days

C. $2\frac{5}{7}$ days D. $2\frac{6}{7}$ days

8. If m men can do $1/n$ of a piece of work in P days, find the expression for the number of persons required to do the whole work in q days?

A. mn/pq B. mnq/p
C. mnp/q D. mp/nq

9. In the above Q. No. 8 if $m = 15$, $n = 4$, $p = 12.5$ and $q = 20$, then the number of persons required to do the same work is:

A. 38 B. 34
C. 30 D. 26

10. A piece of work can be done by 6 men and 5 women in 6 days or 3 men and 4 women in 10 days. In how many days can it be done by 9 men and 15 women?

A. 1 day B. 2 days
C. 3 days D. 4 days

11. X and Y undertook a contract to do a certain job for ₹ 4200. X alone could do the job in 3 weeks and Y alone in 4 weeks. If both of them finished the job working together, in what ratio should money be divided (X : Y)?

A. 3 : 4 B. 4 : 3
C. 1 : 1 D. 2 : 3

12. X and Y did a piece of work together and received ₹ 300. If X alone can do that piece of work in 2 weeks and Y alone in 3 weeks, how should the money be divided between them?

A. X = ₹ 180, Y = ₹ 120
B. X = ₹ 120, Y = ₹ 180
C. X = ₹ 150, Y = ₹ 150
D. X = ₹ 200, Y = ₹ 100

13. A, B and C did a work together and earned ₹ 195. If the ratio of work of A : B : C be as 4 : 6 : 3, the money obtained by C is:

A. ₹ 90 B. ₹ 60

C. ₹ 45 D. ₹ 30

14. To finish a certain job X takes twice as long as Y and Z together and Z three times as long as X and Y together. If X, Y and Z working together complete the job in 6 days, how long would X take to complete the work alone?

A. 16 days B. 18 days

C. 24 days D. 28 days

15. In the above question, how long would Z take to complete the work alone?

A. 16 days B. 18 days

C. 20 days D. 24 days

SOME SELECTED EXPLANATORY ANSWERS

1. C : Work done by A in one day = $\frac{1}{6}$

Work done by B in one day = $\frac{1}{10}$

Work done by (A + B) in one day = $\frac{1}{6}+\frac{1}{10} = \frac{8}{30}$

$\therefore$ A + B together will finish the work in $\frac{30}{8}$ days = $3\frac{6}{8}$ days which is less than 6 days.

2. B : Work done by A and his friend in one day = $\frac{1}{3}+\frac{1}{6}=\frac{3}{6}$

$\therefore$ Both will finish the work in $\frac{6}{3}$ = 2 days

3. D : Work done by X + Y in one day = $\frac{1}{10}$

Work done by X alone in one day = $\frac{1}{15}$

Work done by Y alone in one day = $\frac{1}{10}-\frac{1}{15}=\frac{1}{30}$

$\therefore$ Y alone will finish the work in 30 days.

4. A : Amit alone can do the whole work in $8 \times 2 = 16$ days

$\therefore$ Work done by Amit in one day $= \dfrac{1}{16}$

Aslam alone can do the whole work in $8 \times 3 = 24$ days

$\therefore$ Work done by Aslam in one day $= \dfrac{1}{24}$

Work done by Amit and Aslam in one day $= \dfrac{1}{16} + \dfrac{1}{24} = \dfrac{5}{48}$

$\therefore$ Amit and Aslam will finish the work in $\dfrac{48}{5} = 9.6$ days.

5. C : Work done by X + Y + Z in one day $= \dfrac{1}{8}$

Work done by X + Z in one day $= \dfrac{1}{12}$

Work done by Y in one day $= \dfrac{1}{8} - \dfrac{1}{12} = \dfrac{1}{24}$

$\therefore$ Y alone will finish the work in 24 days.

6. A : $\because$ 24 persons can assemble in 12 days.

$\therefore$ 1 person can assemble in 12×24 days

$\therefore$ 36 persons can assemble in $\dfrac{12 \times 24}{36} = 8$ days

7. D : Work done by X + Y + Z in one day $= \dfrac{1}{8} + \dfrac{1}{10} + \dfrac{1}{8} = \dfrac{7}{20}$

$\therefore$ X + Y + Z will complete the work in $\dfrac{20}{7} = 2\dfrac{6}{7}$ days.

8. C : *m* men can do 1/*n* of work in *p* days

$\therefore$ Number of men required to do the work in one day = *mnp*

Hence, number of men required to do the whole work in *q* days = *mnp/q*.

9. A : $mnp/q = \dfrac{15 \times 4 \times 12.5}{20} = 38.$

10. C :

$$6 \text{ days} \rightarrow 6\,m + 5\,w$$
$$1 \text{ day} \rightarrow 36\,m + 30\,w$$

Similarly,

$$10 \text{ days} \rightarrow 3\,m + 4\,w$$
$$1 \text{ day} \rightarrow 30\,m + 40\,w$$
$$36\,m + 30\,w = 30\,m + 40\,w$$

or, $$6\,m = 10\,w$$

or, $$1\,m = \frac{5}{3}\,w$$

Therefore, $$6\,m + 5\,w = 15\,w$$

and $$9\,m + 15\,w = 30\,w$$

The problem now reduce to

$$15\,w \rightarrow 6 \text{ days}$$

$\therefore$ $$30\,w \rightarrow 6 \times \frac{15}{30} = 3 \text{ days}$$

11. B : Ratio of working capacity of X and Y is 4 : 3

$\therefore$ Ratio of money to be divided = 4 : 3

12. A : Ratio of working capacity of X and Y is 3 : 2

$\therefore$ $$\text{X's share} = \frac{3}{5} \times 300 = ₹\ 180,$$

$$\text{Y's share} = \frac{2}{5} \times 300 = ₹\ 120.$$

13. C : Money obtained byC $= \frac{3}{13} \times 195 = ₹\ 45.$

14. B : 2 times X's daily work = (Y + Z)'s daily work

Adding X's daily work to both sides we get

3 times X's daily work = (X + Y + Z)'s daily work = 1/6

$\therefore$ X's daily work $= \frac{1}{6} \times \frac{1}{3} = \frac{1}{18}$

$\therefore$ X alone can finish the work in 18 days.

15. D : 3 times Z's daily work = (X + Y)'s daily work

Adding Z's daily work to both sides, we get

4 times Z's daily work = (X + Y + Z)'s daily work = 1/6

$\therefore$ Z's daily work $= \frac{1}{6} \times \frac{1}{4} = \frac{1}{24}$

$\therefore$ Z alone can finish the work in 24 days.

10

SPEED, TIME AND DISTANCE

Important Formulae :

$$\text{Distance} = \text{Speed} \times \text{Time}$$

$$\text{Speed} = \frac{\text{Distance}}{\text{Time}}$$

$$\text{Time} = \frac{\text{Distance}}{\text{Speed}}$$

EXERCISE

1. Speed of a moving car is 36 km/hr. Its speed in metres per second is:

A. 10 m/s B. 15 m/s
C. 20 m/s D. 25 m/s

2. Two trains start at the same time from two stations X and Y, 900 km apart; and proceed towards each other at an average speed of 38 and 22 km per hour respectively. They will meet after

A. 12 hours B. 13 hours
C. 14 hours D. 15 hours

3. A scooterist completes a journey in 10 hours, the first half at the rate of 21 km/hr and the second half at the rate of 24 km/hr. The total distance travelled is :

A. 256 km B. 224 km
C. 204 km D. 192 km

4. A train 100 m long is running at the speed of 60 km per hour. Time taken by the train to pass a telegraph post is:

A. 4 sec B. 5 sec
C. 6 sec D. 3 sec

5. A train 150 m long is running at the speed of 90 km/hr. Time taken by the train to pass through a tree is :

A. 3 sec B. 4 sec
C. 6 sec D. 8 sec

6. A train 100 m long is running at the speed of 65 km/hr. Time taken by the train to pass through a man walking at the rate of 5 km/hr in the direction of the train is :

A. 8 sec B. 6 sec
C. 4 sec D. 2 sec

7. A train 100 m long is running at the rate of 55 km/hr. Time taken by the train to pass through a man walking at the rate of 5 km/hr moving in opposite direction is :

A. 10 sec B. 8 sec
C. 6 sec D. 4 sec

8. Two persons start from the same place and walk in the opposite directions at 5 km and 4 km per hour respectively. At the end of 3 hours, distance between them is

A. 12 km B. 15 km
C. 27 km D. 30 km

9. A person starts from a place *P* at 6 A.M. and walks to *Q* at 3 km per hour. Another person starts from *P* at 8 A.M. and follows the first on bicycle at 6 km per hour. Both of them reach *Q* at the same time. The distance from *P* to *Q* is:

A. 12 km B. 10 km
C. 8 km D. 6 km

10. A person can row at the rates of x km/hr up a stream and at the rate of y km/hr down the stream. The rate in still water is:

A. $x+y$ B. $x-y$
C. $\frac{x-y}{2}$ D. $\frac{x+y}{2}$

11. In Q. 10, the rate of flow of stream is :

A. $x+y$ B. $x-y$
C. $y-x$ D. $\frac{y-x}{2}$

12. A person can row down a stream at 6 km/hr and up the same stream at 3 km/hr. His rate in still water is :

A. 9 km/hr B. 4.5 km/hr
C. 1.5 km/hr D. 1.0 km/hr

13. In Q. 12, the rate of flow of the stream is :

A. 1.5 km/hr B. 2.5 km/hr
C. 4.5 km/hr D. 18.0 km/hr

14. A man can row at the rate of 9 km per hr in still water. At what rate can he row against a stream flowing 7 km per hour?

A. 8 km/hr B. 7 km/hr
C. 2 km/hr D. –2 km/hr

15. To walk one kilometre *A* takes m minutes and *B*, n minutes. In one hour, the difference of distance travelled by *A* and *B* is:

A. $m-n$ B. $60m-60n$
C. $\frac{60}{m}-\frac{60}{n}$ D. $\frac{60}{mn}$

EXPLANATORY ANSWERS

1. A : Speed $= \frac{36 \text{ km}}{1 \text{ hr}} = \frac{36000 \text{ m}}{3600 \text{ sec}} = 10$ m/s.

2. D : Distance covered by two trains in 1 hour = 38 + 22 = 60 km.

$$\text{Distance} = 900 \text{ km}$$

$$\text{Time taken} = \frac{900}{60} = 15 \text{ hours.}$$

3. B : Let distance = x km.

Time taken in travelling $\frac{x}{2}$ km at the rate of 21 km/hr

$$= \frac{1}{21} \times \frac{x}{2} = \frac{x}{42} \text{ hr.}$$

Time taken in travelling $\frac{x}{2}$ km at the rate of 24 km/hr

$$= \frac{1}{24} \times \frac{x}{2} = \frac{x}{48} \text{ hr}$$

But $\frac{x}{42} + \frac{x}{48} = 10$

$$\frac{8x + 7x}{336} = 10$$

$$15x = 3360$$

$\Rightarrow$ $x = 224$ km.

4. C : Distance = 100 m

$$\text{Speed} = \frac{60 \text{ km}}{1 \text{ hr}} = \frac{60000 \text{ m}}{3600 \text{ sec}} = \frac{50}{3} \text{ m/sec}$$

$$\text{Time} = \frac{\text{Distance}}{\text{Speed}} = \frac{100}{50/3} = \frac{100 \times 3}{50} = 6 \text{ sec.}$$

5. C : $\text{Speed} = \frac{90 \text{ km}}{1 \text{ hr}} = \frac{90000 \text{ m}}{3600 \text{ sec}} = 25 \text{ m/sec.}$

Distance = 150 m.

$$\text{Time} = \frac{\text{Distance}}{\text{Speed}} = \frac{150}{25} = 6 \text{ sec.}$$

6. B : Net speed = Speed of train – speed of man = 65 – 5 = 60 km/hr

$$\text{Speed} = \frac{60 \text{ km}}{1 \text{ hr}} = \frac{60000 \text{ m}}{3600 \text{ sec}} = \frac{50}{3} \text{ m/s}$$

$$\text{Time} = \frac{\text{Distance}}{\text{Speed}} = \frac{100}{50/3} = \frac{100 \times 3}{50} = 6 \text{ sec.}$$

7. C : Net speed = speed of train + speed of man = 55 + 5 = 60 km/hr

For rest of the answer see Q. 6.

8. C : Since, both the persons are moving in opposite direction and start from the same place, distance them after one hour = 5 + 4 = 9 km.

$\therefore$ Distance after 3 hours = 9 × 3 = 27 km.

9. A : Let distance from P to $Q = x$ km

Speed of first person = 3 km/hr

$$\text{Time taken} = \frac{x}{3} \text{ hr}$$

Speed of second person = 6 km/hr

$$\text{Time taken} = \frac{x}{6} \text{ hr}$$

According to problem, $\frac{x}{3} - \frac{x}{6} = 2$

$$\frac{2x - x}{6} = 2$$

$$x = 12$$

$\therefore$ Distance from P to Q = 12 km.

10. D : Rate in still water = $\frac{x+y}{2}$.

11. D : Rate of flow of stream = $\frac{y-x}{2}$.

12. B : Rate of still water = $\frac{6+3}{2}$ = 4.5 km/hr.

13. A : Rate of flow of stream = $\frac{6-3}{2}$ = 1.5 km/hr.

14. C : Rate of rowing against flowing water

= Rate of rowing of man – Rate of flow of the stream

= 9 – 7 = 2 km/hr.

15. C : Distance travelled by A in 1 hour = $\frac{60}{m}$ km

Distance travelled by B in 1 hour = $\frac{60}{n}$ km

$\therefore$ Difference of distance travelled by A and B in 1 hour = $\frac{60}{m} - \frac{60}{n}$.

11

AVERAGE

EXERCISE

1. The heights of 5 students (in cm) are 140, 135, 142, 138, 140. Their average height is :
   A. 136
   B. 138
   C. 139
   D. 140

2. Marks obtained by 10 students are 22, 35, 37, 38, 29, 27, 34, 36, 28, 34. The average marks are :
   A. 30 B. 31
   C. 32 D. 34

3. Average of class I to class V is 29. Average of class I to class III is 31. Average of class IV to class V is:
   A. 25 B. 26
   C. 27 D. 28

4. The average age of a group of 13 boys is 13 years. When two more boys joined the group, the average rose by 2 years. The sum of the ages of the two new boys is :
   A. 50 years
   B. 30 years
   C. 56 years
   D. 26 years

5. A boy of height 165 cm is replaced by another, which decreases the average height of the group of 34 boys by 1 cm. The height of the new boy is :
   A. 132 cm B. 129 cm
   C. 130 cm D. 131 cm

6. The average of five consecutive even numbers, starting with 2, is:
   A. 4 B. 6
   C. 7 D. 5

7. The average of 4, 5, 3.5, 7.5, 9.5 and 6.5 is :
   A. 6.0 B. 5.2
   C. 5.5 D. 5.0

8. The average of 8 numbers is 12. If each number is increased by 2, the average of the new set of numbers is:
   A. 14 B. 12
   C. 15 D. 13

9. The weights of 5 balls in gms are as under 50, 54, 53, 56, 52. The average weight is :
   A. 53 B. 54
   C. 52 D. 51

10. The lengths of 5 pieces of a string in cms are : 5, 5.2, 6.3, 7.2, 6.3. The average length of a piece is:
    A. 5.8 B. 6.0
    C. 6.1 D. 6.2

EXPLANATORY ANSWERS

1. C : Average height $= \frac{140+135+142+138+140}{5} = \frac{695}{5} = 139.$

2. C : Average marks $= \frac{22+35+37+38+29+27+34+36+28+34}{10}$

$$= \frac{320}{10} = 32.$$

3. B : Total students in class I to V = 29 × 5 = 145

Total students in class I to III = 31 × 3 = 93

Total students in class IV and V = 145 – 93 = 52

Average of class IV and V $= \frac{52}{2} = 26.$

4. C : Total age of 13 boys = 13 × 13 = 169 years

Total age of 15 boys = 15(13 + 2) = 15 × 15 = 225 years

Total age of two new boys = 225 – 169 = 56 years.

5. D : Average decrease in height of 34 boys = 1 cm

Total decrease in height of 34 boys = 34 × 1 = 34 cm

∴ Height of the new boy = 165 – 34 = 131 cm.

6. B : Sum of five consecutive even numbers starting with 2

= 2 + 4 + 6 + 8 + 10 = 30

Average = 30 ÷ 5 = 6.

7. A.

8. A : New average = 12 + 2 = 14.

9. A : Average weight $= \frac{50+54+53+56+52}{5} = \frac{265}{5} = 53.$

10. B : Average length $= \frac{5+5.2+6.3+7.2+6.3}{5} = \frac{30.0}{5} = 6.0.$

12

PARTNERSHIP

EXERCISE

1. *X*, *Y* and *Z* invested in a common business. *X* invested ₹ 6000 for 2 months, *Y* invested ₹ 7000 for 4 months and *Z* invested ₹ 6400 for 5 months. Out of a profit of ₹ 900, *X*'s share is:
   A. ₹ 400 B. ₹ 350
   C. ₹ 150 D. ₹ 110
2. *X*, *Y* and *Z* invested ₹ 2400, ₹ 3600 and ₹ 4800 in a business. Out of a profit of ₹ 1260, *X*'s share is :
   A. ₹ 280 B. ₹ 420
   C. ₹ 560 D. ₹ 140
3. *A*, *B* and *C* invested in a common business. *A* invested ₹ 5000 for 2 months, *B* invested ₹ 6000 for 3 months and *C* invested ₹ 4000 for 5 months. Out of a profit of ₹ 960, *A*'s share is:
   A. ₹ 360 B. ₹ 200
   C. ₹ 400 D. ₹ 300
4. *A*, *B* and *C* invested in a common business. *A* invested ₹ 10000 for 3 months, *B* invested ₹ 15000 for 4 months and *C* invested ₹ 12000 for 5 months. Out of a profit of ₹ 1020, *A*'s share is :
   A. ₹ 204 B. ₹ 408
   C. ₹ 612 D. ₹ 816
5. *X*, *Y* and *Z* invested in a common business. *X* invested ₹ 4000 for 2 months, *Y* invested ₹ 2500 for 4 months and *Z* invested ₹ 3000 for 6 months. Out of a profit of ₹ 1800, *X*'s share is :
   A. ₹ 400 B. ₹ 500
   C. ₹ 800 D. ₹ 900
6. *X*, *Y* and *Z* invested ₹ 4800, ₹ 7200 and ₹ 9600 in a business. Out of a profit of ₹ 2520, *Z*'s share is:
   A. ₹ 280 B. ₹ 560
   C. ₹ 840 D. ₹ 1120
7. *A*, *B* and *C* invested ₹ 600, ₹ 900 and ₹ 1200 in a business. Out of a profit of ₹ 549, *A*'s share is:
   A. ₹ 61 B. ₹ 122
   C. ₹ 183 D. ₹ 244
8. *A*, *B* and *C* invested in a common business. *A* invested ₹ 2000 for 5 months, *B* invested ₹ 1200 for 6 months and *C* invested ₹ 2500 for 3 months. Out of a profit of ₹ 494, A's share is :
   A. ₹ 144 B. ₹ 200
   C. ₹ 150 D. ₹ 300
9. *X*, *Y* and *Z* invested ₹ 10000, ₹ 7200 and ₹ 7500 in a common business. Out of a profit of ₹ 988, *X*'s share is :
   A. ₹ 400 B. ₹ 288
   C. ₹ 300 D. ₹ 247

10. *A*, *B* and *C* invested ₹ 1200, ₹ 1800 and ₹ 2400 in a common business. Out of a profit of ₹ 1098, *A*'s share is :

A. ₹ 244 B. ₹ 586
C. ₹ 488 D. ₹ 366

11. *A* and *B* invested ₹ 30000 and ₹ 34000 in a common business. Out of a profit of ₹ 1600, *A*'s share is :

A. ₹ 800 B. ₹ 750
C. ₹ 850 D. ₹ 900

12. Mohan and Ramesh invested ₹ 8000 and ₹ 1000 respectively in a common business. Out of a profit of ₹ 9630, Mohan's share is:

A. ₹ 3210 B. ₹ 4280
C. ₹ 5350 D. ₹ 6420

13. *X*, *Y* and *Z* invested ₹ 2880, ₹ 3600 and ₹ 1800 in a common business. Out of a profit of ₹ 9600, *X*'s share is :

A. ₹ 3360 B. ₹ 4200
C. ₹ 2100 D. ₹ 6300

14. *A*, *B* and *C* invested ₹ 2400, ₹ 3600 and ₹ 4800 in a common business. Out of a profit of ₹ 981, *A*'s share is :

A. ₹ 109 B. ₹ 218
C. ₹ 327 D. ₹ 436

EXPLANATORY ANSWERS

1. C : *X*'s investment for 1 month = ₹ 6000 × 2 = ₹ 12000
Y's investment for 1 month = ₹ 7000 × 4 = ₹ 28000
Z's investment for 1 month = ₹ 6400 × 5 = ₹ 32000

12000 : 28000 : 32000
3 : 7 : 8

Sum of ratio = 3 + 7 + 8 = 18

$X\text{'s share in the profit} = \frac{3}{18}\times 900 = ₹\ 150.$

2. A :

X		*Y*		*Z*
₹ 2400	:	₹ 3600	:	₹ 4800
2	:	3	:	4

Sum of ratio = 2 + 3 + 4 = 9

$X\text{'s share in the profit} = \frac{2}{9}\times 1260 = ₹\ 280.$

3. B : *A*'s investment for 1 month = ₹ 5000 × 2 = ₹ 10000
B's investment for 1 month = ₹ 6000 × 3 = ₹ 18000
C's investment for 1 month = ₹ 4000 × 5 = ₹ 20000

Ratio = 10000 : 18000 : 20000
5 : 9 : 10

Sum of ratio = 5 + 9 + 10 = 24

$A\text{'s share in the profit} = 960\times\frac{5}{24} = ₹\ 200.$

4. A : A's investment = ₹ 10000 × 3 = ₹ 30000

B's investment = ₹ 15000 × 4 = ₹ 60000

C's investment = ₹ 12000 × 5 = ₹ 60000

Ratio = 30000 : 60000 : 60000

1 : 2 : 2

Sum of ratio = 1 + 2 + 2 = 5

A's share in the profit = ₹ $1020 \times \frac{1}{5}$ = ₹ 204.

5. A : X's investment = ₹ 4000 × 2 = ₹ 8000

Y's investment = ₹ 2500 × 4 = ₹ 10000

Z's investment = ₹ 3000 × 6 = ₹ 18000

X : Y : Z = 8000 : 10000 : 18000

4 : 5 : 9

Sum of ratio = 4 + 5 + 9 = 18.

X's share in the profit = $\frac{4}{18} \times 1800$ = ₹ 400.

6. D :

X		Y		Z
4800	:	7200	:	9600
2	:	3	:	4

Sum of ratio = 2 + 3 + 4 = 9

Z's share in the profit = $\frac{4}{9} \times 2520$ = ₹ 1120.

7. B :

A		B		C
600	:	900	:	1200
2	:	3	:	4

Sum of ratio = 2 + 3 + 4 = 9

A's share in the profit = $\frac{2}{9} \times 549$ = ₹ 122.

8. b : A's investment = ₹ 2000 × 5 = ₹ 10000

B's investment = ₹ 1200 × 6 = ₹ 7200

C's investment = ₹ 2500 × 3 = ₹ 7500

Ratio = 10000 : 7200 : 7500

100 : 72 : 75

Sum of ratio = 100 + 72 + 75 = 247

A's share in the profit = $\frac{100}{247} \times 494$ = ₹ 200.

9. A :

X		*Y*		*Z*
10000	:	7200	:	7500
100	:	72	:	75

Sum of ratio = 100 + 72 + 75 = 247

X's share in the profit = $\frac{100}{247} \times 988$ = ₹ 400.

10. A :

A		*B*		*C*
1200	:	1800	:	2400
2	:	3	:	4

Sum of ratio = 2 + 3 + 4 = 9

A's share in the profit = $\frac{2}{9} \times 1098$ = ₹ 244.

11. B :

A		*B*
30000	:	34000
15	:	17

Sum of ratio = 15 + 17 = 32

A's share in the profit = $\frac{15}{32} \times 1600$ = ₹ 750.

12. B : Mohan's investment = ₹ 8000

Ramesh's investment = ₹ 10000

Ratio = 8000 : 10000 = 4 : 5

Sum of ratio = 4 + 5 = 9

Mohan's share in the profit = $\frac{4}{9} \times \text{Rs.}9630$ = ₹ 4280.

13. A :

X		*Y*		*Z*
2880	:	3600	:	1800
8	:	10	:	5

Sum of ratio = 9 + 10 + 5 = 23

X's share in the profit = $\frac{8}{23} \times 9660$ = ₹ 3360.

14. B :

A		*B*		*C*
2400	:	3600	:	4800
2	:	3	:	4

Sum of ratio = 2 + 3 + 4 = 9

A's share in the profit = $\frac{2}{9} \times 981$ = ₹ 218.

13

MIXTURE AND ALLIGATION

1. Rule of Alligation:

$$\frac{\text{Amount of Cheaper ingredient}}{\text{Amount of Dearer ingredient}} = \frac{\text{Cost price of Dearer} - \text{Mean Price}}{\text{Mean Price} - \text{Cost Price of Cheaper}}$$

Here cost price of unit quantity of the mixture is called the *Mean Price*. The above rule may be represented schematically as under:

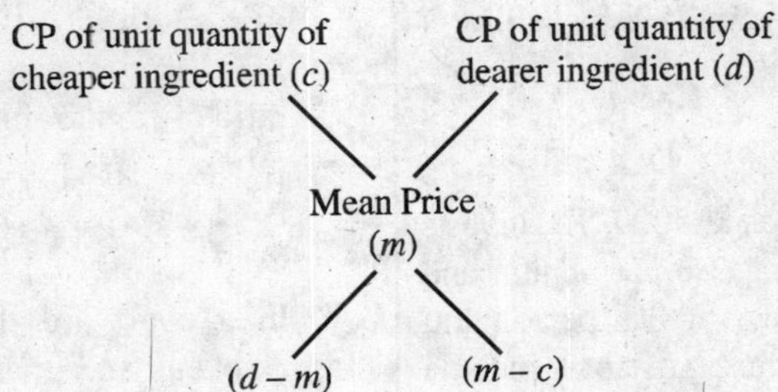

(Cheaper quantity) : (Dearer quantity) = $(d - m) : (m - c)$

This relationship is very helpful in solving problems on mixture involving percentage values, rates, prices, speeds etc.

2. m gm of sugar solution has x % sugar in it. To increase the sugar content in the solution to y %,

$$\text{quantity of sugar need to be added} = \frac{m(y-x)}{100-y}$$

3. A vessel contains x litres of liquid A. y litres are withdrawn and replaced by liquid B. Next y litres of the mixture is withdrawn and again replaced by liquid B.
This operation is repeated n times.

$$\frac{\text{Quantity of liquid A left after } n\text{th operation}}{\text{Whole quantity of liquid A initially present}} = \left(\frac{x-y}{x}\right)^n \text{ or } \left(1-\frac{y}{x}\right)^n$$

EXERCISE

1. Two vessels A and B contain mixture of milk and water in the ratio 4 : 1 and 9 : 11 respectively. They are mixed in the ratio of 3 : 2. Find the ratio of milk : water in the resulting mixture.
   A. 34 : 16 B. 33 : 17
   C. 16 : 34 D. 17 : 33
2. In what ratio must water be added to spirit to gain 25% by selling it at cost price?
   A. 1 : 4 B. 4 : 1
   C. 3 : 4 D. 4 : 3
3. A person has ₹ 5000. He invests a part of it at 3% per annum and the remainder at 8% per annum simple interest. His total income in 3 years is ₹ 750. Find the sum invested at different rates of interest.
   A. ₹ 2000 and ₹ 3000
   B. ₹ 2500 and ₹ 2500
   C. ₹ 3000 and ₹ 2000
   D. ₹ 2750 and ₹ 2250
4. A person covers a distance of 100 kms in 10 hours, partly by walking at 7 km/hr and rest by running at 12 km/hr. Find the distance covered in each part.
   A. 48 kms B. 72 kms
   C. 108 kms D. 124 kms
5. A vessel contains 80 litres of milk. 16 litres of milk was taken out of the vessel and replaced by water. Then 16 litres of mixture was withdrawn and again replaced by water. The operation was repeated for third time. How much milk is now left in the vessel?
   A. 96.40 litres
   B. 50.36 litres
   C. 40.96 litres
   D. 32.76 litres
6. If 4 kg of an alloy made of 1/4th iron and rest is mixed with 6 kg of another alloy made of 2/3rd iron and rest tin, find the ratio of iron to tin in the resultant mixture.
   A. 1 : 1 B. 2 : 1
   C. 1 : 2 D. 3 : 2
7. In a courtyard there are many chickens and goats. If heads are counted, it comes to 100 but when legs are counted, it comes to 320. Find the number of chickens and goats in the courtyard.
   A. 20, 50 B. 30, 70
   C. 40, 60 D. 50, 50
8. A container is full of milk. One-third of milk is taken out of it and replaced by same quantity of water. Then again one-third of the mixture is taken out of it and replaced by the same quantity of water. The process is repeated 4 times. If 16 litres of milk is left in the container at the end of 4th operation, find the capacity of the container.
   A. 76 litres B. 81 litres
   C. 82 litres D. 85 litres

9. The cost of type-I rice is ₹ 15 per kg and type-II is ₹ 20 per kg. If both type I and type II are mixed in the ratio of 2 : 3, then find the price per kg of the mixed variety.

A. ₹ 19.50
B. ₹ 19
C. ₹ 18.50
D. ₹ 18

10. A cask full of wine from which 8 litres are drawn and is then filled with water. This operation is performed three more times. The ratio of quantity of wine left in the cask to that of the water is 16 : 81. How much wine did the cask hold originally?

A. 42 litres B. 32 litres
C. 24 litres D. 18 litres

EXPLANATORY ANSWERS

1. B: Fraction is *Milk* *Water*

A: $\frac{4}{5}$ $\frac{1}{5}$

B: $\frac{9}{20}$ $\frac{11}{20}$

$(3A + 2B) = A \text{ and } B : \left(\frac{12}{5}+\frac{9}{10}\right) \left(\frac{3}{5}+\frac{11}{10}\right)$

$\frac{33}{10}$ $\frac{17}{10}$

So, Ratio of milk : water in the resulting mixture = 33 : 17.

2. A: Let cost price of spirit be Re. 1 per litre.

Then SP of mixture = Re. 1 per litre

Gain = 25%

So, CP of mixture $= 1 \times \frac{100}{125} = \text{Re. } \frac{4}{5}$

We assume that CP of water is zero.

Using alligation rule on cost price,

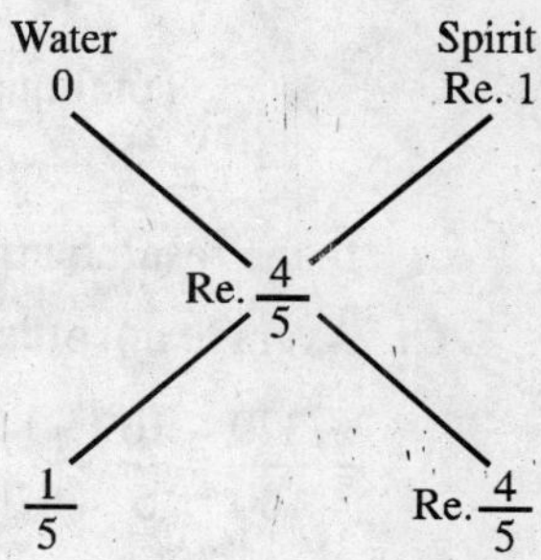

Water should be mixed to spirit in the ratio $\frac{1}{5} : \frac{4}{5}$ or 1 : 4.

3. C: Average rate of interest $= \dfrac{100 \times 750}{5000 \times 3} = 5\%$ per annum

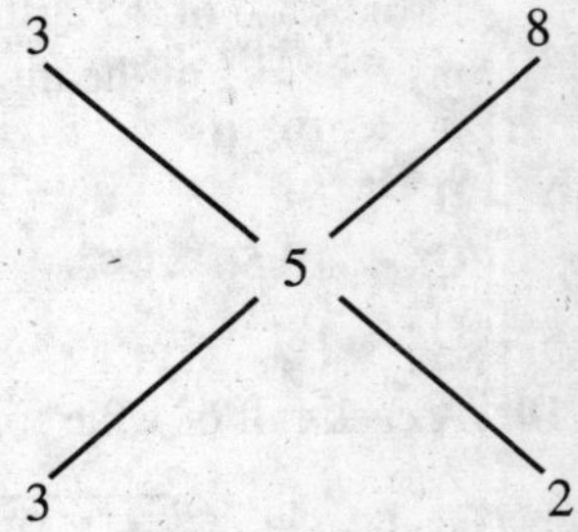

Investment at 3% per annum

$= \dfrac{3}{3+2} \times 5000 = ₹\ 3000$

Investment at 8% per annum

$= \dfrac{2}{3+2} \times 5000 = ₹\ 2000.$

4. B: Average speed $= \dfrac{100}{10} = 10$ km/hr.

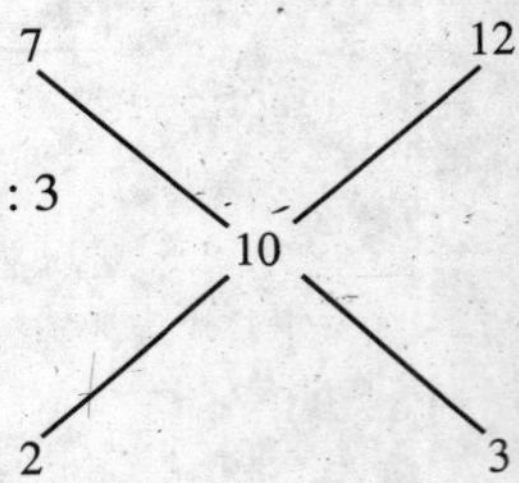

Ratio of time taken at 7 km/hr to 12 km/hr = 2 : 3

Time taken at 7 km/hr $= \dfrac{2}{2+3} \times 10 = 4$ hrs.

Distance covered at 7 km/hr = 7 × 4 = 28 km.

Distance covered at 12 km/hr = 100 – 28 = 72 km.

5. C: Amount of milk left $= 80\left(1-\dfrac{16}{80}\right)^3 = 80\left(\dfrac{4}{5}\right)^3$

$80 \times \dfrac{64}{125} = 40.96$ litres.

6. A: Total quantity of iron $= 4\left(\dfrac{1}{4}\right) + 6\left(\dfrac{2}{3}\right) = 1 + 4 = 5$ kg.

Total quantity of tin $= (4+6) - 5$

$= 5$ kg.

In the resultant mixture, iron : tin = 5 : 5 or 1 : 1.

7. C: Average no. of legs per head

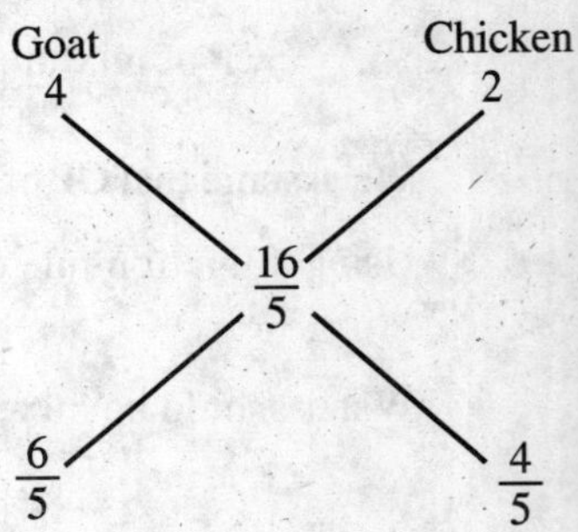

$= \dfrac{320}{100} = \dfrac{16}{5}$

or, 3 : 2

No. of goats $= \dfrac{3}{3+2} \times 100 = 60$

No. of chickens = 100 – 60 = 40.

8. B: Let capacity of the container be x litre; then

$$x(1-1/3)^4 = 16 \Rightarrow x\left(\frac{2}{3}\right)^4 = 16 \quad \Rightarrow x \times \frac{16}{81} = 16 \quad \therefore\ x = 81 \text{ litres}$$

9. D: Let the price per kg of mixed variety be ₹ x; then

By the rule of alligation,

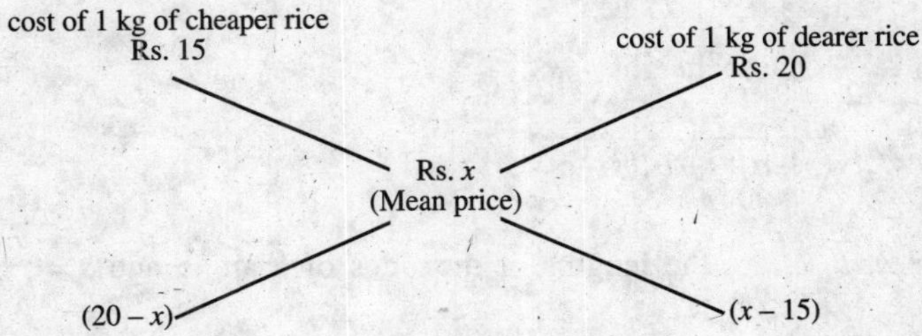

$$\text{Now, } \frac{20-x}{x-15} = \frac{2}{3} \quad \Rightarrow 60 - 3x = 2x - 30 \quad \Rightarrow 5x = 90 \ \therefore\ x = ₹\ 18$$

10. C: Let x litres wine cask hold originally, then

$$\frac{x\left(1-\frac{8}{x}\right)^4}{x} = \frac{16}{81} \Rightarrow \left(1-\frac{8}{x}\right)^4 = \left(\frac{2}{3}\right)^4 \Rightarrow \left(1-\frac{8}{x}\right) = \frac{2}{3}$$

$$\Rightarrow \frac{8}{x} = 1 - \frac{2}{3} \quad \Rightarrow \frac{8}{x} = \frac{1}{3} \quad \therefore\ x = 24 \text{ litres}$$

14

MENSURATION

Triangle

1. Perimeter = 3 × side (Equilateral triangle)
2. Area $= \frac{1}{2} \times \text{base} \times \text{height}$, or

   Area $= \sqrt{s(s-a)(s-b)(s-c)}$

   where *a, b, c,* are the lengths of the sides of triangle and $s = \frac{a+b+c}{2}$

Equilateral Triangle : All three sides are equal in length and all three angles are equal to 60°.

$$\text{Area} = \frac{\sqrt{3}}{4} \times (\text{Side})^2$$

Isosceles Triangle : Two sides are equal in lengths.

1. Area $= \frac{b}{4}\sqrt{4a^2 - b^2}$

   where a = lengths of equal sides $\qquad$ b = length of unequal side
2. In an isosceles right triangle,

   (a) Hypotenuse $= \sqrt{2} \times \text{congruent side (a)}$

   (b) Area $= \frac{1}{2} \times a^2$

   (c) Perimeter $= \sqrt{2} \times a\left(\sqrt{2} + 1\right)$

Rectangle :

1. Area = length(l) × breadth(b)
2. Perimeter = $2(l + b)$
3. Diagonal $= \sqrt{l^2 + b^2}$

Square :

1. Area = $(\text{Side})^2$
2. Perimeter = 4 × side
3. Diagonal = $\text{side} \times \sqrt{2}$

Parallelogram: Area = Base × Height.

Trapezium : Area = $\frac{1}{2} \times \text{Height} \times$ (Sum of parallel sides). Here, height is the distance between the two parallel sides.

Rhombus :

1. Area = $\frac{1}{2} \times \text{Product of diagonals}$
2. Side = $\sqrt{\left(\frac{d_1}{2}\right)^2 + \left(\frac{d_2}{2}\right)^2}$, where d_1 and d_2 are diagonals
3. Perimeter = 4 × side

Quadrilateral : Area = $\frac{1}{2} \times$ One diagonal × (Sum of perpendicular to it from the opposite vertices) = $\frac{1}{2} \times d \times (a+b)$

Circle :

1. Diameter = 2 × Radius
2. Area = $\pi r^2 = \frac{\pi}{4} d^2$; where d = diameter = $\sqrt{\frac{4A}{\pi}}$
3. Circumference = $2\pi r = \pi d$
4. Radius = $\frac{\text{Circumference}}{2\pi} = \frac{\sqrt{\text{Area}}}{\pi}$
5. Length of an Arc = $\frac{\theta}{360°} \times 2\pi r$
6. Area of sector = $\frac{\theta}{360°} \times \pi r^2 = \frac{1}{2} \times \text{Arc} \times r$

Polygon :

1. Interior angle + Exterior angle = 180°
2. Each interior angle = $\left(\frac{2n-4}{n}\right) \times 90°$

where n = number of sides

3. Sum of Exterior angles = 360°
4. Perimeter = Number of sides × Length of side.
5. For an equilateral triangle of side 'a'

   (a) radius of inscribed circle $=\dfrac{a}{2\sqrt{3}}$

   and side of the triangle $= 2\sqrt{3}r$,

   (b) radius of circumcircle $= \dfrac{a}{\sqrt{3}}$

6. Area of regular polygon $=\dfrac{1}{2}$(No. of sides) (Radius of the inscribed circle)

7. Area of regular hexagon $= \dfrac{3\sqrt{3}}{2}(\text{side})^2 = 2.598\ (\text{side})^2$

8. Area of a regular octagon $= 2\left(\sqrt{2}+1\right)(\text{side})^2 = 4.828\ (\text{side})^2$

9. Area of quadrilateral, $A = \sqrt{s(s-a)(s-b)(s-c)(s-d)}$

   where, $s = \dfrac{a+b+c+d}{2}$

VOLUME AND SURFACE AREA OF SOLIDS

Cuboid : A cuboid has six faces, each one a ractangle. It has 12 edges. For example, a rectangular brick.

Let Length = l, Breadth = b and Height = h, then,

1. Volume = (Length × Breadth × Height)
2. Whole Surface Area = $2(lb + bh + lh)$
3. Diagonal $= \sqrt{l^2 + b^2 + h^2}$
4. Area of 4 walls of a room $= 2 \times h\ (l + b)$

Cube : In a cube, Length = Breadth = Height

1. Volume $= (l)^3$
2. Length $= \sqrt[3]{\text{Volume}}$
3. Whole Surface Area $= 6\ l^2$
4. Diagonal $= l \times \sqrt{3}$
5. Lateral Surface Area $= 4\ l^2$

Cylinder :

1. Volume = $\pi r^2 h$
2. Curved Surface Area = $2\pi rh$
3. Total Surface Area = $2\pi r(r + h)$
   where r = radius, h = height

Spherical Cell :

1. Volume = $\frac{4}{3}\pi\left(R^3 - r^3\right)$
2. Total Surface Area= $4\pi(R^2 - r^2)$
   where R = Outer radius
   r = Inner radius

Sphere :

1. Volume = $\frac{4}{3}\pi r^3$
2. Surface Area = $4\pi r^2$

Semi-sphere :

1. Volume = $\frac{2}{3}\pi r^3$
2. Curved surface area = $2\pi r^2$
3. Total surface area = $3\pi r^2$

Cone :

1. Slant height (l) = $\sqrt{r^2 + h^2}$
2. Volume = $\frac{1}{3}\pi r^2 h$
3. Curved surface area = πrl
4. Total surface area = $\pi r(l + r)$
5. If the depth of the frustum of a cone be k and the radii of its ends are r_1 and r_2, then
   (i) Slant height of the frustum of a cone
   $$= \sqrt{k^2 + (r_1 - r_2)^2}$$
   (ii) Curved surface of the frustum = $\pi(r_1 + r_2)\, l$.
   (iii) Volume = $\frac{\pi k}{3}\left(r_1^2 + r_1 r_2 + r_2^2\right)$

EXERCISE

1. What is the area of a circle whose radius is equal to the side of a square whose perimeter is 112 metres?
A. 176 sq m
B. 2504 sq m
C. 284 sq m
D. None of these

2. The sum of the circumference of a circle and the perimeter of a rectangle is 132 cm. The area of the rectangle is 112 sq cm and breadth of the rectangle is 8 cms. What is the area of the circle?
A. 616 sq cm
B. 540 sq cm
C. 396 sq cm
D. Cannot be determined

3. The total area of a circle and a rectangle is equal to 1166 sq cm. The diameter of the circle is 28 cm. What is the sum of the circumference of the circle and the perimeter of the rectangle if the length of the rectangle is 25 cm?
A. 186 cm
B. 182 cm
C. 184 cm
D. Cannot be determined

4. What would be the cost of laying a carpet on a floor which has its length and breadth in the respective ratio of 32 : 21 and where its perimeter is 212 feet, if the cost per square foot of laying the carpet is ₹ 2.5?
A. ₹ 6,720
B. ₹ 5,420
C. ₹ 7,390
D. None of these

5. A triangle's perimeter is 25 cms. Which of the following may be true or is a possibility?
(*a*) The sides are 7 cms., 7 cms. and 11 cms.
(*b*) It is an equilateral triangle.
(*c*) The value of sides can be in integer only.
A. Only (*a*)
B. Only (*a*) and (*b*)
C. Only (*c*)
D. Only (*b*) and (*c*)

6. What will be the cost of building a fence around a circular field with area equal to 18,634 sq. metres; if the cost of building the fence per metre is ₹ 365?
A. ₹ 1,76,660 B. ₹ 68,01,410
C. ₹ 2,43,250 D. ₹ 56,60,220

7. The area of a square is 196 sq cms whose side is half the radius of a circle. The circumference of the circle is equal to breadth of a rectangle. If perimeter of the rectangle is 712 cm. What is the length of the rectangle?
A. 196 cm B. 186 cm
C. 180 cm D. 190 cm

8. The circumference of a circular plot is 484 metres Find out the area of that circular plot—
A. 15246 metre^2
B. 18634 metre^2
C. 20328 metre^2
D. 13552 metre^2

9. A room measures 22 dm by 16 dm. I wish to buy a carpet for the floor leaving an uncarpeted margin 2 dm wide along each of the shorter sides of the room and a margin 0.5 dm wide along each of the longer sides of the room. If the price of the carpet is ₹ 500 per sq. metre, what is the cost of the whole carpet required?

A. ₹ 500 B. ₹ 2700
C. ₹ 2000 D. ₹ 1350

10. A paper is in the form of a rectangle ABCD where AB = 22 cm and BC = 14 cm. A semi-circular portion with segment BC as a diameter is cut off. Find the area of remaining paper.

A. 231 cm^2 B. 213 cm^2
C. 321 cm^2 D. 200 cm^2

11. How many plants can be put in a circular flower bed whose circumference is 880 dm allowing 35 dm^2 for each plant?

A. 880 B. 1760
C. 1000 D. 1500

12. An athletic track 14 m wide consists of two straight sections 120 m long joining semi-circular ends whose inner radius is 35 m. Calculate the area of the track :

A. 5670 m^2 B. 7065 m^2
C. 5670 m^2 D. 7056 m^2

13. A square park has each side of 100 m. At each corner of the park, there is a flower bed in the form of a quadrant of radius 14 m. Then the area of the remaining part of the park is :

A. 9384 m^2 B. 9834 m^2
C. 9000 m^2 D. 8900 m^2

14. The length of minute hand of a clock is 14 cm. Then the area swept by the minute hand in one minute.

A. 10 m^2 B. 12.26 m^2
C. 20.26 m^2 D. 10.26 m^2

15. Find the area of ring between two concentric circles whose circumference are 77 cm and 55 cm.

A. 770 cm^2 B. 321 cm^2
C. 231 cm^2 D. 230 cm^2

16. A rectangle water reservoir is 10.8 metres long and 3.75 metres wide at base. Water flows into it at the rate of 18 m per sec. through the pipe having the cross section 7.5 cm × 4.5 cm. Then the height to which the water will rise in the reservoir in 30 minutes is :

A. 7.2 m B. 2.7 m
C. 3.7 m D. 7.3 m

17. A rectangular sheet of 44 cm × 18 cm is rolled along its length and a cylinder is formed. Then the volume of cylinder is :

A. 7227 cm^2 B. 7272 cm^2
C. 2727 cm^2 D. 2772 cm^2

18. How many metres of cloth 5 metre wide will be required to make a conical tent, the radius of whose base is 7 metre and height is 24 metre?

A. 100 m B. 110 m
C. 550 m D. 55 m

19. The surface area of a sphere whose volume is 4851 cubic metres is :

A. 1386 m^2 B. 1380 m^2

C. 1286 m^2 D. 3186 m^2

20. A hollow sphere of external and internal diameter 4 cm and 2 cm respectively, is melted into a cone of base diameter 8 cm. Then the height of the cone is :

A. 12 cm B. 14 cm

C. 20 cm D. 24 cm

21. The diamensions of a metallic rod are 19 cm × 4 cm × 2 cm and each side of a metallic cube is 4 cm. Both are melted and recast into a new cube. Find the length of edge of cube so formed.

A. 4 cm B. 5 cm

C. 6 cm D. 7 cm

22. An agricultural field is in the form of a rectangle of length 35 metres and width 15.4 metres. A pit 5.5 metres long, 4 metres wide and 2.5 metres deep is dug in the corner of the field and the earth taken out of the pit is spread uniformly over the remaining area of the field. The extent to which the level of the field has been raised is :

A. 16.6 cm B. 10.6 cm

C. 16.1 cm D. 6.10 cm

23. The side of a square exceeds the side of the another square by 4 cm and the sum of areas of two squares is 400 sq. cm. Find the dimensions of the square.

A. 8 cm, 12 cm

B. 10 cm, 14 cm

C. 12 cm, 16 cm

D. 14 cm, 18 cm

24. The cost of levelling a rectangular field at the rate of 85 paise per square metre is ₹ 624.75. Then the perimeter of the field if its sides are in the ratio of 5 : 3 is :

A. 35 m B. 21 m

C. 112 m D. 49 m

25. The diagonal of a rectangular field is 15 m and its area is 108 sq. m. What will be the total expenditure in fencing the field at the rate of ₹ 5 per metre?

A. ₹ 441 B. ₹ 420

C. ₹ 210 D. ₹ 120

26. The minute hand of a clock is 10 cm long. The area of the face of the clock described by the minute hand between 9 AM and 9.35 AM is :

A. 140 cm^2 B. 183.3 cm^2

C. 180 cm^2 D. 175.3 cm^2

27. The length of a rectangular plot is 60% more than its breadth. If the difference between the length and the breadth of that rectangle is 24 cm, what is the area of that rectangle?

A. 2400 sq. cm

B. 2480 sq. cm

C. 2560 sq. cm

D. Data inadequate

28. The area of a rectangle is 460 square metres. If the length is 15% more than the breadth, what is the breadth of the rectangular field?

A. 15 metres
B. 26 metres
C. 34.5 metres
D. None of these

29. The ratio between the length and the breadth of a rectangular field is 3 : 2. If only the length is increased by 5 metres, the new area of the field will be 2600 sq. metres. What is the breadth of the rectangular field?

A. 40 metres
B. 60 metres
C. 65 metres
D. Cannot be determined

30. If the length and breadth of a rectangular plot be increased by 50% and 20% respectively, then how many times will its area be increased?

A. $1\frac{1}{3}$ B. 2
C. $3\frac{2}{5}$ D. None of these

31. The length of a rectangle is decreased by r%, and the breadth is increased by $(r + 5)$%. Find r, if the area of the rectangle is unaltered.

A. 5 B. 8
C. 10 D. 20

32. The length and breadth of the floor of the room are 20 feet and 10 feet respectively. Square tiles of 2 feet length of different colours are to be laid on the floor. Black tiles are laid in the first row on all sides. If white tiles are laid in the one-third of the remaining and blue tiles in the rest, how many blue tiles will be there?

A. 16 B. 24
C. 32 D. 48

33. A park square in shape has a 3 metre wide road inside it running along its sides. The area occupied by the road is 1764 square metres. What is the perimeter along the outer edge of the road?

A. 576 metres
B. 600 metres
C. 640 metres
D. Data inadequate

34. What will be the length of the diagonal of that square plot whose area is equal to the area of a rectangular plot of length 45 metres and breadth 40 metres?

A. 42.5 metres
B. 60 metres
C. 75 metres
D. Data inadequate

35. The length of one pair of opposite sides of a square is increased by 5 cm on each side; the ratio of the length and the breadth of the newly formed rectangle becomes 3 : 2. What is the area of the original square?

A. 25 sq. cm B. 81 sq. cm
C. 100 sq. cm D. 225 sq. cm

36. What will be the ratio between the area of a rectangle and the area of a triangle with one of the sides of the rectangle as base and a vertex on the opposite side of the rectangle?

A. 1 : 2
B. 2 : 1
C. 3 : 1
D. None of these

37. A cow is tethered in the middle of a field with a 14 feet long rope. If the cow grazes 100 sq. ft. per day, then approximately what time will be taken by the cow to graze the whole field?

A. 2 days B. 6 days
C. 18 days D. 24 days

38. A circular ground whose diameter is 35 metres, has a 1.4 m broad garden around it. What is the area of the garden in square metres?

A. 160.16
B. 176.16
C. 196.16
D. None of these

39. The cost of the paint is ₹ 36.50 per kg. If 1 kg of paint covers 16 square feet, how much will it cost to paint outside of a cube having 8 feet each side?

A. ₹ 692 B. ₹ 768
C. ₹ 876 D. ₹ 972

40. The capacity of a cylindrical tank is 246.4 litres. If the height is 4 metres, what is the diameter of the base?

A. 1.4 m B. 2.8 m
C. 14 m D. 28 m

EXPLANATORY ANSWERS

1. D: ∵ Radius of the circle $= \dfrac{112}{4} = 28$ m

∴ Area of the circle $= \dfrac{22}{7}\times 28\times 28 = 2464$ m^2.

2. A: Length of the rectangle $= \dfrac{112}{8} = 14$ cm.

∴ Perimeter of the rectangle = 2(14 + 8) = 44 cm.

∴ Circumference of the circle = 132 – 44 = 88 cm.

∴ $r = \dfrac{88\times 7}{2\times 22} = 14$ cm

∴ Area of the circle $= \dfrac{22}{7}\times 14\times 14 = 616$ sq cm.

3. B: From question—

$\because$ Diameter of the circle = 28 cm.

$\Rightarrow$ Area of the circle = $\frac{22}{7} \times (14)^2$ = 616 cm^2

$\therefore$ Area of the rectangle = 1166 – 616 = 550 cm^2

$\Rightarrow$ Breadth of the rectangle = $\frac{550}{25}$ = 22 cm.

$\therefore$ Required sum $= 2 \times \frac{22}{7} \times (14) + 2(25 + 22)$

= 88 + 94 = 182 cm.

4. A: Length of the floor = $\frac{212 \times 32}{2 \times (32 + 21)}$ = 64 ft.

and breadth the floor = $\frac{64 \times 21}{32}$ = 42 ft.

$\therefore$ Area of the floor = 64 × 42 = 2688 sq. ft.

$\therefore$ Reqd. cost = ₹ 2688 × 2.5 = ₹ 6720.

5. A: Only statement A may be true or possibility.

6. A: Area of the circular field = 18634 m^2

$\therefore$ πr^2 = 18634

$\therefore$ $r^2 = 18634 \times \frac{7}{22}$ = 5929

$\therefore$ r = 77 m

$\therefore$ Length of the fence $= 2 \times \frac{22}{7} \times 77$ = 484 m

$\therefore$ Total cost = 484 × 365 = ₹ 176660.

7. C: One side of the square = $\sqrt{196}$ = 14 cm

$\therefore$ Radius of the circle = 28 cm

$\therefore$Circumference of the circle = $2 \times \frac{22}{7} \times 28$ = 176 cm

$\therefore$Breadth of the rectangle = 176 cm

$\therefore$Length of the rectangle = $\frac{712}{2} - 176$ = 356 – 176 = 180 cm.

8. B: Let r be the radius of the circular plot then from problem,

$\because$ The circumference of the circular plot = 484 m

$$\Rightarrow \quad 2\pi r = 484$$

$$r = 484 \times \frac{7}{22} \times \frac{1}{2} = 77 \text{ metres}$$

$\therefore$ Area of the circular plot $= \pi r^2 = \frac{22}{7} \times (77)^2 = 18634 \text{ m}^2$.

9. D.

10. A: Area of the whole paper ABCD = 22 × 14 = 308 cm^2

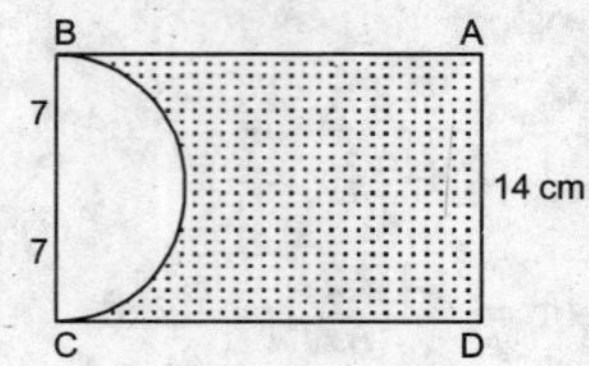

Radius of the semi-circle $= \frac{1}{2} \times 14 \text{ cm} = 7 \text{ cm}$

$\therefore$ Area of the semi-circle $= \frac{1}{2}\pi r^2 = \frac{1}{2} \times \frac{22}{7} \times 7 \times 7 = 77 \text{ cm}^2$

$\therefore$ Area of the remaining part of the paper

$$= 308 \text{ cm}^2 - 77 \text{ cm}^2 = 231 \text{ cm}^2.$$

11. B: Circumference of flower bed = 880 dm

$$\Rightarrow \quad 2\pi r = 880 \text{ dm}$$

$$\Rightarrow \quad r = \frac{880}{2\pi} \text{ dm} = \frac{880 \times 7}{2 \times 22} = 140 \text{ dm}$$

Area of flower bed $= \pi r^2 = \frac{22}{7} \times (140)^2 \text{ dm}^2$

$\therefore$ Required number of plants

$$= \frac{\frac{22}{7} \times 140 \times 140}{35} \text{ dm}^2$$

$$= \frac{22}{7} \times \frac{140 \times 140}{35} = 1760.$$

12. D.

13. A: Area of each quadrant $= \frac{\theta}{360} \times \pi r^2$

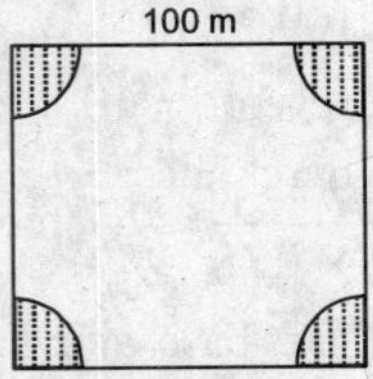

$= \frac{90}{360} \times \frac{22}{7} \times 14 \times 14 \text{ m}^2 = 154 \text{ m}^2$

$\therefore$ Area of 4 quadrants $= 154 \times 4 \text{ m}^2 = 616 \text{ m}^2$

Area of park $= (100)^2 = 10{,}000 \text{ m}^2$

Hence area of the remaining part of the park

$= 10{,}000 - 616 = 9{,}384 \text{ m}^2$.

14. D: Length of minute hand of clock $= r = 14$ cm

Central angle covered in 1 minute $= \frac{360}{60} = 6°$

$\therefore$ Area swept in one minute = Area of sector with central angle 6°

$$= \frac{\theta}{360} \times \pi r^2 = \frac{6}{360} \times \frac{22}{7} \times 14 \times 14$$

$$= \frac{154}{15} = 10.26 \text{ cm}^2.$$

15. C: Let R be the radius of outer circle and r the radius of inner circle.
Circumference of outer circle = 77 cm

$\therefore 2\pi R = 77 \Rightarrow R = \frac{77}{2\pi} = \frac{77 \times 7}{2 \times 22} = \frac{49}{4}$ cm

Circumference of inner circle = 55 cm

$\therefore \quad 2\pi r = 55 \quad \Rightarrow r = \frac{55}{2\pi} = \frac{55 \times 7}{2 \times 22} = \frac{35}{4}$ cm

$\therefore \quad$ Area of ring $= \pi(R^2 - r^2)$

$$= \frac{22}{7} \times \left(\frac{49}{4} + \frac{35}{4}\right)\left(\frac{49}{4} - \frac{35}{4}\right) = 231 \text{ cm}^2$$

16. B: Volume of water that flows in one second

$= (18 \times 0.075 \times 0.045)\ m^3$

Volume of water that flows in 30 minutes

$= 18 \times 0.075 \times 0.045 \times 30 \times 60$

$= 109.35\ m^3$.

Area of the base of the reservoir $= 10.8 \times 3.75\ m^2$

$\therefore$ Height of water $= \dfrac{109.35}{10.8 \times 3.75} = 2.7$ metres.

17. D: Let r cm be the radius of the base and h cm be the height.

Then, $h = 18$ cm.

Now, circumference of the base = Length of the sheed

$\Rightarrow$ Circumference = 44 cm

$\Rightarrow \quad 2\pi r = 44$

$\Rightarrow \quad 2 \times \dfrac{22}{7} \times r = 44$

$\Rightarrow \quad r = 7$ cm

Volume of the cylinder= $\pi r^2 h\ cm^3$

$= \dfrac{22}{7} \times (7)^2 \times 18\ cm^3$

$= 2772\ cm^3$

18. B: Slant height, $l = \sqrt{r^2 + h^2}$

$= \sqrt{7^2 + 24^2} = 25$ metres

Area of curved surface of cone $= \pi rl$

$= \dfrac{22}{7} \times 7 \times 25 = 550\ m^2$

$\therefore$ Area of the cloth required $= 550\ m^2$

$\therefore$ Length of the cloth $= \dfrac{550}{5} = 110$ metres.

19. A.

20. B.

21. C: Volume of the metallic rod $= 19 \times 4 \times 2 = 152$ cu.cm.

Volume of the cube $= 4^3 = 64$ cu. cm.

Total volume of both after melting them

$= 152 + 64 = 216$ cu.cm.

$\therefore$ Volume of new cube = 216 cu. cm.

$\Rightarrow$ Side = 6 cm.

22. B.

23. C: Let S_1 and S_2 be the two squares. Let the side of the square S_1 be x cm. Then the side of the square $S_2 = (x + 4)$ cm.

$\therefore$ Area of square $S_1 = x^2$

and, Area of square $S_2 = (x + 4)^2$

$\therefore$ From question,

$\Rightarrow x^2 + (x + 4)^2 = 400$

Solving the equation,

$\Rightarrow x = -16$ and 12

But x cannot be negative

$\therefore$ Side of the square $S_1 = 12$ cm

$\therefore$ that of square $S_2 = x + 4 = 12 + 4 = 16$ cm.

24. C: Area of the field $= \left(\dfrac{\text{Total cost}}{\text{Rate/metre}^2}\right)$

$= \dfrac{624.75}{0.85} = 735$ sq. metres

Let the length and breadth of the field be $5x$ and $3x$ metres respectively.

Then, its area $= 5x \times 3x = 15x^2$ sq. metres

$\therefore 15x^2 = 735$

$\Rightarrow x^2 = \dfrac{735}{15} = 49$

$\Rightarrow x = 7$

$\therefore$ Length $= 5x = 5 \times 7 = 35$ metres

and breadth $= 3x = 3 \times 7 = 21$ metres

$\therefore$ Perimeter $= 2\,(35 + 21) = 112$ metres.

25. C.

26. B: Angle described by minute hand in 60 minutes = 360°

Angle described by minute hand in 35 minutes $= \dfrac{360}{60} \times 35 = 210°$

$\therefore$ The required area swept by the minute hand = Area of sector $r = 10$ cm

and, $\theta = 210°$

$$= \frac{22}{7} \times 10 \times 10 \times \frac{210}{360}$$

$$= 183.3 \text{ cm}^2.$$

27. C: Let breadth = x cm. Then, length = $\left(\frac{160}{100}x\right)$ cm = $\frac{8}{5}x$ cm.

So, $\frac{8}{5}x - x = 24 \Rightarrow \frac{3}{5}x = 24$

$\Rightarrow x = \left(\frac{24 \times 5}{3}\right) = 40.$

$\therefore$ Length = 64 cm, Breadth = 40 cm.

Area = (64×40) cm^2 = 2560 cm^2.

28. D: Let breadth = x metres. Then, length = $\left(\frac{115x}{100}\right)$ metres.

$\therefore x \times \frac{115x}{100} = 460 \Rightarrow x^2 = \left(\frac{460 \times 100}{115}\right) = 400$

$\Rightarrow x = 20.$

29. A: Let length = $(3x)$ metres and breadth = $(2x)$ metres.

Then, $(3x + 5) \times 2x = 2600$

$\Rightarrow 6x^2 + 10x - 2600 = 0$

$\Rightarrow 3x^2 + 5x - 1300 = 0$

$\Rightarrow (3x + 65)(x - 20) = 0$

$\Rightarrow x = 20.$

$\therefore$ Breadth = $2x$ = 40 m.

30. D:

31. D: Let original length = x and original breadth = y.

Then, original area = xy.

$$\text{New area} = \left[\frac{(100 - r)}{100} \times x\right]\left[\frac{(105 + r)}{100} \times y\right]$$

$$= \left[\left(\frac{10500 - 5r - r^2}{10000}\right)xy\right]$$

$\therefore \left(\frac{10500 - 5r - r^2}{10000}\right)xy = xy \Rightarrow r^2 + 5r - 500 = 0$

$\Rightarrow (r + 25)(r - 20) = 0 \Rightarrow r = 20.$

32. A: Area left after laying black tiles = [(20 – 4) × (10 – 4) sq. ft = 96 sq. ft.

Area under white tiles = $\left(\frac{1}{3}\times 96\right)$ sq. ft = 32 sq. ft

Area under blue tiles = (96 – 32) sq. ft = 64 sq. ft

Number of blue tiles = $\frac{64}{(2\times 2)} = 16.$

33. B: Let the length of the outer edge be x metres. Then, length of the inner edge = $(x - 6)$ m.

$$\begin{aligned}
\therefore \quad x^2 - (x - 6)^2 &= 1764 \\
\Rightarrow \quad x^2 - (x^2 - 12x + 36) &= 1764 \\
\Rightarrow \quad 12x &= 1800 \\
\therefore \quad x &= 150. \\
\therefore \quad \text{Required perimeter} &= (4x)\text{ m} = (4 \times 150)\text{ m} \\
&= 600\text{ m.}
\end{aligned}$$

34. B: Area = (45 × 40) m^2 $\Rightarrow \frac{1}{2} \times (\text{diagonal})^2 = 1800$

$\Rightarrow$ diagonal = 60 m.

35. C: Let original length of each side = x cm.

Then, its area = (x^2) cm^2.

Length of rectangle formed = $(x + 5)$ cm and its breadth = x cm.

$\therefore \frac{x+5}{x} = \frac{3}{2} \Rightarrow 2x + 10 = 3x \Rightarrow x = 10.$

$\therefore$ Original length of each side = 10 cm and its area = 100 cm^2.

36. B: Area of rectangle = lb sq. units.

Area of the triangle = $\frac{1}{2}lb$ sq. units.

$\therefore$ Required ratio = $lb : \frac{1}{2}lb = 2 : 1.$

37. B: Area of the field grazed = $\left(\frac{22}{7} \times 14 \times 14\right)$ sq. ft

$= 616$ sq. ft.

Number of days taken to graze the field = $\frac{616}{100}$ days = 6 days (approx.).

38. D: Radius of the ground = 17.5 m.

Radius of inner circle = (17.5 – 1.4) m = 16.1 m.

Area of the garden = $\pi \times [(17.5)^2 - 16.1)^2]$ m^2

$= \left[\frac{22}{7} \times (17.5 + 16.1)(17.5 - 16.1)\right]$ m^2

$= \left(\frac{22}{7} \times 33.6 \times 1.4\right)$ m^2 = 147.84 m^2.

39. C: Surface area of the cube = (6×8^2) sq. ft = 384 sq. ft.

Quantity of paint required = $\left(\frac{384}{16}\right)$ kg = 24 kg.

$\therefore$ Cost of painting = ₹ (36.50 × 24) = ₹ 876.

40. D: Volume of the tank = 246.4 litres = 246400 cm^3.

Let the radius of the base be r cm. Then,

$$\left(\frac{22}{7} \times r^2 \times 400\right) = 246400 \Rightarrow r^2 = \left(\frac{246400 \times 7}{22 \times 400}\right) = 196 \Rightarrow r = 14.$$

$\therefore$ Diameter of the base = $2r$ = 28 cm.

15

ALGEBRAIC IDENTITIES

It is the branch of mathematics that uses letters and symbols to represent variable quantities and numbers, and to express generalizations about them.

SOME IMPORTANT FORMULAE

A. $a^2 - b^2 = (a + b)(a - b)$
B. $(a + b)^2 = a^2 + 2ab + b^2$
C. $(a - b)^2 = a^2 - 2ab + b^2$
D. $a^3 + b^3 = (a + b)(a^2 - ab + b^2)$
E. $a^3 + b^3 = (a + b)^3 - 3ab(a + b)$
F. $a^3 - b^3 = (a - b)(a^2 + ab + b^2)$
G. $a^3 - b^3 = (a - b)^3 + 3ab(a - b)$
H. $(a + b)^2 = (a - b)^2 + 4ab$
I. $(a - b)^2 = (a + b)^2 - 4ab$
J. $a^3 + b^3 + c^3 - 3abc = (a + b + c)(a^2 + b^2 + c^2 - ab - bc - ca)$
K. If $a + b + c = 0$, then $a^3 + b^3 + c^3 = 3abc$

EXERCISE

1. If $x = 12$ and $y = 4$, the value of $(x+y)^{x/y}$ will be:

A. 4096 B. 3896
C. 4196 D. 5086

2. If $x = 9$, $y = \sqrt{17}$, then the value of $\left(x^2 - y^2\right)^{-1/2}$ will be:

A. 2^{-4} B. 2^2
C. 3^{-3} D. 2^{-3}

3. If $x + y = 2z$, then the value of $\left(\frac{x}{x-z} + \frac{z}{y-z}\right)$ will be:

A. 1 B. 4
C. 3/2 D. 2

4. If $x + y + z = 0$, then the value of $\frac{(x+y)(y+z)(z+x)}{xyz}$ will be:

A. –3 B. –2
C. 0 D. –1

5. If $x + \frac{1}{x} = 3$, the value of $x^4 + \frac{1}{x^4}$ will be:

A. 49 B. 47
C. 37 D. 42

6. If $x^2 + y^2 + z^2 = 115$ and $xy + yz + zx = 27$, then the value of $x + y + z$ will be:

A. ± 15 B. ± 13
C. ± 17 D. ± 19

7. If $x = 17$, $y = 15$ and $z = 13$, then the value of $x^2 + y^2 + z^2 - 2xy - 2xz - 2yz$ will be:

A. 111 B. 109
C. 121 D. 120

8. If $x + y = 1$, then the value of $x^3 + y^3 + 3xy$ will be:

A. 1 B. 4
C. 3 D. 7

9. What will be the value of $x^3 + y^3 + z^3 - 3xyz$ if $x + y + z = 16$ and $xy + yz + zx = 78$?

A. 352 B. 452
C. 342 D. 360

10. Which of the following is equivalent to $(x^4 + y^4)(x^2 + y^2)(x + y)(x - y)$?

A. $x^8 - y^8$
B. $x^{10} - y^{10}$
C. $x^6 - y^6$
D. $x^{12} - y^{12}$

11. If $x^2 = y + z$, $y^2 = z + x$ and $z^2 = x + y$, then the value of $\left(\frac{1}{x+1}+\frac{1}{y+1}+\frac{1}{z+1}\right)$ will be?

A. 4 B. 3
C. 1 D. 2

12. If $2x = a + 3$, then what will be the value of $8x^3 - 18ax$?

A. $a^3 + 27$ B. $a^3 - 27$
C. $a^3 + 25$ D. $a^3 - 36$

13. If $x + y = 8$ and $x - y = 2$, then the value of $x^2 + y^2$ will be:

A. 38 B. 40
C. 42 D. 34

14. If $a^2 + b^2 = 30$ and $a - b = 6$, then the value of ab will be:

A. –3 B. –5
C. 2 D. –6

15. If $a + b + c = 15$ and $a^2 + b^2 + c^2 = 77$, the what will be the value of $ab + bc + ca$?

A. 22 B. 74
C. 20 D. 18

EXPLANATORY ANSWERS

1. A: $(x+y)^{x/y} = (12+4)^{12/4} = (16)^3 = 4096.$ $[\because x = 12, y = 4]$

2. D: $(x^2 - y^2)^{-1/2} = (81-17)^{-1/2}$

$$= (64)^{-1/2} = \frac{1}{\sqrt{64}} = \frac{1}{8} = 2^{-3}.$$

3. A: $\because x + y = 2z \Rightarrow x - z = z - y = -(y - z)$

$$\therefore \frac{x}{x-z}+\frac{z}{y-z}=\frac{x}{-(y-z)}+\frac{z}{y-z}=\frac{z-x}{y-z} = 1.$$ $[\because x - z = z - y]$

4. D: $\because$

$$x + y + z = 0 \Rightarrow x + y = -z$$
$$x + y + z = 0 \Rightarrow y + z = -x$$

and $x + y + z = 0 \Rightarrow z + x = -y$

$$\therefore \quad \frac{(x+y)(y+z)(z+x)}{xyz} = \frac{-z.-x.-y}{xyz} = -1.$$

5. B:

6. B: $\because (x + y + z)^2 = x^2 + y^2 + z^2 + 2\,(xy + yz + zx)$

$\therefore (x + y + z)^2 = 115 + 2 \times 27$

$= 115 + 54 = 169$

$\therefore \; (x + y + z) = \sqrt{169} = \pm\, 13.$

7. C: The given expression is equivalent to $(x - y - z)^2$

$\therefore \quad (x - y - z)^2 = (17 - 15 - 13)^2$

$= (-11)^2 = 121.$

8. A: $\because \quad (x + y)^3 = x^3 + y^3 + 3xy\,(x + y)$

$\therefore \quad (1)^3 = x^3 + y^3 + 3xy \times 1$

$\therefore \quad 1 = x^3 + y^3 + 3xy.$

9. A: $\because (x + y + z) = 16 \Rightarrow (x + y + z)^2 = (16)^2$

$= x^2 + y^2 + z^2 + 2(xy + yz + zx) = 256$

$\therefore x^2 + y^2 + z^2 + 2\times78 = 256 \Rightarrow x^2 + y^2 + z^2$

$= 256 - 156 = 100$

$\therefore \; x^3 + y^3 + z^3 - 3xyz = (x + y + z)\,[(x^2 + y^2 + z^2) - (xy + yz + zx)]$

$= 16[100 - 78]$

$= 16 \times 22 = 352.$

10. A: $\because (x^4 + y^4)(x^2 + y^2)(x + y)(x - y)$

$= (x^4 + y^4)(x^2 + y^2)(x^2 - y^2)$

$= (x^4 + y^4)(x^4 - y^4)$

$= x^8 - y^8.$

11. C:

12. A: $\because 2x = a + 3$

$\Rightarrow \quad (2x)^3 = (a + 3)^3$

$\therefore \quad 8x^3 = a^3 + 27 + 3 \times a \times 3(a + 3)$

$= a^3 + 9a^2 + 27a + 27$

and $\quad 18ax = 9a \times 2x$

$= 9a \times (a + 3) = 9a^2 + 27a$

$\therefore \quad 8x^3 - 18ax = a^3 + 9a^2 + 27a + 27 - 9a^2 - 27a$

$= a^3 + 27.$

13. D: $\because x^2 + y^2 = \dfrac{(x+y)^2 + (x-y)^2}{2}$

$$= \frac{(8)^2 + (2)^2}{2} = \frac{64+4}{2} = \frac{68}{2} = 34.$$

14. A: $\because \quad (a-b)^2 = a^2 + b^2 - 2ab$

$$\Rightarrow \quad ab = \frac{a^2+b^2-(a-b)^2}{2}$$

$$= \frac{30-(6)^2}{2}$$

$$= \frac{30-36}{2} = \frac{-6}{2} = -3.$$

15. B: $\because \; (a+b+c)^2 = a^2 + b^2 + c^2 + 2(ab + bc + ca)$

$$\therefore \quad ab + bc + ca = \frac{(a+b+c)^2-\left(a^2+b^2+c^2\right)}{2}$$

$$= \frac{(15)^2-77}{2} = \frac{225-77}{2}$$

$$= \frac{148}{2} = 74.$$

16

SURDS

Given a number, it is not always possible to find some whole number which when multiplied by itself will give the given number. In other words all given numbers are not perfect square numbers. For example, square root of 9, *i.e.,* $\sqrt{9}$ is 3, which is a whole number. But square root of 15, *i.e.,* $\sqrt{15}$ = 3.873, which is not a whole number.

Hence square roots of natural numbers which are not perfect squares are not rational numbers. These are irrational numbers and are called **Surds**. For example, $\sqrt{3}$, $\sqrt{7}$, $2+\sqrt{11}$, $4+\sqrt{13}$ ..... etc. are **Surds**.

Given below are a few formulas which are quite helpful in solving the problems related to surds:

1. $\sqrt{a}\times\sqrt{a}=a$

2. $\sqrt{a}\times\sqrt{b}=\sqrt{ab}$

3. $\left(\sqrt{a}+\sqrt{b}\right)^2 = a + b + \sqrt[2]{ab}$

4. $\left(\sqrt{a}-\sqrt{b}\right)^2 = a + b - \sqrt[2]{ab}$

5. $x\sqrt{a}+x\sqrt{b}=x\left(\sqrt{a}+\sqrt{b}\right)$

6. $\dfrac{1}{\sqrt{a}+\sqrt{b}}=\dfrac{1}{\sqrt{a}+\sqrt{b}}\times\dfrac{\sqrt{a}-\sqrt{b}}{\sqrt{a}-\sqrt{b}}=\dfrac{\sqrt{a}-\sqrt{b}}{a-b}$

7. $\dfrac{1}{\sqrt{a}-\sqrt{b}}=\dfrac{1}{\sqrt{a}-\sqrt{b}}\times\dfrac{\sqrt{a}+\sqrt{b}}{\sqrt{a}+\sqrt{b}}=\dfrac{\sqrt{a}+\sqrt{b}}{a-b}$

8. $a+\sqrt{b} = c+\sqrt{d} \Rightarrow a = c$ and $b = d$

9. $\sqrt{2}$ = 1.41421, $\sqrt{3}$ = 1.73205, $\sqrt{5}$ = 2.23607,

$\sqrt{6}$ = 2.4494

$\sqrt{7}$ = 2.64575, $\sqrt{8}$ = 2.82842, $\sqrt{10}$ = 3.16227,

$\sqrt{11}$ = 3.31662

EXERCISE

1. What will be the value of $\frac{1}{\sqrt{3}}$ upto 3 decimal places?
A. 0.577 B. 0.477
C. 0.673 D. 0.575

2. If $\sqrt{2}$ = 1.4122, the value of $\frac{1}{2}\left(\frac{\sqrt{2}-1}{\sqrt{2}+1}\right)$ is:
A. .0768 B. .0658
C. .0858 D. .0458

3. If $\sqrt{1936}=44$, the value of $\sqrt{19.36}+\sqrt{0.1936}$ + $\sqrt{.001936}$ upto 3 decimal places will be:
A. 5.679 B. 4.884
C. 9.884 D. 6.778

4. Value of $\frac{\sqrt{2}-1}{\sqrt{2}+1}$ upto 3 decimal places will be:
A. 0.172 B. 0.158
C. 0.176 D. 0.188

5. $\sqrt[3]{8^4}$ is equivalent to:
A. 15 B. 9
C. 16 D. 25

6. If $\sqrt{6}$ = 2.45, the value of $\sqrt{\frac{2}{3}}+3\sqrt{3/2}$ will be equivalent to:
A. 3.942 B. 4.492
C. 4.942 D. 9.345

7. $\sqrt{72}$ is equivalent to:
A. $3\sqrt{5}$ B. $6\sqrt{2}$
C. $8\sqrt{2}$ D. $7\sqrt{3}$

8. What will be the value of $\left(\sqrt{80}+3\times\sqrt{245}-\sqrt{125}\right)$?
A. $18\sqrt{5}$ B. $20\sqrt{5}$
C. $22\sqrt{5}$ D. $28\sqrt{2}$

9. Value of $\left(\frac{\sqrt{5}+\sqrt{3}}{\sqrt{5}-\sqrt{3}}\right)$ will be equivalent to :
A. $4+\sqrt{15}$ B. $3-\sqrt{15}$
C. $2+\sqrt{15}$ D. $4-\sqrt{15}$

10. The expression $\left(\frac{\sqrt{7}+\sqrt{5}}{\sqrt{7}-\sqrt{5}}\right)$ is equivalent to:
A. $6-\sqrt{35}$ B. $2+\sqrt{35}$
C. $4-\sqrt{35}$ D. $6+\sqrt{35}$

EXPLANATORY ANSWERS

1. A: $\because\ \frac{1}{\sqrt{3}}=\frac{1}{\sqrt{3}}\times\frac{\sqrt{3}}{\sqrt{3}}=\frac{\sqrt{3}}{3}=\frac{1.732}{3}=0.577$.

2. C: $\because\ \frac{1}{2}\left(\frac{\sqrt{2}-1}{\sqrt{2}+1}\right)=\frac{1}{2}\times\frac{\sqrt{2}-1}{\sqrt{2}+1}\times\frac{\sqrt{2}-1}{\sqrt{2}-1}=\frac{1}{2}\times\frac{\left(\sqrt{2}-1\right)^2}{\left(\sqrt{2}\right)^2-1^2}$

$$= \frac{1}{2} \times \frac{2+1-2\sqrt{2}}{2-1} = \frac{1}{2} \times \frac{3-2\sqrt{2}}{1} = \frac{1}{2} \times (3-2\times 1.4142)$$

$$= \frac{1}{2} \times 0.1716 = .0858$$

3. B: $\because \sqrt{1936} = 44 \Rightarrow \sqrt{19.36} = 4.4$

$\Rightarrow \sqrt{0.1936} = 0.44$

$\Rightarrow \sqrt{.001936} = .044$

$\therefore \sqrt{19.36} + \sqrt{0.1936} + \sqrt{.001936}$

$= 4.4 + 0.44 + .044 = 4.884.$

4. A: $\because \frac{\sqrt{2}-1}{\sqrt{2}+1} = \frac{\sqrt{2}-1}{\sqrt{2}+1} \times \frac{\sqrt{2}-1}{\sqrt{2}-1} = \frac{\left(\sqrt{2}-1\right)^2}{\left(\sqrt{2}\right)^2 - (1)^2} = \frac{2+1-2\sqrt{2}}{2-1}$

$$= \frac{3-2\sqrt{2}}{1} = 3 - 2 \times 1.414 = 0.172.$$

5. C: $\sqrt[3]{8^4} = (8)^{\frac{4}{3}} = \left(2^3\right)^{\frac{4}{3}} = 2^{3\times\frac{4}{3}} = 2^4 = 16 \cdot$

6. B: $\because \sqrt{\frac{2}{3}} + 3\sqrt{\frac{3}{2}} = \frac{\sqrt{2}}{\sqrt{3}} \times \frac{\sqrt{3}}{\sqrt{3}} + 3 \times \frac{\sqrt{3}}{\sqrt{2}} \times \frac{\sqrt{2}}{\sqrt{2}}$

$$= \frac{\sqrt{6}}{3} + \frac{3\sqrt{6}}{2} = \sqrt{6}\left[\frac{1}{3} + \frac{3}{2}\right] = \sqrt{6} \times \frac{11}{6} = \frac{11}{6} \times 2.45 = 4.492 .$$

7. B: $\because \sqrt{72} = \sqrt{6\times 6\times 2} = \sqrt{6^2 \times 2} = 6\sqrt{2} \cdot$

8. B: $\because \sqrt{80} + 3 \times \sqrt{245} - \sqrt{125}$

$= \sqrt{16\times 5} + 3\times\sqrt{49\times 5} - \sqrt{25\times 5}$

$= 4\sqrt{5} + 21\sqrt{5} - 5\sqrt{5} = 20\sqrt{5} \cdot$

9. A: $\because \dfrac{\sqrt{5}+\sqrt{3}}{\sqrt{5}-\sqrt{3}} = \dfrac{\sqrt{5}+\sqrt{3}}{\sqrt{5}-\sqrt{3}} \times \dfrac{\sqrt{5}+\sqrt{3}}{\sqrt{5}+\sqrt{3}}$

$$= \frac{\left(\sqrt{5}+\sqrt{3}\right)^2}{\left(\sqrt{5}\right)^2-\left(\sqrt{3}\right)^2} = \frac{5+3+2\sqrt{15}}{5-3}$$

$$= \frac{8+2\sqrt{15}}{2} = 4+\sqrt{15}$$

10. D: $\because \dfrac{\sqrt{7}+\sqrt{5}}{\sqrt{7}-\sqrt{5}} = \dfrac{\sqrt{7}+\sqrt{5}}{\sqrt{7}-\sqrt{5}} \times \dfrac{\sqrt{7}+\sqrt{5}}{\sqrt{7}+\sqrt{5}}$

$$= \frac{\left(\sqrt{7}+\sqrt{5}\right)^2}{\left(\sqrt{7}\right)^2-\left(\sqrt{5}\right)^2}$$

$$= \frac{7+5+2\sqrt{35}}{7-5} = \frac{12+2\sqrt{35}}{2} = 6+\sqrt{35}.$$

17

TRIANGLES AND ITS VARIOUS KINDS

Properties of geometrical figures:

(*i*) **Equilateral triangle:** All sides are equal.

(*ii*) **Isosceles triangle:** Two sides are equal.

(*iii*) **Rhombus:** All sides are equal and no angle is a right angle, but diagonals are at right angles and unequal.

(*iv*) **Square:** All sides are equal and each angle is right angle. The diagonals are also equal.

(*v*) **Parallelogram:** Opposite sides are parallel and equal, diagonals bisect each other.

(*vi*) **Rectangle:** Opposite sides are equal and each angle is a right angle, diagonals are equal.

Co-ordinates of standard points:

(*i*) *Centroid of a triangle:*

The point is the intersection of the medians. This point divides each median in the ratio 2 : 1, its co-ordinates are

$$G_1\left(\frac{x_1+x_2+x_3}{3}, \frac{y_1+y_2+y_3}{3}\right)$$

(*ii*) *Incentre of a triangle:*

This is the centre of the circle which touches the sides of a given triangle, it is the point of intersection of the internal bisectors of the angles of the triangle, its co-ordinates are given by the formula

$$I=(x,y) \text{ where } x=\frac{ax_1+bx_2+cx_3}{a+b+c}$$

$$y=\frac{ay_1+by_2+cy_3}{a+b+c}$$

where (a, b, c) are the lengths of the triangle

(*iii*) *Orthocentre of a triangle:*

The point H is the intersection of the altitudes.

(*iv*) The points O, G, H are collinear and G divides OH in the ratio 1 : 2.

EXERCISE

1. The points A (12, 8), $B(-2, 6)$ and C (6, 0) are vertices of :

A. right angled triangle
B. isosceles triangle
C. equilateral triangle
D. None of these

2. The points (1, 1) (–1, –1) and $(-\sqrt{3}, \sqrt{3})$ are the angular points of a triangle, then the triangle is:

A. right angled
B. isosceles
C. equilateral
D. None of these

3. Two vertices of a triangle are the points (1, 4) and (7, 2). Its centroid is the point (5, 3), then the third vertex is :

A. (3, 7) B. (7, 3)
C. (1, 1) D. (0, 0)

4. Let the vertices of a triangle be (0, 0), (3, 0) and (0, 4), then its orthocentre is :

A. (0, 0)
B. $\left(1, \frac{4}{3}\right)$
C. $\left(\frac{3}{2}, 2\right)$
D. None of these

5. Distance of (2, 3) from origin is:

A. 2 B. 5
C. –1 D. $\sqrt{13}$

6. Find the values of y for which the distance between the points P(2, –3) and Q(10, y) is 10 units.

A. 8, 2 B. –9, 3
C. –9, 5 D. –8, 2

7. The centroid of the triangle whose vertices are A(4, –6), B(3, –2) and C(5, 2) is :

A. 3, 2 B. 4, 1
C. 4, –2 D. 4, 3

8. If (7, 3), (6, 1), (8, 2) and (P, 4) are the vertices of a parallelogram taken in order then the value of P is :

A. 4 B. 6
C. 7 D. 9

9. If the vertices of rhombus are (3, 0), (4, 5), (–1, 4) and (–2, –1) taken in order then area of rhombus is :

A. 20 square units
B. 24 square units
C. 22 square units
D. 26 square units

10. Find the value of P for which the points A(–1, 3), B(2, P) and C(5, –1) are collinear :

A. 3 B. 1
C. 2 D. 4

EXPLANATORY ANSWERS

1. A: $BC^2 + CA^2 = AB^2$.

2. C: $BC^2 = CA^2 = AB^2$.

3. B: $5 = \frac{\Sigma x}{3},\ 3 = \frac{\Sigma y}{3}$.

4. A: The two altitudes *i.e.*, *x*-axis and *y*-axis of ΔOAB meet at origin.

5. D:

$AB = \sqrt{(2-0)^2 + (3-0)^2} = \sqrt{4+9} = \sqrt{13}$

6. B: $\because$ PQ = 10

$\Rightarrow \sqrt{(10-2)^2 + (y+3)^2} = 10$

$\sqrt{64 + y^2 + 9 + 6y} = 10$

Squaring both sides,

$y^2 + 6y - 27 = 0$

$\Rightarrow y^2 + 9y - 3y - 27 = 0$

$\Rightarrow y(y + 9) - 3(y + 9) = 0$

$\Rightarrow (y + 9)(y - 3) = 0$

$\Rightarrow y = -9, y = 3$

$\therefore y = -9, 3$

7. C:

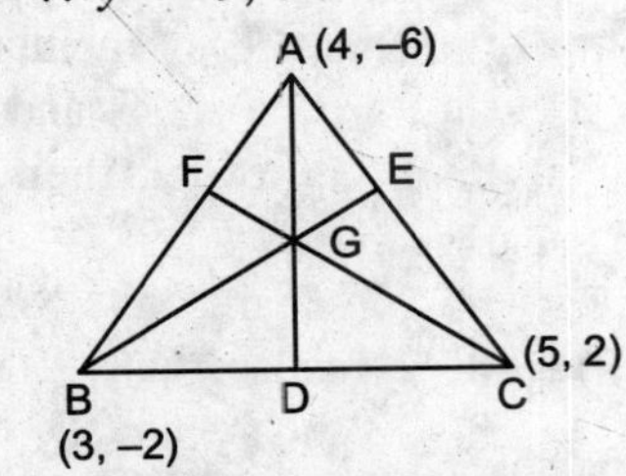

The centroid of the triangle G(*x*, *y*)

$= G\left(\frac{4+3+5}{3}, \frac{-6-2+2}{3}\right)$

$= G(4, -2)$

8. D:

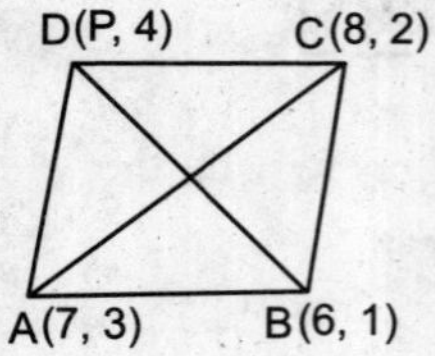

We know that the diagonals of a parallelogram bisect each other. Mid-point of AC and BD coincide.

Hence, $\left(\frac{7+8}{2}, \frac{3+2}{2}\right) = \left(\frac{6+P}{2}, \frac{1+4}{2}\right)$

$\Rightarrow \quad \left(\frac{6+P}{2}, \frac{5}{2}\right) = \left(\frac{15}{2}, \frac{5}{2}\right)$

Equating the x-co-ordinate, we get

$$\frac{6+P}{2} = \frac{15}{2} \Rightarrow P = 9$$

9. B: We know that area of rhombus

$$= \frac{1}{2} \times AC \times BD = \frac{1}{2} \times \sqrt{(-1-3)^2 + (4-0)^2} \times \sqrt{(-2-4)^2 + (-1-5)^2}$$

$$= \frac{1}{2}\sqrt{32} \times \sqrt{72} = \frac{1}{2} \times 4\sqrt{2} \times 6\sqrt{2}$$

$$= \frac{1}{2} \times 48 = 24 \text{ square units.}$$

10. B: Points A, B, C are collinear

$\Rightarrow$ Area of $\Delta ABC = 0$

$$\frac{1}{2}[-1\,(P + 1) + 2(-1 - 3) + 5(3 - P) = 0$$

$$\Rightarrow \frac{1}{2}[-6P + 6] = 0 \Rightarrow 3P = 3 \Rightarrow P = 1.$$

18

SIMILARITY OF TRIANGLES

Two triangles are said to be similar, if

(*i*) their corresponding angles are equal and

(*ii*) their corresponding sides are in the same ratio (*i.e.* proportional).

Also, we know that :

(*i*) If corresponding angles of two triangles are equal, then they are known as equiangular triangles.

(*ii*) Two line segments are divided proportionally when the ratio of the lengths of the segments of one of them is equal to the ratio of the lengths of the segments of the other.

EXERCISE

1. Two similar triangles have
A. equal sides
B. equal areas
C. equal angles
D. None of these

2. Two congruent triangles have
A. proportional sides
B. equal sides
C. equal corresponding sides
D. equal corresponding angles

3. Which of the following is false for two congruent triangles
A. Corresponding angles are equal.
B. Two sides and included angles are equal.
C. Corresponding sides are equal.
D. Two angles and one side are equal.

4. If the sides of a triangle are 8 cm, 12 cm and 15 cm then the angle is
A. Right angle
B. Obtuse angle
C. Acute angle
D. None of these

5. If two triangles are on the same base and between the parallel lines then they will be
A. equilaterals
B. right angled
C. equal in area
D. congruent

6. If the three heights of a traingle are equal then it is
A. right angled triangle
B. obtuse angled triangle
C. equilateral triangle
D. None of these

7. If two corresponding sides and the angle between them of a traingle are equal to another triangle. Then the angles are :

A. congruent but not similar
B. similar but not congruent
C. neither congruent nor similar
D. congruent and similar.

8. Ratio of areas of two similar triangles is equal to :

A. ratio of squares of the corresponding altitudes
B. ratio of squares of corresponding medians.
C. Either (A) or (B)
D. (A) and (B) both

9. If the areas of two similar triangles are equal then the triangles :

A. are congruent
B. have equal length of corresponding sides
C. (A) and (B)
D. None of these

10. Two isosceles triangles have equal vertical angles and their areas are in the ratio of 9 : 25 then the ratio between their corresponding heights is :

A. 5 : 3 B. 25 : 9
C. 3 : 5 D. 16 : 9

EXPLANATORY ANSWERS

1. C: equal angles
2. C: equal corresponding sides
3. D: Two angles and one side are equal.
4. C: Acute angle
5. C: equal in area
6. C: equilateral triangle
7. C: neither congruent nor similar
8. D: (A) and (B) both
9. C. (A) and (B)
10. C: According to equestion

$$\angle A = \angle D \text{ and } \frac{ar(\Delta ABC)}{ar(\Delta DEF)} = \frac{9}{25}$$

Since, $AB = AC$ (given) ....(*i*)

$DE = DF$ (given) ....(*ii*)

Dividing (*i*) by (*ii*)

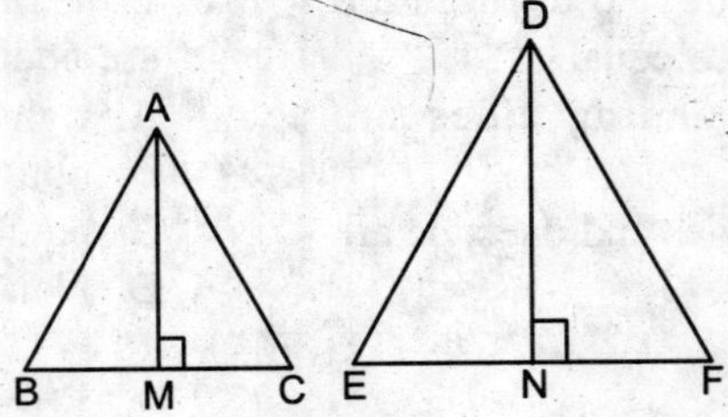

$$\frac{AB}{DE} = \frac{AC}{DF} \qquad ...(iii)$$

Hence, $\Delta ABC \sim \Delta DEF$ [By SAS criterion of similar Δs]

In ΔAMC and ΔDNF

$\angle AMC = \angle DNF = 90°$

$\angle C = \angle F$ (because $\Delta ABC \sim \Delta DEF$)

$\therefore \angle AMC \sim DNF$ (By AA Criterion of similar Δs)

$$\therefore \quad \frac{AC}{DF} = \frac{AM}{DN}$$

$$\text{and,} \quad \frac{ar\,(\Delta\,ABC)}{ar\,(DEF)} = \frac{AC^2}{DF^2} = \frac{AM^2}{DN^2}$$

$$\therefore \quad \frac{AM^2}{DN^2} = \frac{9}{25} \Rightarrow \frac{AM}{DN} = \frac{3}{5}$$

Hence required ratio = 3 : 5

19

CIRCLE AND TANGENTS

A circle is a set of those points in a plane that are at a given constant distance from a given fixed point in the plane. The fixed point is called the **centre of the circle** and the constant distance of every point on the circle from its centre of called the **radius of the circle**.

The fixed point O is called its centre and the constant distance r is called the radius.

Diameter is the longest chord of the circle.

Secant

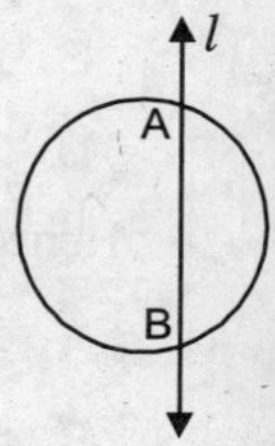

A line which interesects a circle in two distinct points is called a **secant** of the circle. In the fig. the line l intersects the circle in two distinct points A and B. The line l is a secant to the circle.

Tanget

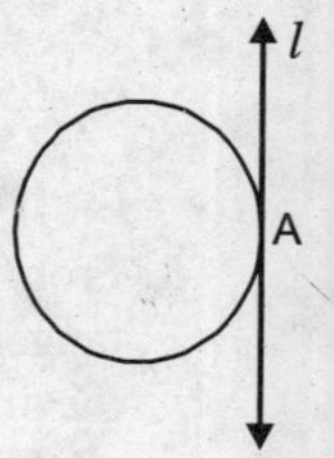

A tangent to a circle is a line that intersects the circle at exactly one point.

The point at which it meets the circle is called its point of contact and the line (tangent) is said to touch the circle at this point. In the figure, the line l meets the circle at only point A. Here A is the point of contact.

EXERCISE

1. PQ is a diameter and PQRS is a cyclic quadrilateral. If $\angle PSR$ = 150°, then measure of $\angle RPQ$ is :

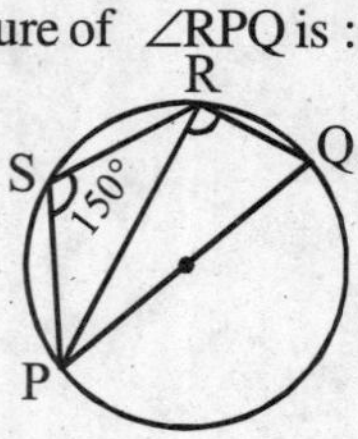

A. 90°

B. 60°

C. 30°

D. None of these

2. Determine the value of x in the figure given below.

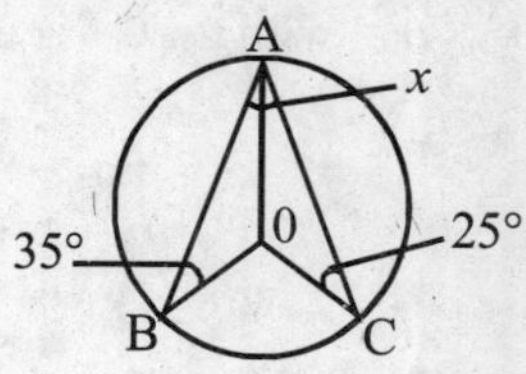

A. 35°

B. 25°

C. 30°

D. 60°

3. O is the centre of the circle. If $\angle OAB = 30°$ and $\angle OCB = 40°$, find $\angle AOC$.

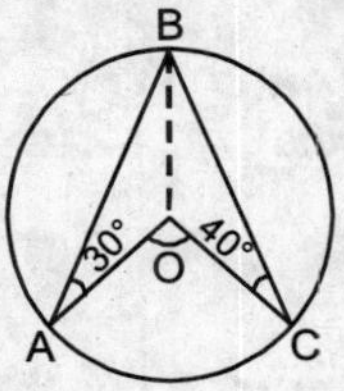

A. 120°

B. 140°

C. 110°

D. 130°

4. In fig. if $\angle ACB = 40°$, $\angle DPB = 120°$, then find *y*.

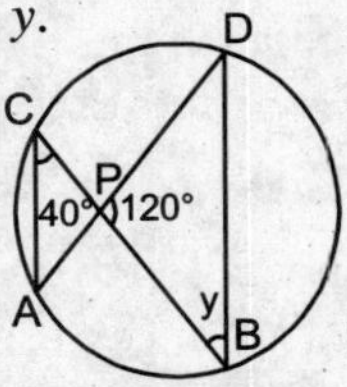

A. 10°

B. 20°

C. 15°

D. 25°

5. In the fig. if $\angle BDC = 30°$, $\angle CBA = 110°$, then find BCA.

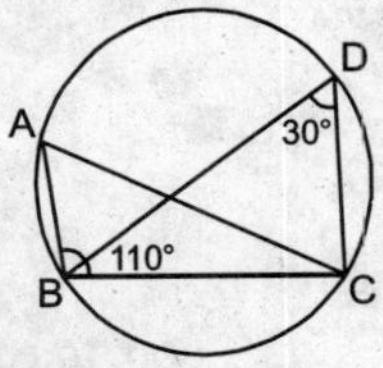

A. 20°

B. 40°

C. 35°

D. 60°

6. From a point Q, the length of the tangent to a circle is 24 cm and the distance from the centre is 25 cm. The radius of the circle is

A. 7 cm B. 12 cm

C. 15 cm D. 24.5 cm

7. In the given figure, if TP and TQ are the two tangents to a circle with centre O and that $\angle POQ = 110°$, then $\angle PTQ$ is equal to

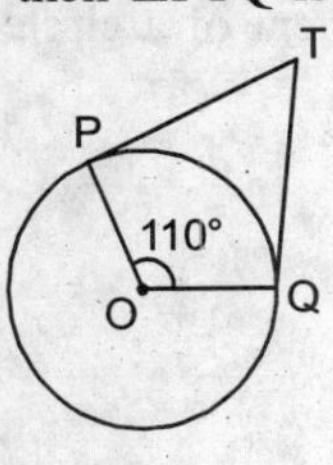

A. 60°

B. 70°

C. 80°

D. 90°

8. If tangents PA and PB from a point P to a circle with centre O are inclined to each other at angle of 80°, then $\angle POA$ is equal to

A. 50°

B. 60°

C. 70°

D. 80°

9. In Fig., a circle touches all the four sides of a quadrilateral ABCD whose sides AB = 6 cm, BC = 7 cm and CD = 4 cm. Find AD

A. 2 cm

B. 5 cm

C. 3 cm

D. 4 cm

10. If AB, AC, PQ are tangents in the figure and AB = 5 cm. The perimeter of ΔAPQ is

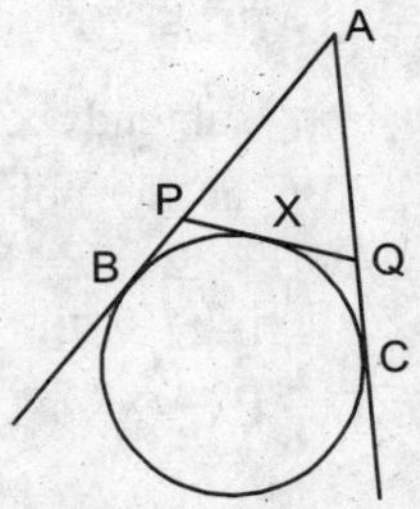

A. 8 cm

B. 6 cm

C. 10 cm

D. 5 cm

EXPLANATORY ANSWERS

1. B: $\angle PQR = 180° - 150° = 30°$

$\angle PRQ = 90°$ (Angle of a semicircle)

$\angle RPQ + 90° + 30° = 180°$

$\Rightarrow \angle RPQ = 60°$

2. D: $\angle OAB = \angle OBA \left(\because OA = OB\right)$

$\angle OAB = 35°$

Similarly, $\angle AOC = 25°$

$\therefore \quad \angle x = 35° + 25° = 60°$

3. B: O is the centre of the circle,

$\angle OAB = 30°$, $\angle OCB = 40°$. join OB

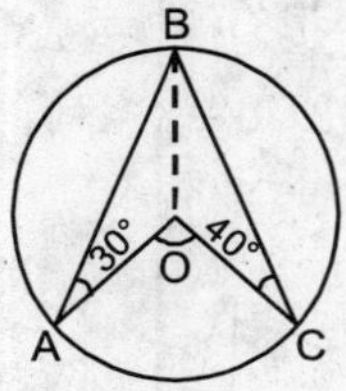

In ΔOAB,

$\therefore$ OA = OB (radii of the same circle)

$\therefore \angle OBA = \angle OAB = 30°$ ($\angle s$ opp. to equal sides of a Δ) ...(*i*)

Similarly, $\angle OBC = \angle OCB = 40°$ ...(*ii*)

Adding equations (*i*) and (*ii*), we get

$\angle OBA + \angle OBC = 30° + 40°$

$\Rightarrow \angle ABC = 70°$

$\because \widehat{AC}$ subtends $\angle AOC$ at the centre and ΔABC at any point on the circumference

$\angle AOC = 2 \times \angle ABC$

$= 2 \times 70° = 140°$

4. B: $\angle D = \angle C$ [$\because$ $\angle s$ in the same segment of a circle are equal]

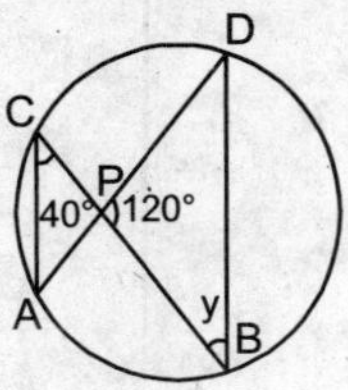

But $\angle C = 40°$ (Given)

$\therefore \angle C = 40°$

In Δ BPD, we have

$\angle BPD + \angle D + \angle B = 180°$ [$\because$ sum of three $\angle s$ of $a\ \Delta = 180°$]

$\Rightarrow 120° + 40° + y = 180°$

$\Rightarrow y = 180° - 160° = 20°$.

5. B: $\angle BAC = \angle BDC$ ($\angle$s in the same segment)

$= 30°$ (given)

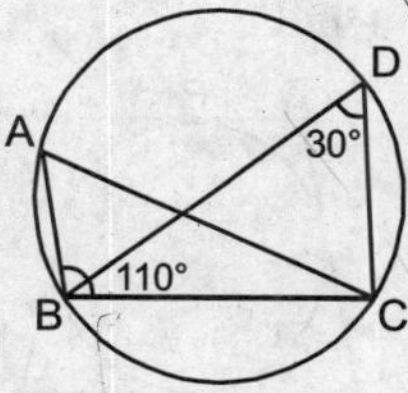

$\angle BAC + \angle CBA + \angle BCA = 180°$ ($\angle$s of ΔABC)

$\Rightarrow 30° + 110° + \angle BCA = 180°$

$\Rightarrow \angle BCA = 180° - 30° - 110° = 40°$

6. A: In rt. $\angle d\ \Delta$OTQ,

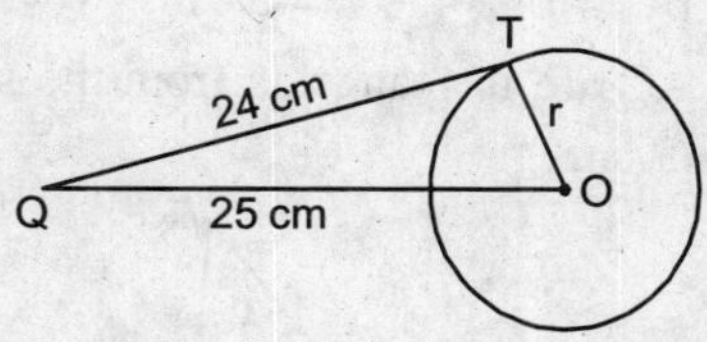

$OT = \sqrt{OQ^2 - OT^2}$

$= \sqrt{25^2 - 24^2} = \sqrt{625 - 576}$

$= \sqrt{49} = 7$ cm.

7. B: Since $\angle POQ + \angle PTQ = 180°$ [$\because \angle OPT = 90°, \angle OQT = 90°$]

$\Rightarrow 110° + \angle PTQ = 180°$

$\Rightarrow \angle PTQ = 180° - 110° = 70°$.

8. A: Since $\angle APB = 80°$

$\angle AOB = 180° - 80° = 100°$

$\angle PAO = \angle PBO = 90°$

Since OP bisects $\angle AOB$

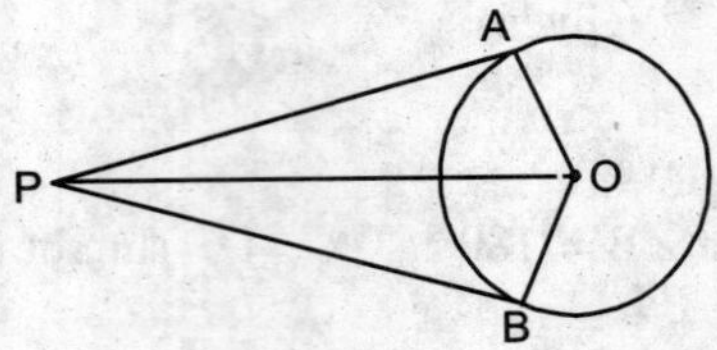

$$\angle AOP = \frac{1}{2}(100^\circ) = 50^\circ$$

i.e. $\angle POA = 50^\circ$.

9. C: AD = AS + DS = AP + DR [∵ AS = AP and DS = DR]

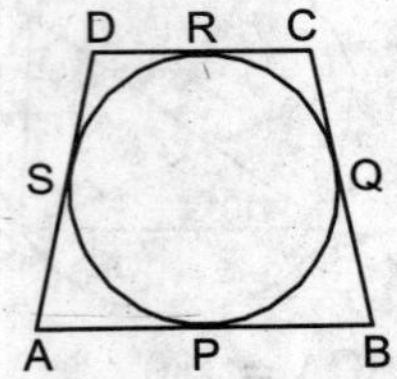

= (AB – BP) + (CD – RC)
= AB + CD – (BP + RC)
= AB + CD – (BQ + CQ) [∵ BP = BQ, RC = CQ]
= AB + CD – BC = 6 + 4 – 7 = 3 cm.

10. C: Since AB and AC are the tangents from the same point A

∴ AB = AC = 5 cm

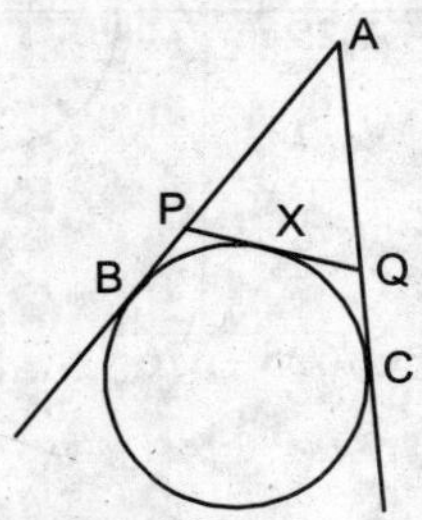

Similarly, BP = PX and XQ = QC

Perimeter of ΔAPQ = AP + AQ + PQ

= AP + AQ + (PX + XQ)

= (AP + PX) + (AQ + XQ)

= (AP + BP) + (AQ + QC)

= AB + AC = 5 + 5 = 10 cm.

20

TRIGONOMETRY

Trigonometric Ratios of Angles

There are six trigonometric ratios — sine, cosine, tangent, cotangent, secant and cosecant—upon which trigonometry is based.

ΔABC is a right- angled triangle in which $\angle ACB = \theta$. The side AB is opposite to an angle θ and is called **opposide side**. BC is the **adjacent side** in relation to angle θ; AC is the **hypotenuse**.

The six trigonometric ratios of the acute angle θ are defined as follows :

$$\sin\theta = \frac{p}{h} = \frac{AB}{AC} \qquad \cos\theta = \frac{b}{h} = \frac{BC}{AC}$$

$$\tan\theta = \frac{p}{b} = \frac{AB}{BC} \qquad \cot\theta = \frac{b}{p} = \frac{BC}{AB}$$

$$\sec\theta = \frac{h}{b} = \frac{AC}{BC} \qquad \text{cosec}\theta = \frac{h}{p} = \frac{AC}{AB}$$

IMPORTANT FORMULAE

A. (*i*) $\tan\theta = \frac{\sin\theta}{\cos\theta} = \frac{1}{\cot\theta}$ (*ii*) $\cot\theta = \frac{\cos\theta}{\sin\theta} = \frac{1}{\tan\theta}$

(*iii*) $\sec\theta = \frac{1}{\cos\theta}$ (*iv*) $\text{cosec}\theta = \frac{1}{\sin\theta}$

B. (*v*) $\sin^2\theta + \cos^2\theta = 1$

$\sin^2\theta = 1 - \cos^2\theta \Rightarrow \sin\theta = \sqrt{1-\cos^2\theta}$

$\cos^2\theta = 1 - \sin^2\theta \Rightarrow \cos\theta = \sqrt{1-\sin^2\theta}$

(*vi*) $1 + \tan^2\theta = \sec^2\theta$

$\sec^2\theta - \tan^2\theta = 1$

$\sec^2\theta - 1 = \tan^2\theta$

(*vii*) $1 + \cot^2\theta = \operatorname{cosec}^2\theta$

$\operatorname{cosec}^2\theta - \cot^2\theta = 1$

$\operatorname{cosec}^2\theta - 1 = \cot^2\theta$

C. (*viii*) $\sin(90 - \theta) = \cos\theta$

(*ix*) $\cos(90 - \theta) = \sin\theta$

(*x*) $\tan(90 - \theta) = \cot\theta$

(*xi*) $\cot(90 - \theta) = \tan\theta$

(*xii*) $\sec(90 - \theta) = \operatorname{cosec}\theta$

(*xiii*) $\operatorname{cosec}(90 - \theta) = \sec\theta$

D. (*i*) $\sin(A \pm B) = \sin A \times \cos B \pm \cos A \times \sin B$

(*ii*) $\cos(A \pm B) = \cos A \times \cos B \mp \sin A \times \sin B$

E. (*i*) $\sin 2\theta = 2\sin\theta \cdot \cos\theta$

(*ii*) $\cos 2\theta = \cos^2\theta - \sin^2\theta$

$= 1 - 2\sin^2\theta = 2\cos^2\theta - 1$

(*iii*) $\tan 2\theta = \dfrac{2\tan\theta}{1-\tan^2\theta}$

F. (*i*) $\sin 3\theta = 3\sin\theta - 4\sin^3\theta$

(*ii*) $\cos 3\theta = 4\cos^3\theta - 3\cos\theta$

T-Ratios of Standard Angles

θ	**0°**	**30°**	**45°**	**60°**	**90°**
$\sin\theta$	0	$\frac{1}{2}$	$\frac{1}{\sqrt{2}}$	$\frac{\sqrt{3}}{2}$	1
$\cos\theta$	1	$\frac{\sqrt{3}}{2}$	$\frac{1}{\sqrt{2}}$	$\frac{1}{2}$	0
$\tan\theta$	0	$\frac{1}{\sqrt{3}}$	1	$\sqrt{3}$	∞
$\cot\theta$	∞	$\sqrt{3}$	1	$\frac{1}{\sqrt{3}}$	0
$\sec\theta$	1	$\frac{2}{\sqrt{3}}$	$\sqrt{2}$	2	∞
$\operatorname{cosec}\theta$	∞	2	$\sqrt{2}$	$\frac{2}{\sqrt{3}}$	1

HEIGHT AND DISTANCE

Our common use for trigonometry is to measure heights and distance that are either awkward or impossible to measure by ordinary means. One of the biggest triumphs of trigonometry is being able to find the size of an object or the distance to an object (such as the moon) without going to the object. In trigonometry, we develop methods for measuring sides and angles as well as for solving related applied problems. Because of the extensive use of these concepts, trigonometry is considered one of the most practical and relevant branches of mathematics.

The Angle of Elevation

If a person is looking up at an object, the acute angle measured from the horizontal to a line of sight observation of the object is called the angle of elevation.

In the given figure, α is the angle of elevation.

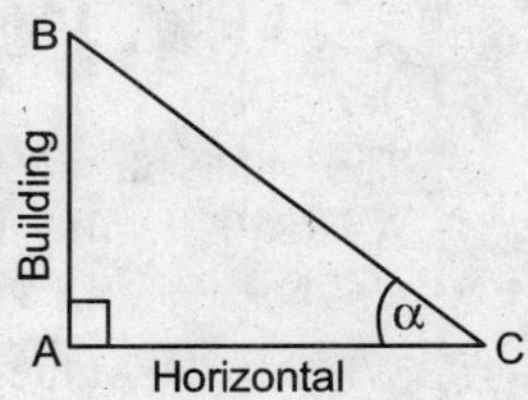

The Angle of Depression

The angle β for a point below a horizontal line is the angle formed by the horizontal line and the observer's line of sight through the point. In the following figure, β is the angle of depression.

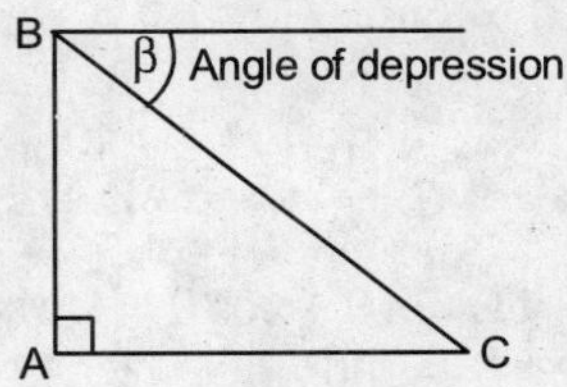

EXERCISE

1. If $2 \tan \theta = 1$, find the value of

$$\frac{3\cos\theta + 2\sin\theta}{2\cos\theta - \sin\theta}$$

A. $\frac{8}{3}$ B. $\frac{5}{3}$

C. $\frac{2}{3}$ D. 2

2. $\cos^2 72° + \cos^2 18° = ?$

A. 0 B. 1

C. –1 D. 2

3. $3 \tan^2 30° + \sec^4 45° - \tan^2 60°$ is equal to :

A. 0 B. 1

C. 2 D. 3

4. The value of $\frac{\sin 10°}{\cos 80°}$ is :

A. 0 B. 1

C. 2 D. 3

5. If $\theta = 45$ then $\frac{2\tan\theta}{1+\tan^2\theta}$ is :

A. 1 B. 0

C. 2 D. 3

6. If $\theta = 30°$ then $\cos 2\theta$ is :

A. 0 B. 1

C. $\frac{1}{2}$ D. $\frac{\sqrt{3}}{2}$

7. What is the value of $\sin^2 35° + \sin^2 55°$?

A. 0 B. 1

C. $\frac{1}{2}$ D. 2

8. The value of tan 45° × cot 45° is :

A. 0 B. 1

C. 2 D. $\frac{1}{2}$

9. The value of sin(90° – θ) is :

A. cos θ B. sin θ

C. –cos θ D. None of these

10. What is the value of sin 30° × cosec 30°

A. 1 B. 0

C. $\frac{1}{2}$ D. 2

11. sin θ + cos θ = 1 where θ = ...

A. 30° B. 45°

C. 60° D. 90°

12. tan 45° × tan 82° is

A. 1 B. 0

C. 2 D. 3

13. The angle of elevation of the top of a tower from a point on the ground, which is 30 m away from the foot of the tower is 30°. The height of the tower is :

A. $8\sqrt{3}$ m B. $9\sqrt{3}$ m

C. $10\sqrt{3}$ m D. $12\sqrt{3}$ m

14. A kite is flying at a height of 60 m above the ground. The string attached to the kite is temporarily tied to a point on the ground. The inclination of the string with the ground is 60°. Find the length of the string, assuming that there is no slack in the string.

A. $40\sqrt{3}$ m B. $30\sqrt{3}$ m

C. $20\sqrt{3}$ m D. $10\sqrt{3}$ m

15. From a point on the ground, the angles of elevation of the bottom and top of a transmission tower fixed at the top of a 20 m high building are 45° and 60° respectively. The height of the tower is :

A. $25(\sqrt{3}-1)$ m

B. $20(\sqrt{3}-1)$ m

C. 20 m

D. 10 m

16. Two poles of equal heights are standing opposite to each other on either side of a road, which is 100 metres wide. From a point between them on the road, the angles of elevation of their tops are 30° and 60°. The height of each pole is

A. 44 m B. 43.25 m

C. 50 m D. 40.5 m

17. The angle of elevation of the top of a hill at the foot of a tower is 60° and the angle of elevation of top of the tower from the foot of the hill is 30°. If the tower is 50 m high, then the height of the hill is :

A. 148 m B. 150 m

C. 152 m D. 160 m

18. The angles of elevation of the top of a tower from two points a and b from the base and in the same straight line with it are complementary. The height of the tower is :

A. ab B. $\sqrt{ab}$

C. a^2b^2 D. None of these

19. The angles of elevation of the top of a tower from two points at the distances of 4 m and 9 m from the base of the tower and in the same straight line with it are complementary. The height of the tower is :

A. 8 m B. 5 m

C. 6 m D. 4 m

20. The value of $\frac{\tan 49°}{\cot 41°}$ is :

A. 1 B. 2

C. 0 D. 3

EXPLANATORY ANSWERS

1. A: $\frac{3\cos\theta + 2\sin\theta}{2\cos\theta - \sin\theta} = \frac{3\frac{\cos\theta}{\cos\theta} + 2\frac{\sin\theta}{\cos\theta}}{2\frac{\cos\theta}{\cos\theta} - \frac{\sin\theta}{\cos\theta}}$

[Dividing both the numerator and denominator by cos θ]

$= \frac{3 + 2\tan\theta}{2 - \tan\theta} = \frac{3 + 2 \times \frac{1}{2}}{2 - \frac{1}{2}}$ [Given 2 tan θ = 1 ∴ tan θ = $\frac{1}{2}$]

$= \frac{3+1}{3/2} = 4 \times \frac{2}{3} = 2\frac{2}{3}$.

2. B: $\cos^2 72° + \cos^2 18° = \cos^2 (90 - 18°) + \cos^2 18°$

$= \sin^2 18° + \cos^2 18° = 1$.

3. C: $3\left(\frac{1}{\sqrt{3}}\right)^2 + (\sqrt{2})^2 - (\sqrt{3})^2$

$= 3 \times \frac{1}{3} + 4 - 3 = 2$.

4. B: $\frac{\sin 10°}{\cos(90° - 10°)} = \frac{\sin 10°}{\sin 10°} = 1$.

5. A: $\frac{2\tan 45°}{1 + \tan^2 45°} = \frac{2 \times 1}{1+1} = \frac{2}{2} = 1$.

6. C: $\cos 2(30°) = \cos 60° = \frac{1}{2}$.

7. B: $\sin^2 35° + \sin^2(90° - 35°)$

$= \sin^2 35° + \cos^2 35° = 1.$ $[\because \sin^2\theta + \cos^2\theta = 1]$

8. B: $\tan 45° \times \cot 45° = 1 \times 1 = 1.$

9. A: $\sin (90° - \theta) = \cos \theta.$

10.A: $\sin 30° \times \text{cosec } 30° = \frac{1}{2}\times\frac{2}{1}=\frac{1}{1}=1.$

11.D: Put $\theta = 90°$ then $\sin \theta + \cos \theta = \sin 90° + \cos 90° = 1 + 0 = 1.$

12.A: $\tan 45° \times \tan 8° \cdot \tan (90° - 8°)$

$= \tan 45° \times \tan 8° \times \cot 8° = 1 \times 1 = 1.$

13.C: Let AB be the tower. The angle of elevation of the top A of the tower from a point C on the ground which is 30 metres away from the foot of the tower is 30°.

$\therefore \quad \angle ACB = 30°$

and $\quad BC = 30$ m.

From right ΔABC, we have

$$\frac{AB}{BC} = \tan 30°$$

$$\Rightarrow \quad AB = BC \tan 30° = 30 \times \frac{1}{\sqrt{3}} = 10\sqrt{3} \text{ m.}$$

14.A: Let AB = height of kite = 60 m and the inclination of the string AC is 60°.

From right-angled ΔABC, we have

$$\frac{AC}{AB} = \text{cosec } 60°$$

$$\Rightarrow \quad \frac{AC}{60} = \frac{2}{\sqrt{3}} \Rightarrow AC = 60 \times \frac{2}{\sqrt{3}} = 40\sqrt{3} \text{ m.}$$

15.A: Let AB = 20 m be the building and AC be the transmission tower fixed at the top of building. From a point D on the ground, the angle of elevation of the bottom and top of transmission tower are 45° and 60°.

$\therefore \angle ADB = 45°$ and $\angle CDB = 60°$

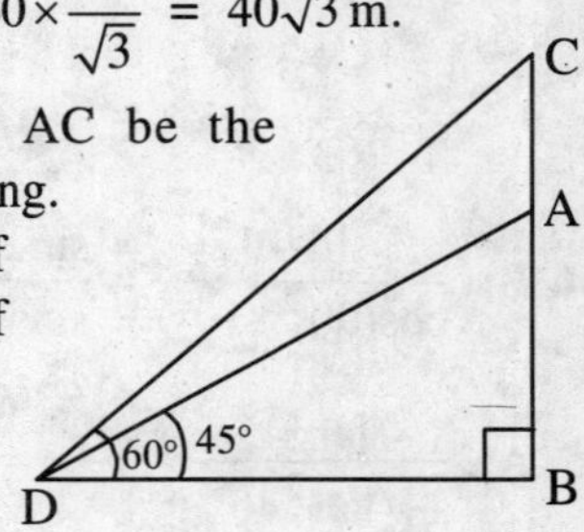

From right ΔABD, we have

$$\frac{AB}{BD} = \tan 45° = 1$$

$\therefore$ AB = BD

$\Rightarrow$ BD = 20 m [$\because$ AB = 20 m]

From right-angled ΔCBD, we have

$$\frac{BC}{BD} = \tan 60°$$

$\Rightarrow$ $BC = BD \tan 60°$

$$= 20 \times \sqrt{3} = 20\sqrt{3}\,\text{m}$$

Now $AC = BC - AB = 20\sqrt{3} - 20$

$$= 20(\sqrt{3} - 1)\,\text{m}.$$

Hence the height of the tower = $20(\sqrt{3} - 1)$ m.

16.B: Let AB and CD be the two poles of equal height *h* metres standing on either side of the road AC = 100 metres.

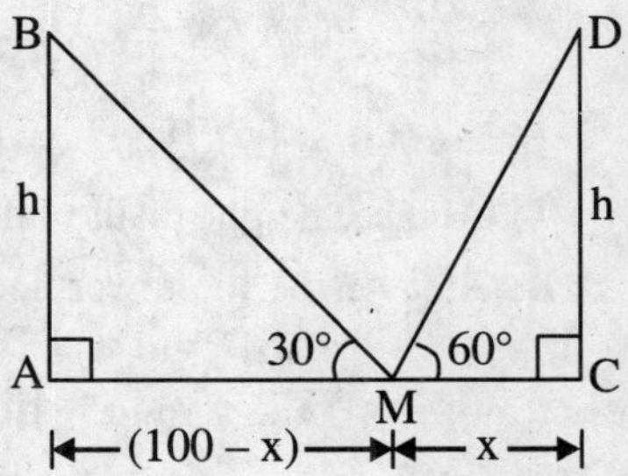

Let M be the point at which the poles AB, CD subtend angles of 30° and 60° respectively.

Let CM = x metres so that

AM = $(100 - x)$ metres

In right-angled ΔMCD, $\frac{h}{x} = \tan 60°$

$\Rightarrow$ $h = x\sqrt{3}$ ...(*i*)

In right-angled ΔMAB,

$$\frac{h}{100 - x} = \tan 30° \Rightarrow \frac{h}{100 - x} = \frac{1}{\sqrt{3}}$$

$\Rightarrow$ $h\sqrt{3} = 100 - x \Rightarrow (x\sqrt{3})\sqrt{3} = 100 - x$

$$3x = 100 - x$$

$$4x = 100;\ x = 100 \div 4 = 25\text{ m}$$

$\therefore$ From (*i*), $h = x\sqrt{3} = 25 \times 1.73 = 43.25$ m

Hence, distance of point M from C = 25 m and distance of point from A = (100 – 25)m = 75 m. Height of each pole = 43.25 m.

17.B: Let AB be the hill and CD the tower.

$$\angle BDA = 60° \text{ and } \angle DBC = 30°$$

$$CD = 50 \text{ m.}$$

Let AB = h metres

In right-angled ΔADC,

$$\frac{CD}{BD} = \tan 30°$$

$$\Rightarrow \quad BD = \frac{CD}{\tan 30°}$$

$$= CD \cot 30°$$

$$\Rightarrow \quad BD = 50\sqrt{3} \text{ metres}$$

Now in right-angled ΔABD, we have

$$\frac{AB}{BD} = \tan 60° \Rightarrow AB = BD \tan 60°$$

$$\Rightarrow AB = (50\sqrt{3})\sqrt{3} = 150 \text{ m.}$$

Hence, height of the hill is 150 m.

18.B: Let AB be the tower and C and D be the two points such that BD = a and BC = b.

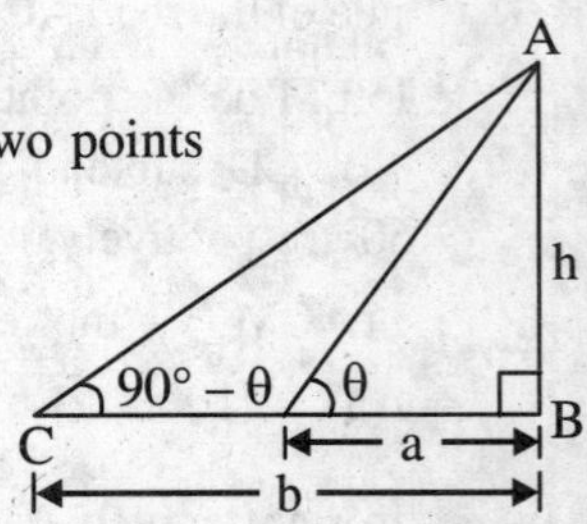

If ∠BDA = θ, then ∠BCA = 90° – θ

Now in right-angled ΔABD,

$$\frac{AB}{BD} = \tan\theta \Rightarrow \frac{h}{a} = \tan\theta$$

$$\therefore \quad h = a \tan\theta \qquad \text{...}(i)$$

In right-angled ΔABC,

$$\frac{AB}{BC} = \tan(90° - \theta) = \cot\theta$$

$$\Rightarrow \quad \frac{h}{b} = \cot\theta \Rightarrow h = b\cot\theta \qquad \text{...}(ii)$$

multiplying (i) and (ii), we get

$$h^2 = ab\tan\theta\cot\theta = ab\tan\theta \times \frac{1}{\tan\theta} = ab.$$

$$\therefore \quad h = \sqrt{ab}.$$

19.C: Let AB be the tower and C and D be the two points such that BD = 4 m and BC = 9 m.

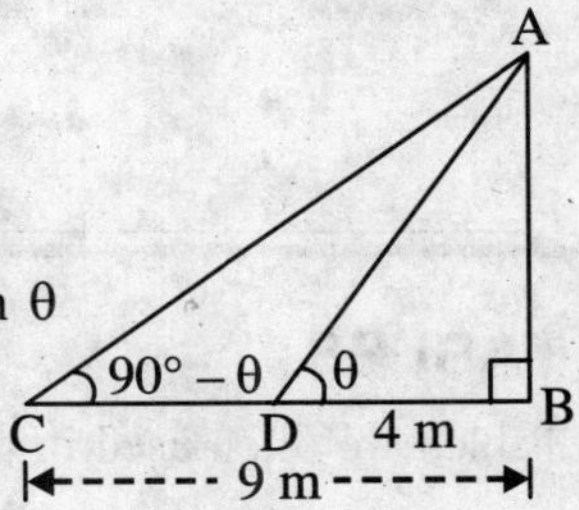

If ∠BDA = θ, then ∠BCA = 90° – θ

Now in right-angled ΔABD,

$$\frac{AB}{BD} = \tan\theta \Rightarrow \frac{h}{4} = \tan\theta$$

$$\therefore \qquad h = 4\tan\theta \quad ...(i)$$

In right-angled ΔABC,

$$\frac{AB}{BC} = \tan(90° - \theta) = \cot\theta$$

$$\Rightarrow \qquad \frac{h}{9} = \cot\theta \Rightarrow h = 9\cot\theta \qquad ...(ii)$$

multiplying (*i*) and (*ii*), we get

$$h^2 = 36\tan\theta\cot\theta = 36\tan\theta \times \frac{1}{\tan\theta} = 36.$$

$$\therefore \qquad h = \pm\sqrt{36} = 6 \text{ m}.$$

20.A: $\frac{\tan 49°}{\cot 41°} = \frac{\tan(90° - 41°)}{\cot 41°} = \frac{\cot 41°}{\cot 41°} = 1$ $\quad$ [∵ tan(90° – θ) = cot θ]

21

DATA TABLES

TABLES

Tables are often used in reports, magazines and newspaper to present as set of numerical data. It is one of the easiest and most accurate ways of presenting data. One of the main purposes of tables is to make complicated information easier to understand. Hence, the advantage of presenting data in a table is that one can see the information at a glance. We present below an example of tabular presentation of annual expenditure of 5 families for last 5 years.

Annual Expenditure of 5 families (in ₹ Thousands)

Years → Families ↓	2008	2009	2010	2011	2012
A	35	50	55	60	70
B	40	60	65	75	80
C	45	50	70	80	95
D	30	40	45	50	75
E	50	55	60	70	90

Essentials of a Tables:

(*i*) **Title:** Heading of the table

(*ii*) **Stub:** The section of the table containing row headings in called Stub.

(*iii*) **Column Captions :** The heading of each column is designated as column caption.

(*iv*) **Body**

(*v*) **Footnotes**

(*vi*) **Source**

EXERCISE

Directions (Qs. 1 to 4) : *Study the table carefully and answer the following questions.*

Division of students based on commercial streams

Stream	Department			
	Art		Science	
	Girls	Boys	Girls	Boys
1. Business management	25	45	25	65
2. Typewriting	23	186	20	32
3. Casting	25	120	12	58
4. Typewriting & casting	12	100	3	5

1. If 60% girls and 70% Boys are passed in their respective streams, then what is the total pass per cent?

A. 58 B. 66
C. 54 D. 62

2. What is the percentage difference between total number of students from Business management and casting and number of students from typewriting.

A. 44 B. 66
C. 33 D. 55

3. What is the percentage of boys in costing stream from art department?

A. 27 B. 10
C. 18 D. 15

4. What is percentage difference between total number of boys and girls?

A. 321 B. 280
C. 308 D. 250

Directions (Qs. 5 to 9) : *Study the following table to answer these questions.*

Average Hourly Wage (in ₹) by Age Group

Years	18 – 20 years		21 – 23 years	
	Male	Female	Male	Female
2007	15.1	15.1	29.7	25.1
2008	12.4	13.4	21.0	19.1
2009	10.0	13.8	14.7	16.9
2010	11.0	13.4	18.0	20.5
2011	21.2	16.3	29.1	32.7
2012	15.0	21.0	32.1	33.9

5. In 2011, for the 21-23 years age group, the wages for the females was approximately what per cent of that of the males?

A. 220 B. 30
C. 85 D. 110

6. What was the difference between the average wages of males and of females for the 21 – 23 years age group?

A. 0.80 B. 0.60
C. 0.40 D. 0.20

7. In how many years was the wage for the females higher than that of males in both the age groups?

A. Three B. Four
C. Two D. One

8. In the age group of 18–20 years, in which year was the wage-disparity maximum?
A. 2010 B. 2011
C. 2009 D. 2012

9. In the age group of 21–23 years, in which year was the wage-disparity minimum?
A. 2008 B. 2012
C. 2009 D. 2007

Directions (Qs. 10 to 15) : *Answer these questions on the basis of the data given in the following table indicating the trend in sales of four companies. The amounts given are in lakhs of rupees :*

Year	Name of the Company			
	Dowby	Alpha	Baron	Celia
2004	12.00	2.00	18.50	12.00
2005	10.00	5.00	15.00	16.00
2006	18.00	7.50	16.50	15.00
2007	20.00	11.50	14.50	36.00
2008	25.00	15.00	50.00	48.00

10. Which company has shown consistently an increasing sales average?
A. Alpha B. Baron
C. Celia D. Dowby

11. The cumulative sales of all the companies put together in 2005 was how much of the sales of 2008?
A. $\frac{3}{7}$ B. $\frac{2}{5}$
C. $\frac{1}{4}$ D. $\frac{1}{3}$

12. What was the average sales of Baron over the 5 years?
A. 22.90 B. 21.90
C. 23.90 D. 20.90

13. Which company faced a decline in sales in 2007 over its previous year?
A. Alpha B. Baron
C. Celia D. Dowby

14. The ratio of the highest turnover of any company in any year to the lowest turnover of any company in any year is
A. 25 B. 15
C. 2.5 D. 0.25

15. How many companies had the same turnover in the same year?
A. 1 B. 2
C. 3 D. 4

EXPLANATORY ANSWERS

1. D:

2. A: Number of students in Business management stream = 160
and number of students in typewriting = 261
Number of students in casting = 215

$$\text{Required percent} = \left(\frac{160+215-261}{261}\right)\times 100 = 44\% \text{ (Approx).}$$

3. A: $\text{Required percent} = \frac{(25+120)}{536}\times 100 = 27\%.$

4. A: Total number of boys = 45 + 65 + 186 + 32 + 120 + 58 + 100 + 5 = 611
Total number of girs = 25 + 23 + 25 + 12 + 25 + 20 + 12 + 13 = 145

Required per cent = $\left(\frac{611-145}{145}\right)\times 100$ = 321%.

5. D: Required percentage = $\frac{32.7}{29.1}$ × 100 = 112.37 ≈ 110%.

6. B:

7. A:

Year	Wage for male 18-20 years + 21-23 years	Wage for female 18-20 years + 21 – 23 years
2007	₹ 44.8	₹ 40.2
2008	₹ 33.4	₹ 32.5
2009	₹ 24.7	₹ 30.7
2010	₹ 29.0	₹ 33.9
2011	₹ 50.3	₹ 49.0
2012	₹ 47.1	₹ 54.9

Hence, in three years the wage of females was higher than that of male.

8. D: In 2012 wage for male (18-20 years) was ₹ 15.0 white wage for female was ₹ 21.0. Obviously it is maximum wage disparity.

9. B: In 2012 wage for male (21-23 years) was ₹ 32.1 white wage for female was ₹ 33.9. Obviously it is minimum wage-disparity.

10. A: Of course, Alpha has shown consistently increasing sales average.

11. C:

Year	Total Sales of all the Companies	Cumulative Sales
2004	44.50	44.50
2005	46.00	90.50
2006	57.00	147.50
2007	82.00	229.00
2008	138.00	367.50

Let, 90.50 = K × 367.50

⇒ $K = \frac{90.50}{367.50} = \frac{181}{735} \approx \frac{1}{4}$.

12. A: $\frac{18.50+15.00+16.50+14.50+50.00}{5} = \frac{114.50}{5} = 22.90$.

13. B: Obviously, Baron faced a decline in sales.

14. A: $\frac{50}{2} = 25$

15. B: In 2004, Celia and Dowby.

22

BAR GRAPHS

BAR GRAPHS

Given quantity of a bar graph can be compared by the height or length. A bar graph can have either vertical or horizontal bars. You can compare different quantities or the same quantity at the different times. The bars may be placed adjacent to each other or may be separated from each other by spaces depending upon the problem.

For Illustration:

Registration of New Vehicles in Delhi (in thousands)

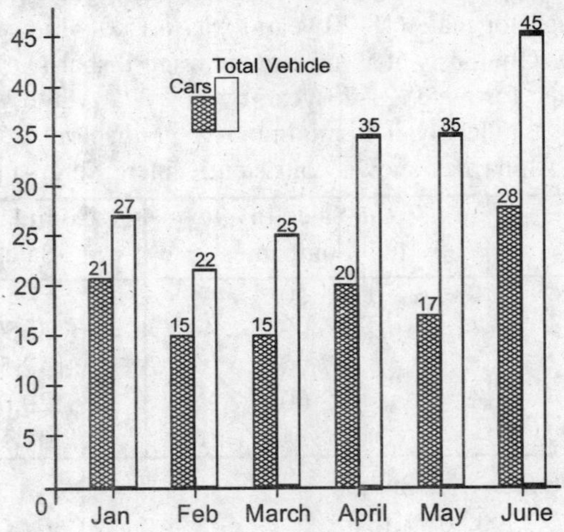

CUMULATIVE GRAPH

These are usually bar or line graphs where the height of the bar or line is divided up proportionally among various quantities presented in the graph. The representation of quantities may be done in terms of either percentage of the total or in absolute figures. These are also called sub-divided graphs. Thus, cumulative graph may be conveniently used for making comparisons.

For Illustration:

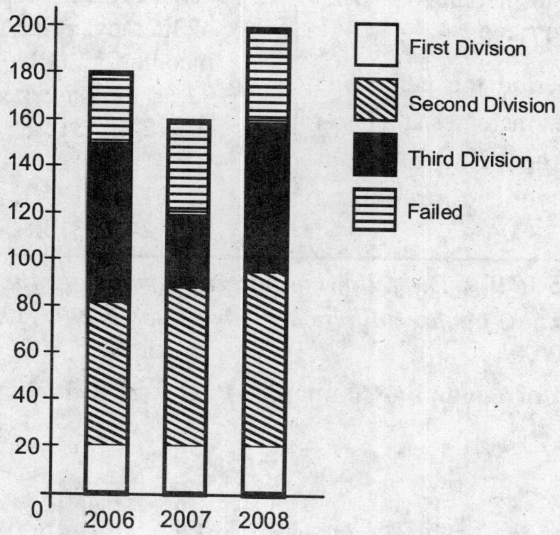

EXERCISE

Directions (Qs. 1 to 4) : *Study the following bar graph giving Economic Indices for the period 1961-62 to 2001-02 to answer these questions.*

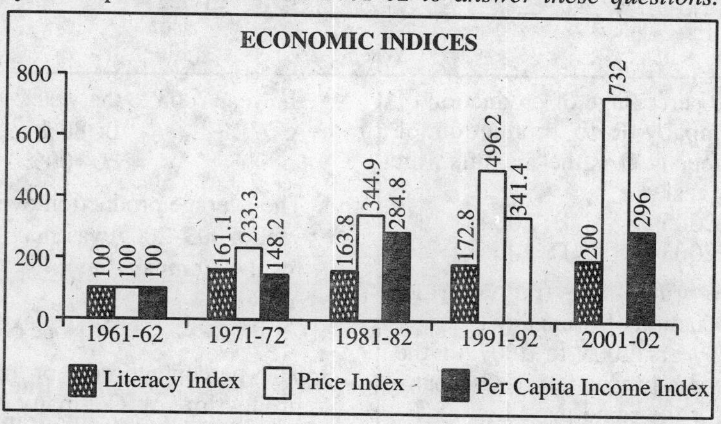

1. What is the average annual percentage increase in literacy index from 1961-62 to 2001-02?

A. 25% B. 15.8%

C. 18.3% D. 4.9%

2. Of the three economic indices which index for which period shows the maximum percentage increase as compared to the previous period?

A. Literacy, 1971-72
B. Price, 2001-02
C. Per capita income, 1981-82
D. Price, 1971-72

3. In which period the per capita income index increases at a faster rate than the price index as compared to the preceding period?

A. 1971-72 B. 2001-02
C. 1981-82 D. 1991-92

4. What are the respective indices of literacy, price and per capita income for 2001-02 taking 1971-72 as the base period?

A. 124.1, 313.8, 200
B. 313.8, 124, 201
C. 313.8, 124.1, 190
D. 124.1, 313.8, 194

Directions (Qs. 5 to 9) : *The following bar graph indicates the production of sugar (in lakh tonnes) by three different sugar companies P, Q and R over the years 2003 to 2007.*

Production of Sugar by Companies P, Q and R during 2003–2007.

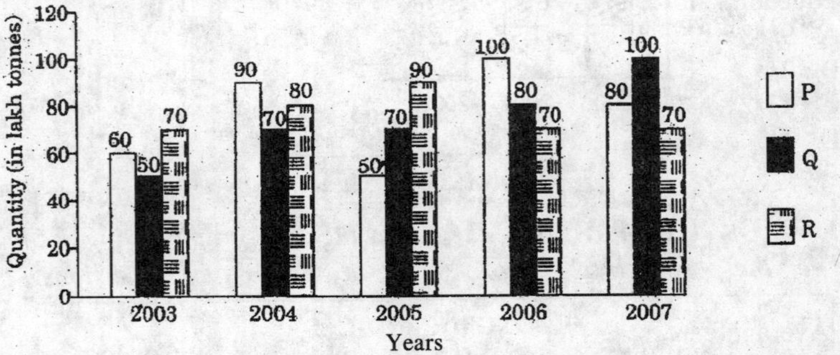

5. The percentage of production of Company R to production of Company Q is the maximum in the year

A. 2005 B. 2004
C. 2003 D. 2006

6. The ratio of the average production of Company P during the years 2005 to 2007 to the average production of Company Q for the same period is

A. 15 : 17 B. 23 : 25
C. 27 : 29 D. 9 : 11

7. The percentage increase in production of Company Q from the year 2003 to the year 2007 is

A. 60% B. 80%
C. 90% D. 100%

8. The average production over the years 2003–2007 was maximum for the Company(ies)

A. R B. Q
C. P D. None of these

9. The percentage rise or fall in production of Company Q as compared to the previous year is the maximum in the year

A. 2006 B. 2005
C. 2004 D. 2007

Directions (Qs. 10 to 13) : *Study the following graph to answer these questions.*

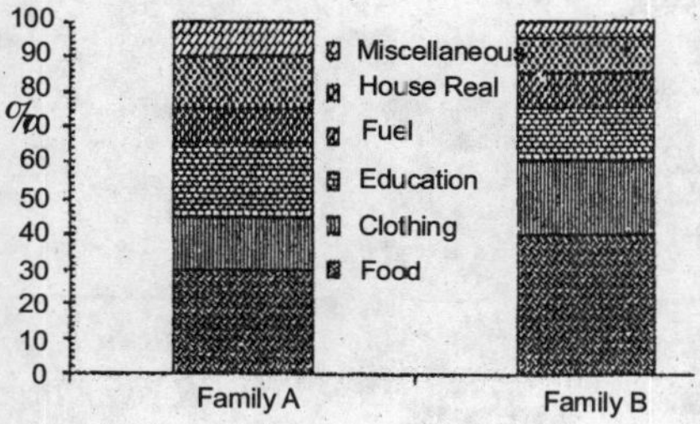

10. What fraction of the total expenditure is spent on education in family A?

A. 9/13
B. 2/3
C. 13/21
D. 1/5

11. If the total expenditure of family B is ₹ 10,000, then money spent on clothes by this family during the years is

A. ₹ 2,000 B. ₹ 600
C. ₹ 200 D. ₹ 6,000

12. If the total annual expenditure of family A is ₹ 30,000, the money spent on food, clothes and house rent is

A. ₹ 21,000 B. ₹ 18,000
C. ₹ 18,500 D. ₹ 15,000

13. What percentage is B's expenditure on food over A's expenditure on food, taking equal total expenditure?

A. 133.33% B. 70%
C. 10% D. 75%

EXPLANATORY ANSWERS

1. A: Average percentage increase = $\frac{200-100}{4}$ = 25%.

2. D: Price index of 1971-72 shows 133.3% increase which is maximum.

3. C:

Years	Per Capita Income Index	Price Index
71-72	48.20%	133.30%
81-82	67.88%	47.83%
91-92	19.87%	43.87%
01-02	Negative	47.52%

According to above table in 81-82. The Per capita income index increases at faster rate than the price index.

4. A:

5. C: In 2003, required percentage = $\frac{70}{50}\times 100 = 140\%$

In 2004, required percentage = $\frac{80}{70}\times 100 = 114.2\%$

In 2005, required percentage = $\frac{90}{70} \times 100 = 128.57\%$

Thus, in 2003 required percentage was maximum.

6. B: Required ratio = (50 + 100 + 80) : (70 + 80 + 100)
= 230 : 250 = 23 : 25

7. D: Required increase percentage

$$= \frac{100-50}{50} \times 100 = 100\%$$

8. A: Obviously that is R.

9. D: Obviously that year is 2007.

10. D: Required ratio = $\frac{20}{100} = \frac{1}{5}$.

11. A: Money spend on clothes by family B = $1000 \times \frac{20}{100}$ = ₹ 2000.

12. B: Required expenditure = $30000 \times \frac{(30+15+15)}{100}$ = ₹ 18000.

13. A: Required percentage = $\frac{40}{30} \times 100$ = 133.33%.

23

FREQUENCY POLYGON

FREQUENCY POLYGON

Frequency Polygon are used to show how a quantity changes continuously. If the line goes up, the quantity is increasing; if the line goes down, the quantity is decreasing; if the line is horizontal, the quantity is not changing.

For Illustration:

Demand and Production of rubber (in thousand tons) in various years

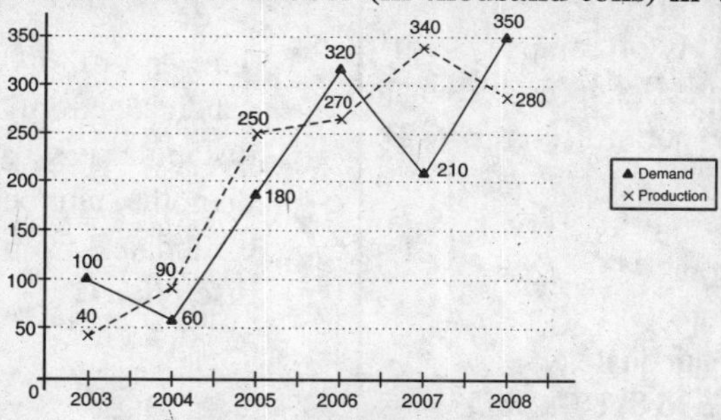

EXERCISE

Directions (Qs. 1 to 4) : *Study the given graph carefully to answer these questions.*

The following graph shows the ratio of imports to exports by two companies A and B over the years.

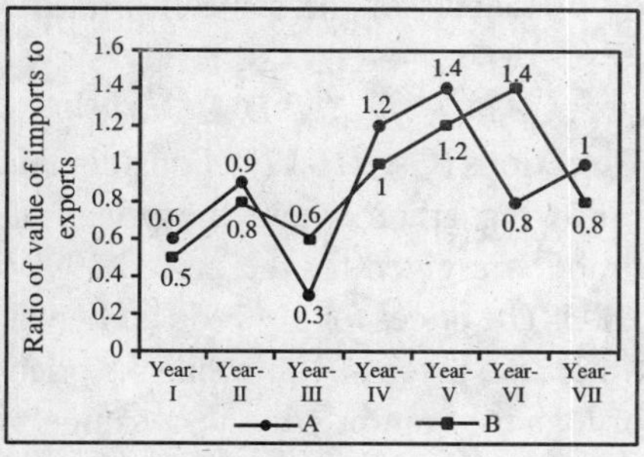

1. If the imports of company A in Year – VI were ₹ 10.40 crore, what were the exports of company A in the same year?

A. 13 crore B. 12.75 crore

C. 12.50 crore D. 13.75 crore

2. It is supposed that Imports – Exports = ‘x’ for company A in Year-I and the imports of company A in Year-I were ₹ 3.6 crore, and it is also supposed that Imports – Exports = ‘a’ for company B in Year-V and the exports of company B in Year-V were ₹ 5 crore. What is the relationship between 'a' and 'x'?

A. x > a B. x = a

C. a > x D. x ≠ a

3. If the exports of company B in Year-III were ₹ 2.19 crore, what were the imports of company B in the same year?

A. 3.65 crore

B. 1.314 crore

C. 1.214 crore

D. 1.414 crore

4. If the imports of company A in Year-V were ₹ 8.40 crore, what were the exports of company B in Year-VII?

A. 6 crore

B. 7.40 crore

C. 7.20 crore

D. Data inadequate

Directions (Qs. 5 to 8) : *The following graph shows the number of successful candidates from different schools (A to F) in different disciplines. Study the graph carefully to answer these questions.*

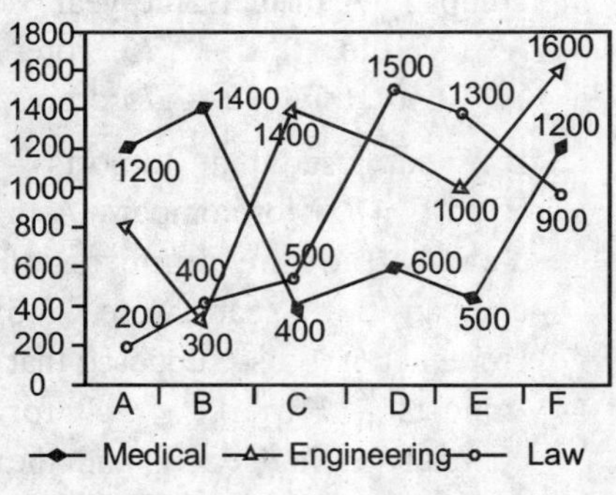

5. In which of the following institutes is the difference between the number of successful candidates in Engineering and that in Medical discipline the maximum?

A. F B. C

C. B D. D

6. The total number of successful candidates from Medical discipline is approximately what per cent more than that from Law?

A. 8% B. 15%

C. 12% D. 10%

7. The number of successful candidates from F in Engineering discipline is what per cent more than the number of successful candidates from A in Medical discipline?

A. 30% B. 25%

C. $33\frac{1}{3}\%$ D. 20%

8. In which of the following institutes is the sum of the number of successful candidates in Engineering and Law disciplines 50% of the number of Medical students of the same institute?

A. C B. E

C. D D. B

Directions (Qs. 9 to 12) : Consider the following graph where the prices of timber are given for the period 1997-2003. The prices for plywood and sawn timber are given in ₹/m^3 while the price of logs is given in ₹/tonne. Assume 1 ton is equal to 1,000 kg and one cu.m of log weigh 800 kg.

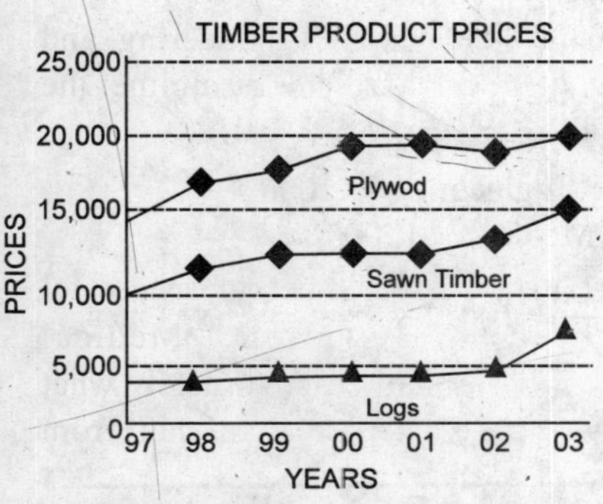

9. Which product had the largest percentage increase in price per cubic meter over the 7-year period ?

A. Sawn timber
B. Logs
C. Plywood
D. None of these

10. The maximum increase in price per cubic metre for any product over any two successive years was :

A. ₹ 2,500 B. ₹ 3,125
C. ₹ 2,000 D. ₹ 4,125

11. In 2003, the total sales of the company measured in cubic metres was made up of 40% plywood, 30% sawn timber and 30% logs. The average realisation per cubic metre in 2003 was closest to :

A. ₹ 16,500 B. ₹ 13,500
C. ₹ 15,000 D. ₹ 18,000

12. In 2004, the prices of plywood, sawn timber and logs went up by 5%, 1% and 10%, respectively, and the total sales were made up of 40% plywood, 30% sawn timber and 30% logs. The average realisation per cubic metre in 2004 was closest to :

A. ₹ 15,500 B. ₹ 16,500
C. ₹ 14,500 D. ₹ 18,500

EXPLANATORY ANSWERS

1. A:

2. C: $x = ₹\ 3.6 \text{ crore} - ₹\ \frac{3.6}{0.6} \text{ crore} = -₹\ 2.4 \text{ crore}$

$a = ₹\ 5 \text{ crore} \times 1.2 - ₹\ 5 \text{ crore} = ₹\ 1 \text{ crore}$

Thus, $a > x$.

3. B: Required exports = ₹ 2.19 crore × 0.6 = ₹ 1.314 crore.

4. D: There is no relation between imports of company A in year-V and exports of company B in year-VIII and the given data is not sufficient to answer the question.

5. B:

Institute	Required difference
A	1200 – 800 = 400
B	1400 – 300 = 1100
C	1400 – 400 = 1000
D	1200 – 600 = 600
E	1000 – 500 = 500
F	1600 – 1200 = 400.

6. D: Total number of successful candidates in Medical = 5300, Law = 4800

Required percentage = $\frac{5300 \times 4800}{4800} \times 100$ = 10.4% = 10%.

7. C: Successful candidates from F in Engineering = 1600
Successful candidates from A in Medical = 1200

Required percentage = $\frac{1600 - 1200}{1200} \times 100$

$= \frac{100}{3} = 33\frac{1}{3}\%$.

8. D:

	A	B	C	D	E	F
Medical	1200	1400	400	600	500	1200
Engineering	800	300	1400	1200	1000	1600
Law	200	400	500	1500	1300	900

Hence, in B the total number of successful candidates of Engineering and Law is 50% of the number of candidates of Medical.

9. B: Increase in plywood = $\frac{(20,000 - 14000)}{14000} \times 100 = 42.86\%$

Increase in Sawn Timber = $\frac{15000 - 10000}{10000} \times 100 = 50\%$

Increase in Logs = $\frac{\frac{7500}{1.25} - \frac{4000}{1.25}}{\frac{4000}{1.25}} \times 100$ = 87.5%

Hence, Logs had the largest increase in prices.

10. A: In plywood during 97 to 98 the price rise is about ₹ 2500 and it is maximum.

11. C: 40% of ₹ 20000 = $20000 \times \frac{40}{100}$ = ₹ 8000

30% of ₹ 15000 = $15000 \times \frac{30}{100}$ = ₹ 4500

30% of ₹ 7500 = $7500 \times \frac{30}{100}$ = ₹ 2250

Total = ₹ 8000 + ₹ 4500 + ₹ 2250 = ₹ 14750 ≈ ₹ 15000.
Hence, correct answer in C

12. A:

24
PIE CHARTS

PIE CHARTS

These are used to show the share of various sectors in the total. They usually show the percentage share of each sector in the whole (taken as 100%). In such representation the total quantity in question is distributed over a total angle of 360°. The area of each sector is proportional to the relative frequency of the class represented by the sector.

$$\text{Sector angle} = \frac{\text{Class frequency}}{\text{Total frequency}} \times 360°$$

For Illustration:

Distribution of Expenditure of a family

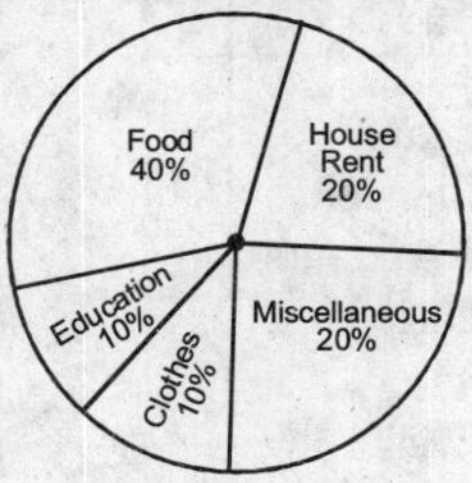

EXERCISE

Directions (Qs. 1 to 4) : *Study the pie-chart carefully to answer the questions that follow:*

Percentage-wise Break up of Students in terms of Specialization in MBA

TOTAL NUMBER OF STUDENTS = 8000

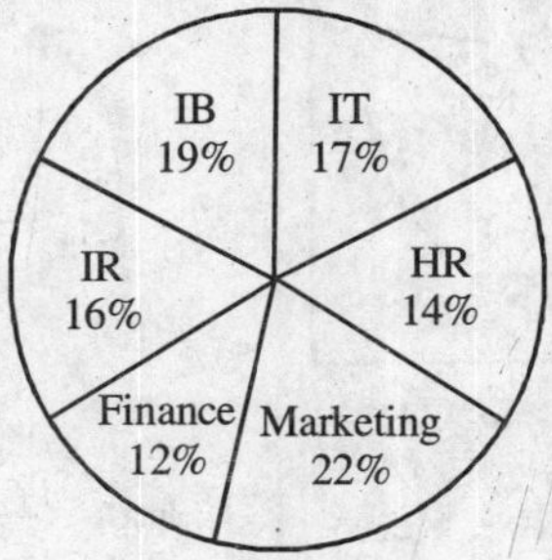

1. What is the total number of students having specialization in IR, Marketing and IT?
   A. 4640 B. 4080
   C. 4260 D. 4400

2. Students having IB as specialization forms **approximately** what per cent of students having Marketing as specialization?
   A. 116 B. 86
   C. 124 D. 74

3. What is the total number of students having IB as specilization?
   A. 1520 B. 1280
   C. 1360 D. 1120

4. What is the respective ratio of the students having Finance as specialization to that of students having HR as specialization?
   A. 11 : 19 B. 18 : 13
   C. 6 : 7 D. 12 : 21

Directions (Qs. 5 to 8) : *Study the graph below to answer these questions.*

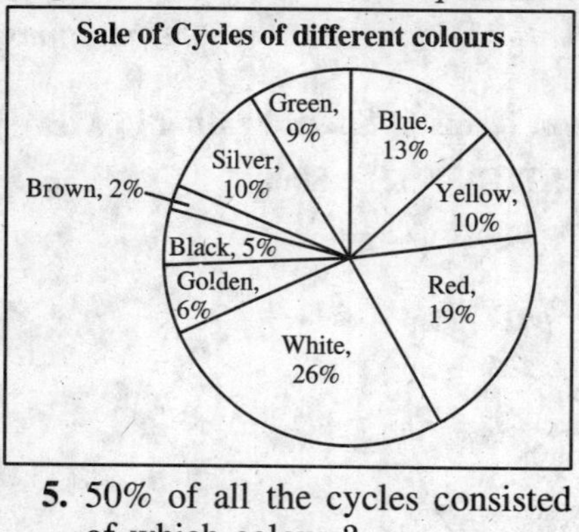

5. 50% of all the cycles consisted of which colours?
   A. Black, Golden, Blue, Red
   B. Blue, Black, Red, Silver
   C. White, Golden, Blue, Black
   D. Golden, Green, Black, White

6. Cycles of which colour when increased by two per cent and then combined with that of red cycles will make 30 per cent of the total?
   A. Golden
   B. Blue
   C. Black
   D. None of these

7. If in certain period the total production of all cycles was 95400 then how many more blue cycles were sold than green?
   A. 2580 B. 3618
   C. 2850 D. 3816

8. Cycles of which colour are 20% less popular than white coloured cycles?
   A. Black
   B. Golden
   C. Blue
   D. None of these

Directions (Qs. 9 to 12) : *Study the pir-chart below to answer these questions. The chart gives the composition of solar radiation.*

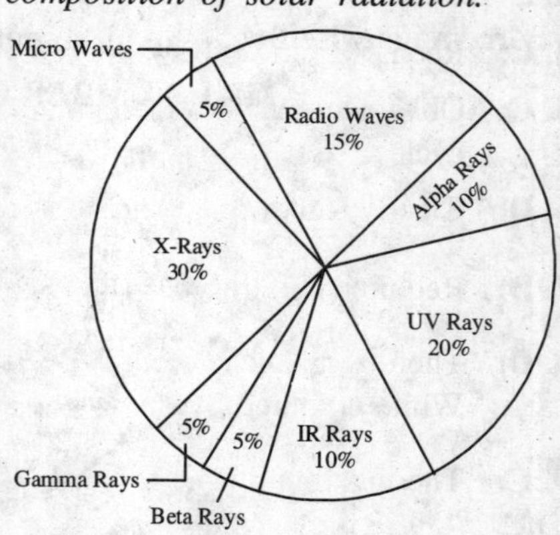

Total sun rays received in one minute = 3600 units

9. If the human body can withstand a maximum of 9720 units of IR rays when exposed to the sun continuously, then what is the maximum time in minutes that any person could stand in the sun without crossing the threshold limit of IR rays?

A. 23 B. 19

C. 27 D. 29

10. The amount of Beta rays in 10 minutes of the sun rays is how many times the amount of IR rays in 3 minutes of the sun rays?

A. 1.44 B. 1.33

C. 1.66 D. None of these

11. How many minutes of exposure to the sun in a day would be enough to ensure that the body receives enough amount of Vitamin D, given that the body requires 40 units of Vitamin D every day and that 30 units of Beta rays generate one unit of Vitamin D?

A. $5\frac{1}{3}$ B. $5\frac{2}{3}$

C. $6\frac{1}{3}$ D. $6\frac{2}{3}$

12. The amount of Alpha rays received in two minutes is how much more/ less than the amount of Radio waves received in 4 minutes?

A. 1320 units more

B. 1200 units less

C. 1440 units less

D. 1600 units more

EXPLANATORY ANSWERS

1. D:

2. B: Required percentage $= \frac{19}{22} \times 100 = 86.36\% \approx 86\%$

3. A: Required number of Students $= \frac{19}{100} \times 8000 = 1520$

4. C: Required ratio = 12 : 14 = 6 : 7

5. C: Obviously, White, Golden, Blue and Black colours consists 50% of cycles.

6. D: Clearly, there is no such colours.

7. D: Required difference $= 95400 \times \frac{(13-9)}{100} = 954 \times 4 = 3816.$

8. D: There is no such coloured cycle which is exactly 20% less popular than White coloured cycles.

9. C: The maximum time $= \frac{9720}{\frac{3600 \times 10}{100}} = 27.$

10. D:

11. D: 40 units of vitamin D generate from

$$= 40 \times 30 = 1200 \text{ units of } \beta\text{-rays}$$

The amount of β-rays received in 1 min.

$$= \frac{5}{100} \times 3600 = 180 \text{ units}$$

$$\text{Hence, required time} = \frac{1200}{180} = 6\frac{2}{3} \text{ min.}$$

12. C: The amount of a-rays received in 2 min.

$$= \frac{10}{100} \times 3600 \times 2 = 720 \text{ units}$$

The amount of radio waves received in 4 min.

$$= \frac{15}{100} \times 3600 \times 4 = 2160 \text{ units}$$

Required difference = 2160 – 720 = 1440 units less.

25

MISCELLANEOUS QUESTIONS

1. When three right hand side digits of a number are 1,000 the number is divisible by:
   A. 4
   B. 5
   C. 9
   D. All the above

2. When the two right hand side digits of a number are 100, the number is divisible by:
   A. 2
   B. 4
   C. 5
   D. All the above

3. When the last digit of a number is 5, the number is divisible by:
   A. 3
   B. 5
   C. 25
   D. All the above

4. The H.C.F. of the product of first six odd numbers and the product of first six even numbers is:
   A. 45 B. 40
   C. 34 D. 30

5. $1\frac{1}{2}+\frac{1}{7}\times 10\frac{1}{2}-2\frac{1}{3}\div 1\frac{3}{4}$ of $1\frac{1}{3}$ is equal to:
   A. 1 B. 2
   C. 3 D. 4

6. $6\frac{1}{2}-\left[5\frac{1}{2}-\left\{4\frac{1}{2}-\left(3\frac{1}{2}-\overline{2\frac{1}{2}-\frac{1}{2}}\right)\right\}\right]$ is equal to:
   A. 4 B. 3
   C. 2 D. 1

7. $\frac{1}{2}+\frac{2}{3}/\frac{3}{7}-\frac{1}{6}$ is equal to:
   A. $5\frac{4}{11}$ B. $3\frac{5}{11}$
   C. $4\frac{5}{11}$ D. $7\frac{6}{21}$

8. The sum of $\frac{1}{2}$, $\frac{1}{4}$, $\frac{1}{8}$ of a number is 28. The number is:
   A. 24 B. 28
   C. 32 D. 36

9. If 20 men can finish a piece of work in 10 days, how many persons can finish the same job in 4 days?
   A. 20 B. 30
   C. 40 D. 50

10. If 15 men can finish a job in 20 days, 25 men will finish the same job in:
    A. 8 days B. 12 days
    C. 16 days D. 12 days

EXPLANATORY ANSWERS

1. D: For example, consider the number 1000. The multiples of 1000 are 125 and 8, while the multiples of 125 and 8 are 5 and 4. Hence, the number is divisible by 4, 5 as well as 8.

2. D.

3. B.

4. A: First six odd numbers are 1, 3, 5, 7, 9, 11

Product of first six odd numbers = $1 \times 3 \times 5 \times 7 \times 9 \times 11$

$= 1 \times 3 \times 5 \times 7 \times 3 \times 3 \times 11$

First six even numbers are 2, 4, 6, 8, 10, 12

Product of first six even numbers = $2 \times 4 \times 6 \times 8 \times 10 \times 12$

$= 2 \times 2 \times 2 \times 2 \times 3 \times 2 \times 2 \times 2 \times 2 \times 5 \times 2 \times 2 \times 3$

The common factors are 3, 3, 5.

$\therefore$ H.C.F. = $3 \times 3 \times 5 = 45$.

5. B: $$1\frac{1}{2}+\frac{1}{7}\times 10\frac{1}{2}-2\frac{1}{3}\div 1\frac{3}{4} \text{ of } 1\frac{1}{3} = \frac{3}{2}+\frac{1}{7}\times\frac{21}{2}-\frac{7}{3}\div\frac{7}{4} \text{ of } \frac{4}{3}$$

$$= \frac{3}{2}+\frac{3}{2}-\frac{7}{3}\div\frac{7}{3} = \frac{3}{2}+\frac{3}{2}-\frac{7}{3}\times\frac{3}{7} = \frac{3}{2}+\frac{3}{2}-1 = \frac{3}{2}+\frac{1}{2} = 2.$$

6. A: $$6\frac{1}{2}-\left[5\frac{1}{2}-\left\{4\frac{1}{2}-\left(3\frac{1}{2}-\overline{2\frac{1}{2}-\frac{1}{2}}\right)\right\}\right]$$

$$= \frac{13}{2}-\left[\frac{11}{2}-\left\{\frac{9}{2}-\left(\frac{7}{2}-2\right)\right\}\right] = \frac{13}{2}-\left[\frac{11}{2}-\left\{\frac{9}{2}-\frac{3}{2}\right\}\right]$$

$$= \frac{13}{2}-\left[\frac{11}{2}-3\right] = \frac{13}{2}-\frac{5}{2} = 4.$$

7. C: $$\frac{1}{2}+\frac{2}{3}/\frac{3}{7}-\frac{1}{6} = \frac{7}{6}/\frac{11}{42} = \frac{7}{6}\times\frac{42}{11} = \frac{49}{11} = 4\frac{5}{11}.$$

8. C: Let the number be x.

$$\therefore \frac{x}{2}+\frac{x}{4}+\frac{x}{8} = 28, \text{ or } \frac{7}{x} = 28 \qquad \therefore x = \frac{28\times 8}{7} = 32.$$

9. D: Work can be finished in 10 days by 20 men

Work can be finished in 1 day by 20×10 men

Work can be finished in 4 days by $\dfrac{20\times 10}{4}$ = 50 men.

10. B: 15 men can finish the job in 20 days

25 men can finish the job in $\dfrac{20\times 15}{25}$ = 12 days.

GENERAL KNOWLEDGE & GENERAL AWARENESS

NATIONAL SYMBOLS

STATE EMBLEM

State Emblem of India is an adaptation from the Sarnath Lion Capital of Ashoka. It was adopted by the Government of India on January 26, 1950. In the adapted form, only three lions are visible, the fourth being hidden from the view. The wheel (Dharma Chakra) appears in relief in the centre of the abacus with a bull on the right and a horse on the left.

The bell-shaped lotus has been omitted. The words ''Satyameva Jayate'' meaning ''Truth alone triumphs'' are inscribed below the Emblem in Devanagari script.

NATIONAL FLAG

The National Flag of India is a horizontal tricolour of deep saffron (Kesari), white and dark green in equal proportion. In the centre of the white band there is a wheel in navy blue colour. It has 24 spokes. The ratio of the length and the breadth of the flag is 3 : 2. Its design was adopted by the Constituent Assembly of India on July 22, 1947.

NATIONAL ANTHEM

Rabindranath Tagore's song 'Jana-gana-mana' was adopted by the Constituent Assembly as the National Anthem of India on January 24, 1950.

Jana-gan-mana-adhinayaka jaya he, Bharata-bhagya-vidhata
Punjab-Sindh-Gujarat-Maratha-Dravida-Utkala-Banga
Vindhya-Himachala-Yamuna-Ganga Uchhala-jaladhi-taranga.
Tava subha name jage, Tava subha asisa mange, Gahe tava jaya gatha,
Jana-gana-mangala-dayak, jaya he Bharata bhagya vidhata,
Jaya he, jaya he, jaya he, Jaya jaya jaya, jaya he.

NATIONAL SONG

Bankim Chandra Chatterji's 'Vande Mataram' which was a source of inspiration to the people in their struggle for freedom, has been adopted as National Song. It has an equal status with the National Anthem.

Vande Mataram
Sujalam, suphalam, malayaja-shitalam,
Shasya shyamalam, Mataram
Shubhrajyotsna,pulkita yaminim,
Phulla kusumita drumadalashobhinim,
Subhasinim sumadhura—bhashinim,
Sukhadam, Varadam, Mataram.

NATIONAL CALENDAR

It is based on the Saka era with Chaitra as its first month and a normal year of 365 days. It was adopted from March 22, 1957. Dates of the national calendar have a permanent correspondence with dates of Gregorian calendar as Chaitra I falls on March 22 in a normal year and March 21 in a leap year. In official communications, both Saka and Gregorian calendar dates are written. Months of the national calendar are Chaitra, Vaishakha, Jaishtha, Ashada, Shravan, Bhadra, Ashvina, Kartika, Margashirsha, Pausha, Magha and Phalguna.

NATIONAL ANIMAL

The magnificent tiger — Panthera tigris (Linnaeus) is the national animal of India. Tiger is found in several parts of the country and is known for its grace, strength, agility and enormous power. 'Project Tiger' was launched in 1973 to check their dwindling population in India.

NATIONAL BIRD

The Indian Peacock — Pavo Christatus (Linnaeus) is the national bird of India. It is a colourful, swan-sized bird with a fan-shaped crest of feathers on its head and a long-slander neck. The male species is more colourful with blue breast and a spectacular bronze-green train of around 200 elongated feathers.

National Flower—Lotus
National Tree—Banyan
National Fruit—Mango
National Currency—Rupee '₹' (One Rupee = 100 Paise)
National Aquatic Animal—Dolphin

BOOKS AND AUTHORS

Name of Book	Author
Ain-e-Akbari	Abul Fazal
Anand Math	Bankim Chandra Chatterjee
An Unknown Indian	Nirad C. Chaudhuri
Arthshastra	Kautilya
Coolie	Mulk Raj Anand
Das Kapital	Karl Marx
Discovery of India	Jawaharlal Nehru
Eternal India	Mrs. Indira Gandhi
Godan	Prem Chand
Gitanjali	Rabindranath Tagore
Gora	Rabindranath Tagore
Geet Govinda	Jayadeva
Harsha Charit	Bana Bhatta
Hindu View of Life	Dr. S. Radhakrishnan
India Wins Freedom	Maulana Abul Kalam Azad
Jobs of Millions	V.V. Giri
Jungle Book	Rudyard Kipling
Kamayani	Jai Shankar Prasad
Kadambari	Bana Bhatta
Life Divine	Sri Aurobindo
Last days of Netaji	G.D. Khosla
Les Miserables	Victor Hugo
Mahabharat	Veda Vyas
Macbeth	William Shakespeare
Mein Kempf	Hitler
Meghduta	Kalidas
Mother (Maa)	Maxim Gorky
Mother India	Katherine Mayo
My Experiments with Truth	Mahatma Gandhi

Name of Book	Author
My Presidential Years	R. Venkataraman
Neeti Shatak	Bhartrihari
Nehru and His Vision	Dr. K.R. Narayanan
Old Man and the Sea	Ernest Hemingway
One World	Wendell Wilkie
Panchtantra	Vishnu Sharma
Paradise Lost	John Milton
Ramayana	Valmiki (in Sanskrit)
Raghuvansham	Kalidas
Rajtarangini	Kalhan
Ram Charit Manas	Tulsi Das
Abhijnan Shakuntalam	Kalidas
Satanic Verses	Salman Rushdie
Saket	Maithili Sharan Gupta
Speed Post	Shobha De
The God of Small Things	Arundhati Roy
Treasure Island	R.L. Stevenson
Twelfth Night	William Shakespeare
Train to Pakistan	Khuswant Singh
Uttara Ram Charitra	Bhava Bhuti
Vanity Fair	W.M. Thackeray
War and Peace	Leo Tolstoy
Wealth of Nations	Adam Smith
Wake up India	Annie Besant

INVENTIONS AND DISCOVERIES

Geographical Discoveries

Discovery	Discoverer
America	Columbus
Brazil	Cabral
North Pole	Robert Peary
Everest (Conquered)	Tabie Junko
Planetary Motion	Kepler
Hawaiian Islands	Captain Cook
South Pole	Amundsen
Solar System	Copernicus

Chemistry and Physics

Discovery	Discoverer
Atom Bomb	Otto Hahn
Atomic Theory	Dalton
Atomic Numbers	Moseley
Cosmic Rays	R.S. Millikan
Dynamite	Alfred Nobel
Electrons Theory	Bohr
Electricity (current)	Volta
Electric Telegraphy (Code)	S. Morse
Gravitation	Newton
Gas Light	Murdock
Oxygen	J. Priestly
Photography	L. Daguerre
Printing for the blind	Louis Braille
Radium	Madame Curie
Telegraph	Samuel Morse
Television	J.L. Baird
Telephone	Graham Bell
Wireless	G. Marconi
X-rays	W.K. Roentgen

Mechanical

Discovery	Discoverer
Aeroplane	Wright Brothers
Bicycle	Macmillan
Computer	Charles Babbage
Dynamo	Michal Faraday
Diesel Engine	Rudolf Diesel
Engine (Railway)	Stephenson
Fountain Pen	Waterman
Gramophone	Edison
Locomotive Power of Steam	James Watt
Helicopter	Brequet
Life Boat	Henry Greathead
Microscope	Z. Jansen
Printing Press	Gutenberg
Revolver	Colt
Sewing Machine	Elias Howe
Thermometer	Fahrenheit
Transistor	W. Shockley
Typewriter	Sholes
Telescope	Hans Lippershey
Tank (Military)	Swinton

Medical

Discovery	Discoverer
Antiseptic Surgery	Lord Joseph Lister
Bacteria	Leeuwenhock
Circulation of Blood	William Harvey
Homoeopathy (Discovered)	Hahnemann
Insulin	F. Banting
Penicillin	Alexander Flemming
Malaria Parasite	Dr. Ronald Ross
Stethoscope	Laennec
Vitamins	Funk
Anti-Rabies Treatment	Pasteur

General

Discovery	Discoverer
Nylon	Carouthers
Science of Geometry	Euclids

WORLD'S GEOGRAPHICAL SURNAMES

• City of Sky-scrapers—New York • City of Seven Hills—Rome • City of Dreaming Spires—Oxford • City of Golden Gate—San Francisco • City of Magnificent Buildings—Washington D.C. • City of Eternal Springs—Quito (S. America) • China's Sorrow—Hwang Ho • Cockpit of Europe—Belgium • Dark Continent—Africa • Emerald Isle—Ireland • Eternal City—Rome • Empire City—New York • Forbidden City—Lhasa (Tibet) • Garden City—Chicago • Gate of Tears—Strait of Bab-el-Mandeb • Gift of the Nile—Egypt • Granite City—Aberdeen (Scotland) • Hermit Kingdom—Korea • Herring Pond—Atlantic Ocean • Holy Land—Jerusalem • Island Continent—Australia • Islands of Cloves—Zanzibar • Isle of Pearls—Bahrein (Persian Gulf) • Key to the Mediterranean—Gibralter • Land of Cakes—Scotland • Land of Golden Fleece—Australia • Land of Maple Leaf—Canada • Land of Morning Calm—Korea • Land of Midnight Sun—Norway • Land of the Thousand Lakes—Finland • Land of the Thunderbolt—Bhutan • Land of White Elephant—Thailand • Land of Thousand Elephants—Laos • Land of Rising Sun—Japan • Loneliest Island—Tristan De Gunha (Mid-Atlantic) • Manchester of Japan—Osaka • Pillars of Hercules—Strait of Gibraltar • Pearl of the Antilles—Cuba • Playground of Europe—Switzerland • Quaker City—Philadelphia • Queen of the Adriatic—Venice • Roof of the World—The Pamirs, Central Asia • Sugar bowl of the world—Cuba • Venice of the North—Stockholm • Windy City—Chicago • Whiteman's grave—Guinea Coast of Africa • Yellow River—Huang Ho (China) • Sickman of Europe—Turkiye.

CURRENCIES OF DIFFERENT COUNTRIES

Country	Currency	Country	Currency
Australia	Australian Dollar	Poland	Zloty
Bangladesh	Taka	Spain	Euro
Belgium	Euro	Indonesia	Rupiah
Britain	Pound (Sterling)	Iraq	Dinar
Myanmar	Kyat	Italy	Euro
Canada	Canadian Dollar	Japan	Yen
Germany	Euro	Mexico	Peso
Iran	Rial	Netherland	Euro
India	Rupee	European Union	Euro
Ceylon	Rupee	Sweden	Krone
China	Yuan	Switzerland	Swiss Franc
Czech Republic	Koruna	Turkiye	Lira
Denmark	Krone	U.A.E.	Dirham
France	Euro	U.S.A.	Dollar
Pakistan	Rupee	Russia	Rouble

CAPITAL OF COUNTRIES

Country	Capital	Country	Capital
Austria	Vienna	Kenya	Nairobi
Afghanisatan	Kabul	Kuwait	Kuwait
Algeria	Algiers	Laos	Vientiane
Angola	Luanda	Lebanon	Beirut
Australia	Canberra	Mexico	Mexico City
Argentina	Buenos Aires	Malaysia	Kualalumpur
Bangladesh	Dhaka	Morocco	Rabat
Belgium	Brussels	Mozambique	Maputo
Bolivia	Lapaz	New Zealand	Welington
Bulgaria	Sofia	The Netherlands	Amsterdam
Bhutan	Thimpu	Panama	Panama City
Brazil	Brasilla	Portugal	Lisbon
Canada	Ottawa	Poland	Warsaw
China	Beijing	Sri Lanka	Colombo
Cyprus	Nicosia	Sweden	Stockholm
Columbia	Bagota	Switzerland	Bern
Denmark	Copenhegan	Sudan	Khartoum
Ethiopia	Addis Ababa	Sierre	Leone
Finland	Helsinki	South Africa	Capetown
France	Paris	Saudi Arabia	Riyadh
Germany	Berlin	Spain	Madrid
Greece	Athens	Thailand	Bangkok
Guatemala	Guatemala City	Turkiye	Ankara
Hungary	Budapest	Russia	Moscow
Iran	Tehran	Azerbaijan	Baku
India	New Delhi	Armenia	Yerevan
Indonesia	Jakarta	Latvia	Riga
Iraq	Baghdad	Ukrain	Kiev
Italy	Rome	U.S.A.	Washington
Ireland	Dublin	U.K.	London
Japan	Tokyo	Egypt	Cairo
Combodia	Phnom Penh	Vietnam	Hanoi
Korea (North)	Pyong Yang	Zambia	Lusaka
Korea (South)	Seoul		

INDIAN CITIES AND THEIR RIVERS

City	State/UT	River	City	State/UT	River
Agra	U.P.	Yamuna	Patna	Bihar	Ganga
Ahmedabad	Gujarat	Sabarmati	Prayagraj	U.P.	Confluence of the Ganga, Yamuna, and invisible Saraswati
Alwaye	Kerala	Periyar			
Kolkata	West Bengal	Hooghly			
Cuttack	Odisha	Mahanadi			
Delhi	Delhi	Yamuna	Srinagar	J & K	Jhelum
Haridwar	Uttarakhand	Ganga	Surat	Gujarat	Tapti
Kanpur	Uttar Pradesh	Ganga	Tiruchirapally	Tamil Nadu	Kaveri
Ludhiana	Punjab	Sutlej	Ujjain	Madhya Pradesh	Shipra
Lucknow	Uttar Pradesh	Gomati	Vijayawada	Andhra Pradesh	Krishna
Nasik	Maharashtra	Godavari	Varanasi	Uttar Pradesh	Ganga

WONDERS OF THE WORLD

Seven Wonders of the Ancient World: (1) the Pyramids of Egypt, built in approximately 2700 BC; (2) the Hanging Gardens at Babylon; (3) the temple of Artemis at Emphesus; (4) the statue of Zeus at Olympia; (5) the tomb of Mausolus at Halicarnassus, built in nearly 350 BC; (6) the Colossus of Rhodes, built in nearly 280 BC; (7) the Pharos Lighthouse at Alexandria.

Seven Wonders of the Medieval World: (1) the Colosseum of Rome; (2) the Great Wall of China; (3) the Porcelain Tower of Nanking; (4) the Mosque at St. Sophia (Constantinople); (5) Stonehenge; (6) the Catacombs of Rome; (7) the Leaning Tower of Pisa.

Seven New Wonders of the World: (1) Taj Mahal of Agra (India); (2) Pyramid at Chichen Itza (Mexico); (3) Machu Picchu (Peru); (4) Statue of Christ The Redeemer (Brazil); (5) Great Wall of China; (6) Roman Colosseum, Italy; (7) Ruins of Petra, Jordan.

STATES & UT's OF INDIA (CAPITALS, PRINCIPAL LANGUAGES)

States/UT's	Capitals	Principal Languages
Andhra Pradesh	Amaravati	Telgu and Urdu
Arunachal Pradesh	Itanagar	Monpa, Adi, Nissi etc.
Assam	Dispur	Assamese and Bengali
Bihar	Patna	Hindi and Maithili
Chattishgarh	Raipur	Hindi
Goa	Panaji	Konkani
Gujarat	Gandhi Nagar	Gujarati
Haryana	Chandigarh	Hindi
Himachal Pradesh	Shimla	Hindi and Pahari
Jharkhand	Ranchi	Hindi
Kerala	Thiruvananthpuram	Malayalam
Karnataka	Bengluru	Kannada
Madhya Pradesh	Bhopal	Hindi
Maharashtra	Mumbai	Marathi
Meghalaya	Shillong	Khashi, Jayantia and Garo
Manipur	Imphal	Manipuri
Mizoram	Aizawl	Mizo and English
Nagaland	Kohima	Naga, Assamese and English
Odisha	Bhubaneshwar	Odiya
Punjab	Chandigarh	Punjabi
Rajasthan	Jaipur	Hindi, Rajasthani
Sikkim	Gangtok	Sikkimese and Gorkhali
Tamil Nadu	Chennai	Tamil
Tripura	Agartala	Bengali, Tripuri and Manipuri
Uttar Pradesh	Lucknow	Hindi
Uttarakhand	Dehradun	Hindi
West Bengal	Kolkata	Bengali
Telangana	Hyderabad	Telgu and Urdu

States/UT's	Capitals	Principal Languages
Jammu & Kashmir	Srinagar	Kashmiri, Dongri, Urdu, Dardi and Pahari
Andaman and Nicobar Islands	Shri Vijaya Puram	Hindi, Nicobarese, Bengali, Malayalam, Tamil, Telugu
Chandigarh	Chandigarh	Hindi, Punjabi, English
Dadar and Nagar Haveli and Daman and Diu	Daman	Gujarati, Hindi
Delhi	Delhi	(Hindi, Punjabi)
Lakshadweep	Kavaratti	Malayalam
Puducherry	Puducherry	Tamil, Telugu, Malayalam, English and French
Ladakh	Leh	Ladakhi, Pahari

HIGH COURTS IN INDIA

Name	Year	Territorial Jurisdiction	Seat
Allahabad	1866	Uttar Pradesh	Prayagraj (Bench at Lucknow)
Andhra Pradesh	2019	Andhra Pradesh	Amaravati
Bombay	1862	Maharashtra, Goa, Dadar and Nagar Haveli and Daman and Diu	Mumbai (Benches at Nagpur, Panaji and Sambhaji Nagar)
Calcutta	1862	West Bengal and Andaman & Nicobar	Kolkata (Circuit Benches at Shri Vijaya Puram and Jalpaiguri)
Chhattisgarh	2000	Chhattisgarh	Bilaspur
Delhi	1966	Delhi	Delhi
Gauhati	1948	Assam, Nagaland, Mizoram and Arunachal Pradesh	Guwahati (Benches at Kohima, Aizawl and Itanagar)
Gujarat	1960	Gujarat	Ahmedabad
Himachal Pradesh	1971	Himachal Pradesh	Shimla
Jammu & Kashmir and Ladakh	1928	Jammu & Kashmir, Ladakh	Srinagar and Jammu
Jharkhand	2000	Jharkhand	Ranchi
Karnataka	1884	Karnataka	Bengaluru (Circuit Benches at Dharwar and Gulbarga)
Kerala	1958	Kerala & Lakshadweep	Ernakulam
Madhya Pradesh	1956	Madhya Pradesh	Jabalpur (Benches at Gwalior and Indore)
Madras	1862	Tamil Nadu & Puducherry	Chennai (Bench at Madurai)
Orissa	1948	Odisha	Cuttack
Patna	1916	Bihar	Patna
Punjab and Haryana	1966	Punjab, Haryana and Chandigarh	Chandigarh
Rajasthan	1949	Rajasthan	Jodhpur (Bench at Jaipur)
Sikkim	1975	Sikkim	Gangtok
Uttarakhand	2000	Uttarakhand	Nainital
Tripura	2013	Tripura	Agartala
Meghalaya	2013	Meghalaya	Shillong
Manipur	2013	Manipur	Imphal
Telangana	2019	Telangana	Hyderabad

HILL STATION

Station	State
1. Almora, Mussoorie Nainital	Uttarakhand
2. Cherrapunji (Shillong), Khasi Hills (Shillong)	Meghalaya
3. Ooty, Kodaikanal Yereaud	Tamil Nadu
4. Dalhousie, Kassauli	Himachal Pradesh
5. Darjeeling	West Bengal
6. Gulmarg, Srinagar	Jammu & Kashmir
7. Mahabaleshwar	Maharashtra
8. Mt. Abu	Rajasthan
9. Panchmarhi	Madhya Pradesh
10. Ranchi	Jharkhand

FAMOUS NATIONAL PARKS

1.	Corbett National Park	:	Nainital, Uttarakhand
2.	Dudhwa National Park	:	Lakhimpur Kheri, Uttar Pradesh
3.	Kaziranga National Park	:	Jorhat, Assam
4.	Kanha National Park	:	Jabalpur, Bhedaghat, Madhya Pradesh
5.	Gir National Park	:	Rajkot, Junagarh, Gujarat
6.	Guindy National Park	:	Guindy, Chennai, Tamil Nadu
7.	Nagairhole National Park	:	Coorg, Karnataka
8.	Bandipur National Park	:	Mysore, Karnataka

FAMOUS NATIONAL WILDLIFE SANCTUARIES

1.	Dachigam Wildlife Sanctuary	:	Srinagar, Jammu and Kashmir
2.	Sariska	:	Alwar, Rajasthan
3.	Hazaribagh Wildlife Sanctuary	:	Hazaribagh, Jharkhand
4.	Mudhumali Wildlife Sanctuary	:	Mudhumalia, Nilgiri, Tamil Nadu
5.	Periyar Wildlife Sanctuary	:	Idukki, Kottayam, Kerala

HOLY PLACES IN INDIA

1.	Amarnath	Jammu and Kashmir	8.	Mathura	Uttar Pradesh
2.	Ayodhya	Uttar Pradesh	9.	Puri	Odisha
3.	Badrinath	Uttarakhand	10.	Rameswaram	Tamil Nadu
4.	Dwarka	Gujarat	11.	Tirupati	Andhra Pradesh
5.	Haridwar	Uttarakhand	12.	Ujjain	Madhya Pradesh
6.	Kancheepuram	Tamil Nadu	13.	Varanasi	Uttar Pradesh
7.	Kedarnath	Uttarakhand	14.	Bodh Gaya	Bihar

SPORTS

Terms Associated With Sports :

Cricket : Ashes, Bye, Bodyline, Bowling, Break, Cover-point, Creases, Chinaman, Chucker, Drive, Duck, Follow on, Googly, Hit-Wicket, Hat-trick, Leg-before-wicket, Leg break, Leg-bye, Maiden over, No ball, Night-watchman, Runner, Run-out, Stumped, Silly-point, Slip.

Football : Handball, Corner kick, Dribble, Free Kick, Hat-trick, Off-side, Penalty Kick, Try, Throw in, Wembley.

Hockey : Bully, Carry, Corner kick, Corner, Penalty stroke, Off-side, Penalty, Roll in scoop, Sticks, Sudden death, Striking circle, Short Corner, Scoop, Tie-breaker, Under-cutting, Hat-trick.

Tennis : Backhand drive, Deuce, Fault, Half-volley, Net, Let, Volley, Smash, Service.

Billiards : Break, Cannons, Cue, Pot, Jigger, Scratch, In Bauk, In, Off.

Bridge : Dummy, Finesse, Grand-slam, Little Slam, Revoke, Ruff slam, Trump, Tricks, Vulnerable.

Volley Ball : Booster, Love, Service, Volley, Smasher.
Badminton : Smash, Drop, Let.
Chess : Check, Checkmate, Gambit, State-mate.
Golf : Bogy, Caddie, Hole, Links, Stymie, Tee, Put.
Polo : Chukker, Mallet, Bunder.
Baseball : Bunting, Diamond, Pitcher, Put-out, Strike, Home.
Boxing : Knockout, Punch, Upper-cut, Jab, Hook.

FAMOUS TROPHIES

Agha Khan Cup	Hockey
Beighton Cup	Hockey
Corbillion Cup	World Table Tennis (Women)
Davis Cup	Lawn Tennis
Duleep Trophy	Cricket
Durand Cup	Football
Ezra Cup	Polo
I.F.A. Shield	Football
Irani Cup	Cricket (India)
Jayalaxmi Cup	Table Tennis (Women)
Lady Rattan Tata Trophy	Hockey (Women)
Nehru Cup	Hockey (India)
Obaidullah Cup	Hockey
Ranji Trophy	Cricket (India)
Rangaswamy Cup	Hockey (India)
Rovers Cup	Football (India)
Santosh Trophy	Football (India)
Subroto Cup	Football
Thomas Cup	Badminton
Uber Cup	Badminton (Women)
Wellington Trophy	Rowing (India)

BIGGEST, LARGEST, TALLEST OF THE WORLD

Largest Desert	Sahara (Africa)
Rainiest Place	Mowsynram near Cherrapunjee (Meghalaya, India)
Biggest Ocean	Pacific Ocean
Deepest Ocean	Pacific Ocean
Largest Mammal	Whale
Fastest Animal	Cheetah
Lightest Substance	Hydrogen gas
Longest River	Nile
Highest Waterfalls	Salto Angel Falls (Venezuela)

Tallest Animal	Giraffe
Largest Bird (Land)	Ostrich
Hardest Mineral	Diamond
Largest Delta	Sunderbans (W.B. India)
Longest Day	June, 21
Shortest Day	December, 22
Biggest Army	People's Liberation Army, China
Largest Salt Water Lake	Caspian Sea
Highest Mountain Peak	Everest (8848 metre high)
Longest Wall	Great Wall of China
Largest Peninsula	Arabia
Largest Planet	Jupiter
Smallest Continent	Australia
Largest Lake	Caspian Sea
Deepest Lake	Baikal, 3200 ft.
Finest Harbour	Sydney Harbour
Smallest Planet	Mercury
Largest Continent	Asia
Planet nearest to the Sun	Mercury
Highest Building	Burj Khalifa, Dubai
Country Biggest	Russia (17075000 sq. km.)
Electorate, Largest	India (over 90 crores)
Longest Epic	Mahabharat
Island, Biggest in the World	Greenland
Population, Largest	China
Longest Railway Platform	Shree Siddharoodha Swamiji Railway Station, Hubballi, Karnataka (India)
Swimming Course	English Channel

FIRST IN INDIA

Governor General of Independent India — Lord Mountbatten
Indian Commander-in-chief of free India — General K.M. Cariappa
Cosmonaut — Sq. Ldr. Rakesh Sharma
Field Marshal — S.H.F.J. Manekshaw
Indian Governor General of Indian Union — C. Rajagopalachari
Indian I.C.S. Officer — Satyendra Nath Tagore
Indian to swim across English Channel — Mihir Sen
Indian Women to swim across English Channel — Miss Arti Saha
Chief of Defence Staff — Gen. Bipin Rawat

Man to climb Mount Everest	— Tenzing Norgay
Man to climb Mount Everest without Oxygen	— Phu Dorjee
Man to climb Mount Everest twice	— Nwang Gombu
Nobel Prize Winner	— Rabindra Nath Tagore
President of Indian National Congress	— W.C. Banerjee
President of Indian Republic	— Dr. Rajendra Prasad
Talkie Film	— Alam Ara (1931)
Test Tube Baby (Documented)	— Indira
Viceroy of India	— Lord Canning
Woman Minister of Indian Union	— Rajkumari Amrit Kaur
Woman Governor	— Mrs. Sarojini Naidu
Woman President of Indian National Congress	— Dr. Annie Besant
Woman Prime Minister	— Mrs. Indira Gandhi
Woman Speaker of a State Assembly	— Mrs. Shanno Devi
Prime Minister of India	— Pt. Jawaharlal Nehru
Muslim President of Indian Union	— Dr. Zakir Hussain
Speaker of Lok Sabha	— G.V. Mavlankar
Women to Climb Mount Everest	— Bachhendri Pal
Woman Judge in Supreme Court	— Mrs. Meera Sahib Fatima Biwi
Women Chief Justice of a High Court	— Smt. Leela Seth
The First Indian Weightlifter to Win bronze medal in Olympics	— Karnam Malleshwari (Sydney, in 2000)
World Chess Champion	— Vishwanathan Anand
India's First Woman Merchant Navy Officer	— Sonali Banerjee
The First Woman Air Vice-Marshal	— P. Bandopadhyaya
The First Indian to be appointed as United Nations Civilian Police Advisor	— Ms. Kiran Bedi
The First Women to be appointed Deputy Governor of Reserve Bank of India	— K.J. Udeshi
The First Indian Lady to win a medal in World Athletic Championship	— Anju Bobby George
The First Sikh Prime Minister of India	— Dr. Manmohan Singh

IMPORTANT DAYS

15th January	—	Army Day
26th January	—	Republic Day
30th January	—	Leprosy Eradication Day/ Martyr's Day
28th February	—	National Science Day
8th March	—	International Women's Day
15th March	—	World Consumer's Day
21st March	—	World Disabled Day

5th April	—	National Marine Day
7th April	—	World Health Day
18th April	—	World Heritage Day
22nd April	—	International Earth Day
Ist May	—	Worker's Day
3rd May	—	International Sun Day
21st May	—	Anti-Terrorism Day
24th May	—	Commonwealth Day
31st May	—	World No Tobacco Day
5th June	—	World Environment Day
21st June	—	International Yoga Day
26th June	—	International Day against Drug Abuse
11th July	—	World Population Day
15th August	—	Independence Day
24th August	—	Sanskrit Day
5th September	—	Teacher's Day
8th September	—	World Literacy Day
29th September	—	World Tourism Day
1st October	—	World Elder's Day
6th October	—	World Animal Day
8th October	—	Air Force Day
10th October	—	National Solidarity Day
16th October	—	World Food Day
24th October	—	U.N. Day
14th November	—	Children's Day
19th November	—	National Integration Day
26th November	—	Law Day
1st December	—	World AIDS Day
4th December	—	Navy Day
7th December	—	Flag Day
10th December	—	Human Rights Day

PARLIAMENTS OF IMPORTANT COUNTRIES

Afghanistan	—	Shora
Britain	—	Parliament House of Commons, House of Lords
Denmark	—	Folketing
The Netherlands	—	States General
India	—	Sansad
Israel	—	Knesset

Iran	—	Majlis
Ireland	—	Airetann
Iceland	—	Althing
Japan	—	Diet
Norway	—	Storting
Russia	—	Supreme Soviet
Spain	—	Cortes
Sweden	—	Riksdag
U.S.A.	—	Congress Senate
Germany	—	Bundestag

MINERAL RESOURCES OF THE WORLD

Mineral	Largest Producers		
Petroleum	Saudi Arabia	Russia	USA
Mica	China	Russia	India
Manganese	South Africa	USA	Brazil
Silver	Peru	China	Mexico
Gold	China	Australia	USA
Aluminium	China	Russia	Canada
Iron Ore	China	Brazil	Australia
Coal	China	U.S.A.	India

WORLD'S LARGEST PRODUCERS

Articles	Producers	Articles	Producers
Carpets	Iran	Rice	China
Cheese	USA	Rubber	Thailand
Cocoa	Cote D'Ivoire	Silk	China
Coffee	Brazil	Steel	China
Copper	Chile	Sugar	Brazil
Cotton	China	Tea	China
Diamonds	Russia	Tin	China
Jute	India	Wheat	China
		Wool	Australia

TEN LARGEST COUNTRIES AND THEIR AREAS

Rank by Area	Country	Area (sq. km.)	Rank by Area	Country	Area (sq. km.)
1.	Russia	17,075,400	6.	Australia	7,686,848
2.	Canada	9,976,139	7.	India	3,287,263
3.	China	9,561,000	8.	Argentina	2,776,889
4.	U.S.A.	9,363,123	9.	Kazakhstan	2,724,900
5.	Brazil	8,511,965	10.	Algeria	2,381,741

PARLIAMENT

Parliament is the national legislature of the Indian Union. It consists of two Houses known as the Council of States or the Rajya Sabha and the House of People or Lok Sabha. The President is an integal part of Parliament.

Rajya Sabha: The Rajya Sabha is the Upper House of the Parliament and it is constituted of representatives from the States or the Constituent units of the Indian Union. It is a permanent body, one third of its members retiring after every two years. Its maximum strength is 250. Out of these, twelve members are nominated by the President from well-known personalities in the realm of Science, Art, Literature and Social Service. Rest of 238 representatives of the States and Union Territories are elected. Rajya Sabha at present consists of 245 members.

Lok Sabha: The Lok Sabha whose life is five years, is the Lower House of Parliament and comprises of members directly elected by the people. The House of the people (Lok Sabha) at present consists of 543 members directly elected from the states and Union Territories. By the 104th amendment, 2019 of the Constitution the reservation for two members of the Anglo-Indian Community by President have been abolished. The House of the People shall continue for five years (unless sooner dissolved) from the date of its meeting and no longer and the expiry of the said period of 5 years shall operate as dissolution of the House.

PRESIDENT

The President is the Constitutional head of the Republic of India. He is more or less the titular head of the executive. Really speaking, he is the constitutional head but not the real executive.The real power is vested in the hands of the Council of Ministers.

Qualifications: (*i*) Indian citizen, (*ii*) age not less than 35 years, (*iii*) should have qualification for election to Lok Sabha, (*iv*) should not hold any office of profit, (*v*) should not be a Member of Parliament or State Legislature.

Powers: He makes appointments to all the constitutional posts. He can address either House of Parliament and dissolve Lok Sabha. All Bills passed by Parliament must receive his assent to become an Act. He issues ordinances when Parliament is not in session. No Money Bill can be introduced in Lok Sabha without his recommendation. He can grant pardon, reprieve or remit punishment and he can commute death sentences, can declare national emergency, state emergency and financial emergency.

Term and Emolument: The President holds the office for a period of five years. He is eligible for re-election. He draws a fixed salary. He is also entitled to rent free official residence called Rashtrapati Bhawan.

VICE-PRESIDENT

The Vice-President acts as the ex-officio Chairman of the Council of States (Rajya Sabha). He is elected by an electoral college consisting of the members of both Houses of Parliament in accordance with the system of proportional representation by means of the single transferable vote. He must be a citizen of India, not less than 35 years of age, and should be eligible for election as a member of the Council of States. Disputes in connection with election of a president or a vice-president are to be a dealt with in accordance with Article-71. Such disputes shall be decided by the Supreme Court.

PRIME MINISTER

The Constitution lays down that there shall be a Council of Ministers headed by the Prime Minister to aid and advise the President in the exercise of his functions. The Prime Minister is the head of the Cabinet. Other Ministers are appointed by the President on his advice. He is the leader of the majority party in the Lok Sabha.

THE SOLAR SYSTEM: SOME FACTS

Number of Planets: 8—Mercury, Venus, Earth, Mars, Jupiter, Saturn, Uranus and Neptune.

Largest most

Massive planet .... Jupiter
Brightest planet .... Venus
Brightest star .... Sirius
Fastest orbiting planet .... Mercury
Longest (Synodic) day .... Mercury
Planet with largest moon .... Jupiter
Greatest average density .... Jupiter
Tallest mountain .... Mars
Strongest magnetic fields ... Jupiter
Most circular orbit .... Venus
Shortest (synodic) day .... Jupiter
Hottest planet .... Venus
No moons .... Mercury, Venus
Planet with moon with most eccentric orbit .... Neptune
Lowest average density ...... Saturn
Deepest Oceans .... Jupiter
Greatest amount of liquid on the surface .... Earth

THE EARTH: FACTS AND DATA

Composition of the Earth: Aluminium (0.4%), Sulphur (2.7%), Silicon (13%), Oxygen (28%), Calcium (1.2%), Nickel (2.7%), Magnesium (17%), Iron (35%)

Surface area	:	510100500 sq km
Land Surface (29.1%)	:	148950800 sq km
Ocean Surface (70.9%)	:	361149700 sq km
Type of water	:	97% salt, 3% fresh
Total area of water	:	382672000 sq km
Equatorial diameter	:	12753 km

Equatorial Circumference	:	40066 km
Polar Circumference	:	39992 km
Polar diameter	:	12710 km
Equatorial radius	:	6376 km
Polar radius	:	6335 km
Mass	:	5.976×10^{24} kg
Mean distance from the Sun	:	149407000 km
Earth's orbit speed (around sun)	:	107320 kmph
Period of Revolution (round the sun)	:	365 days 5 hrs 48 min. 45.51 seconds
Time of Rotation (on its axis)	:	23 hrs 56 min 4.09 seconds
Inclination of the axis (to the plane of the ecliptic)	:	23°27'

PRINCIPAL MOUNTAIN PEAKS OF THE WORLD

Mountains	Height in Metres	Range	Date of First Ascent
1. Mount Everest	8,848	Himalayas	May 29, 1953
2. K-2 (Godwin Austen)	8,611	Karakoram	July 31, 1954
3. Kanchenjunga	8,597	Himalayas	May 25, 1955
4. Lhotse	8,511	Himalayas	May 18, 1956
5. Makalu I	8,481	Himalayas	May 15, 1955
6. Dhaulagiri I.	8,167	Himalayas	May 13, 1960
7. Mansalu I	8,156	Himalayas	May 9, 1956
8. Chollyo	8,153	Himalayas	Oct. 19, 1954
9. Nanga Parbat	8,124	Himalayas	July 3, 1953
10. Annapurna I	8,091	Himalayas	June 3, 1950
11. Gasherbrum I	8,068	Karakoram	July 5, 1958
12. Broad Peak I	8,047	Karakoram	June 9, 1957
13. Gasherbrum II	8,034	Karakoram	July 7, 1956
14. Shisha Pangma (Gosainthan)	8,014	Himalayas	May 2, 1964
15. Gasherbrum III	7,952	Karakoram	Aug. 11, 1975

POPULAR NICK NAMES OF SOME FAMOUS PERSONALITIES

Andhra Kesari	T. Prakasam
Anna	C.N. Anna Durai
Bang Bandhu	Sheikh Mujibur Rehman
Bapu	Mahatma Gandhi
Bard of Avon	William Shakespeare
Chachaji	Jawaharlal Nehru
Desh Bandhu	C.R. Das
Frontier Gandhi	Khan Abdul Gaffar Khan
Fuhrer	Adolf Hitler
G.B.S.	George Bernard Shaw
Grand Old Man of India	Dadabhai Naoroji
Grand Old Man of Britain	Gladstone
Guru Dev	Rabindra Nath Tagor
Guruji	M.S. Golwalkar
Iron Man of India	Sardar Patel
Lok Nayak	Jayaprakash Naraya
Lady with the Lamp	Florence Nightingale
Lal, Bal, Pal	Lala Lajpat Rai, B Gangadhar Tilak, Bipin Chand Pal

Little Corporal	Napoleon Bonaparte	Netaji	Subhash Chandra Bose
Lokmanya	Bal Gangadhar Tilak	Nightingale of India	Sarojini Naidu
Mahamana	Pt. Madan Mohan Malaviya	Panditji	Jawaharlal Nehru
Maid of Orleans	Joan of Arc	Punjab Kesari	Lala Lajpat Rai
Maiden Queen	Queen Elizabeth I	Shastriji	Lal Bahadur Shastri
Missile Man	A.P.J. Abdul Kalam	Uncle Ho	Ho Chi Minh
Man of Destiny	Napoleon Bonaparte	Wizard of the North	Walter Scott

FAMOUS INTERNATIONAL ORGANISATIONS, HEADQUARTERS AND YEAR OF ESTABLISHMENT

International Organisations	*Headquarters*	*Year of Establishment*
United Nations Organisations (U.N.O.)	New York	1945
International Monetary Fund (I.M.F.)	Washington D.C.	1945
World Health Organisation (W.H.O.)	Geneva	1948
Food & Agricultural Organisation (FAO)	Rome	1945
International Labour Organisation (ILO)	Geneva	1919
UNESCO	Paris	1946
International Court of Justice	The Hague	1946
Universal Postal Union (UPU)	Berne	1874
International Civil Aviation Organisation (ICAO)	Montreal	1944
UNIDO	Vienna	1966
International Atomic Energy Agency (IAEA)	Vienna	1957
International Finance Corporation (IFC)	Washington	1956
United Nations Development Programme (UNDP)	New York	1965
UNICEF	New York	1946
International Maritime Organisation (IMO)	London	1958
World Meteorological Organisation (WMO)	Geneva	1950
International Telecommunication Union (ITU)	Geneva	1865
Arab League	Cairo	1945
Commonwealth of Nations	London	1949
World Trade Organisation (WTO)	Geneva	1995
International Development Association (IDA)	Washington D.C.	1960
International Bank for Reconstruction and Development (IBRD)	Washington D.C.	1944
World Intellectual Property Organisation (WIPO)	Geneva	1967
Organisation of Islamic Conference (OIC)	Jeddah (Saudi Arabia)	1971
European Union	Brussels	Changed form of EEC Established in 1958
Red Cross	Geneva	1863
Interpol	Lyon	1923
Asian Development Bank (ADB)	Manila	1966
North Atlantic Treaty Organisation (NATO)	Brussels	1949
Association of South East Asian Nations (ASEAN)	Jakarta	1967

HIGHEST HONOURS OF SOME COUNTRIES

Country	Highest Honour	Country	Highest Honour
India	Bharat Ratna	Britain	Member of British Empire, Victoria Cross
Pakistan	Nishan-e-Pakistan	Japan	Order of Moulovenice Sun
Kuwait	Mubarak-Al-kabir Medal	Denmark	Order of Diana Brog
Saudi Arabia	Shah Abdul Aziz Medal	France	Legend of Honour
Argentina	The Order of Sona Martin	America	Presidential Medal of Freedom
Nicaragua	Augusto-Caesar Sandino Order	Germany	Pore Lee Merit Iron Cross
Vietnam	The order of the Golden Star	The Netherlands	The Order of Lion of the Netherlands
Hungary	The Order of Banner		

ART AND CULTURE

☞ **Classical Dances**

Dance	State	Famous Artists
Bharat Natyam	Tamil Nadu	Yamini Krishnamurthy, Rukmini Devi Arundale, Swapna Sundari, Sonal Mansingh, Vaijanti Mala, Mrinalini Sarabhai, Chandralekha, Indrani, Ram Gopal, Bal Saraswati
Kathakali	Kerala	Gopinath, K.K. Nayar, Kunju-Kurup, T.K. Chandu
Kuchipudi	Andhra Pradesh/ Telangana	Sapna Sundari, Raja Reddy, Shobha Nayar, Radha Reddy, Vedantam Satyanarayan, Vimpanti Chinna Satyam.
Kathak	North India	Birju Maharaj, Gopi Krishna, Shambhu Maharaj, Sitara Devi, Vishnu Sharma, Durga Lal, Shobhana Narayan
Odissi	Odisha	Kelucharan Mahapatra, Indrani Rehman, Madhavi Mudgal, Pratima Bedi, Samyukta Panigrahi, Sonal Mansingh, Debudas
Manipuri	Manipur	Uday Shankar, Bipin Singh, Suryamukhi, Darohra Jhaveri

☞ **Famous Folk Dances**

State/UT	Folk Dance
Andhra Pradesh/ Telangana	Dandari, Banjara
Assam	Bihu, Keli Gopal, Sataria
Bihar	Chhau, Magahi, Durga dance
W. Bengal	Kirtan, Kalatri, Asweabadh, Brita, Kalidance
Chhattisgarh	Saila, Karama, Bhagoria
Gujarat	Garba, Rasalila, Tippani, Dandia
Haryana	Damyal, Lahoor
Himachal Pradesh	Dussehra dance, Hikat, Notio
Jammu & Kashmir	Dumhal
Jharkhand	Jhau, Ghumakudia, Jadur, Sarhul, Soharai, Karama, Vaima, Loojhari, Jat-Jatin, Vidayat
Karnataka	Yakshagan, Dolu Kunitha

State/UT	Folk Dance
Kerala	Mohini Attam, Padayuni
Madhya Pradesh	Lota Nritya, Jawara
Maharashtra	Tamasha, Dahi Handi, Go Deepak Dindi
Manipur	Dhol Cholam
Meghalaya	Nongakarem
Nagaland	Bamboo dance
Odisha	Chhau, Maya Shabari, Dalach
Punjab	Gidda, Bhangra, Panihari
Rajasthan	Thumar, Kathaputali, Tera Ta
Tamil Nadu	Terukalathu, Kabalatam, Kargam, Pulivesham
Tripura	Hazagiri
Uttar Pradesh	Rasalila, Nautanki, Tha Dhurang, Jhumela, Huraka, B
Uttarakhand	Kajari, Karan
Goa	Dhode Modini

MUSIC

Main Schools of Classical Music

- There are two main schools of classical music, namely, the Hindustani and the Carnatic. The Hindustani school of classical music is in vogue in north-western India, eastern India and northern parts of the South India.

Musical Instruments

- *They are:* Tabla, Mridangam, Pakhawaj, Chandai, Dholak, Veena, Sitar, Sarod, Gootuvadhyam, Sarangi, Flute, Nadaswaram, Shehnai, Shringi and Turahi.

FAMOUS INTERNATIONAL AIR SERVICES

Air Service	Name of Country	Air Service	Name of Country
Air India	India	Pan American World Airways	America
British Overseas Airways Corporation	Britain	Lufthansa Airlines	Germany
		Iraqi Airways	Iraq
Trans World Airlines	America	National Airlines	Iran
Russian Airlines	Russia	Quantas Airlines	Australia
Japan Airlines	Japan	Hong-Kong Airlines	Hong-Kong
Pakistan International Airlines	Pakistan	Egypt Airlines	Egypt
Malaysia Airlines	Malaysia	Slovak Airlines	Slovakia
Royal Nepal Airlines	Nepal	S.I.A.	Singapore
Swiss Airways	Switzerland	Garuda Airways	Indonesia
Air France	France	Bangladesh Viman Sewa	Bangladesh
Kuwait Airways	Kuwait	Air Lanka	Sri Lanka
K.L.M. Royal Airlines	The Netherlands (Holland)	Elitalia Airlines	Italy
		Air Canada	Canada

FAMOUS RELIGIONS, FOUNDERS, HOLY BOOKS & PLACES OF WORSHIP

Religion	Founder	Holy Books	Place of Worship
Hinduism	Hinduism has no one Founder. (This religion is based upon the religion of original Aryan Settlers)	Ramayan, Vedas, Puranas and Geeta	Temple
Sikh	Guru Nanak Dev	Guru Grantha Sahib	Gurdwara
Christianity	Jesus Christ	Bible	Church
Islam	Prophet Mohammed	Koran (Quran)	Mosque
Parsi	Zoroaster	Zend Avesta	Fire Temple
Jainism	Adinath Rishavdev	Jain Granth	Jain Temple
Buddhism	Gautam Buddha	Tripitaka	Buddha Temple
Jew	Moosa	Torah	Synagogue

INTELLIGENCE AGENCIES OF SOME PROMINENT COUNTRIES

Country	Intelligence Agency	Country	Intelligence Agency
India	Research & Analysis Wing (RAW), Intelligence Bureau (I.B.),Central Bureau of Investigation (C.B.I.)	Russia	K.G.B. (Komitel Gosudars-tvennoy Bezopasnosty) (Committee for State Security)
Pakistan	Inter Service Intelligence (I.S.I.)	Canada	Security Intelligence Service
U.S.A.	Central Intelligence Agency, Federal Bureau of Investigation	S. Africa	Bureau of State Security
		Iran	Sabak
Britain	Military Intelligence (M.I.)-5 and 6, Special Branch, Ultra, Joint Intelligence Organisation	Iraq	Al-Mukhabarat
		Australia	Australian Security and Intelligence Organisation
Israel	Mosad	France	S.D.E.C.E.
Egypt	Mukhabarat	Spain	C.E.S.I.D.
Japan	Nicho	Cuba	D.G.I.

SOME PROMINENT RACES OF THE WORLD

Races	Country	Races	Country
Veddas	Sri Lanka	Tartars	Siberia
Somaid	West Siberia	Baddu	Arab's Desert
Masai	East Africa	Semang	Malaysia
Muree	New Zealand	Eskimo	Canada, Tundra Region
Yakoot	Russian Tundra	Lapps	European Tundra
Papuans	New Guyana	Hausa	Nigeria
Pygmy	Congo Basin	Kirghiz	Steppes (Russia)
Bantu	Central and South Africa	Bushman	Kalahari Desert
		Red Indian	North America

FAMOUS STRAITS OF THE WORLD

Strait	Between	Country
Malacca Strait	Andaman Sea and South China Sea	Indonesia
Palk Strait	Mañnar and Bay of Bengal	India-Sri Lanka
Magellan Strait	Pacific and South Atlantic Ocean	Chile
Dover Strait	English Channel and North Sea	England-France
Berring Strait	Berring Sea and Chukasi Sea	Alaska-Russia
Sugaroo Strait	Japan Sea and Pacific Ocean	Japan
Sunda Strait	Java and Indian Ocean	Indonesia
Gibralter Strait	Mediterranean Sea and Atlantic Ocean	Spain
Harmuj Strait	Persia and Bay of Oman	Oman-Iran
Hudson Strait	Bay of Hudson and Atlantic Ocean	Canada

FAMOUS NEWSPAPERS OF THE WORLD

Newspaper	Place of Publishing	Language
Daily News	New York (America)	English
Guardian	London (Britain)	English
Pravada	Moscow (Russia)	Russian
Al-Ahram	Cairo (Egypt)	Arabic

Newspaper	Place of Publishing	Language
Merdeca	Jakarta (Indonesia)	Indonesian
Times	London (Britain)	English
People's Daily	Beijing (China)	Chinese
New Statesman	Britain	English
Daily Mirror	Britain	English
Hindu, Hindustan, Times of India, Tribune, Statesman, Indian Express, Economic Times	India	English
Hindustan, Nav Bharat Times, Dainik Bhaskar, Dainik Jagaran, Punjab Kesari	India	Hindi

IMPORTANT BOUNDARY LINES

Boundary Line	Countries	Boundary Line	Countries
Durand Line	Pakistan and Afghanistan	24th Parallel	India-Pakistan
Hindenberg Line	Germany-Poland	17th Parallel	The line which defined the boundary between North Vietnam and South Vietnam before the two were united.
Maginot Line	France and Germany		
Mannerhein Line	Russia-Finland		
Mc Mahon Line	India-China		
Order Niesse Line	Germany-Poland	38th Parallel	North Korea and South Korea
Radcliff Line	India-Pakistan		
Seigfrid Line	Germany-France	49th Parallel	U.S.A. and Canada

SIGNALS/SIGNS AND MEANING

Signal/Sign	Meaning	Signal/Sign	Meaning
Red Triangle	Family Planning	White Flag	Treaty or Surrender
Red Cross	Medical Help	Yellow Flag	Vehicles with patients of contagious diseases
Red Light	Danger, 'Stop' for the movement of vehicles	Two Bones across with a Skull	Danger of electricity
Green Light	Go	Half mast flown Flag	National mourning
Olive Branch	Peace	Lotus and culture	Sign of civilization
White Pigeon or Dove	Peace	Wheel (Chakra)	Sign of Progress
Black Strip on Arm	(i) Opposition (ii) Sorrow	A blind folded woman with scale in hand	Sign of Justice
Black Flag	Opposition		
Red Flag	(i) Danger (ii) Revolution	Reversed flown flag	National calamity

NATIONAL EMBLEMS OF IMPORTANT COUNTRIES

Country	National Emblem	Country	National Emblem
America	Golden Rod	New Zealand	Kiwi, Fern Southern Cross
Australia	Kangaroo		
Ireland	Shamrock	Norway	Lion
Italy	White Lily	Nepal	Kukri
Israel	Candelabrum	Pakistan	Crescent
Iran	Rose	Poland	Eagle
Canada	White Lily	France	Lily
Great Britain	Rose	Belgium	Lion
Chile	Candor and Huemul	Bangladesh	Water Lily
Germany	Corn Flower	Mongolia	The Soyombo
Japan	Chrysanthemum	Russia	Double headed eagle
Zimbabwe	Zimbabwe Bird	Lebanon	Cedar Tree
Denmark	Beach	Sudan	Secretary Bird
Turkiye	Crescent and Star	Syria	Eagle
The Netherlands	Lion	India	Lioned Capital

REGION WISE POPULATION

Region	Population (2021)	World Share (in percentage)
Asia	4,584,249,616	59.1%
Africa	1,375,397,882	17.4%
Europe	747,142,309	9.8%
Latin America and the Caribbean	651,321,069	8.4%
Northern America	373,076,833	4.8%
Oceania	41,663,096	0.5%

COMPUTER

The computer is the system of that electronic device through which various informations are processed on the basis of a definite set of instructions called program and mathematical (numerical) and non-mathematical both types of informations are processed.

The first mechanical computer was composed or fabricated by Blaise Pascal in 1642 and it is called Pascalene. But in 1833, Charles Babbage first time conceived an automatic calculator or computer. Charles Babbage is called the father of modern computer. Herman made an electronic tabulating machine based on punch cards which operates automatically.

In 1937, first mechanical computer mark-I was fabricated by Howard Akeen.

The most outstanding contribution in the development of modern computer goes to John Wan Newmaan who brought the 2nd revolution in the area of computer in 1951. He discovered EDVAC (Electronic Discrete Variable Automatic Computer) and utilised the stored program and the binary number system in the computer.

FUNCTIONS OF COMPUTER

1. Collection and composition (input) of datas;
2. Storage of datas.
3. Processing of datas.
4. Retrieval or output of the proccessed informations and datas.

UNITS OF COMPUTER

1. Input unit.
2. Central processing unit–CPU.
3. External Memory unit.
4. Output unit.

The CPU of the computer is called brain of the computer and sometimes CPU is also called Micro Processor of the computer. The data is entered through the input unit in the computer and through the central processing unit with the help of External Memory Unit datas are arranged and processed. Ultimately by the output unit these datas or informations are issued or released.

PARTS OF COMPUTER

- **Monitor :** The monitor of the computer is like a television in which the picture appears in the form of doted points on the screen and these are called pixcels.
- **Hard Disc and Floppy Disc :** The Hard Disc is the permanent disc in the computers while the Floppy Disc is the disc utilised when datas or informations are to be transferred from one computer to another.
- **Mouse :** The mouse of the computer is like the remote control of TV through which computer is directly regulated or controlled without utilising the key-board.
- **Printer :** The printer is a device which prints any documents or processed informations of the computer.

SOME HIGH LEVEL LANGUAGES

1. **FORTRAN :** This language was developed for solving the mathematical formulae very quickly and conveniently.
2. **COBOL :** This language was developed for the commerical purposes. For the processing of this language a group of sentences is selected called paragraph and all paragraphs composed are called a section, while all sections composed are called a division.

3. **BASIC :** In basic a definite part of the prescribed instruction is only inserted in the computer.
4. **ALGOL :** This was basically fabricated and designed for the complex algebraic calculations.
5. **PASCAL :** It is an amplified and modified form of ALGOL.
6. **COMAL :** This computer language is used for the students of secondary level.
7. **LOGO :** This language is used for children and kids for drawing Graphic line diagrams.
8. **PROLOG :** This language is developed in 1973 in France and this language is used for Artificial Intelligence which is capable and equivalent to the logical program.
9. **FORTH :** This language was invented by Charles Mure which is frequently used in all types of the works in the computer.

COMPUTER VIRUS

The computer virus is an electronic code which is used to abolish or erradicate the inclusive informations or programs of the computer. Some important computer viruses are Micheleanjalo, Dork Avangor, kilo, filip, Macmug, Scores, Casecade, Jeruslem, Date crime, Coloumbs crime, Internet virus, Pachcom, Pach EXE, COM-EXE, Marizuana, C-brain, bloody, Chenge Mungu and Desi etc.

COMPUTER NETWORKING

There are two types of networkings which are usually occur—Local Area Networking (LAN) and Wide Area Networking (WAN). By LAN all the computers of the same buildings are connected like the computers of university premises, computers of offices etc.

By WAN all the comptuers of a large area are connected like the computers of all the offices of a city or town etc. In India a very large computer network namely INDONET has been installing through which all the main towns and cities has to be interlinked.

COMPUTER TERMINOLOGY

- **Bit :** The bit is a unit of measurement of the electronic data. One bit is either 0 or 1 but not both. On composing 8 bits, 1 byte is formed.
- **Bug :** The Bug is the error in the computer program or system and its eradication is called Debug.
- **Byte :** Total eight bits compose a byte. Thus 8 bits = 1 byte.
- **CD-ROM :** A CD like of music CD in which data can be stored substantially called CD-ROM. In a CD with comparison to floppy extremely more datas can be stored but one problem in it is that one time recorded data can not be deleted or modified.

- **Chip :** It is a thin slice on which by a special mechanism a circuit is designed which is normally made from Silicon.
- **Memory System :** The place where computer data and program are temporarily kept is called Memory system. Usually memory is implied from RAM.
- **Modem :** The device which converts digital signals into analogue signals and vice-versa is called Modem.
- **RAM :** It is Random Access Memory (a place) where datas to be processed are kept temporarily and it is unstable memory.
- **ROM :** It is Read Only Memory and it is stable or Non-valatile memory which doesn't ended after power off.
- **Scanner :** It is a device through which graphic image is transformed to digital image and the scanners are of usually two types one desktop and another hand operating.

PROGRAMING

Computers perform phenomenal feats of calculation, but they do not do so in a complicated way. They actually carry out very simple operations, such as addition and subtraction. They achieve their fantastic computing power by carrying out these operations at incredible speed.

The programme, or set of instructions for operating the computer, is therefore written as a sequence of very simple steps. (See box below) Several computer languages have been developed for different applications, including BASIC, COBOL, FORTRAN and PASCAL. Writing programmes is very skilled and time-consuming work. But for most typical computer applications ready-written programmes are available, called "packages".

☞ How A Programme Works

Without a programme to tell it what to do and how to do it, a computer is unable to function. If, for example, you wanted to know how many times the word 'the' appears in this paragraph, or in the whole book, it would not be enough merely to put the text into a computer and then ask it how many times the word appears. For the computer to accomplish the calculations it has to be told what to do in simple steps. The instructions might be:

1. Scan the text until a space followed by 'T' or 't' is found.
2. If the next letter is not 'h', go back to step 1.
3. If the letter is 'h', is the next letter 'e'?
4. If not, go back to step 1. If it is, go to step 5.
5. If 'e' is followed by a space, add 1 to the total.
6. Go back to step 1.

A full computer programme for this operation would need to be broken down into even more simple steps, but a series of such programmes could enable a computer to analyse any amount of text in great detail.

DEFENCE

The Supreme Command of the Armed Forces is vested in the hands of the President of the Country. The responsibility for national defence, however, rests with the Cabinet. All important questions having a bearing on defence are decided by the Cabinet Committee on Political Affairs, which is presided over by the Prime Minister. The Defence Minister is responsible to Parliament for all matters concerning the Defence Services. All the administrative and operational control of Armed Forces are exercised by the Ministry of Defence. The three services – Army, Navy and Air Force function through their respective service headquarters headed by the chief of Staff. The post of the Chief of Defence Staff (CDS) was created in 2019.

COMMISSIONED RANKS IN DEFENCE SERVICES

Army	Navy	Air Force
General	Admiral	Air Chief Marshal
Lieutenant-General	Vice-Admiral	Air Marshal
Major-General	Rear-Admiral	Air Vice-Marshal
Brigadier	Commodor	Air Commodor
Colonel	Captain	Group Captain
Lieutenant-Colonel	Commander	Wing Commander
Major	Lt.Commander	Squadron Leader
Captain	Lieutenant	Flight Lieutenant
Lieutenant	Sub-Lieutenant	Flying Officer

INTERNAL SECURITY ORGANISATIONS OF INDIA

S. No.	Name of Organisation	Year of Creation	Headquarters
1.	Assam Rifles (A.R.)	1835	Shillong
2.	Central Reserve Police Force (C.R.P.F.)	1939	New Delhi
3.	National Cadet Corps (N.C.C.)	1948	New Delhi
4.	Territorial Army	1948	In different States
5.	Indo-Tibetan Border Police	1962	New Delhi
6.	Home Guard	1962	In different States
7.	Coast Guard	1978	New Delhi
8.	Border Security Force (B.S.F.)	1965	New Delhi
9.	Central Industrial Security Force (C.I.S.F.)	1969	New Delhi
10.	National Security Guard	1984	New Delhi
11.	Police	—	In different States

COMMANDER-IN-CHIEFS

1.	General Sir Rob Lockhart	Aug. 15, 1947 — Dec. 31, 1947
2.	General Sir Roy Bucher	Jan. 1, 1948 — Jan. 14, 1949
3.	General K. M. Cariappa	Jan. 15, 1949 — Jan. 14, 1953
4.	General Maharaj Rajendra Sinhji	Jan. 15, 1953 — March 31, 1955

FIRST INDIAN CHIEFS OF STAFF OF INDIAN FORCES

1. General Maharaj Rajendra Sinhji (Army Staff)	April 1, 1955 — May 14, 1955
2. Vice Admiral R.D. Katari (Naval Staff)	April 22, 1958 — June 4, 1962
3. Air Marshal S. Mukherjee (Air Staff)	April 01, 1954 — Nov. 08, 1960

ARMY INSTITUTES

1.	Sainik Schools upto +2 Level	33 places in India
2.	Rashtriya Indian Military College (prepare for entrance to N.D.A)	Dehradun
3.	National Defence Academy (three services)	Khadakwasla, Pune
4.	Indian Military Academy (Army)	Dehradun
5.	Officers Training Academy (3 services) Short Courses	Chennai
6.	National Defence College	New Delhi
7.	The College of Combat	Mhow
8.	The College of Military Engineering	Kirkee
9.	Military College of Telecommunication Engineering	Mhow
10.	The armoured Corps Centre and School	Ahmed Nagar
11.	The School Artillery	Deolali
12.	The Infantry School	Mhow and Belgaum
13.	College of Material Management	Jabalpur

AIR FORCE INSTITUTIONS

Air Force Academy	Hyderabad
Helicopter Training School	Hakimpet
Flying Instructors School	Tambaram, Chennai
The College of Air Warfare	Secunderabad
Air Force Administrative College	Coimbatore
Air Force Technical College	Jalahalli

DEFENCE PRODUCTION UNITS

1.	Bharat Dynamites Ltd.	Hyderabad
2.	Praga Tools	Hyderabad
3.	Mishra Dattu Nigam	Hyderabad
4.	Bharat Electronics Ltd.	Bengaluru
5.	Bharath Earthmovers Ltd.	Bengaluru
6.	Heavy Vehicles Ltd.	Avadi, Chennai
7.	Garden Reach Ship Builders and Engineers Ltd.	Kolkata
8.	Mazagaon Dock	Mumbai

9.	Goa Shipyard	Marmugao
10.	Hindustan Shipyard Ltd.	Vishakhapatnam
11.	Hindustan Aeronautics Ltd.	Bengaluru, Hyderabad, Nasik, Koraput, Kanpur, Lucknow

☞ Indian Army Commands

Command	HQ Location	Command	HQ Location
Eastern Command	Kolkata	Western Command	Chandigarh
Northern Command	Udhampur	Southern Command	Pune
Central Command	Lucknow	Training Command	Shimla
South-Western Command	Jaipur		

☞ Indian Air Force Commands

Command	HQ Location	Command	HQ Location
Western Air Command	New Delhi	South-Western Air Command	Gandhinagar
Central Air Command	Prayagraj	Eastern Air Command	Shillong
Southern Air Command	Thiruvananthapuram	Training Command	Bengaluru

☞ Indian Navy Commands

Command	HQ Location	Command	HQ Location
Eastern Naval Command	Vishakhapatnam	Western Naval Command	Mumbai
Southern Naval Command	Kochi		

☞ Missile and Other Weapons

Name	Class	Range
✶ Agni I	SRBM	850 km
✶ Agni II	MRBM	2500 km
✶ Agni III	IRBM	3500 km-5500 km
✶ Agni IV *or* Agni II Prime	IRBM	4000 km
✶ Agni V	ICBM	5000 km-6000 km
✶ Agni VI	ICBM	8000 km-10000 km
✶ Agni 3SL	ICBM	5200 km-11600 km
✶ Dhanush	SRBM	350 km
✶ Nirbhay	Subsonic Cruise Missile	1000 km

Name	Class	Range
✶ Brahmos	Supersonic Cruise Missile	290 km
✶ Brahmos 2	Hypersonic Cruise Missile	290 km
✶ Prithvi I	SRBM	150 km
✶ Prithvi III	SRBM	350 km
✶ Sagarika	SLBM	700 km-2200 km
✶ Shaurya	TBM	700 km-2200 km
✶ Astra	Air to Air Missile	80 km-100 km

INDIA

1. For how long did Kurukshetra War continue?
A. 20 days B. 30 days
C. 18 days D. 26 days

2. Where is Hawa Mahal located?
A. Jaipur B. Lucknow
C. Bikaner D. Jaisalmer

3. The battle of wandiawash was fought in:
A. 1760
B. 1726
C. 1818
D. 1857

4. Who was the Governor general of India during Sepoy Mutiny?
A. Lord Dalhousie
B. Lord Canning
C. Lord Cornwallish
D. Lord Bentinck

5. Fort William in West Bengal was built in the name of?
A. William Blake
B. William Taylor
C. William III
D. William

6. Which of the following transferred his capital from Dhaka to Murshidabad?
A. Mir Qasim
B. Mir Zafar
C. Murshid Quli Khan
D. Alibardi Khan

7. East India Company was established in
A. 1600 B. 1708
C. 1702 D. 1710

8. By which war was British rule in India established firmly?
A. Battle of Buxar
B. Battle of Wandiwash
C. Battle of Plassey
D. None of these

9. 'Do or Die' Movement is otherwise known as
A. Civil Disobedience Movement
B. Non-cooperation Movement
C. Quit India Movement
D. Khilafat Movement

10. Gandhiji's Satyagraha revolt was initiated against
A. Rowlatt law
B. Partition of Bengal
C. Anti people policy of the British
D. Drain of Wealth

11. First session of Indian National Congress was held in
A. Bombay B. Pune
C. Lucknow D. Dehradun

12. Indus Valley People worshipped the God ......?
A. Pashupati Shiva
B. Agni
C. Mother Goddess
D. All of these

13. The first real emperor of India was
A. Alexander
B. Ashoka
C. Samudragupta
D. Akbar

14. Which of the following Vedas is the oldest?
A. Sam Veda B. Yajur Veda
C. Atharva Veda D. Rig Veda

15. The first general election in India was held in the year
A. 1951 B. 1952
C. 1956 D. 1948

16. Who was the first Female President of the Indian National Congress?
A. Sucheta Kriplani
B. Annie Besant
C. Vijay Lakshmi Pandit
D. Indira Gandhi

17. Who accompanied Bhagat Singh to bomb at the Central Legislature in Delhi?
A. Chandrasekhar Azad
B. Baghajatin
C. Batukeswar Dutta
D. Paramchand

18. Who founded 'Swadesh Bandhav Samity'?
A. Aswini Kumar Dutta
B. Pulin Das
C. Surya Sen
D. Barindra Ghosh

19. The tourism phrase 'Paradise Unexplored' is associated with
A. Jammu & Kashmir
B. North East India
C. Chhattisgarh
D. Uttarakhand

20. Amir Khusro was the Court Poet of
A. Balban
B. Alauddin Khilji
C. Ghiyasuddin Tughluq
D. Akbar

21. Who wrote 'Ramcharita Manas'?
A. Banabhatta
B. Kalidasa
C. Sandhyakara Nandi
D. Tulsi Das

22. Who is known as the 'Father of Modern India'?
A. Rammohan Roy
B. Jawaharlal Nehru
C. Mahatma Gandhi
D. W.C. Banerjee

23. Who wanted Indian National Congress to be 'a safety valve'?
A. A.O. Hume
B. Lord Lytton
C. W.C. Banerjee
D. Surendra Nath Banerjee

24. Who founded 'Indian Association'?
A. Surendra Nath Banerjee
B. Bipin Chandra Pal
C. Barindra Ghosh
D. W. C. Banerjee

25. The Civil Service was brought into existence in India by
A. Warren Hastings
B. Cornwallis
C. Dalhousie
D. Ripon

26. Permanent Settlement was a feature of
A. Zamindari System
B. Mahalwary System
C. Ryotwari System
D. None of above

27. The Gurumukhi script was introduced by
A. Guru Amardas
B. Guru Ramdas
C. Guru Angad
D. Guru Nanak

28. The Rowlatt Act was passed in the year
A. 1916 B. 1918
C. 1919 D. 1921

29. Chandragupta Maurya defeated
A. Poros B. Alexander
C. Seleukas D. Ambhi

30. Supreme Court in India was established in Calcutta in
A. 1771 B. 1774
C. 1775 D. 1776

31. Fakir Mohan Senapati is the famous literary figure of
A. Manipuri B. Odia
C. Maithili D. Telgu

32. The first radio-programme in India was broadcast by Radio Club of Bombay in:
A. 1924 B. 1923
C. 1926 D. 1927

33. On 26 June, 1975, which Indian President declared a State of Emergency?
A. Neelam Sanjeeva Reddy
B. Zakir Hussain
C. V. V. Giri
D. Fakhruddin Ali Ahmed

34. In India, the first state to institute a Human Rights Commission is
A. A.P. B. Kerala
C. W. Bengal D. Rajasthan

35. Which is the highest literate state of India?
A. Kerala
B. Mizoram
C. Sikkim
D. Arunachal Pradesh

36. The Union Territory which became part of India on August 16, 1962 is
A. Goa
B. Daman
C. Puducherry (Pondicherry)
D. Andaman Island

37. The 'Vikram Sarabhai Space Centre' is located at
A. Bengaluru
B. Hyderabad
C. Chennai
D. Thiruvananthapuram

38. The first film actor to be nominated to Rajya Sabha was
A. Ashok Kumar
B. Dilip Kumar
C. Jeevan
D. Prithviraj Kapoor

39. The first Indian Institute of Technology was set up in India in 1950 at
A. Kolhapur B. Kanpur
C. Kharagpur D. Bangalore

40. Which state has the maximum forest cover amongst all Indian States and Union Territories?
A. T.N. B. A.P.
C. M.P. D. U.P.

41. The first ruler in India to mint rupee, a silver coin was
A. Sher Shah Suri
B. Akbar
C. Shahjahan
D. Alauddin Khilji

42. Manas Wildlife Sanctuary housing tigers is in
A. Sikkim
B. Assam
C. Karnataka
D. Arunachal Pradesh

43. Surat is located on the banks of
A. Tapti B. Narmada
C. Godavari D. Yamuna

44. Indira Awas Yojna was launched in
A. 1987 B. 1984
C. 1986 D. 1988

45. The headquarters of Southern Command of Indian Army is in
A. Pune B. Hyderabad
C. Chennai D. Bangalore

46. If the President of India wants to submit his resignation, to whom, would he submit his resignation?
A. Speaker of the Lok Sabha
B. Chief Justice of Supreme Court
C. Vice President
D. Prime Minister

47. 'Akash' is India's .
A. Air to air missile
B. Anti-tank guided missile
C. Surface to surface missile
D. Surface to air missile

48. Tapti river originates from
A. Amarkantak
B. Panchmarhi
C. Trimbakeshwar
D. Satpura range

49. The first municipal corporation in India was established in Madras in
A. 1687 B. 1699
C. 1685 D. 1690

50. How many Postal Index Number (PIN) zones India has been divided into?
A. 6 B. 7
C. 9 D. 8

51. RAW (Research and Analysis Wing) works under
A. Ministry of Home
B. Ministry of Personnel
C. PMO
D. Cabinet Secretariat

52. The Lodi dynasty was founded in 1451 by
A. Ibrahim Lodi
B. Sikandar Lodi
C. Bahlol Lodi
D. None of these

53. In which state is Ghana Bird Sanctuary located?
A. U.P. B. M.P.
C. Rajasthan D. Assam

54. Which state of India touches the boundary most other states?
A. A.P. B. M.P.
C. Assam D. U.P.

55. Which of the Mughal rulers promoted painting most?
A. Babar B. Akbar
C. Jahangir D. Shahjahan

56. The High Courts in India were first established at
A. Calcutta and Madras
B. Calcutta, Madras and Bombay
C. Lucknow, Calcutta and Delhi
D. Madras and Bombay

57. The total number of High Courts in India is
A. 18 B. 13
C. 22 D. 25

58. Both Mahavira and Buddha preached during the reign of
A. Ajatashatru
B. Uday

C. Bimbisara
D. Nandivardhan

59. The first woman film actress who was nominated to the Rajya Sabha?
A. Vyajanthi Mala
B. Madhubala
C. Meena Kumari
D. Nargis Dutt

60. Who gave the slogan 'India for Indians'?
A. Mahatma Gandhi
B. Raja Rammohan Ray
C. Dayanand Saraswati
D. Swami Vivekanand

61. Of the following revolutionaries, who died of 63 days' hunger strike?
A. Chandrashekhar Azad
B. Rasbihari
C. Jatindra Nath Das
D. Sukhdev

62. Who founded the first Women's University in India?
A. Mahamana Malviya
B. Dhondo Keshav Karve
C. Iswarchand Vidyasagar
D. Lala Hardayal

63. The journal published by Mahatma Gandhi in South Africa was
A. Young India
B. Truth
C. Indian Opinion
D. Justice

64. The Satellite Tracking and Ranging Station is located at
A. Bhopal
B. Sriharikota
C. Thiruvananthapuram
D. Kavalur

65. Sarnath is in the state of:
A. UP B. MP
C. Kerala D. Gujarat

66. The Guru who founded the 'Khalsa' was
A. Har Rai
B. Har Kishan
C. Teg Bahadur
D. Govind Singh

67. The famous 'Lucknow Pact' was signed between the Congress and the Muslim League in
A. 1913 B. 1914
C. 1915 D. 1916

68. Who among the following was the first recipient of Bharat Ratna?
A. C. Rajagopalachari
B. Dr. Zakir Hussain
C. Rajendra Prasad
D. Jawaharlal Nehru

69. Buddhist, Hindu and Jain rockcut caves exist in
A. Ajanta B. Ellora
C. Elephanta D. Nasik

70. Who was known as the mother of Indian revolutionaries?
A. Sister Nivedita
B. Annie Besant
C. Madame Cama
D. Matangini

71. The founder of Muslim League was
A. Liaqat Ali
B. Shukat Ali
C. Nawab Salimullah
D. M.A. Jinnah

72. Who of the following is known as 'Deshbandhu'?
A. Chandra Shekhar
B. Chitranjan Das
C. A. O. Hume
D. Annie Besant

73. The Chauri-Chaura episode took place on
A. 1st February, 1922
B. 2nd February, 1922
C. 5th February, 1922
D. 6th February, 1922

74. About 30 per cent of India's area lies in the three states of
A. Rajasthan, Uttar Pradesh and Andhra Pradesh
B. Madhya Pradesh, Andhra Pradesh and Gujarat
C. Rajasthan, Madhya Pradesh and Maharashtra
D. Maharashtra, Andhra Pradesh and Uttar Pradesh

75. The richest state in replenishable groundwater resource is
A. Andhra Pradesh
B. Madhya Pradesh
C. Uttar Pradesh
D. West Bengal

76. Goa became India's .... State
A. 25th B. 24th
C. 26th D. 27th

77. In which State would you find Jim Corbet National Park?
A. Assam
B. Uttar Pradesh
C. Maharashtra
D. Uttarakhand

78. Jharia mines are situated in which of the following States?
A. Jharkhand
B. West Bengal
C. Bihar
D. Odisha

79. 'Sardar Sarovar' project is in which of the following States?
A. Rajasthan B. Haryana
C. Uttar Pradesh D. Gujarat

80. The new name of Rajasthan canal is
A. Gandhi canal
B. Indira Gandhi canal
C. Jawahar canal
D. Subhash canal

81. Which of the following lakes in Rajasthan is saline?
A. Ana Sagar B. Pichola
C. Sambhar D. Jaisamand

82. In which state is the district of Udham Singh Nagar situated?
A. Punjab
B. Uttarakhand
C. Uttar Pradesh
D. Rajasthan

83. Which amongst the following States has the highest population density as per census 2011?
A. Kerala
B. Madhya Pradesh
C. Uttar Pradesh
D. Bihar

84. Which one among the following states is smallest in area?
A. Andhra Pradesh
B. Gujarat
C. Karnataka
D. Tamil Nadu

85. In which State is Nalsarovar Bird Sanctuary located?

A. Maharashtra B. Odisha
C. Gujarat D. Rajasthan

86. Which of the following is the 28th State of India?
A. Jharkhand
B. Uttarakhand
C. Chhattisgarh
D. Gorakhaland

87. In which State is Ghana Bird Sanctuary located?
A. U.P. B. M.P.
C. Assam D. Rajasthan

88. Which of the following States does not have border with China?
A. Uttarakhand B. U.P.
C. H.P. D. Sikkim

89. What is the capital of the state of Chhattisgarh?
A. Raipur B. Patna
C. Jamshedpur D. Bokaro

90. With which State would you associate the festival of Dev Devali?
A. Bihar
B. West Bengal
C. Uttar Pradesh
D. Maharashtra

91. Areawise, which is the smallest State in India?
A. Goa B. Sikkim
C. Manipur D. Tripura

92. The capital of Lakshdweep is
A. Aizwal B. Port Blair
C. Kavaratti D. Agartala

93. The famous Kanha Wildlife Sanctuary is located in the State of
A. Assam
B. Bihar
C. Madhya Pradesh
D. Karnataka

94. Which one of the following State is most populous?
A. Odisha
B. Uttar Pradesh
C. Maharashtra
D. Bihar

95. Bhangra is a folk dance of
A. Punjab
B. Madhya Pradesh
C. Odisha
D. Assam

96. Kaziranga Animals Sanctuary is situated in the State of
A. Assam
B. Uttar Pradesh
C. Madhya Pradesh
D. Rajasthan

97. Konark temple is situated in the State of
A. Odisha
B. Kerala
C. Madhya Pradesh
D. Andhra Pradesh

98. The State which produces maximum Bauxite in India is
A. Rajasthan
B. Kerala
C. Odisha
D. West Bengal

99. Lumbini, the birth place of Gautam Buddha is in
A. Bihar
B. Sikkim
C. Nepal
D. Uttar Pradesh

100. Which of the following is the least densely populated State?

A. Sikkim
B. Meghalaya
C. Mizoram
D. Arunachal Pradesh

101. "Dudhawa National Park" is situated in
A. Madhya Pradesh
B. Bihar
C. Uttar Pradesh
D. Karnataka

102. Sandal wood is found in
A. Tamil Nadu
B. Himachal Pradesh
C. Karnataka
D. Maharashtra

103. The chief producer of 'Jute' in India is
A. West Bengal B. Karnataka
C. Tamil Nadu D. Assam

104. Thar Ghat and Bhor Ghat are the important passes in
A. Kerala
B. Maharashtra
C. Gujarat
D. Rajasthan

105. The famous monolithic statue of Jain Saint Bahubali is situated in the state of
A. Andhra Pradesh
B. Bihar
C. Karnataka
D. Tamil Nadu

106. Which port of India is the largest exporter of marine products?
A. Kochi
B. Vizag
C. Kolkata
D. Chennai

107. 'Mettur Dam' is constructed on which river?
A. Sutlej
B. Mahanadi
C. Cauvery
D. Krishna

108. Goa was liberated from the Portuguese in
A. 1964 B. 1961
C. 1963 D. 1962

109. The State which accounts for more than 90 per cent of total rubber production in India is
A. Karnataka
B. Kerala
C. Tamil Nadu
D. Andhra Pradesh

110. Which one of the following States has no common border with UP?
A. Punjab
B. Haryana
C. Madhya Pradesh
D. Uttarakhand

111. Name the State in which the Hirakud Dam is located?
A. Odisha B. Karnataka
C. U.P. D. Gujarat

112. Panna in Madhya Pradesh is associated with
A. Manganese B. Mica
C. Copper D. Diamond

113. The holy city Hardwar is in which State?
A. Uttar Pradesh
B. Haryana
C. Bihar
D. Uttarakhand

114. According to the census of 2011 the only State in India that shows excess of females over males is
A. Uttar Pradesh
B. Kerala
C. Maharashtra
D. Jammu & Kashmir

115. Which States share the Tungabhadra multipurpose project?
A. Karnataka and Madhya Pradesh
B. Odisha and Madhya Pradesh
C. Andhra Pradesh and Karnataka
D. Tamil Nadu and Andhra Pradesh

THE WORLD

116. What is the name of China's News Agency?
A. China News Services
B. China Times
C. New China News Agency
D. New China Report

117. Which country's government report is known as yellow book?
A. France B. Britain
C. Italy D. Germany

118. 'ASEAN' stands for
A. Academy of South-East Asian Nations
B. Association of South-East African Nations
C. Association of South-East Asian Nations D. None of the above

119. Which one of the following countries, is not a member of the G-7 Group?
A. France B. Italy
C. Spain D. Germany

120. 'LTTE' stands for
A. Lankan Tigers for Tamil Eelam
B. Liberation Tigers for Tamil Eelam
C. Lankan Troops for Tamil Empire
D. None of the above

121. G-15 is
A. An organisation of the developed countries of the World
B. An organisation of the developed countries of Europe
C. An organisation of the developing countries of Asia
D. An organisation of the developing countries of the World

122. 123 Agreement is between these countries
A. Indo-US
B. Indo-Russia
C. Indo-Pak
D. Indo-China

123. In which year was the new currency 'Euro' introduced?
A. 1996 B. 1997
C. 1998 D. 1999

124. The Longest day in southern Hemisphere is
A. 22 June
B. 22 December
C. 21 March
D. 22 September

125. 'Great Barrier Reef' is situated near
A. South America
B. Europe
C. Australia
D. Africa

126. The largest city of Europe is
A. Paris B. Belgium
C. London D. Vienna

127. The largest producer of Rubber in the world is
A. Malaysia B. Indonesia
C. Thailand D. Phillipines

128. The biggest producer of ships in the world is
A. U.S.A. B. Germany
C. South Korea D. Japan

129. Kimberlay mine in South Africa is the world's largest mine of
A. Gold B. Silver
C. Diamond D. Pearl

130. Maoris are the original inhabitants of
A. Greenland B. Canada
C. New Zealand D. Java Island

131. The largest producer of Tin in the world is
A. China
B. South Africa
C. Namibia
D. Ethiopia

132. UN Day is observed on
A. December 10
B. October 24
C. September 15
D. July 10

133. 'Levanter' is a
A. Bird
B. Wind
C. Place
D. None of these

134. Capetown is a famous port known of the export of
A. Textiles B. Gold
C. Petrol D. Rubber

135. The currency of Bhutan is:
A. Ngultrum B. Yuan
C. Rupiah D. Shekel

136. 'Escudo' is the currency of
A. Singapore B. Slovakia
C. Ecuador D. Portugal

137. 'Swahili' is the official language of
A. New Zealand
B. Kenya
C. Latavia
D. None of the above

138. The first country which hosted the modern Olympics was
A. U.S.A.
B. England
C. Greece
D. None of the above

139. The pre-Korean war border between South Korea and North Korea is called
A. 49th parallel
B. 35th parallel
C. 38th parallel north
D. 17th parallel

140. International Date Line passes through which of the following?
A. Atlantic Ocean
B. Black Sea
C. Mediterranean Sea
D. Pacific Ocean

141. Where is the headquarters of Asian Development Bank?

A. Jakarta B. Manila
C. Singapore D. Bangkok

142. 'World AIDS Day' is observed on
A. January 1 B. April 1
C. September 1 D. December 1

143. The following is not a member of the European Union
A. Turkiye B. Cyprus
C. Slovakia D. Ireland

144. The most drought-prone country of the world is
A. Australia B. Egypt
C. Iraq D. Mexico

145. The first Guinness Book of World Records appeared in the year
A. 1950 B. 1954
C. 1960 D. 1963

146. The Secretary General of UNO is appointed by
A. The General Assembly
B. The Security Council
C. The International Court of Justice
D. The General Assembly on the recommendations of the security council

147. Which of the following countries is a member of OPEC?
A. Britain B. Russia
C. Kuwait D. Mexico

148. Where was the first Non-Aligned Summit (NAM) Meet held?
A. New Delhi B. Cairo
C. Belgrade D. Havana

149. Which one of the following is the capital of Cambodia?
A. Ho Chi Minh City
B. Janoi
C. Semarong
D. Phnom Penh

150. Which one among the following administers the International Development Association?
A. UNDP B. UNIDO
C. IFAD D. IBRD

151. The Americans are also known as
A. Kiwis
B. Yankees
C. Tories
D. None of the above

152. The term fascism is mainly associated with
A. Germany B. Italy
C. Spain D. France

153. Paris is situated on the river
A. Danube B. Seine
C. Tiber D. Avon

154. The first person to enter into space was
A. Valentina Tereshkova
B. Bdward H. White
C. Yuri Gagarin
D. Alan Shepard

155. Which of the following is International body?
A. IBRD B. IFC
C. IDA D. All of these

156. Yen is the currency of
A. Japan B. USA
C. Canada D. U.K.

157. When is the 'International Women's Day' observed?
A. March 8 B. February 14
C. May 10 D. October 2

158. Diamond Harbour and Salt Lake Cities are situated in
A. California B. Florida
C. Hong Kong D. Kolkata

159. The largest natural gas reserves are found in
A. Russia
B. Antarctica
C. Senegal
D. South Africa

160. The headquarters of APEC (Asia Pacific Economic Cooperation) is situated at
A. Kuala Lumpur B. Singapore
C. Lima D. Santiago

161. Which of the following countries leads space launch tally?
A. Russia B. USA
C. Japan D. E.U.

162. The 1st Lady Prime Minister in the world was
A. Golda Meir
B. Srimavo Bhandarnaike
C. Indira Gandhi
D. Margrett Thatcher

163. The strait which separates Asia from North America is
A. Berring strait
B. Palk Strait
C. Strait of Gibralter
D. Strait of Malacca

164. In World War I (1914-1918) Central Powers did not include
A. Serbia B. Turkiye
C. Bulgaria D. Austria

165. Which of the following is a land locked sea?
A. Timor Sea
B. Aral Sea
C. Greenland Sea
D. None of the above

166. Airoflat (Airways) belongs to
A. Australia B. Hong Kong
C. Russia D. Poland

167. The sobriquet—'Little Corporal' is associated with
A. Napolean
B. Lal Bahadur Shastri
C. Gladstone
D. C.F. Andrews

168. 'Orange Book' is the official publications of the government of
A. Poland B. France
C. Netherlands D. Belgium

169. Who is considered as 'Father of Australia'?
A. Izaak Walton
B. Sir Edmund Barton
C. George Caley
D. Jeremy Bentham

170. The old name of Zimbabwe is
A. Northern Rhodesia
B. Southern Rhodesia
C. New Hebrindes
D. Christiana

171. Who is credited with the 'first round the world' non-stop flight?
A. James Gallagher
B. John A Macready
C. Steve Fossett
D. Oakkley Kelly

172. Atacama desert is located in
A. Europe
B. South Africa
C. South America
D. Asia

173. Ndjamena is the capital of
A. Sudan B. Albania
C. Bulgaria D. Chad

174. Grand National Assembly is the parliament of
A. Turkiye B. Venezuela
C. Nauru D. Zambia

175. The world's smallest republic is
A. Monaco B. Hong Kong
C. Vetican City D. Nauru

176. Magna Carta was signed in
A. 1250 AD B. 1215 AD
C. 1295 AD D. 1280 AD

177. International Police Organisation—Interpol was created in
A. 1925 B. 1923
C. 1930 D. 1931

178. Kampuchea is the old name of
A. Burkina Faso B. Cambodia
C. Benin D. Laos

179. Which of the following is known as land of cakes?
A. Scotland
B. Switzerland
C. Germany ·
D. None of these

180. Who is called the 'Father of Railways'
A. James Watt
B. Izzak Walton
C. E.A. Pal
D. George Stephenson

181. During Second World War the Prime Minister of England was
A. C.R. Attlee
B. Winston Churchill
C. James Callaghan
D. Edward Heath

182. What is called as the 'Roof of the world'?
A. Indira Point
B. Kanchenjunga
C. Pamir Knot
D. Indira Col

183. Which among the following is called 'The Land of Morning Calm'?
A. Canada B. Thailand
C. Korea D. Myanmar

184. Tagalog is a native tongue of which country?
A. Italy B. Philippines
C. Germany D. Australia

185. The unification of East and West Germany took place in
A. 1990 B. 1991
C. 1993 D. 1994

186. Which city is the capital of Myanmar?
A. Mandalay B. Moulmein
C. Nay Pyi Taw D. Pegu

187. The headquarters of the Green Peace International are located at
A. Amsterdam B. Canberra
C. Ottawa D. Nagasaki

188. The grassland of Argentina is known as:
A. Pampas
B. Campos
C. Savanna
D. None of the above

189. 'Sick Man of Europe' is the nick name of
A. Serbia B. Rome
C. Turkiye D. Italy

190. Which is the currency of Myanmar?
A. Kyat B. Lira
C. Boht D. Dollar

191. The United Nations University is located at
A. Tokyo B. Geneva
C. New York D. Washington

192. When is the Earth Day celebrated?
A. April 7 B. April 22
C. June 5 D. April 8

193. Which of the following is situated in Paris?
A. Statue of Liberty
B. Eiffel Tower
C. Victoria Memorial
D. Leaning Tower of Pisa

194. Human Rights day is celebrated on
A. 10 December
B. 1 December
C. 4 December
D. 3 December

195. Which one of the following is not correctly matched?
A. China–Shanghai
B. Canada–Ottawa
C. Australia–Canberra
D. Russia–Moscow

196. The headquarter of World Trade Organisation (WTO) is located at
A. Rome
B. New York
C. Geneva
D. Washington DC

197. Which of the following countries is not a member of SAARC?
A. Nepal B. China
C. Pakistan D. India

198. Where is SAARC secretariat situated?
A. Islamabad
B. Colombo
C. New Delhi
D. Kathmandu

199. What is the activity of the INTERPOL?
A. Central record keeping agency of the international crimes
B. Investigative agency of the UN
C. An organisation to coordinate the police activities of the participating nations
D. A terrorist outfit

200. The six official languages of the UN are Russian, Chinese, English, French, Spanish and
A. Hindi B. Urdu
C. Arabic D. Japanese

201. What does SAPTA stands for?
A. South Asian Preferential Trade Agreement
B. South Asian Post Trade Agreement
C. SAARC Preferential Trade Agreement
D. SAARC Prevention Trade Agreement

202. The Association of South East Asian Nations (ASEAN) has its headquarters at
A. Manila
B. Jakarta
C. Kuala Lumpur
D. Bangkok

203. The normal term of office of UN Secretary General is
A. 3 years B. 4 years
C. 5 years D. 6 years

204. Which one of the following is the most urbanised country of South Asia?
A. Bhutan B. India
C. Pakistan D. Sri Lanka

205. Which of the following is NOT a permanent member of the UN Security Council?

A. Germany B. France
C. Great Britain D. China

206. The first Secretary General of the United Nations was
A. Mrs. Vijay Lakshmi Pandit
B. Trygve Lie
C. Dag Hammarskjoeld
D. U. Thant

207. Who was the first Indian to be the President of U.N. General Assembly?
A. Natwar Singh
B. V.K. Krishna Menon
C. Smt. Vijay Laxmi Pandit
D. Romesh Bhandari

208. Where is the headquarters of the International Court of Justice?
A. The Hague (Netherlands)
B. Paris (France)
C. Rome (Italy
D. Washington (USA)

209. How many Judges are there in the International Court of Justice?
A. 9 B. 10
C. 11 D. 15

210. When was the United Nations Organisation founded?
A. 20th October, 1945
B. 11th November, 1944
C. 24th October, 1945
D. 26th June, 1945

211. The headquarters of the Organisation of Petroleum Exporting Countries is at
A. Teheran B. Vienna
C. Abu Dhabi D. Doha

212. How many members does the Security Council of UN have?
A. 10 B. 15
C. 16 D. 20

213. Which country is not a member of ASEAN?
A. Indonesia B. India
C. Singapore D. Philippines

214. Which country contributes the main share of greenhouse gases emission?
A. China B. USA
C. Japan D. India

215. The headquarters of the UNO is located in
A. Washington B. New York
C. Philadelphia D. Chicago

GENERAL POLITY

216. Which of the following States does not have a Legislative Council?
A. Uttar Pradesh
B. Maharashtra
C. Bihar
D. Urrarakhand

217. Who takes the decision to hold elections to the Panchayats?
A. Election Commission
B. State Government
C. Central Government
D. District Magistrate

218. According to the Indian Constitution, which of the following has been given Residual Powers?
A. States

B. States and Centre
C. Centre
D. Local Bodies

219. How many Schedules are there in the Indian Constitution?
A. 8 Schedules
B. 10 Schedules
C. 12 Schedules
D. 15 Schedules

220. India has borrowed the Provisions of Directive Principles of State Policy from which country?
A. Great Britain
B. United States of America
C. Ireland
D. China

221. Which President of India remained in office for two terms?
A. Dr. S. Radha Krishnan
B. Dr. Rajendra Prasad
C. Dr. K. R. Narayanan
D. Dr. Neelam Sanjeeva Reddy

222. Which is the permanent House of Parliament in India?
A. House of the People
B. Council of States
C. Legislative Assembly of States
D. None of these

223. Fundamental duties are included through
A. 17th Amendment
B. 42nd Amendment
C. 52nd Amendment
D. 44th Amendment

224. Which one of the following is not a function of the Indian Parliament?
A. To participate in the election of the President
B. To make laws
C. To pass the budget
D. To punish the Judges of High Courts

225. In which year Ladakh become a Union Territory?
A. 2017 B. 2019
C. 2018 D. 2020

226. What is the required quorum of the Members of Rajya Sabha?
A. 1/4 of all members present and voting
B. 1/5 of all members
C. 1/10 of all members
D. 1/2 of all members

227. Who is 'The Guardian of the Constitution of India?
A. The President
B. The Prime Minister
C. The Supreme Court
D. The Parliament

228. By which Article of the Constitution the Fundamental Rights of Indian Citizens can be suspended?
A. Article–356 B. Article–365
C. Article–359 D. Article–374

229. In a unitary form of government the powers of the unit are derived from the
A. Constitution
B. Centre
C. Judiciary
D. None of the above

230. Which of the following word is not included in the Preamble of the Indian Constitution?

A. Secular B. Democratic
C. Federal D. Sovereign

231. What is the procedure to remove the deadlock between Lok Sabha and Rajya Sabha over a Bill?
A. The President convenes a joint sitting of both Houses
B. The Supreme Court decides the issue
C. The President decides the issue
D. The Speaker decides the issue

232. Ashok Mehta Committee was constituted by which Government?
A. Nehru's Government
B. Morarji's Government
C. Chandra Shekhar's Government
D. Rajiv Gandhi's Government

233. Which was the first State after independence to implement Panchayati Raj?
A. Maharashtra B. Rajasthan
C. Uttar Pradesh D. Bihar

234. Which one of the following Articles about Fundamental Rights is directly related to the exploitation of Children?
A. Article–17 B. Article–19
C. Article–23 D. Article–24

235. Consider the following statements and select the correct answer from the codes given at the end
1. A Money Bill cannot be introduced in the Rajya Sabha.
2. Rajya Sabha can reject a Money Bill.
3. Money Bill must be returned to Lok Sabha within 14 days by the Rajya Sabha.
4. There is a provision for joint sitting of the Lok Sabha and the Rajya Sabha in case of disagreement over a Money Bill.

Codes:
A. 1 and 2 are correct
B. 3 and 4 are correct
C. Only 4 correct
D. 1 and 3 are correct

236. The First Finance Commission was constituted in the year
A. 1956 B. 1953
C. 1952 D. 1951

237. Which one of the following Amendments of the Constitution has given Delhi the status of National Capital Territory?
A. 61st B. 69th
C. 71st D. 79th

238. The President of India can be removed from his office only on the ground of
A. Proved misbehaviour
B. Incapability
C. Violating the Constitutions
D. Disobedience of the Parliament

239. Which one of the following States has only one representative each in Lok Sabha?
A. Manipur, Meghalaya
B. Himachal Pradesh, Jammu and Kashmir
C. Arunachal Pradesh, Tripura
D. Mizoram, Nagaland

240. The candidate for the Office of the President must be sponsored by at least

A. 10 electors B. 20 electors
C. 50 electors D. 15 electors

241. Who among the following is known as the guardian of the 'Public Purse' in India?
A. The Comptroller and Auditor General
B. The President
C. The Minister of Finance
D. The Parliament

242. Which of the following countries enjoys a federal form of government?
A. China B. USA
C. Cuba D. Belgium

243. Which of the following countries has an unwritten constitution?
A. UK B. USA
C. Pakistan D. India

244. Although Union List, State List and Concurrent List cover the entire legislative business, yet there may be an item not mentioned anywhere. Who will legislate on that item?
A. Parliament only
B. State Legislature only
C. Both A and B
D. Neither A nor B

245. The most important feature of the Indian Parliament is that
A. It is the Union Legislature in India
B. It also comprises of the President
C. It is bicameral in nature
D. The Upper House of the Parliament is never dissolved

246. The 3-tier of the Panchayati Raj System consists of
A. Gram Sabha, Anchal Panchayat, Panchayat Samiti
B. Janapad Panchayat, Taluka Panchayat, Anchal Panchayat
C. Gram Panchayat, Block and Panchayat Samiti, Zilla Parishad
D. Gram Sabha, Panchayat Samiti, Zilla Parishad

247. A Financial Emergency can be declared by applying
A. Article–360 B. Article–361
C. Article–370 D. Article–371

248. How many times the President of India can seek re-election to his post?
A. Once
B. 2 times
C. 3 times
D. Any number of times

249. Match List-I with List-II and select the correct answer using the code given below the Lists

List-I

(*a*) MP (*b*) President
(*c*) Vice-President (*d*) Speaker

List-II

1. Elected by an Electoral College
2. Elected by the Parliament
3. Elected by the Lok Sabha
4. Elected by adult voting

Codes:

	(*a*)	(*b*)	(*c*)	(*d*)
A.	1	2	3	4
B.	2	3	4	1
C.	3	4	1	2
D.	4	1	2	3

250. Which of the following appointments is NOT made by the President of India?
A. Speaker of the Lok Sabha
B. Chief Justice of India
C. Chief of Air Staff
D. Chief of Army

251. Minimum age of the candidate for contesting Lok Sabha-election is
A. 25 years B. 21 years
C. 30 years D. 35 years

252. Chief Justice of High Court is appointed by
A. Prime Minister
B. Governor
C. Chief Justice of India
D. President, at the advice of Chief Justice of India and the Governor of the concerned state

253. All the following are Fundamental Rights guaranteed by the Indian Constitution except
A. The right to equality
B. The right against exploitation
C. The right to adequate means of livelihood
D. The right to freedom of religion

254. The total number of members in the legislative Council of a state cannot exceed
A. One-fourth of the total number of members of the Legislative Assembly
B. One-third of the total number of members of the Legislative Assembly
C. One-sixth of the total number of members of the Legislative Assembly
D. No such limit has been fixed

255. Which of the following countries has an Unwritten Constitution?
A. USA B. India
C. Pakistan D. UK

256. How many languages have been recognised by the Constitution?
A. 13 B. 14
C. 15 D. 22

257. Gangtok is the capital of
A. Sikkim B. Nagaland
C. Meghalaya D. Manipur

258. Money bills can be introduced in the State Legislature with the prior consent of
A. The Speaker
B. The Chief Minister
C. The Governor
D. The President

259. The NITI Aayog of India is
A. A statutory body
B. An advisory body
C. A constitutional body
D. An independent and autonomous body

260. The Attorney-General of India is appointed by
A. The Chief Justice of India
B. The Prime Minister
C. The President of India
D. The UPSC

261. The President of India can nominate to the Rajya Sabha

A. 6 members
B. 9 members
C. 12 members
D. 15 members

262. Which of the following States/ Union Territories have a common High Court?
A. Uttar Pradesh and Bihar
B. Punjab and Jammu and Kashmir
C. Punjab, Haryana and Chandigarh
D. Assam and Bengal

263. The most controversial amendment passed during the emergency was
A. 43rd B. 41st
C. 42nd D. 44th

264. The Union Cabinet is responsible to
A. The Rajya Sabha and the Lok Sabha
B. The President of India
C. The Lok Sabha only
D. The Electorate

265. The Governor of a State in India is
A. Directly elected by the people of the State
B. Appointed by the Prime Minister
C. Appointed by the President
D. Appointed by the State Chief Minister

266. The total number of members of the Legislative Council can in no case be less than
A. 40
B. 60
C. 50
D. No minimum strength has been fixed

267. The right to vote in India is given to all people on the basis of
A. Education B. Age
C. Property D. Religion

268. The maximum strength of the Legislative Assembly of a State is
A. 450 B. 500
C. 400 D. 525

269. The 84th Amendment Act has frozen the total number of existing seats in the Lok Sabha on the basis of 1971 census. They shall remain unaltered till the first census to be taken after the year
A. 2010 B. 2015
C. 2021 D. 2026

270. Match List-I with List-II and select the correct answer using the codes given below the lists:

List-I

(*a*) Public Accounts Committee
(*b*) Committee on Petitions
(*c*) Joint Committee on Stock Market-Scam
(*d*) Department Committees

List-II

1. Adhoc Committee
2. Standing Committee
3. Financial Committee
4. Functional Committee

Codes:

	(*a*)	(*b*)	(*c*)	(*d*)
A.	1	4	3	2
B.	2	3	4	1
C.	3	4	1	2
D.	4	2	1	3

271. The Provisions related to Official Language of India can be amended by

A. Simple majority
B. Minimum 2/3 majority
C. Minimum 3/4 majority
D. Cannot be amended

272. Match List-I with List-II and select the correct answer using the codes given below the lists:

List-I
(Officers)

(*a*) Vice-President of India
(*b*) Comptroller and Auditor General of India
(*c*) Solicitor General of India
(*d*) Attorney General of India

List-II
(Institutions)

1. Public Accounts Committee
2. Meetings of Lok Sabha
3. Rajya Sabha
4. Supreme Court
5. Committee on Public Undertakings

Codes:

	(*a*)	(*b*)	(*c*)	(*d*)
A.	3	1	4	2
B.	2	3	4	1
C.	4	2	3	1
D.	1	4	2	3

273. The Indian Parliament cannot legislate on a subject of State-list unless

1. The President of India directs it to do so.
2. The Rajya Sabha passes a resolution that it is necessary to do so in national interest.
3. The Speaker of the Vidhan Sabha certifies that the legislation is necessary.
4. There is national Emergency.

Considering the above statements, select the correct answer from the codes given below:

Codes:

A. 1, 2 and 3 B. 2, 3 and 4
C. 1 and 2 D. 2 and 4

274. Prior sanction of the President of India is required before introducing the bill, in the Parliament on

1. Formation of a new State.
2. Affecting taxation in which States are interested.
3. Altering the boundaries of the States.
4. Money bill.

Considering the above statements, select the correct answer from the codes given below:

Codes:

A. 1, 2, and 3
B. 2, 3 and 4
C. 1, 2 and 4
D. All of the above

275. Which of the following statements about the Vice-President of India are not correct?

1. In order to be Vice-President a person must be qualified for election as a member of the House of the People.
2. A member of the State Legislature can seek election to that Office.

3. The term of the Office of the Vice-President is the same as that of the President
4. He can be removed through a formal impeachment.

Choose the correct answer from the codes given below:

Codes:

A. 1 and 2 B. 2 and 3
C. 1 and 4 D. 3 and 4

276. The stages in the normal financial legislation include

1. Presentation of the budget
2. Discussion on the budget
3. Passing of Appropriation Bill
4. Vote on Account
5. Passing of the Finance Bill

Choose the correct answer from the codes given below:

Codes:

A. 1, 2 and 3
B. 1, 3 and 4
C. 1, 2, 3 and 4
D. 1, 2, 3 and 5

277. The Tenth Schedule of Indian Constitution deals with

A. Anti-defection Legislation
B. Panchayati Raj
C. Land Reforms
D. Distribution of powers between the Union and States

278. Who among the following can participate in the proceedings of both the Houses of Parliament?

A. Vice-President
B. Solicitor-General
C. Chief-Justice
D. Attorney-General

279. In case the post of President of India falls vacant and there is also no Vice-President, then who among the following would be the acting President?

A. Vice-Chairman of Rajya Sabha
B. Attorney-General of India
C. Lok Sabha Speaker
D. Chief Justice of Supreme Court

280. Which one of the following describes India a Secular State?

A. Fundamental Rights
B. Preamble to the Constitution
C. 9th Schedule
D. Directive Principles

281. Which one of the following statements about the State Governors is NOT true?

A. He is a part of the State Legislature
B. He can pardon a sentence of death
C. He does not appoint judges of the State High Court
D. He has no emergency powers

282. Which of the following constitutional amendment integrated Sikkim as a full-fledged State of the Indian Union?

A. 34th B. 35th
C. 36th D. 37th

283. Which of the following Indian States has no Panchayati Raj institution?

A. Assam B. Tripura
C. Kerala D. Nagaland

284. Which one of the following States has the highest number of reserve seats for the Scheduled Tribes in the Lok Sabha?

A. Bihar
B. Uttar Pradesh
C. Madhya Pradesh
D. Gujarat

285. Match List-I with List-II and select the correct answer using the codes given below the lists:

List-I

(*a*) Article–164 (*b*) Article–155
(*c*) Article–75 (*d*) Article–54

List-II

1. Appointment of the State Chief Minister and Council of Ministers.
2. Appointment of the Governor.
3. Appointment of the Union Prime Minister and Council of Ministers.
4. Election of the President of India.
5. Composition of Legislative Assemblies.

Codes:

	(*a*)	(*b*)	(*c*)	(*d*)
A.	1	2	3	4
B.	1	2	4	5
C.	2	1	3	5
D.	2	1	4	5

286. Which one of the following is the subject of Concurrent List?
A. Police
B. Criminal matters
C. Radio and Television
D. Foreign affairs

287. Which one of the following is the period for the Legislative Council to detain the ordinary bills?
A. 3 months B. 4 months
C. 6 months D. 14 days

288. Which one of the following is correct about the Supreme Court regarding its Judgement?
A. It can change the judgement
B. It cannot change the judgement
C. Only the Chief-Justice of India can change the judgement
D. Only the Ministry of Law can change the judgment

289. Which one of the following is the most important element of the state?
A. Flag
B. Capital
C. Sovereignty
D. Head of the government

290. Which among the following is the correct expression of the term 'Secular' in India?
A. India has many religions
B. Indians have religious freedom
C. To follow the religion depends upon the will of an individual
D. There is no religion of the State in India

291. How many Sessions of the Indian Constituent Assembly were conducted for the formulation of Indian Constitution?
A. 7 B. 11
C. 12 D. 15

292. Which among the following is/are appointed by the President of India?
1. Vice-Chairman of the NITI Aayog
2. Chairman of the Finance Commission
3. Chief Minister of the Union Territories

Select the correct answer by using the following codes:

Codes:

A. Only 2 is correct
B. 2 and 3 are correct
C. 1 and 3 are correct
D. Only 1 is correct

293. Which one of the following Indian States does not keep its own High Court?

A. Odisha
B. Sikkim
C. Himachal Pradesh
D. Goa

294. Which is not correct about a parliamentary form of government?

A. The executive is responsible to the legislature
B. The head of the State can dissolve the lower house of the legislature
C. The executive is a part of the legislature
D. All the ministers are the members from the lower house of the legislature

295. Which constitutional amendment was made in India regarding the Urban local government?

A. 73 B. 74
C. 75 D. 76

296. The Indian Constitution is

A. Very rigid
B. Rigid
C. Flexible
D. Rigid and flexible

297. Article 17 of the Indian Constitution

A. Abolishes untouchability
B. Grants right to equality
C. Protects individual's freedom
D. Grants right to constitutional remedies

298. A candidate to be eligible for the membership of Rajya Sabha should not be less than

A. 21 years B. 25 years
C. 30 years D. 35 years

299. A subject is said to be concurrent list when a law can be passed on it by

A. The President and Prime Minister
B. The Central Government
C. The State Government
D. The Central and State Government

300. When a Money Bill is passed by the Lok Sabha, but not returned by the Rajya Sabha within 14 days of its receipt, then

A. It cannot become an Act
B. It is deemed to have been passed by both the Houses
C. It is again referred to the Rajya Sabha
D. It is again referred to the Lok Sabha

301. One may lose citizenship if he

A. Maintains trade with a foreign country
B. Visits foreign countries
C. Has correspondence with foreign people
D. Takes political shelter in a foreign country

302. Which one of the following is not the power of the President of India?

A. To appoint and dismiss the members of Lok Sabha
B. To appoint and dismiss the ambassadors
C. To dissolve Lok Sabha
D. To declare emergency

303. Indian Constitution was prepared in
A. 2 years 11 months
B. 2 years 11 days
C. 2 years 18 days
D. 2 years 11 months 18 days

304. Which of the following is not included in the preamble to the Indian Constitution?
A. Justice-social, economic and political
B. Education to men, women and children
C. Liberty of thought, expression, faith and worship
D. To promote equality of status and opportunity to all

305. Of the following, which statement regarding Directive Principles is incorrect?
A. They aim at creating tolerable conditions of work
B. They emphasize the need of establishment of a welfare State
C. They can be enforced through law
D. They are the guidelines for government

306. Fundamental rights can be suspended by
A. President
B. Vice-President
C. Prime Minister
D. Speaker of Lok Sabha

307. Supreme Court in India has to work according to the
A. President
B. Prime Minister
C. Parliament
D. Constitution

308. Which of the following subjects is not included in the Union List?
A. Defence B. Income tax
C. Railways D. Sales tax

309. Which of the following features doesnot help the Indian Constitution in becoming unitary in character?
A. Division of powers
B. Single citizenship
C. Single election commission
D. Residuary powers with the centre

310. Which of the following writs or orders is passed by the Supreme Court or a High Court to ascertain the validity of appointment of a person on a certain post?
A. Habeas corpus
B. Prohibition
C. Quo warranto
D. Mandamus

311. Which one of the following is a regional political party?
A. Congress B. BJP
C. CPI D. Akali Dal

312. Which one of the following is enforceable in a court of law?
A. Preamble
B. Fundamental rights
C. Fundamental duties
D. Directive principles

313. Which one of the following is not an essential qualification for appointment as a Governor?
A. He should be a domicile of that state
B. He should be a citizen of India
C. He must have completed the age of thirty five
D. He must not be a member of either House or Parliament

314. The President of India does not appoint
A. The Prime Minister
B. The Chief Election Commissioner
C. The Chief Minister in a State
D. The Chief Justice of a High Court

315. According to which part of the Indian Constitution was the Panchayati Raj started
A. I part B. II part
C. III part D. IV part

316. Indian Constitution for the S.C. and S.T. provides
A. List system
B. Separate electoral system
C. Communal vote system
D. Joint electorate with reservation of seats

317. The Ex-Officio Chairman of the NITI Aayog is
A. President
B. Vice-President
C. Prime Minister
D. Minister for Planning

318. Who among the following is not appointed in the State by the Governor?
A. Speaker of Vidhan Sabha
B. Chief Minister
C. Chairman of State P.S.C.
D. Other Ministers

319. The members of the Rajya Sabha are
A. Directly and indirectly elected
B. Directly elected and nominated
C. Indirectly elected and nominated
D. Only nominated

320. Which of the following is the lowest civil court?
A. The court of a sub-judge
B. The court of a third class Magistrate
C. The court of a Munsif
D. The court of a Naib Tehsildar

321. The Supreme Court of India has exclusive original jurisdiction in regard to
A. Writ petitions
B. Civil cases
C. Criminal cases
D. Centre-State disputes

322. Which is not true in India in the following
A. The centre can make laws from the State list
B. The centre can make laws from the concurrent list
C. The State can make laws from the Union list
D. The State can make laws from the concurrent list

323. The joint session of both the Houses of Parliament is presided over by
A. The President
B. The Vice-President

C. The Prime Minister
D. The Speaker

324. In case of a conflict between the Parliament and the State legislature over a subject in the concurrent list
A. The law of Parliament will prevail
B. The law of State legislature will prevail
C. The law of both will prevail
D. The Supreme Court will decide the matter

325. The ordinance issued by the President must be approved by the Parliament within
A. Six weeks of its issue
B. Six weeks of the re-assembly of the Parliament
C. Six months of its issue
D. Two months of the reassembly of the parliament

326. The President can be impeached by
A. Absolute majority of the Parliament
B. Two third majority of Parliament and State legislatures
C. Two third majority of each House of Parliament
D. Simple majority of the Parliament

327. The judges of Supreme Court can be removed by
A. The Chief Justice of India
B. The Prime Minister
C. The President
D. The Parliament

328. Lok Sabha is not more powerful than 'Rajya Sabha' in the following
A. Legislative matters
B. Executive matters
C. Financial matters
D. Amendment of the Constitution

329. The minimum age required for the member of Legislative Council is
A. 25 years B. 30 years
C. 35 years D. 40 years

330. Which of the election campaigns is illegal in India?
A. Delivering speeches during the polling hours
B. Propaganda on loudspeakers etc.
C. Wall paintings, posters, flags etc.
D. Door to door canvassing by the candidate

ECONOMIC SCENARIO

331. Which region has the maximum concentration of Iron and Steel industries?
A. Shillong Plateau
B. Chota Nagpur Plateau
C. Deccan Plateau
D. Malwa Plateau

332. Capital formation in an economy depends on
A. Total income
B. Total demand
C. Total savings
D. Total production

333. If the tax rate increases with the higher level of Income, it shall be called
A. Proportional tax
B. Progressive tax
C. Lump sum tax
D. Regressive tax

334. New capital issue is placed in
A. Secondary market
B. Grey market
C. Primary market
D. Black market

335. Who appoints a banking Ombudsman?
A. President of India
B. Finance Ministry
C. Supreme Court of India
D. Reserve Bank of India

336. Prime cost is equal to
A. Variable cost plus administrative cost
B. Variable cost plus fixed costs
C. Variable cost only
D. Fixed cost only

337. The main focus of first five year plan was
A. Agricultural Development
B. Industrial Development
C. Sustainable Development
D. Over all Development

338. Bank deposits that can be withdrawn without notice are called
A. Account payee deposits
B. Fixed deposits
C. Variable deposits
D. Demand deposits

339. An expenditure that has been made and cannot be recovered is called
A. Variable cost
B. Opportunity cost
C. Sunk cost
D. Operational cost

340. The practice of selling goods in a foreign country at a price below their domestic selling price is called
A. Diplomacy
B. Discrimination
C. Dumping
D. Double pricing

341. If the cash reserve ratio is lowered by the RBI, it's impact on credit creation will be
A. Increase it
B. Decrease it
C. No impact
D. None of the other

342. Indian Development Forum (IDF) was earlier known as
A. Aid India Consortium
B. Aid India Bank
C. World Bank
D. None of the above

343. It will be true to classify India as
A. A food-deficit economy
B. A labour-surplus economy
C. A trade surplus economy
D. A capital surplus economy

344. Modvat is related to
A. Sales Tax B. Wealth Tax
C. Income Tax D. Excise Duty

345. The twelfth plan's main objective was
A. Removal of poverty
B. Longterm Development
C. Growth with social-justice
D. Development of minorities

346. Rainbow revolution is related with
A. Green-revolution
B. White-revolution
C. Blue-revolution
D. All the above

347. The term 'Orange Economy' is referred to:
A. Creative Economy
B. Orange Farming
C. Food Processing Industry
D. Silk Industry

348. The period of plan-holiday in India was
A. 1962-65 B. 1966-69
C. 1969-72 D. 1972-75

349. The 'Rolling Plan' concept in national planning was introduced by
A. Indira Gandhi
B. The National Front Government
C. The Janata Government
D. Rajiv Gandhi

350. Second Green-revolution will be related with
A. HYVS
B. Wheat
C. Rice
D. Bio-technology

351. Fiscal-deficit is
A. Total expenditure—Total receipts
B. Revenue expenditure—Revenue receipts
C. Capital expenditure—Capital receipts—Borrowings
D. Sum of budget deficit and Govt's market borrowings and Liabilities

352. The impact of Green Revolution was felt most in the production of
A. Wheat B. Rice
C. Pulses D. Oil Seeds

353. The largest producer of Saffron in India is
A. Tamilnadu
B. West Bengal
C. Jammu and Kashmir
D. Kerala

354. Which of the following is related to 'Yellow Revolution'?
A. Fishery
B. Foodgrains production
C. Milk production
D. Oilseeds production

355. Under which Five Year Plan did agriculture register a negative growth?
A. Third B. Fifth
C. Seventh D. Ninth

356. Which of the following is not a speculator in the Stock Exchange?
A. Bull B. Bear
C. Broker D. Stag

357. The largest public sector Commercial bank of India is the
A. Bank of India
B. Reserve Bank of India
C. State Bank of India
D. Union Bank of India

358. The development of tourism and hotel industry in India is the function of
A. I.A.A.I. B. I.T.D.C.
C. I.T.C. D. H.I.C.

359. For a developing country like India small scale and cottage industries should be encouraged primarily because they
A. Equalise wealth distribution
B. Generate large employment
C. Produce at lower cost
D. Require lower capital investment

360. Which of the following items is most significant item of Indian imports in terms of value at present?
A. Machinery and Transport equipments
B. Pearls and precious stones
C. Electronics and computers
D. Petrol and petroleum products

361. The apex bank for industrial credit in India is
A. RBI B. NABARD
C. ICICI D. IDBI

362. The prominent function of the Central Statistical Organisation is
A. To determine the money supply
B. To collect national income estimates
C. To collect employment details
D. To determine prices

363. Planning and control are related in such a way that
A. Planning preceeds control
B. Control preceeds planning
C. Both are concurrent
D. Both go hand in hand with each other in a cyclical manner

364. 'Gresham's Law' states that
A. Good money drives away bad money out of circulation
B. Bad money drives away good money out of circulation
C. Good money promotes bad money in the system
D. Bad money promotes good money in the system

365. National income refers to
A. Money value of goods and services produced in a country during a year
B. Money value of stocks and shares of a country during a year
C. Money value of capital goods produced by a country during a year
D. Money value of consumer goods produced by a country during a year

366. Which of the following taxes is levied by the Union and collected and appropriated by the States?
A. Service tax
B. Stamp duties
C. Estate duty
D. Passenger and goods tax

367. Which of the following is not shared by the Centre and the States?
A. Income tax
B. Excise duty
C. Corporation duty
D. Sales tax

368. Expenditure on which of the following is not considered as an investment in the theory of income determination?
A. Factory construction

B. A computer
C. Increase in stocks of unsold goods
D. Stocks or shares in a joint stock company

369. With what aspect of commerce are "Bull" and "Bear" associated?
A. Banking
B. E-Commerce
C. International trade
D. Stock market

370. FDI means—
A. Foreign Direct Investment
B. Full Dog Cost
C. Full Direct Cost
D. Finance Institute

371. Which of the following state has been announced as 'a state of total organic farming'?
A. Sikkim B. Karnataka
C. Kerala D. Punjab

372. Which amongst the following is one of the books by Bill Gates?
A. Business At the Speed of Thought
B. The Google Story
C. Net and Internet
D. The World is Flat

373. Many times we read a term 'Free Market' in newspapers. What does it mean?
[Pick up the correct statement(s)]
1. It is a market where pricing is driven by the laws of supply and demand.
2. In free market things are available without restraints of the government.
3. In such markets goods are free from extraneous influences such as tariff or quotas.

A. Only 1
B. Only 2
C. Only 3
D. 1 and 2 both

374. Earlier it was thought safe to allow each financial institution to carry out only one type of financial service. But now banks are selling shares, insurance companies can sell banking services. These new financial conglomerates are colloquially referred to as
A. Multinationals
B. Financial supermarkets
C. Market regulators
D. Brand Promoters

375. Which of the following is the purpose owing to which banks have created Investment Fluctuation Reserves (IFR)? This will help them in managing
A. Interest rate risk
B. CRR
C. SLR
D. Foreign Currency Accounts

376. Which of the following organizations has created an 'Investor Protection Fund', which is funded by fines and penalties collected by the organization itself from various clients?
A. SEBI
B. IDBI
C. IRDA
D. None of these

377. Which of the following is a programme to provide electric connections to those living below poverty line?
A. MPLADS
B. Kutir Jyoti
C. Ganga Kalyan Yojana
D. Sangam Yojana

378. Which among the following is core industry?
A. Iron and Steel
B. Cement
C. Both A and B
D. Railway

379. Who propounded the 'market law'?
A. Adam Smith
B. J.B. Say
C. T.R. Malthus
D. David Ricardo

380. National income is based on the
A. Total revenue of the state
B. Production of goods and services
C. Net profit earned and expenditure made by the state
D. The sum of all factors of incomes

381. 'Utility' in economics means the capacity to
A. Provide comforts
B. Earn an income
C. Satisfy human wants
D. Satisfy human motives

382. Labour welfare does not include
A. Education facilities
B. Health facilities
C. Housing facilities
D. Quick promotion in job

383. 'Sellers market' denotes a situation where
A. Commodities are available at competitive rates
B. Demand exceeds supply
C. Supply exceeds demand
D. Supply and demand are evenly balanced

384. "Legal Tender Money" refers to
A. Cheques
B. Drafts
C. Bills of exchange
D. Currency notes

385. The sum total of incomes received for the services of labour, land or capital in a country is called
A. Gross domestic product
B. National income
C. Gross domestic income
D. Gross national income

386. The measurement of poverty line is based on the criteria of
A. Their dwelling houses
B. The nature of employment
C. Coloric consumption
D. Level of education

387. Capital is that wealth
A. Which is used for the production of wealth
B. Which is kept in boxes and lockers
C. Which is buried in the land
D. Which is stored for consumption

388. The poverty line has been defined in the
A. Seventh Five–Year Plan
B. Sixth Five–Year Plan

C. Eighth Five–Year Plan
D. Fifth Five–year Plan

389. Perfect market means there are
A. Many sellers and many buyers
B. A few sellers and a few buyers
C. A few sellers and many buyers
D. A few buyers and many sellers

390. A hard currency is the one
A. Whose external value is increasing
B. Which can be acquired only with official permission
C. Which can be obtained only against sale of gold
D. Which is really accepted in international transactions

391. Which of the following is not a Central Government Tax?
A. Income Tax
B. Customs Duty
C. Land Revenue
D. Corporation Tax

392. Who is called the father of White Revolution?
A. Dr. Kurien Verghese
B. Nanjunda Swamy
C. M.S. Swaminathan
D. U.R. Rao

393. The major source of revenue in India is through
A. Direct Taxes
B. Indirect Taxes
C. Internal Borrowings
D. External Borrowings

394. The Reserve Bank of India was established in
A. 1927 B. 1935
C. 1947 D. 1949

395. Finance Commission is appointed by
A. Prime Minister
B. President of India
C. Ministry of Finance
D. NITI Aayog

396. Which of the following groups suffer the most from inflation?
A. Debtors
B. Creditors
C. Business class
D. Holders of real assets

397. Which one of the following is not an example of indirect tax?
A. Sales tax
B. Excise duty
C. Customs duty
D. Expenditure tax

398. The major aim of devaluation is to
A. Encourage imports
B. Encourage exports
C. Encourage both exports and imports
D. Discourage both exports and imports

399. Which one of the following taxes is not shared by the central Government with the States?
A. Union excise duties
B. Estate duty
C. Customs duty
D. Income tax

400. NAFED is connected with
A. Animal husbandry
B. Conservation of fuels
C. Agricultural marketing
D. Agricultural implements

401. Planning Commission was constituted in
A. June 1949
B. October 1951
C. March 1950
D. None of these

402. Which of the following is an organization of Software and Service Companies?
A. NASDAQ B. NASSCOM
C. NCSA D. NCAER

403. Tata Iron and Steel Company is situated in
A. Bihar B. Jharkhand
C. Odisha D. West Bengal

404. NABARD stands for
A. National Bank of Agriculture and Regional Development
B. National Bank for Agriculture and Rural Development
C. National Bureau of Aeronautical Research and Development
D. None of these

405. 'Bottle neck inflation' means
A. No rise in prices despite increase in aggregate demand
B. Rise in prices without increase in the aggregate demand
C. Decline in prices due to increase in aggregate demand
D. None of these

406. The main cause of International Trade is
A. Equal cost difference
B. Absolute cost difference
C. Comparative cost difference
D. Equal and comparative cost difference

407. Which one of the following taxes is not shared by the Central Government with the States?
A. Union excise duties
B. Customs duty
C. Income tax
D. Estate duty

408. A dualistic economy is one in which
A. both rich and poor people co-exist side by side
B. it has both foreign trade and internal trade
C. industry and agriculture exist side by side
D. modern sector and traditional sector exist side by side

409. Whose signatures are found on the 10 rupee note in India?
A. Prime Minister of India
B. President of India
C. Finance Minister of India
D. Governor, Reserve Bank of India

410. "Green Revolution" began in India during the year
A. 1967-68 B. 1966-67
C. 1968-69 D. 1969-70

GENERAL SCIENCE

411. In the blood group 'O' the antigen present is
A. A B. B
C. A and B D. No antigen

412. The time-period of a pendulum on the moon
A. Decreases
B. Increases

C. Remains the same
D. Is zero

413. The human ear is sensitive to sound intensity ranging from
A. 200 to 300 db
B. 300 to 400 db
C. 500 to 600 db
D. 0 to 180 db

414. A solar eclipse occurs when the
A. Sun comes between the earth and the moon
B. Moon comes between the sun and the earth
C. Earth comes between the sun and the moon
D. Sun comes between the earth and the star

415. The Angstrom unit measures
A. Temperature
B. Electric current
C. Time
D. Wavelength

416. We can hold a pen due to the
A. Force of gravity
B. Force of friction
C. Force of weight
D. Work done by our muscles

417. One calorie of energy is equivalent to
A. 0.42 joule B. 4.2 joule
C. 42 joule D. 420 joule

418. Metals, when exposed to electromagnetic radiations, emit
A. Electrons
B. Protons
C. Neutrons
D. Alpha particles

419. Which one of the following is a super cooled liquid?
A. Mercury B. Bromine
C. Glass D. Ice-cream

420. Haemoglobin is an Iron-containing
A. Nucleic acid B. Protein
C. Antibody D. Hormone

421. Green flames given out by the burning of firework is due to the presence of
A. Sodium B. Barium
C. Potassium D. Calcium

422. Which one of the following is not a function of protein ?
A. Building up of tissues
B. Catalysing some reactions
C. Growth of bones
D. Repair of torn tissues

423. Metal used for galvanising iron is
A. Mercury B. Aluminium
C. Copper D. Zinc

424. An example of a synthetic rubber is
A. Neoprene B. Nylon
C. Rayon D. Polyester

425. The metal which is called Quick Silver is
A. Silver B. Aluminium
C. Mercury D. Lead

426. What forms the largest part of most diets?
A. Nucleic acid
B. Proteins
C. Carbohydrates
D. Lipids

427. Acid present in Tamarind is
A. Citric acid B. Acetic acid
C. Tartaric acid D. Oxalic acid

428. Which of the following diseases is caused by a viral infection?
A. Typhoid B. Cholera
C. Common cold D. Tetanus

429. If the blood group of one parent is AB and that of the other O, the possible blood group of their child would be
A. A or B
B. A or B or O
C. A or AB or O
D. A or B or AB or O

430. How many bones are there in the human body?
A. 187 B. 287
C. 206 D. 306

431. Dinosaurs were
A. Mammals that became extinct
B. Large herbivorous creatures which gave rise to hippopotamus species
C. Egg-laying mammals
D. Reptiles that became extinct

432. Sweat glands in mammals are primarily concerned with
A. Removal of excess salts
B. Excretion of nitrogenous wastes
C. Thermoregulation
D. Sex-attraction

433. The vitamin that helps to prevent infections in the human body is
A. Vitamin A B. Vitamin B
C. Vitamin C D. Vitamin D

434. The normal RBC count in adult male is
A. 5.5 million B. 5.0 million
C. 4.5 million D. 4.0 million

435. A storm is predicted if atmospheric pressure
A. Rises suddenly
B. Rises gradually
C. Falls suddenly
D. Falls gradually

436. The gas which turns into liquid at the lowest temperature among the following is
A. Hydrogen B. Oxygen
C. Helium D. Nitrogen

437. An egg sinks in soft water but floats in a concentrated solution of salt because
A. Egg absorbs salt from the solution and expands
B. Albumin dissolves in salt solution and egg becomes lighter
C. The density of salt solution exceeds the density of eggs
D. Water has high surface tension

438. What should a person on a freely rotating turn table do to decrease his (angular) speed?
A. Bring his hands together
B. Raise his hands up
C. Spread his hands outwards
D. Sit down with raised hands

439. Gunpowder consists of a mixture of
A. Sand and TNT
B. TNT and charcoal
C. Nitre, sulphur and charcoal
D. Sulphur, sand and charcoal

440. Which of the following is the sweetest sugar?
A. Sucrose B. Glucose
C. Fructose D. Maltose

441. In nuclear reactors, graphite is used as a/an

A. Fuel B. Lubricant
C. Moderator D. Insulator

442. Which of the following celestial bodies contains abundant quantities of helium-3, a potential source of energy ?
A. Earth B. Moon
C. Venus D. Saturn

443. Among the following which fruit is a rich source of iron?
A. Jamun B. Karonda
C. Loquat D. Guava

444. Vitamin which promotes wound healing is
A. Vitamin B B. Vitamin C
C. Vitamin A D. Vitamin D

445. Bauxite is an ore of
A. Aluminium B. Boron
C. Lead D. Silver

446. Which of the following methods is used to determine the age of the earth ?
A. Carbon dating
B. Germanium dating
C. Uranium dating
D. All the above

447. Name the gas which under normal conditions produces pollution in the atmosphere?
A. Carbon monoxide (CO)
B. Carbon dioxide (CO_2)
C. Nitrogen (N_2)
D. Oxygen (O_2)

448. Electron-volt is the unit for
A. Energy
B. Charge of electron
C. Potential difference
D. Power

449. An atom bomb is based on the principle of
A. Nuclear fission
B. Nuclear fusion
C. Nuclear spallation
D. None of these

450. Titan is the largest moon or satellite of
A. Mars B. Venus
C. Jupiter D. Saturn

451. The most toxic metal pollutant of the automobile exhaust is
A. Copper B. Lead
C. Cadmium D. Mercury

452. Which of the following disease is caused by a virus?
A. Diphtheria B. Malaria
C. Cholera D. Hepatitis

453. If the circumference of a circle is increased by 50% then the area will be increased by
A. 50% B. 100%
C. 125% D. 225%

454. The term 'Siamese Twins' is used for
A. Twins in which there is one male and one female
B. Twins in which both are females
C. Twins suffering from a common disease of siam
D. Twins physically attached to each other

455. Every solar eclipse takes place on
A. full moon only
B. new moon only
C. both A and B
D. neither A nor B

456. The atmosphere is heated mainly by
A. Insolation
B. Conduction
C. Radiation
D. Convection

457. An antibiotic is
A. A chemical synthesised by a human cell against a micro-organism
B. A chemical synthesised by a micro-organism against another micro-organisms
C. A substance produced by blood cells against bacteria
D. A substance produced by blood cells against infection

458. Laws of heredity was put forward by
A. Mendel B. Mendeleev
C. Pavlov D. Koch

459. A device used for converting a.c. into d.c. is called
A. Transformer B. Rectifier
C. Induction oil D. Dynamo

460. Heart murmur indicates a
A. Defective valve
B. Poor oxygenation
C. Dislocation of the heart
D. Improper development of muscles

461. Which one of the following can be synthesized by Liver?
A. Vitamin-A B. Vitamin-E
C. Vitamin-D D. Vitamin-K

462. Fluid part of blood devoid of corpuscles is called
A. Tissue fluid B. Plasma
C. Serum D. Lymph

463. The language used in writing the scientific name of animals is
A. French B. Latin
C. German D. Dutch

464. Energy of Ultra-violet rays is greater than
A. Infra-red rays
B. Gamma rays
C. X-rays
D. Cosmic rays

465. Polythene is polymer of
A. Ethylene B. Propylene
C. Acetylene D. Aniline

466. Ripe grapes contain
A. Fructose B. Sucrose
C. Galactose D. Glucose

467. Which is used for settling muddy water?
A. Common salt
B. Common alum
C. Aluminium powder
D. Bleaching powder

468. Rayon is made from
A. Plastic B. Gasoline
C. Petroleum D. Cellulose

469. Which one of the following is pure water?
A. Rain water
B. Filter water
C. Tubewell water
D. Distilled water

470. Which silver salt is used for making film for photography?
A. Silver bromide
B. Silver chloride
C. Silver sulphate
D. Silver nitrate

471. The instrument used to measure the speed of the wind is

A. Altimeter
B. Anemometer
C. Chronometer
D. Dosimeter

472. Which is widely used in the plastic industry for manufacturing bakelite ?
A. Ethyl alcohol B. Phenol
C. Orth-cresol D. Catechol

473. To an astronaut sky appears
A. White B. Rich blue
C. Light blue D. Dark

474. A hydrogen balloon floats up because of
A. Air pressure decreases with decrease in height
B. Air pressure decreases with decrease in weight
C. Weight of the balloon is less than the weight of air displaced by it
D. The pressure inside the balloon is more than the pressure outside it

475. Who defined the law of gravitation ?
A. Newton B. Archimedes
C. Galileo D. Faraday

476. The metal used to make lightning conductors is
A. Iron B. Aluminium
C. Copper D. Zinc

477. Radioactive decay of uranium produces
A. Arsenic B. Bismuth
C. Lead D. Tin

478. Cancer is caused by activation of genes
A. Regulatory genes
B. Oncogenes
C. Structural genes
D. Jumping genes

479. The biochemical processes taking place in the body is known as
A. Anabolism
B. Catabolism
C. Metabolism
D. None of the above

480. The weight of a body on the surface of the earth is 10 kg. Its weight at the centre of the earth is
A. 0 kg B. 5 kg
C. 10 kg D. Infinite

481. Which of the following is not a stimulant?
A. Caffeine
B. Barbiturates
C. Cocaine
D. Amphetamines

482. Which one of the following is not an electromagnetic wave?
A. Radiowave
B. X-ray
C. Visible light
D. Sound wave

483. The instrument used for measuring blood pressure is called
A. Barometer
B. Sphygmomanometer
C. Tonometer
D. None of the above

484. Most patients hospitalised for mental disorders suffer from
A. Neurosis
B. Depression

C. Hysteria
D. Schizophrenia

485. Flowers without petals are pollinated by
A. Bees B. Birds
C. Butterflies D. Wind

486. The ingredient that assists clotting of blood is
A. Vitamin A B. Folic acid
C. Vitamin D D. Vitamin K

487. RNA of retrovirus can produce DNA by
A. DNA polymerase
B. RNA polymerase
C. Endonuclease
D. Reverse transcriptase

488. Stimulating the occipital area of the brain produces sensations of
A. Vision B. Taste
C. Motion D. Touch

489. Complete loss of memory is termed
A. Trauma B. Amnesia
C. Coma D. Paranesia

490. How many sets of valves does a human heart have
A. Four B. Three
C. Two D. One

491. The cells which are responsible for the production of antibodies are
A. Red blood cells
B. Neutrophils
C. Lymphocytes
D. Platelets

492. The source of the enzyme diastase is
A. Salivary gland
B. Stomach
C. Liver
D. Pancreas

493. Mycoplasma is associated with a disease that affects the organs of
A. Respiration
B. Excretion
C. Reproduction
D. Digestion

494. Which one of the following has the highest value of specific heat?
A. Glass B. Copper
C. Lead D. Water

495. The device used for locating submerged objects under sea is
A. Sonar B. Radar
C. Laser D. Maser

496. The metal whose electrical conductivity is more, is
A. Copper B. Aluminium
C. Silver D. Lead

497. What happens to a liquid, when the vapour pressure equals the atmospheric pressure?
A. The liquid cools
B. The liquid boils
C. No change
D. The liquid evaporates

498. Seaweeds are important source of
A. Fluorine B. Chlorine
C. Bromine D. Iodine

499. In nuclear reactor, heavy water is used as
A. Coolant
B. Fuel
C. Moderator
D. Atomic smasher

500. Which one of the following pairs is correctly matched?

A. Tetanus–BCG
B. Tuberculosis–ATS
C. Malaria–Chloroquin
D. Scurvy–Thiamin

501. Tear gas used by the police to disperse the mob contains
A. Carbon dioxide
B. Chlorine
C. Ammonia
D. Hydrogen sulphide

502. The speed of sound is
A. 760 mile/hour
B. 100000 mile/hour
C. 250 mile/hour
D. 1000 mile/hour

503. Haemoglobin is a type of
A. Respiratory pigment
B. Carbohydrate
C. Vitamin
D. None of these

504. Which one of the following diseases is not caused by Virus?
A. Polio B. Jaundice
C. Small Pox D. Diphtheria

505. A needle sinks in water whereas a ship made of iron floats on it because
A. The edge of the needle is pointed
B. The ship is flat
C. The ship is driven by powerful engine
D. Specific gravity of the needle is greater than that of water displaced by it

506. The cloudy nights are warmer than clear nights because
A. The clouds prevent radiation of heat from the ground and the air
B. Clouds absorb sunlight in the day and radiate the same in night
C. Clouds make the atmosphere damp and generate heat
D. The clouds obstruct the movement of air which creates heat

507. Who invented pressure cooker
A. Robert Boyle
B. Guillet
C. Thomson
D. None of these

508. Which one of the following human organs is less susceptible to harmful radiations?
A. Eyes B. Heart
C. Brain D. Lungs

509. Which one of the following is essential for plants to produce their food?
A. Oxygen
B. Starch
C. Carbon dioxide
D. Proteins

510. The organ of the human body directly affected by the disease of Hepatitis is
A. Liver B. Lungs
C. Heart D. Brain

511. What is the function of a Pacemaker?
A. It decreases the heart beat
B. It regulates heart beat
C. It increases heart beat
D. It accelerates blood supply to heart

512. Thiamine is
A. Vitamin C B. Vitamin B_2
C. Vitamin B_6 D. Vitamin B_1

513. Doctors, Artists and Sculptors use calcium sulphate which is popularly known as
A. Quick lime
B. Lime stone
C. Bleaching powder
D. Plaster of Paris

SPORTS

514. 'Subroto Cup' is associated with which game/sports?
A. Hockey B. Football
C. Basketball D. Badminton

515. 'Rovers Cup' is associated with
A. Football B. Hockey
C. Lawn Tennis D. Basketball

516. India's oldest Football Tournament is
A. Durand Cup
B. Santosh Trophy
C. I.F.A. Shield
D. None of the above

517. Who was the first Indian to win Asian Snooker championship?
A. Geet Sethi
B. S. Jagtiani
C. Wilson Jones
D. Yasin Merchant

518. National sports day is celebrated on
A. August 29
B. September 29
C. August 18
D. September 18

519. Aryana Sabalenka, famous Tennis Player is from—
A. Belarus
B. China
C. France
D. South Africa

520. Who is called the architect of the modern Olympics?
A. Dimitrias Vikelas
B. Juan Samaranch
C. Baron de Pierre Coubertin
D. Count Henni de Banllet Latour

521. Formula-1 is associated with
A. Ice Hockey
B. River rafting
C. Motor racing
D. None of the above

522. Who amongst the following is Chess player of International repute?
A. Refael Nadal
B. Abhinav Bindra
C. Glen McGrath
D. D. Gukesh

523. The first Indian Cricketer to score a Century was
A. Kapil Dev
B. Lala Amarnath
C. Sachin Tendulkar
D. M.A. Pataudi

524. Which of the following cups is not associated with the game of football?
A. Subroto Cup
B. Agha Khan Cup
C. Durand Cup
D. Rovers Cup

525. Which country hosts the Azlan Shah Cup Hockey tournament?
A. Malaysia B. Indonesia
C. Pakistan D. UAE

526. With which of the following games is Narain Kartikeyan associated?
A. Boxing
B. Billiards
C. Golf
D. Motor Racing

527. Keenan stadium is located at
A. Jamshedpur B. Cuttack
C. Patna D. Ranchi

528. Deodhar Trophy is related to which sport?
A. Volleyball B. Football
C. Cricket D. Tennis

529. Duleep Trophy is associated with
A. Tennis B. Cricket
C. Football D. Hockey

530. How many rings are there in the Olympic flag?
A. 6 B. 5
C. 4 D. 8

531. Saina Nehwal plays which of the following games?
A. Lawn Tennis B. Badminton
C. Chess D. Swimming

532. 'LBW' is the term associated with the game of
A. Cricket B. Hockey
C. Tennis D. Football

533. Santosh Trophy is associated with the game of
A. Cricket B. Football
C. Hockey D. Tennis

534. Which of the following is a Cricket related term?
A. Push in B. Scissor Kick
C. Hook D. Smash

535. The game of 'chess' is said to have originated in
A. China B. Iran
C. Indonesia D. India

536. With which game is the 'Agha Khan Cup' associated?
A. Football B. Cricket
C. Badminton D. Hockey

537. Which of the following terms is associated with the game of 'Golf'?
A. Revoke B. Scratch
C. Bogey D. Mallet

538. Which of the following International Tennis Tournaments is held on grass court?
A. US Open
B. French Open
C. Wimbledon
D. Australian Open

539. In which International Championship, 'Thomas Cup' is given
A. Football B. Cricket
C. Badminton D. Tennis

540. 'Gambit' is related to which among the following sports?
A. Carrom B. Bridge
C. Chess D. Billiards

541. The term 'Grandmaster' is used in which of these games?
A. Chess B. Judo
C. Bridge D. Karate

542. In the game of Volleyball, the number of players on each side is
A Eight B. Five
C. Seven D. Six

543. The term "Cue" is associated with which game?
A. Hockey B. Football
C. Billiards D. Cricket

544. With which game is Neeraj Chopra Associated?
A. Basketball
B. Javelin Throw
C. Chess
D. Tennis

545. How many players are there in each side in the game of Netball?
A. 7 B. 6
C. 9 D. 11

546. 'Uber Cup' is associated with which of the following?
A. Tennis B. Badminton
C. Chess D. Cricket

547. Where is the annual Australian Open Tennis tournament held?
A. Sydney B. Melbourne
C. Canberra D. Brisbane

548. The Olympic Motto is
A. Health is wealth
B. Promote Universal brotherhood
C. Faster, Higher, Stronger
D. Excellence is the goal

549. The term 'Tee' is associated with which of the following sports?
A. Polo
B. Table Tennis
C. Golf
D. Judo

550. Which Indian sportsman is known as Hockey Wizard throughout the world?
A. A.B. Subbiah
B. Jude Felix
C. Dhyan Chand
D. Ajitpal Singh

551. When did India become World Cricket Champion?
A. 1980 B. 1982
C. 1983 D. 1986

552. "Googly" is associated with:
A. Cricket
B. Table-Tennis
C. Hockey
D. Billiards

553. With which game are the terms bull's eye, muzzle and plug associated?
A. Shooting B. Solitaire
C. Billiards D. Rowing

554. Who is the first Indian to take a hat trick in an international test?
A. Kapil Dev
B. Jasu Patel
C. Harbhajan Singh
D. B.S. Chandrashekhar

555. Who was declared by Wisden as "The Best Indian Bowler of the Century" (20th Century)?
A. Kapil Dev
B. B.S. Chandrashekhar
C. B.S. Bedi
D. Subhash V. Gupte

556. "Jab" and "Parry" are terms used in which sport?
A. Wrestling
B. Boxing
C. Billiards
D. Weightlifting

557. First Commonwealth Games were held in:
A. London B. Sydney
C. Perth D. Hamilton

558. Davis Cup is associated with the sport of
A. Tennis
B. Football
C. Cricket
D. Hockey

559. The term 'breast stroke' is associated with:
A. Skating
B. Croquet
C. Swimming
D. Rifle Shooting

560. What is the National Game of the USA?
A. Cricket
B. Baseball
C. Soccer
D. Billiards

561. Manu Bhaker is associated with
A. Hockey
B. Shooting
C. Golf
D. Badminton

562. 'Merdeka Cup' is associated with
A. Golf
B. Football
C. Squash
D. Hockey

563. Who among the following has become the first woman in the world to swim across seven seas?
A. Shikha Tandon
B. Bula Chowdhury
C. Amanda Beard
D. Arti Saha

ART, CULTURE AND LITERATURE

564. 'Tamasha' is the famous folk form of musical theatre in
A. Bihar
B. Punjab
C. Maharashtra
D. Uttar Pradesh

565. 'Paryushan Parv' is celebrated by
A. Buddhists
B. Hindus
C. Jains
D. Sikhs

566. The Book 'Mother India' was written by
A. Catherine Mayo
B. Lala Lajpat Rai
C. Bal Gangadhar Tilak
D. Bipin Chandra Pal

567. Which one of the following pairs is correctly matched?
A. Madhya Pradesh – Kuchipudi
B. Kerala – Kathakali
C. Andhra Pradesh – Bharat Natyam
D. Tamil Nadu – Kathak

568. Which of the following is a kind of Japanese form of flower arrangement?
A. Ikebana
B. Sionara
C. Siukina
D. Tikiwasi

569. 'Ghumar' is a folk dance of
A. Madhya Pradesh
B. Tamil Nadu
C. Rajasthan
D. Kerala

570. From which upanishad the words "Satyamev Jayate" have been taken?
A. Mandukopnishad
B. Kathopanishad
C. Chhandogyopanishad
D. None of these

571. Upanishads are books on
A. Religion
B. Yoga
C. Law
D. Philosophy

572. The Rigveda contains
A. Rituals to be adopted by people

B. Hymns in honour of the gods
C. Yagnas to be performed
D. History of the Vedic period

573. In which language was the Shrimad Bhagavad Gita originally written?
A. Sanskrit
B. Apabharamsa
C. Prakrit
D. Pali

574. Tripitakas are the sacred books of the
A. Jains B. Hindus
C. Muslims D. Buddhists

575. Purushasukta is found in the
A. Bhagavad Gita
B. Rigveda
C. Manusmriti
D. Atharva Veda

576. Amjad Ali Khan is a maestro with which instrument?
A. Violin B. Sitar
C. Sarod D. Sarangi

577. Which actor played the role of Mahatma Gandhi in the film Gandhi?
A. Shah Rukh Khan
B. Paresh Rawal
C. Ben Kingsley
D. Abhijit

578. Which language is spoken by the people of Tripura?
A. Bengali B. Telugu
C. Assamese D. Malayalam

579. The collection of Buddha's teachings are
A. Buddha Charita
B. Sutta Pitak
C. Abhidhamma Pitak
D. Vinay Pitak

580. 'Tera Tali' is the folk dance of
A. Kerala
B. Rajasthan
C. Madhya Pradesh
D. Tamil Nadu

581. 'Bonsai' is the Japanese art of
A. Painting
B. Growing small trees
C. Making dolls
D. Arranging flowers

582. 'Ramayanam', the Tamil version of the great epic Ramayana was made by
A. Kamban
B. Avvaiyar
C. Ilangovadigal
D. None of the above

583. Gangaur festival is held in honour of
A. Saraswati B. Ganesh
C. Parvati D. Radha

584. Who among the following is known as Dhumketu in Gujarati Literature?
A. Kaniyalal Munshi
B. Gourishanker Joshi
C. Ramanlal Desai
D. Zaverchand Meghani

585. Where is the highest in the world 'Vishwa Shanti Stup' in Bihar?
A. Vaishali B. Nalanda
C. Rajgeer D. Patna

586. Which of the following dances is not a Classical dance?
A. Kathakali B. Garba
C. Odissi D. Manipuri

587. In the world of Hindi Cinema, who was affectionately called as 'Dada Moni'?

A. Balraj Sahani
B. Prithviraj Kapoor
C. Ashok Kumar
D. Utpal Dutt

588. Who is the Director of the film "Elizabeth : The Golden Age Cast"?
A. Ramanand Sagar
B. Ram Gopal Verma
C. Karan Johar
D. Shekhar Kapur

589. Which of the following is a classical dance form of Andhra Pradesh?
A. Kathakali
B. Bharatnatyam
C. Odissi
D. Kuchipudi

590. Pt. Shiv Kumar Sharma is an exponent of
A. Mandolin B. Santoor
C. Sitar D. Veena

591. With which musical instrument is Zakir Hussain associated
A. Sitar B. Tabla
C. Guitar D. Veena

592. Which of the following is not correctly matched?
A. Bhangra – Punjab
B. Bihu – Nagaland
C. Garba – Gujarat
D. Tamasha – Maharashtra

593. Leonardo da Vinci, who is famous for his great masterpiece 'Monalisa' was a painter from
A. England B. France
C. Italy D. Germany

594. Which Raga is supposed to have emanated from the throat of Lord Shiva and sung prior to dawn for invoking violity?
A. Raga Vilavala
B. Raga Dipaka
C. Raga Vibhasa
D. Raga Bhairvi

595. 'Pongal' festival is celebrated in the month of
A. March B. September
C. October D. January

596. 'Bhogali Bihu' is a festival of
A. Assam B. Odisha
C. Gujarat D. Rajasthan

597. Classical dance having its roots in Tamil Nadu is
A. Kathakali
B. Kathak
C. Kuchipudi
D. Bharat Natyam

598. 'Kathak' is the shastriya dance of which area?
A. North India
B. Kerala
C. Andhra Pradesh
D. Tamil Nadu

599. Which one of the following is essentially a solo dance?
A. Kathak
B. Kuchipudi
C. Mohiniattam
D. Manipuri

600. Match the artists and their Art forms:

(*a*) Jatin Das	1. Painting
(*b*) V.G. Jog	2. Sculpture
(*c*) Sonal Mansingh	3. Odissi dance
(*d*) Manjit Bawa	4. Violin

	(a)	(b)	(c)	(d)
A.	3	2	1	4
B.	4	2	1	3
C.	1	3	4	2
D.	2	4	3	1

601. 'Pulitzer' prizes are awarded to Americans for excellence in
A. Films
B. Social work
C. Journalism
D. Medicine

602. When was the Nobel Prize started?
A. 1901 C. 1934
B. 1905 D. 1900

603. 'Bharat Ratna' Award was given for the first time in
A. 1956 B. 1957
C. 1952 D. 1954

604. Saraswati Samman is awarded by
A. K.K. Birla Foundation
B. Government of India
C. Bharatiya Jnanpith
D. Sahitya Academy

605. Who was the first Asian to win a Nobel Prize?
A. Hideki Yuka
B. Har Gobind Khurana
C. C.V. Raman
D. Rabindranath Tagore

606. The highest Gallantry Award given in India is
A. Ashok Chakra
B. Mahavir Chakra
C. Param Vir Chakra
D. None of these

607. On which day every year National Awards for Teachers are announced?
A. September 5
B. November 14
C. November 19
D. August 15

608. Dronacharya Awards are given
A. to outstanding athletes
B. to outstanding coaches
C. for best performance in archery
D. for invention in science

609. Dr. C.V. Raman was awarded Nobal Prize in
A. Chemistry B. Literature
C. Physics D. Medicine

610. The first recipient of Major Dhyan Chand Khel Ratna Award is
A. Leander Peas
B. Viswanathan Anand
C. Kapil Dev
D. Limba Ram

611. The highest civilian award in India is
A. Bharat Ratna
B. Padam Vibhushan
C. Padam Bhushan
D. Padma Shri

612. Which of the following Indians awarded 'Legion D Award' the highest civilian award of France?
A. Satyajit Ray
B. Pandit Ravi Shankar
C. Lok Nayak Jayaprakash
D. J.L. Nehru

613. Dhanvantari Awards are given for the best performance in the field of
A. Medical Sciences
B. Nuclear Sciences
C. Economics
D. Space Research

614. Nobel Prizes are not given for which of the following fields?
A. Music B. Chemistry
C. Peace D. Physics

615. Dadasaheb Phalke Award is given for:
A. Drama
B. Social welfare
C. Films
D. Literature

616. In which year Nehru Award for International understanding was instituted?
A. 1969 B. 1984
C. 1964 D. 1966

617. Who among the following has not been awarded the Bharat Ratna?
A. Indira Gandhi
B. Mahatma Gandhi
C. Sardar Patel
D. Radhakrishnan

618. Which one of the following is the second highest Civilian award in India?
A. Padma Shri
B. Bharat Ratna
C. Padma Bhushan
D. Padma Vibhushan

619. 'Victory Medal' is awarded in:
A. the USA B. the UK
C. Russia D. France

620. National film Awards were instituted in the year
A. 1954 B. 1950
C. 1961 D. 1969

621. In which year was the Nobel Prize for Economics announced for the first time?
A. 1969 B. 1901
C. 1919 D. 1970

622. Borlaug Award was instituted for recognising outstanding contribution in the field of
A. agriculture B. ecology
C. journalism D. medicine

623. Jesse Owens Global Award is given in the field of
A. Literature B. Journalism
C. Science D. Sports

624. Nobel Alfred Bernhard after whom Nobel Prizes are given was
A. Engineer
B. Chemist
C. Both A and B
D. Doctor

625. Who was the first winner of Nehru Award for International Understanding?
A. Martin Luther King
B. Mother Teresa
C. U. Thant
D. Dr. Jonas Salk

626. The famous book 'Gita Gôvind' is written by
A. Banabhatt B. Jaydev
C. Mirabai D. Kalidas

627. 'Ain-e-Akbari' was written by
A. Firista B. Ibn Batuta
C. Abul Fazl D. Birbal

628. Who wrote "Vande Mataram"?
A. Rabindra Nath Tagore
B. Sumitra Nandan Pant
C. Bankim Chandra Chatterji
D. Vivekanand

629. Who among the following is the author of 'Das Capital'?

A. Lenin
B. J.M. Keynes
C. Robert Owen
D. Karl Marx

630. 'Panchatantra' was written by
A. Jai Dev
B. Ved Vyas
C. Bhavbhuti
D. Vishnu Sharma

631. Patanjali is well known for the Compilation of
A. Yoga Sutra
B. Panchatantra
C. Brahma Sutra
D. Ayurveda

632. Who among the following has written the book, 'The Wings of Fire: An Autobiography'?
A. K.R. Narayanan
B. Sobha De
C. A.B. Vajpayee
D. A.P.J. Abdul Kalam

633. Who compiled the 'Adi Granth'?
A. Guru Nanak
B. Guru Ramdas
C. Guru Arjun Dev
D. Guru Gobind Singh

634. The famous book 'Anandmath' was authored by
A. Rabindranath Tagore
B. Bankim Chandra Chattopadhyaya
C. Sarojini Naidu
D. Sri Aurobindo

635. Which one of the following pairs is not correctly matched?
A. Mudrarakshasa : Visakhadatta
B. Rajtarangini : Kalhana
C. Kadambari : Bana Bhatta
D. Ratnavali : Bilhana

636. 'Harry Potter and the Deathly Hallows' is written by
A. Robert Ludlum
B. J.K. Rowling
C. Sidney Sheldon
D. Spencer Johnson

637. 'Arthashastra' was written by
A. Kalidas
B. Kautilya
C. R.K. Narayan
D. Bana Bhatt

638. Name the author of book "The Post Office (Dak Ghar)"?
A. R.K. Narayan
B. Rabindra Nath Tagore
C. Prem Chand
D. Krishan Chandra

639. Who wrote the nursery rhyme, "Twinkle, twinkle, little star"?
A. Lovelace
B. Ann Taylor
C. William Ross Wallace
D. William Shakespeare

640. Ashtadhyayi is a book written by
A. Panini
B. Patanjali
C. Vishnu Sharma
D. None of these

641. Prithviraj Raso was written by:
A. Kalhan
B. Chand Bardai
C. Bhavbhuti
D. Bule Shah

642. The book 'Prison Diary' was written by
A. Mahatma Gandhi
B. V.D. Savarkar
C. Jai Prakash Narayan
D. Morarji Desai

643. "Runs and Ruins" is written by
A. Nawab Pataudi
B. Vivian Richards
C. Clive Lloyd
D. Sunil Gavaskar

644. Who is the author of the book, 'The God of Small Things'?
A. Ali Sardar Jafri
B. Vikram Chandra
C. Padma Seth
D. Arundhati Roy

645. India-2020 is a book written by
A. Montek Singh Ahluwalia
B. A.P.J. Abdul Kalam
C. G. Ganeshan
D. Indra Kumar Gujral

DEFENCE

646. When was the foundation of BSF laid?
A. 1965 B. 1970
C. 1910 D. 1950

647. The first indigenously assembled T90S Battle Tank has been named
A. Arjun B. Bhima
C. Bhisma D. Tarang

648. First Indian Commander-in-Chief was
A. Gen. K.S. Thimayya
B. Gen. K.M. Kariappa
C. S.H.F.J. Manekshaw
D. None of the above

649. Navy week is celebrated in India during the
A. 1st week of October
B. 1st week of November
C. 1st week of December
D. 1st week of March

650. Sukhoi Deal was signed between
A. India and Russia
B. India and China
C. India and Germany
D. India and Nepal

651. India's first Defence University is set up in
A. Uttar Pradesh
B. Madhya Pradesh
C. Punjab
D. Haryana

652. Astra Missile is
A. Surface to surface missile
B. Surface to air missile
C. Air to surface missile
D. Air to air missile

653. Army war college is situated at
A. Gurgaon B. Pune
C. Jabalpore D. Mhow

654. The Indian Navy does not have
A. Eastern Naval Command
B. Western Naval Command
C. Northern Naval Command
D. Southern Naval Command

655. Aircraft carrier Admiral Gorshkov purchased from Russia has been renamed
A. INS Vikramaditya
B. INS Mysore
C. NNS Virat
D. None of the above

656. Russia's highest military decoration is known as
A. Military cross
B. Medal for valour

C. Victory medal
D. Order of the Patriotic war

657. National Defence Academy is located at
A. Secundrabad
B. Khadakvasla
C. Kochi
D. Dehradun

658. Which among the following is anti tank missile
A. Agni B. Akash
C. Nag D. Arjun

659. The supreme commander of Armed forces is
A. President
B. Prime Minister
C. Field Marshal
D. General

660. Arjun is the name given to
A. Tank B. Submarine
C. Missile D. Aircraft

661. The Vijayanta Tanks are manufactured at
A. Avadi B. Bangalore
C. Kanpur D. Patna

662. Which of the following pairs is not correct?
A. Agni – Surface to surface missile
B. Prithvi – Surface to air missile
C. Akash – Surface to air missile
D. Trishul – Surface to air missile

663. Army Day is celebrated in India every year on
A. January 1
B. January 15
C. February 1
D. February 15

664. Indian Air Force was established in the year
A. 1932 B. 1947
C. 1857 D. 1950

665. Indian Military Academy is situated in
A. Pune B. Dehradun
C. Patna D. Jabalpur

666. The first India-made frigate is
A. INS Vikrant B. INS Kukri
C. INS Udaigiri D. INS Nilgiri

667. The name of India's first aircraft carrier is
A. INS Kukri
B. INS Nilgiri
C. INS Vikrant
D. INS Himgiri

668. Pinaka is a
A. Multi-barrel rocket system
B. Long range missile
C. Piolet-less aircraft
D. None of these

669. The flag ship of the Indian Navy is
A. INS Vikramaditya
B. INS Nilgiri
C. INS Udaigiri
D. INS Dunagiri

670. The highest rank in the Indian Army is of
A. General
B. Major General
C. Captain
D. Brigadier General

671. The Headquarter of Assam Rifles is in
A. Dispur B. Shillong
C. Kohima D. Aizawl

672. The Army Headquarters is in
A. New Delhi B. Kolkata
C. Pune D. Patna

673. The Territorial Army was organised in
A. August 1947
B. October 1949
C. January 1948
D. December 1950

674. Which one of the following is associated with the manufacture of guided missiles?
A. Bharat Electronics Limited
B. Hindustan Aeronautics Limited
C. Bharat Dynamics Limited
D. Bharat Earth Movers Limited

675. 'Trishul' is a
A. Short range surface to air missile
B. Surface to surface tactical battle field missile
C. Medium range surface to air missile
D. Marine accoustic research ship

676. Air Force Academy is located in
A. Kakinada
B. Coimbatore
C. Hyderabad
D. Mumbai

677. The missile Agni-II of India is a
A. Nuclear missile
B. Surface to air missile
C. Surface to surface missile
D. Surface to sea missile

678. Where is the Naval Air Station "Garud" situated?
A. New Delhi B. Kochin
C. Chennai D. Dehradun

THE UNIVERSE

679. The average diameter of the earth is approximately
A. 25,000 km B. 18,500 km
C. 12,754 km D. 16,360 km

680. The circumference of the earth is
A. 60,000 km B. 40,067 km
C. 55,230 km D. 48,660 km

681. How many days does the earth take to complete a circle around the sun?
A. 365 B. $365\frac{1}{2}$
C. $365\frac{1}{4}$ D. 370

682. The earth's movement on its orbit is from
A. West to East
B. East to West
C. North to South
D. South to North

683. Sun has a temperature of about
A. 6000°C B. 8000°C
C. 7000°C D. 10000°C

684. Which planet appears red?
A. Mercury B. Venus
C. Mars D. Saturn

685. Lunik II was
A. First space vehicle to sample moon's crust
B. First space vehicle to softland on moon
C. First rocket to hit moon
D. First robot to reach moon

686. Light takes how much time to reach the earth from the sun
A. 400 seconds
B. 20 seconds
C. 8 minutes
D. 8 seconds

687. What is a light year?
A. A year in which there is constant light
B. A year in which the gravitational pull is less than normal value of 'G'
C. The distance traversed by the light in one year
D. A unit of time (that earth takes to go round the sun)

688. Days and nights are caused due to the earth's
A. Rotation
B. Revolution
C. Gravitational pull
D. Nearness to the sun

689. The moon has got a diameter of about
A. 5045 km B. 3476 km
C. 4009 km D. 2345 km

690. First Indian to reach International Spae Station (ISS) is:
A. Sq. Ldr. Mahesh Dutta
B. Gr. Capt. Shubanshu Shukla
C. Col. Ashutosh Narayan
D. None of these

691. Lunar Eclipse is caused when
A. The sun and the moon and the earth are in a line
B. The earth comes between the sun and the moon
C. The sun and the earth are on lither side of the moon
D. The sun comes between the earth and the moon

692. Apart from the sun and the moon, the brightest object in the sky is
A. The North Star
B. Mercury
C. Venus
D. Mars

693. The rings of Saturn are
A. Solid sheets of rock
B. Composed of billions of ice covered rock particles
C. Liquid
D. Gaseous

694. The planets shine because
A. they emit light
B. they are illuminated by nearby stars
C. they reflect light reaching them from the sun
D. they reflect light reaching them from the earth

695. The nearest planet to the earth is
A. Mercury B. Saturn
C. Venus D. Jupiter

696. Satellites have discovered that the earth is
A. Exactly round
B. Exactly oval
C. Orange shaped
D. Pear shaped

697. How many times larger the sun is as compared with the earth?
A. 1000 times
B. 10,000 times
C. 1,00,000 times
D. None of the above

698. Which of the following is not a planet of the sun?

A. Neptune B. Moon
C. Venus D. Mercury

699. The earth is inclined to the plane of its Orbit at an angle of
A. $56\frac{1}{2}°$ B. 80°
C. $66\frac{1}{2}°$ D. 45°

700. Which planet is nearest to sun?
A. Jupiter B. Mercury
C. Mars D. Venus

701. The vast and hot gaseous mass is called
A. Sun B. Earth
C. Moon D. Planet

702. In which year did man first step out on the moon?
A. 1961 B. 1965
C. 1969 D. 1971

703. Which of the following is the heaviest planet in the solar system?
A. Earth B. Jupiter
C. Mars D. Saturn

704. A planet is formed when there is
A. Light and Air
B. Light and Water
C. Light, Water and Soil
D. Light, Water and Air

705. The biggest satellite of the Solar System, Ganimyd is the satellite of which planet?
A. Saturn B. Jupiter
C. Neptune D. Mars

706. Which is the brightest planet in the Solar System?
A. Jupiter B. Mercury
C. Uranus D. Venus

707. Which planet is referred to both as the ''Morning Star and the Evening Star''?
A. Saturn B. Venus
C. Jupiter D. Mercury

708. Triton is a satellite of
A. Jupiter B. Mercury
C. Uranus D. Neptune

709. Which is the fastest orbiting planet in the solar system?
A. Mars B. Mercury
C. Jupiter D. Venus

710. Which among the following is known as blue planet?
A. Earth B. Jupiter
C. Venus D. Saturn

711. Which is the hottest planet in the Solar System?
A. Jupiter B. Saturn
C. Venus D. Uranus

712. The duration of day at the equator is
A. 11 hours B. 14 hours
C. 16 hours D. 12 hours

713. The first ever robot spacecraft to probe planet Venus was named
A. Galileo B. Magellan
C. Newton D. Challenger

714. First Indian to reach space is
A. Sq. Ldr. Rakesh Sharma
B. Wg. Comd. Ramesh Sharma
C. Cal. Yuri Gagarin
D. None of the above

715. The satellite of the earth is
A. Alpha B. Triton
C. Titan D. Moon

716. Alpha, Beta, Gama, Delta and Epsilon rings are found in

A. Saturn B. Uranus
C. Neptune D. Jupiter

717. Halley's comet reappears in every
A. 76 years B. 75 years
C. 77 years D. 100 years

718. The cosmic year is related to
A. Earth
B. Sun
C. Moon
D. None of the above

GEOGRAPHY

719. Which one of the following is correctly matched?
A. Maharashtra–Paradwip
B. Karnataka–Tuticorin
C. Tamil Nadu–Mangalore
D. Gujarat–Kandla

720. Match List-I with List-II and select the correct answer from the code given below the lists

List-I	List-II
(*a*) Ankaleshwar	1. Cement
(*b*) Manduadih	2. Aeronautics
(*c*) Bangalore	3. Diesel Locomotive
(*d*) Katni	4. Petroleum

Codes:

	(*a*)	(*b*)	(*c*)	(*d*)
A.	4	1	2	3
B.	1	2	3	4
C.	2	3	4	1
D.	4	3	2	1

721. Pochampad irrigation project lies over the
A. Kosi river
B. Mahanadi
C. Krishna river
D. Godavari river

722. Jawaharlal Nehru Port is a satellite port of
A. Chennai B. Kolkata
C. Mumbai D. Mangalore

723. Which one of the following cities is not situated on a river bank ?
A. Ahmedabad B. Bhopal
C. Cuttack D. Gorakhpur

724. 'Kayal' stands for
A. Tarai Plains
B. Logoons of Kerala
C. Ganga Delta
D. Regur of Deccan Plateau

725. The river flowing through rift valley in India is
A. Mahanadi
B. Narmada
C. Kaveri
D. Subarnarekha

726. The State which is leading producer of pulses in India is
A. Uttar Pradesh
B. Rajasthan
C. Madhya Pradesh
D. Maharashtra

727. Which one of the following vegetational species has the largest area coverage in India?
A. Sal B. Sheesham
C. Teak D. Deodar

728. Zawar mines of Udaipur are famous for
A. Iron-ore B. Mica
C. Zinc D. Manganese

729. Which one of the following is not correctly matched?
A. Patratu – Jharkhand
B. Talchir – Odisha
C. Ramagundam – Tamil Nadu
D. Singrauli – Uttar Pradesh

730. On which of the following river the Tulbul project is located?
A. Beas B. Jhelum
C. Ravi D. Satluj

731. Tehri Dam is located at the confluence of which of the following rivers?
A. Ganga and Ramganga
B. Alaknanda and Mandakini
C. Alaknanda and Bhagirathi
D. Bhagirathi and Bhilangana

732. Match List-I with List-II and select the correct answer from the code given below

List-I *(Steel Producer)*	**List-II** *(Source of Iron-ore)*
(*a*) Bhadrawati	1. Kemangundi
(*b*) Bhilai	2. Guru Mahisani
(*c*) Jamshedpur	3. Gua
(*d*) Kulti-Asansol	4. Rajhara

Codes:

	(*a*)	(*b*)	(*c*)	(*d*)
A.	1	4	2	3
B.	1	2	3	4
C.	1	3	4	2
D.	2	3	4	1

733. Which one of the following river basins of India has the maximum annual water yield?
A. Ganga
B. Brahmaputra
C. Indus
D. Godavari

734. Which one of the following is not associated with the Chambal Valley Project ?
A. Gandhi Sagar
B. Rana Pratap Sagar
C. Jawahar Sagar
D. Govind Sagar

735. Which of the following rock formations of India is the richest in fossil content?
A. Vindhyan B. Siwalik
C. Gondwana D. Cuddapah

736. The largest producer of raw wool in India is
A. Jammu and Kashmir
B. Andhra Pradesh
C. Karnataka
D. Rajasthan

737. The largest producer of milk in India is
A. Uttar Pradesh B. Rajasthan
C. Punjab D. Gujarat

738. Tsunamis are mainly produced by
A. Subaerial earthquakes
B. Submarine earthquakes
C. Cyclones
D. Tides

739. Which one of the following is not correctly matched?
A. Khasis – Meghalaya
B. Lepcha – Sikkim
C. Angamis – Manipur
D. Toda – Tamil Nadu

740. Ghatshila is famous for
A. Copper B. Bauxite
C. Uranium D. Coal

741. Which one of the following lakes of the world covers largest area?

A. Baikal B. Titicaca

C. Chad D. Nicaragua

742. Chena cultivation is found in

A. Cambodia

B. Indonesia

C. Sri Lanka

D. Philippines

743. Which desert of the following is the habitat of Bushman?

A. Sahara B. Kalahari

C. Atacama D. Arab

744. Which one of the following States has built the famous Gandhi Sagar across the Chambal river?

A. Rajasthan

B. Maharashtra

C. Uttar Pradesh

D. Madhya Pradesh

745. Which one of the following is correct?

The Palghat Gap serves inland communications from

A. Madurai to Thiruvananthapuram

B. Chennai to Kochi

C. Pune to Mumbai

D. Bengaluru to Mangalore

746. Which one of the following pairs is not correctly matched?

Headquarters of Railway Zone	City
A. South Western	Hubli
B. North Western	Jaipur
C. Western	Mumbai
D. Central	Jabalpur

747. The Great Barrier Reef is located in which country ?

A. Chile B. Australia

C. USA D. Indonesia

748. River Luni originates near Pushkar and drains into which one of the following?

A. Rann of Kachchh

B. Arabian Sea

C. Gulf of Cambay

D. Lake Sambhar

749. Which of the following seas/gulfs are connected by the Suez Canal?

A The Mediterranean Sea and the Red Sea

B Gulf of Oman and the Red Sea

C The Mediterranean Sea and the Gulf of Oman

D Persian gulf and the Arabian Sea

750. What is the other name for the equatorial rain forests?

A. Llanos B. Campos

C. Gran Chaco D. Selvas

751. Which of the following straits is not in Asia?

A. Malacca Strait

B. Bass Strait

C. Formosa Strait

D. Molucca Strait

752. Match the List-I with the List-II and select the correct answer using the codes given below the Lists

List-I *(Centre of Economic Activity)*	List-II *(Country)*
(*a*) Edmonton	1. Australia
(*b*) Kimberley	2. South Africa
(*c*) Cardiff	3. UK
(*d*) Cairns	4. Canada

Codes:

	(*a*)	(*b*)	(*c*)	(*d*)
A.	1	2	3	4
B.	4	3	2	1
C.	1	3	2	4
D.	4	2	3	1

753. Which one of the following cities is located on the banks of the river Lawrence?

A. Chicago B. Detroit
C. Montreal D. Vancouver

754. Which one of the following national parks is located near Chamoli ?

A. Dudhwa National Park
B. Great Himalayan Park
C. Jim Corbett National Park
D. Nanda Devi National Park

755. The reservoir G.B. Pant Sagar is located on which river?

A. Betwa B. Ghaghara
C. Kosi D. Rihand

756. Among the following forest types in India, which one occupies the largest area?

A. Tropical wet evergreen forest
B. Tropical moist deciduous forest
C. Sub-tropical dry evergreen forest
D. Montane wet temperate forest

757. Match the List-I with the List-II and select the correct answer using the codes given below the Lists

List-I ***(Sea)***	**List-II** ***(Country)***
(*a*) Banda Sea	1. China
(*b*) Sulu Sea	2. Indonesia
(*c*) Tasman Sea	3. New Zealand
(*d*) Yellow Sea	4. Philippines

Codes:

	(*a*)	(*b*)	(*c*)	(*d*)
A.	2	4	3	1
B.	2	3	4	1
C.	1	4	3	2
D.	1	3	4	2

758. The famous 'Gir' forests are located in

A. Karnataka B. Assam
C. Gujarat D. Kerala

759. In which of the following grouping of States of India is rubber grown on a commercial scale?

A. Maharashtra – Gujarat– Madhya Pradesh
B. Kerala – Tamil Nadu – Karnataka
C. Sikkim – Arunachal Pradesh – Nagaland
D. Odisha – Madhya Pradesh – Maharashtra

760. Gandak is a joint project of

A. Bihar and UP
B. Bihar and Jharkhand
C. Bihar and Odisha
D. UP and Madhya Pradesh

761. Which one of the following planets has no moon?

A. Mars B. Neptune
C. Mercury D. Earth

762. The standard time of India is

A. $5\frac{1}{2}$ hours ahead of GMT

B. $4\frac{1}{2}$ hours behind of GMT

C. 4 hours ahead of GMT

D. $5\frac{1}{2}$ hours behind of GMT

763. Black Forests are found in
A. France
B. Germany
C. Czechoslovakia
D. Rumania

764. The Earth rotates on its axis at an inclination of

A. $23\frac{1}{2}°$ B. $22\frac{1}{2}°$

C. $21\frac{1}{2}°$ D. 20°

765. Which of these harbours is not a natural harbour ?
A. Chennai B. Mumbai
C. Cochin D. Paradip

766. The seeds of certain plants fail to germinate if they do not pass through the digestive tract of fruit-eating birds. This is due to
A. Hibernation
B. Seed coat impermeability
C. Infertility
D. Vegetative reproduction

767. Tuvalu is an island situated in
A. Pacific ocean
B. Atlantic ocean
C. Indian ocean
D. None of these

768. Which of the following is a land locked sea?
A. North Sea
B. Aral Sea
C. Timor Sea
D. Red Sea

769. In India the Negrito race is found in
A. Puducherry
B. Lakshadweep
C. Andman and Nicobar
D. Southern Tamil Nadu

770. The Khonds tribal group live in
A. Kerala
B. Jammu & Kashmir
C. Jharkhand
D. Odisha

771. Which one of the following peaks is the highest?
A. Nanda Devi
B. Kanchenjunga
C. Godwin Austen
D. Nanga Parbat

772. Which one of the following is the correct order in which the following cities are located from West to East?
A. Alwar–Gorakhpur–Ranchi–Bhagalpur
B. Bhagalpur–Ranchi–Alwar–Gorakhpur
C. Ranchi–Alwar–Bhagalpur–Gorakhpur
D. Gorakhpur–Bhagalpur–Ranchi–Alwar

773. Which waterway separates India from Sri Lanka?
A. Eight Degree Channel
B. Palk Strait
C. Ten Degree Channel
D. Andaman Sea

774. Which of the following divides India into Northern and Southern parts?
A. Equator

B. Tropic of Cancer
C. Tropic of Capricorn
D. Arctic Circle

775. Where is the International Advanced Research Centre for Powder metallurgy and New Materials (ARCI) located?
A. Bengaluru
B. Hyderabad
C. Coimbatore
D. Machilipatnam

776. How many hours of daylight does the equator experience on September equinox?
A. 8 hours B. 9 hours
C. 10 hours D. 12 hours

777. The four largest planets of the Solar System in decreasing sizes are
A. Jupiter, Mercury, Saturn and Uranus
B. Mercury, Jupiter, Saturn and Neptune
C. Jupiter, Saturn, Uranus and Neptune
D. Jupiter, Mercury, Saturn and Neptune

778. Which of the following produces maximum crude petroleum in India at present?
A. Assam
B. Gujarat
C. Off-shore Bombay High
D. Coastal Tamil Nadu

779. India is one of the largest producers of manganese is in the world along with
A. China and Russia
B. Brazil and Russia
C. Australia and U.S.A.
D. South Africa and U.S.A.

780. Which of the following rivers makes an estuary?
A. Kaveri B. Krishna
C. Narmada D. Ganga

781. Baltora glacier is located in
A. Karakoram ranges
B. Pamir plateau
C. Shivalik
D. Alps

782. Which one of the following is not a tributary of the river Godavari?
A. Manjra B. Wardha
C. Pranhita D. Koyna

783. The International Date Line is the
A. 180° Longitude
B. $88\frac{1}{2}$ East Longitude
C. Equator
D. 0° Longitude

784. Which of the following countries has highest percentage of land under cultivation?
A. China B. U.S.A.
C. Canada D. India

785. In atmosphere the lowermost layer is
A. Troposphere
B. Exosphere
C. Ionosphere
D. Stratosphere

786. Comets revolve around the
A. Earth B. Venus
C. Sun D. Jupiter

787. In which of the following is the Great Barrier Reef located?
A. Coral Sea

B. Solomon Sea
C. Bismarck Sea
D. Arafura Sea

788. Which is the largest canal of the world?
A. Suez canal
B. Panama canal
C. Kra canal
D. Grand canal

789. The largest producer of fish in the world is
A. China B. Japan
C. USA D. India

790. Which of the following ports is not situated at Pacific coast?
A. Vancouver
B. Los Angeles
C. San Francisco
D. Miami

791. How much is the area of India?
A. 32,87,263 sq. km
B. 99,76,140 sq. km
C. 95,97,000 sq. km
D. 31,40,200 sq. km

792. Which is the southern-most point of India?
A. Kanyakumari
B. Goa
C. Indira point
D. Rameshwaram

793. Which river is known as the 'Sorrow of Bihar'?
A. Kosi B. Chambal
C. Gandak D. Son

794. In which state are the Mahadeo hills located?
A. Bihar
B. Rajasthan
C. Madhya Pradesh
D. Chhattisgarh

795. The 'Kalabaisakhis' originate during
A. Winter season
B. Rainy season
C. Period of retreating monsoon
D. Summer

796. Which state of India is the largest producer of Iron ore?
A. Karnataka
B. Odisha
C. Jharkhand
D. Madhya Pradesh

797. Which mineral is known as 'Black Gold'?
A Iron ore
B. Bauxite
C Coal
D. Manganese

798. Which food grain occupies the largest cropped area in India?
A. Maize B. Wheat
C. Rice D. Sugarcane

799. Which of the following is a cash crop?
A. Rice B. Wheat
C. Jowar D. Sugarcane

800. Which of the following states is the leading producer of sugarcane in India?
A. Uttar Pradesh
B. Madhya Pradesh
C. Punjab
D. Bihar

801. Which state is the largest producer of tea in India?
A. Assam
B. West Bengal
C. Kerala
D. Karnataka

802. Which state of India is the largest producer of diamond?
A. Madhya Pradesh
B. Chhattisgarh
C. Jharkhand
D. Rajasthan

803. Hemas are mainly found in
A. Congo
B. Japan
C. Turkiye
D. South Africa

804. Which one of the following is not a habitat of the Santhals?
A. West Bengal
B. Odisha
C. Jharkhand
D. Punjab

805. Which state of India has the highest percentage of scheduled tribe population?
A. Mizoram
B. Nagaland
C. Meghalaya
D. Assam

806. Which continent has the highest growth of population?
A. Africa
B. South America
C. Europe
D. Asia

807. Which is India's first oil refinery?
A. Digboi
B. Panipat
C. Trombay
D. Vishakhapatnam

808. Which is the most universal mode of transport?
A. Road Transport
B. Rail Transport
C. Ocean Transport
D. None of these

809. Match the List-I with the List-II and select the correct answer using the codes given below the Lists

List-I (Reservoir)	List-II (State)
(*a*) Stanley Reservoir	1. Karnataka
(*b*) Koyna Reservoir	2. Maharashtra
(*c*) Jalaput Reservoir	3. Odisha
(*d*) Bhadra Reservoir	4. Tamil Nadu

Codes:

	(*a*)	(*b*)	(*c*)	(*d*)
A.	1	2	3	4
B.	1	3	2	4
C.	4	3	2	1
D.	4	2	3	1

810. Match the List-I with the List-II and select the correct answer using the codes given below the Lists

List-I (Irrigation/ Power Projects)	List-II (Location)
(*a*) Malprabha	1. Andhra Pradesh
(*b*) Kakrapara	2. Karnataka
(*c*) Srisailam	3. Gujarat
(*d*) Bhima	4. Maharashtra

Codes:

	(*a*)	(*b*)	(*c*)	(*d*)
A.	4	1	3	2
B.	2	1	3	4
C.	4	3	1	2
D.	2	3	1	4

811. The hills that have the Dodda Bettah Peak are:

A. Nilgiri
B. Annamalai
C. Palani
D. Kutralam

812. The busy port of Rotterdam is situated in

A. The Netherlands
B. Belgium
C. Denmark
D. Germany

813. Which one of the following descriptions denotes the phenomenon of El Nino?

A. A violent rotating column of air extending from a thunderstorm to the ground
B. The deflection of the ocean currents in the northern and southern hemispheres due to the rotation of Earth
C. The Anomalous widespread warming of the sea surface of the tropical east and central Pacific Ocean
D. The revolving tropical storms of the Caribbean and Gulf of Mexico

814. Match the List-I with the List-II and select the correct answer using the codes given below the Lists

List-I *(Country)*	**List-II** *(Capital City)*
(*a*) Argentina	1. Buenos Aires
(*b*) Brazil	2. Caracas
(*c*) Peru	3. Lima
(*d*) Venezuela	4. Sao Paulo

Codes:

	(*a*)	(*b*)	(*c*)	(*d*)
A.	1	3	4	2
B.	1	4	3	2
C.	2	3	4	1
D.	2	4	3	1

815. Match the List-I with the List-II and select the correct answer using the codes given below the Lists

List-I *(Sea)*	**List-II** *(Country)*
(*a*) Adriatic Sea	1. Bulgaria
(*b*) Baltic Sea	2. Italy
(*c*) North Sea	3. Poland
(*d*) Black Sea	4. United Kingdom

Codes:

	(*a*)	(*b*)	(*c*)	(*d*)
A.	2	4	3	1
B.	2	3	4	1
C.	1	2	4	3
D.	1	4	2	3

816. Among the following States, which one has the highest amount of Nickel Ore resources?

A. Chhattisgarh
B. Jharkhand
C. Karnataka
D. Odisha

817. The famous petronas Twin Towers are located in

A. China
B. Japan
C. Malaysia
D. Indonesia

818. Match the List-I with the List-II and select the correct answer using the codes given below the Lists.

List-I *(Irrigation Project)*	List-II *(River)*
(*a*) Mettur	1. Kaveri
(*b*) Onkareshwar	2. Narmada
(*c*) Joyakwadi	3. Godavari
(*d*) Farrakka	4. Ganga

Codes:

	(*a*)	(*b*)	(*c*)	(*d*)
A.	1	2	3	4
B.	4	2	1	3
C.	3	2	4	1
D.	1	3	2	4

HEALTH AND HYGIENE

819. Digestion of food starts in
A. Mouth B. Liver
C. Stomach D. Intestine

820. By taking the pulse rate of the human body, a doctor determines
A. Heartbeat
B. Functioning of heart valves
C. The amount of blood in body
D. The condition of liver

821. The smallest living thing that can cause disease in the human body is
A. Flea B. Bacteria
C. Protozoa D. Virus

822. Which of the following is essentially required to digest the food in stomach?
A. Air B. Water
C. Enzyme D. Mineral

823. Polio is a disease caused due to
A. Bacterial infection
B. Viral infection
C. Protozoal infection
D. Food poisoning

824. Excessive intake of alcohol damages a person's
A. Kidney
B. Liver
C. Stomach
D. All the above to a certain degree

825. Pasteurization of milk means
A. Heating of milk upto 100°C
B. Heating of milk at 62°C
C. Cooling of milk at 100°C
D. Cooling of milk upto 0°C

826. Ranikhet disease affects
A. Dogs B. Cows
C. Poultry D. Sheep

827. Wisdom teeth appear in a human being between
A. 17 and 20 years of age
B. 30 and 40 years of age
C. 10 and 17 years of age
D. 4 and 8 years of age

828. Which of the following is a genetically transmitted disease?
A. Myopia
B. Long Sightedness
C. Colour Blindness
D. Night Blindness

829. Dialysis is
A. The same process as osmosis
B. The diffusion of sugar molecules through water
C. The process involved in the diffusion of some sugar molecules through a membrane

D. The evaporation of surplus sugar

830. Iron is essential for

A. To form haemoglobin and RBC

B. To maintain the general health

C. To carry oxygen to the tissues of the body

D. All the above

831. In human body, quantity of water is about

A. 10% B. 20%

C. 65% D. 80%

832. The urine of a man contain mainly

A. Urea

B. Sugar

C. Salt

D. None of the above

833. During which season our body needs more fats?

A. Summer season

B. Rainy season

C. Winter season

D. Spring season

834. Deficiency of insulin causes

A. Beri-Beri B. Diabetes

C. Cancer D. Anaemia

835. Which one of the following is a rich source of Vitamin A?

A. Potato tuber

B. Carrot root

C. Onion Bulb

D. Maize Grains

836. For getting instant energy an athlete should take

A. Carbohydrate

B. Protein

C. Vitamin

D. Chewing gum

837. The Amoeba type organisms in the human body, causing malaria and amoebic dysentry are known as

A. Bacteria B. Viruses

C. Fungi D. Protozoans

838. Deficiency of Vitamin A causes

A. Beri-Beri

B. Rickets

C. Scurvy

D. Night Blindness

839. The normal temperature of the human body is

A. 32°C B. 27°C

C. 37°C D. 40°C

840. Which disease of the following is caused by Virus?

A. Typhoid fever

B. Conjunctivitis

C. Malarial Fever

D. Cholera

841. The function of Calcium in our body is

A. To increase the supply of blood to the heart

B. To provide strength to the bones and teeth

C. To provide oxygen to the blood

D. To provide more sugar in our blood

842. What is a fracture?

A. Bleeding

B. Swelling

C. A broken bone

D. Bruising

843. In which unit can we measure food energy?
A. Calorie B. Kelain
C. Joule D. Erg

844. The drug most widely used to relieve pain is
A. Opium B. Aspirin
C. Morphine D. Baralgan

845. Diphtheria and influenza are caused by
A. Bacteria and virus respectively
B. Bacteria
C. Virus and bacteria respectively
D. None of the above

846. Vitamin E deficiency causes
A. Haemophilia
B. Sterlity
C. Falling of hair
D. Weakness

847. Which of the following should be avoided by a heart patient?
A. Bread B. Cream
C. Apple D. Rice

848. Which one of the following blood groups is universal recipient?
A. AB B. A
C. O D. B

849. Triple antigen prevents
A. Whooping cough, Tetanus, Diphtheria
B. Polio, Tetanus, Small-pox
C. Small-pox, Typhoid, Malaria
D. Tetanus, Diphtheria, Malaria

850. What is the normal range of the adult human heart-beat per minute?
A. 50 to 59 B. 60 to 80
C. 81 to 90 D. 91 to 110

851. A person in normal health required per day
A. 1,800 calories
B. 4,000 calories
C. 2,500 calories
D. 3,000 calories

852. 'ELISA' test is done for detection of
A. AIDS B. Kalazar
C. Cancer D. Diabetes

853. Conjunctivitis is a disease of the
A. Lever B. Eyes
C. Kidney D. Heart

854. Weakness and dullness in the body is due to the lack of
A. Fats
B. Proteins
C. Carbohydrates
D. Vitamin

855. Which of the following helps to drive out harmful germs from the body?
A. RBC B. WBC
C. Kidney D. Liver

856. Malaria and Yellow Fever germs are carried by
A. Birds B. Flies
C. Mosquitoes D. Ants

857. Meningitis affect the
A. Eyes B. Skin
C. Brain D. Throat

858. During processing the maximum amount of which food substance is lost
A. Protein
B. Vitamins
C. Fat
D. Carbohydrates

SCIENTIFIC RESEARCH

859. William Harvey is famous for the work in
A. Heart
B. Circulation of blood
C. Biochemistry
D. Neurology

860. Vaccination was used for the first time by
A. Edward Jenner
B. Marie Bichat
C. Robert Brown
D. None of the above

861. Laveran discovered the
A. Malaria germs
B. Bacteria
C. Leprosy bacillus
D. Aspirin

862. Penicillin is discovered by
A. Karl Landsteiner
B. Alaxender Fleming
C. Paul Muller
D. None of the above

863. Small Pox eradicated by
A. Robert Weinberg
B. W.H.O.
C. A group of American scientists
D. UNIDO

864. Fountain Pen was discovered by
A. T.A. Edison
B. W. Murdock
C. L.E. Waterman
D. None of the above

865. NASA stands for
A. National Aeronautical and Space Administration
B. National Aircraft Station of America
C. National Academy of Science and Aeronauticals
D. None of the above

866. The positron is discovered by
A. W.F. Libby
B. C.D. Anderson
C. James Chadwick
D. W. Heisenberg

867. The father of Embryology is
A. S.C. Maheshwari
B. B.M. Johri
C. P. Maheshwari
D. K.G. Mukerji

868. Who studied the living cell for the first time?
A. A.V. Leuwenhock
B. Robert Hooke
C. Robert Brown
D. None of the above

869. The first scientist who observe the cell under the microscope was
A. Schwann
B. Schleiden
C. Robert Hooke
D. None of the above

870. Watson and Crick propounded
A. Cell theory
B. Pollen grain theory
C. Structure of DNA
D. All the above

871. The scientists who formulated the cells theory was
A. Watson & Crick
B. M.J. Schleiden and T. Schwann
C. Rudolph & Virchow
D. None of the above

872. Theory of organic evolution was proposed by
A. Darwin B. Lamark
C. Johansen D. Schwann

873. First Electron microscope was invented by
A. Hallier
B. Zachrias Jansen
C. Knoll and Rusk
D. None of the above

874. Who proposed the first model of cell membrane structure?
A. Robertson
B. Danielli and Darson
C. Both A and B
D. None of the above

875. Who discovered citric acid or tricarboxylic acid cycle?
A. Altman
B. Kolliker
C. H.A. Krebs
D. None of the above

876. Who gave the name chlorophyll?
A. Schimper
B. Dutrochet
C. Haeckel
D. None of the above

877. The nucleus and chromosome were discovered by
A. Robert Brown and Hofmeister
B. Hofmeister
C. Robert Brown
D. W. Waldeyer

878. The important contribution of Wagner is
A. Discovered nucleus
B. Described chromosome
C. Described nucleolus
D. None of the above

879. Match the column-I and column-II

(*a*) Weismann	1. Rust diseases
(*b*) Jacob and Monod	2. Theory of continuity of germplasm
(*c*) K.C. Mehta	3. Operon concept
(*d*) P. Maheshwari	4. Embryology

Select the answer from the following
A. (*a*)-1, (*b*)-2, (*c*)-3, (*d*)-4
B. (*a*)-2, (*b*)-1, (*c*)-3, (*d*)-4
C. (*a*)-3, (*b*)-4, (*c*)-2, (*d*)-1
D. (*a*)-2, (*b*)-3, (*c*)-1, (*d*)-4

880. Mendel is regarded as
A. Father of genetics
B. Father of Botany
C. Father of Lichenology
D. None of the above

881. The father of Indian Lichenology is
A. D.D. Awasthi
B. P. Maheshwari
C. K.G. Mukerji
D. H.G. Khorana

882. Who was the first to obtain hybrid?
A. Carlson B. T. Fairchild
C. Morgan D. Khorana

883. Match the column-I and column-II

(*a*) Formulation of quantum mechanics of atomic theory	1. Atomic Energy Commission, America

(*b*) Explosion of first hydrogen bomb	2. W. Heisenberg
(*c*) Discovery of the electron	3. NASA
(*d*) The skylab	4. J. Thomson

Select the answer from the following

A. (*a*)-2, (*b*)-1, (*c*)-4, (*d*)-3
B. (*a*)-1, (*b*)-2, (*c*)-3, (*d*)-4
C. (*a*)-2, (*b*)-1, (*c*)-3, (*d*)-4
D. (*a*)-1, (*b*)-3, (*c*)-2, (*d*)-4

FUNDAMENTALS OF COMPUTER

884. Which is the part of computer System?
A. Hardware
B. Accounting system
C. Note-book
D. Tools

885. Which is the part of Computer Hardware?
A. Input devices
B. CPU
C. Output devices
D. All of these

886. Which is the main part of Computer System?
A. Input
B. CPU
C. Output
D. All of the above

887. Which is the brain of computer?
A. CPU
B. Input Devices
C. Auxiliary Memory Devices
D. LAN

888. Which is the steps of data processing?
A. Recording data
B. Classification
C. Sorting
D. All of the above

889. Ascending of data is related with
A. Recording of data
B. Sorting
C. Summarising
D. Calculating

890. The Calculator was developed by
A. Franc Boldwin
B. Jacards Loom
C. J. Betty
D. Howard Aiken

891. Hybrid computer is a combination of
A. Analog Computer and Digital Computer
B. Calculator and Laptop
C. Laptop and Abacus
D. Punch Card and Analog Computer

892. Which is the counting devices?
A. Abacus
B. Written Manual
C. Mechanical Calculator
D. All of the above

893. Java is
A. Programming Language
B. Network
C. Calculating devices
D. All of these

894. Which is a Programming Language(s)?
A. COBOL
B. FORTRAN IV
C. Java
D. All of the above

895. Voltage meter is a
A. Analog Computer
B. Digital Computer
C. Language
D. LAN

896. Who is known as father of Computer?
A. Bill Gates
B. Charles Babbes
C. Alan Euning
D. Johan Euring

897. Electricity meter is a .... computer.
A. Microcomputer
B. Hybrid Computer
C. Analog Computer
D. Digital Computer

898. Which is the Microcomputer?
A. Watch
B. Calculator
C. Written Manual
D. Palm Top

899. Who made the first computer programme?
A. Bill Gates
B. Lady Loveless
C. Newman
D. Einstine

900. What is disk storage capacity of Mini Computer?
A. 20 GB B. 40 GB
C. 100 GB D. 1000 GB

901. Laptop is a
A. Microcomputer
B. Hybrid Computer
C. Analog Computer
D. Digital Computer

902. CPU stand for
A. Control Processing Unit
B. Central Processing Unit
C. Common Processing Unit
D. All of these

903. Which is the part of CPU?
A. Control Unit
B. ALU
C. Main Memory
D. All of the above

904. ALU stand for
A. Arithmetic and Logical Unit
B. Art Logical Unit
C. Apple Log Unit
D. Access Logical Unit

905. Which is the part of structure of Micro Processor?
A. ALU B. Register
C. Control Unit D. All of these

906. Keyboard is a
A. Input device
B. Output device
C. LAN
D. Network

907. Which is input device?
A. Mouse B. Punch Card
C. Scanner D. All of these

908. Number Keys are
A. 0, 1 and 3 B. F1 to F12
C. Enter D. Shift

909. Which of the followings is Control Keys?
A. Enter B. Shift
C. Esc D. All of these

910. Match the following

List-I *(Keyboard)*	**List-II** *(Type of Keys)*
(*a*) Number Keys	1. 0
(*b*) Alphabet Keys	2. B
(*c*) Edit Keys	3. Page Down
(*d*) Control Keys	4. Lock

Codes:

	(*a*)	(*b*)	(*c*)	(*d*)
A.	1	2	3	4
B.	3	1	2	4
C.	3	1	4	2
D.	1	4	3	2

911. Which is Editing Key of Computer?
A. Page up B. Page Down
C. Delete D. All of these

912. Which is the Symbol Keys of Keybord?
A. ? B. %
C. @ D. All of these

913. Which is the eye of the Computer?
A. Scanner B. Punch Card
C. Mouse D. All of these

914. OMR is
A. Option Multiple Report
B. Optical Mark Reader
C. Open Mark Reader
D. All of these

915. The Bar Coding has the
A. 10 digit B. 100 digit
C. 1000 digit D. 1 digit

916. Plotter is a
A. Input device
B. LAN
C. Language
D. Output device

917. Which is the output device?
A. Printer B. VDV
C. Plotter D. All of these

918. The plotter may be used in
A. Graphics and Artists
B. Accounting
C. Recording
D. Sorting

919. RAM is a
A. Computer Memory
B. Network
C. Language
D. Programme

920. Which is the Primary Memory of the Computer?
A. RAM B. ROM
C. PROM D. All of these

921. Which is the full form of ROM?
A. Read only Memory
B. Read on Memory
C. Roal only Memory
D. Role on Memory

922. The personal Computer is
A. Desktop Mode
B. Notebook Computer
C. Plam Computer
D. All of the above

923. Which is the component of Computer System?
A. Hardware B. Software
C. Users D. All of these

924. Which is the Hardware of Personal Computer?
A. Input and Output Device
B. Processor
C. Memory
D. All of these

925. Which is the output device of Personal Computer?

A. Speaker
B. Monitor
C. Printer
D. All of the above

926. Which is the input device of Personal Computer?
A. Microphone
B. Digital Camera
C. Touch Pad
D. All of these

927. Control bus is an
A. Electronic Path
B. Computer
C. Network
D. Memory

928. Which is a Semiconductor Memory of Computer?
A. Cache Memory
B. RAM
C. ROM
D. All of these

929. Which is the Secondary Memory of Computer?
A. RAM
B. ROM
C. Cache Memory
D. Magnetic

930. Bus is a
A. Network Topology
B. Memory
C. Cost
D. Planning

931. Which is the short form of Local Area Network?
A. LAN B. MAN
C. WAN D. RAM

932. LAN Topology contains
A. Bus B. Star
C. Ring D. All of these

933. Which is the feature of Internet?
A. www B. Telenet
C. Channels D. All of these

EMINENT PERSONALITIES

934. Tulsi Das lived during the reign of:
A. Babar B. Shahjahan
C. Aurangzeb D. Akbar

935. Who among the following was not an astronomer?
A. Bana Bhatt
B. Varahamihira
C. Arya Bhatta
D. Bhaskaracharya

936. M K Gandhi was born on October 2. Another famous Indian also born on this day-was:
A. Sardar Patel
B. Lal Bahadur Shastri
C. Rabindra Nath Tagore
D. Bhagat Singh

937. Megasthenese was:
A. a Chinese ambassador at the court of Chandragupta
B. a Greek philosopher
C. the envoy of Seleucus at the court of Chandragupta
D. a Greek Geometrician traveller

938. Charak was a renowned:
A. Historian
B. Physician
C. Minister
D. Astronomer

939. Who founded the Indian National Congress?

A. W C Bennerjee
B. A O Hume
C. Sardar Patel
D. Subhash Chandra Bose

940. According to a document recovered by the Archives Deptt. of Punjab Government, Tansen, before joining the court of Akbar was associated with the court of:
A. Maharaja Banur
B. Maharaja Udaipur
C. Maharaja Rewa
D. Maharaja Jodhpur

941. 'Father of History' is the name given to:
A. Herodotus
B. Megasthenese
C. John Rey
D. Ibn Batuta

942. The first US President who visited India, was:
A. J.F. Kennedy
B. D Eisenhower
C. Jimmy Carter
D. George Washington

943. The first person who sailed around the world was:
A. Robert Pierre
B. Magellan
C. Captain Cook
D. None of these

944. The 'Servants of India Society' was founded by:
A. Annie Besant
B. Gopalakrishna Gokhale
C. Bal Gangadhar Tilak
D. Dadabhai Naoroji

945. The first PM to have resigned without attending a Parliament session, was:
A. Charan Singh
B. Lal Bahadur Shastri
C. Morarji Desai
D. Indira Gandhi

946. Valentina Tereshkova is famous for being the:
A. first woman pilot
B. first woman in space
C. first woman on the moon
D. first female engineer

947. Who was called by the epithet "Desh Bandhu" during the struggle for freedom?
A. Chittaranjan Das
B. Lala Lajpat Rai
C. M K Gandhi
D. Bhagat Singh

948. C. Funk's name has been associated with the research of which of the following?
A. Vitamins
B. Proteins
C. Minerals
D. Carbohydrates

949. Who defined democracy as a "Government of the people, by the people and for the people?"
A. Ruskin
B. Abraham Lincoln
C. Mahatma Gandhi
D. Aristotle

950. 'Lion of Punjab' is the nickname assigned to:
A. Bipin Chandra Pal
B. Lala Lajpat Rai
C. Sardar Bhagat Singh
D. None of these

951. 'Anna' was the abbreviated name of:

A. C N Annadurai
B. T Prakasam
C. C Rajagopalachari
D. None of these

952. 'Frontier Gandhi' was the nickname of:
A. Mahatma Gandhi
B. Khan Abdul Ghaffar Khan
C. Vinoba Bhave
D. None of these

953. "Freedom is my birth right". Who was the famous, Indian national leader who gave this slogan?
A. Ranade B. Tilak
C. Nehru D. Gandhi

954. Who said: "Give me somewhere to stand, and I will move the world?"
A. Archimedes B. Newton
C. Galileo D. Einstein

955. Who first propounded the Theory of Population?
A. Darwin
B. Mendel
C. Malthus
D. Marshal Ricardo

956. Which one of these was not murdered?
A. Thomas Becket
B. Socrates
C. Julius Caesar
D. Abraham Lincoln

957. Which instrument was played by Bismillah Khan?
A. Flute B. Tabla
C. Shehnai D. Sarod

958. Bismark was:
A. German Democrat of late Nineteenth century, a very influential figure
B. a noted German statesman
C. a great inventor of early 20th century who classified human blood into various groups
D. an Emperor of France before World War I

959. The 'little corporal' is the nickname of:
A. Lal Bahadur Shastri
B. Mahatma Gandhi
C. Napoleon Bonaparte
D. Bismark

960. The Greek philosopher who wrote nothing yet (who) is the most famous and that greatest figure in the world, he was:
A. Marcus Aurelius
B. Plato
C. Aristotle
D. Socrates

961. The name of the world's first black spaceman is:
A. Prensa Latina
B. Arnaldo Amayo Mendez
C. Yury Rumanenko
D. Robert Mendereze

962. Mrs Junko Tabei, who created history on May 16, 1975 by becoming the world's first woman to reach the 8,848 metre (29,002 ft) high Everest peak belongs to which of the following countries?
A. Japan B. Tibet
C. Thailand D. Nepal

963. The first woman President of Indian National Congress was:
A. Indira Gandhi
B. Sarojini Mahishi
C. Annie Besant
D. Vijayalakshmi Pandit

964. Fuehrer is the nickname of:
A. Mussolini
B. Rommel
C. Napoleon
D. Hitler

965. Michael Angelo was a famous artist, poet, painter, sculptor, architect of Italy. He can rightly be called a 'brother' to:
A. Picasso
B. Van Gogh
C. M F Hussain
D. Leonardo da Vinci

966. Bachendri Pal is:
A. the first Indian woman to win a medal in Olympic Games
B. the first Indian woman to climb Mt Everest
C. the first woman pilot of Indian Airlines
D. the first woman IPS officer of India

967. Baden Powell was:
A. a famous poet
B. a famous golf player
C. a Nobel Prize winner scientist
D. founder of boy scouts

968. Who had discovered North America in 1492?
A. Vasco da Gama
B. Columbus
C. John Cabot
D. James Cook

969. The name of the youngest US President who was assassinated in 1963, was:
A. John F Kennedy
B. Abraham Lincoln
C. Thomas Jefferson
D. George Washington

970. J D Rockfeller was:
A. an industrialist
B. a scientist
C. American President
D. world famous navigator

971. Dr Martin Luther King was assassinated in the year:
A. 1963 B. 1965
C. 1966 D. 1968

972. The father of Russian Revolution is:
A. Nikita Khurschev
B. Stalin
C. V I Lenin
D. L I Brezhnev

973. Which of the following British statesman/politician won a Nobel Prize in literature?
A. C Atlee
B. W Churchill
C. Robert Clive
D. Margaret Thatcher

974. Which of the following head of the state won the Nobel Prize for Peace in 2019?
A. Stephen Harber
B. Jacob Zuma
C. Abiy Ahmed Ali
D. Yukio Haloyama

975. The name of India born British author who was issued a death threat (Fatwa) by Ayatollah Khomeini is:
A. Salman Rushdie
B. Pamella Bordes
C. R K Narayan
D. Mira Nayar

976. Satish Gujral is a famous:
A. painter B. architect
C. violinist D. sitarist

977. Ayatollah R. Khomeini was the religious leader of which of the following countries?
A. Iran B. Iraq
C. Saudi Arabia D. Kuwait

978. Which one of the following is popularly known as "Lady with the Lamp"?
A. Mother Teresa
B. Florence Nightingale
C. Sarojini Naidu
D. Isabella Archer

979. Havaiian Islands were discovered in 1778 by the legendary:
A. Captain James Cook
B. John Cabot
C. Christopher Columbus
D. Vasco da Gama

980. Who is called the "Father of Geometry"?
A. Bertrand Russel
B. Aristotle
C. Euclid
D. Archimedes

981. The first human being to land on moon is:
A. Yuri Gagarin
B. Neil Armstrong
C. Rakesh Sharma
D. Robert Medereze

982. The Communist Party of the Chinese People's Republic was founded by:
A. Huo Kua Fenge
B. Chiang Kai Shek
C. Chou-En-Lai
D. Mao-Tse-Tung

983. Who was the first President of USA?
A. Abraham Lincoln
B. Wilson Woodrow
C. George Washington
D. Thomas Jefferson

ANSWERS

1	2	3	4	5	6	7	8	9	10
C	A	A	B	C	C	A	A	C	A
11	**12**	**13**	**14**	**15**	**16**	**17**	**18**	**19**	**20**
A	D	B	D	B	B	C	A	B	B
21	**22**	**23**	**24**	**25**	**26**	**27**	**28**	**29**	**30**
D	A	A	A	B	A	C	C	C	B
31	**32**	**33**	**34**	**35**	**36**	**37**	**38**	**39**	**40**
B	B	D	C	A	C	D	D	C	C
41	**42**	**43**	**44**	**45**	**46**	**47**	**48**	**49**	**50**
A	B	A	C	A	C	D	B	A	C
51	**52**	**53**	**54**	**55**	**56**	**57**	**58**	**59**	**60**
D	C	C	D	C	B	D	C	D	C
61	**62**	**63**	**64**	**65**	**66**	**67**	**68**	**69**	**70**
C	B	C	D	A	D	D	A	B	C

71	72	73	74	75	76	77	78	79	80
C	B	C	C	D	A	D	A	D	B
81	**82**	**83**	**84**	**85**	**86**	**87**	**88**	**89**	**90**
C	B	D	D	C	A	D	B	A	D
91	**92**	**93**	**94**	**95**	**96**	**97**	**98**	**99**	**100**
A	C	C	B	A	A	A	C	C	D
101	**102**	**103**	**104**	**105**	**106**	**107**	**108**	**109**	**110**
C	C	A	B	C	D	C	B	B	A
111	**112**	**113**	**114**	**115**	**116**	**117**	**118**	**119**	**120**
A	D	D	B	C	A	A	C	C	B
121	**122**	**123**	**124**	**125**	**126**	**127**	**128**	**129**	**130**
D	A	D	B	C	C	C	D	C	C
131	**132**	**133**	**134**	**135**	**136**	**137**	**138**	**139**	**140**
A	B	B	B	A	D	B	C	C	D
141	**142**	**143**	**144**	**145**	**146**	**147**	**148**	**149**	**150**
B	D	A	A	B	D	C	C	D	D
151	**152**	**153**	**154**	**155**	**156**	**157**	**158**	**159**	**160**
B	B	B	C	D	A	A	D	A	B
161	**162**	**163**	**164**	**165**	**166**	**167**	**168**	**169**	**170**
B	B	A	A	B	C	A	C	B	B
171	**172**	**173**	**174**	**175**	**176**	**177**	**178**	**179**	**180**
A	C	D	A	D	B	B	B	A	D
181	**182**	**183**	**184**	**185**	**186**	**187**	**188**	**189**	**190**
B	C	C	B	A	C	A	A	C	A
191	**192**	**193**	**194**	**195**	**196**	**197**	**198**	**199**	**200**
A	B	B	A	A	C	B	D	C	C
201	**202**	**203**	**204**	**205**	**206**	**207**	**208**	**209**	**210**
A	B	C	C	A	B	C	A	D	C
211	**212**	**213**	**214**	**215**	**216**	**217**	**218**	**219**	**220**
B	B	B	A	B	D	B	C	C	C
221	**222**	**223**	**224**	**225**	**226**	**227**	**228**	**229**	**230**
B	B	B	D	B	C	C	C	B	C
231	**232**	**233**	**234**	**235**	**236**	**237**	**238**	**239**	**240**
A	B	B	D	D	D	B	C	D	C
241	**242**	**243**	**244**	**245**	**246**	**247**	**248**	**249**	**250**
A	B	A	A	D	C	A	D	D	A
251	**252**	**253**	**254**	**255**	**256**	**257**	**258**	**259**	**260**
A	D	C	B	D	D	A	C	B	C
261	**262**	**263**	**264**	**265**	**266**	**267**	**268**	**269**	**270**
C	C	C	C	C	A	B	B	D	C

271	**272**	**273**	**274**	**275**	**276**	**277**	**278**	**279**	**280**
A	A	D	D	C	D	A	D	D	B
281	**282**	**283**	**284**	**285**	**286**	**287**	**288**	**289**	**290**
B	C	D	C	A	B	A	A	C	D
291	**292**	**293**	**294**	**295**	**296**	**297**	**298**	**299**	**300**
B	A	D	D	B	D	A	C	D	B
301	**302**	**303**	**304**	**305**	**306**	**307**	**308**	**309**	**310**
D	A	D	B	C	A	D	D	A	C
311	**312**	**313**	**314**	**315**	**316**	**317**	**318**	**319**	**320**
D	B	A	C	D	D	C	A	C	C
321	**322**	**323**	**324**	**325**	**326**	**327**	**328**	**329**	**330**
D	C	D	A	B	C	D	D	B	A
331	**332**	**333**	**334**	**335**	**336**	**337**	**338**	**339**	**340**
B	C	B	C	D	A	A	D	C	C
341	**342**	**343**	**344**	**345**	**346**	**347**	**348**	**349**	**350**
A	A	B	D	B	D	A	B	C	D
351	**352**	**353**	**354**	**355**	**356**	**357**	**358**	**359**	**360**
D	A	C	D	A	D	C	B	B	D
361	**362**	**363**	**364**	**365**	**366**	**367**	**368**	**369**	**370**
D	B	D	B	A	B	C	C	D	A
371	**372**	**373**	**374**	**375**	**376**	**377**	**378**	**379**	**380**
A	A	D	B	A	D	B	C	B	B
381	**382**	**383**	**384**	**385**	**386**	**387**	**388**	**389**	**390**
C	D	B	D	D	C	A	D	A	D
391	**392**	**393**	**394**	**395**	**396**	**397**	**398**	**399**	**400**
C	A	B	B	B	B	D	B	C	C
401	**402**	**403**	**404**	**405**	**406**	**407**	**408**	**409**	**410**
C	B	B	B	B	C	B	D	D	A
411	**412**	**413**	**414**	**415**	**416**	**417**	**418**	**419**	**420**
D	B	D	B	D	B	B	A	C	B
421	**422**	**423**	**424**	**425**	**426**	**427**	**428**	**429**	**430**
B	B	D	A	C	C	C	C	A	C
431	**432**	**433**	**434**	**435**	**436**	**437**	**438**	**439**	**440**
D	C	A	B	C	A	C	C	C	C
441	**442**	**443**	**444**	**445**	**446**	**447**	**448**	**449**	**450**
C	D	A	C	A	C	A	C	A	D
451	**452**	**453**	**454**	**455**	**456**	**457**	**458**	**459**	**460**
B	D	D	D	B	C	B	A	B	A
461	**462**	**463**	**464**	**465**	**466**	**467**	**468**	**469**	**470**
A	B	B	A	A	D	B	D	A	A

471	472	473	474	475	476	477	478	479	480
B	B	D	C	A	C	C	B	C	A
481	**482**	**483**	**484**	**485**	**486**	**487**	**488**	**489**	**490**
B	D	B	D	D	D	D	A	B	C
491	**492**	**493**	**494**	**495**	**496**	**497**	**498**	**499**	**500**
C	A	A	D	A	C	B	D	C	C
501	**502**	**503**	**504**	**505**	**506**	**507**	**508**	**509**	**510**
B	A	A	D	D	A	A	D	C	A
511	**512**	**513**	**514**	**515**	**516**	**517**	**518**	**519**	**520**
B	D	D	B	A	A	D	A	A	C
521	**522**	**523**	**524**	**525**	**526**	**527**	**528**	**529**	**530**
C	D	B	B	A	D	A	C	B	B
531	**532**	**533**	**534**	**535**	**536**	**537**	**538**	**539**	**540**
B	A	B	C	D	D	B	C	C	C
541	**542**	**543**	**544**	**545**	**546**	**547**	**548**	**549**	**550**
A	D	C	B	A	B	B	C	C	C
551	**552**	**553**	**554**	**555**	**556**	**557**	**558**	**559**	**560**
C	A	A	C	B	B	D	A	C	B
561	**562**	**563**	**564**	**565**	**566**	**567**	**568**	**569**	**570**
B	B	B	C	C	A	B	A	C	A
571	**572**	**573**	**574**	**575**	**576**	**577**	**578**	**579**	**580**
D	B	A	D	B	C	C	A	B	B
581	**582**	**583**	**584**	**585**	**586**	**587**	**588**	**589**	**590**
B	A	C	B	A	B	C	D	D	B
591	**592**	**593**	**594**	**595**	**596**	**597**	**598**	**599**	**600**
B	B	C	C	D	A	D	A	C	D
601	**602**	**603**	**604**	**605**	**606**	**607**	**608**	**609**	**610**
C	A	D	A	D	C	A	B	C	B
611	**612**	**613**	**614**	**615**	**616**	**617**	**618**	**619**	**620**
A	A	A	A	C	C	B	D	A	A
621	**622**	**623**	**624**	**625**	**626**	**627**	**628**	**629**	**630**
A	A	D	B	C	B	C	C	D	D
631	**632**	**633**	**634**	**635**	**636**	**637**	**638**	**639**	**640**
A	D	C	B	D	B	B	B	B	A
641	**642**	**643**	**644**	**645**	**646**	**647**	**648**	**649**	**650**
B	C	D	D	B	A	C	B	C	A
651	**652**	**653**	**654**	**655**	**656**	**657**	**658**	**659**	**660**
D	D	D	C	A	D	B	C	A	A
661	**662**	**663**	**664**	**665**	**666**	**667**	**668**	**669**	**670**
A	B	B	A	B	D	C	A	A	A

671	672	673	674	675	676	677	678	679	680
B	A	B	C	A	C	C	B	C	B
681	682	683	684	685	686	687	688	689	690
C	A	A	C	C	C	C	A	B	B
691	692	693	694	695	696	697	698	699	700
B	C	B	C	C	D	C	B	C	B
701	702	703	704	705	706	707	708	709	710
A	C	B	A	B	D	B	D	B	A
711	712	713	714	715	716	717	718	719	720
C	D	B	A	D	B	A	B	D	D
721	722	723	724	725	726	727	728	729	730
D	C	B	B	B	C	C	C	C	B
731	732	733	734	735	736	737	738	739	740
D	A	B	D	C	D	A	B	C	A
741	742	743	744	745	746	747	748	749	750
B	C	B	A	B	D	B	A	A	D
751	752	753	754	755	756	757	758	759	760
B	D	C	D	D	B	A	C	B	A
761	762	763	764	765	766	767	768	769	770
C	A	B	A	D	B	A	B	C	D
771	772	773	774	775	776	777	778	779	780
C	A	B	B	B	D	C	C	A	C
781	782	783	784	785	786	787	788	789	790
A	D	A	D	A	C	A	D	A	D
791	792	793	794	795	796	797	798	799	800
A	C	A	C	D	B	C	C	D	A
801	802	803	804	805	806	807	808	809	810
A	A	A	D	A	A	A	A	D	D
811	812	813	814	815	816	817	818	819	820
A	A	C	B	B	D	C	A	A	A
821	822	823	824	825	826	827	828	829	830
D	C	B	D	B	C	A	C	C	D
831	832	833	834	835	836	837	838	839	840
C	A	C	B	B	A	D	D	C	B
841	842	843	844	845	846	847	848	849	850
B	C	A	B	A	B	B	A	A	B
851	852	853	854	855	856	857	858	859	860
C	A	B	A	B	C	C	B	B	A
861	862	863	864	865	866	867	868	869	870
A	B	B	C	A	B	C	A	C	C

871	872	873	874	875	876	877	878	879	880
B	A	B	B	C	B	A	C	D	A
881	882	883	884	885	886	887	888	889	890
A	B	A	A	D	B	A	D	B	A
891	892	893	894	895	896	897	898	899	900
A	D	A	D	A	B	C	D	B	A
901	902	903	904	905	906	907	908	909	910
A	B	D	A	D	A	D	A	D	A
911	912	913	914	915	916	917	918	919	920
D	D	A	B	A	D	D	A	A	D
921	922	923	924	925	926	927	928	929	930
A	D	D	D	D	D	A	A	D	A
931	932	933	934	935	936	937	938	939	940
A	D	D	D	A	B	C	B	B	C
941	942	943	944	945	946	947	948	949	950
A	B	B	B	A	B	A	A	B	B
951	952	953	954	955	956	957	958	959	960
A	B	B	A	C	B	C	B	C	D
961	962	963	964	965	966	967	968	969	970
B	A	C	D	D	B	D	B	A	A
971	972	973	974	975	976	977	978	979	980
D	C	B	C	A	A	A	B	A	C
981	982	983							
B	D	C							